Sophie von Hellermann • *Judgement Day*

Whilst a man is free—cried the corporal,
giving a flourish with his stick thus—

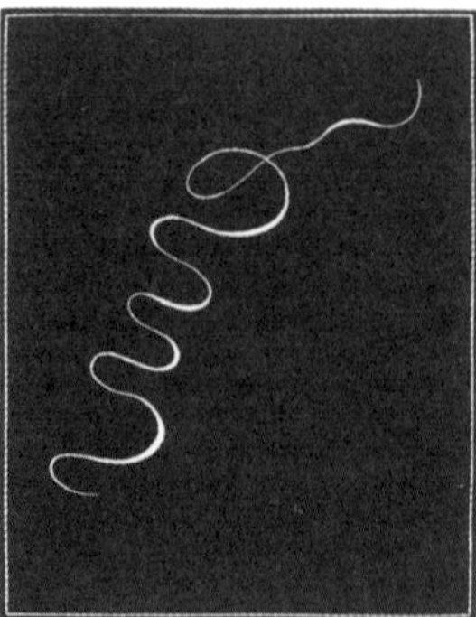

from: The Life and Opinions of Tristram Shandy

Sophie von Hellermann

Judgement Day

KOENIG BOOKS, LONDON

I would like to thank Sabine Brümmer, Peter Willberg, Carol Greene,
Andrew Renton, Emily Speers Mears, Anne Pontégnie, Clemens Krümmel,
Linda Zimmermann, Jochen Link, Franz König, Friederike von Hellermann, Jonathan Viner,
Achim Kukulies, Dietmar Lutz, Rachel Williams, Mark Dickenson, Marc Foxx,
Rodney Hill, Andy Keate, Linn Lühn, Ghislaine Hussenot, Simon Wallis
and everybody else who has generously supported and helped me with this book.

Sophie von Hellermann, February 2006

Dedicated to those waiting outside

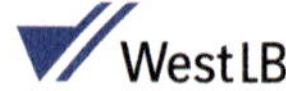

This book has been published with generous support
from WestLB AG on the occasion of the exhibition

Sophie von Hellermann • *Judgement Day*

Neuer Aachener Kunstverein
19 March – 21 May 2006

Chisenhale Gallery, London
6 June – 23 July 2006

Copyright © 2006 Sophie von Hellermann, Koenig Books and the authors
Coordination: Sabine Brümmer
Design: Peter B. Willberg
Copy-editing: Janet Law
Translation: Julien Bismuth, Karl Hoffmann
Printed in Austria by Holzhausen Druck and Medien, Vienna

Photo Credits:
Achim Kukulies, Andy Keate, Stephen White, Oren Slor, Robert Wedemeyer,
Joshua White, Chris Burke, Wendelin Bottländer

First published by Koenig Books London

Koenig Books Ltd.
at the Serpentine Gallery
Kensington Gardens
London W2 3XA

www.koenigbooks.co.uk

Distribution: Buchhandlung Walther König, Ehrenstr.4, 50672 Köln
Tel. ++49 (0)221-205960, Fax ++49 (0)221-2059640, Mail verlag@buchhandlung-walther-koenig.de

Distribution outside Europe: D.A.P. / Distributed Art Publishers Inc., New York NY 10012, USA
Tel. +1 212-6721999, Fax +1 212-627-9484

ISBN 3-86560-057-3

Special edition of 15 + 5 AP with a hand painted cover by Sophie von Hellermann, signed, numbered.
Presented in solander box made by Friederike von Hellermann

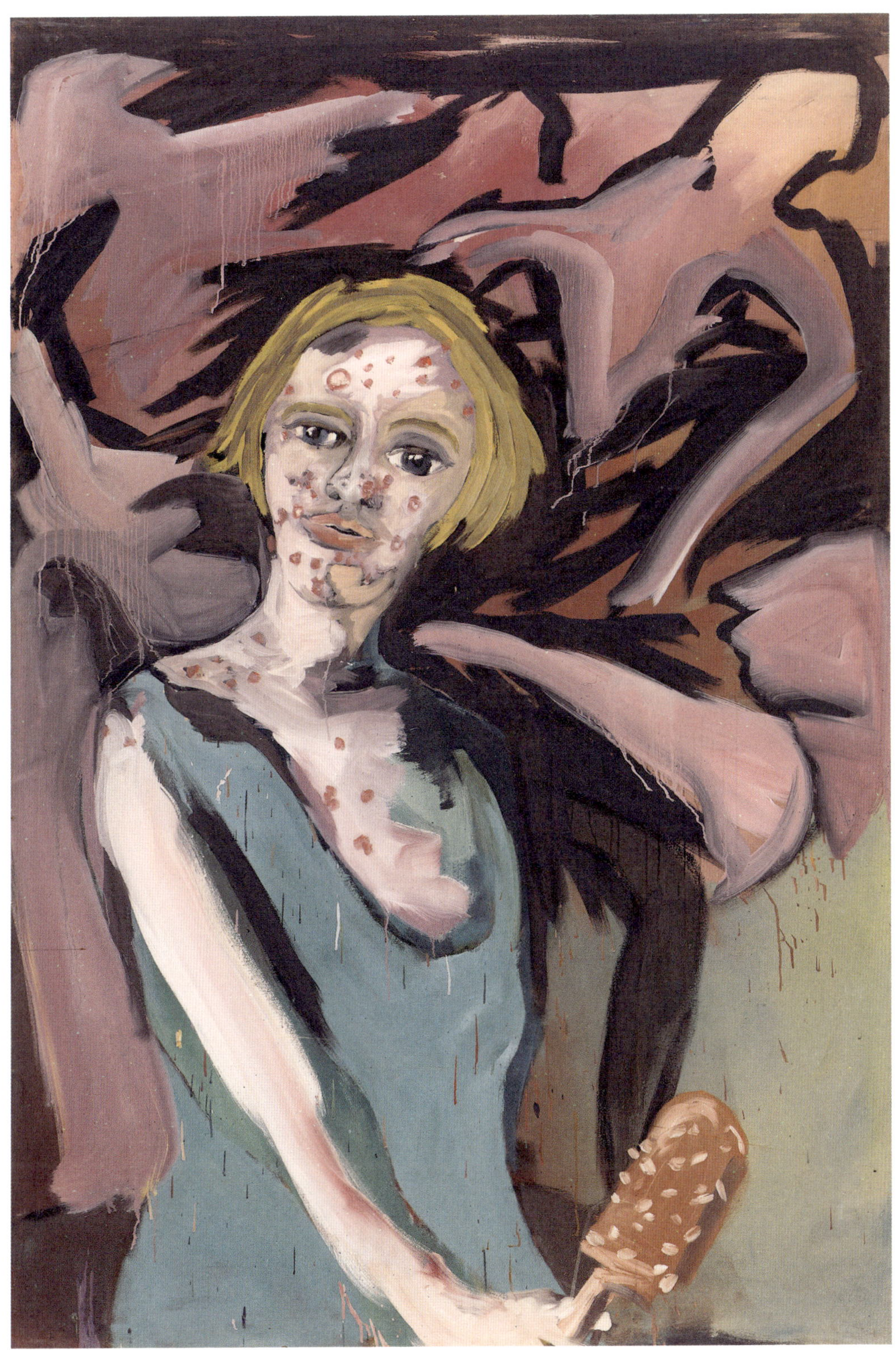

Pickel, 1994

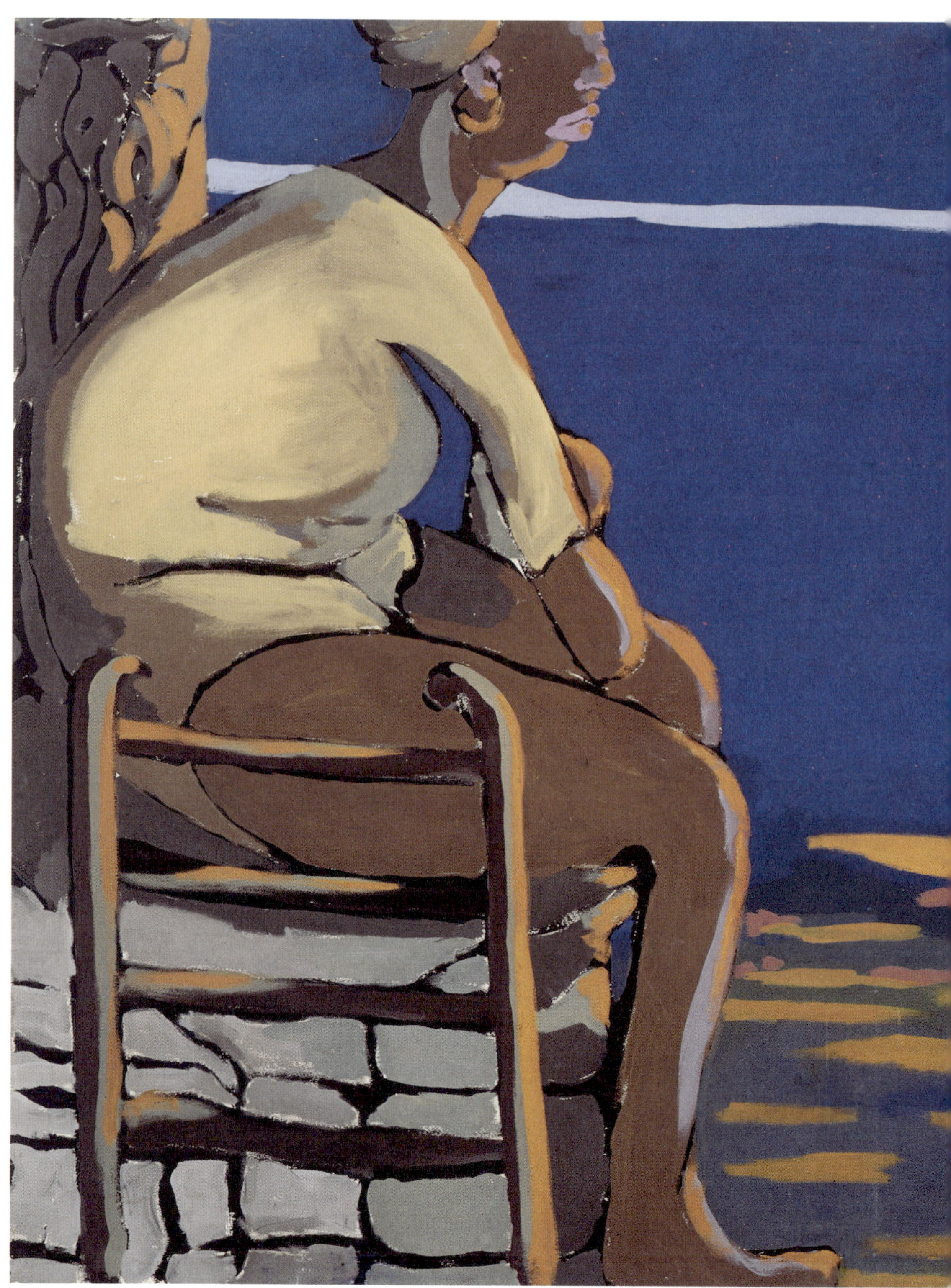

Sitting on the Dock of the Bay, 1994

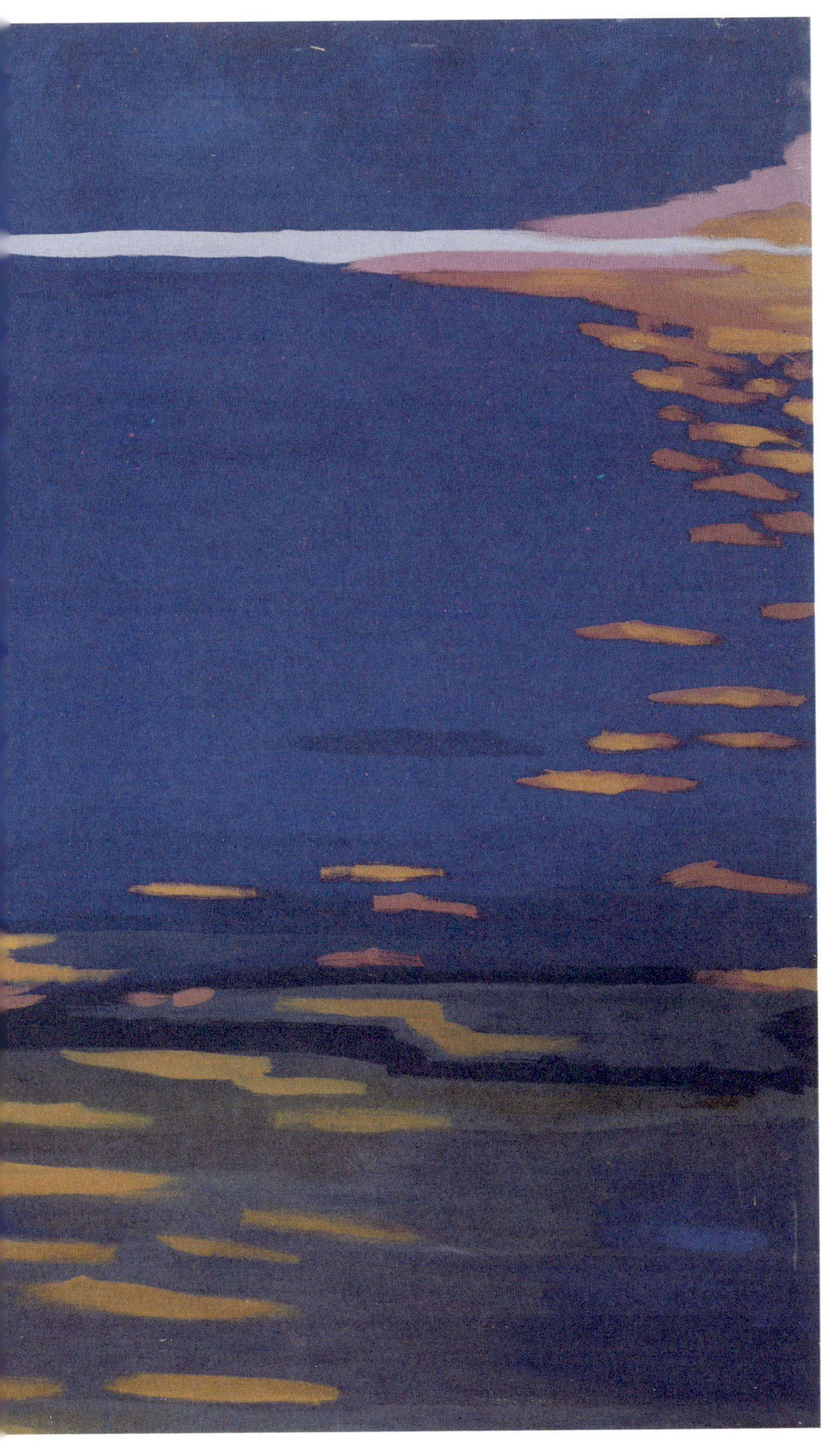

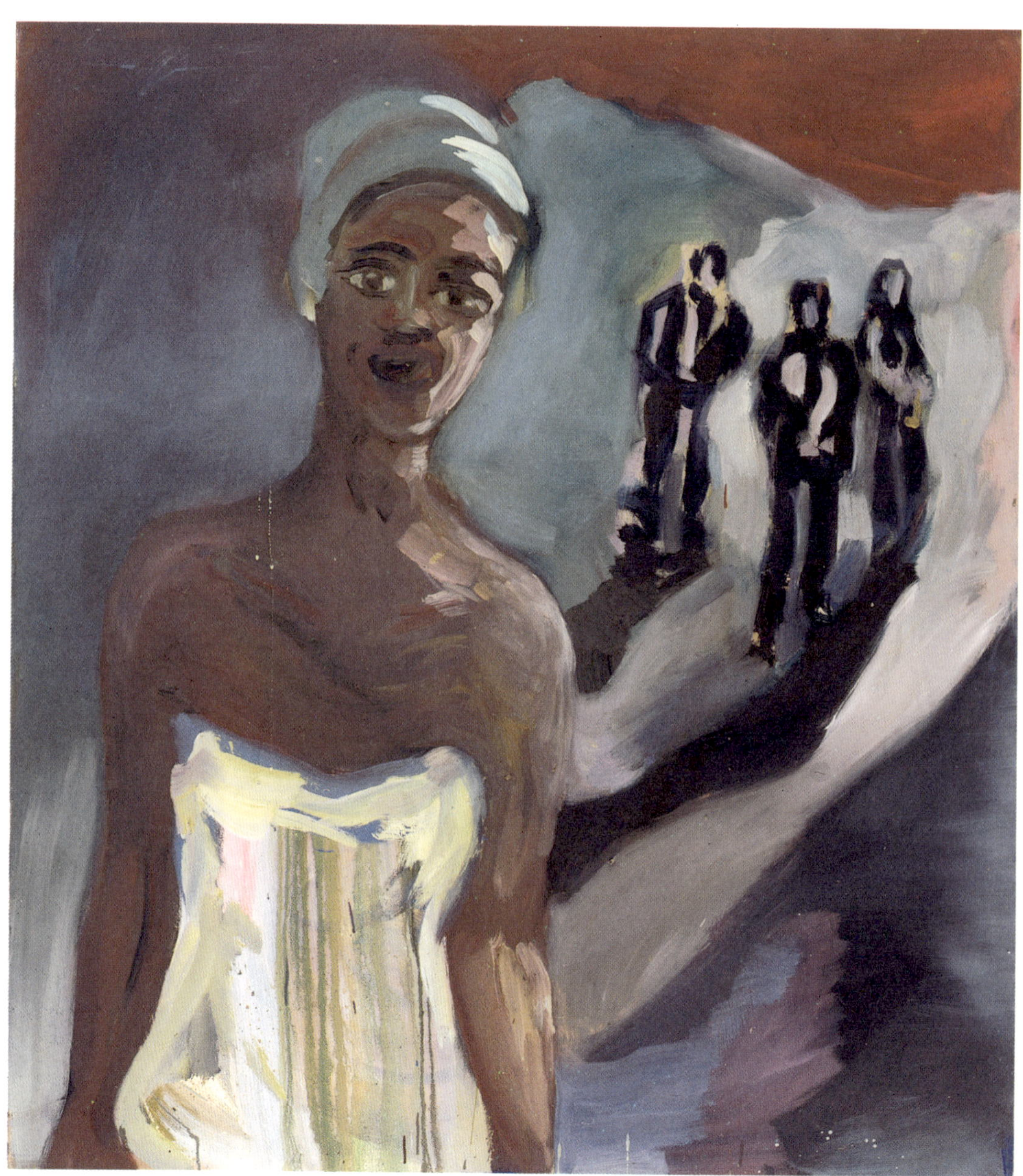

Untitled, 1994

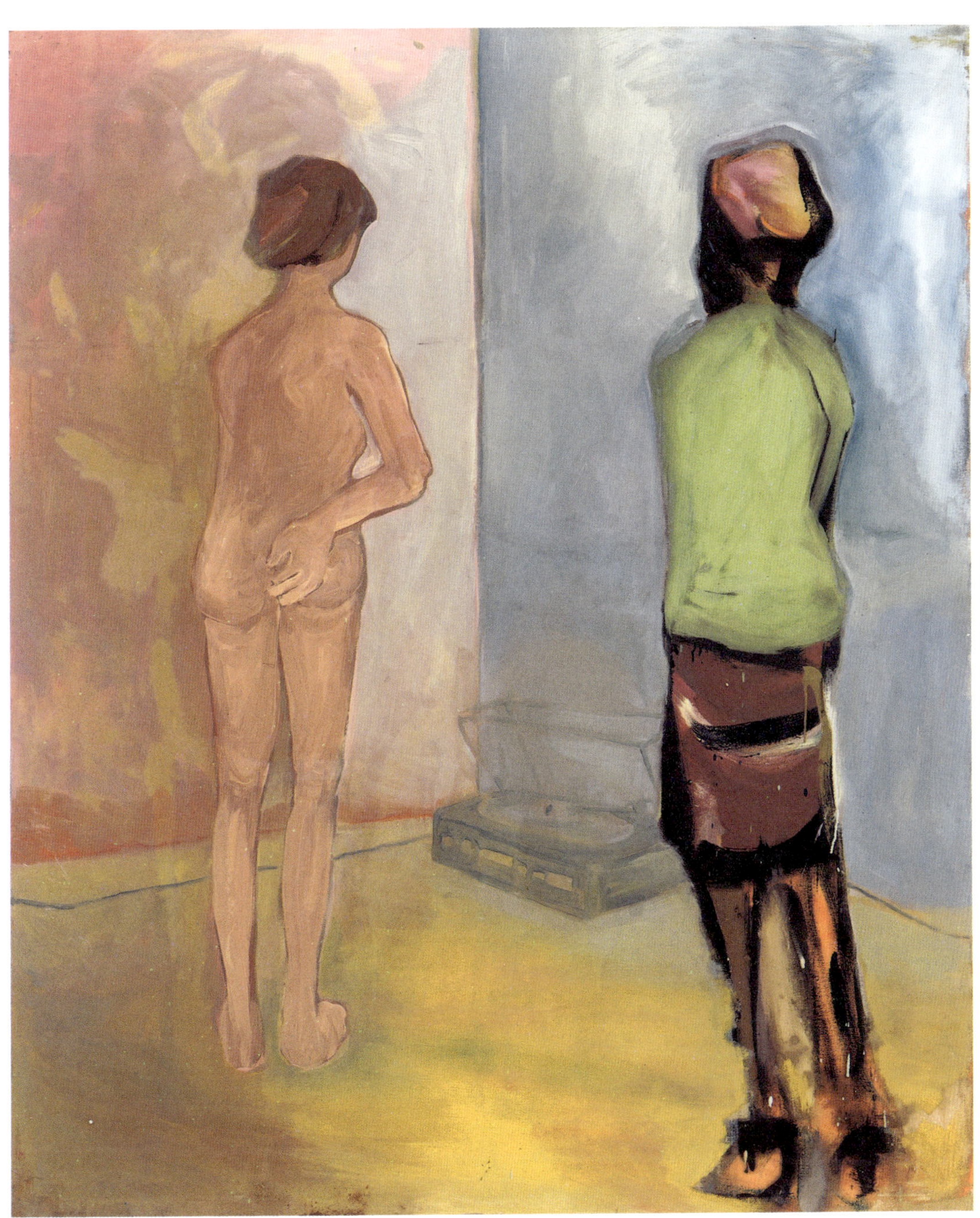

Untitled (for Ann Peebles), 1994

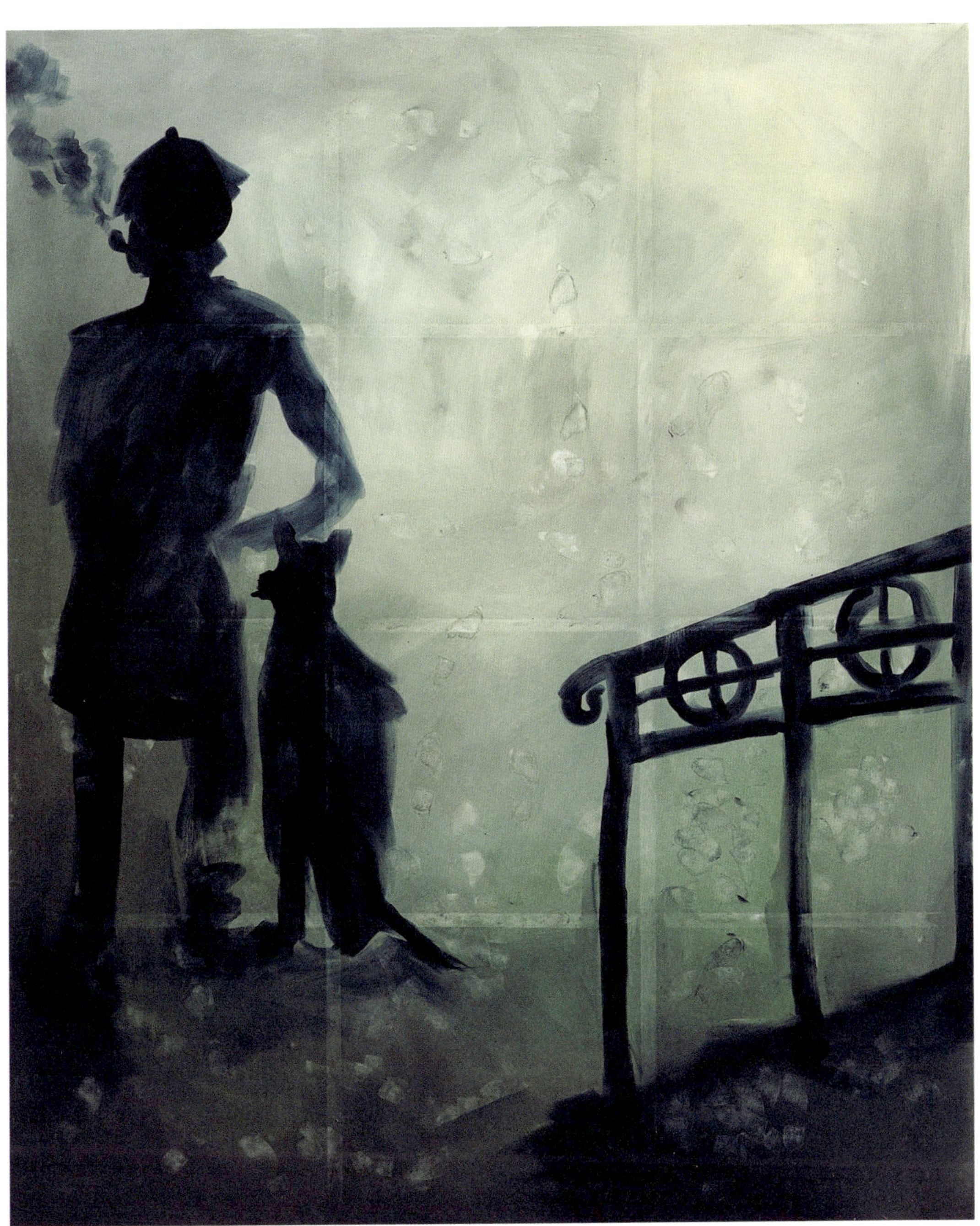

Sherlock Holmes, 1995

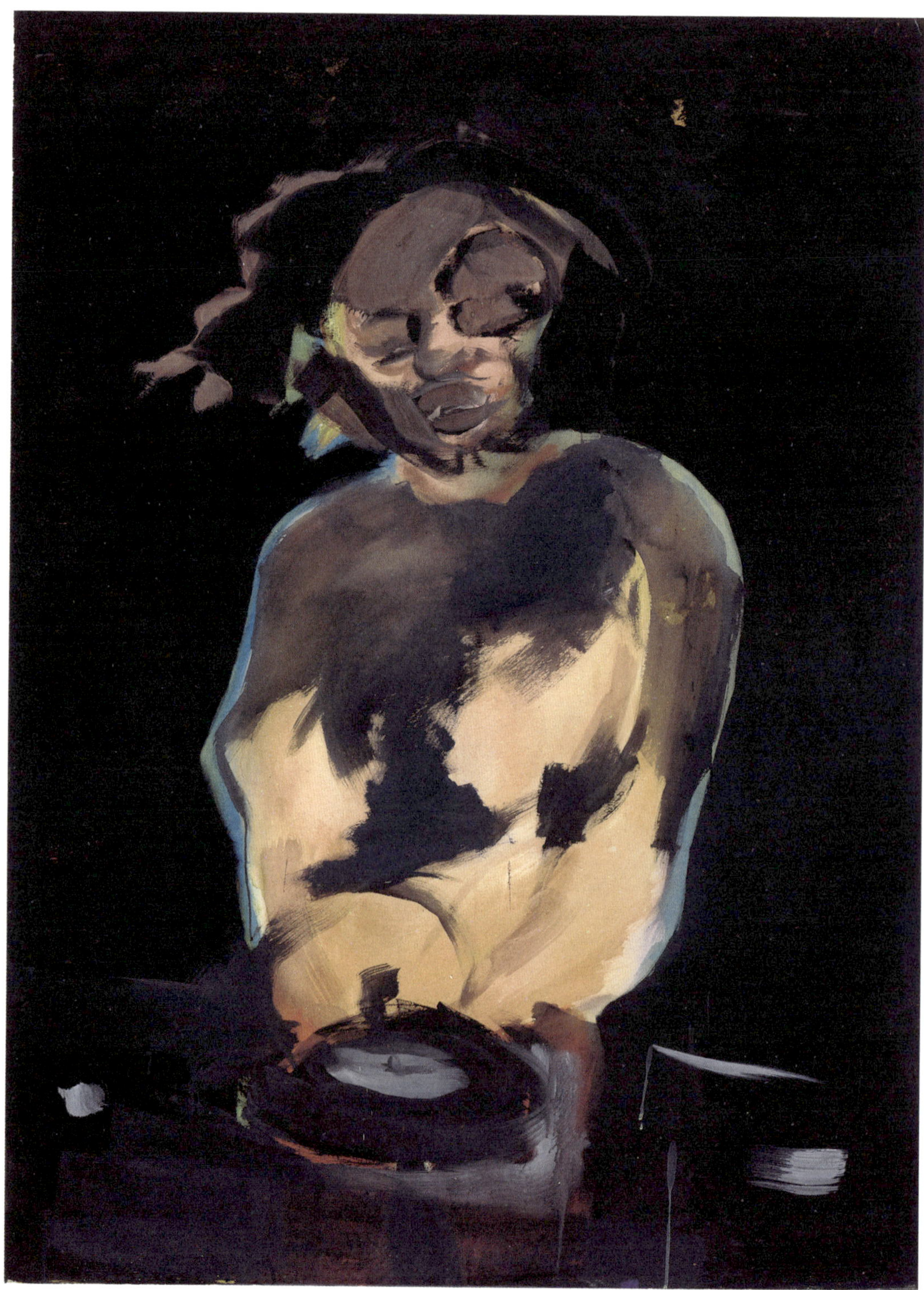

Fabio, 1996

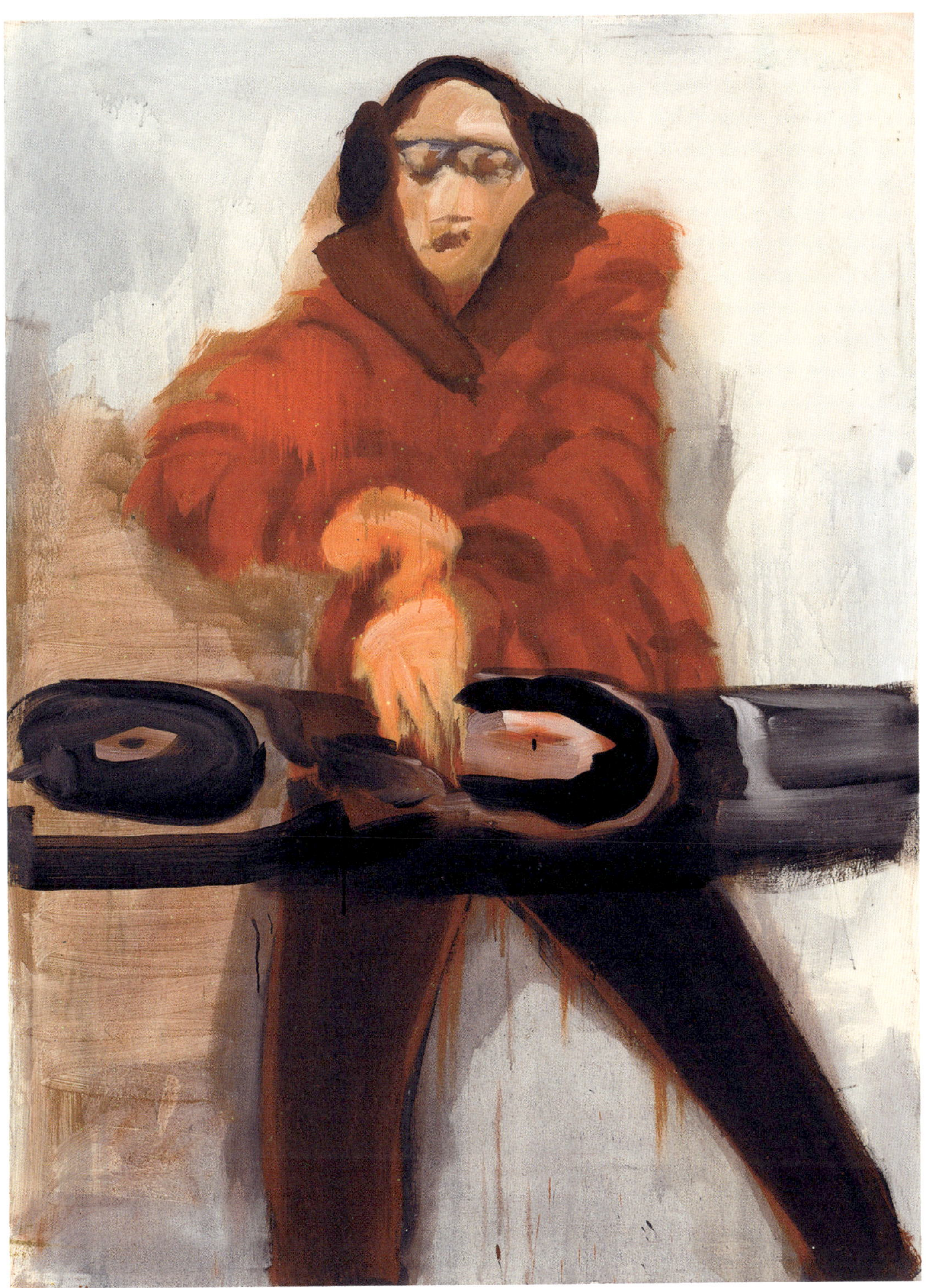

DJ Buzz, 1996

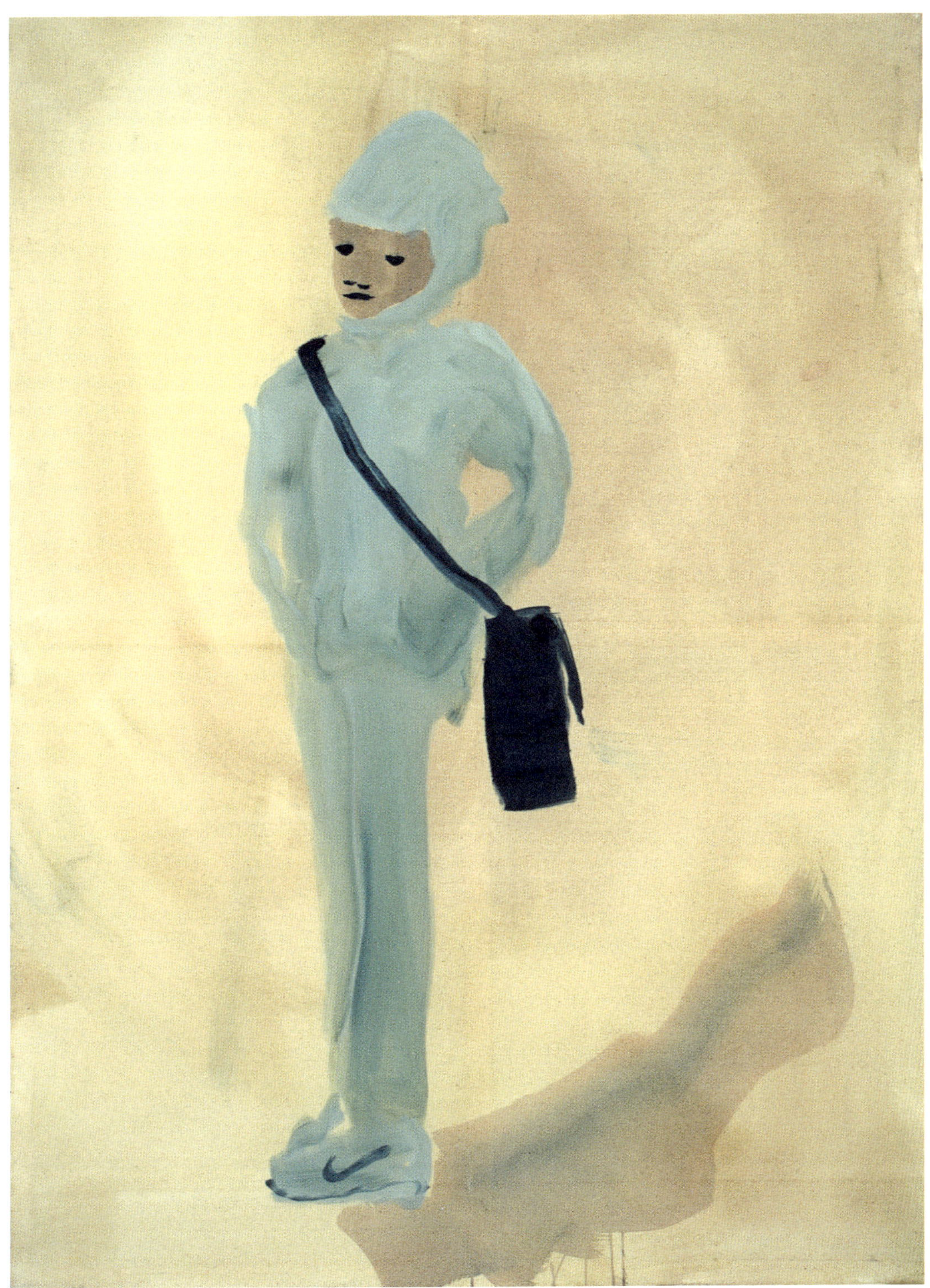

Plattenträger, 1997

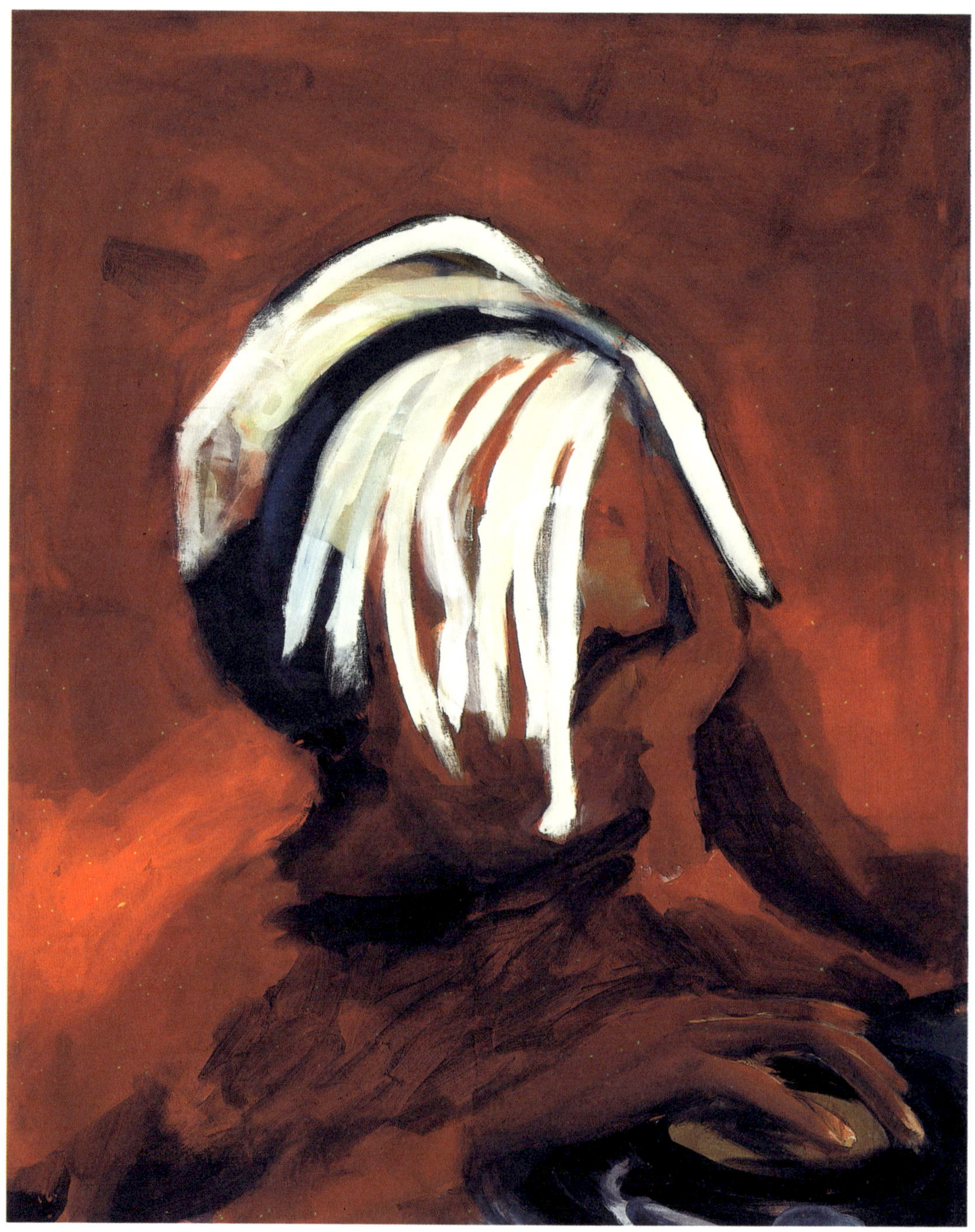

Kemistry, 1997

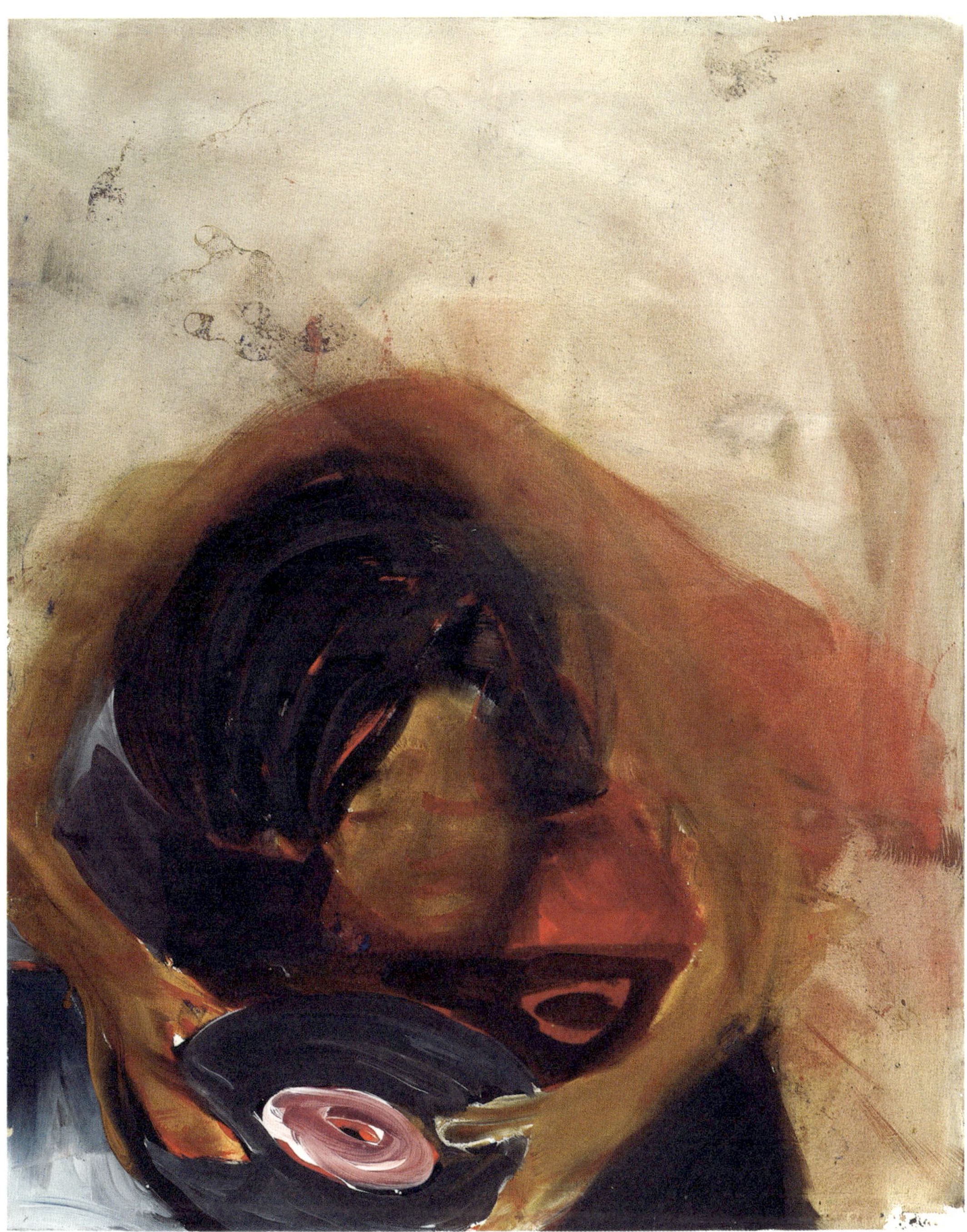

Storm, 1997

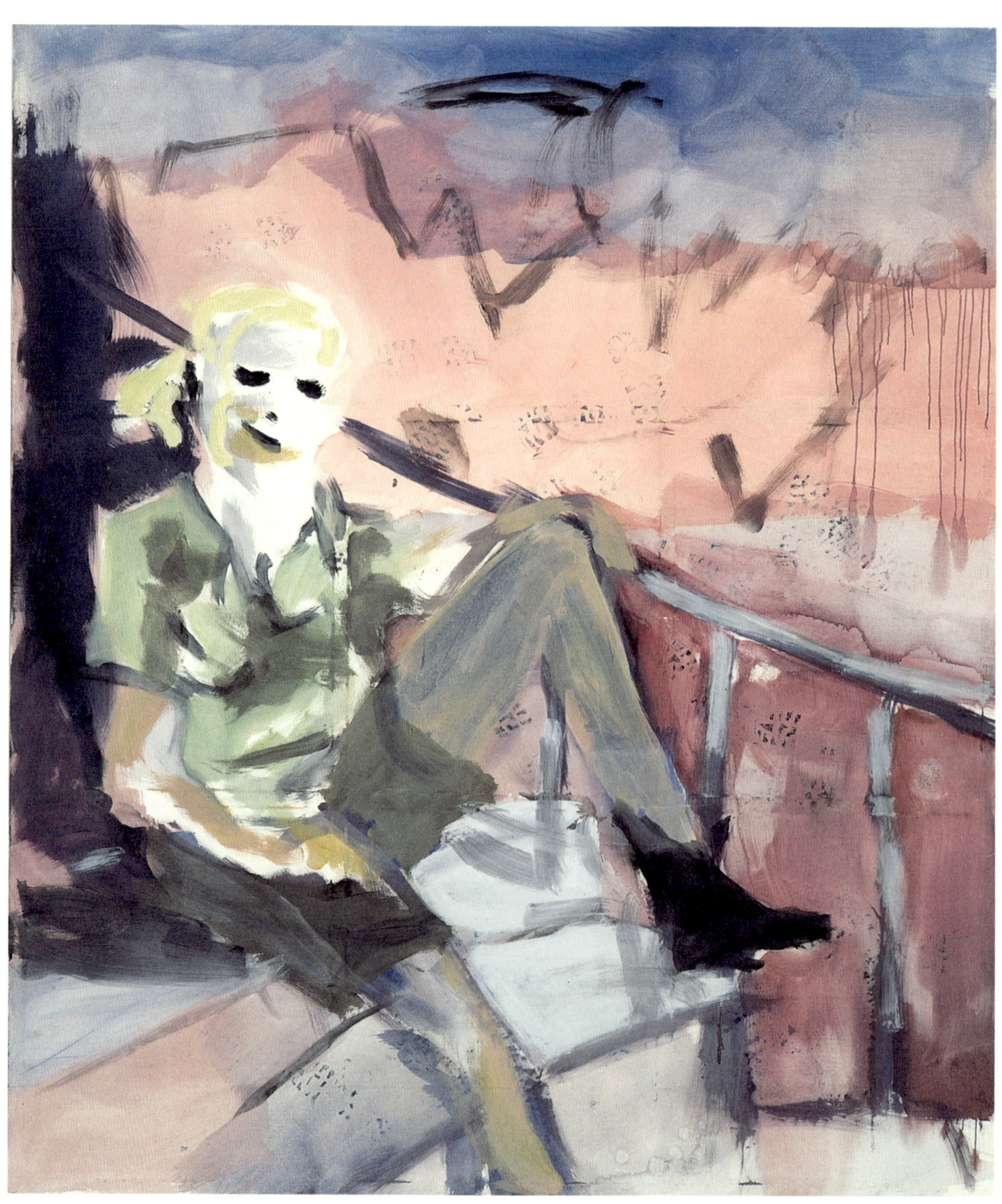

Mädchen auf Treppe, 1998

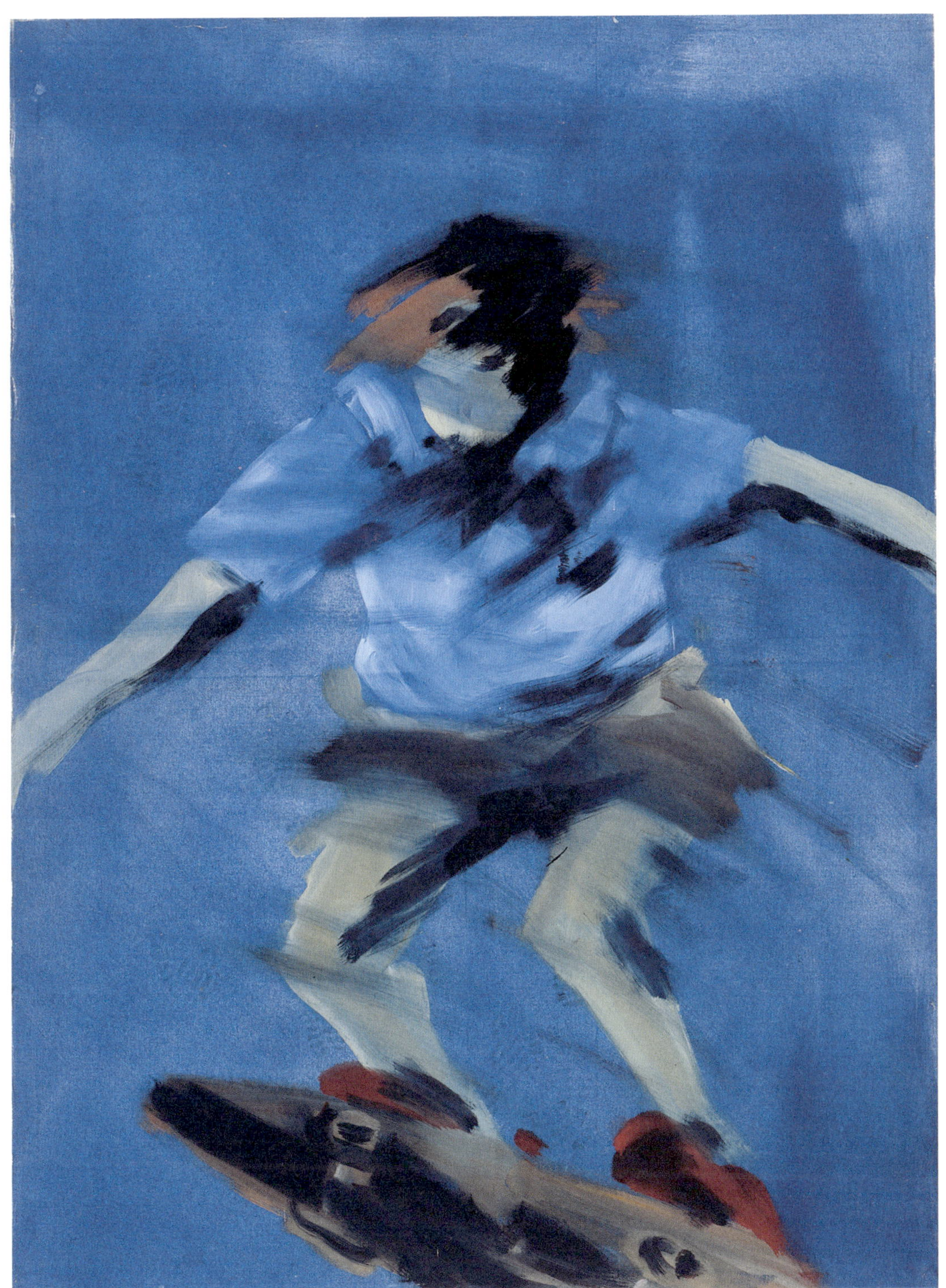

Skateboarder, 1998

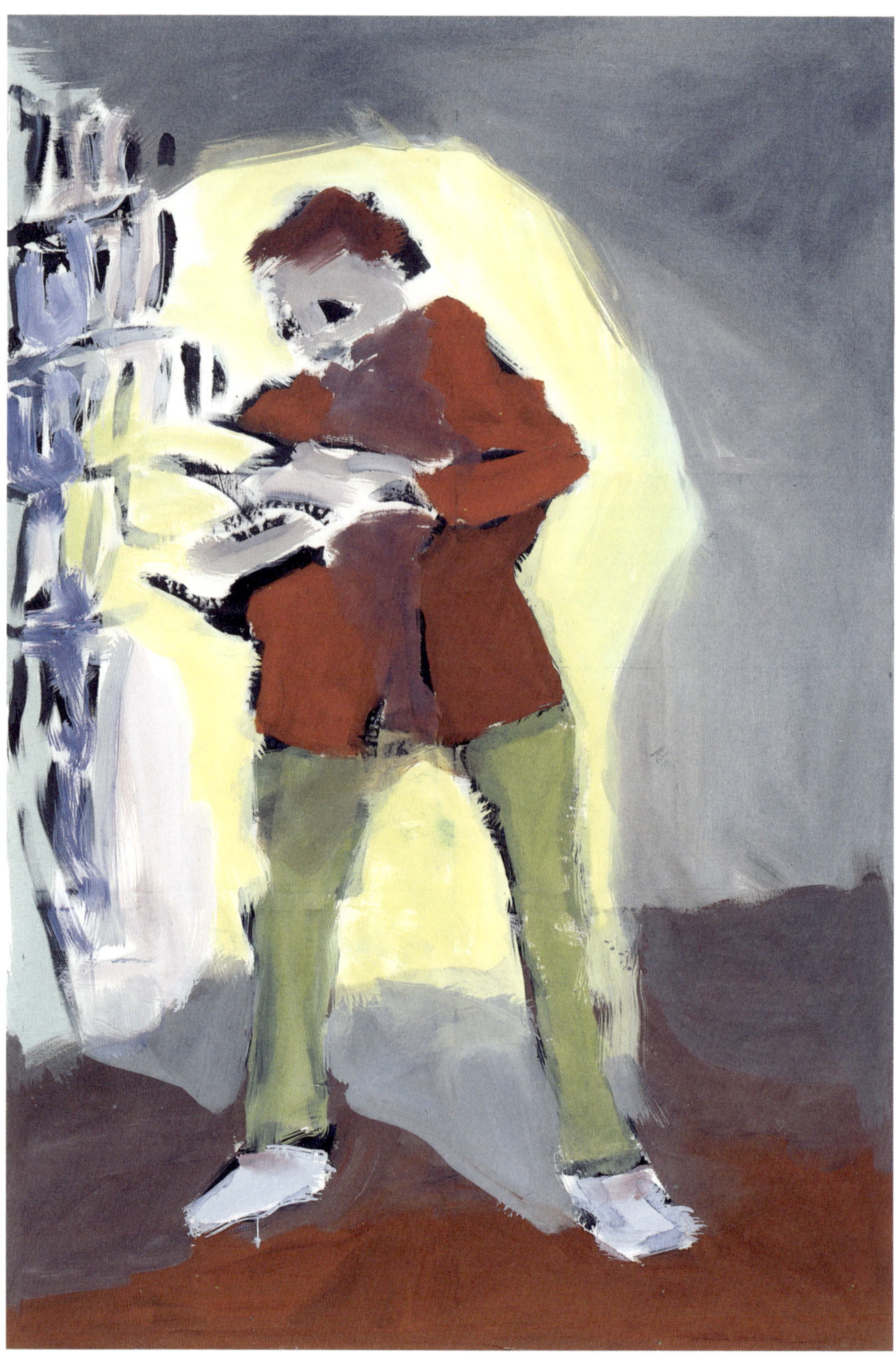

Der Lesende, 1998

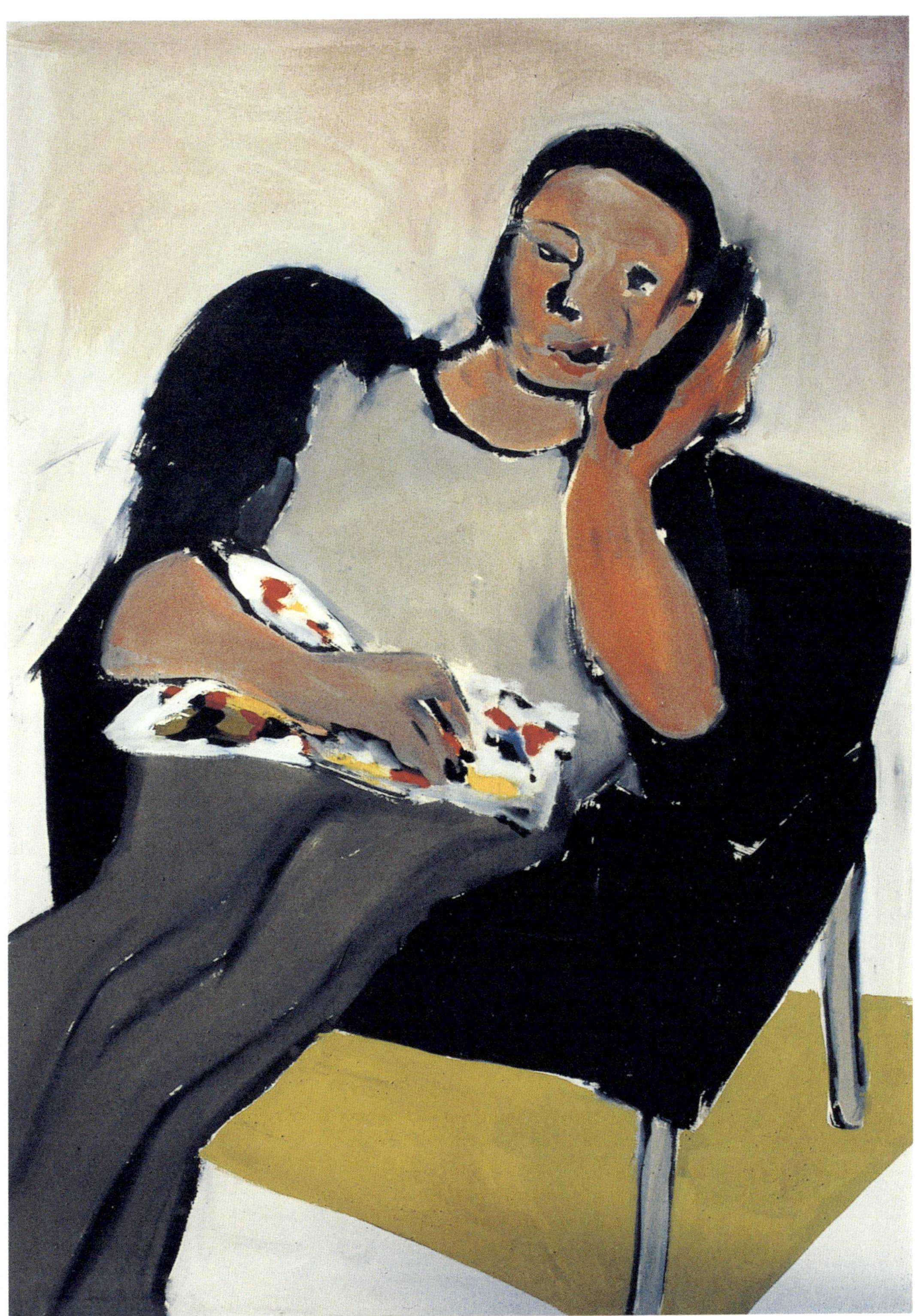

The Young Gallerist, 1998

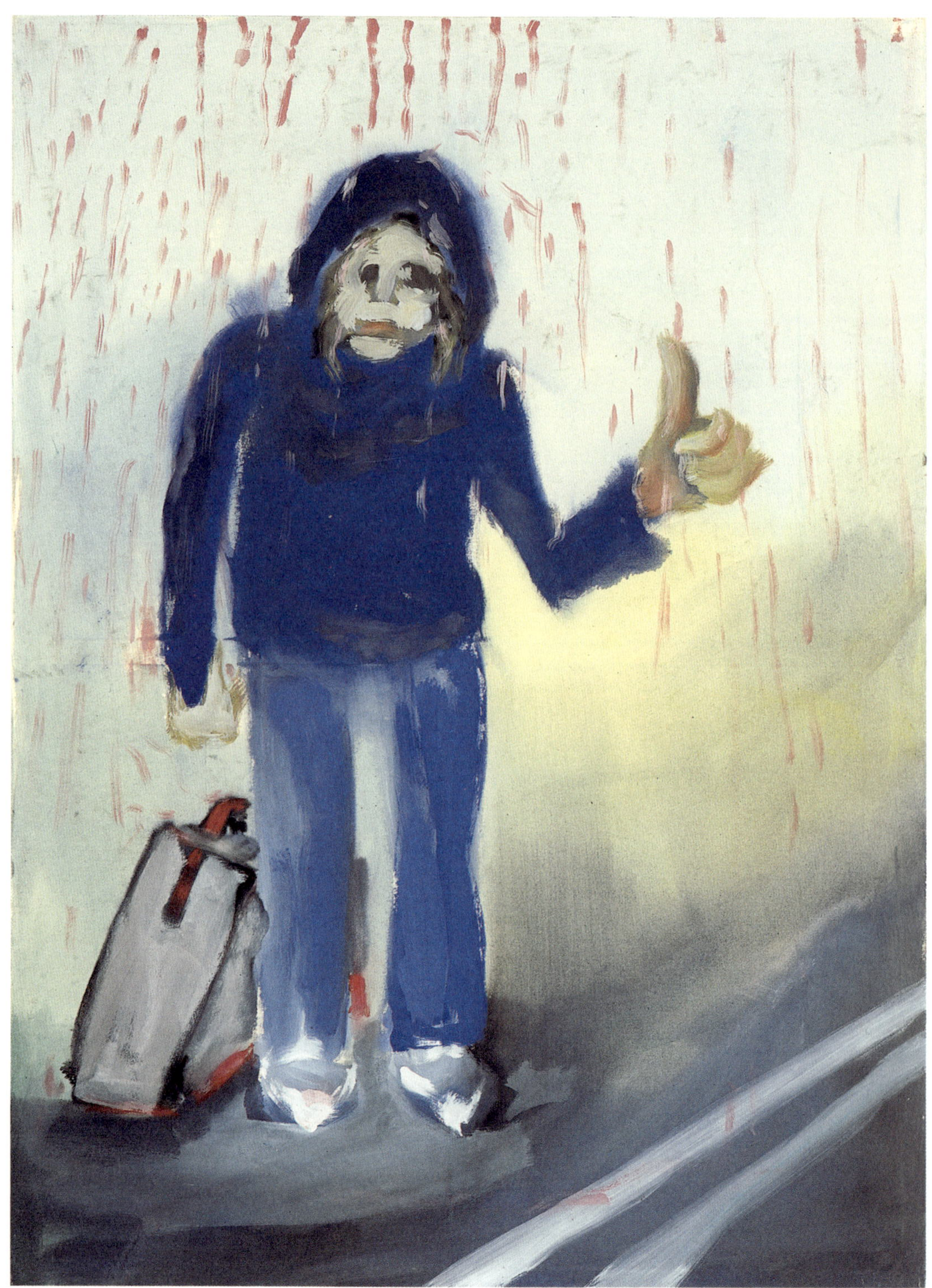

Hitchhiker, 1998

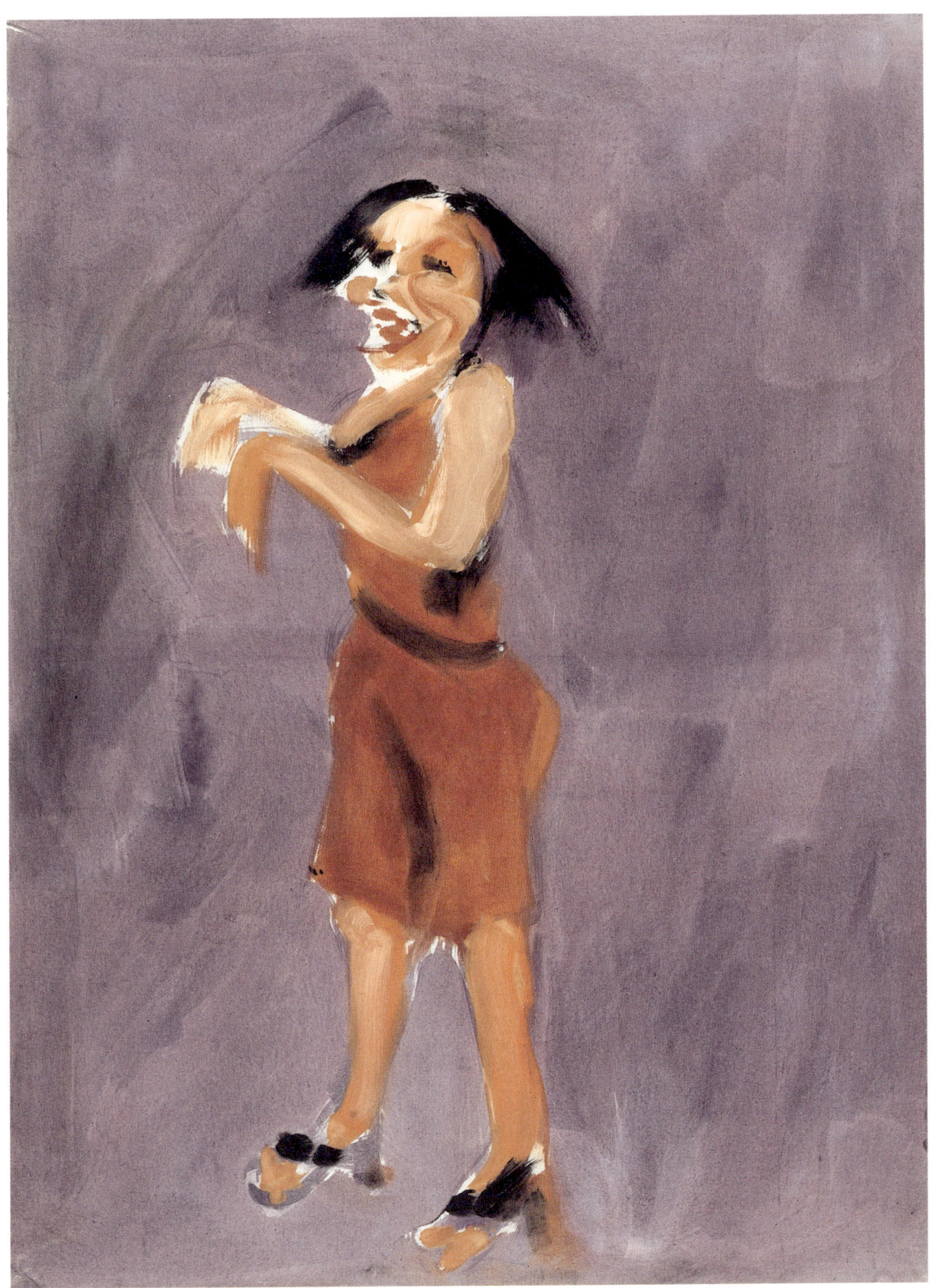

MC Schäfer, 1999

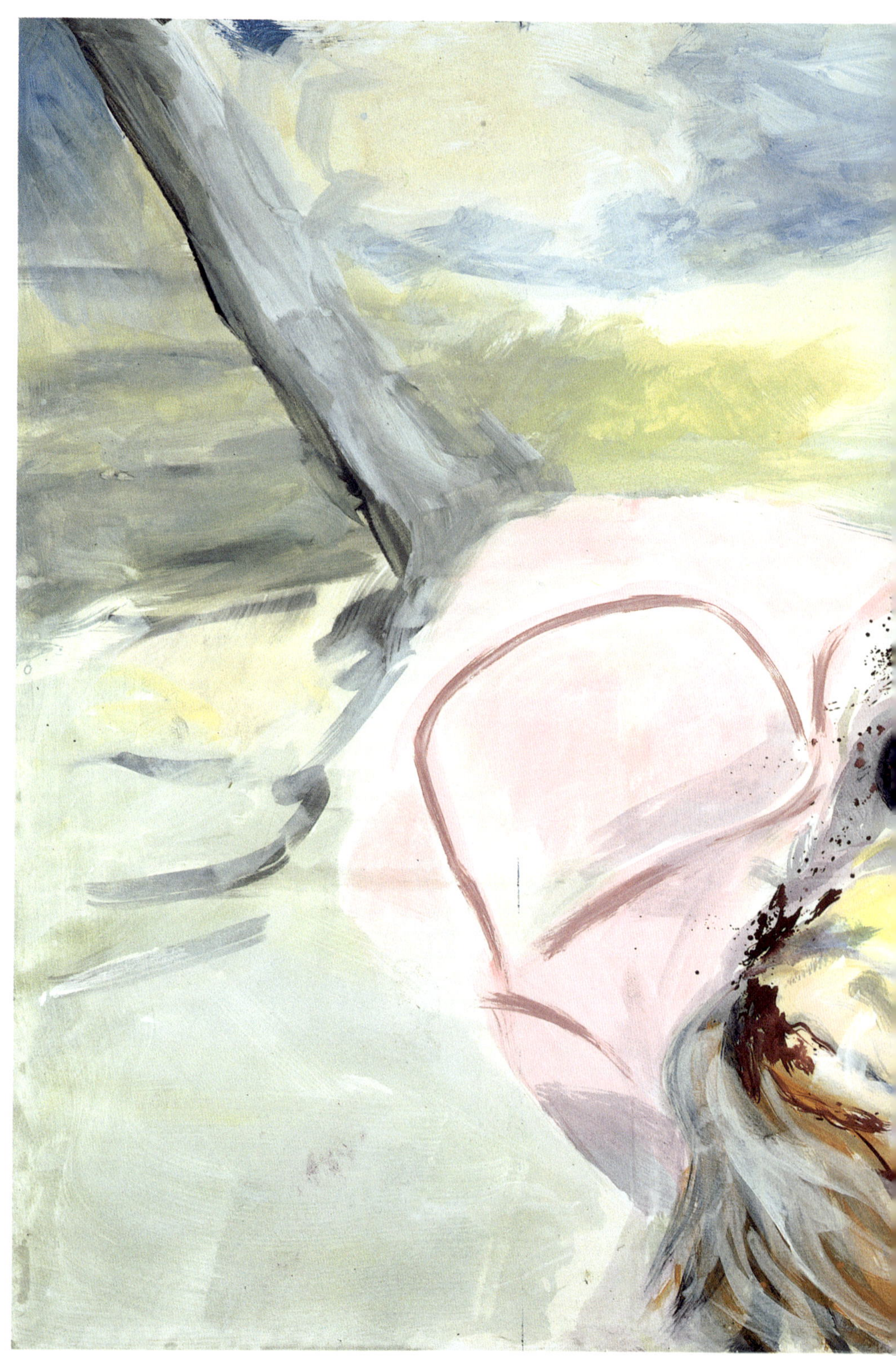

 Car Crash, 1998

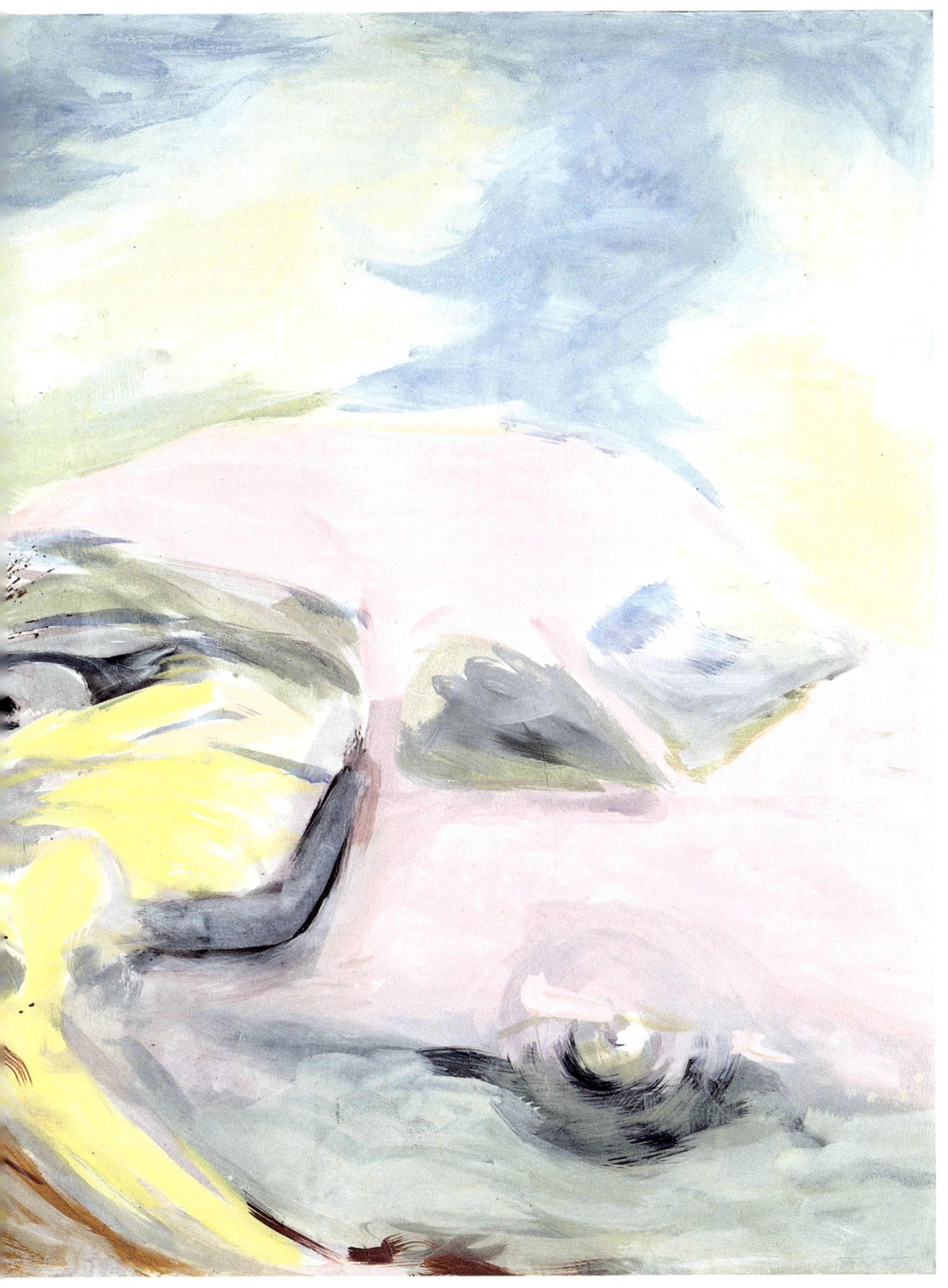

'L'AIR DE RIEN'

To answer the critics who accused him of making simple paintings, Matisse exhibited photographs of his canvases at different stages of completion alongside the finished works, in December 1945 at the Galerie Maeght in Paris, thereby demonstrating the complexity of his working practice. Sixty years and many pictorial revolutions later, critics are still greatly suspicious of facility, or even nonchalance, as displayed in the work of Sophie von Hellermann; indeed, many of the reviews of her exhibitions reveal a general distrust of the 'lightness' of her style. Yet, it is unlikely that she will ever seek to testify to her seriousness using a similar sort of stratagem.

I had seen Sophie von Hellermann's paintings before her 2004 exhibition at the Vilma Gold gallery in London, which I came upon almost by chance. However, it was there that I started to understand her paintings and to like them. In a gallery space that was in the throes of renovation, von Hellermann had installed a series of large-scale works devoted to the final moments of the life of Nico. I did not at first make the connection with the singer, yet the paintings of the tragic but banal adventures of this blonde woman, narrated from one canvas to the next in a style both masterful and negligent, struck me with their audacious fusion of trivial narration and romantic lyricism. The contrast between the monumental scale of her canvases, the licentiousness of her fluid style, and the slight and lightweight subject-matter produced a melancholic drollery which did not in the least compromise the pleasure that von Hellermann seemed to have experienced in painting these pictures, and which she so eloquently managed to convey.

As do other artists of her generation, von Hellermann allows herself to draw from the history of painting and from its progressively acquired liberties in order to trace her singular path. It is not a question, as it was for Kippenberger (often cited as an influence), of deconstructing the modernist project, but rather of 'creating one's own space'.* The modesty of this statement should not lead us to suppose a lack of ambition on von Hellermann's part. From this singular space, she uses painting as an instrument that allows her simultaneously to appropriate and to excuse herself from reality. She does not seek to reproduce the real in order to give an account of it, but to re-invent it in order to better place it under her control. To seek to avoid reproducing the real is not a sign of cowardice, but rather of a form of courage indicated by its exigency and reserve. Each one of Sophie von Hellermann's paintings condenses a story, and contains it perfectly within the limits of the frame, yet it is pierced full of holes from within. These empty spaces imbue her works with their evocative power: a capacity first to absorb the gaze and then to expose both the imagination and the memory to sensation.

The subject-matter of her essentially narrative paintings is at the intersection of a personal and a collective history, without there being any clear boundaries between the two. Given her casualness, some are surprised at her ability to deal with subjects as serious as Einstein and the Red Army Faction. No topic is any more serious than any other for von Hellermann; there is only a contamination and simultaneous construction of the individual and the collective, reality and fiction.

La liseuse de romans [The reader of novels] (1853) is a painting by the romantic *pompier* painter Antoine Wiertz. It depicts a languorous young girl in the nude, book in hand, surrounded by novels discreetly placed by a devil hidden under her bed. This stigmatisation of women lost by or in fictional narratives is still relevant today. Sophie von Hellermann reminds me of this 'reader of novels', albeit one who has now moved to the other side of the easel. Like Karen Kilimnik or Lily van der Stokker before her, she deliberately claims for herself a host of clichés pejoratively linked to femininity: light-mindedness or even frivolity, nonchalance, precosity, absent-mindedness or sentimentality, all of which she assumes under the guise of soft provocation. To this day, gravity, realism, and a certain serious or pragmatic mind-set are the values which determine the critical respect accorded to a work of art. Sophie von Hellermann does not spurn these 'values' out of naïveté or superficiality; rather, she is trying to breach a pictorial tradition which she knows inside out. Rapid execution, a prolific output, a casual style, narratives which blend quotidian life with situations taken from literature or history, a permanent confusion of the trivial and the grandiose – these are the instruments which she uses to transgress the rules of propriety in painting. Yet, she does not display the insignias of rebellion. Instead, with elegance and perversity, she gives her subversive activity an inoffensive and almost charming façade. Behind the young romantic girl hides a pioneer all the more threatening for her ability to fuse seduction and provocation into the same gesture, the same ambiguous and delightful trap.

Anne Pontégnie

* Conversation with Jemima Montagu in Dear Painter, Paint me…, exhibition catalogue (Paris: Éd. Du Centre Pompidou, 2002).

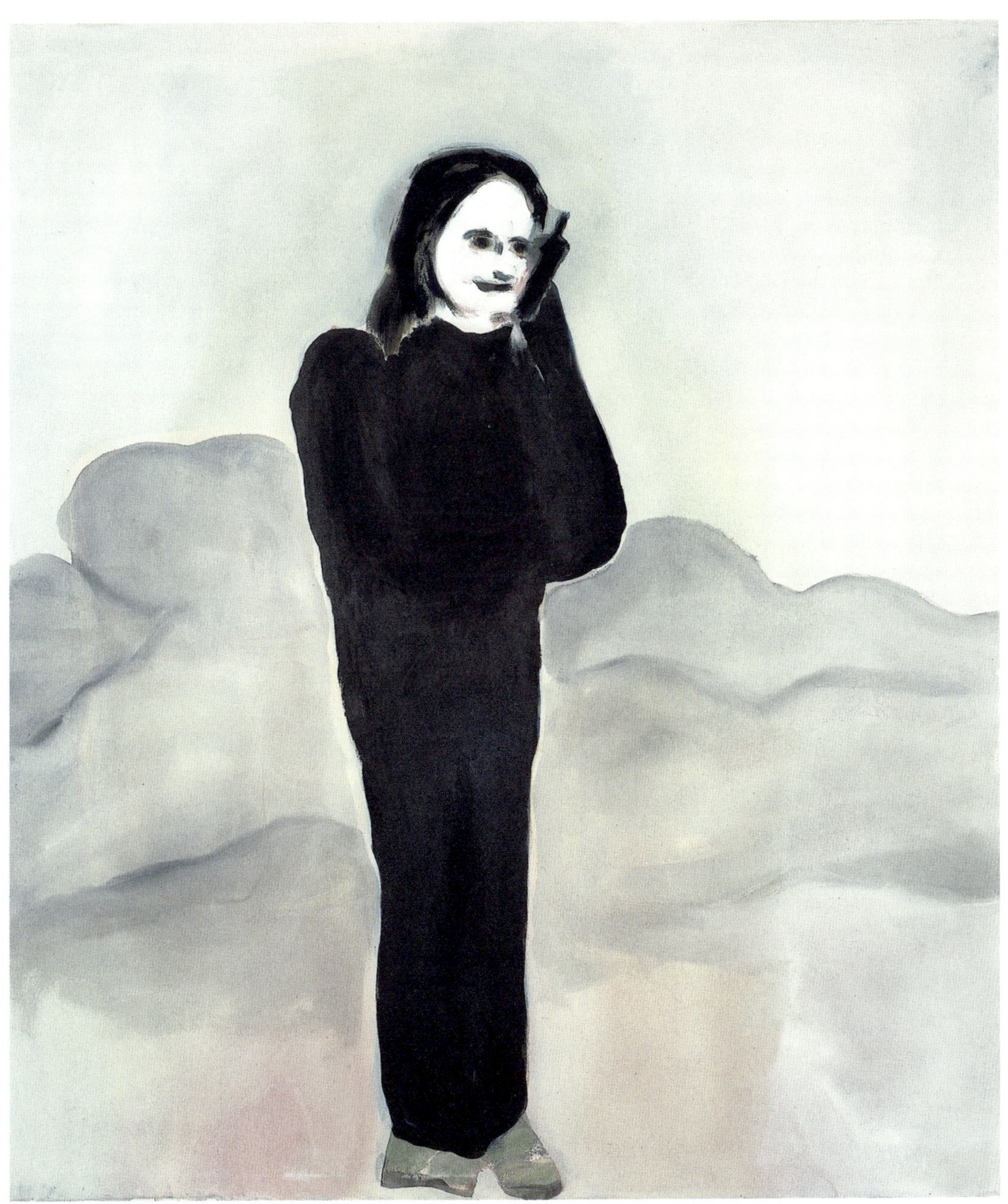

Goth on the Phone, 1999

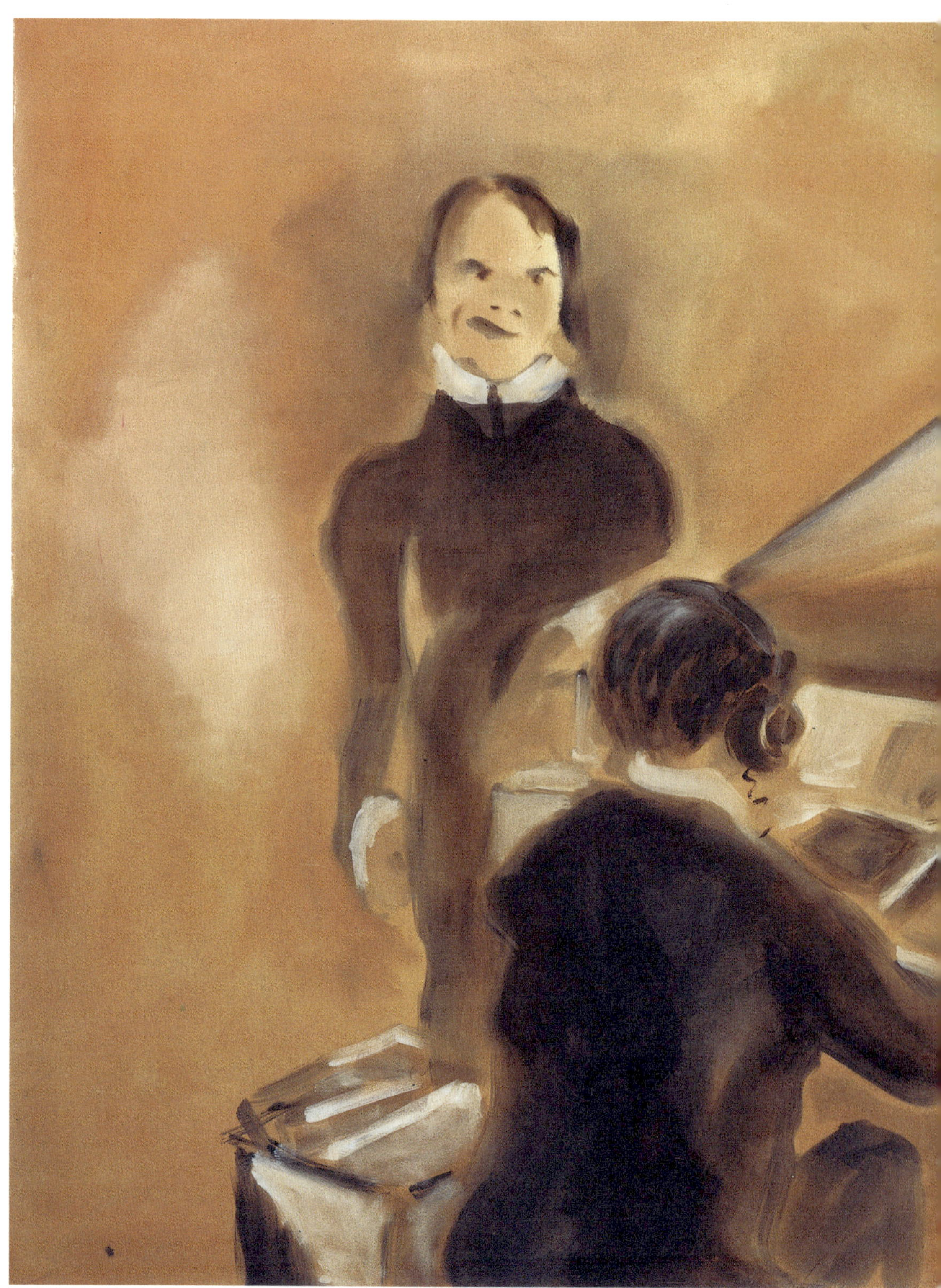

Memory Hotel, 1999

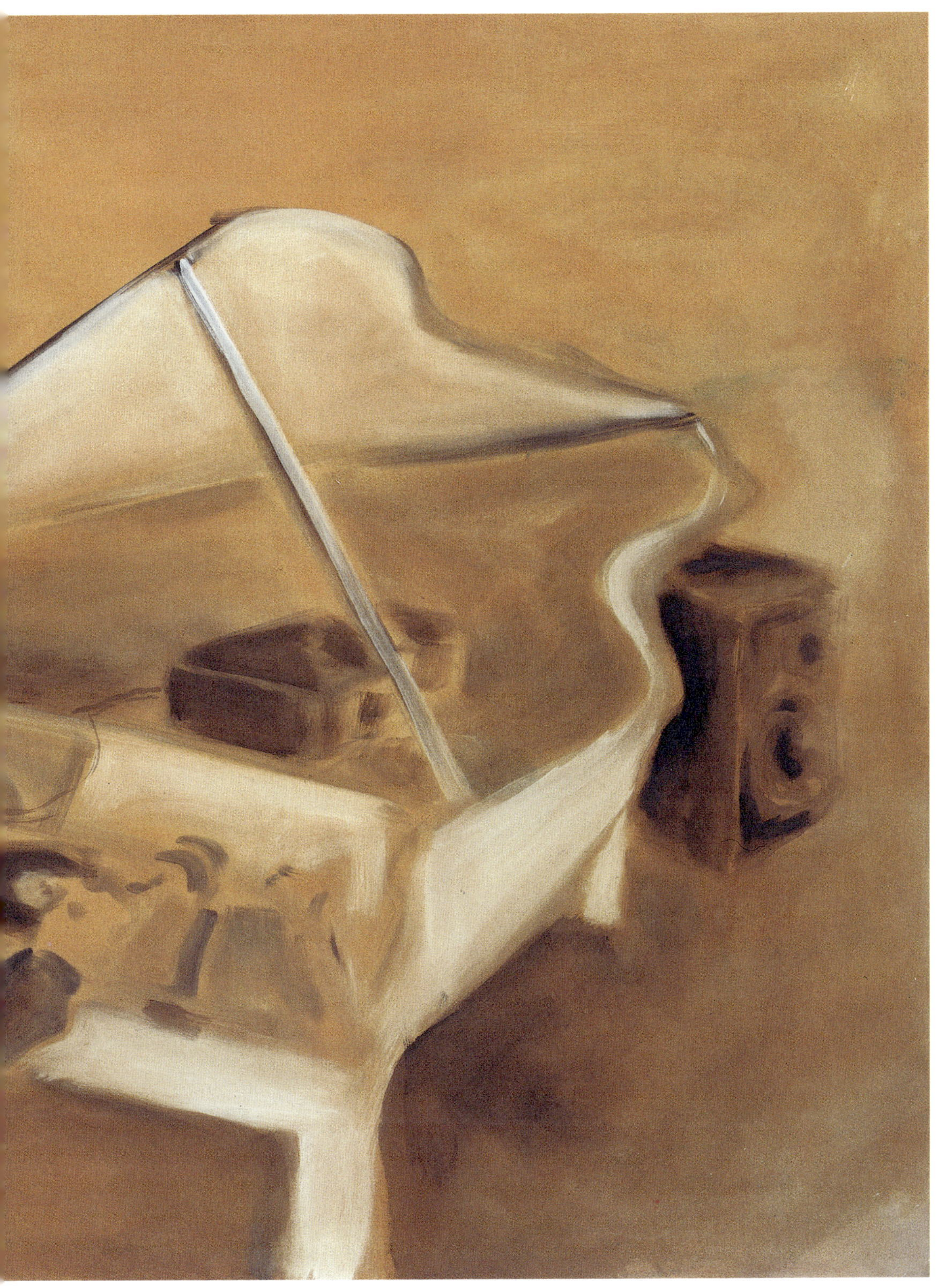

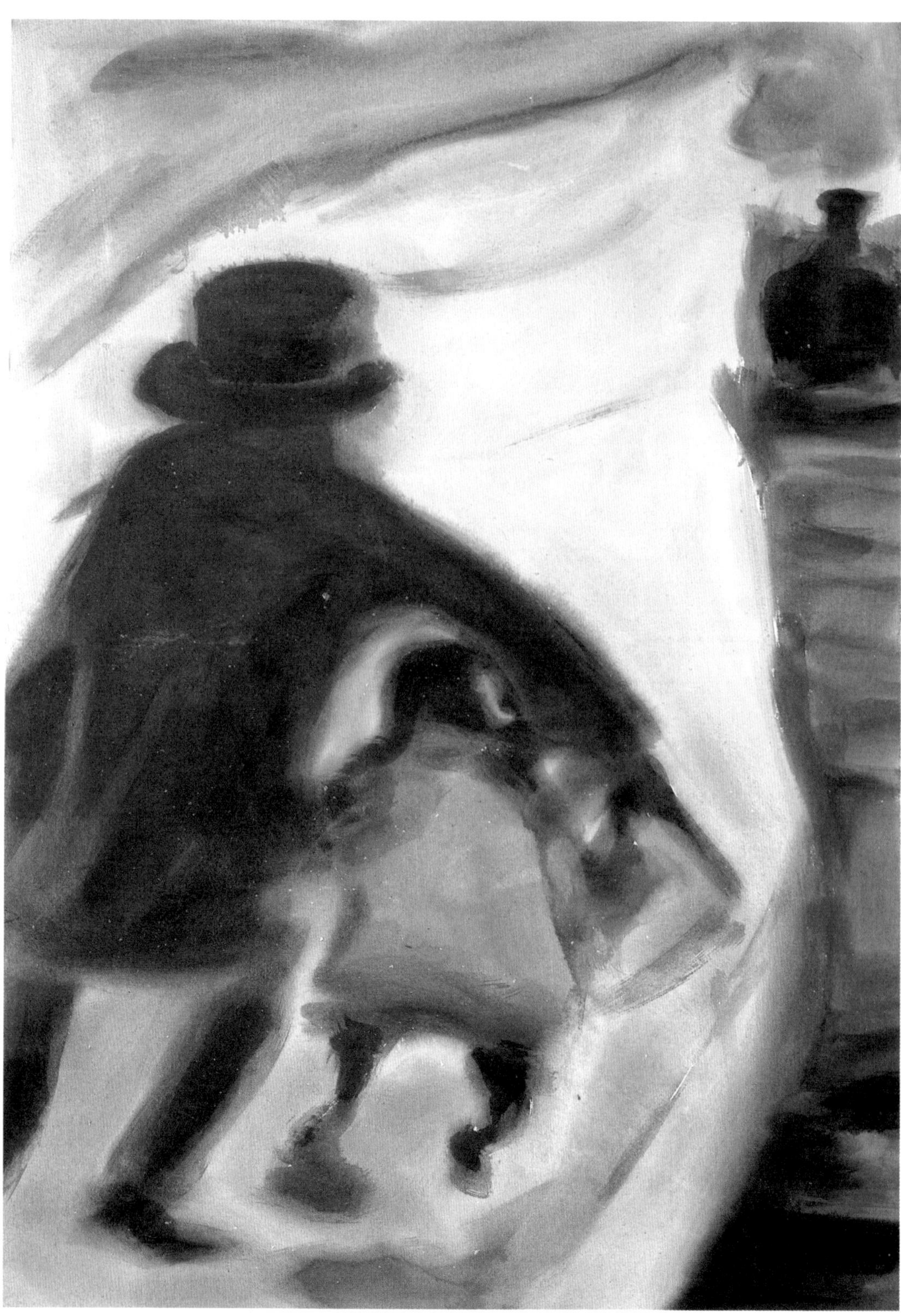

Anastasia at the Station, 2000

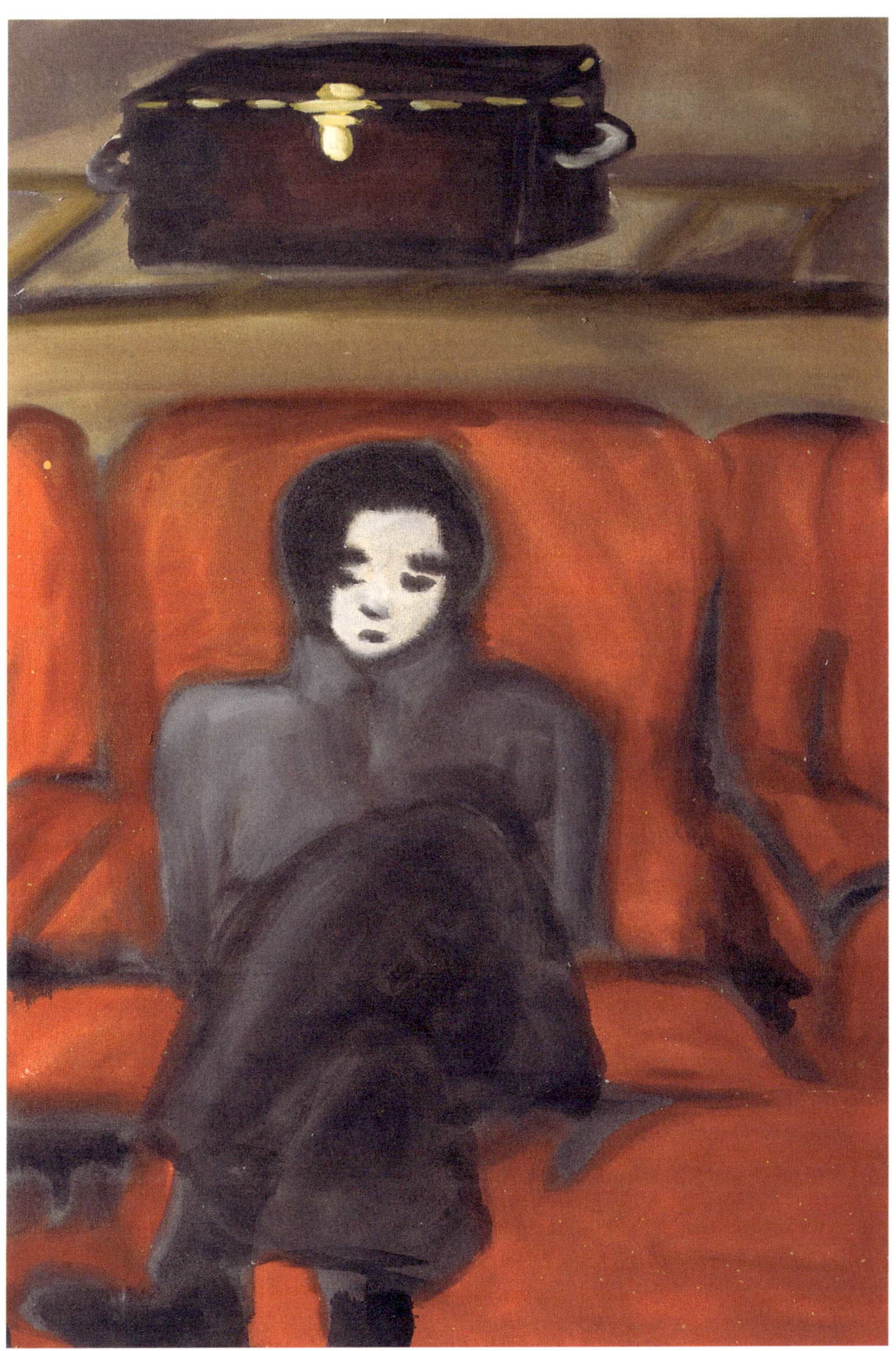

Anastasia on the Train, 2000

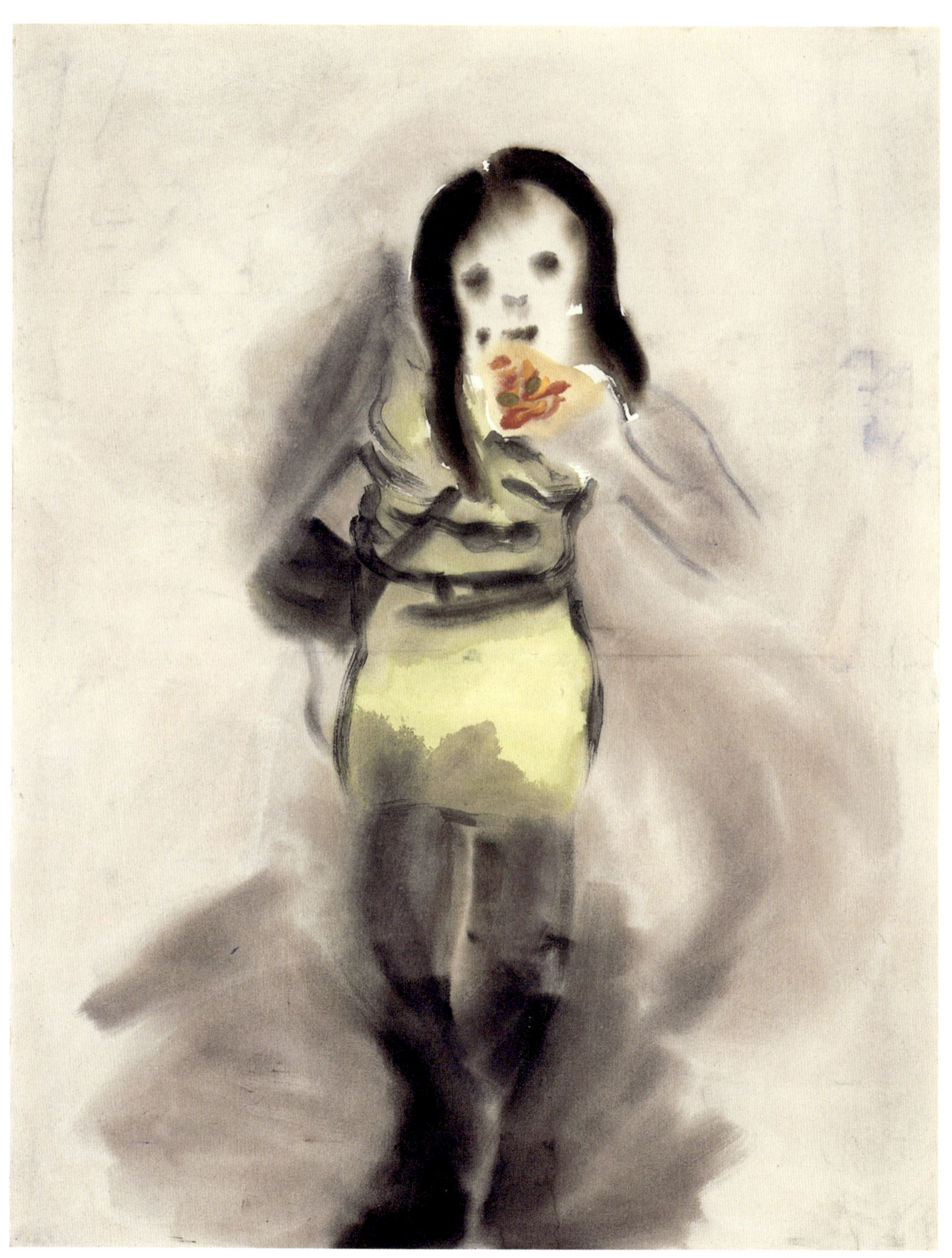

Anastasia in Cleveland, 2000

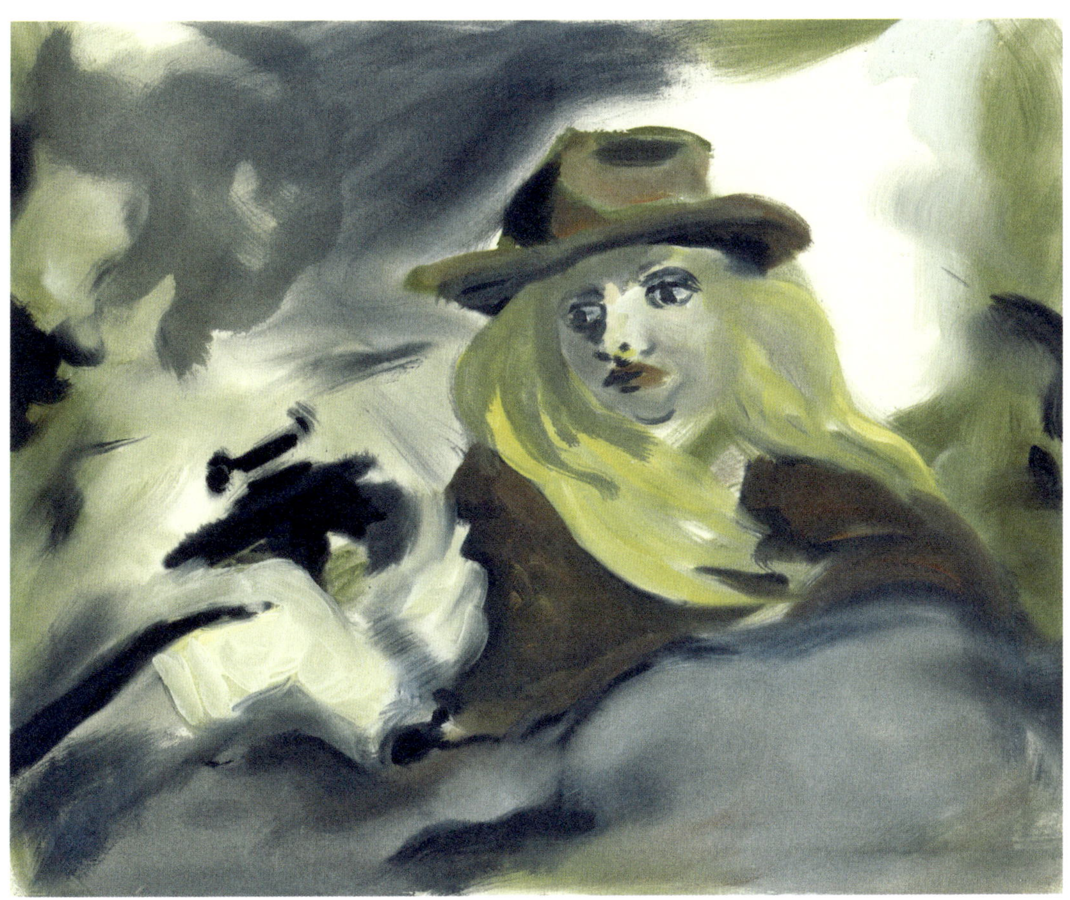

Shoot Him!, 2000

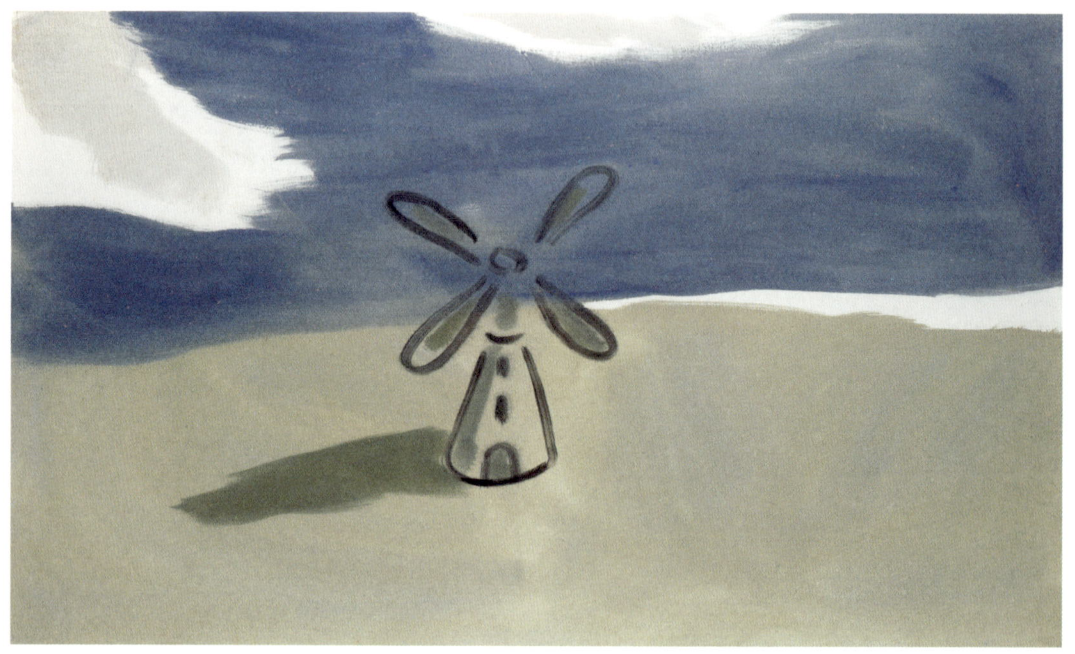

Dutch Landscape, 2001

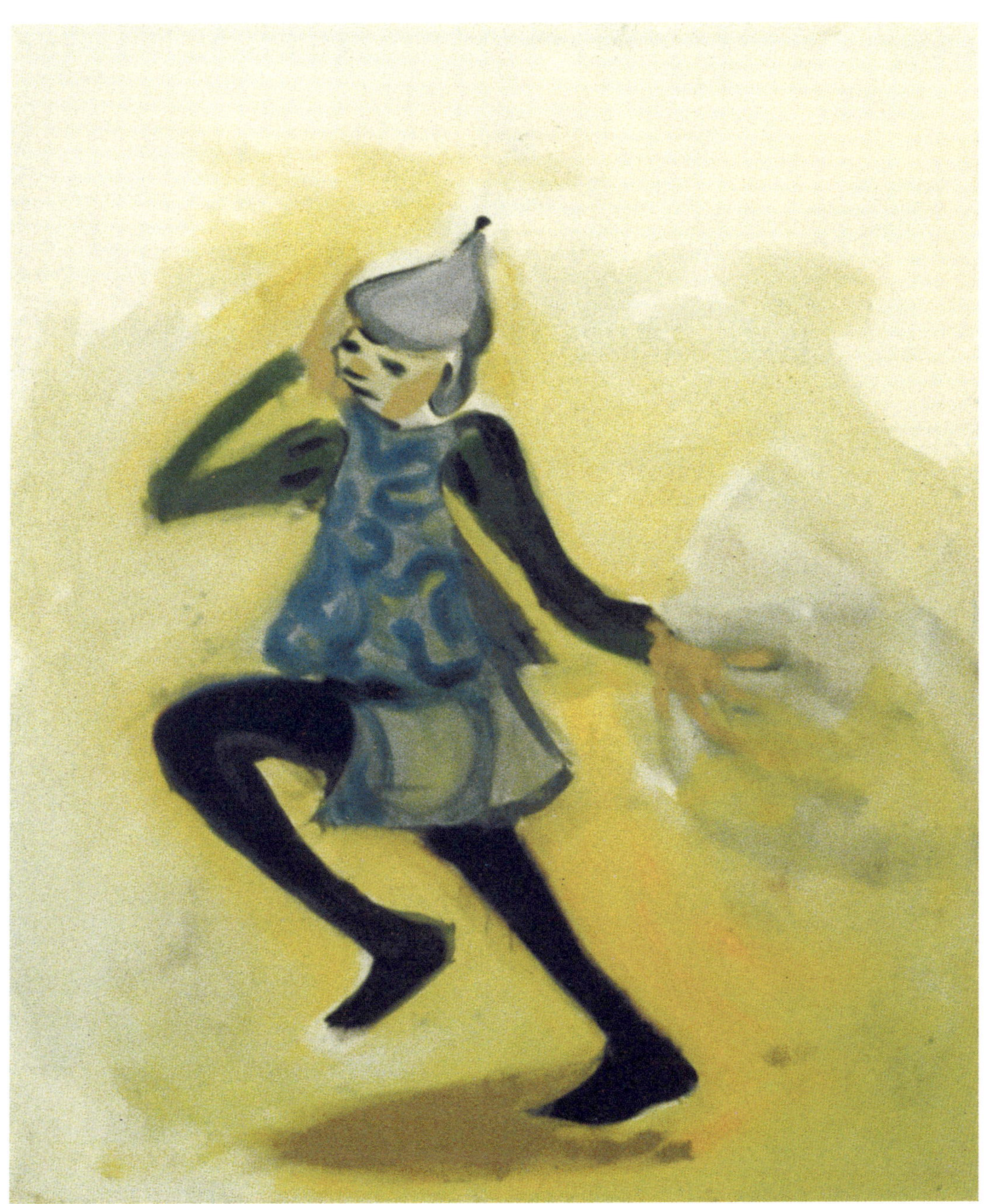

Emotional Rescue, 1999

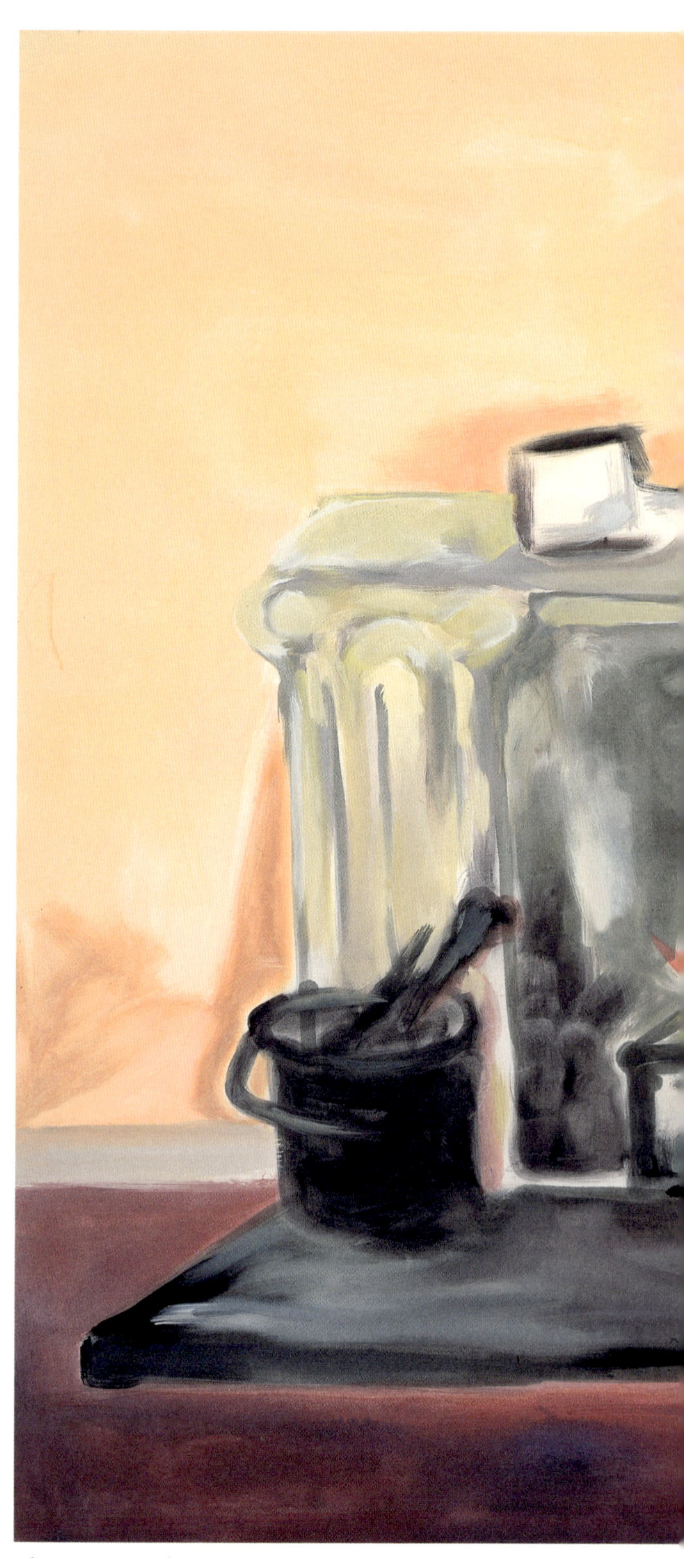

I love Boys, Girls, Music, Art, Pleasure…, 2000

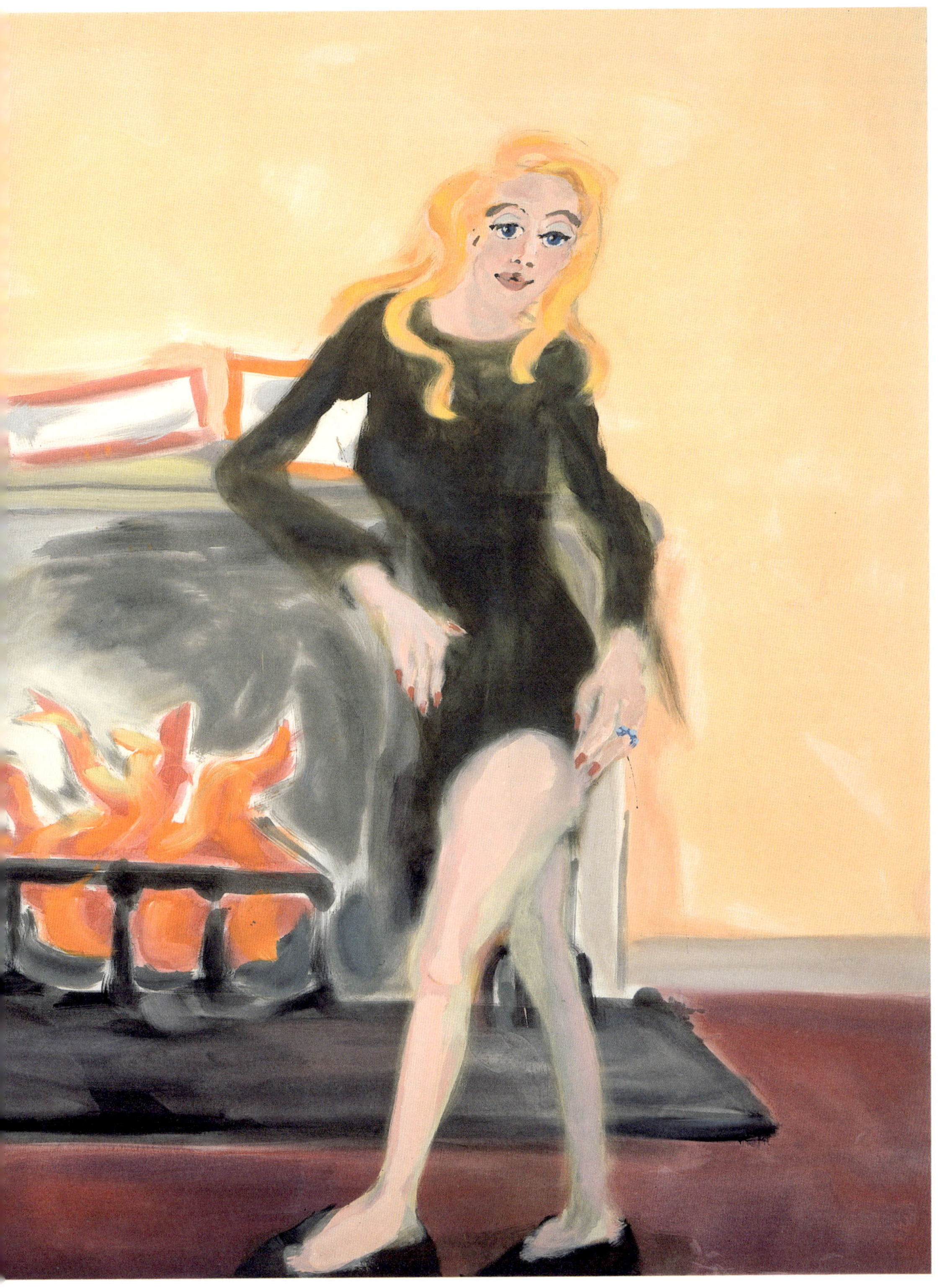

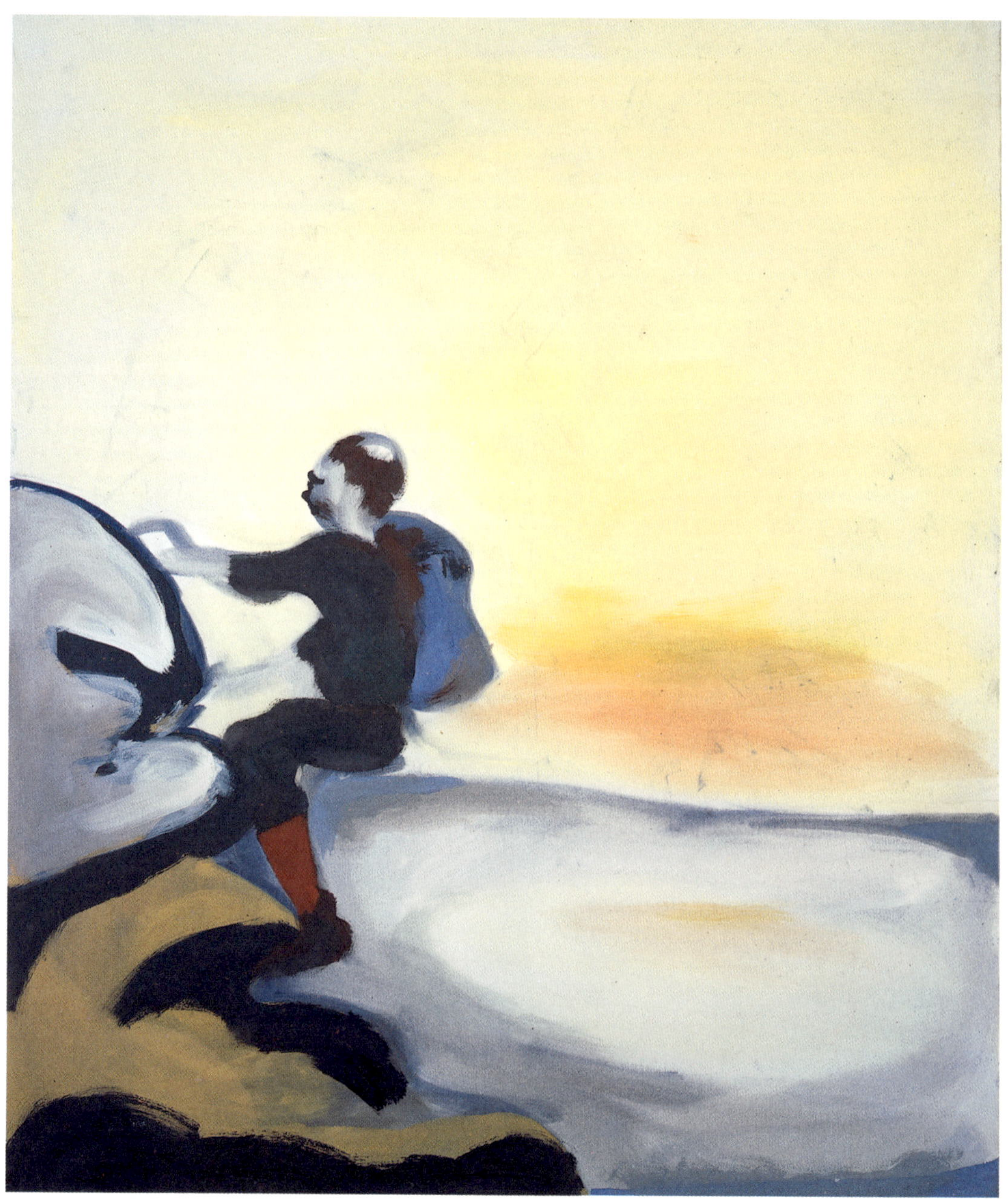

Heidegger, 2000

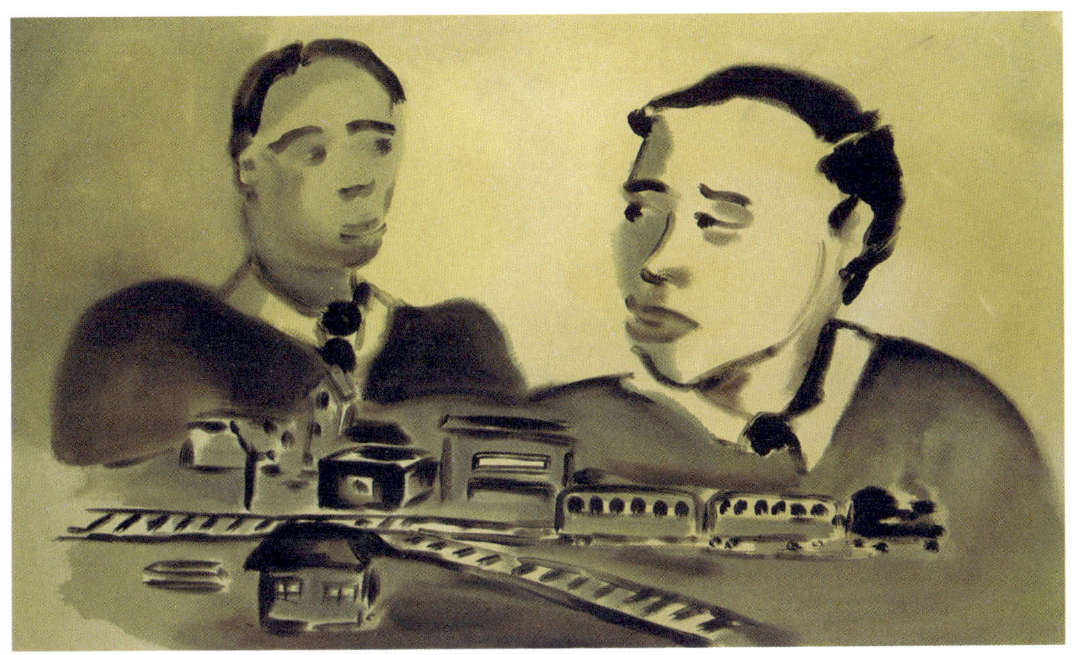

Karl und Franz, 2000

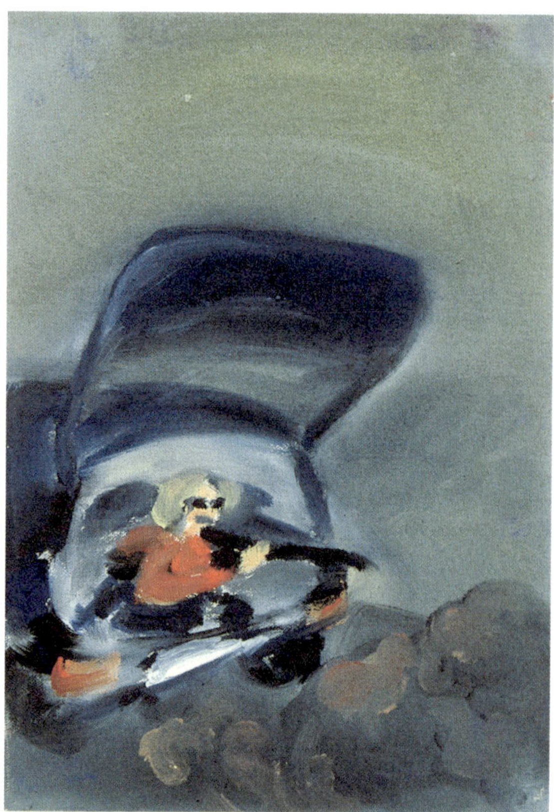

Housewife Terrorism, 2000

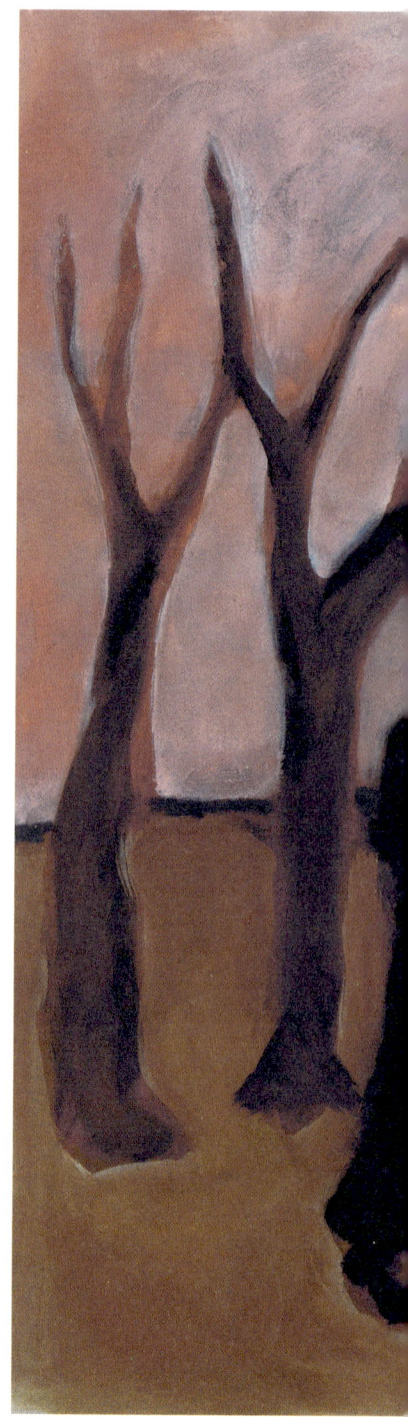

Mourning Electro, 2000

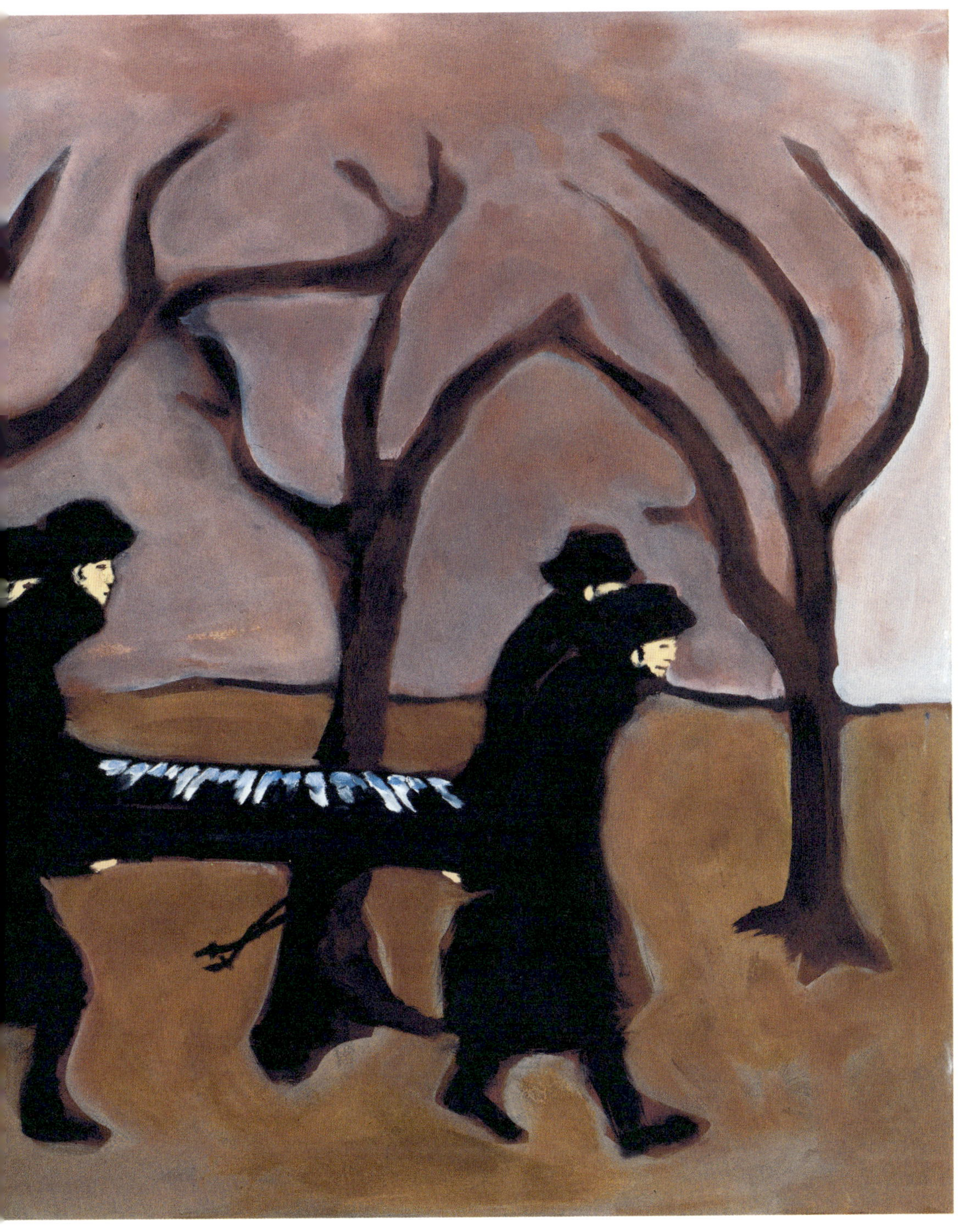

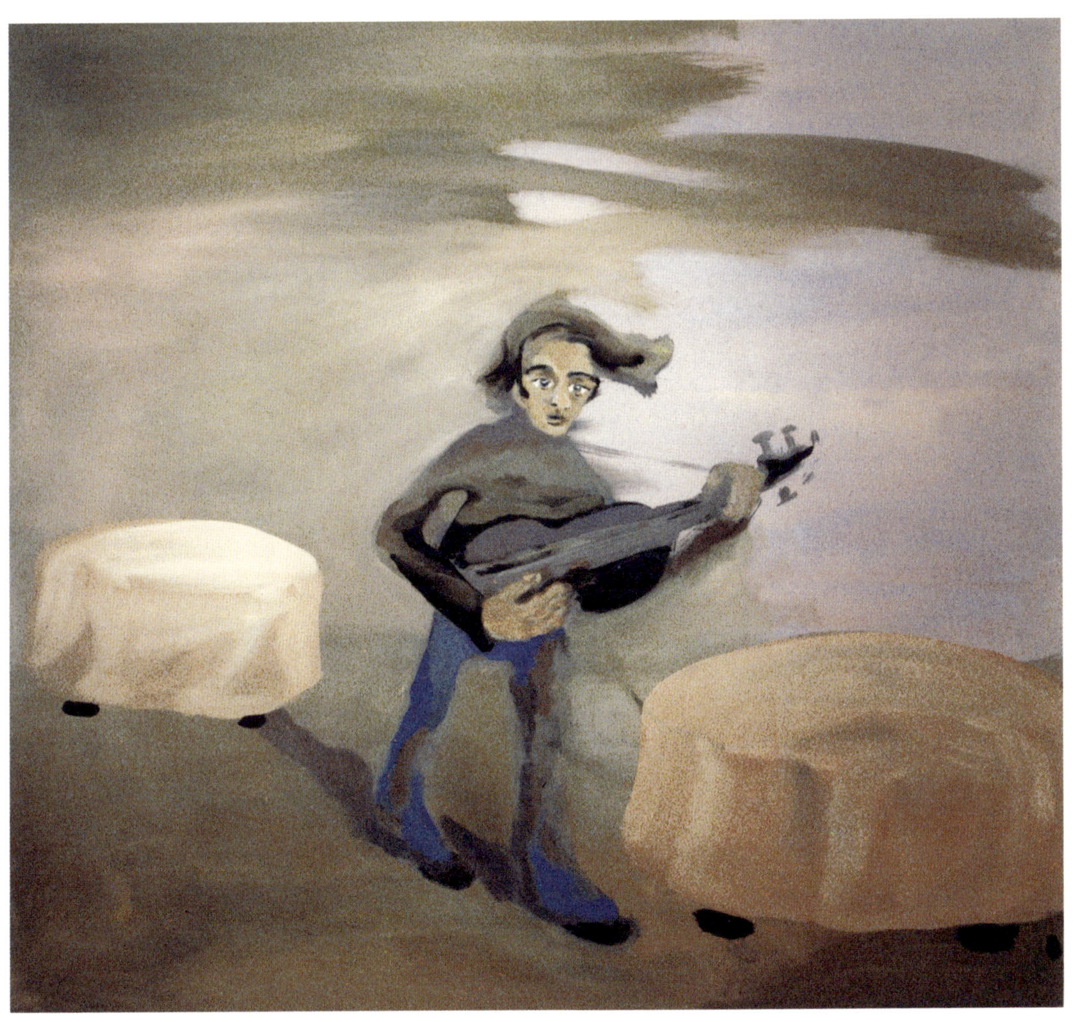

Solo Album, 2000

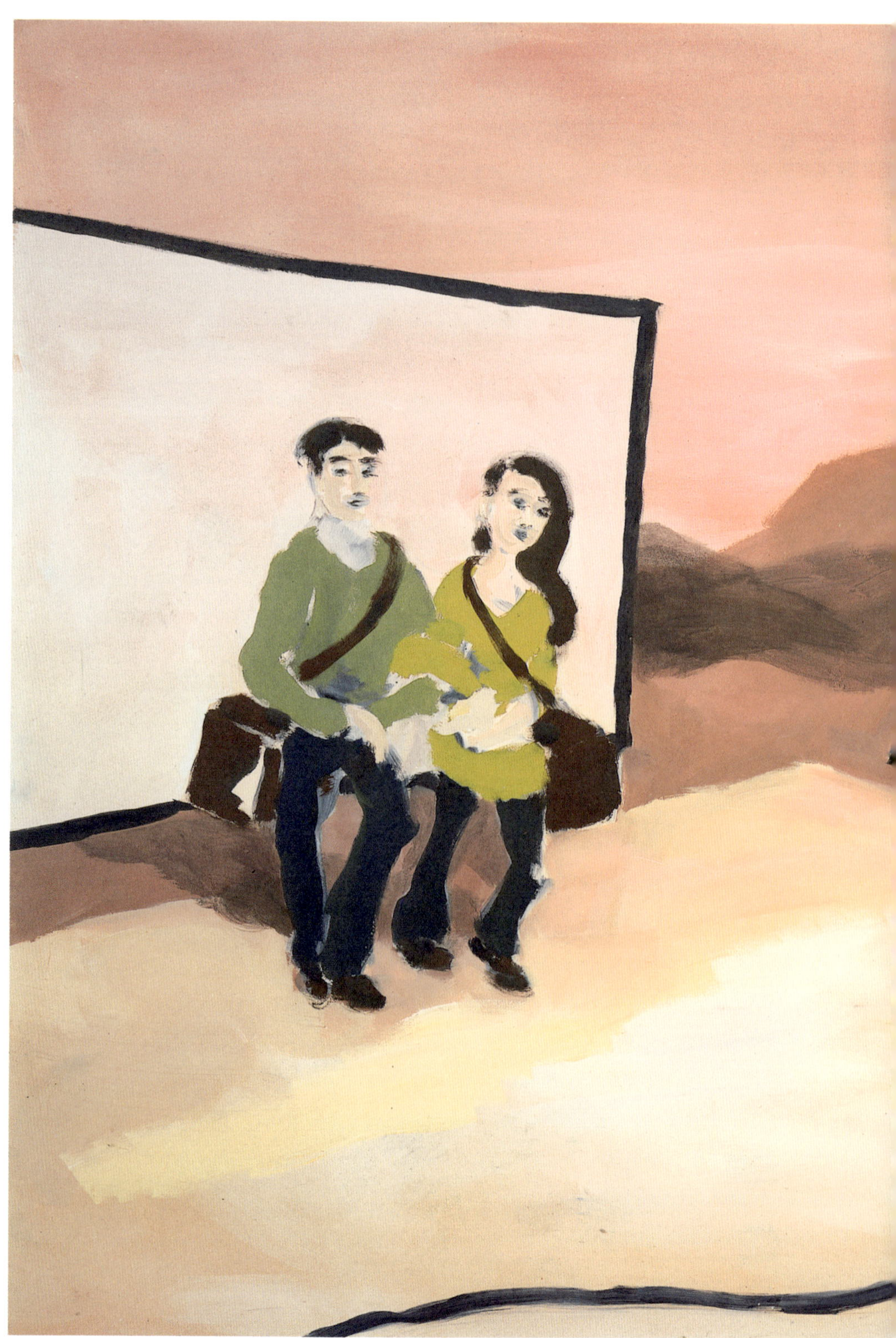

46   *On set go,* 2000

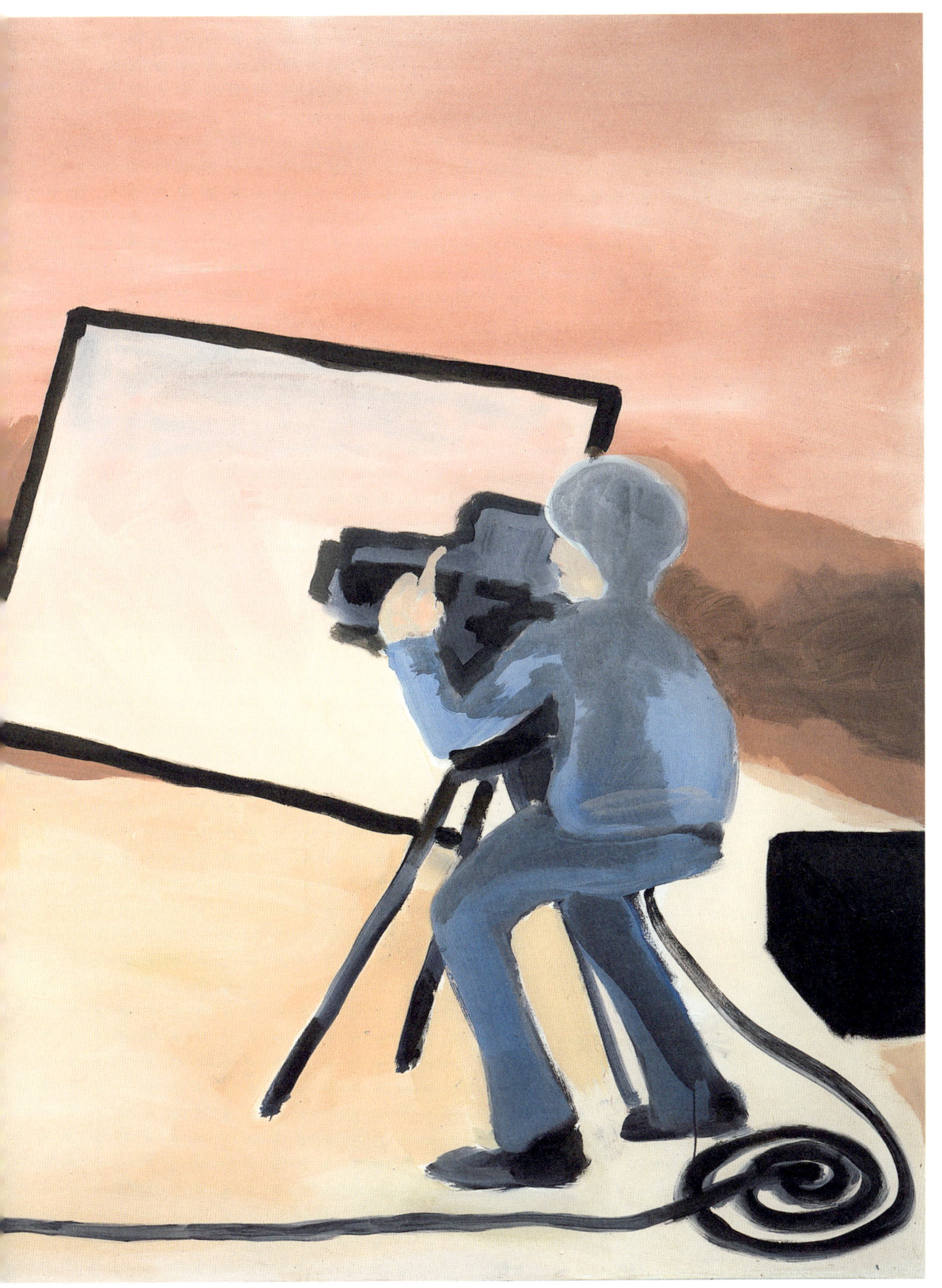

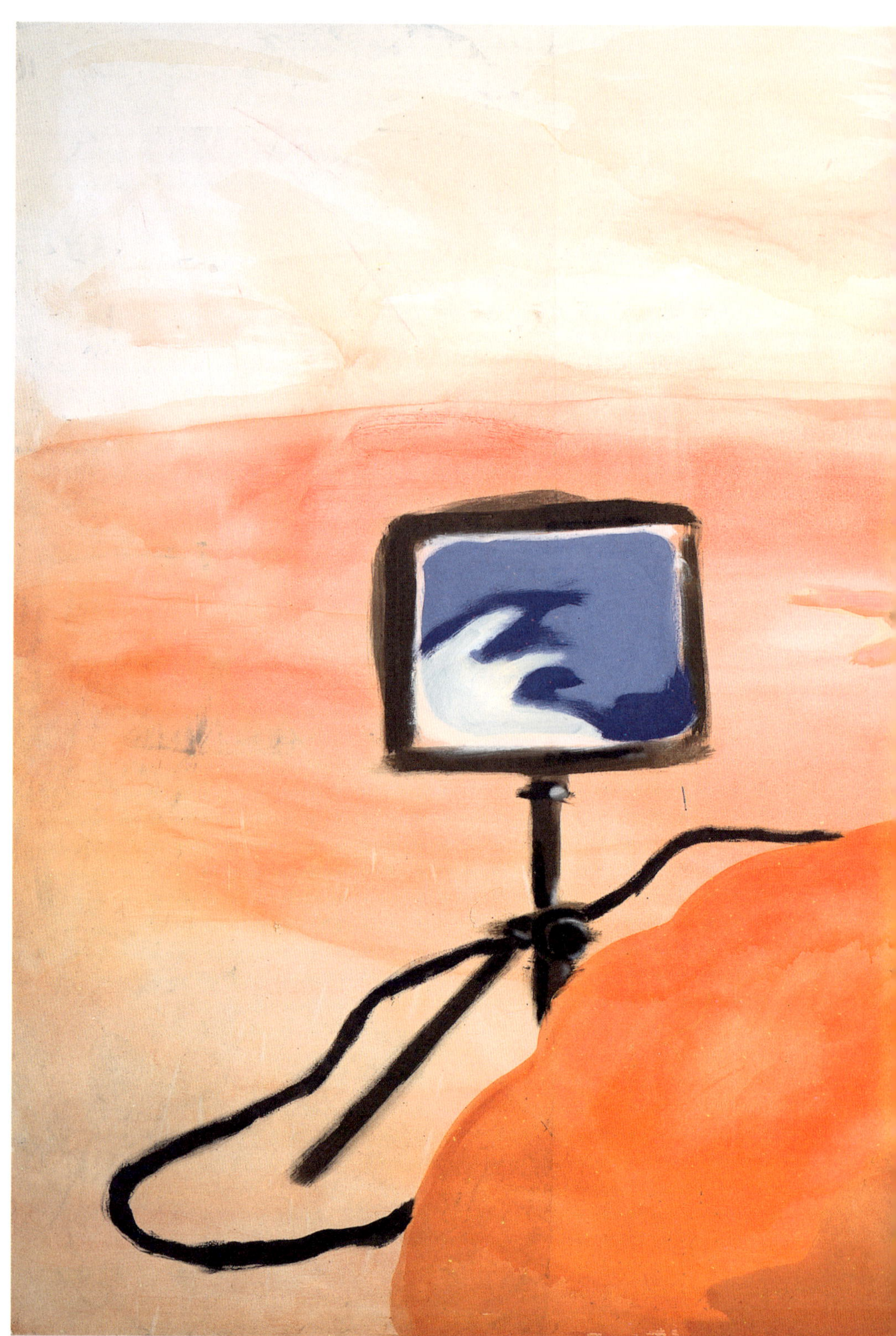

  postproductionerds, 2000

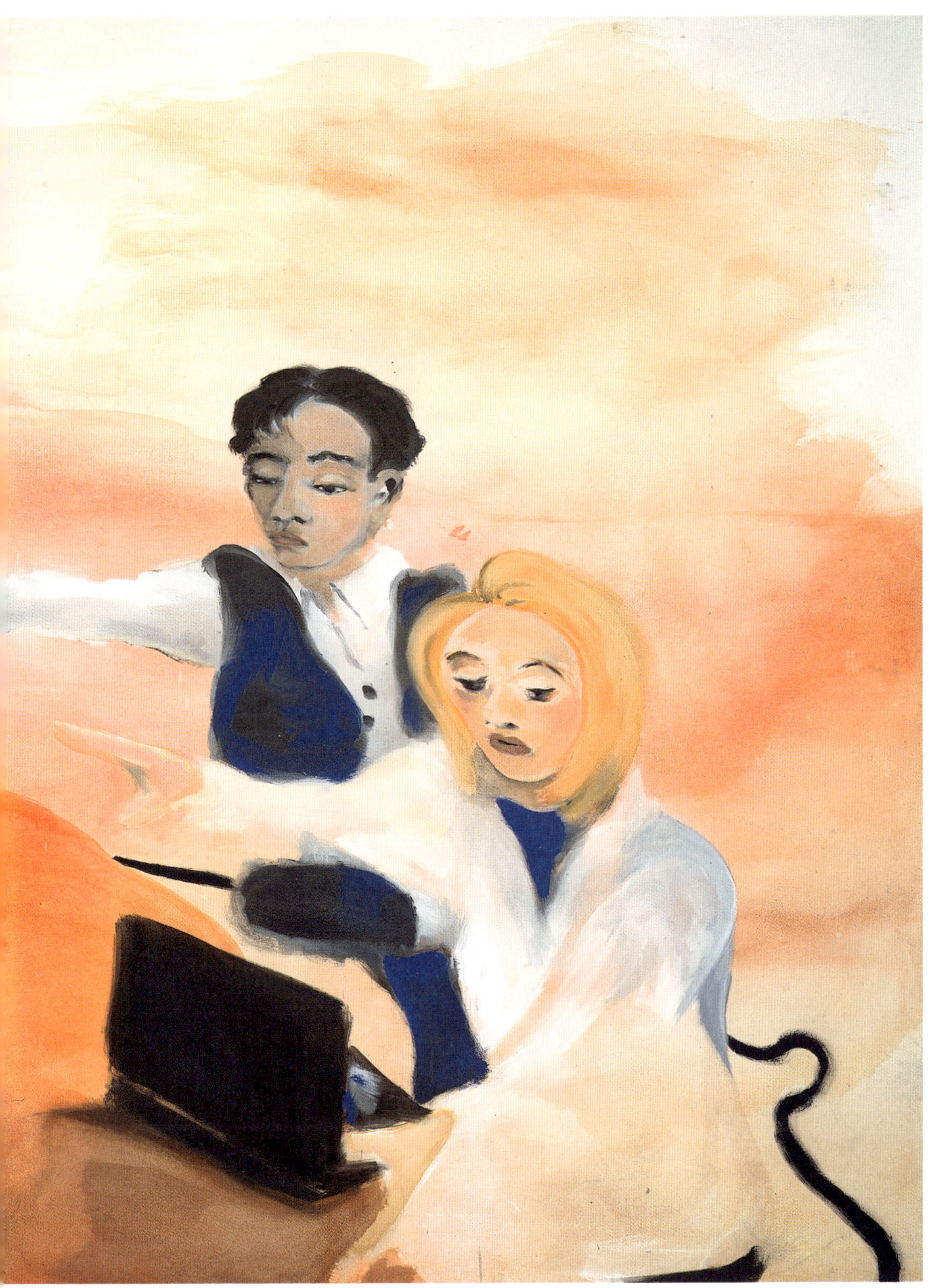

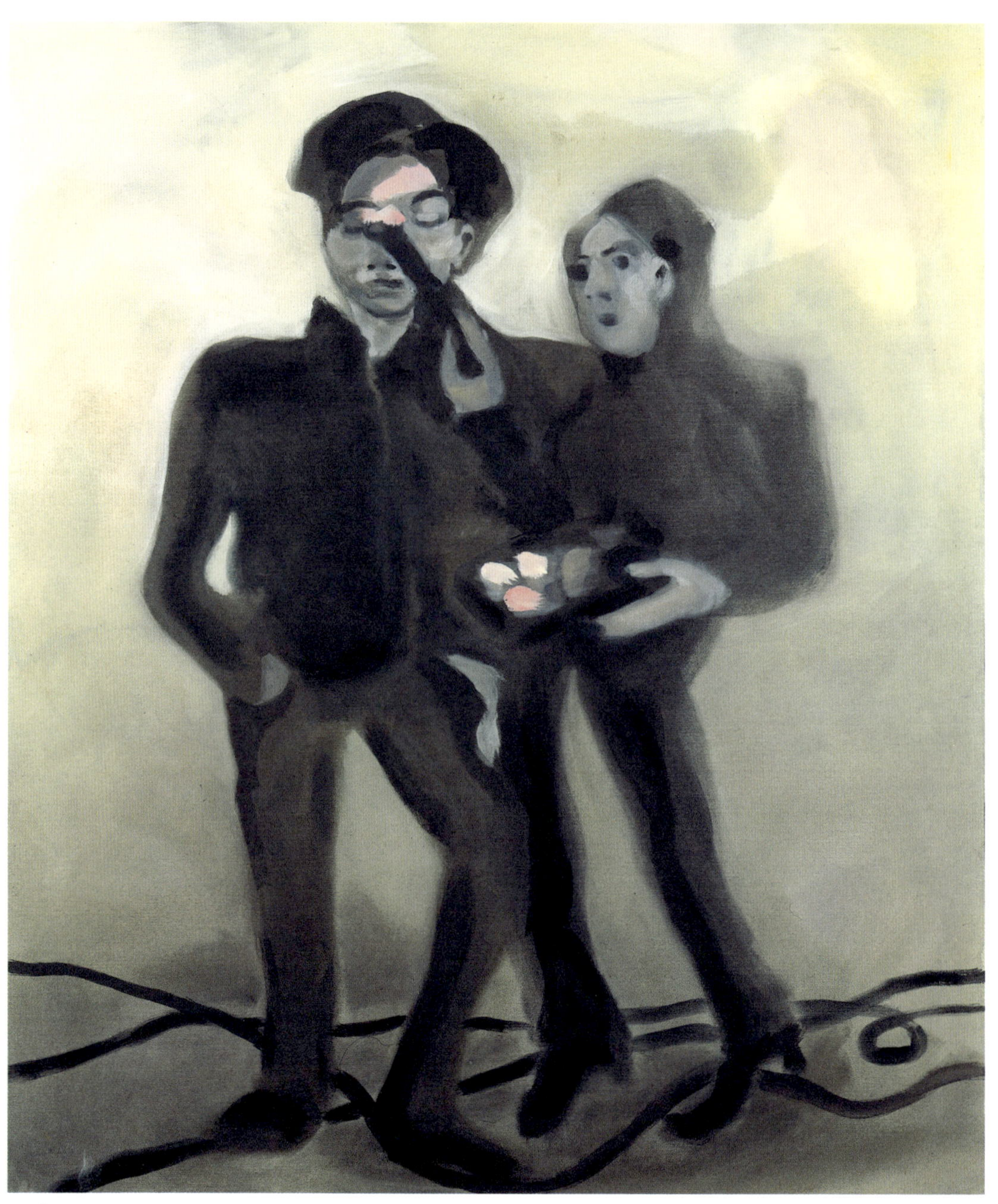

Make-up Artist, 2000

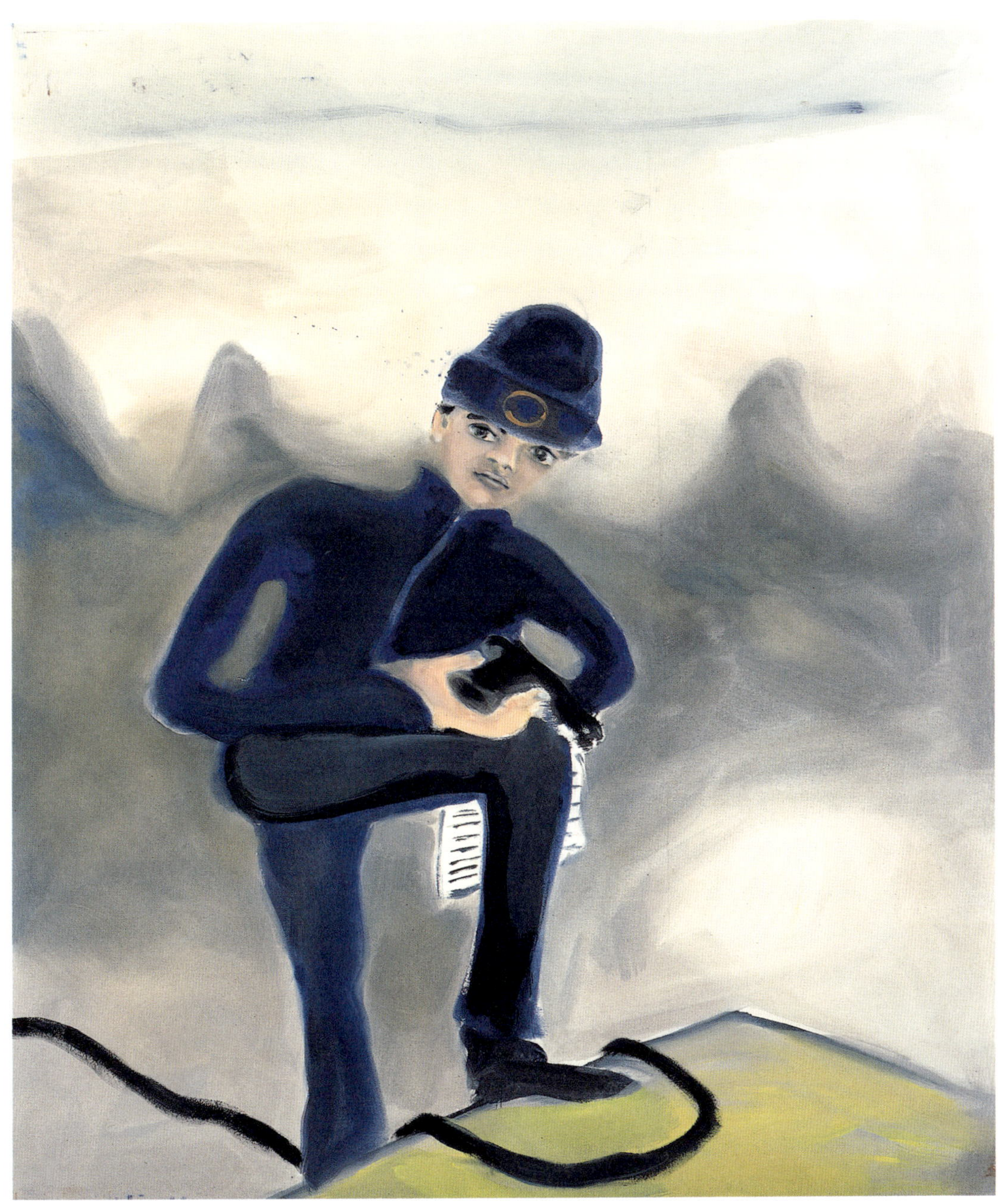

Main Actor I, 2001

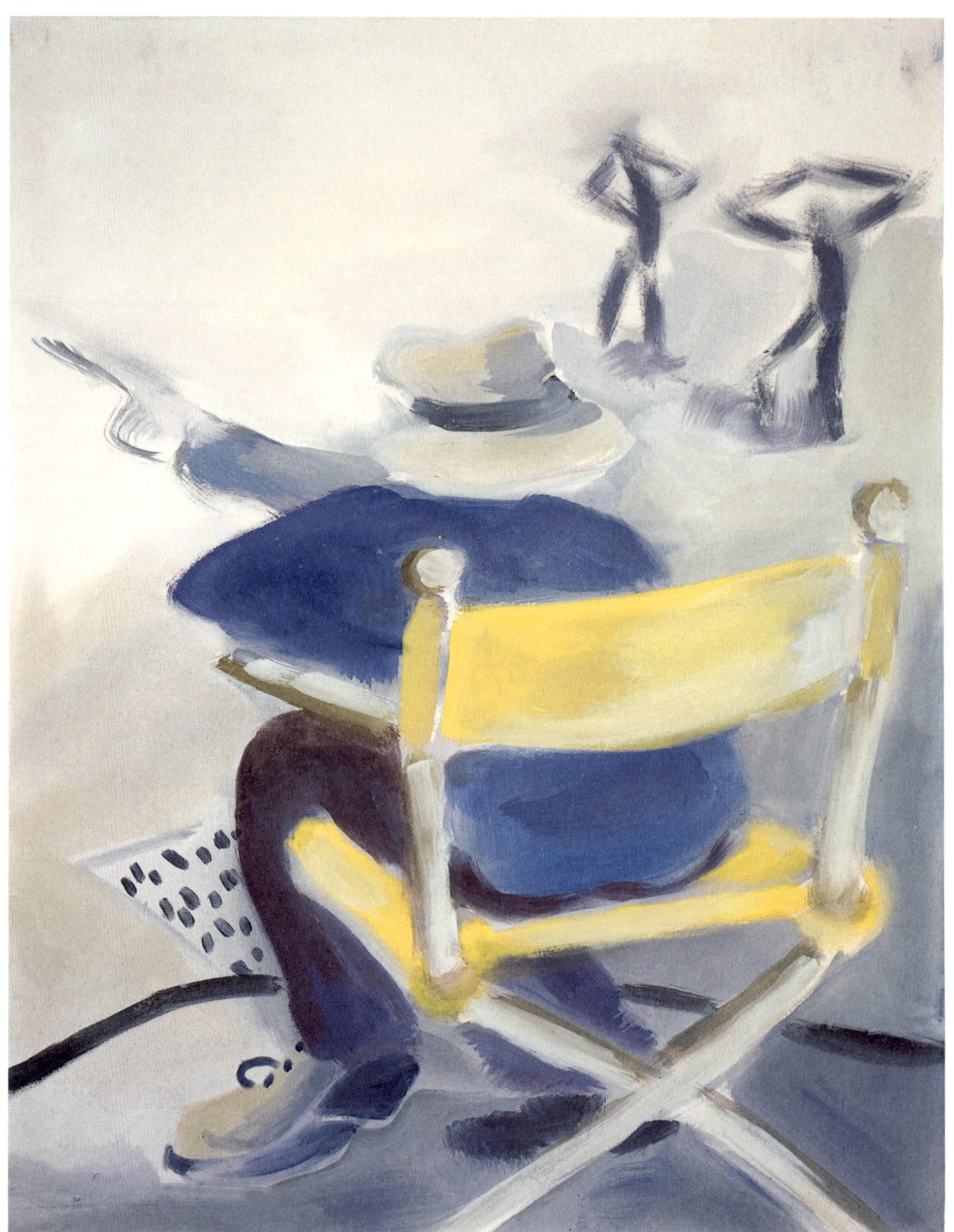

Director, 2001

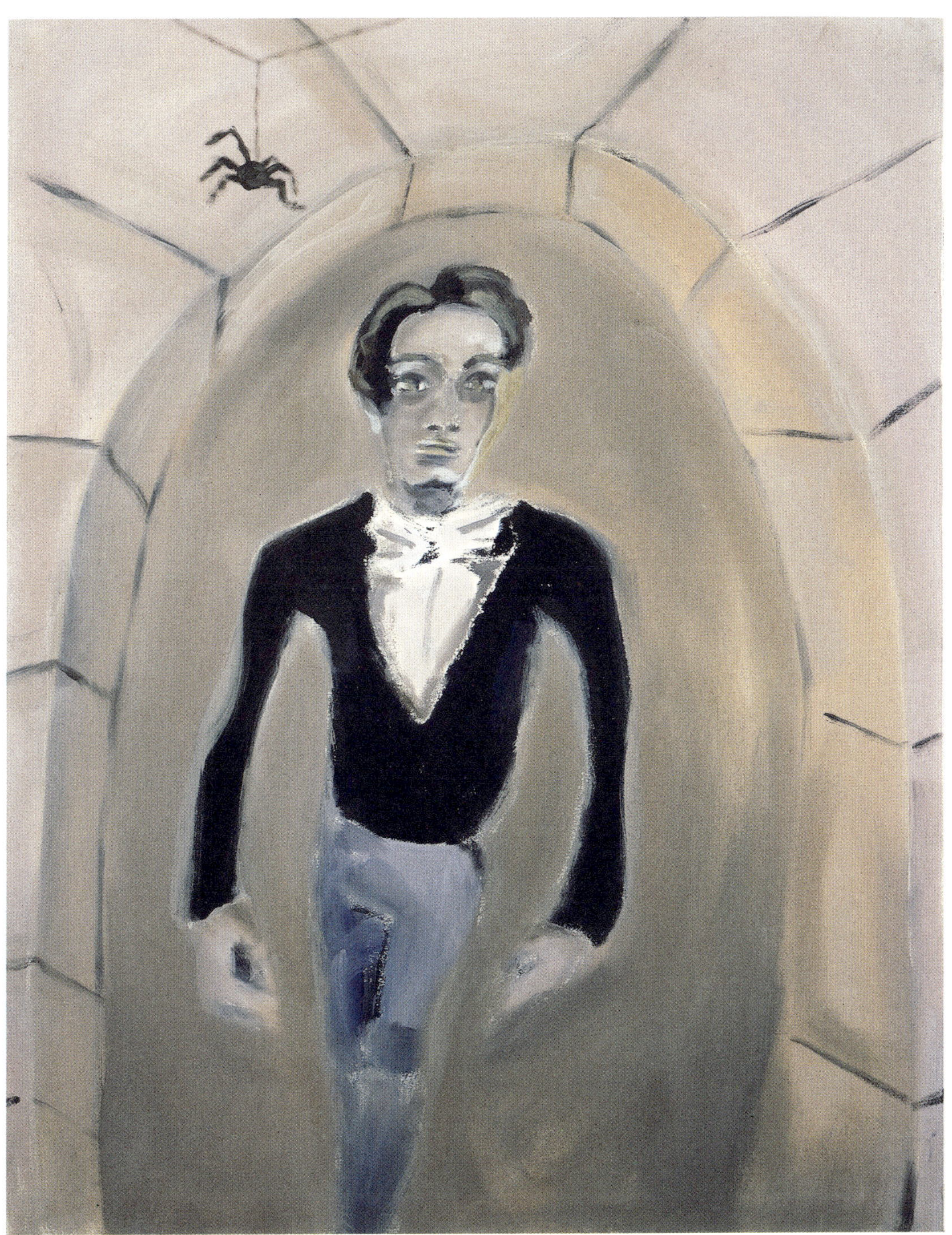

Main Actor II, 2001

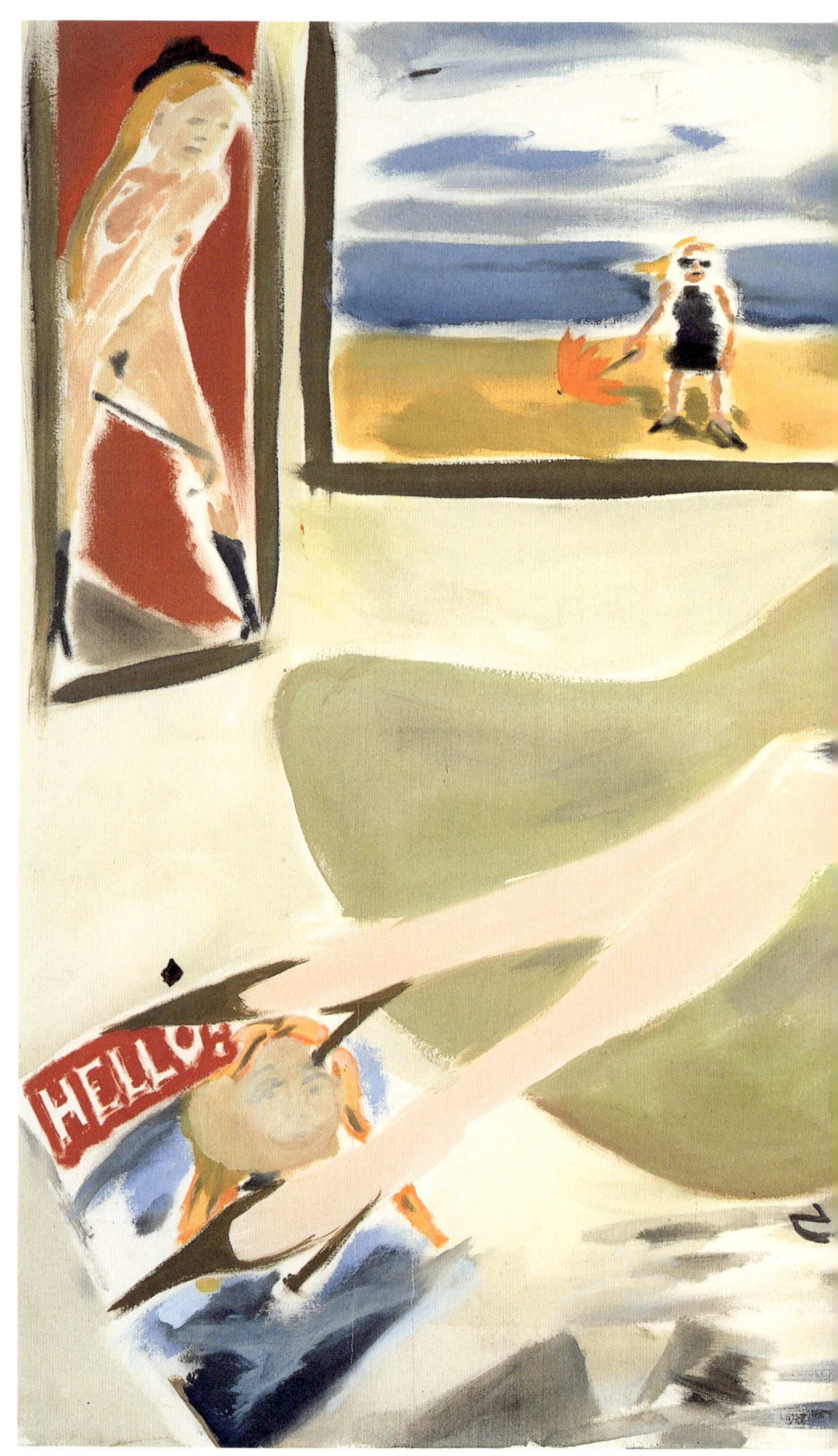

  Leading Lady, 2001

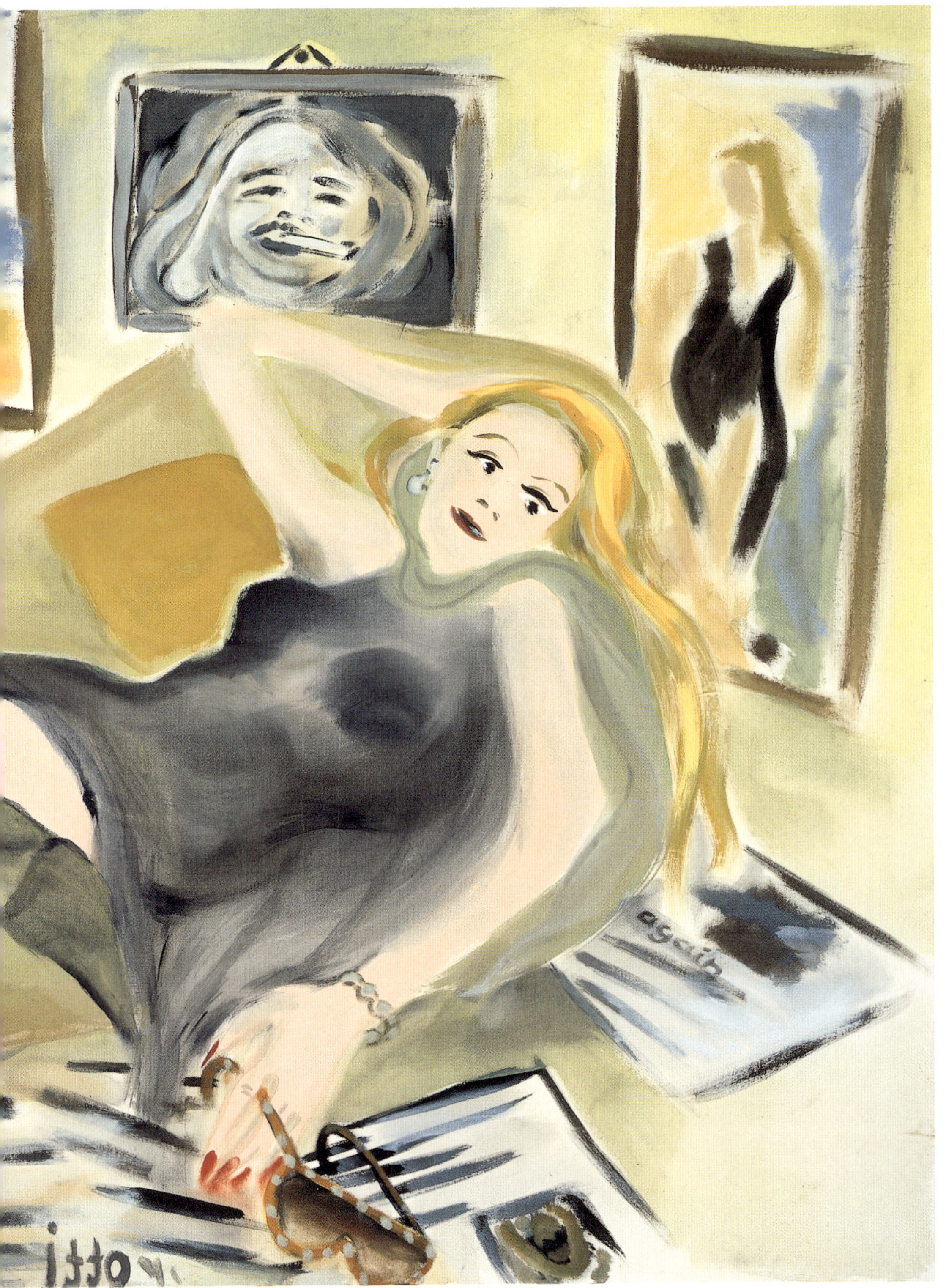

agath
itto 4.

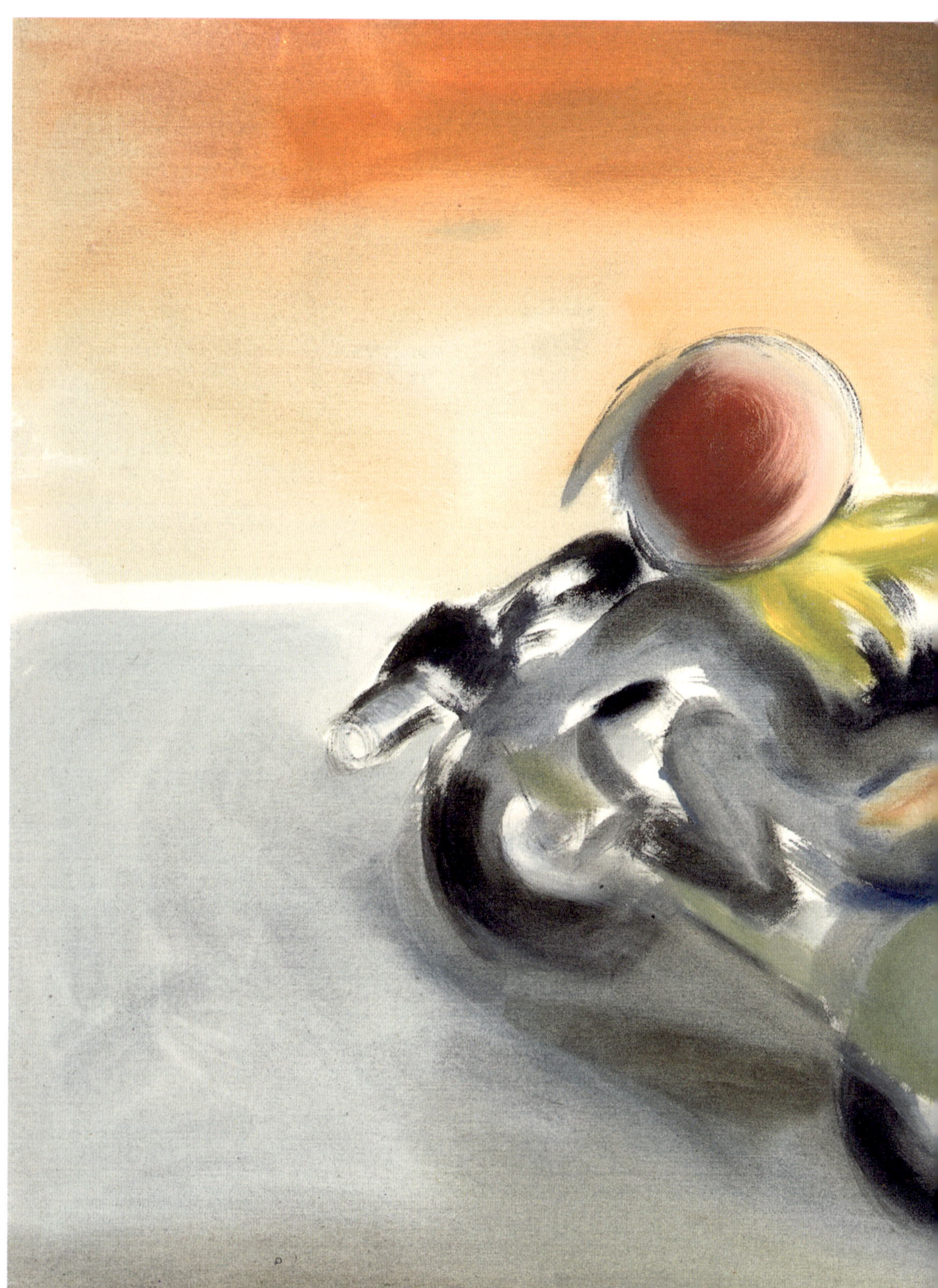

Pizza Taxi, 2001

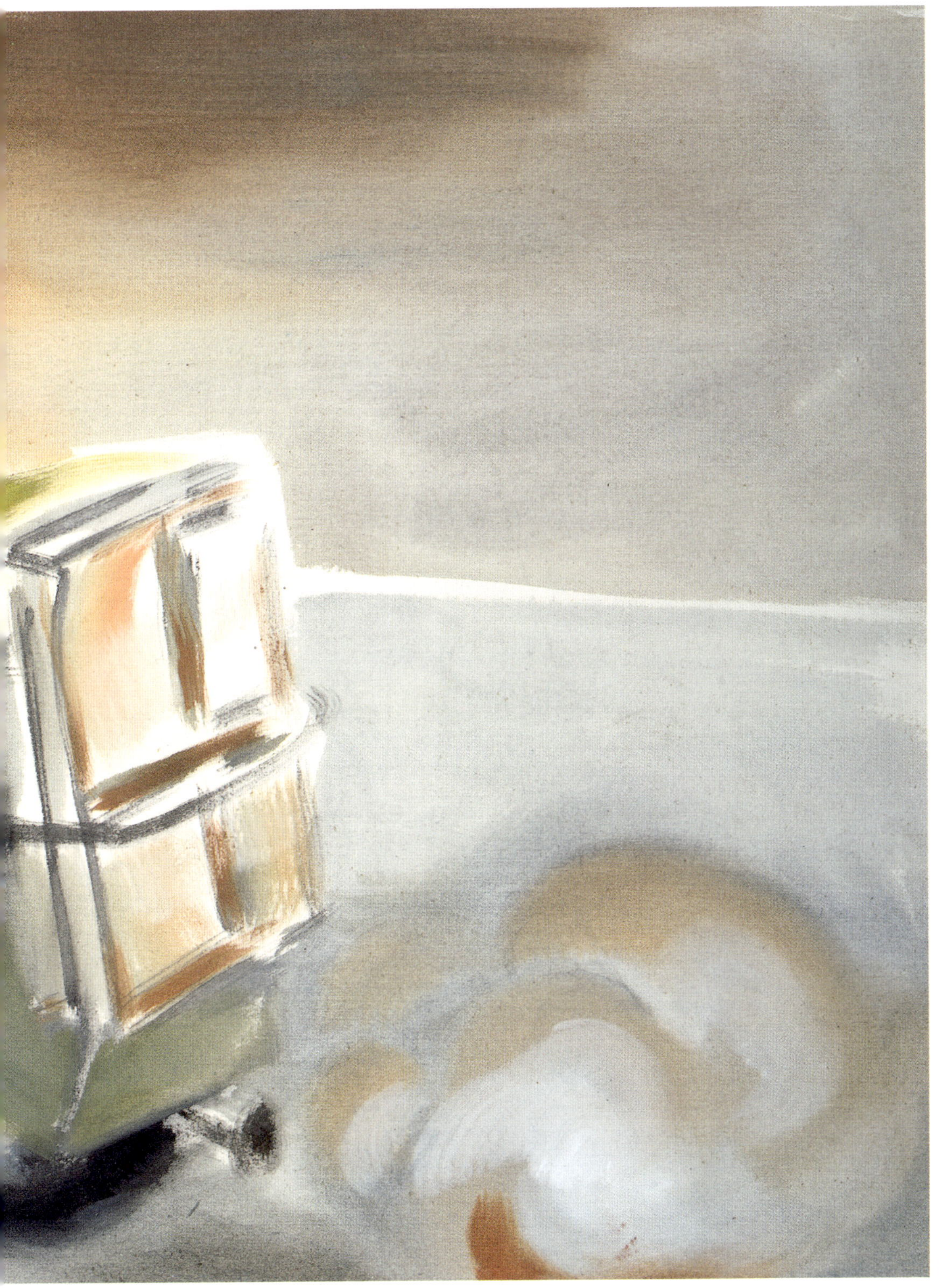

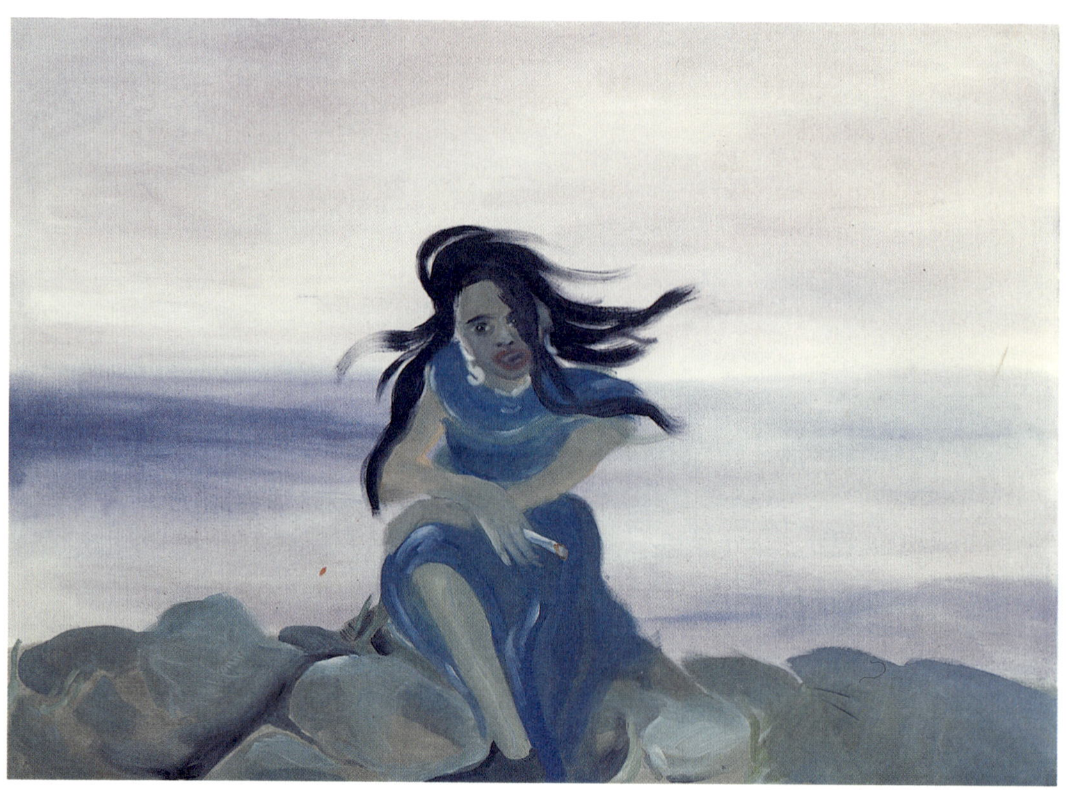

Maxim and Rebecca (diptych), 2001

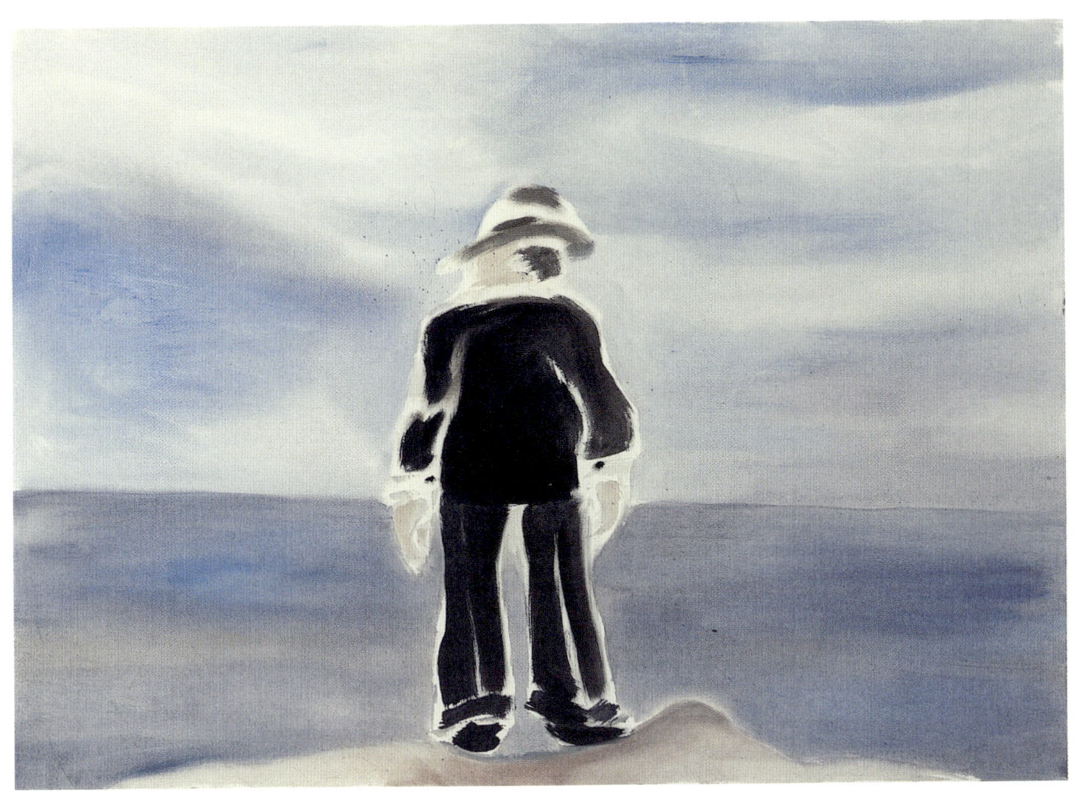

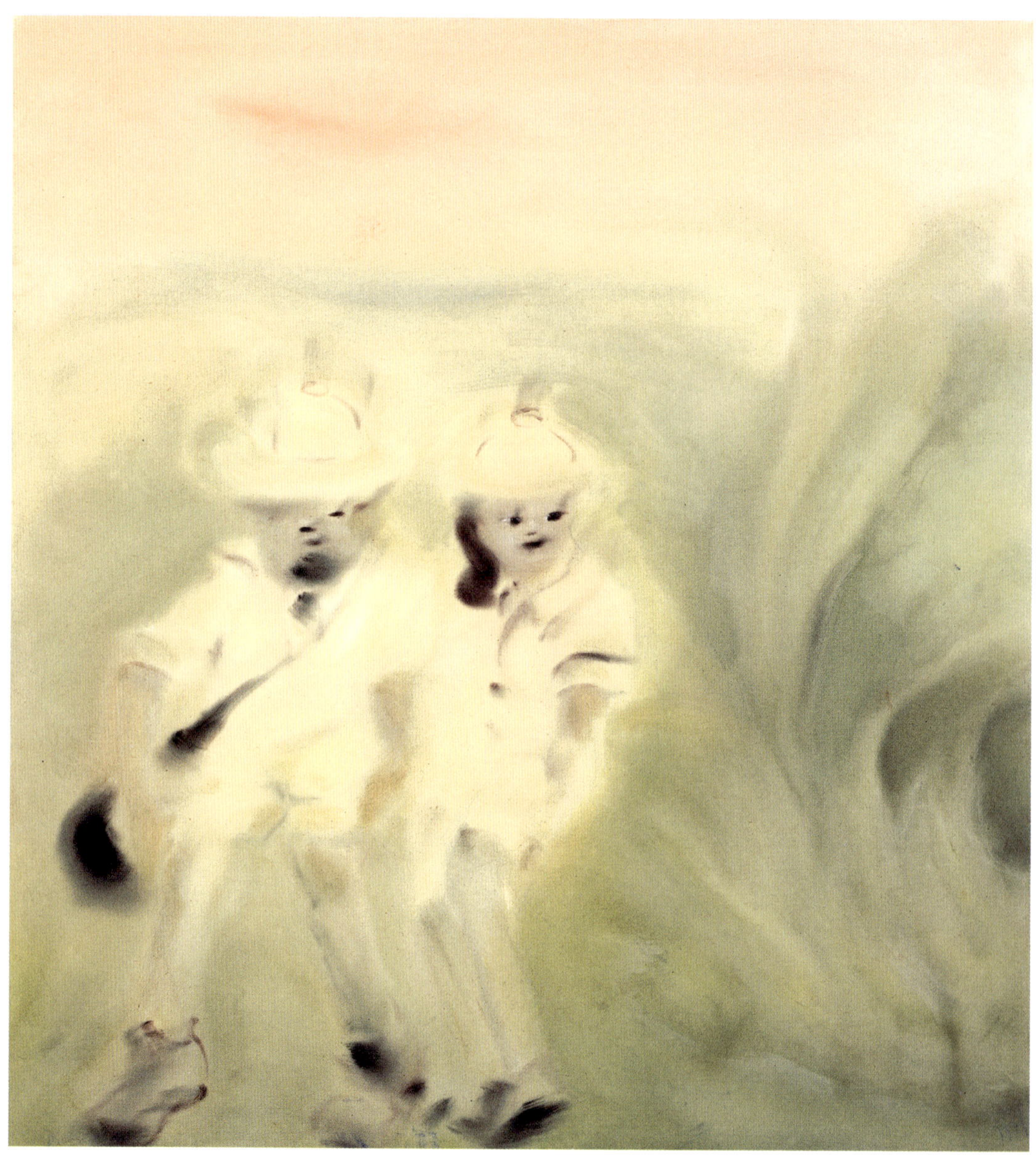

Explorers, 2001

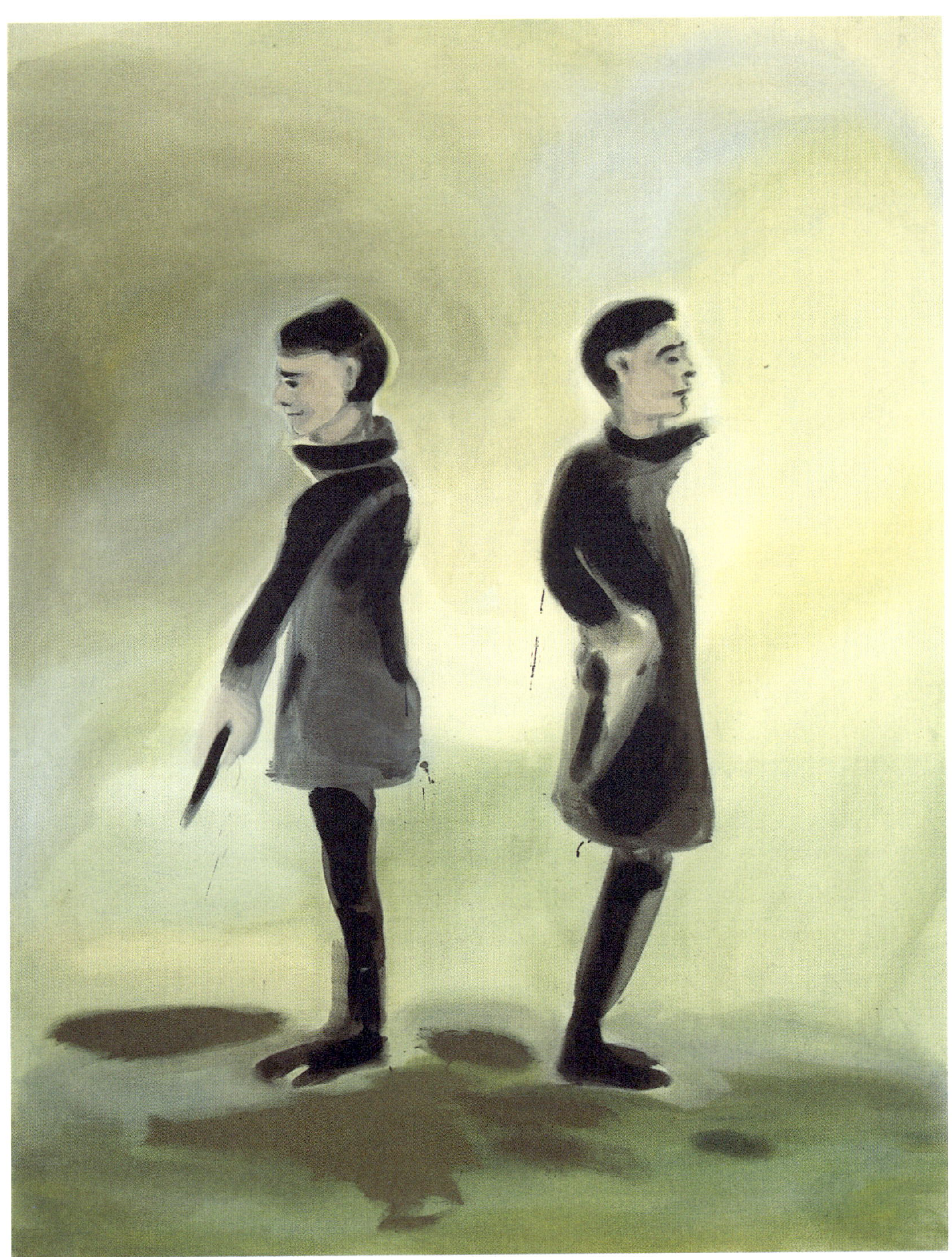

Duellists, 2001

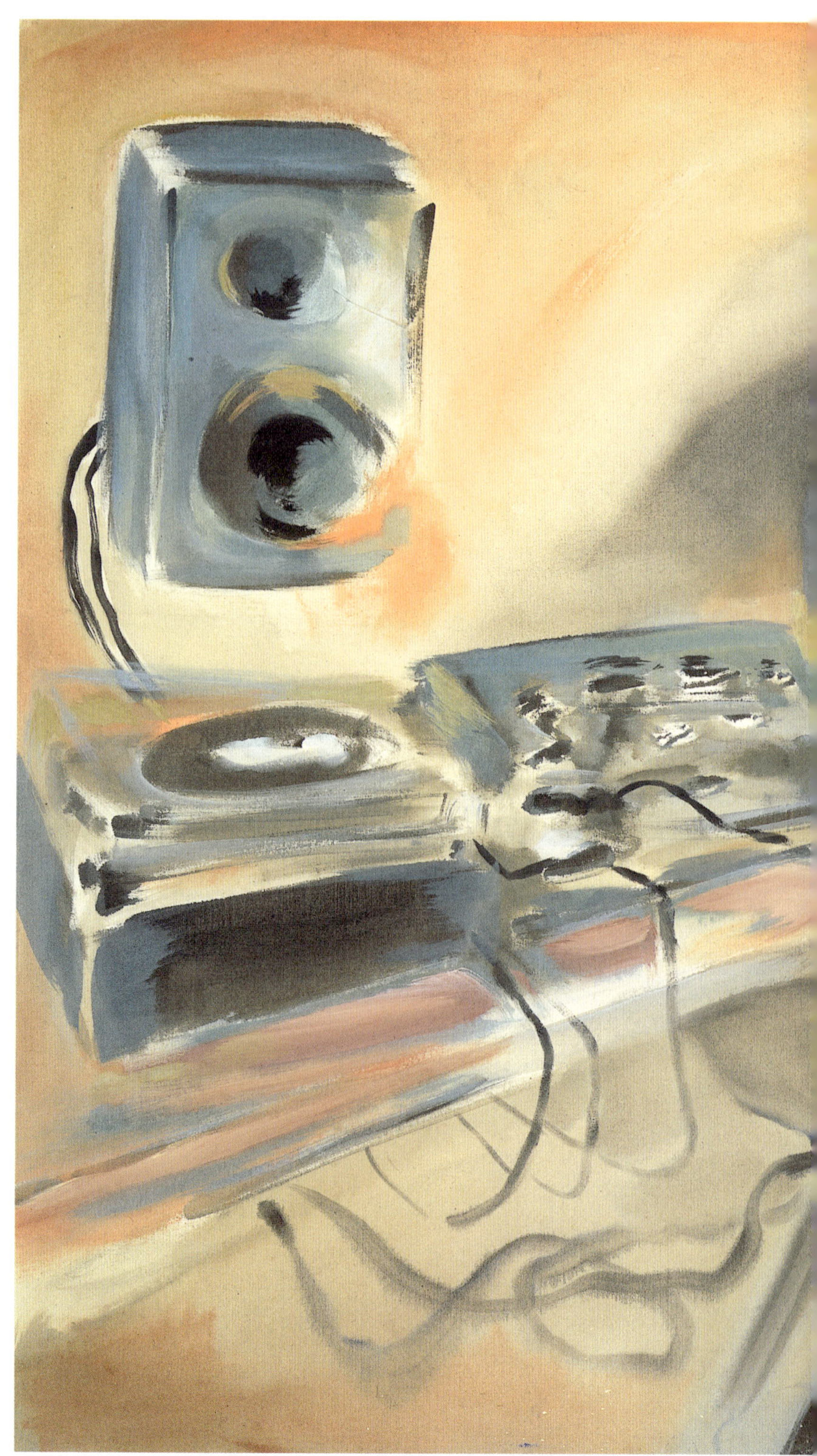

Flesh Records, 2001

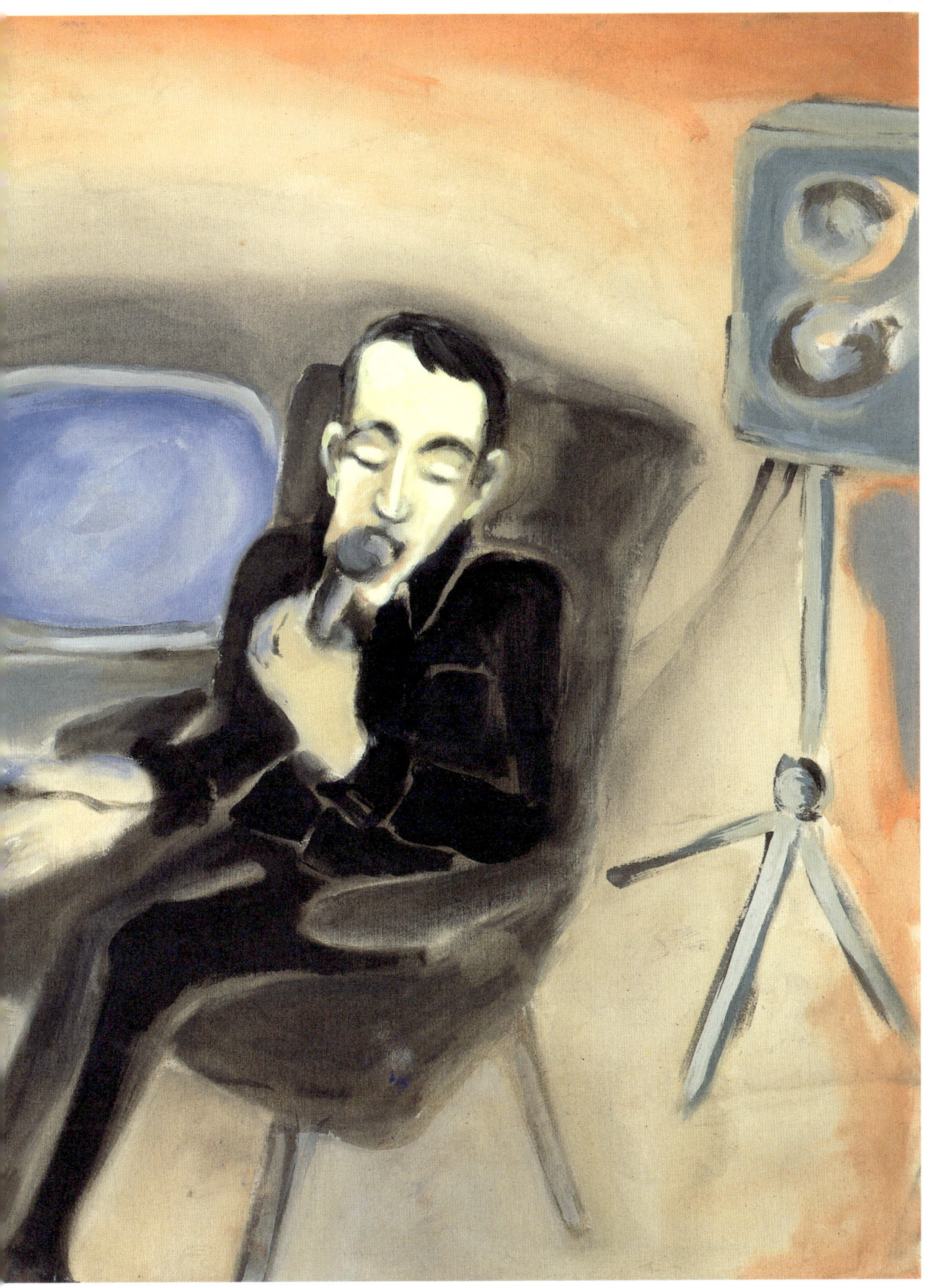

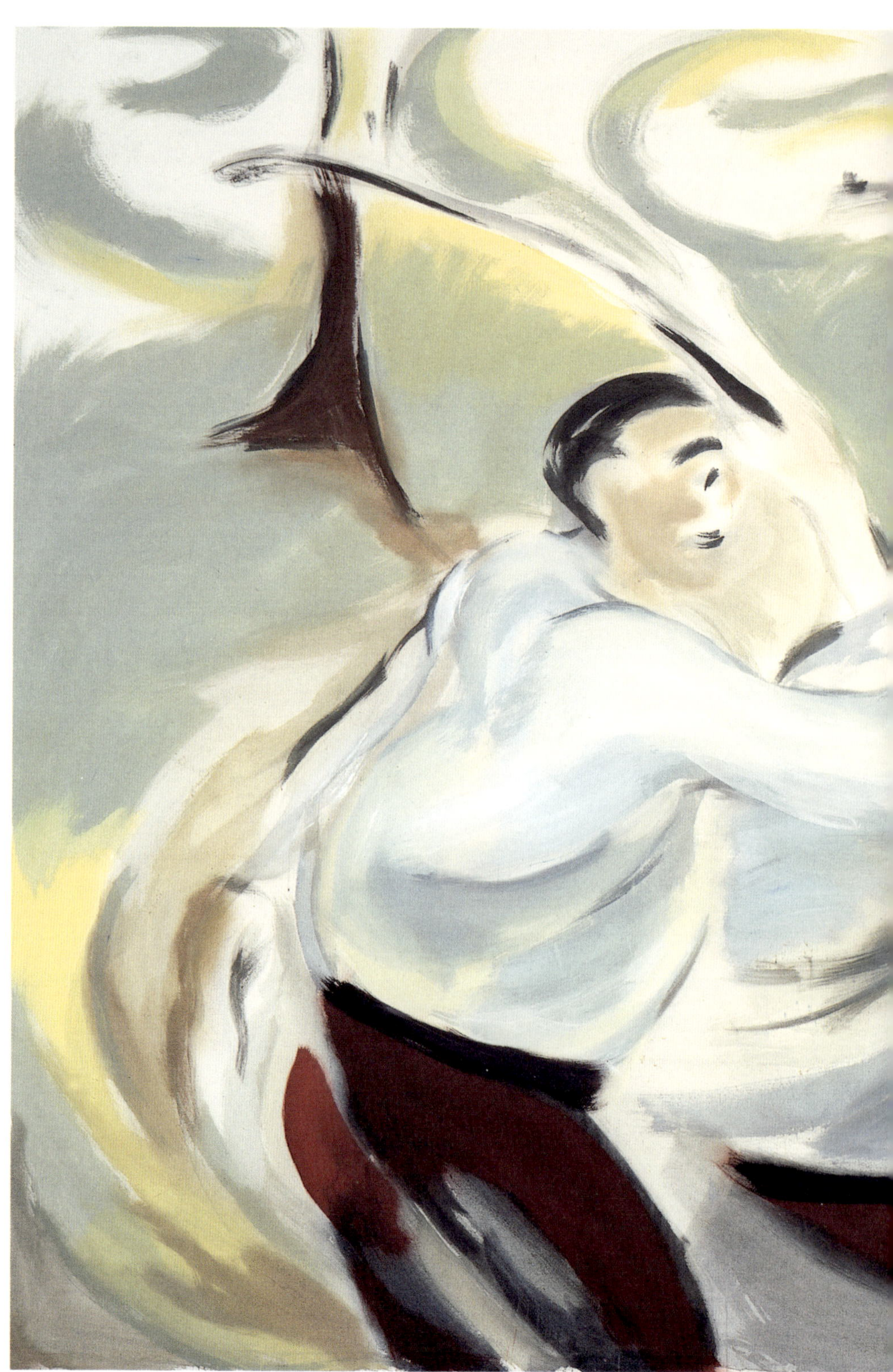

    Belle de Jour, 2001

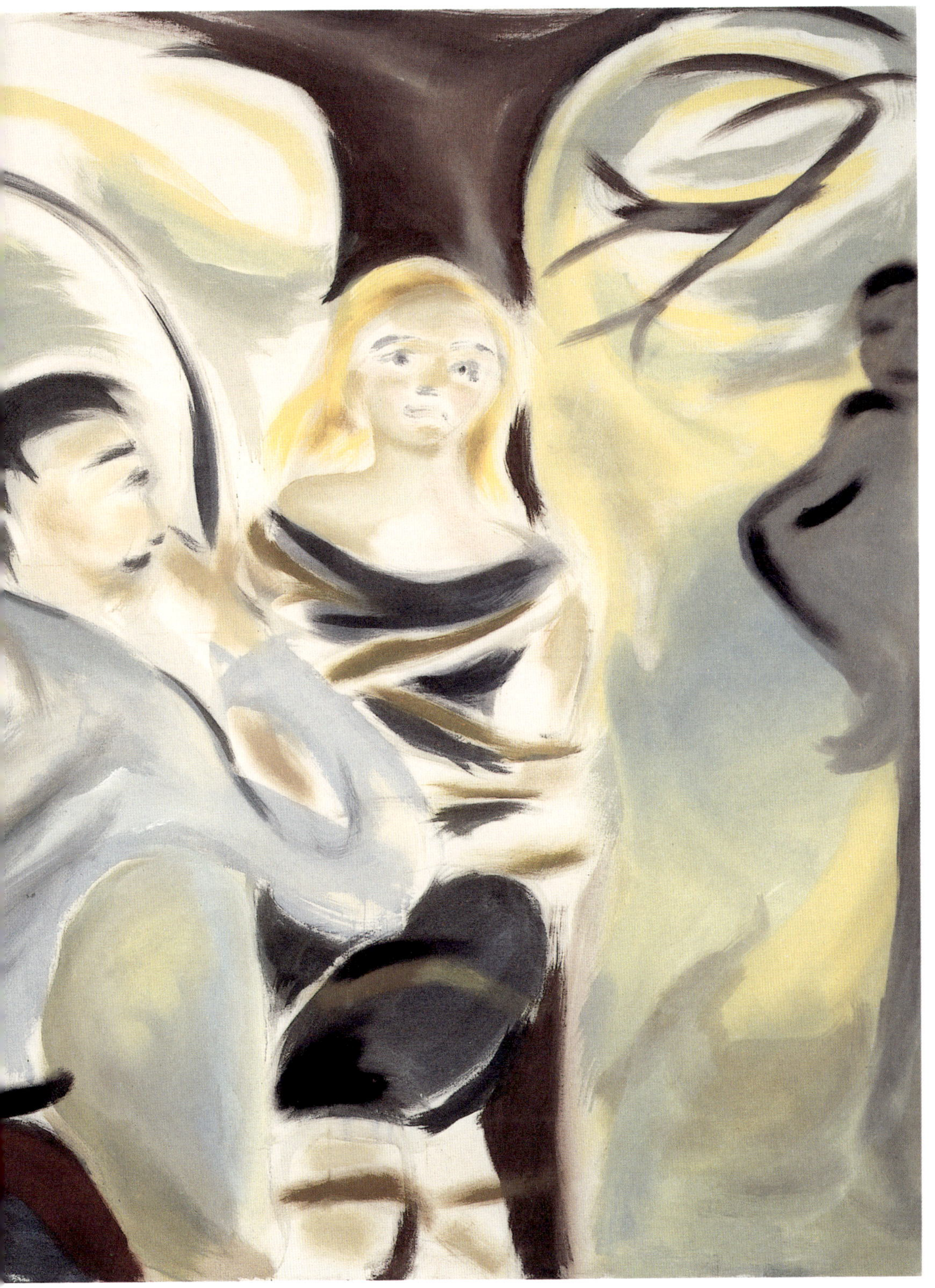

Gustav Metzger, 2001

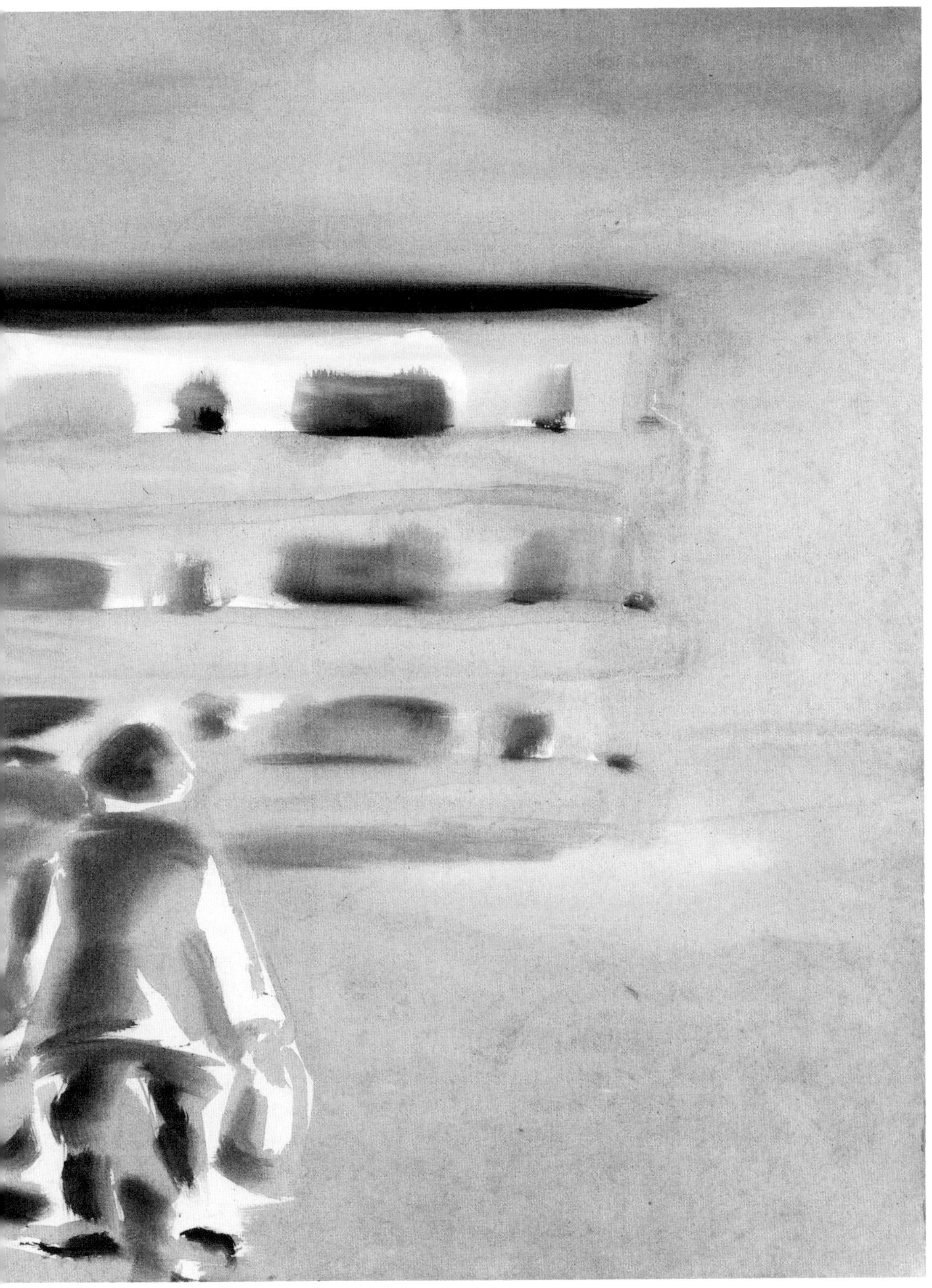

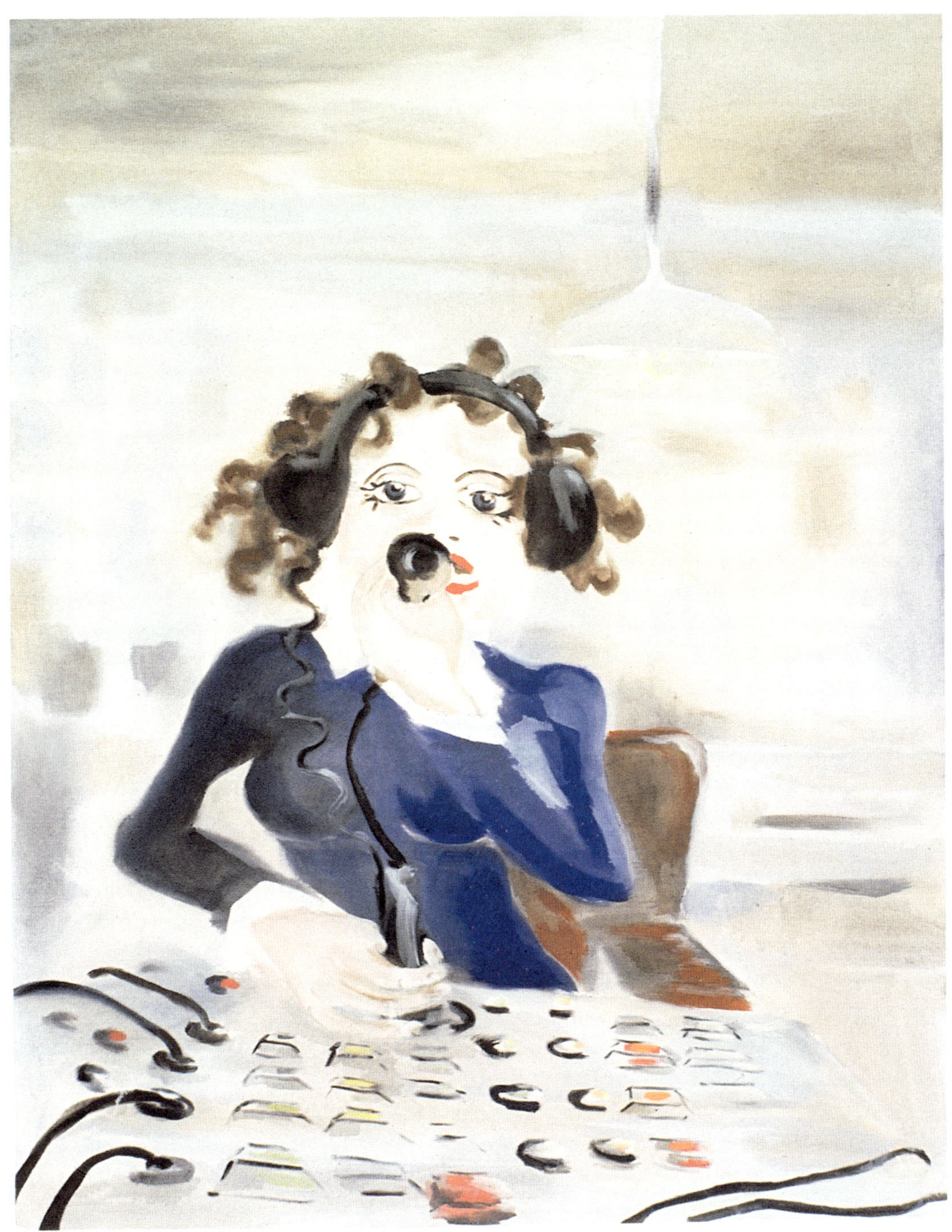

A Matter of Life and Death I, 2001

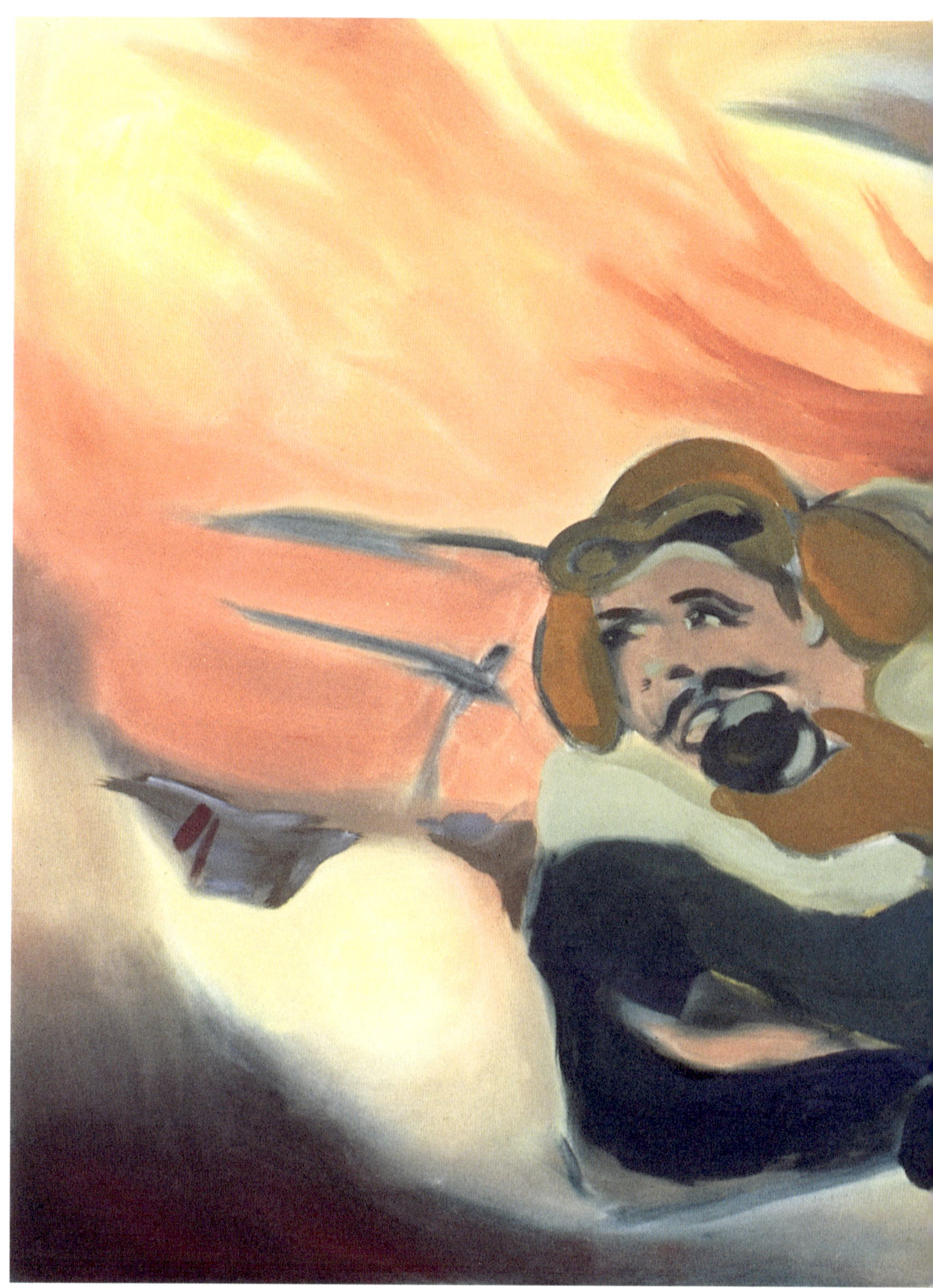

A Matter of Life and Death II, 2001

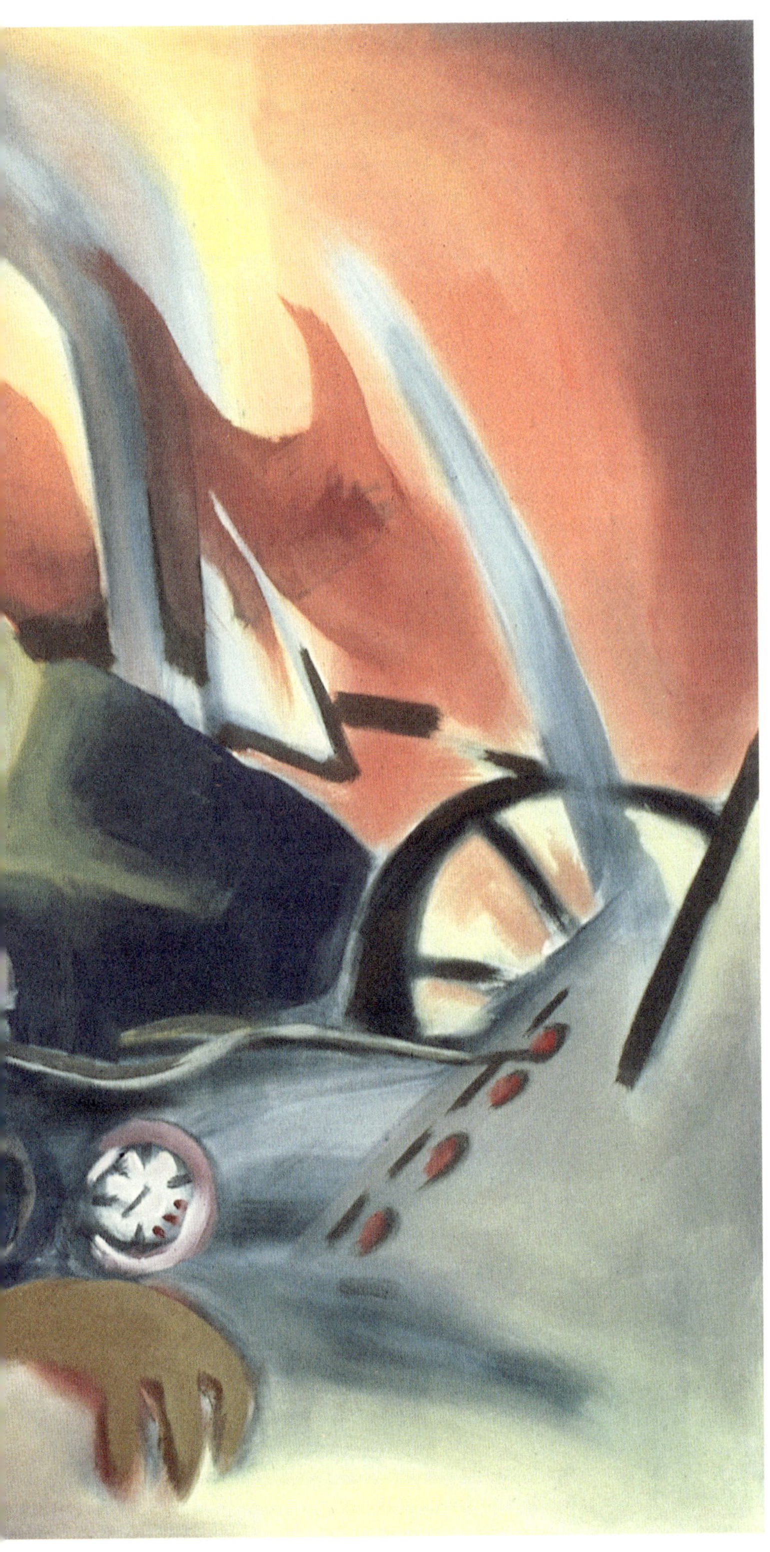

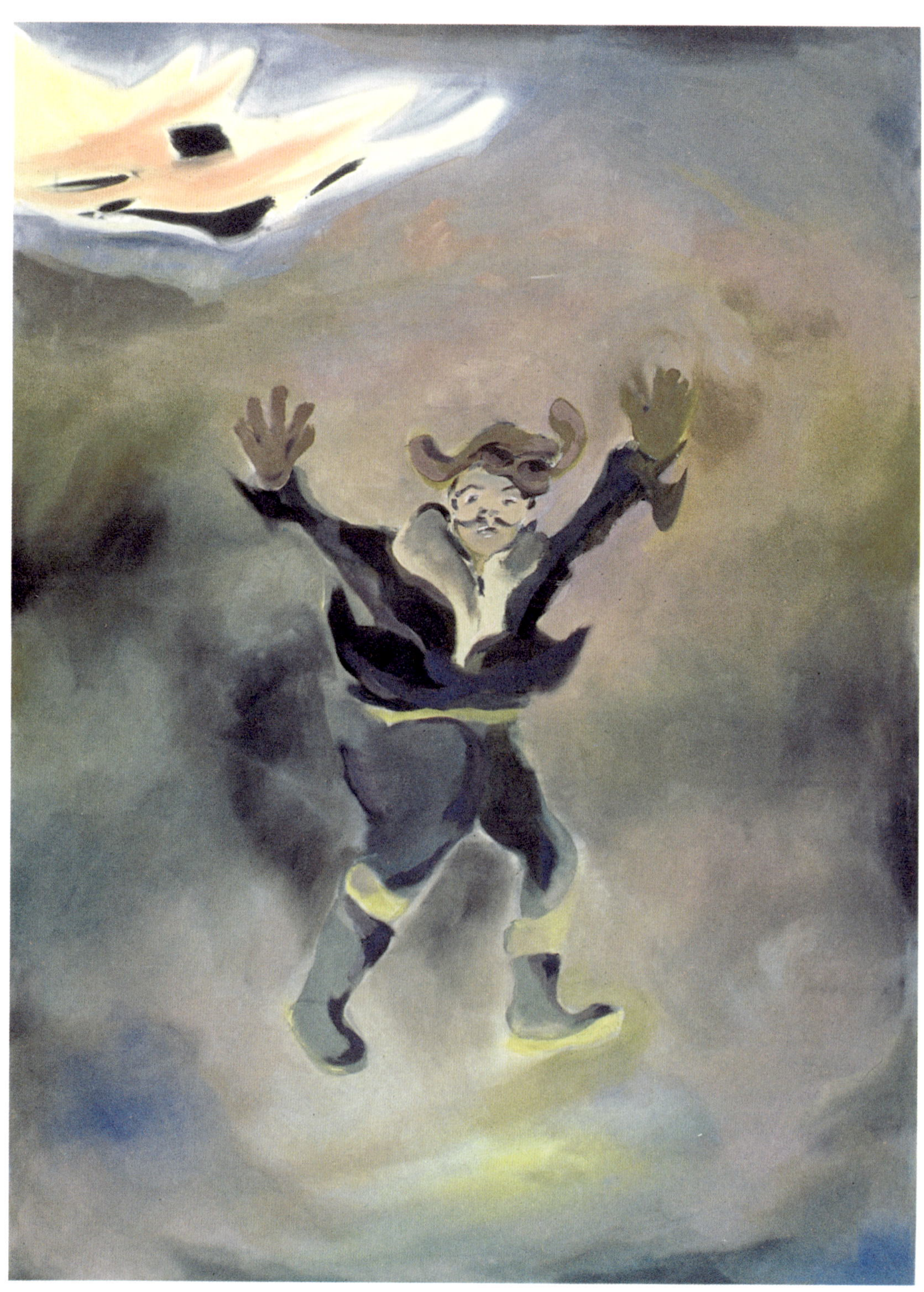

A Matter of Life and Death III, 2001

THE JOKE'S ON YOU
The unexpected sparing of psychological effort

This text is the result of a conversation with Sophie von Hellermann. While we were talking, we watched in close to chronological sequence a slide show of 126 of her paintings documented on a CD. The pictures were created over, roughly, the last ten years and are presented together for the first time in this catalogue. The instrument was a Notebook which displayed a new image, following a fade, about every ten seconds. Of course, this structure of a self-presentation was already connected with a thesis, or a preconception, pertaining to von Hellermann's painting. The set-up of having her pictures 'glide by' in rapid sequence, and in a miniaturised and digitised form, provided a certain riposte to the rather superficial 'image' associated with this kind of painting, which in terms of form and content one can most easily situate between triviality and melodrama. We first viewed the 'Sherlock Holmes' pictures from around 1994/95. The last time I had seen her original pictures was during that period, when I first met her in Düsseldorf. So the computer screen became the medium through which I viewed all of her other paintings.

Sophie von Hellermann mostly works with large-scale, space-filling formats – a decision possibly deriving from the group-dynamic, installation-like aesthetics of her numerous collaborations with members of the 'hobbypopMUSEUM'. These group activities continue, but despite this unusual persistence they are far from being the key to understanding her aesthetic and formal decisions. When looking at her past work, one sees no signs of withdrawal. Sophie von Hellermann's art is conversational; on the pictorial level it provides 'conversation pieces' that regularly stimulate ensuing conversations to take unexpected, self-reflective turns.

As opposed to the rhetoric applied in the pictures, her technique is simple. She uses acrylic paint, mostly on unprimed cotton, sometimes on canvas. There is no finicky playing with layers, no indulging in detail. She stopped using oil ten years ago, saying that it's a lot easier to handle water than turpentine. She continues to use pigments, which she finds more satisfying than ready-made paint. In contrast to the widespread, art-folkloristic notion of intoxicating turpentine smells, she finds water and water-pigment sludge much more, well, sensuous.

Upon taking a closer look at her pictures, it appears to be significant that she is capable of making quick decisions. In graphics, her technique would come closest to that of lithography. Strokes of repentance are excluded. It is admirable that her technical ability rarely admits of weaknesses, nor has it, as in the case of Kippenberger, become so relentless and, as a contextualized gesture, so official, that it can only be realised with the help of assistants. When considering similar painterly techniques, in von Hellermann's case one would single out her use of watercolour, an intermediary form that allows gestural elements while otherwise dealing with light effects and colour gradients. Earlier, she used colour in a much more 'unmixed' way. Now there's the 'watercolour effect' and along with other factors it contributes to emphasising the moody aspect. She wants what she does to appear easy, to be represented by very few elements. She says: 'But that also happens because I use too much water that seeps through. A large part of what I have painted is then gone. In the end, it sometimes looks as if the canvas were carried past the actual events.'

Does this painterly commitment permit competition with other, technological, image media? It is striking that Sophie von Hellermann's paintings frequently depict cameras and TV screens or computer monitors. Although this does not constitute an elaborate iconography requiring hours of discussions, the self-reflective aspect of her painting can perhaps be discerned on this superficial level of motifs. Her handling of size and the increased contingency of the material she utilises give rise to the question of the extent to which she plans a picture. Does she have a complete sketch in her mind beforehand and then sets out to implement it? Is she like Bob Ross (an artist I am reminded of when looking at these watercolour effects), who always starts working with a fixed plan in his head and then has only the not-really-consoling explanation for the viewer that artistic licence allows him the freedom to draw the line this way or that? What does the feeling (or its simulation) of one thing leading to another mean to von Hellermann, when she entrusts herself to the 'enframing' of painting?

Particularly when viewing several of her pictures next to each other, their 'internal' historicity becomes evident. Technical reinvention does not play a role. Precisely because she produces a relatively large number of pictures, she can no longer start from scratch: pictures inevitably relate to earlier pictures. But, then again, I believe that the purely physical difficulty of size becomes clear only when actually facing the original picture. Before I had viewed even half of the slide show, I had the impression that through size (which I can only estimate) von Hellermann takes on responsibility for the ideas she deems 'picture-worthy'. I imagine a prior calculus – or an attempt at it – that assesses the kind of impact a pictorial idea will have depending on its size. She has often demonstrated that a picture can consist of just a few elements – for example, the picture with the candle in front of the turned-off TV and the hand holding a remote control at the lower edge of the picture; or, in *Chum Pain Party I* (2002), where the arm with the hand with the finger touches the light switch. And there are also more complexly structured pictures, such as *Leading Lady* (2001), which just speed by, where she seems to have had difficulty maintaining an economic use of time when painting – so that the individual elements flow into each other and impede each other.

Many of the pictures deal – often by means of literary references – with explicitly ephemeral and sometimes trivial narrative moments, incorporating anecdotal situations. Or with moments that touch on a structural element: one can say for sure that the motorbike deliveryman in *Pizza Taxi* (2001) is not a classical Mercury but by making the typical Generation-X service a major subject, von Hellermann creates a link between 'high' and 'low'. Hence, she is not concerned with the notion of spontaneity but, in most cases, with making comments from the 'outside', whereby painting, for a short while, can become a pizza; a comment, though, which is so flexible that it can more or less choose to whom it is addressed. Apart from that, a better way to approach her pictures is to state what they are not. There is *no* expertise of refined techniques and materials paraded in a Hockneyesque manner – instead, one often encounters a 'wet-in-wet', conspicuously spontaneous, process-oriented form of painting that at first appears to have a lot to do with coming to terms with the large surface. Yet she then always seems to convey the more interesting aspect of grasping a pictorial idea.

There is a lot to be said for initially understanding many of her pictures as the spatializing of various kinds of jokes, albeit with an apparently paralinguistic feeling for implications, cryptic allusions and, upon closer examination, the complexity of what superficially appears simple and trivial. To point out Sophie von Hellermann's linguistic interest is not to indulge in the usual attempt to 'enhance' art by means of academic modes of description. What is indeed required over and above simple observation (for instance, that there is hardly any writing and, if so, then as a problem), is a metaphor for distancing – not necessarily in linguistic terms – to designate the difference between her work and other kinds of picture jokes, such as cartoons, because they hardly have an impact beyond the effects of displacement into the art context. At issue here is a distance that is necessary, in a literal sense, to detach oneself from the idea that a joke ought to be something minute, something secondary, found only in marginalia, that cannot grow to fill the dimensions of a real space, let's say a gallery. I say this to allude to the fact that the kind of joke we are dealing with here is notoriously at odds with the universality inherent in this genre of thought. *The joke's on you.* The dimensional zoom needn't end with the breadth of the wall which can barely accommodate the pictures in stretchers – it *could* become a cosmic joke.

What about the pictures that, as opposed to the way we started out, cannot so easily be set in parallel to the genre of the joke? They also play with the switch of dimensions (the relation of picture size to subject size) and the temporal displacement of the punch-line, using elements of a technique of joking which one finds in Freud. But what becomes clear in von Hellermann's visible mix of culturally quite different references – between Kemistry & Storm and the Brontë sisters, between Guy Fawkes and Rudyard Kipling, between Bianca Jagger and Christa Päffgen – is that they all appear to take part in a world of melodrama, of 'living fast and dying relatively young', which seems to be the counter-world to that of the joke. It is a world of vague homage and belated obituary. Von Hellermann is not interested in celebrities as such; their value is merely rhetorical. What is important here are distances, both those that exist between persons, groups, classes, professions, genders etc., and those between thoughts, ideas and concepts.

Of course, painting, as one of the more flexible techniques, is the playing field of ambiguities per se. This is the reason why the world of the (always punctual) joke consequently develops a natural, systemic appetite for the world of melodrama (which always feels sorry for those who are too late). The joke as the domain of so-called deeper meaning and melodrama as something unambiguous (it points to the inevitable abyss) constitute a juxtaposition that can be temporarily balanced but usually vacillates. New stages of ambiguity and equivocation can thus be found time and again. The hysterically pointed idiom is also important. It not only helps create individual, self-contained paintings, but also makes sure that the pictures start to open up on the sides, as it were, so as to establish comical connections with each other and the space. It doesn't really occur to one to read them in an iconographical way; instead, one starts putting together ensembles and viewing two or three pictures at a time. It then becomes evident that they can get on well with each other. What they really can do is to arrange psychologically difficult dimensional leaps with great 'depths of drop' to unexpectedly simple, pictorially wide-awake and liberating constellations – with each one enabling the distance to be redefined.

A clearly evolving artistic idiom is being elaborated here, but it sets out again and again to disassemble or dissolve a handwriting that tends to become fixed. Von Hellermann does not focus on a 'faux naïf' effect or a 'bad painting' approach, as is the case with many current 'neo-romanticists'. Instead, there are often imported moments that, before completing a picture, allow for doubt. Should this direction be taken or that? This almost constitutional insecurity should not be stylised as an experimental method. Starting with her early pictures in which she sometimes 'replaced' painting by writing parts of a narrative with the brush (in *Düsseldorf* of all places!) and, of course, in motifs such as

Sherlock Holmes, she has repeatedly included a criminological and forensic aspect in the melodramatic fragment. At times her painting itself acquires an investigative trait, and what remains of this is an attitude that views painting as a problem, like a criminal case, but one that perhaps cannot be solved – as one is accustomed to doing when viewing 'masterly' painting.

Clemens Krümmel

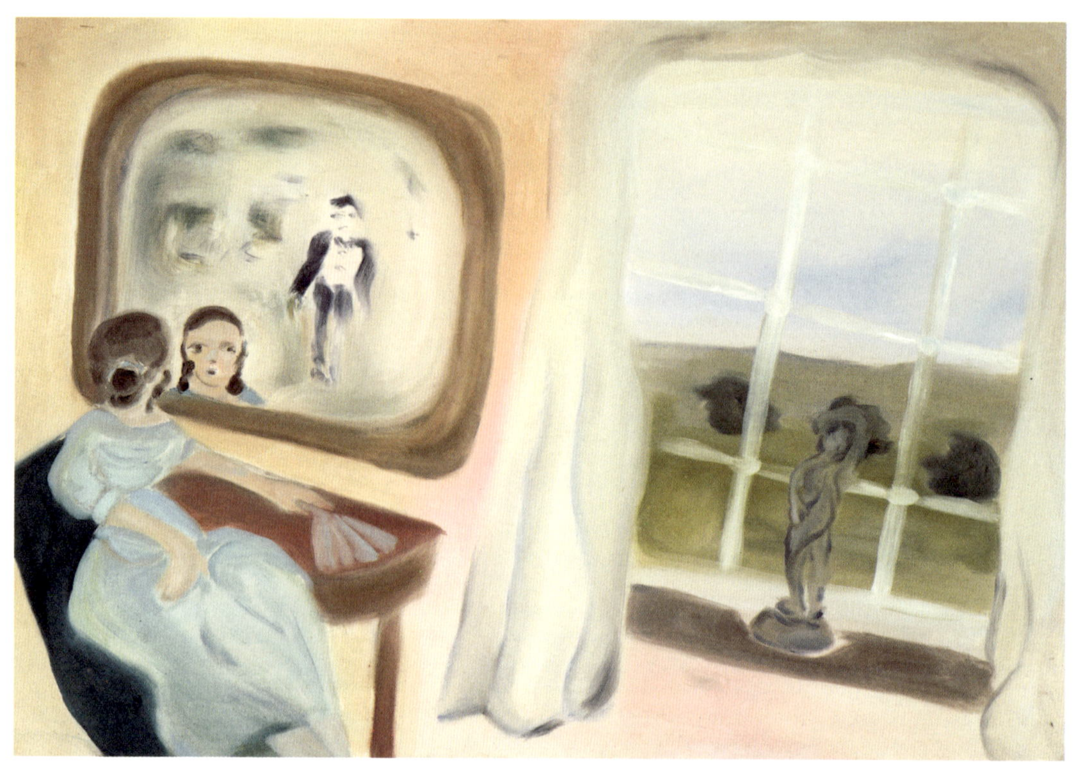

Thou art the man, 2001

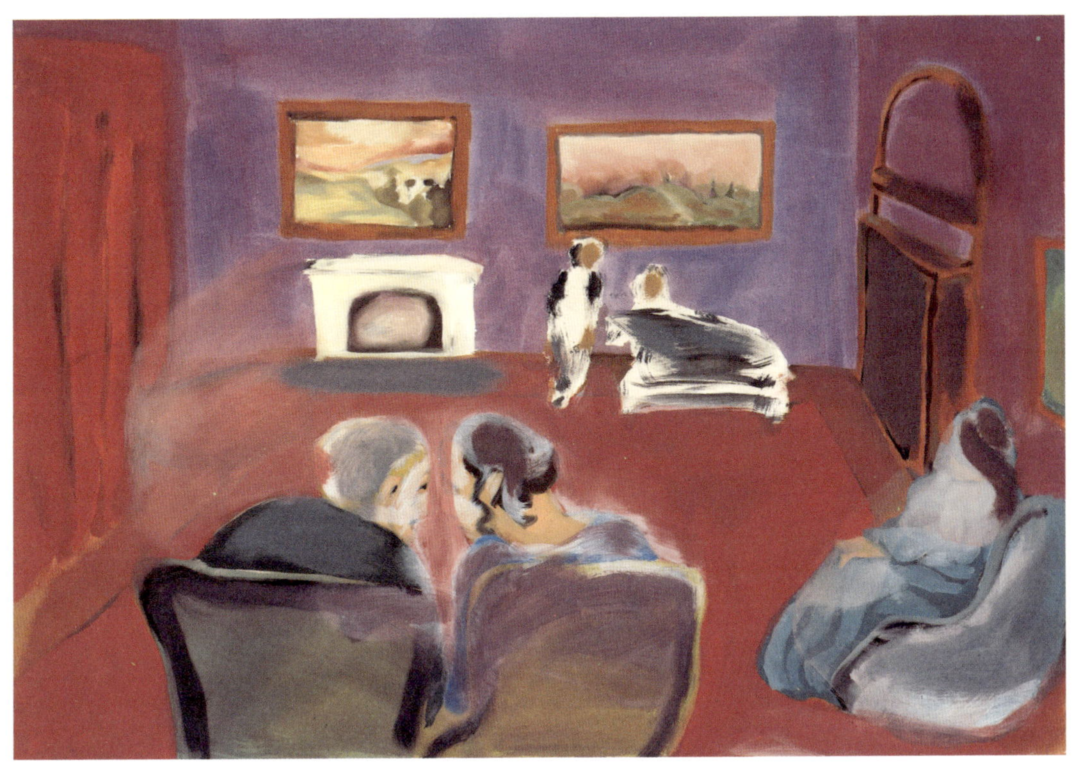

Vusering Hites, 2001

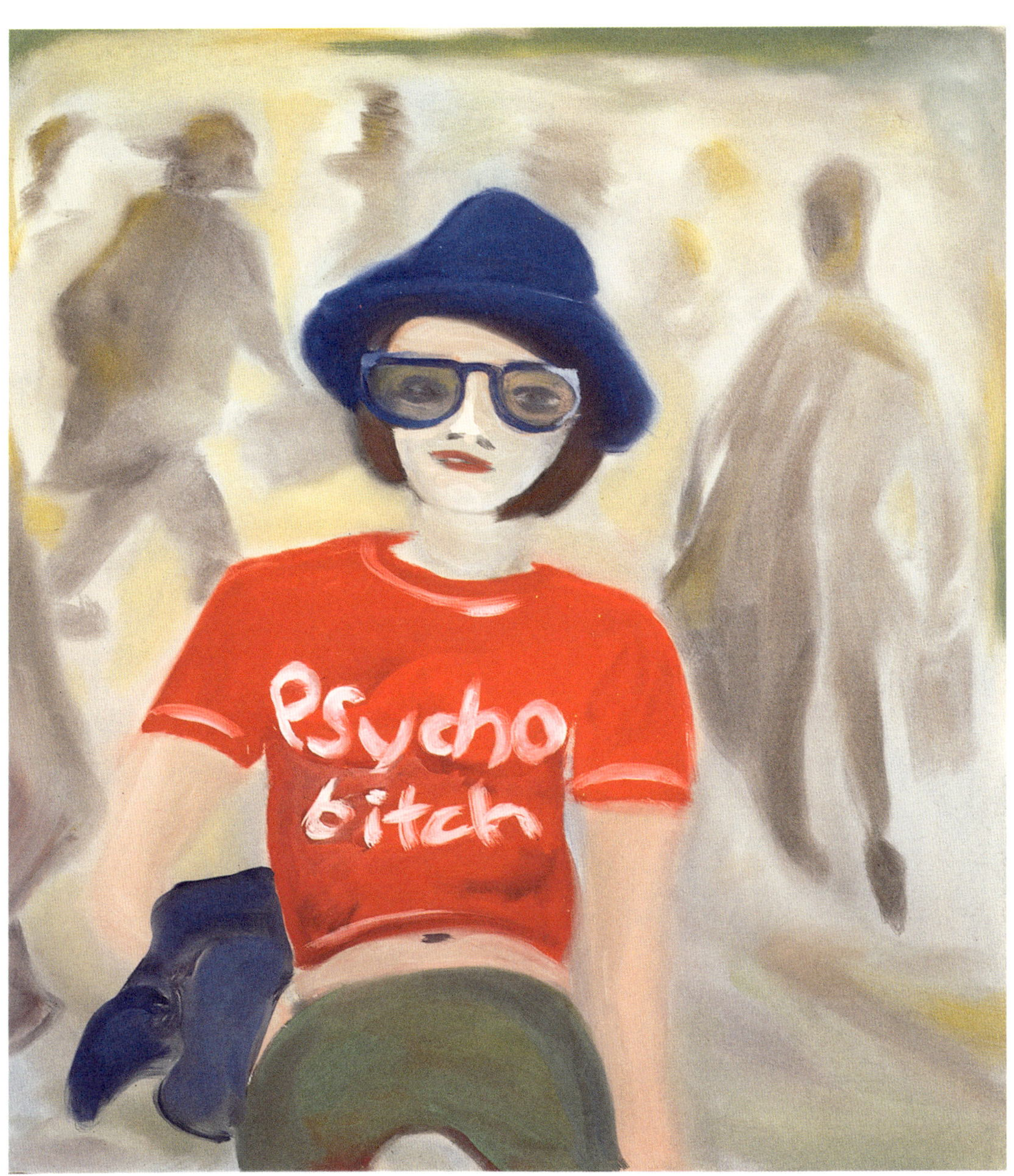

Before I came to live here, 2001

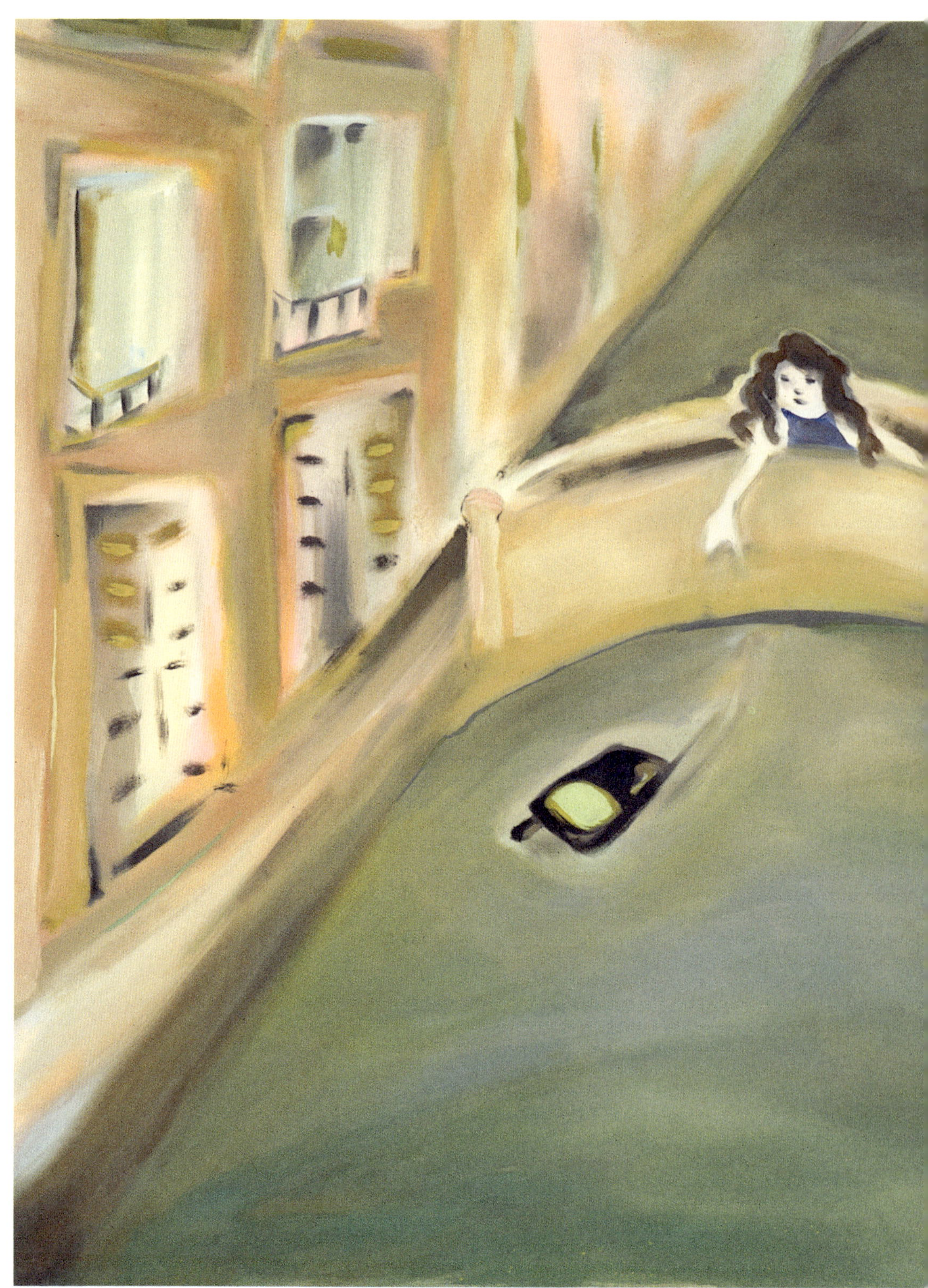

Having no Desire to be Entertained, 2001

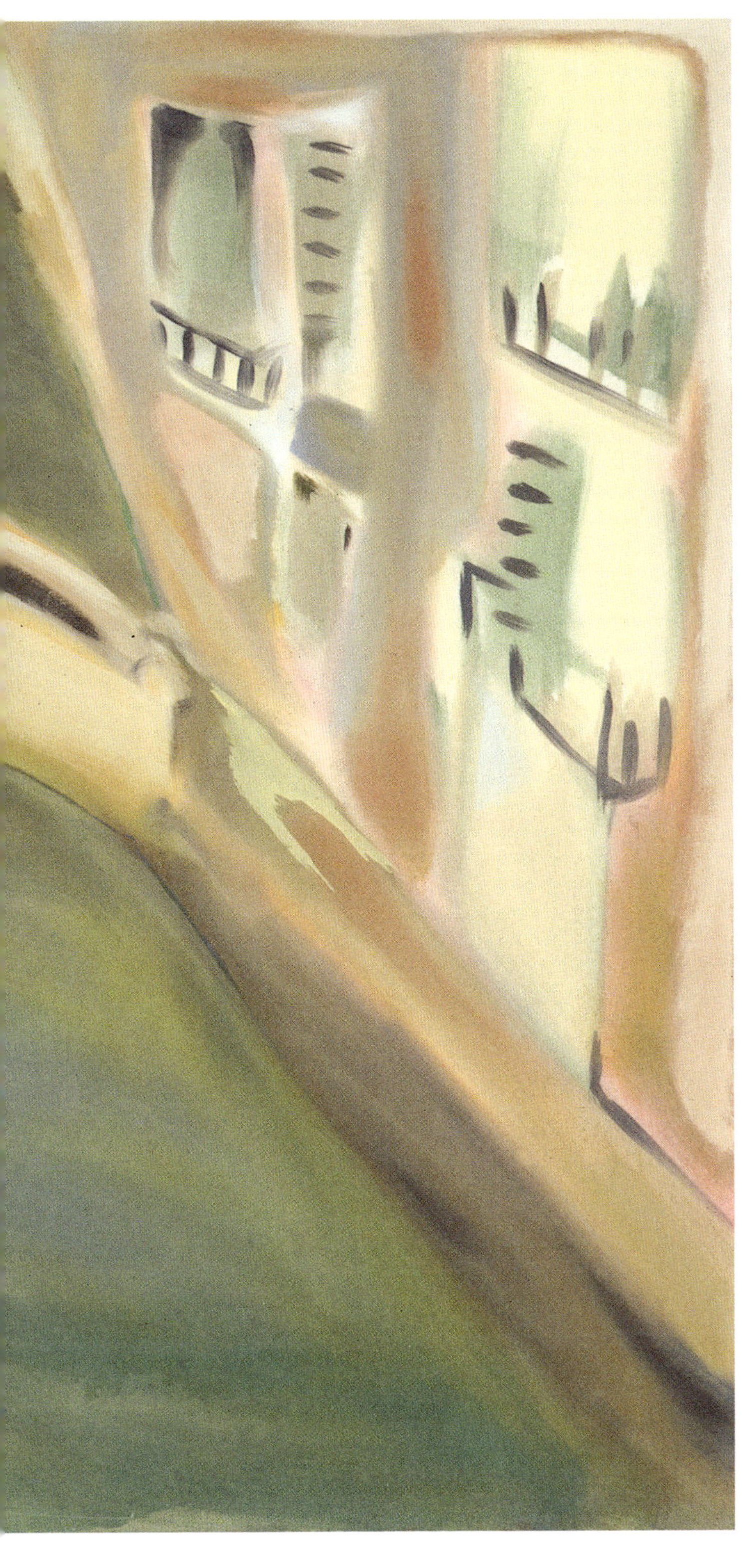

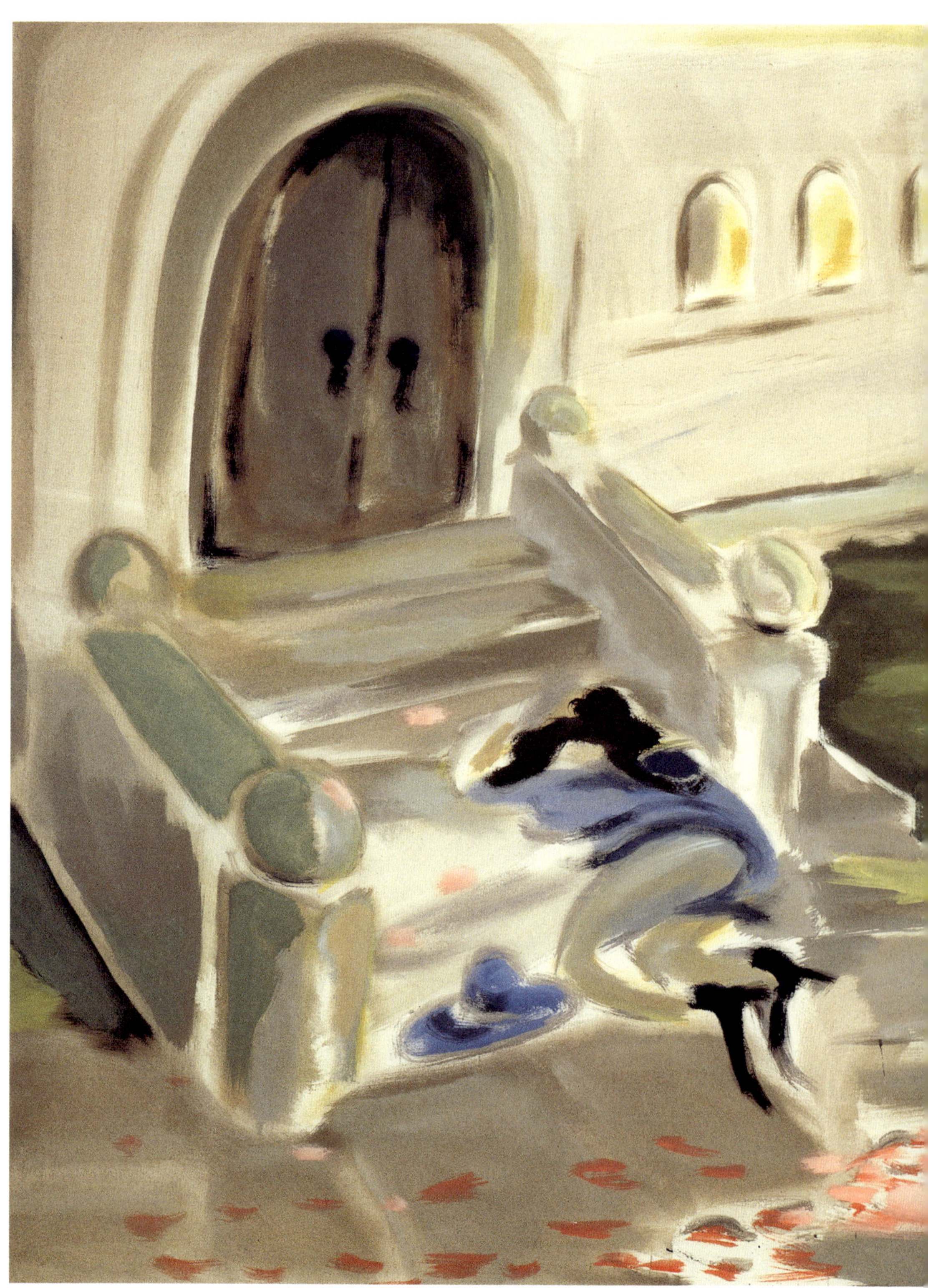

These Things Happened Last Winter, Sir, 2001

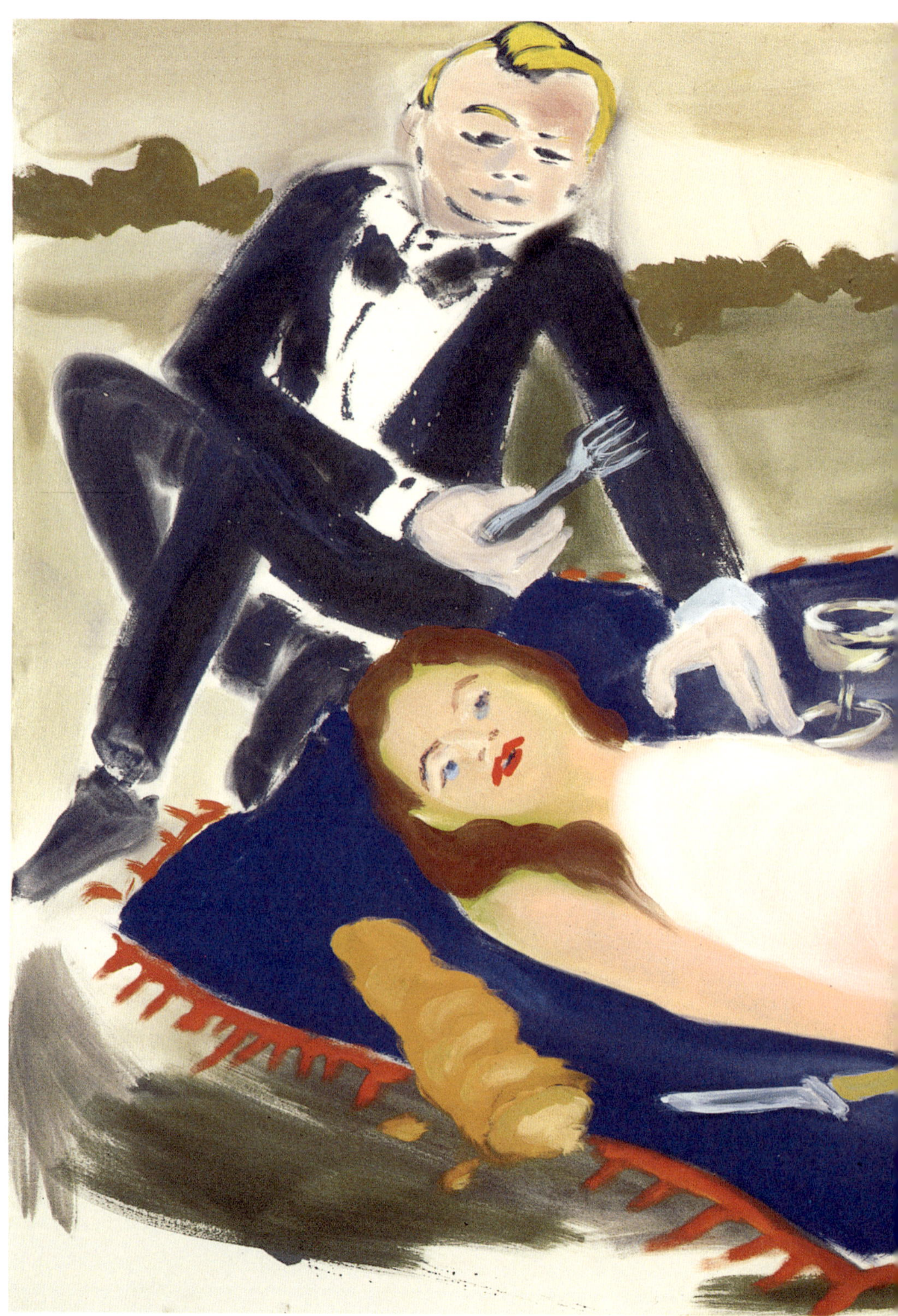

   When He Came…, 2001

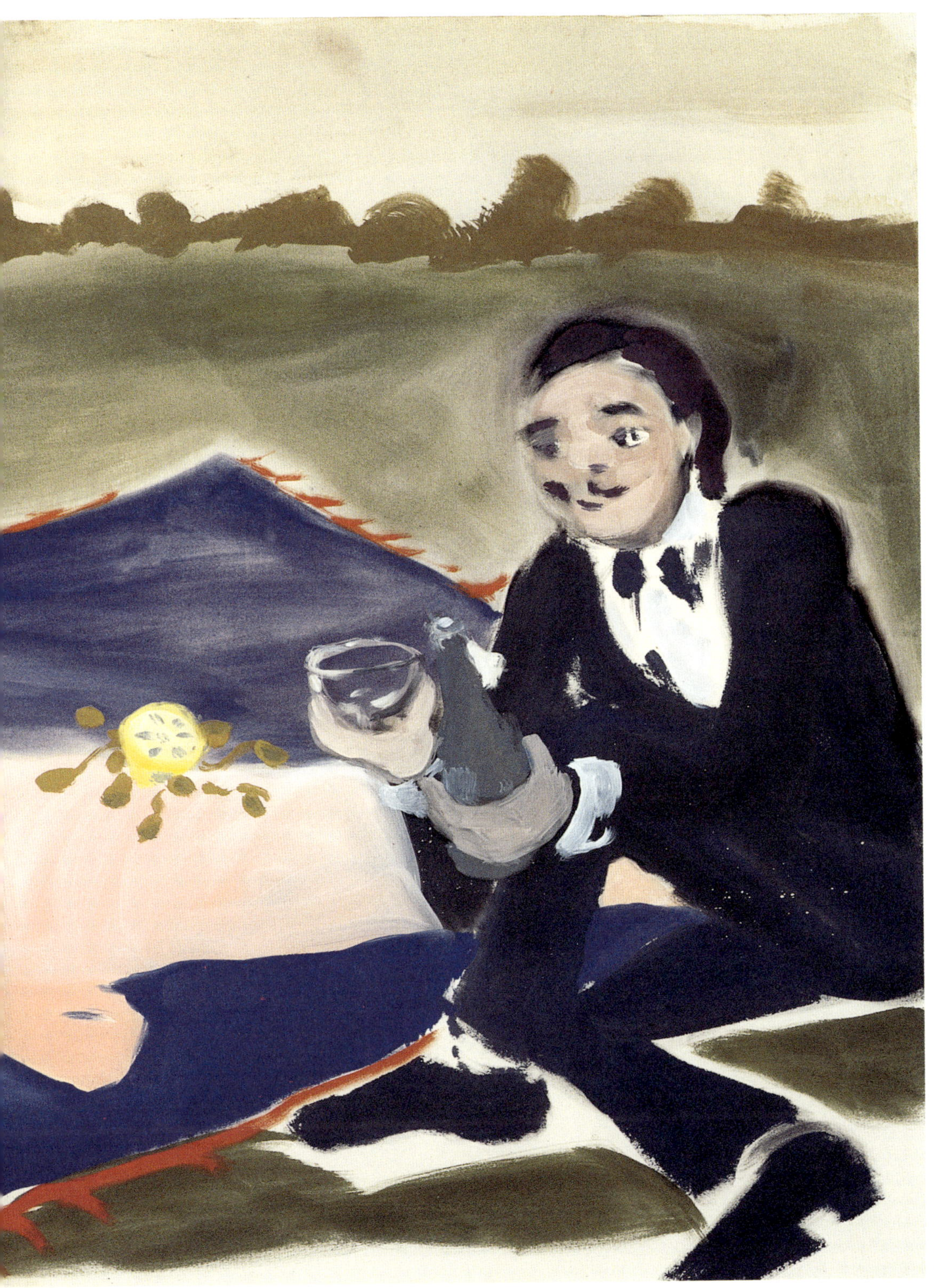

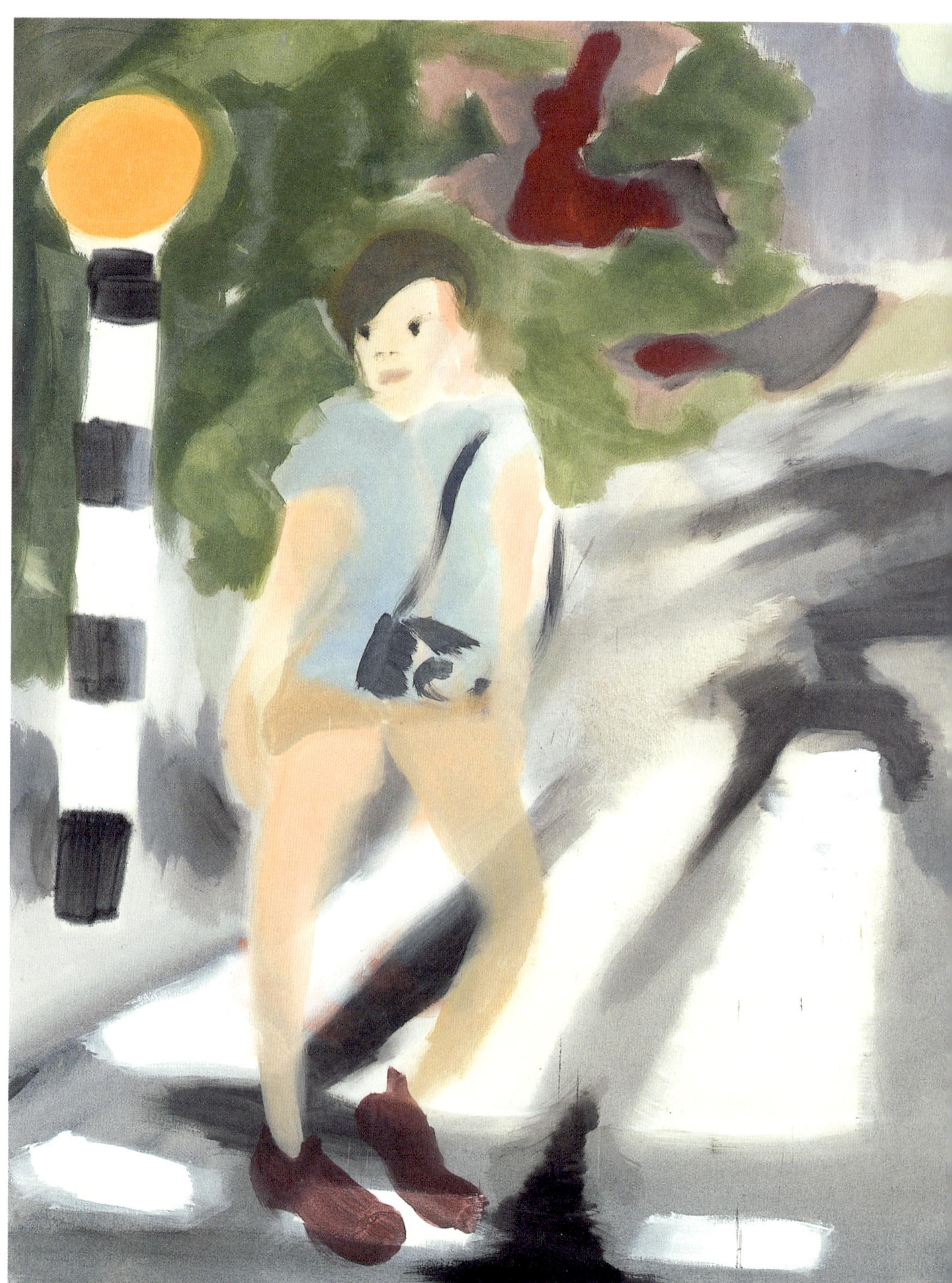

Come Together, 2001

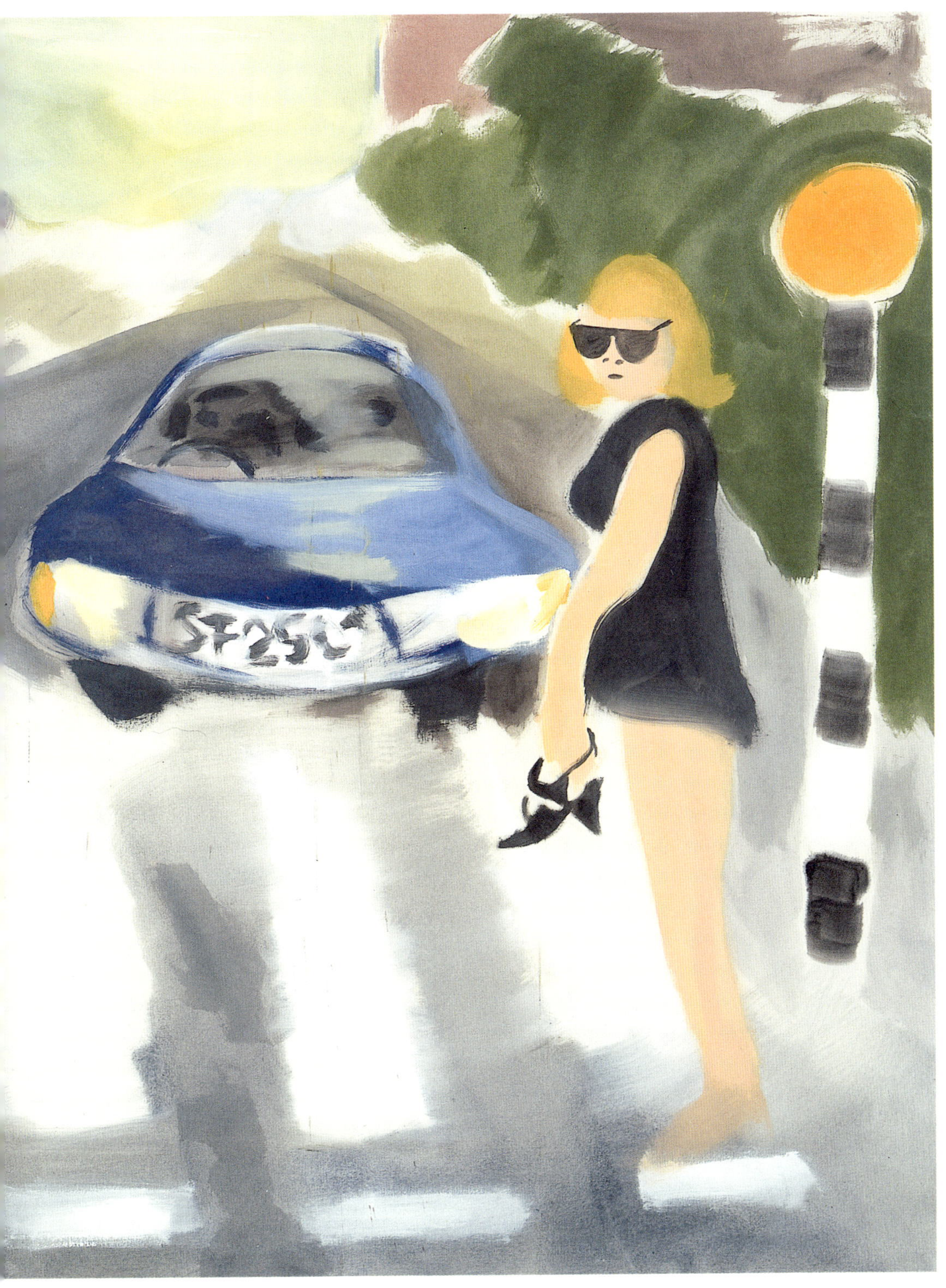
SF25G

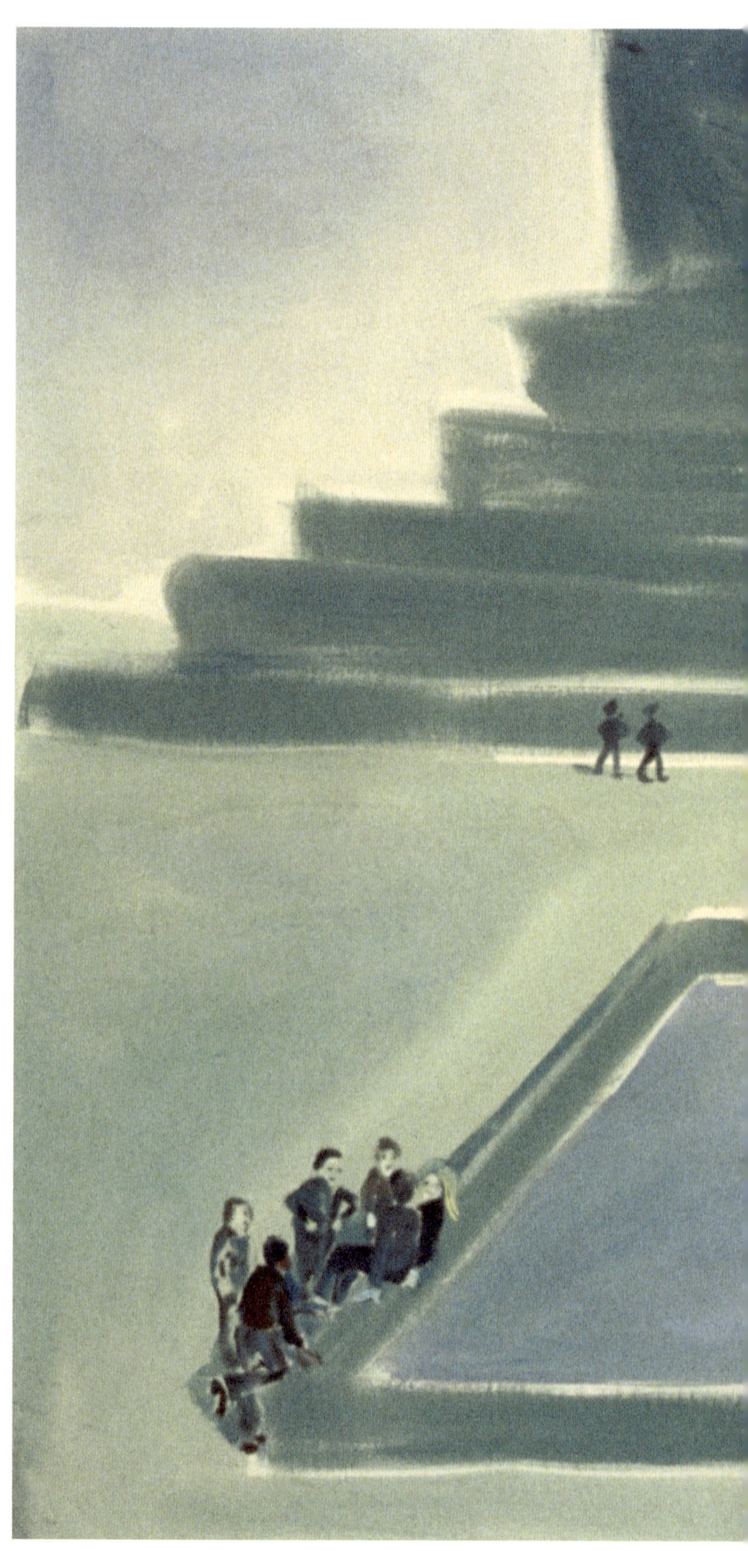

Something, 2001

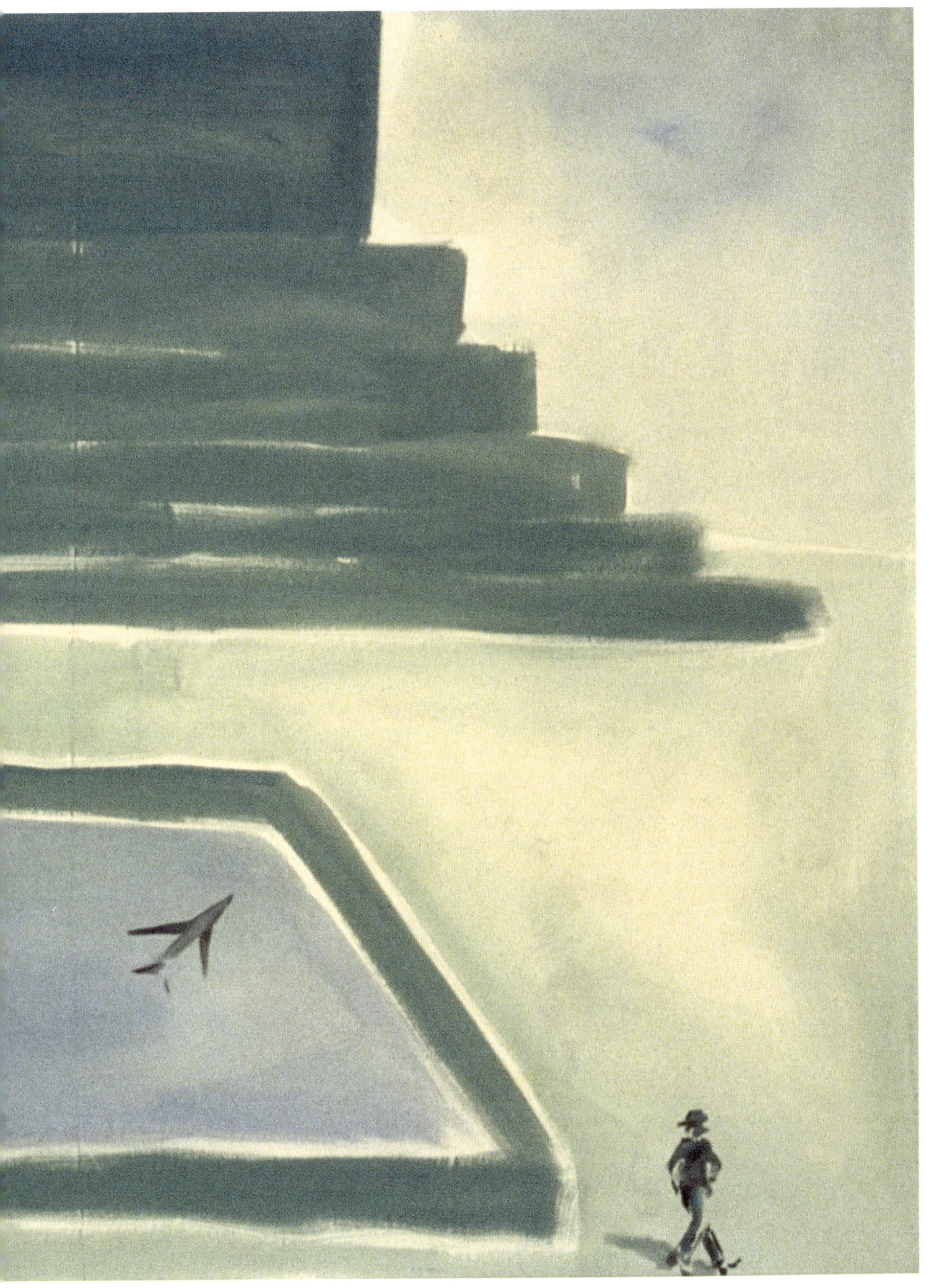

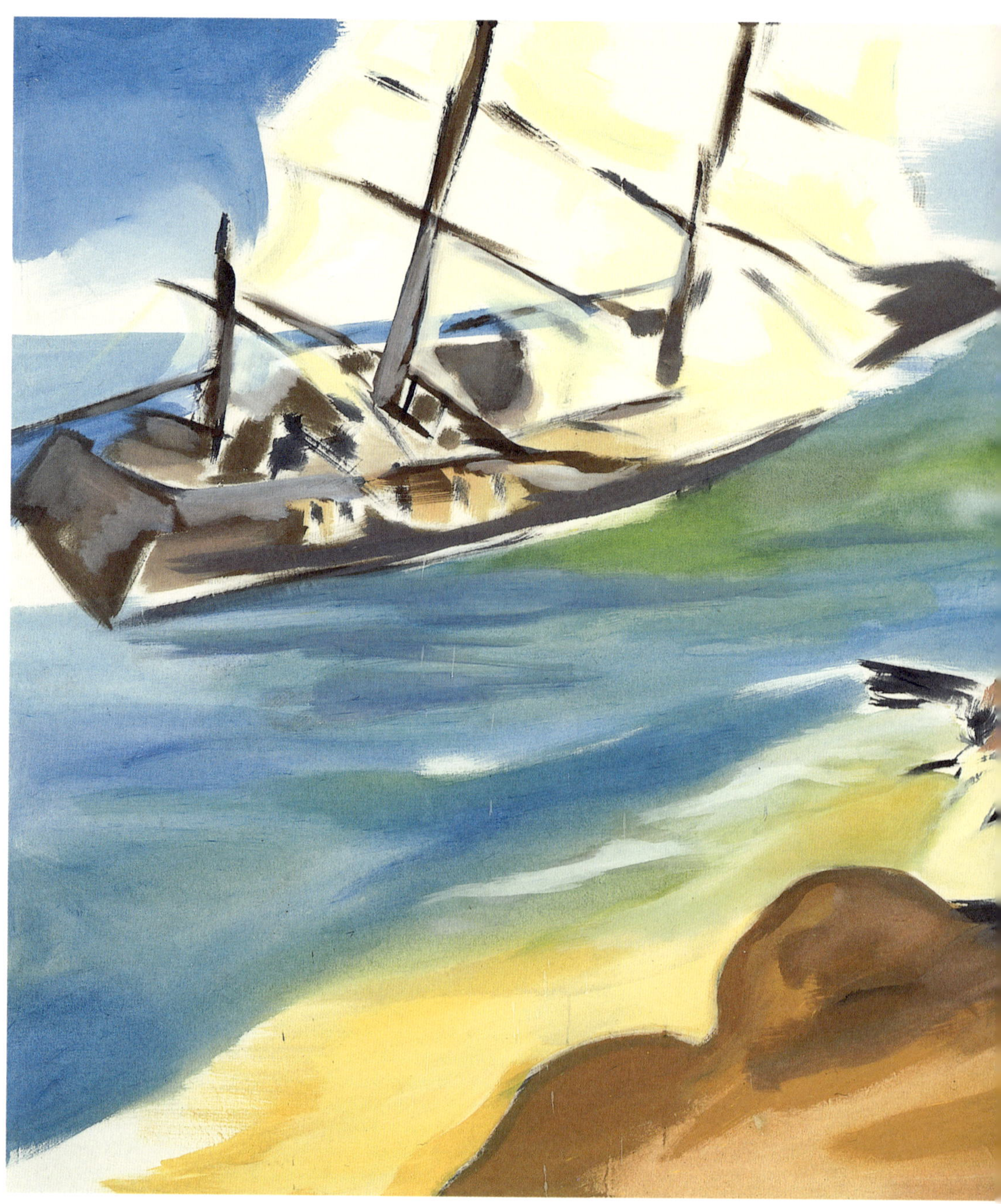

She came in through the bathroom window, 2001

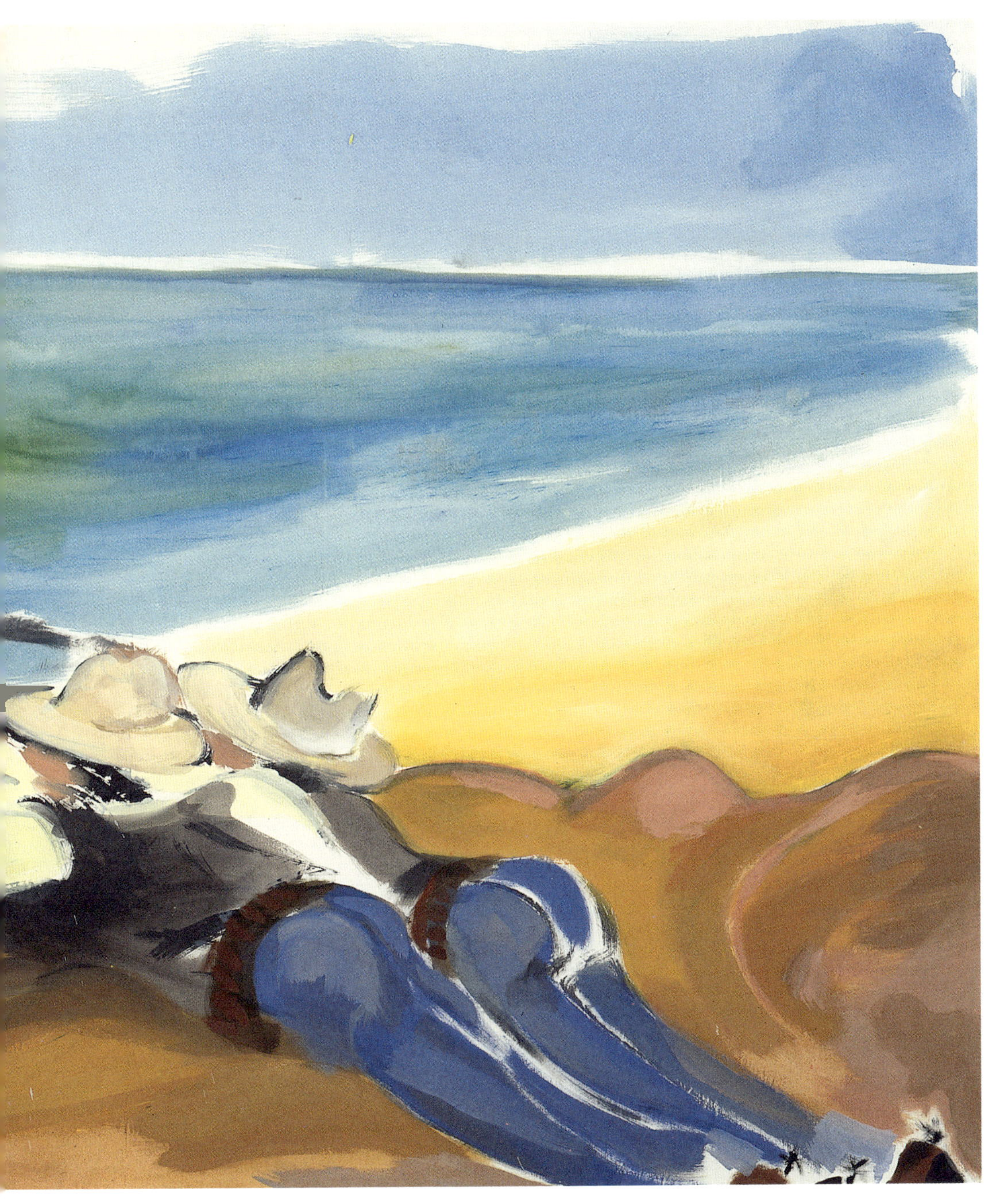

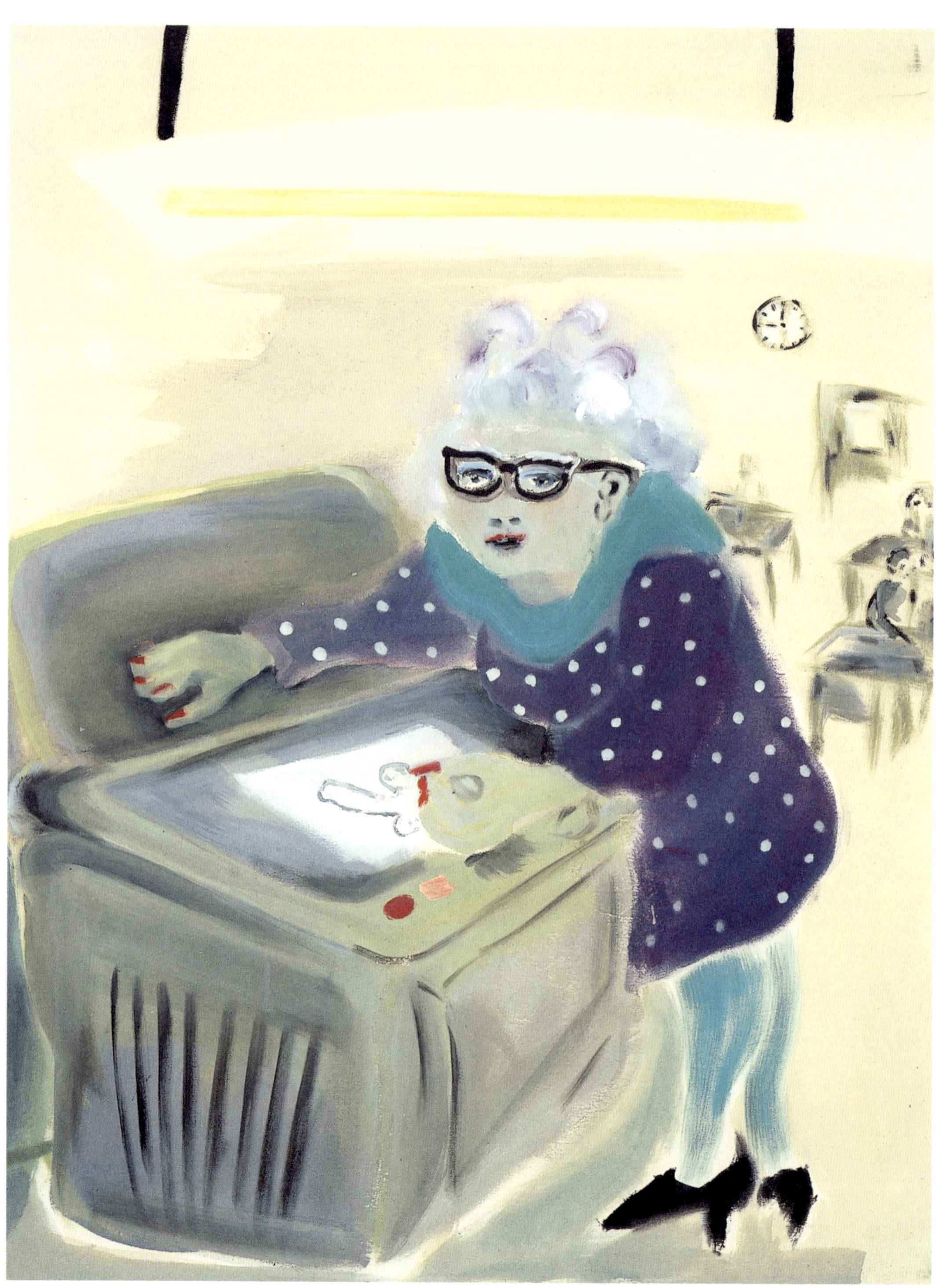

Darling, you never give me your honey, 2001

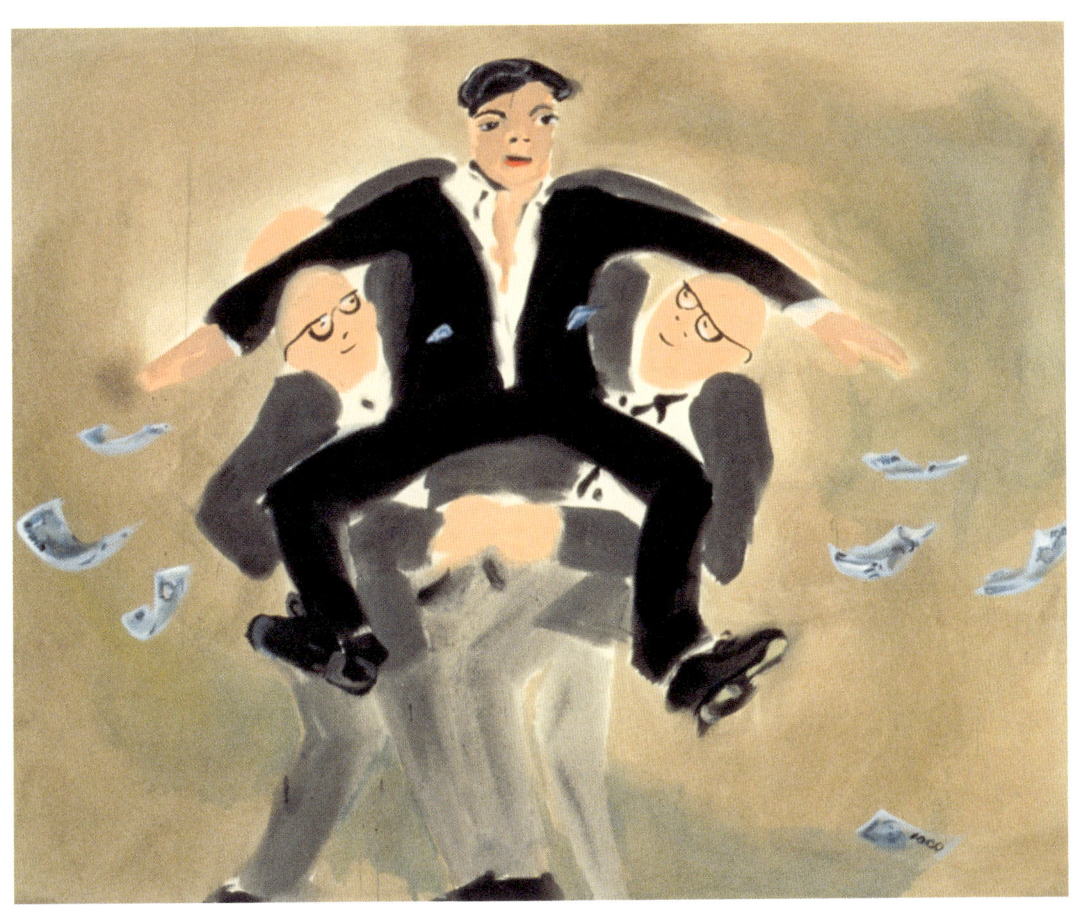

Here comes the Sun, 2001

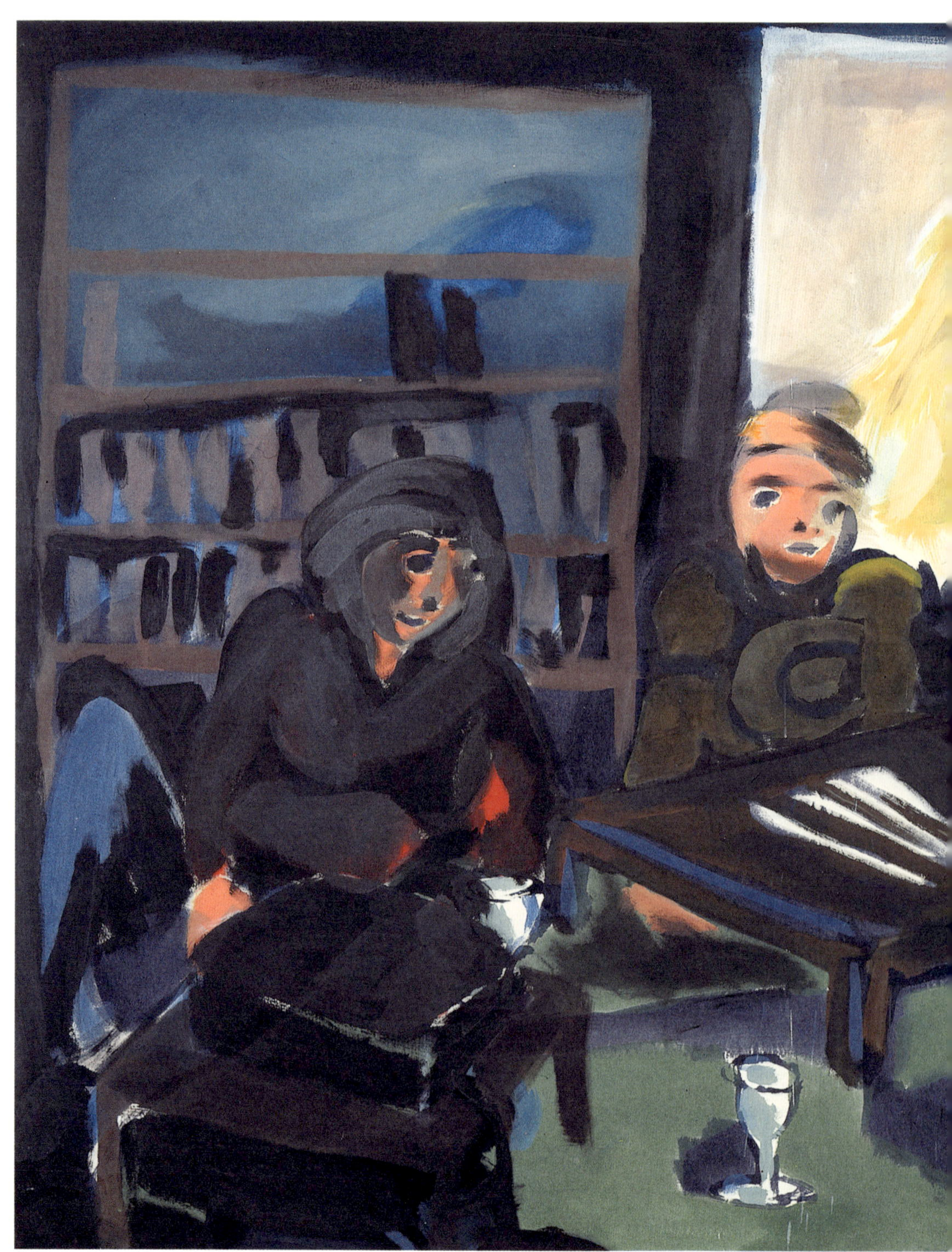

Octopus's Garden, 2001

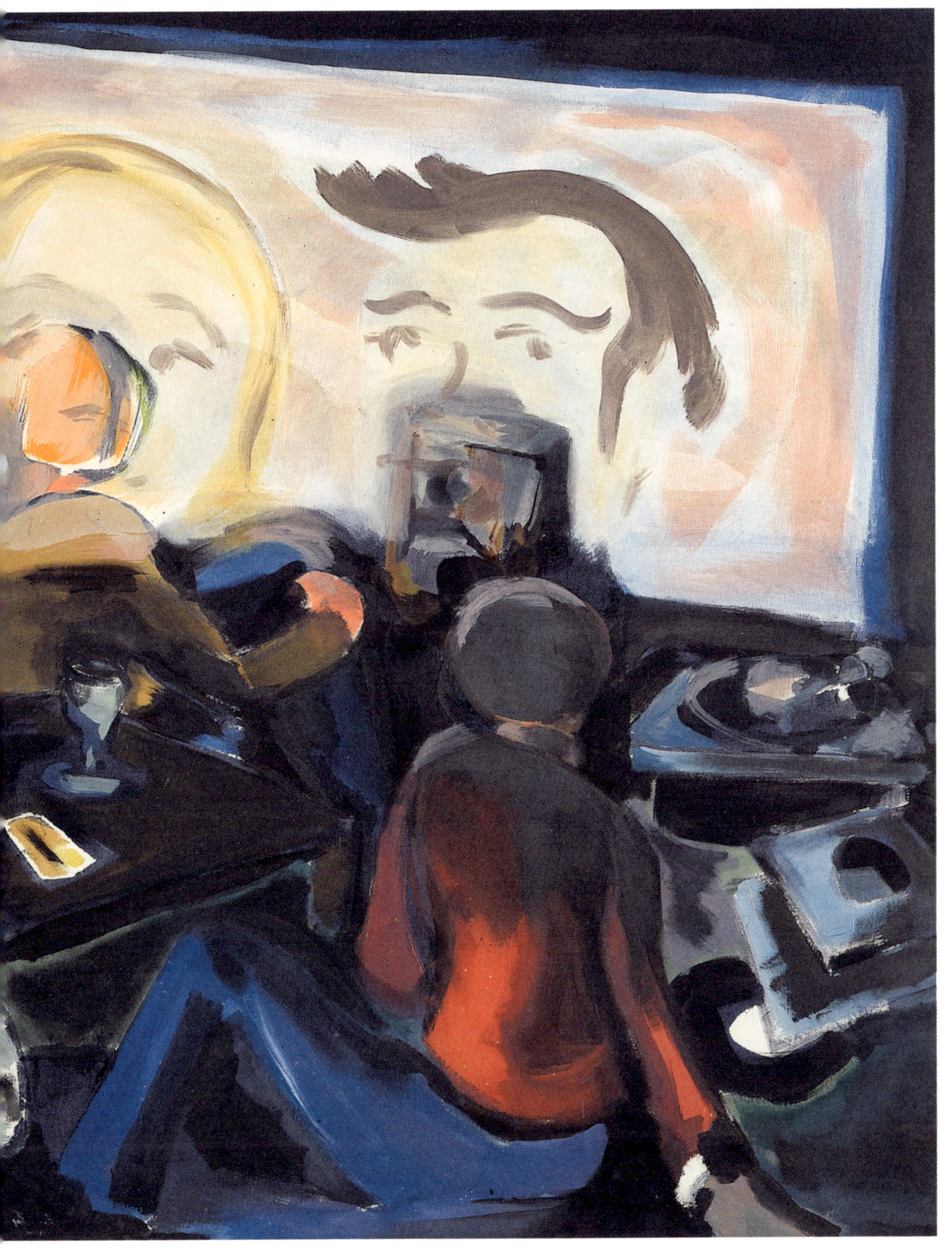

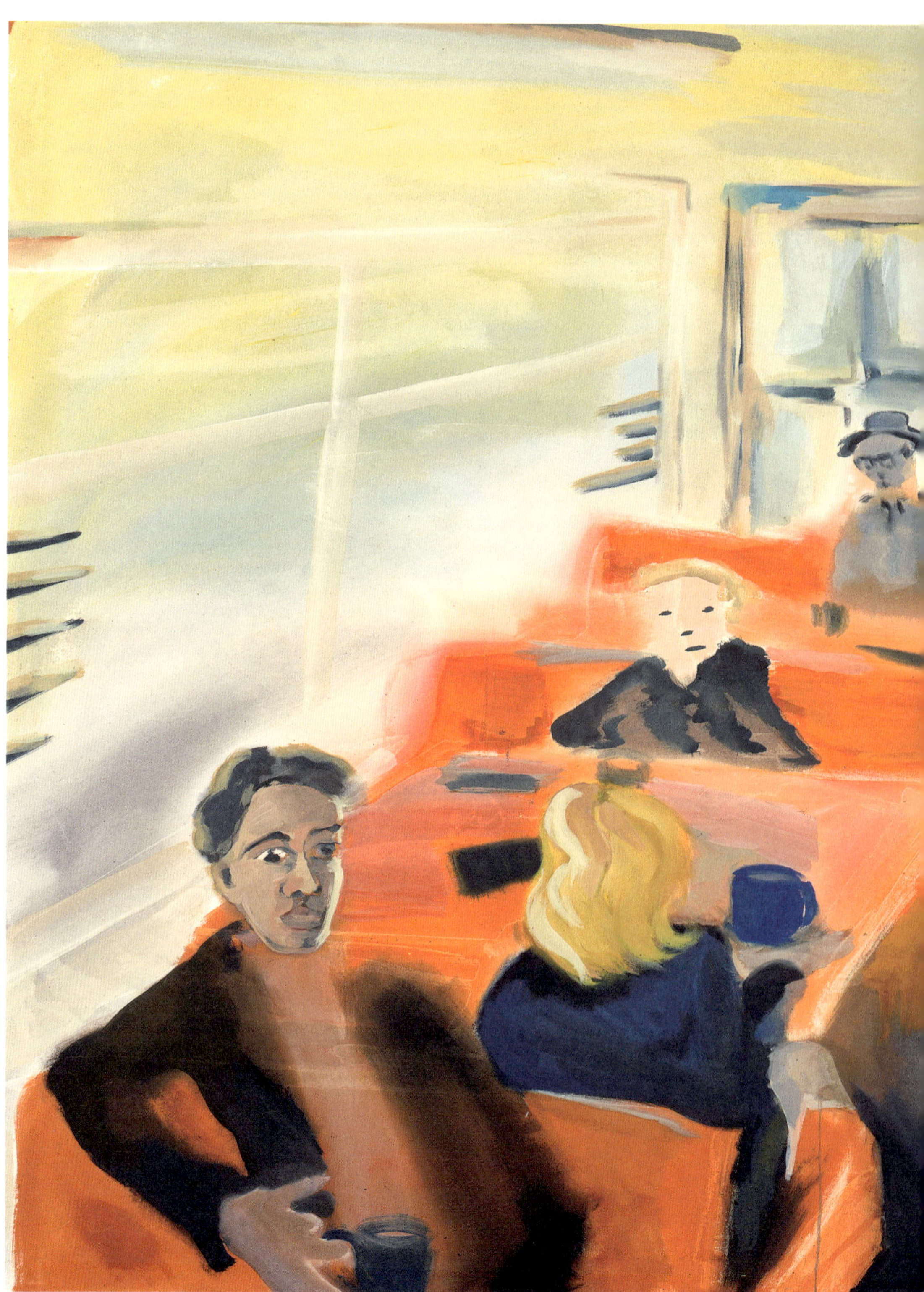

Alice in the Diner, 2001

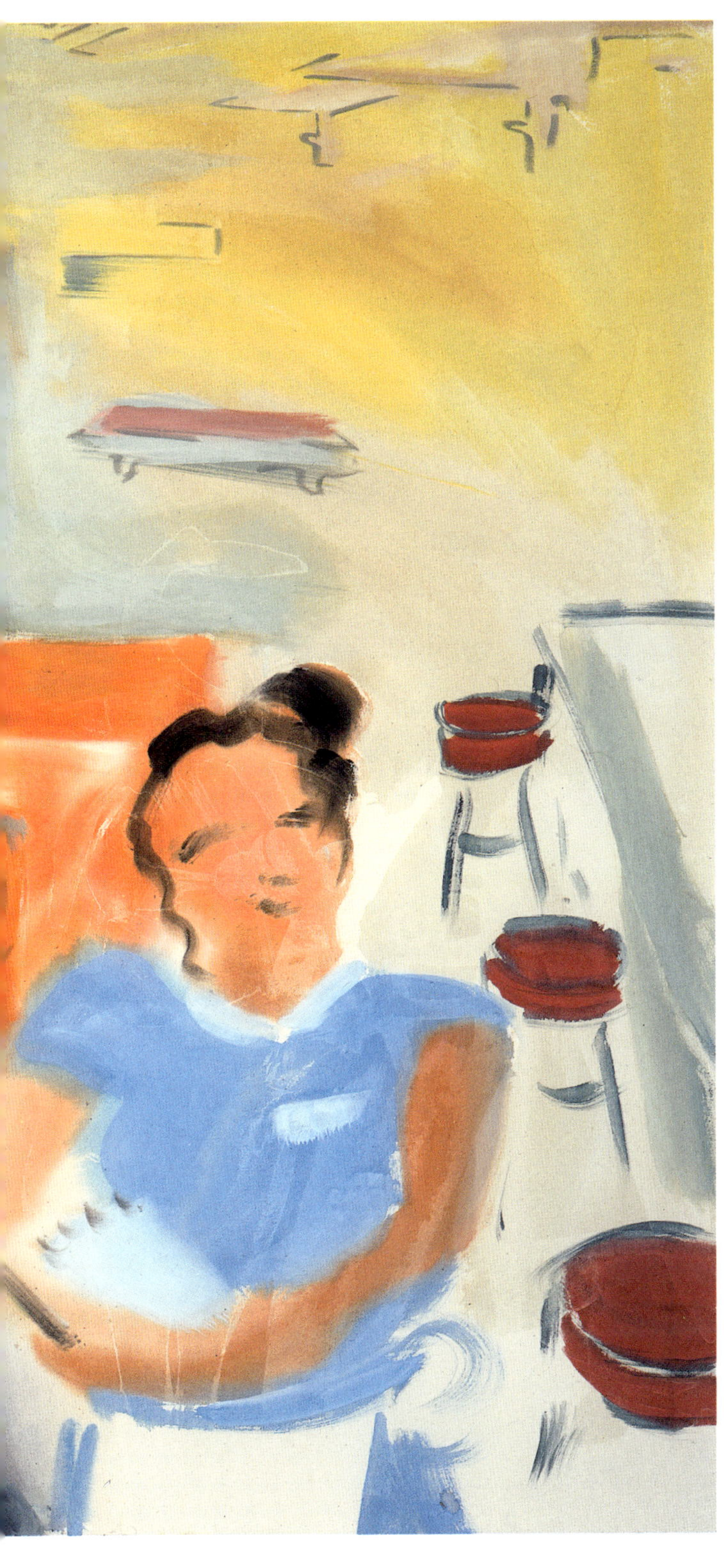

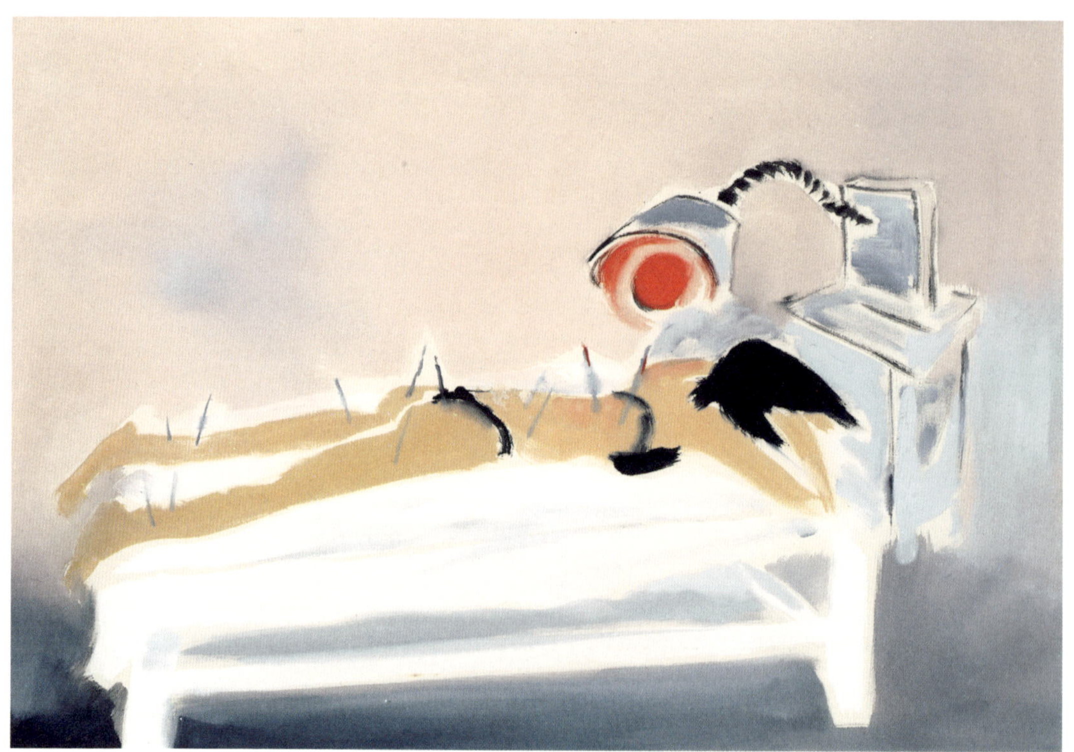

Acupuncture, 2001

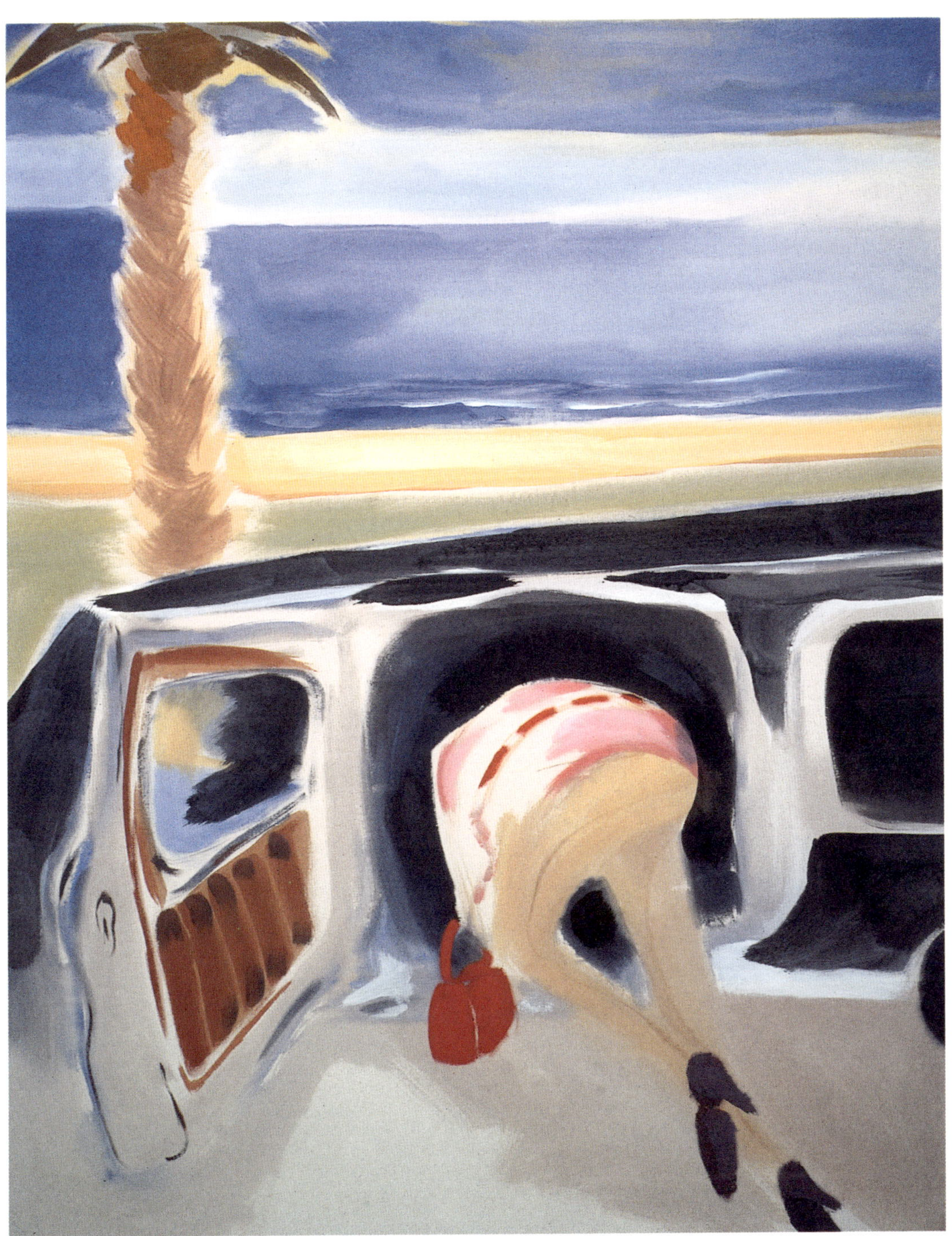

Alice going down the black hole, 2001

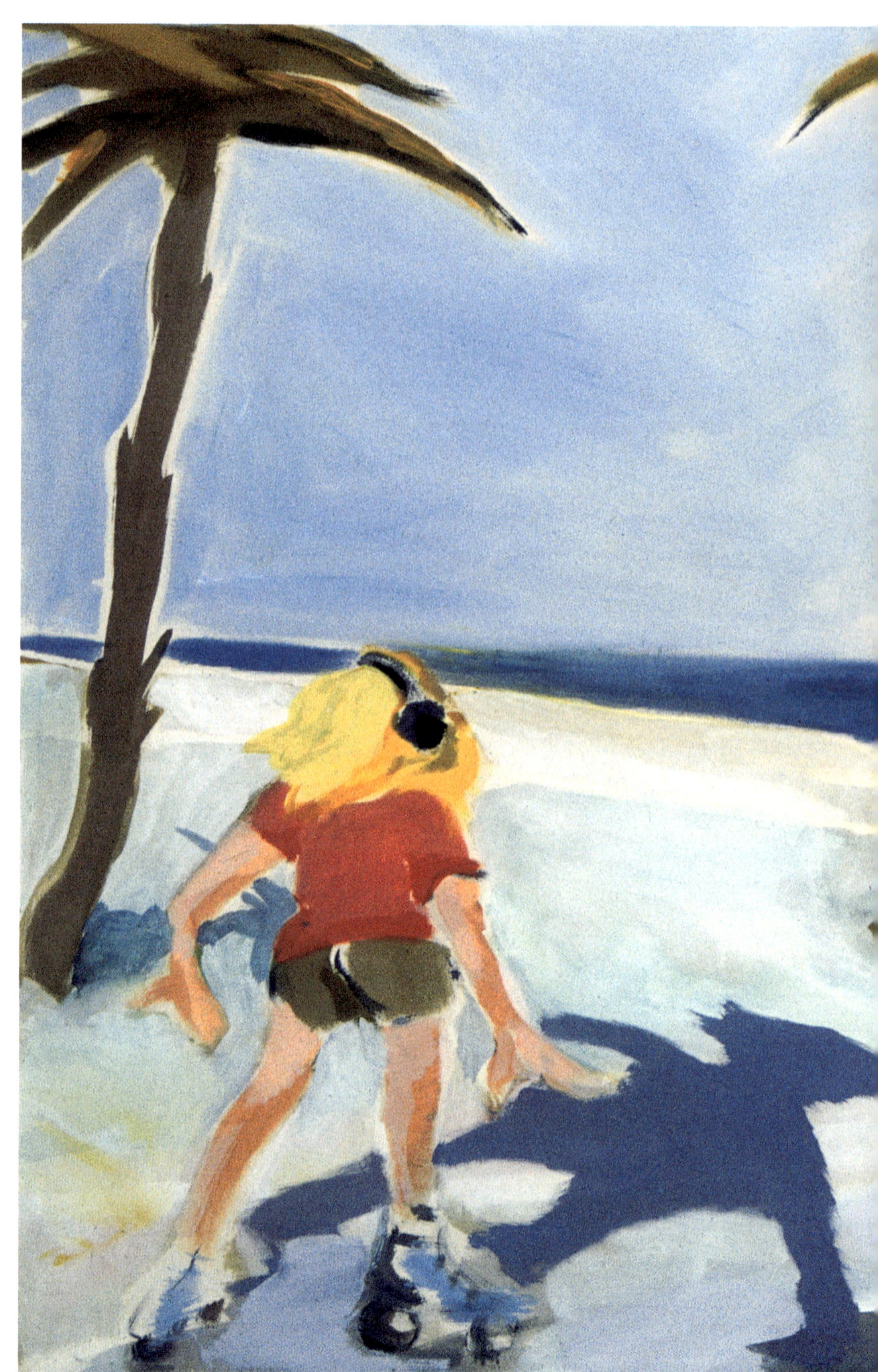

 Skate Board, Santa Monica, 2001

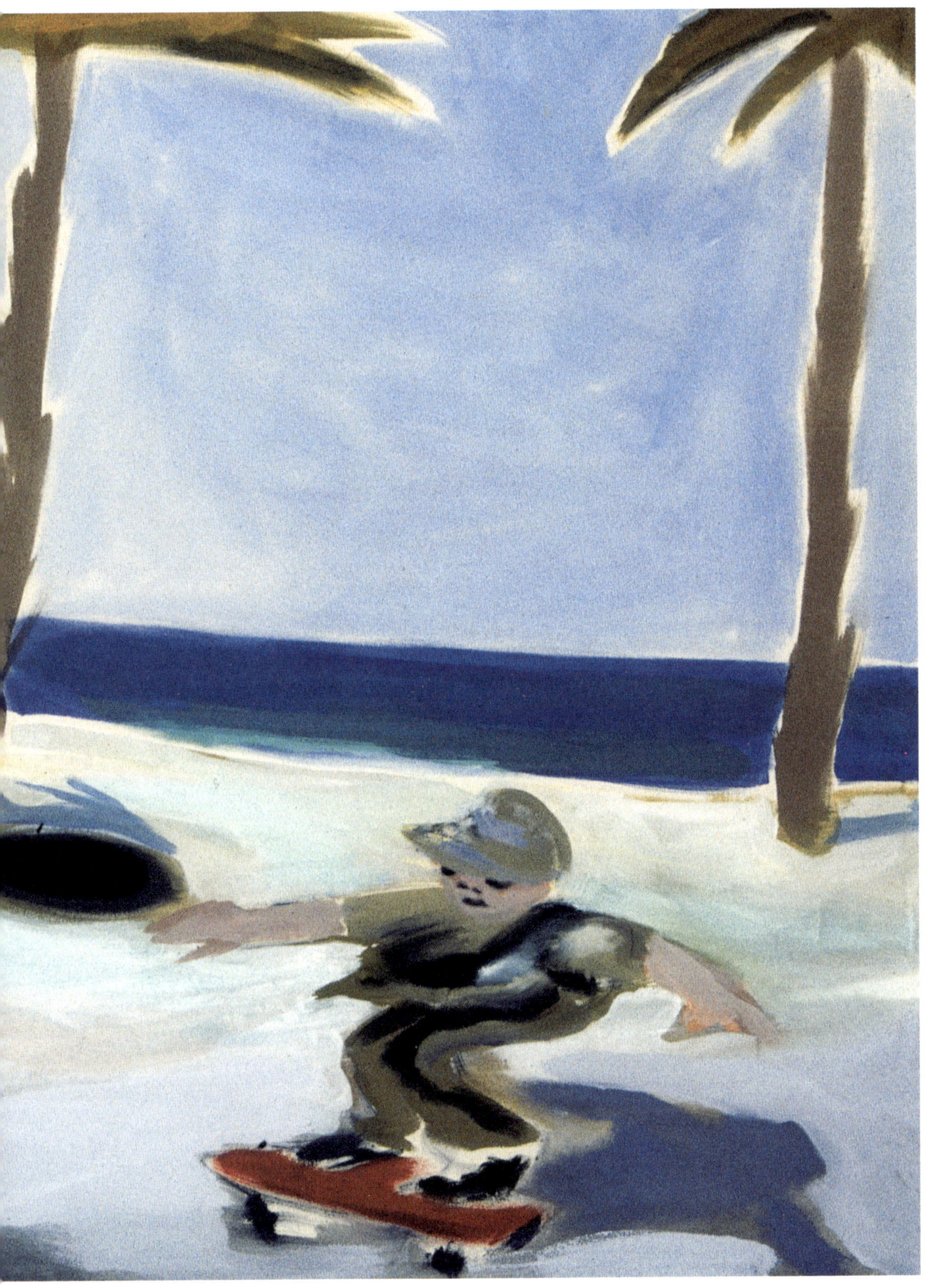

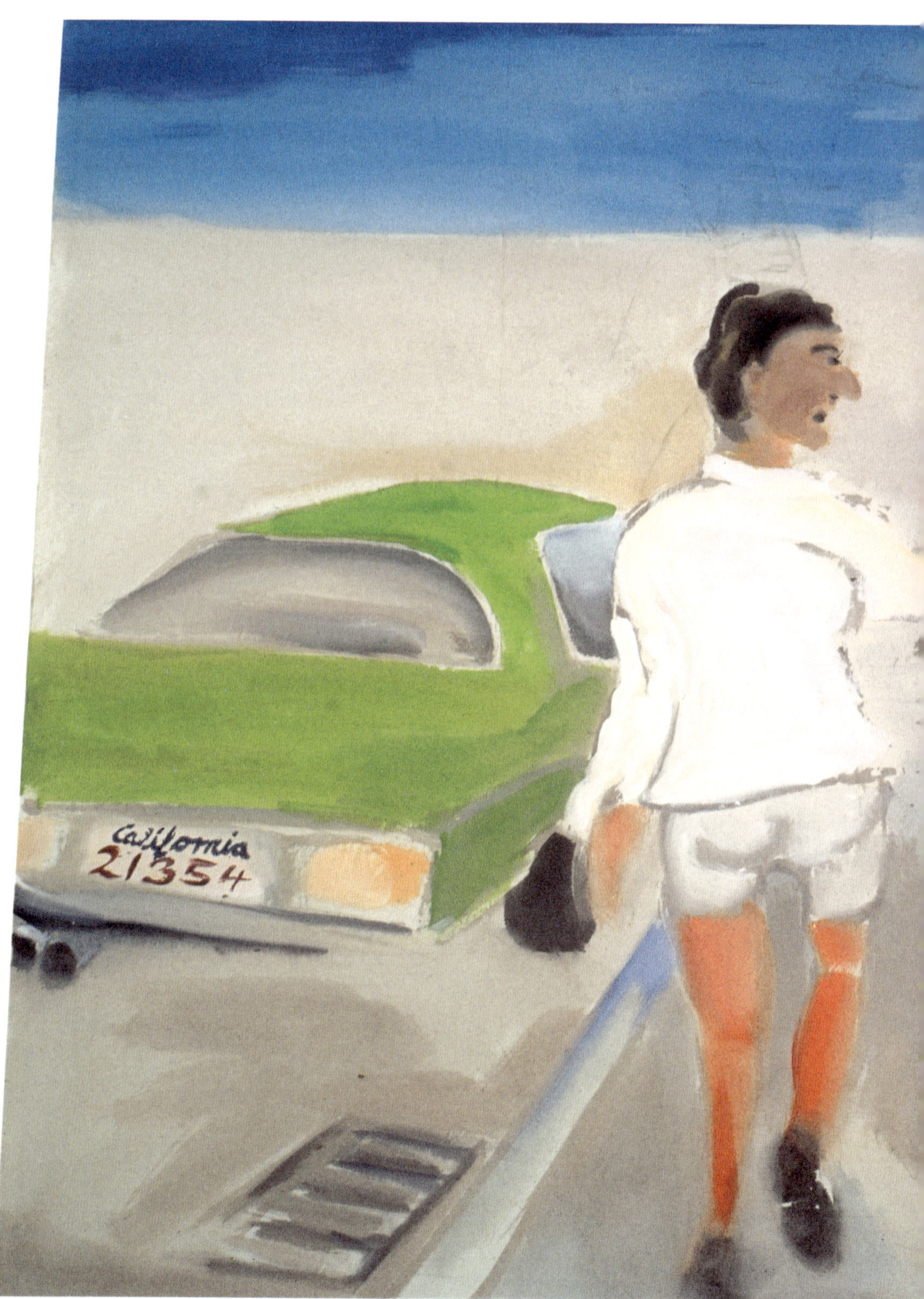

Marc Foxx, 2001

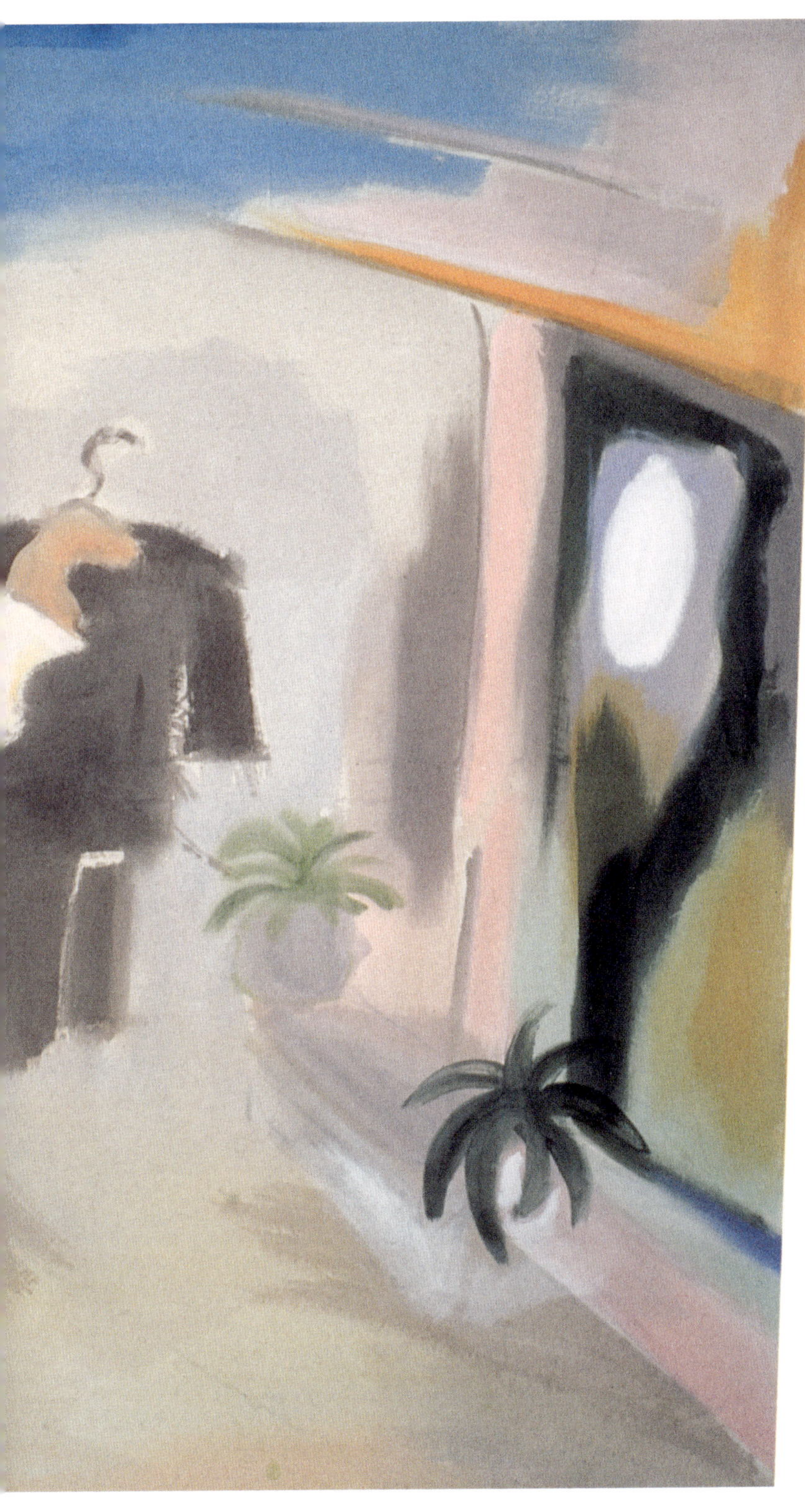

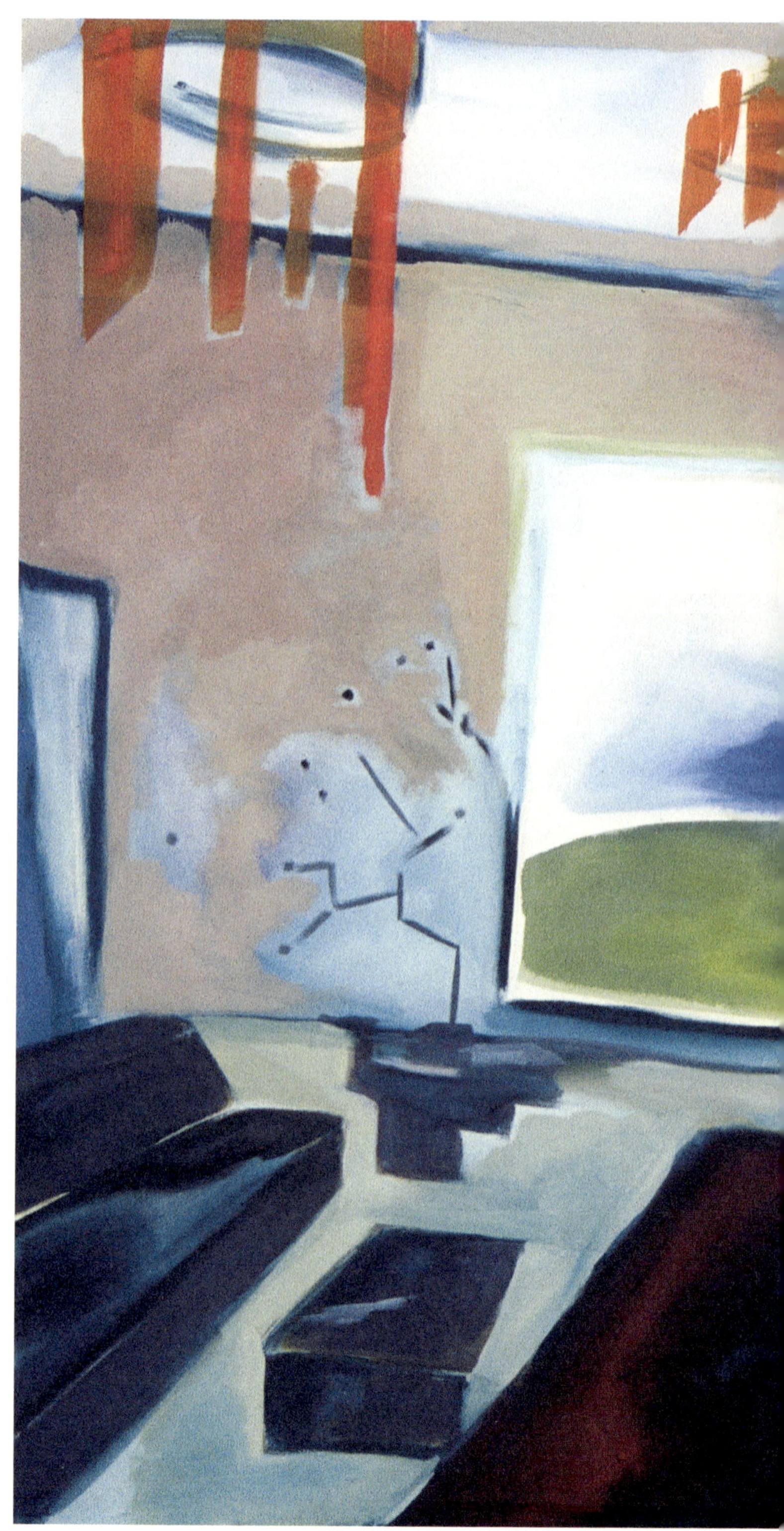

Check In, 2001

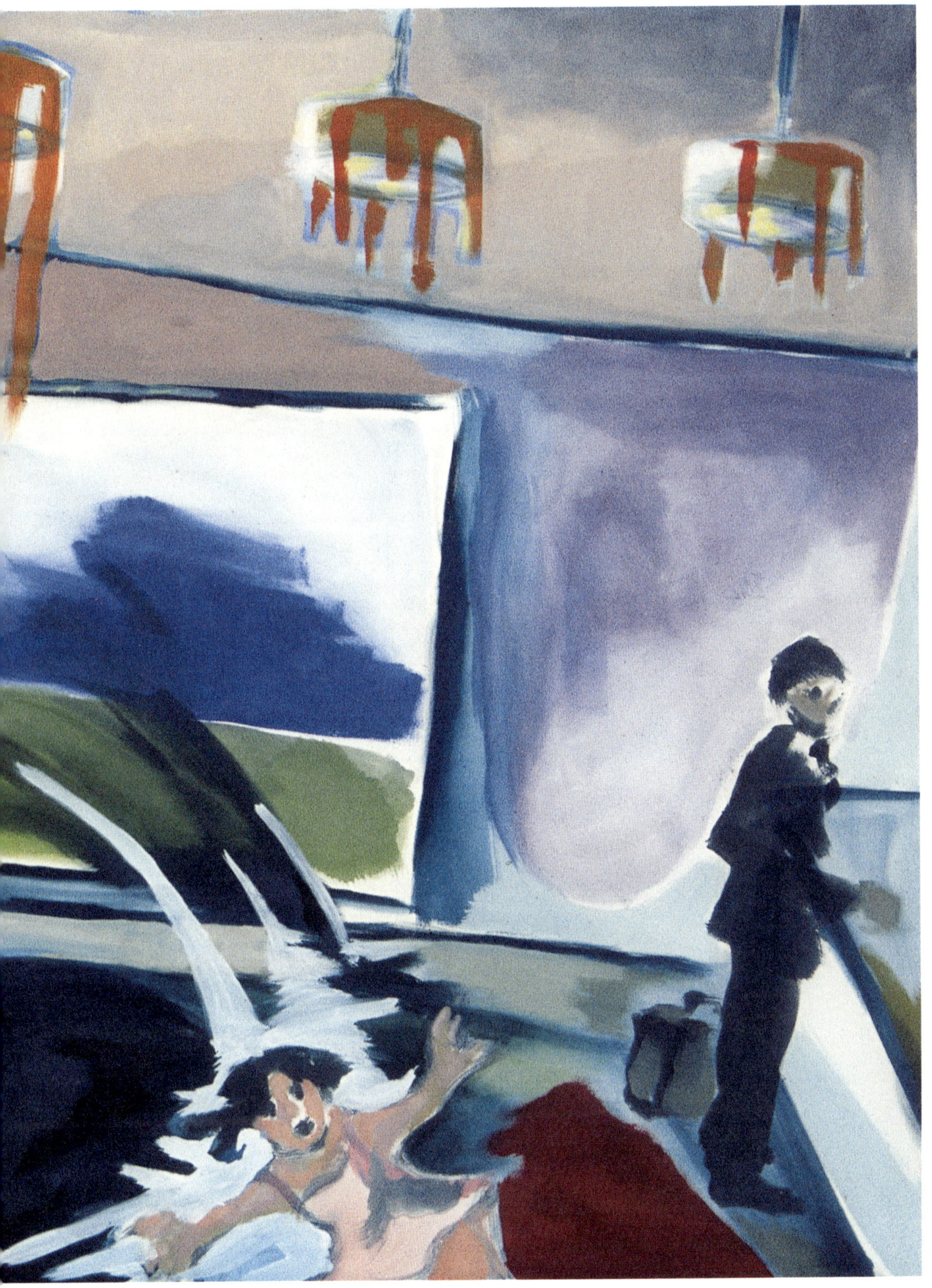

Director's House, 2002

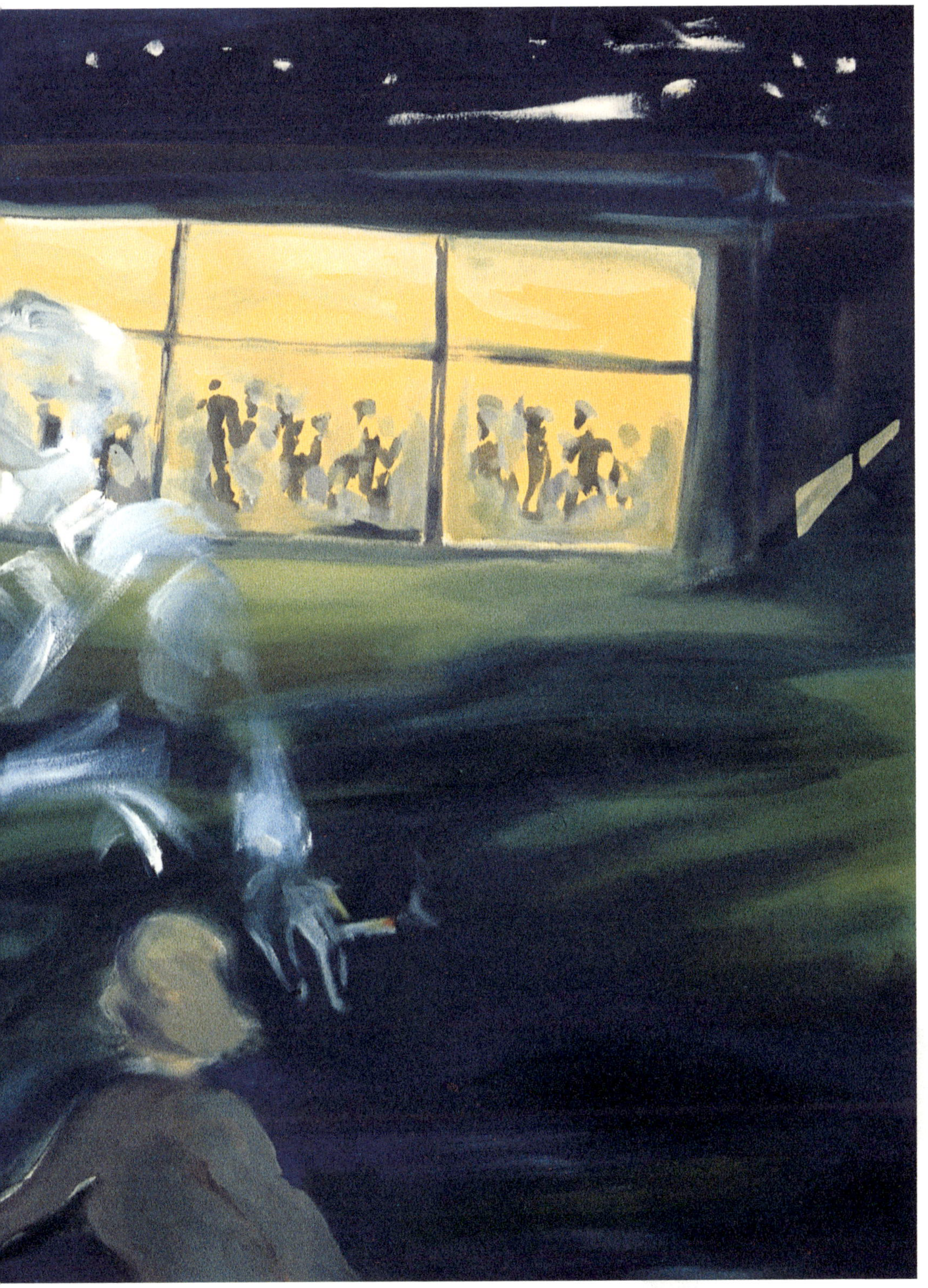

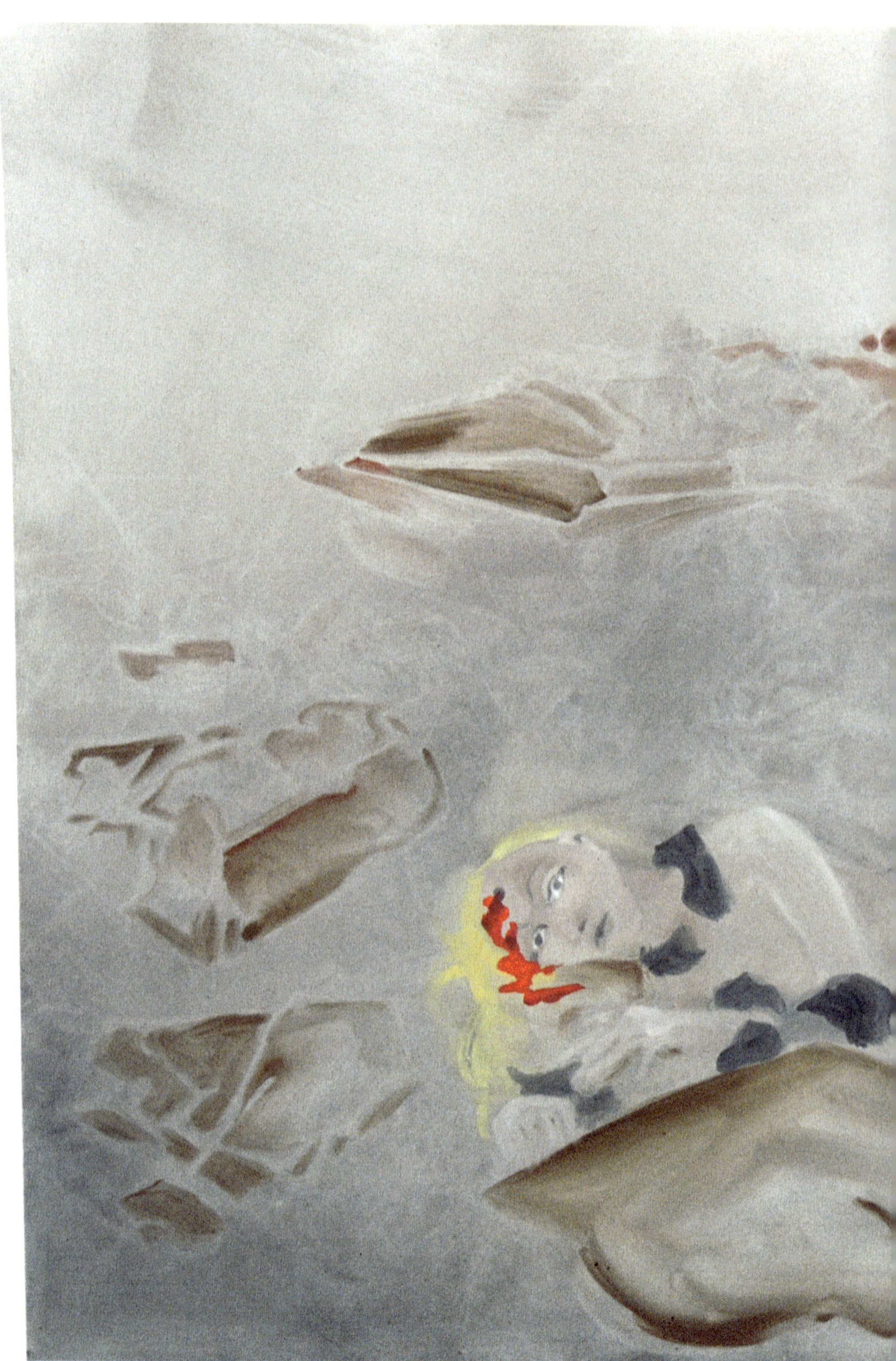

  Really Dead, 2001

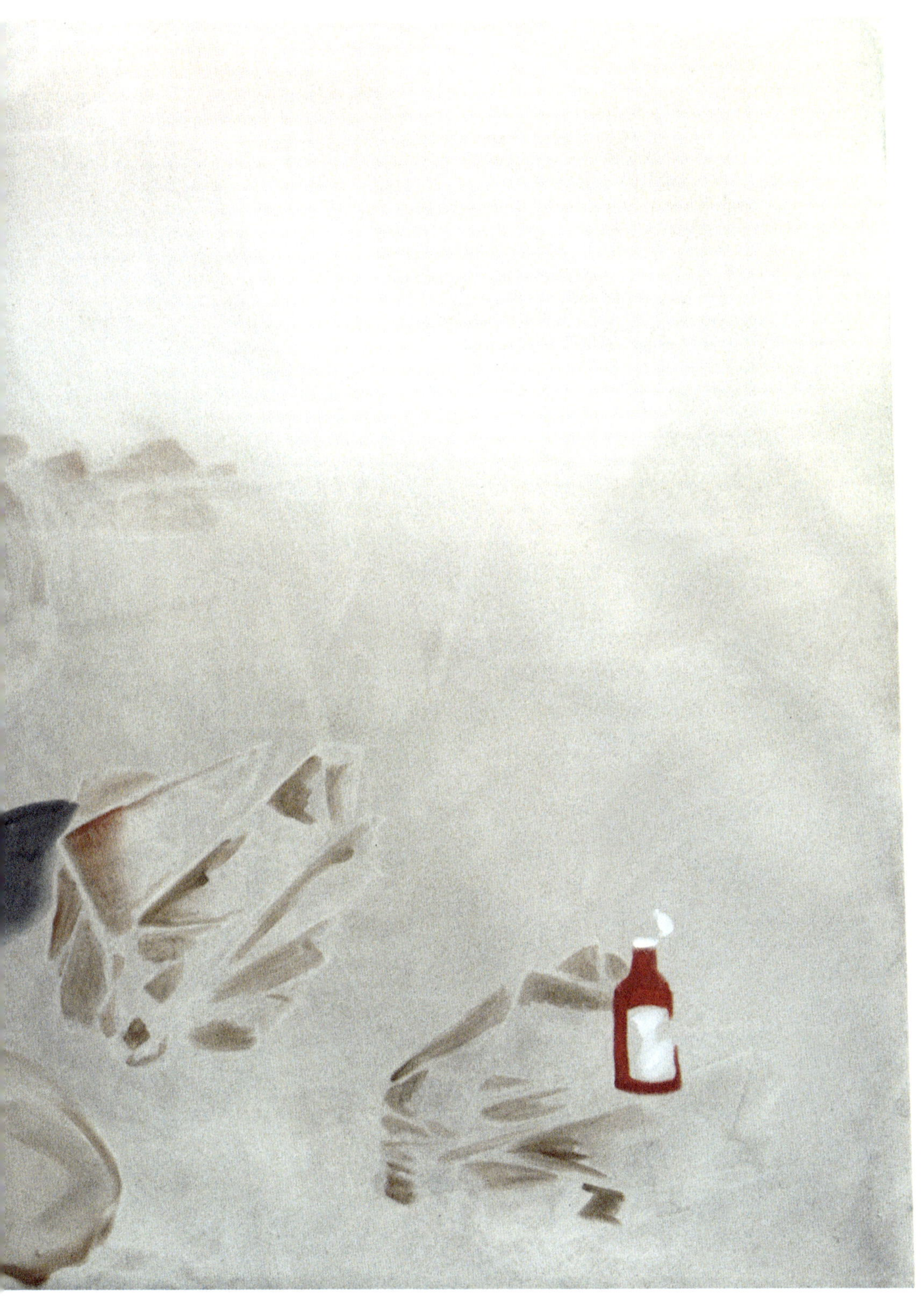

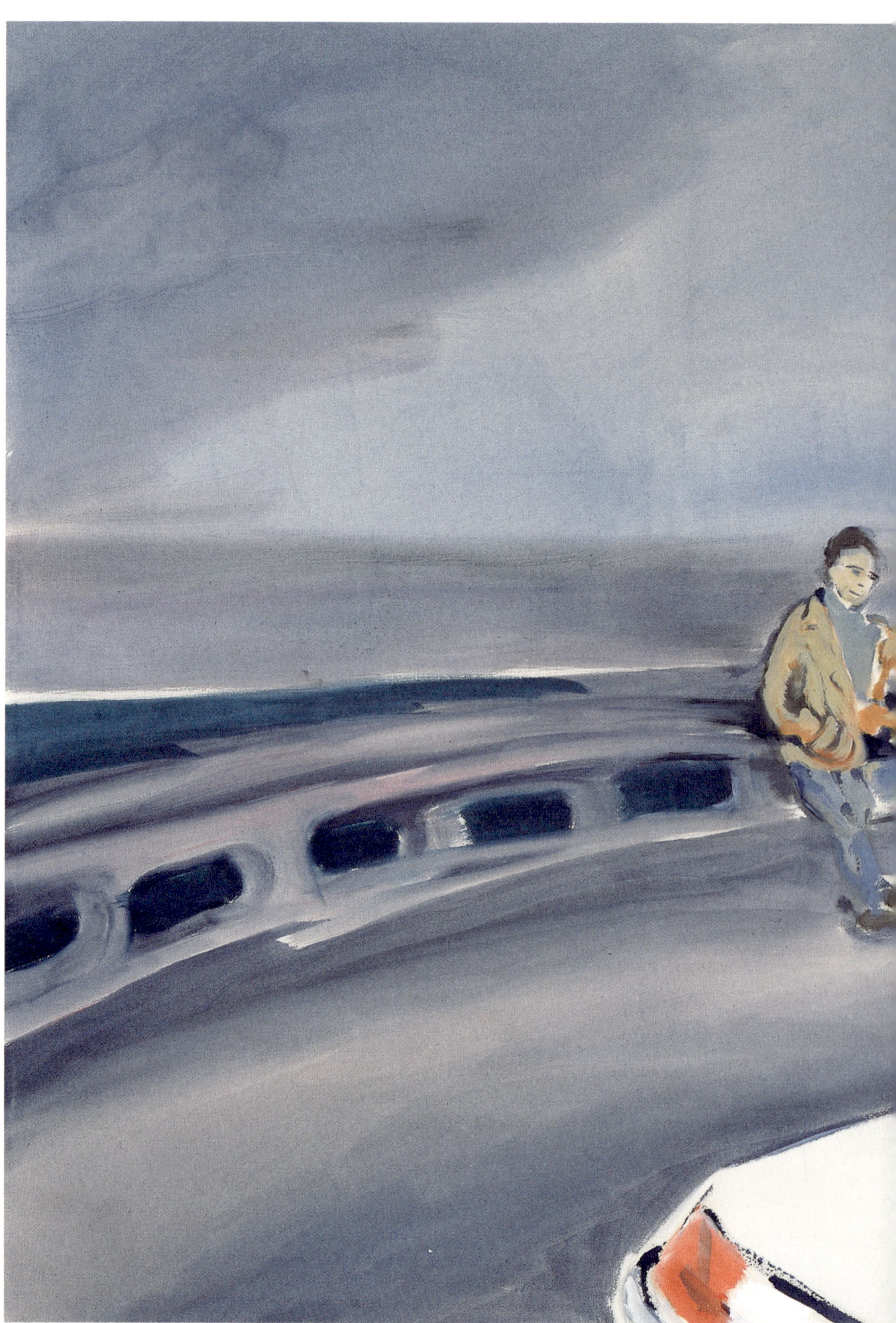

   Dirty Bath Water, 2001

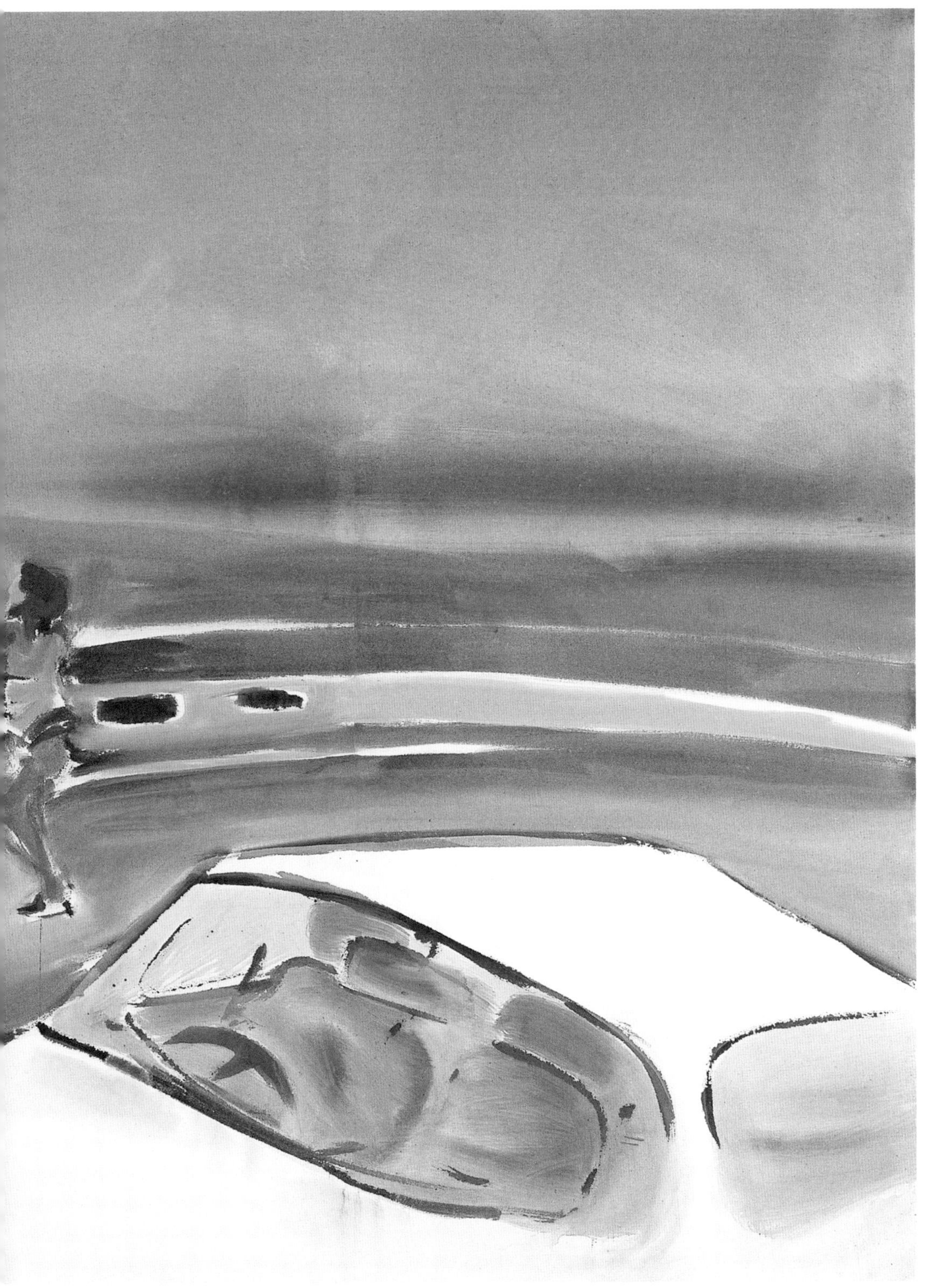

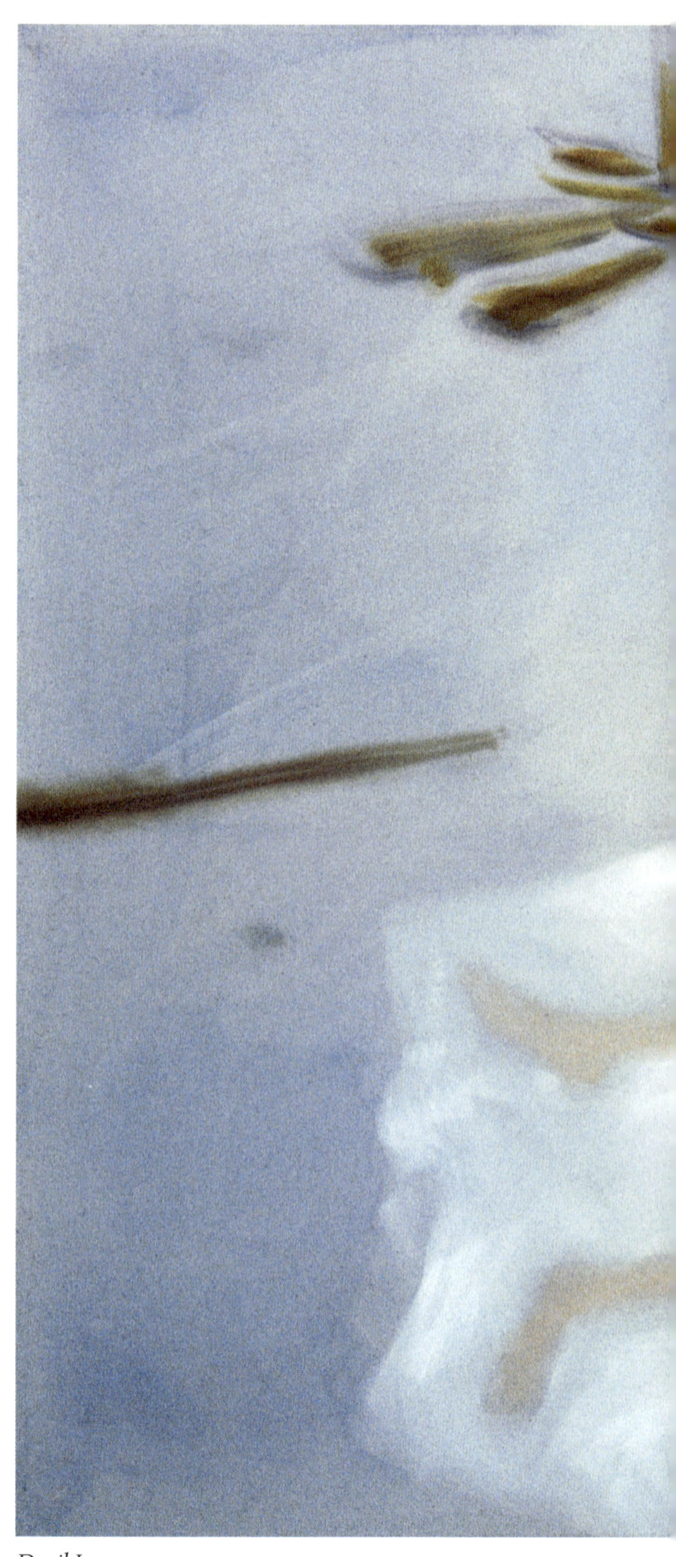

Devil Lovers, 2001

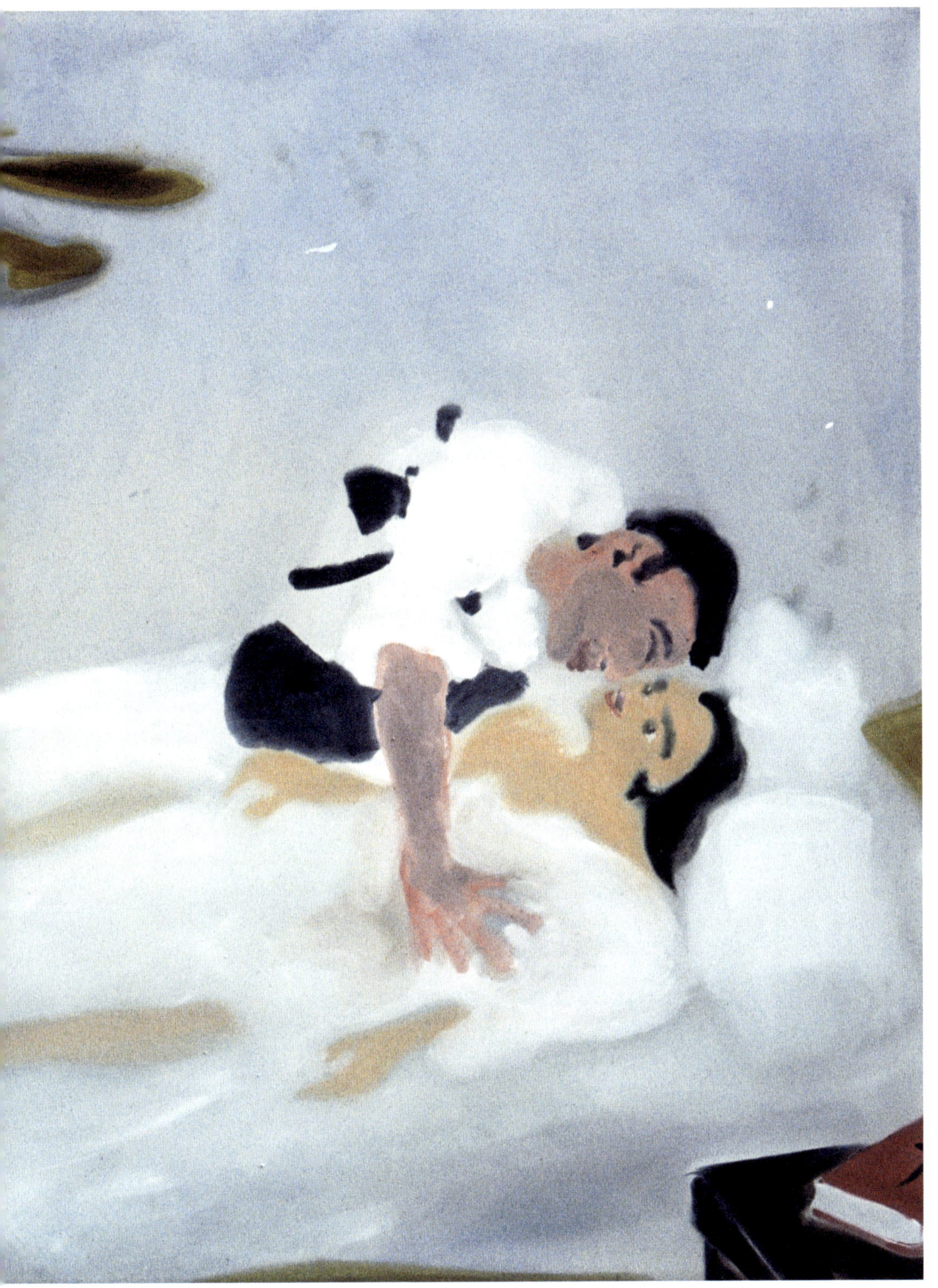

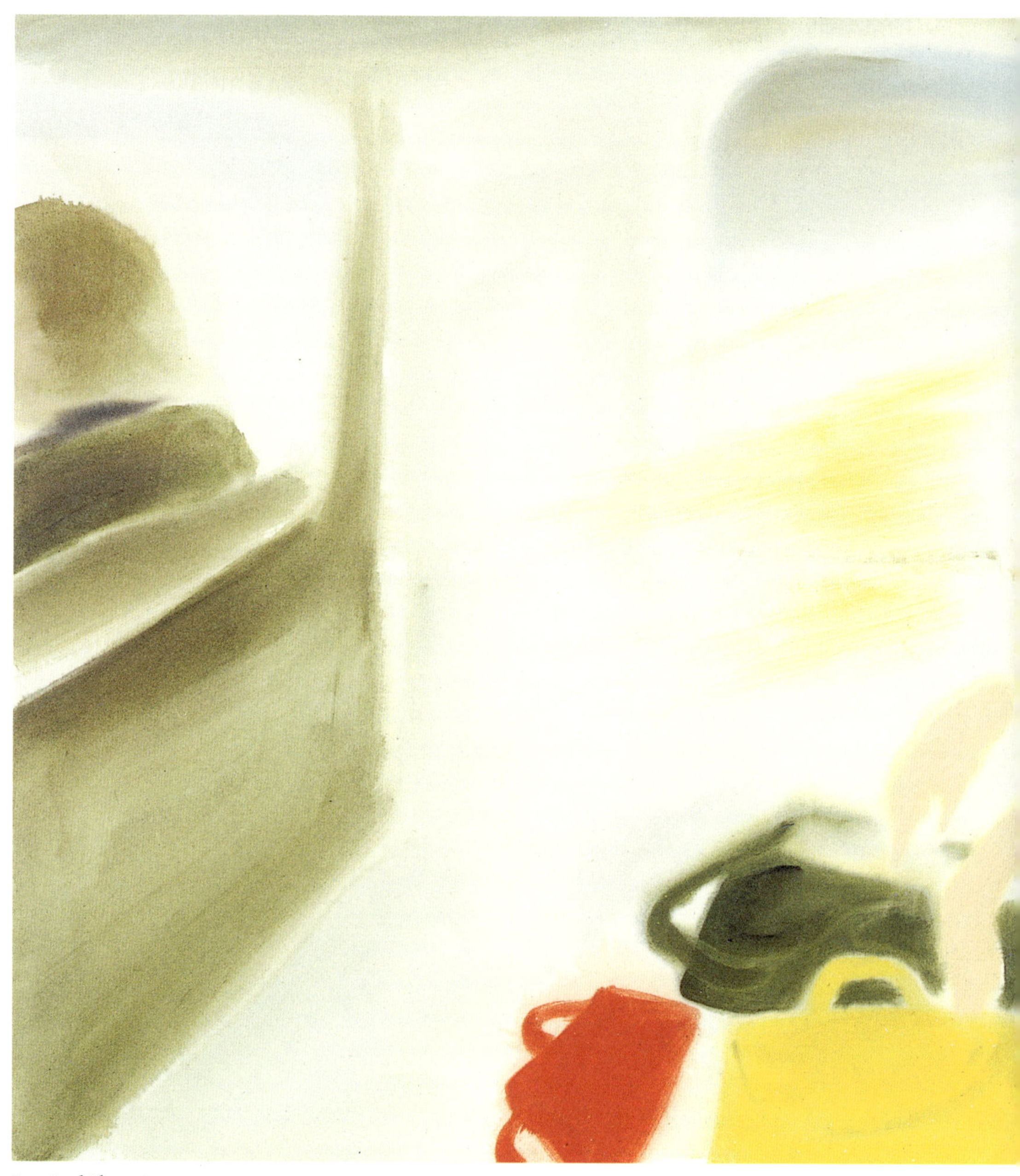

Inspired Shopping, 2002

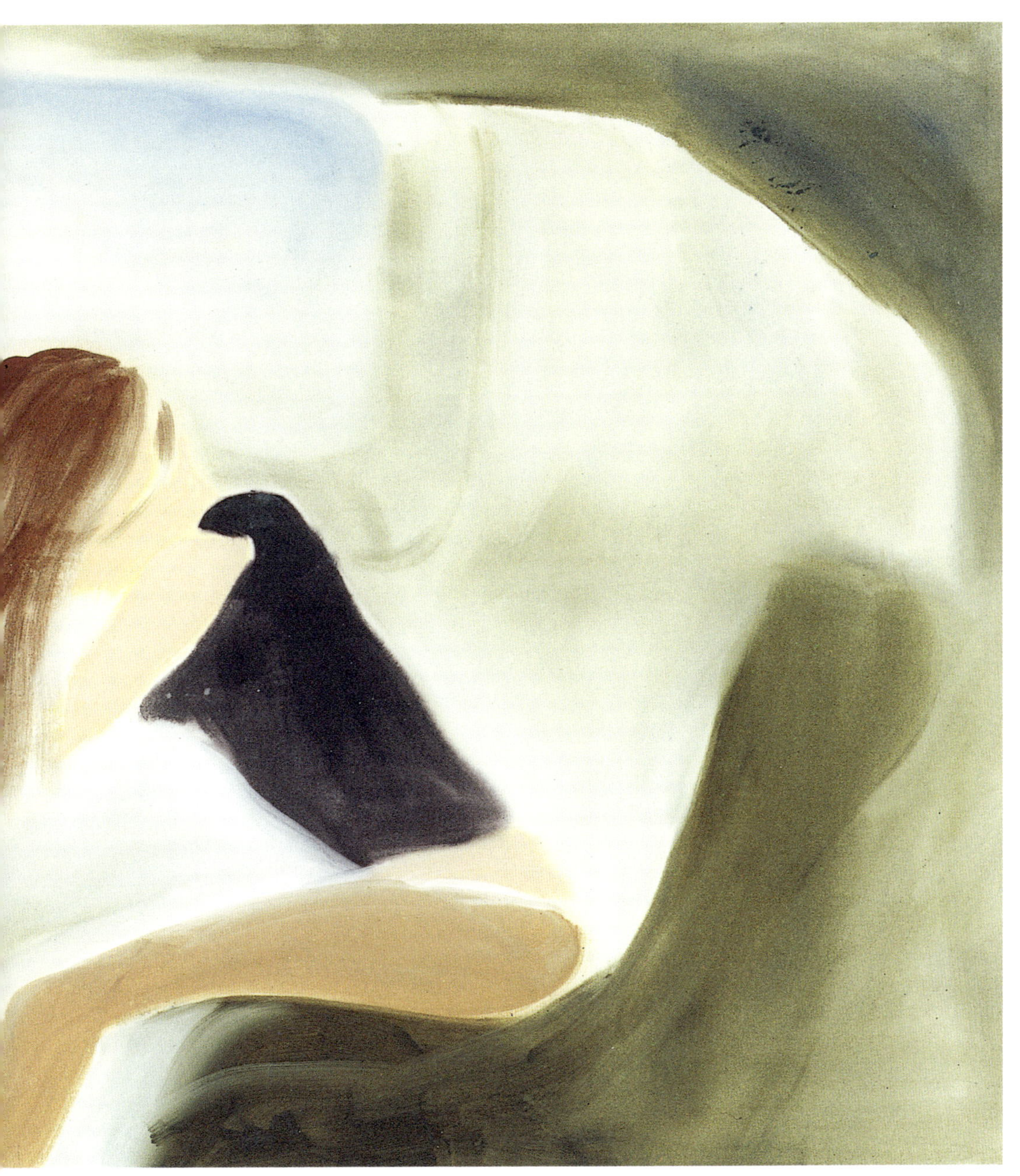

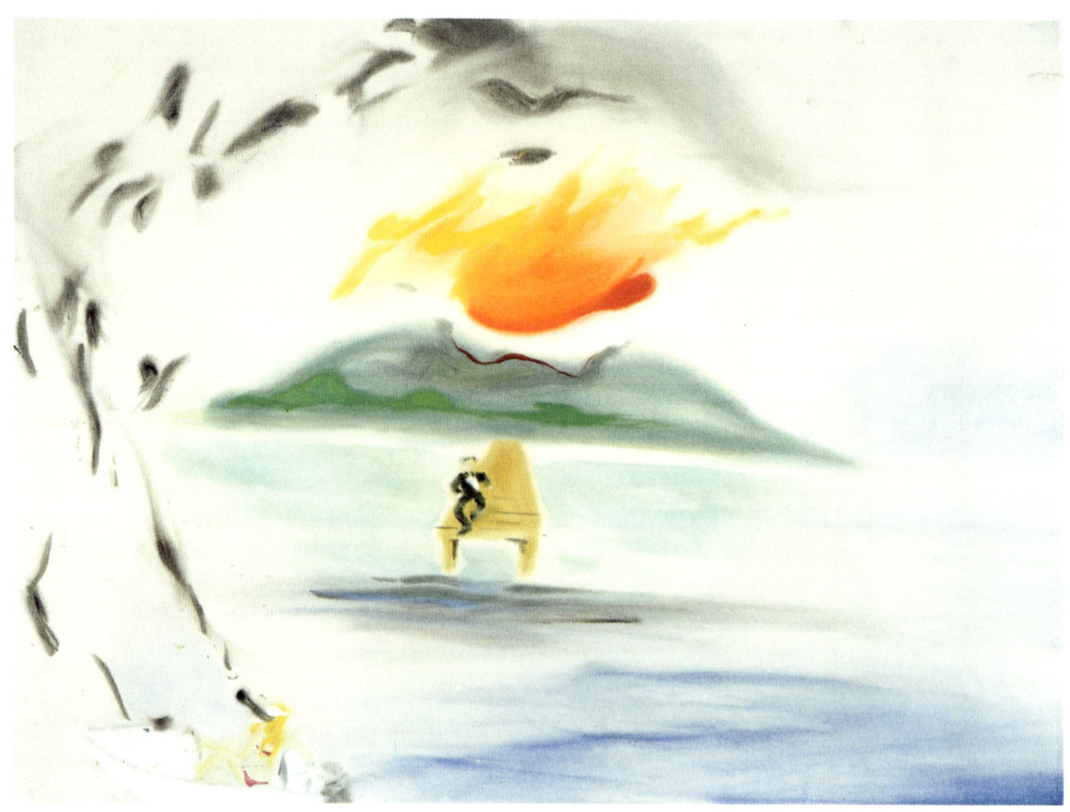

Take Me Baby, 2002

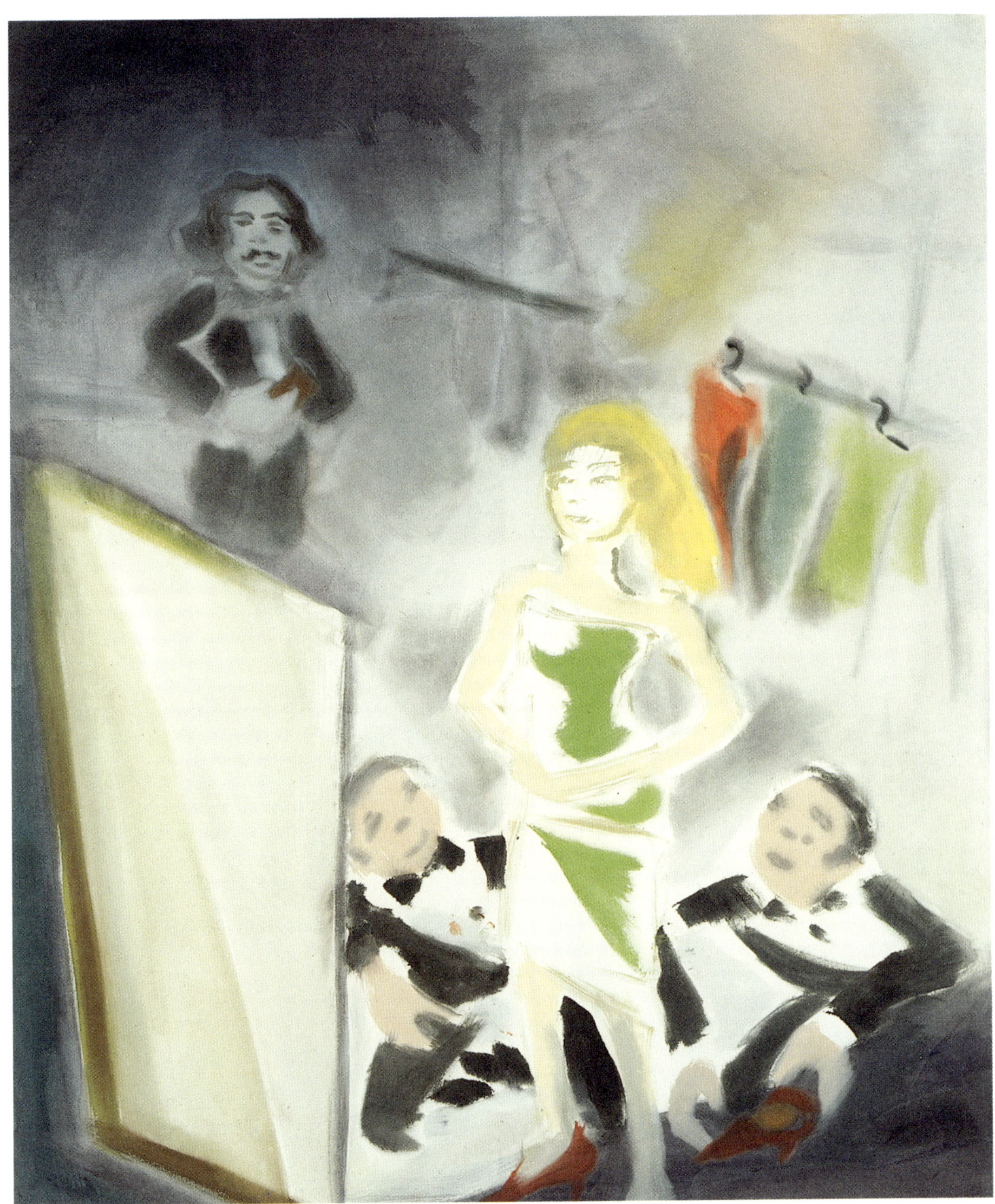

Fitting in Prado, 2002

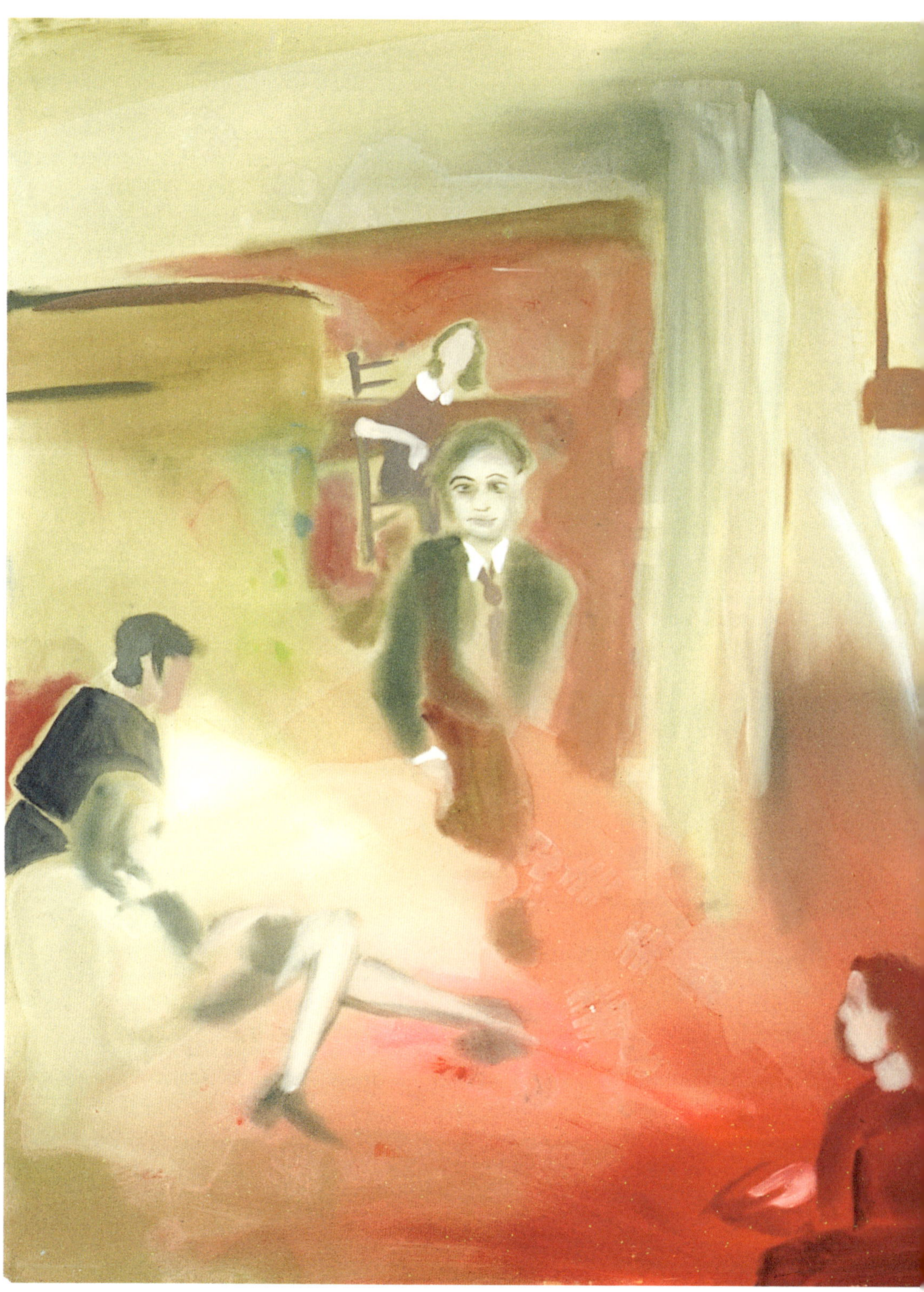

Deco Morons (Bedford Place), 2002

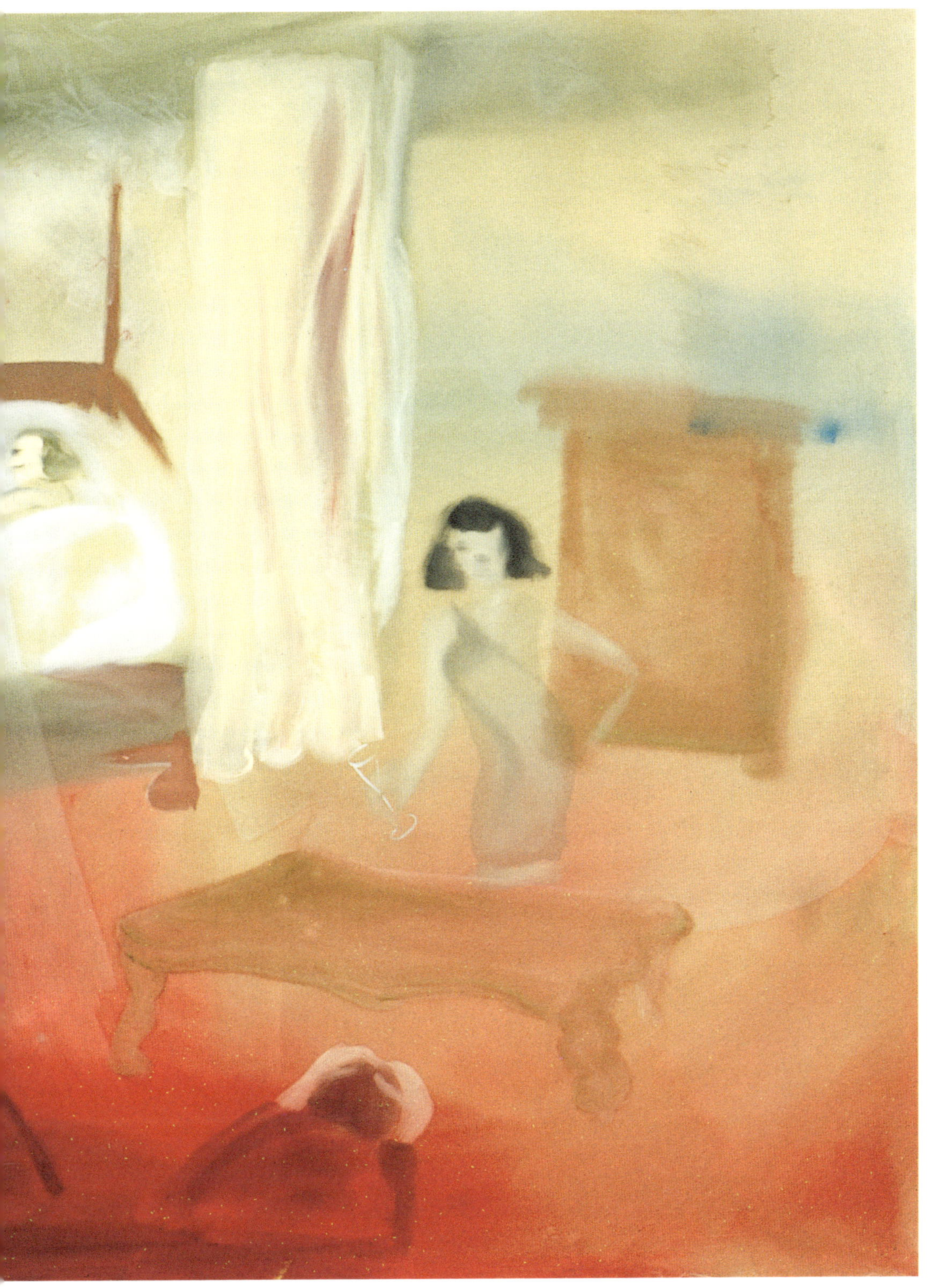

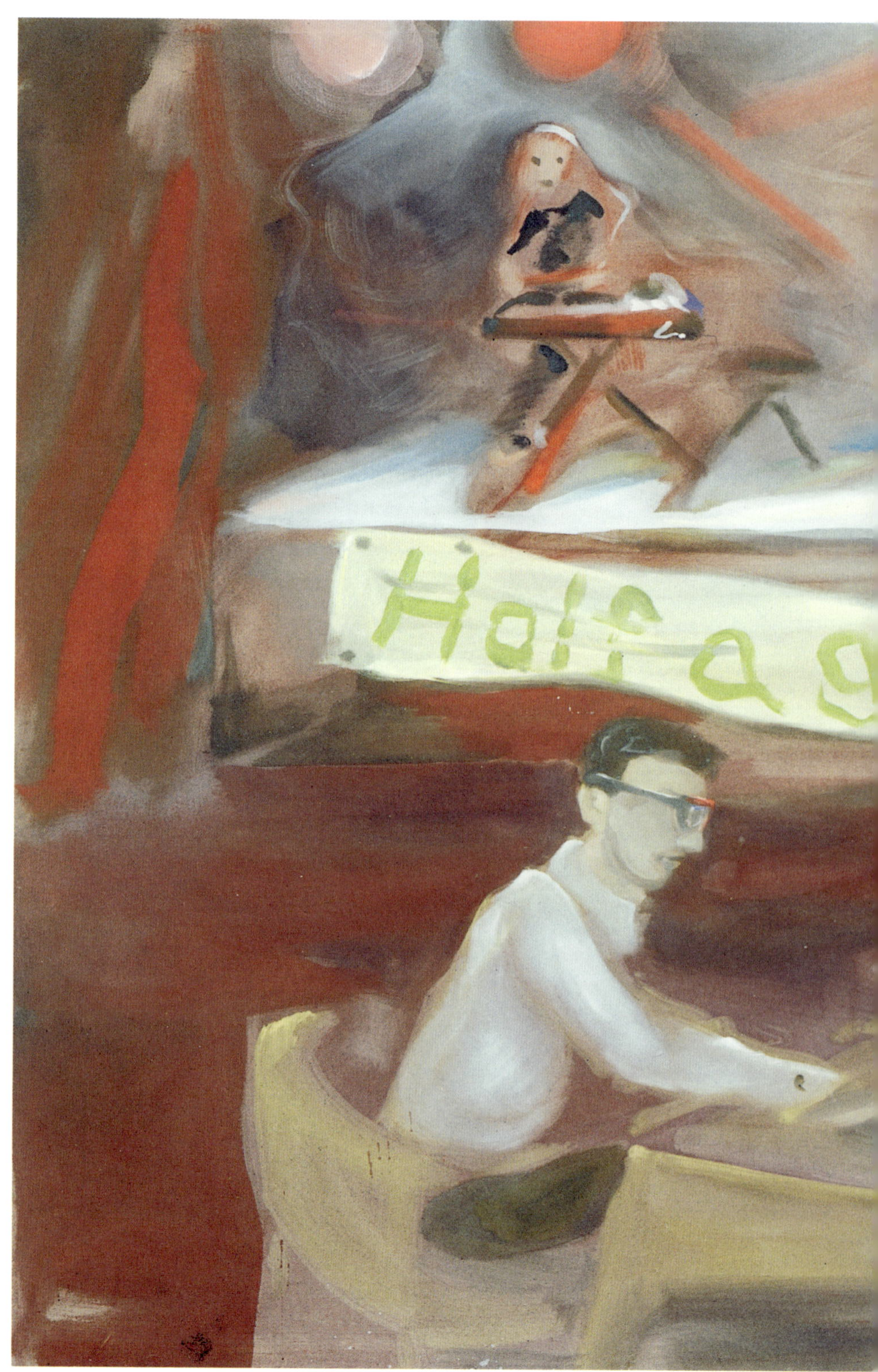

122   *Half a Good Day*, 2002

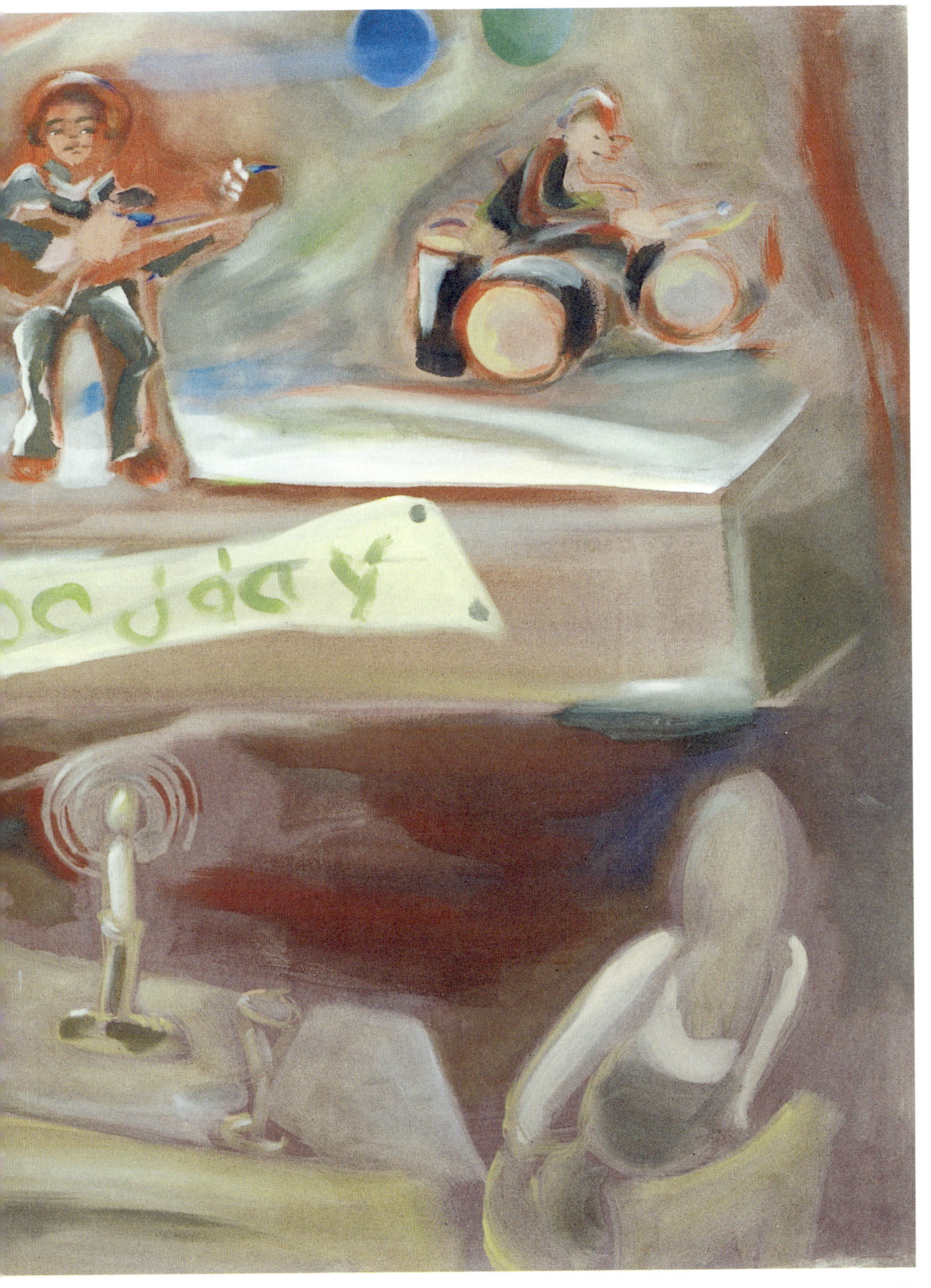
day

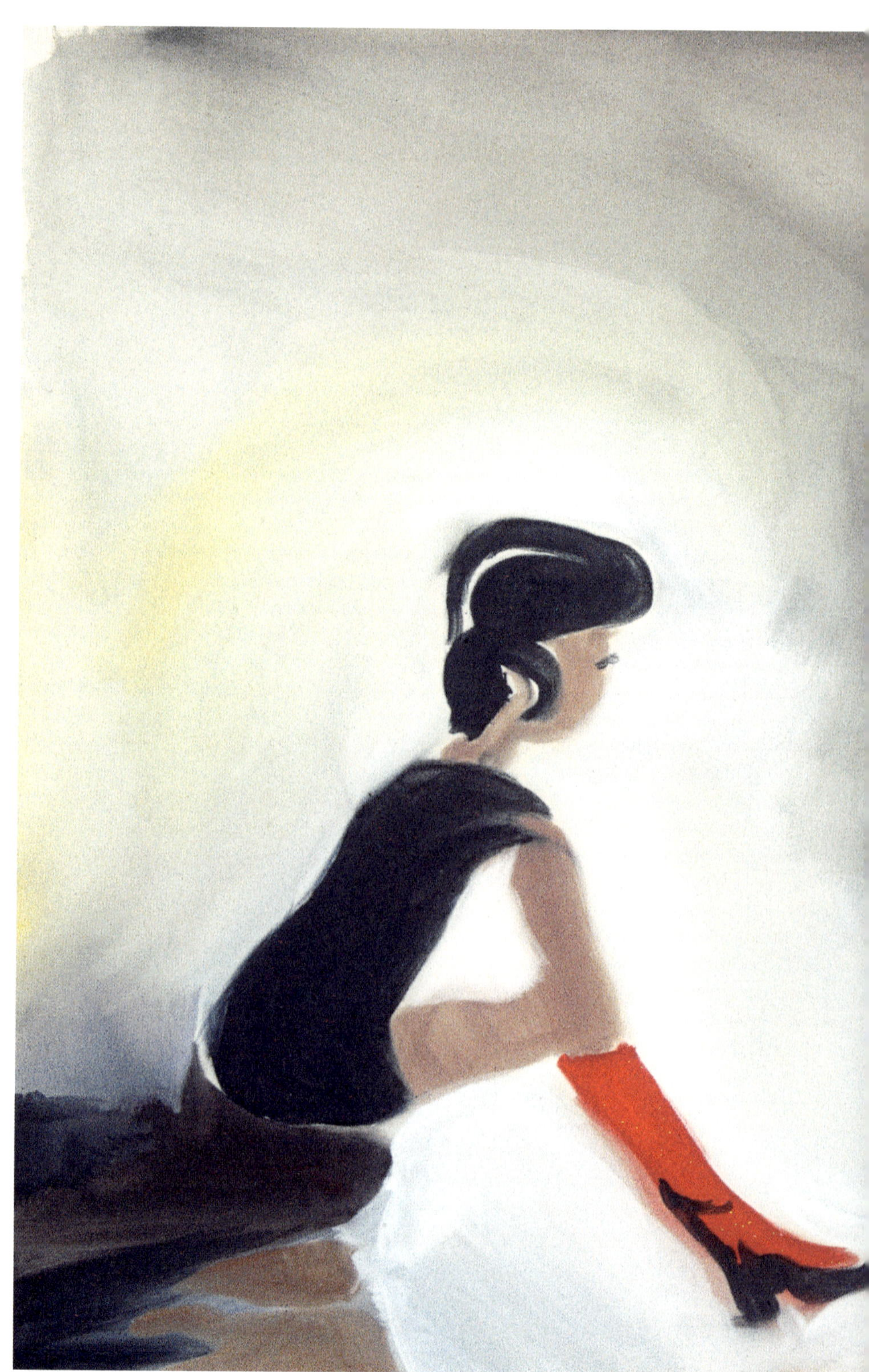

124   *Photo Shoot,* 2002

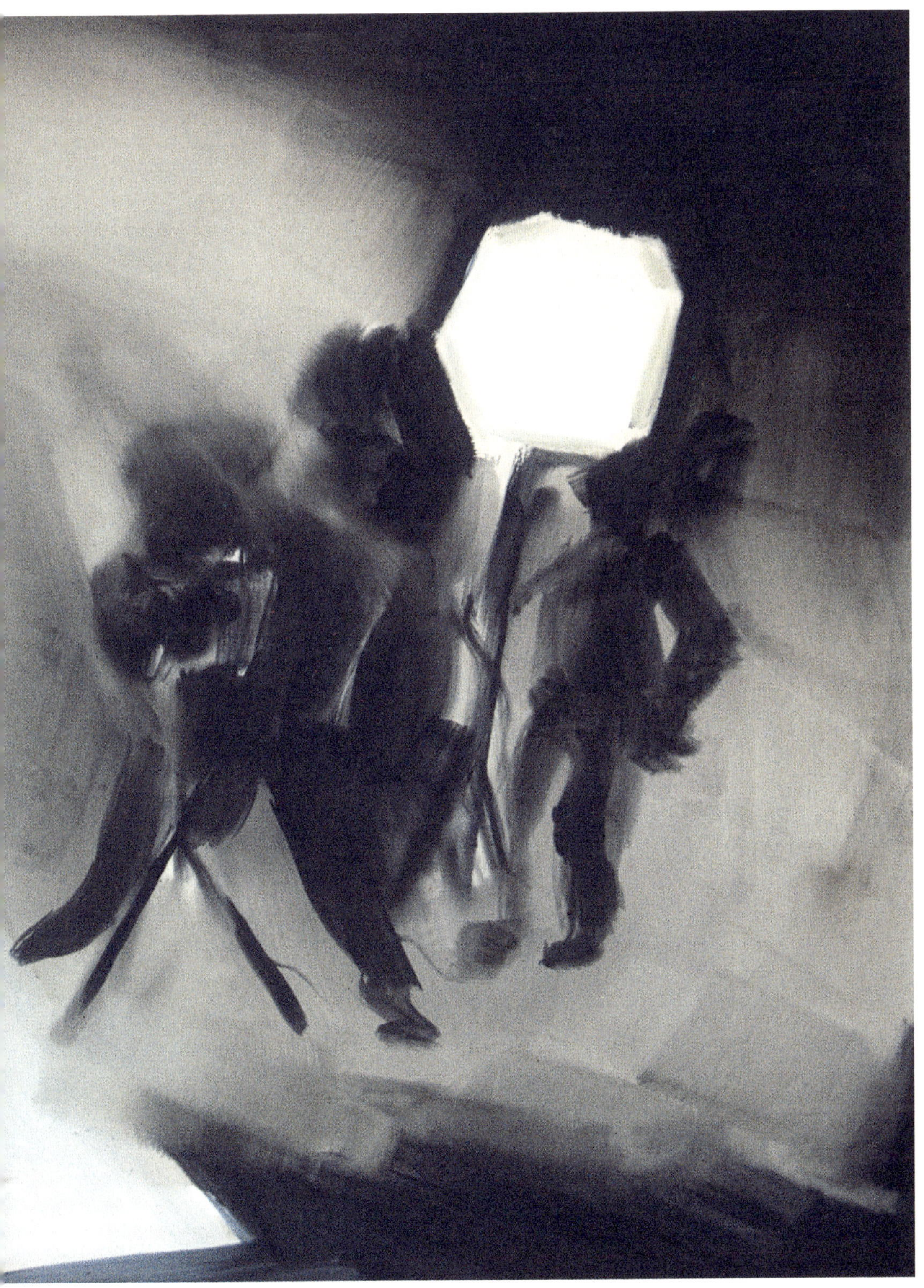

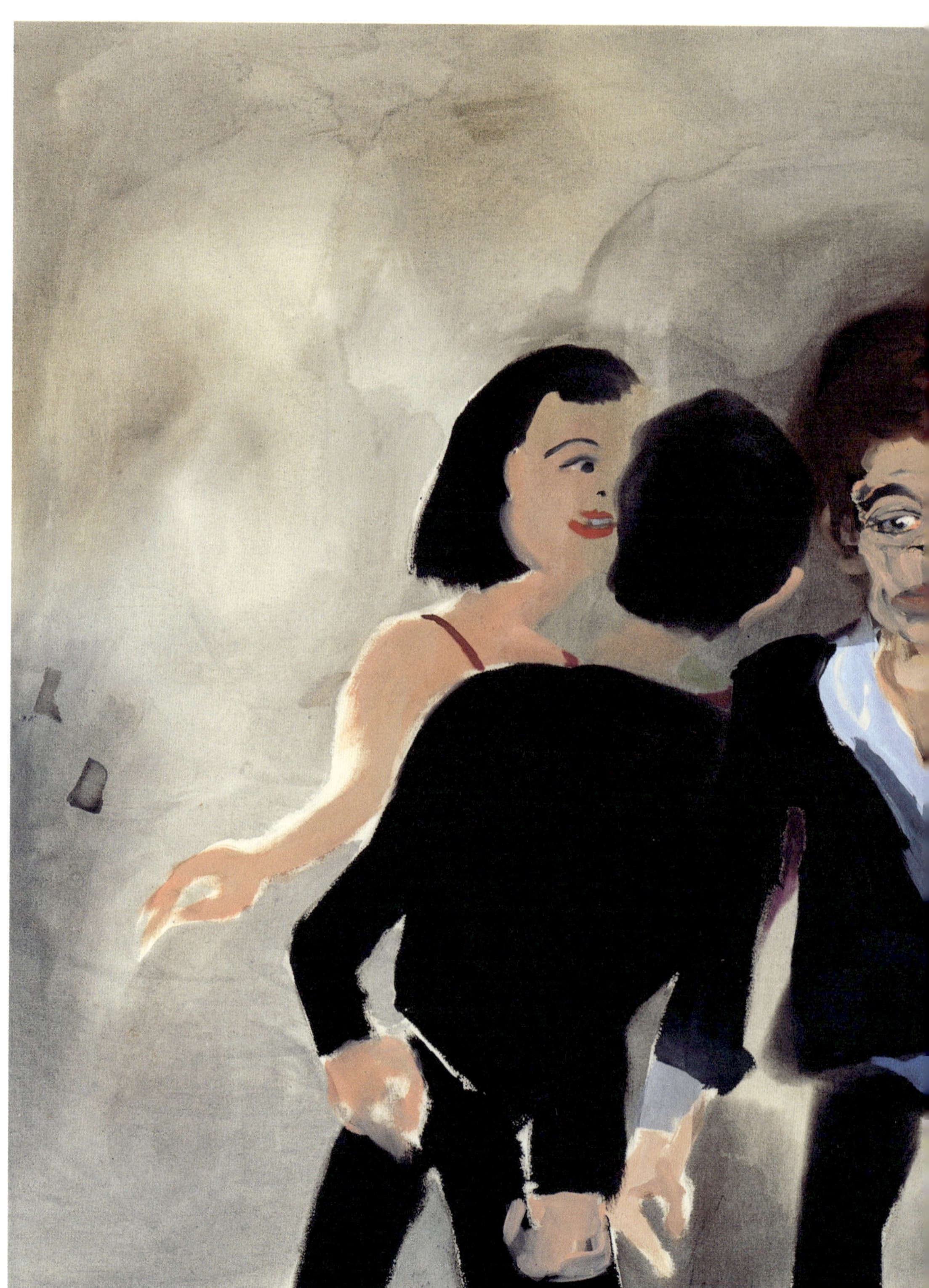

Mick Jagger, 2002

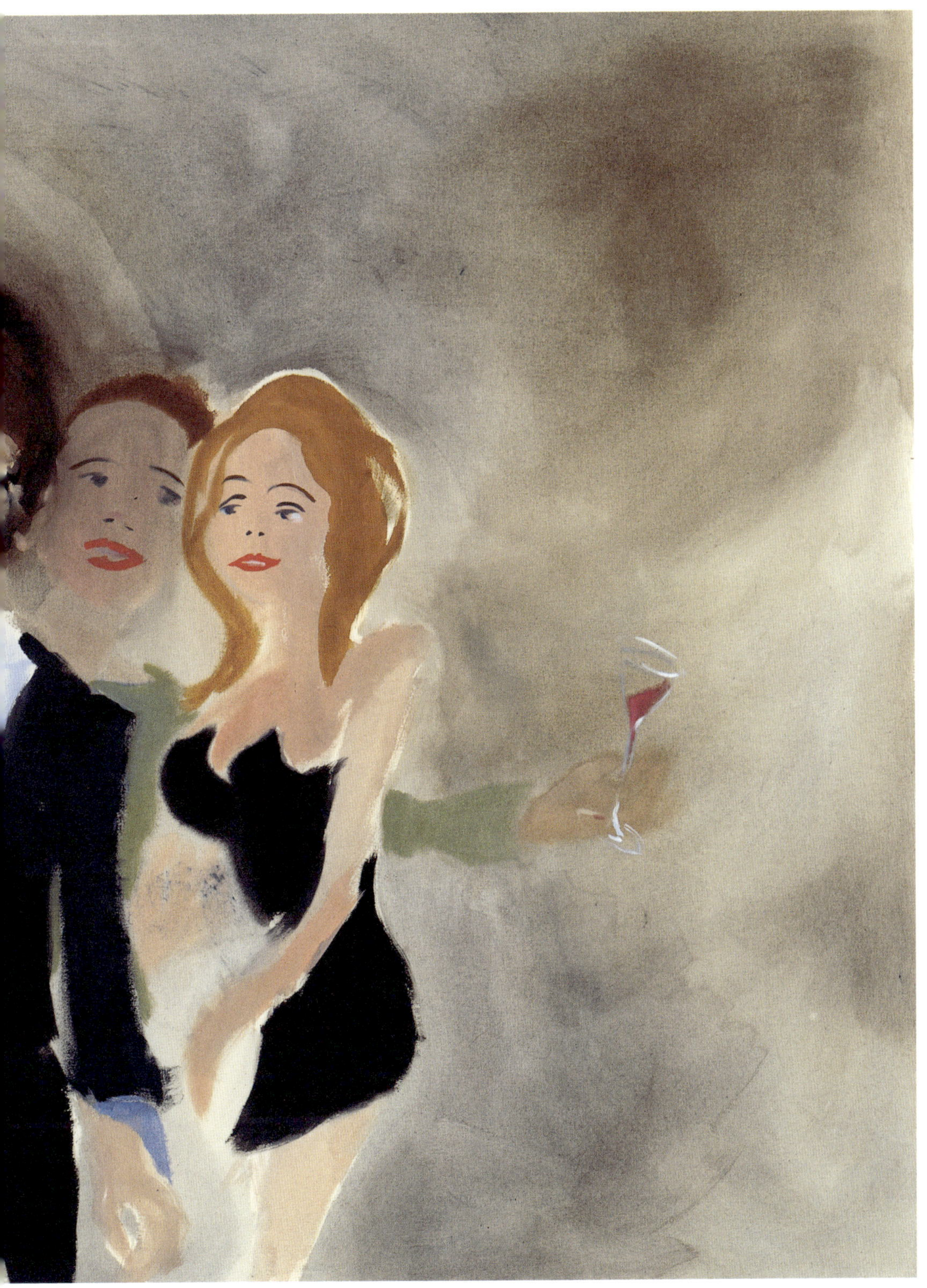

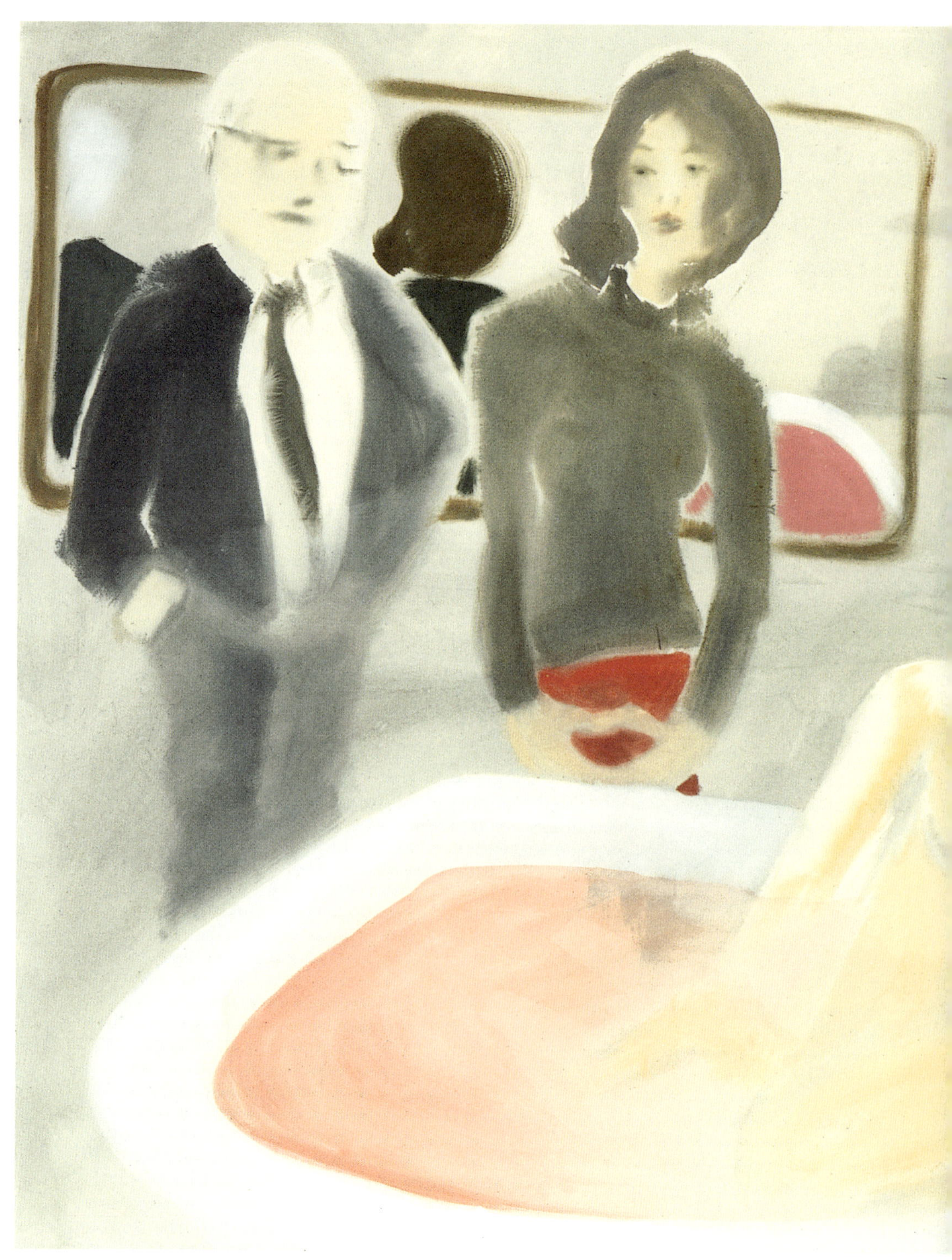

Pink Champagne, 2002

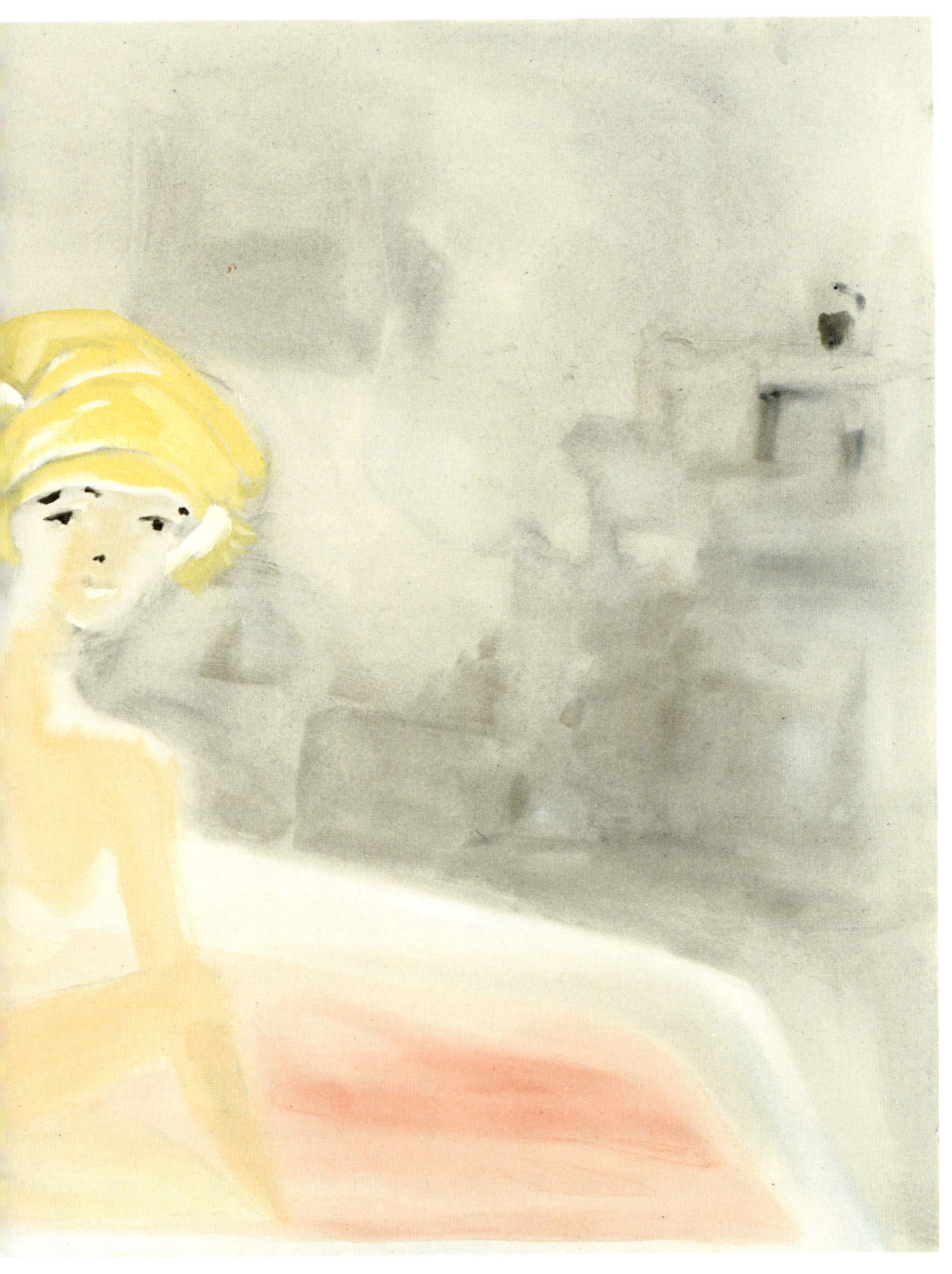

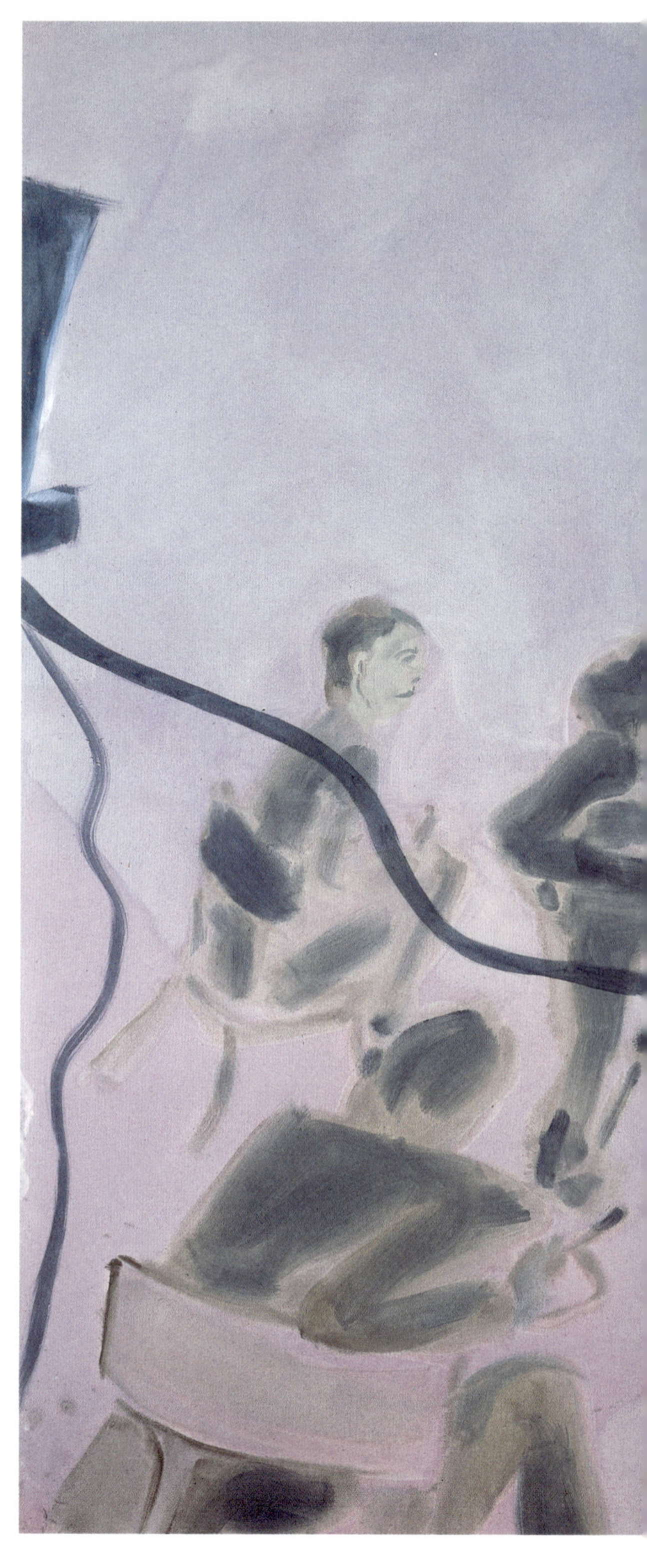

Losing Integrity, 2002

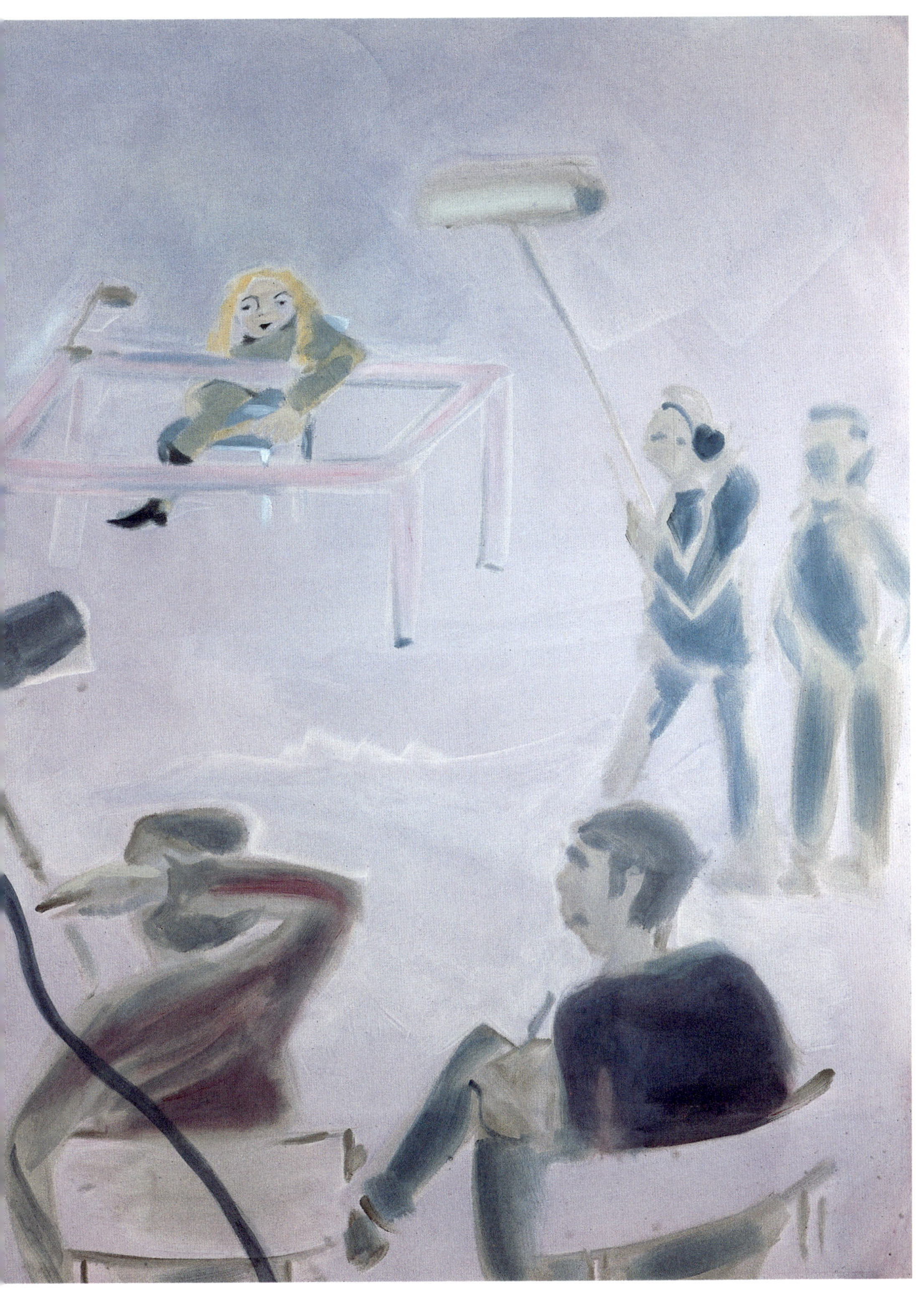

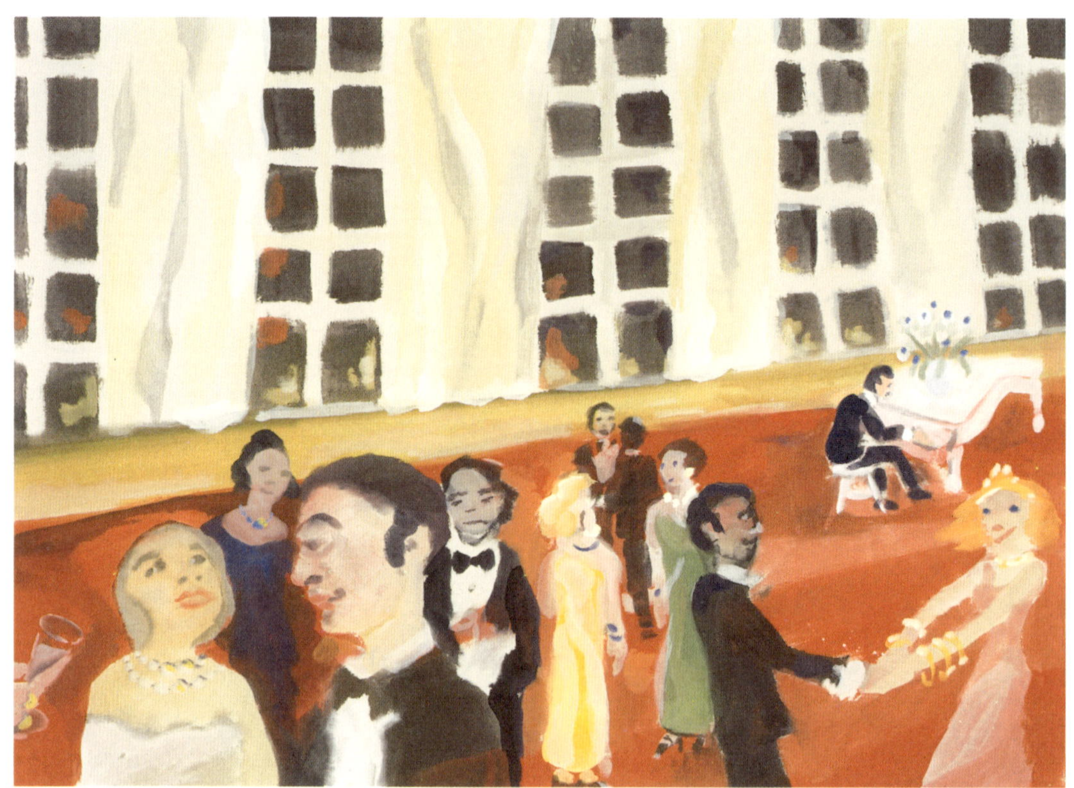

Untitled (Ballroom), 2002

HYSTERIC GLAMOUR

The hysteric, I imagined, entered a transport of physical excess at a moment where she was overcome by the unconscious return of a repressed memory. She was a sort of over-baked woman, flinging herself around and reeking of chaos. Her potential for annoyance was quite high – and if she had made art it would probably have looked like Kiki Smith's.

JOSEPHINE PRYDE, *It Recites* (2005)[i]

For the desire of our witty hysteric (Freud is the one who characterises her as such) – I mean her waking desire; that is, her desire for caviar – is the desire of a woman who is fulfilled and yet does not want to be.

JACQUES LACAN, *Ecrits* (1966)[ii]

What does Bush think about *Roe vs. Wade?*

(punchline at the end of the essay)

SICH AUSEINANDERSETZEN

I am using this invitation to write about Sophie von Hellermann's work as an opportunity to work through some ideas on feminism and glamour in contemporary art. I am particularly interested in the tension between the idea of a new feminist subjectivity and the hysteric's moment, as Josephine Pryde describes it in *It Recites*. Sophie's dreamy paintings of heady scenarios seemed a perversely interesting point of entry precisely because, in a certain sense, they embody the antithesis of the approach to feminism that I favour, which places its focus on the contexts of production and representation. However, might it be possible through a reading of Sophie's work to resurrect the possibility of the hysteric as a critical position?

LADIES OF THE ROPE

Los Angeles, the summer of 2004. In a gallery space with a subdued tone that echoed the overcast sky outside, a painting performed a light skip that momentarily ruptured the sombre atmosphere: *The Theft of the Jaded Goddess* (2004). A black-clad thief scales a rope that snakes down from a domed, glass-paned ceiling. The thief embraces the green sculpture she has just whisked from a pink square of security light.

The painting, and the pun in its title, tipped a debonair wink to the LA setting in which it was displayed. *The Theft*'s frivolousness felt defiantly rebellious, especially since it provoked an ascetic companion to wrinkle his nose. The thief might almost be getting in a couple of good swings on the rope before ascending – and this subterfuge-upon-subterfuge creates a possible space for critical reflection, which mimics the rope's movement of tense and release, snap and slack, as it sways.

As a viewer trying to maintain a position of critical responsibility, how is it possible to *enjoy* Sophie's fantastical paintings, which offer no ready criteria for analysis? The paintings' intense, hysteric glamour actively refuses to stand up to critical analysis. But perhaps this also creates an opportunity to suggest the hysteric as a critical position, to flip her backwards out of her ahistorical moment (be warned: in doing so this essay also performs some interpretative backflips). A refusal to stand up to rigorous categorisation is a strategy for resisting wider, and undesirable, typecasting, as those bigamists the Bernadette Corporation, wedded to both glamour and the Situationists, among others, have demonstrated. Keep in mind here that I use 'glamour' in a slightly trickier way than in its unbiased sense – it is both the magical spell an object (art or not) can cast on us, and the gratuitously sexy danger which that spell (desire) allows.

Hysteric glamour, then. As well as reeking of chaos, I take the hysteric to embody a certain deranged glamour that surfaces now and again in the most critically interrogative situations. In the very obvious awkwardness of its sur-facing, this glamour paradoxically forces its observer to address the issues of sexuality, femininity and subjectivity it appears to elude. That is, these two apparently mutually exclusive approaches (glamour and critical responsibility – aesthetics and politics) feed off each other, provided the hysteric imparts a necessary instability, the snap and slack of the rope as it swings. What lasting effect this instability might have on viewing and/or subjectivity when it sur-faces I am not quite sure, but I hope to be able to propose some possible sug-gestions in the course of this essay and extend the issue outwards to address some broader concerns.

This essay is much more a flinging around of ideas that may or may not get along than a studied 'compare and contrast'. The German term *sich auseinan-dersetzen* sums up best what I aim to do, because it translates literally as 'to-set-them-up-from-out-of-one-another' that is, to implode them into each other. Perhaps in doing so it might become possible to perform a metonymic slip in the style of the *Roe vs. Wade* joke.

(Also, an exploration of subjectivity requires a solipsistic approach that I hope excuses the certain amount of autobiographic detail that slips into the text.)

ISN'T IT FUN.[iii]

A couple of hysteric moments from popular culture: Princess Diana flings herself down the stairs during her pregnancy; a Stepford Wife malfunctions at a garden party and starts to repeat fragments of herself. Princess Di's self-abuse, a purported internalisation of the abuse of the world's most notoriously repressed family, turns into a way out of an apparently inescapable situation when she talks about it with Martin Bashir in a *Panorama* interview – this self-abuse is consequently interpreted in popular mythology as a victorious rebellion. Similarly, the temporary cracking of the Stepford artifice provokes the controlled panic of the Stepford husbands albeit without the (fleetingly) happy ending. The hysteric moment is a tear in the fabric of society that exposes it at its most vulnerable and luridly unpleasant – a dangerously sexy, ambivalent moment just before the hysteric's emotion, sprayed around like so many pheromones, becomes overpowering. Perhaps that moment's volatility offers a more permanent place for the formation of new subjectivity.

The hysteric, according to Lacan reading Freud, suffers from a desire for unfulfilled desire. She does not want to be satisfied (she has everything she needs). She wants caviar. Sound familiar? Her transport of physical symptoms activates a moment of intensely negated self-awareness which I would liken to this critical space of instability, snap and slack. Her hysteria also offers a critical strategy for viewing, in that the abandon it provokes is one of clarity – albeit in a backwards sense of frivolous rebellion, but nevertheless possibly the more subversive for being so flipped. The hysteric has proved to be such a difficult patient throughout history because she eludes easy medical classification, as Gérard Wajcman notes: 'The hysterical subject questions the physician about the symptom that, unexplainably, riddles her body. She presses him for an answer, impelling him to generate the knowledge needed to cure her. While knowledge cannot articulate the hysteric, the hysteric ushers the articulation of knowledge. Intending to talk about hysteria, we found that hysteria made us talk.'[iv] I feel like that about Sophie's paintings.

ISN'T IT FUN. ISN'T IT... FUN.

Men in suits and ties, jackets removed in relaxation, stretch over the flat plane of a billiards table. With its dark green baize light, the *Billiard* (2005) scene conjures the same hazy environment of stealth and glamour in which the patrons of the restaurant whisper in the corner of *Monte Carlo* (2004). The oh-so-sophisticated figure of the *Agent Provocateur* (2004), in purple-and-black harem clothing, smoke ring ascending from her cigarette, might be sitting in a corner. In the distance, *Bianca Jagger* (2004) walks down an airport runway.

Taken at face value, these scenes are an adulatory depiction of a far-away destination populated by 007 and his girls that can be conflated into one great fantasy scenario. In this scenario, gambling, Monte Carlo and everything else exist beyond culpability, in a world of carefree irresponsibility. These scenes are like the arbitrary swells of emotive orchestral sound that constitute the soundtrack of Jean Luc Godard's *Le Mèpris* (1963), as if the soundman, or here the artist, were pressing on/off at random to prompt your empathetic transport.

In *Good Space Girl* (2005), a doe-eyed, voluptuous Anita Ekberg blonde, with toenails painted red and *La Dolce Vita*-style dress, floats in a spaceship. Lack of gravity has its way with her belongings and her champagne bottle, and sends hair, legs and boobs akimbo. The colour of her dress and the inside of the space ship are painted in blocky smudges, like slow burns on your memory or the slightly blurry movement shared by dreams and DVDs playing on cranky computers. For full effect, try watching something as colour-saturated as Todd Haynes's *Far From Heaven* (2002). (These paintings are slippery in form as well as content.) In *Far From Heaven*, the colours of clothing and the autumn leaves exuberantly express what Julianne Moore's troubled housewife can only mask under her pale face. The *Good Space Girl*, on the other hand, welcomes – yes, surrenders to – her hysteric moment. And in doing so she becomes unanalysable, prompting our own puzzling, talk. Sophie's work cannot be taken at face value alone; instead, the paintings invite us to assume the position of the analyst, taking a ride on the transportive swells to a critical space beyond the surface wash of carefree irresponsibility.

PUMP AIR. PUMP AIR

What is the alternative to surrender? There's something much more frightening about numbness. I was very bored that summer in 2004 in LA, with the slightly numb feeling, like having drunk too much coffee, that moving along stretches of highway in air-conditioned cars imparts. Medicating yourself away becomes easy when you're in a culture that encourages numbness (that treats hysteria with easy-to-swallow pills). The snap and slack of the rope, the hysteric moment, on the other hand, keeps things sharp and you on your toes. The lyrics to the Velvet Underground song scattered about this essay describe the verge of numbness quite literally – the song describes anaesthetic being administered to a patient (about to undergo a sex change) – but the threat lies in the subtext: the anaesthesia might not wear off.

Funny, then, how many in this day and age – in medicated LA, and elsewhere too – fear the anaesthesia wearing off. It *seems* easier to operate so. Taking a stand against numbness, Gregg Bordowitz has called for an increase in mortification in art and culture, an increase in drama, in outward expressions of inward despair. For Gregg, mortification serves as a means of taking an activist stance against the fear of death repressively exercised in the name of security in the United States and elsewhere.[v] I mortify myself, then, am utterly ashamed of the current political situation; I am depressed, but angrily, actively so. Such an upfront (hysteric) assumption of affect is urgently necessary.

LADIES OF THE ROPE II

Perhaps when Josephine was thinking about the figure of the hysteric, Jutta Koether's series of *Hysterics* (2000) paintings was on her mind. They depict outlines of female heads bearing only token facial characteristics, on muddied backgrounds, in swirls of washed-out colour. Some faces are crossed out, others have eyes with big bags under them and, in some cases, a blaze of light bursts from their centre. In their nervousness, their wired-ness, they could well be in the middle of one of the hysteric transports of physical excess described by Josephine. In her paintings and installations, Jutta works towards a 'new (feminist) subjectivity' that refuses any fixed, and thus easily typecast, identity. These frazzled representations convey a volatile, shifting position within which it might also be possible to stake a hysteric subjectivity.[vi]

HYSTERIC (HISTORIC) GLAMOUR

I don't want to force an undertone upon the paintings (which elude this 'unpacking' – de-crating), but... no, actually, I do. They are produced within a specific historic context, and we view them from within that context too. The snap and slack of Sophie's paintings, their hysteric moment, *is* historical. Wajcman writes: 'We'll give the name of hysteric to this object which cannot be mastered by knowledge and therefore remains outside of history, even outside its own.' It's a nice idea, but incorrect, in the sense that mastery by knowledge does not determine coercion into history – history is always there.

The need persists for a redefinition of feminism and of subjectivity, which would serve to reassert their importance both for a critical viewing of contemporary art, and on a larger scale. The way in which women are represented still needs to be contested; representations have become thinner, perkier, blonder, more like Paris Hilton (the anti-hysteric, who always presents the same face to the media, the same pose, regardless of the context – i.e. even when fucking). Women in the art world are still confronted by a glass ceiling (a quick, but not peremptory, nod here to the thousands of female gallerinas, curatorial assistants, editorial assistants, who co-ordinate the lives of the few at the top, mostly men; a longer [quizzical?] tilt of the head to those women who have made it up to the top). Fashion – not disconnected from the previous. Sex – etc.

Pressing deeper – we need to stop pushing such a condescending version of Western feminism on parts of the world whose moral structures and social systems are so frequently bombarded with assertions of 'the West knows best'. 'Feminism' gets bandied about like 'democracy' by characters such as Laura Bush – now there's a joke. It should go without saying that both concepts have their own rich forms and traditions in the Orient. A new (feminist) subjectivity is urgent because feminism is being placed in the same precarious position as democracy, as a moral bargaining tool, while those who wield it simultaneously bludgeon it to misrecognition. In terms of the *Roe vs. Wade* joke's metonymic slip: feminism should also always perform that slip, back to the bigger issues with which it is intertwined.

Why a new (feminist) subjectivity? The brackets indicate the persistent need to acknowledge (without stamping one's foot about it) the terms of the debate and its origins, without making it exclusive to women; acknowledging the layers of theory that have accrued since the explosion of the feminist movement in the 1970s, while buying a little more time to root around within the terms, to skip and repeat scratched grooves of a broken record[vii] in the search for newly relevant meaning. (This critique is admittedly played, but did feminism neglect to welcome the hysteric moment?) As Wajcman observes, 'the hysteric ushers the articulation of knowledge' – the hysteric prompts naming by the analyst and in doing so prompts a creation of the world and therefore a subjectivity. Why subjectivity? If the reader will forgive the old trope of recourse to dictionary definitions, here's a Microsoft Word entry: (1) interpretation based on personal opinions or feelings rather than on external facts or evidence. (2) concentration on personal, individual responses in artistic expression. I take this to mean (1) how we take it upon ourselves to conjure and (2) respond to the world. I take it as only a quasi-solipsism: both have collective significance, one's personal subjectivity is likely to influence other personal subjectivities – we interpret ourselves in the hysteric and she slips away from fixed meaning once again.

SHAVED AND HAIRLESS, WHAT WAS SCREAMING NOW
LIES SILENT AND ALMOST SLEEPING

In *Housewife Terrorism* (2000), a woman wearing sunglasses and a red top, her lips a smear of dark lipstick, climbs out of the boot of a car, guns blazing. The purple background goes with the colour of her top, which is the same red as the brake lights on the car – so co-ordinated, darling, you almost don't notice she's packing. *Maaike Schoorel, Hollywood* (2003) makes herself up in the mirror, lifting her mascara to her violet eyes; yellow orbs of light around the mirror give the scene a pearly haze. In the back of a taxi, a woman leans forwards to pull a piece of clothing out of one of her shopping bags and to perform a quick change (*Inspired Shopping,* 2002). She has taken her trousers off. Bags spill over the floor; head down, she searches through them, her reddish hair over her face. A blonde tries on a dress in a mirror; black-tie-wearing shop attendants hover around her like moths (*Fitting in Prado,* 2002).

STRAPPED SECURELY TO THE WHITE TABLE
ETHER CAUSES THE BODY TO WITHER AND WRITHE
NOW COMES THE MOMENT OF GREAT DECISION,
THE DOCTOR'S MAKING HIS FIRST INCISION
DON'T PANIC

In *It Recites*, Josephine uses the figure of the hysteric to make her own slip, from individual to historical. She writes: 'I thought that maybe instead of thinking of an individual hysteric figure, it might be possible to think of hysteria in a time. The hysteria of a time, a time producing hallucinations connected to repressed memories.' Josephine very beautifully elides our historical condition with the hysteric's repressed returning, without going so far as to state what exactly our historical condition is – picking her way daintily around it, perhaps? But taking to heart Gregg Bordowitz's exhortation to mortify yourself as often as you can, here goes: summarised baldly, our historical condition is one in which we have so far proven unable to oppose a war in Iraq, a barbaric occupation of the country by 'coalition forces' and a barbaric resistance. The mainstream media play an Old Faithful role in the dissemination/disruption of information; the left has lost its way, for which it would be wrong to blame only USSR-style communism; there has been a rise in religious fundamentalism of all creeds; a rise in the communications and service economy and a concurrent depersonalisation of communication; we live with global warming; the erosion of basic human rights, and so on. Simulacral collapse seems daily more imminent… yet Sophie's characters nevertheless carry on putting on their make-up and shopping and gambling glamorously and, presumably, eating caviar in a gauze of unreliability, uncertainty – of hysteric glamour.

DON'T PANIC…

What does Bush think about *Roe vs. Wade*?
He doesn't really care how black people get out of New Orleans.

Emily Speers Mears

NOTES

Apologies and thanks to Gregg Bordowitz, John Kelsey, Jutta Koether, Josephine Pryde and Sophie von Hellermann – and of course the Japanese clothing label – for gratuitous misappropriation.

i   Josephine Pryde, *It Recites*, in *Wenn sonst nichts klappt: Wiederholung wiederholen*, ed. Sabeth Buchmann (Hamburg: polypen und b-books verlag, 2005), pp. 52–59.

ii   Jacques Lacan, *Ecrits: A Selection*, 1966. trans. Bruce Fink, Heloise Fink and Russell Grigg. (London: W. W Norton, 2004). For Grigg's notes on Lacan in translation, see lemessager.online.fr/English/lacanintranslation.htm

iii   These headings are taken from the lyrics of the Velvet Underground's *Lady Godiva's Operation* (1968).

iv   Gérard Wajcman, *The Hysteric's Discourse*, 1982, published on lacan.com/hysteric.htm

v   Gregg Bordowitz spoke about mortification in a pair of talks given in New York at Cooper Union and the Whitney Museum of American Art Independent Study Program in the autumn of 2004.

vi   Jutta is also at times a member of the Bernadette Corporation.

vii   I owe this metaphor of 'scratched and skipping grooves' to John Kelsey. It is lifted straight from his essay *Unclaimed Bags Will Be Destroyed*, which appeared in the catalogue to the exhibition *Uncertain States of America* at the Astrup Fearnley Museum of Modern Art, Oslo, 2005.

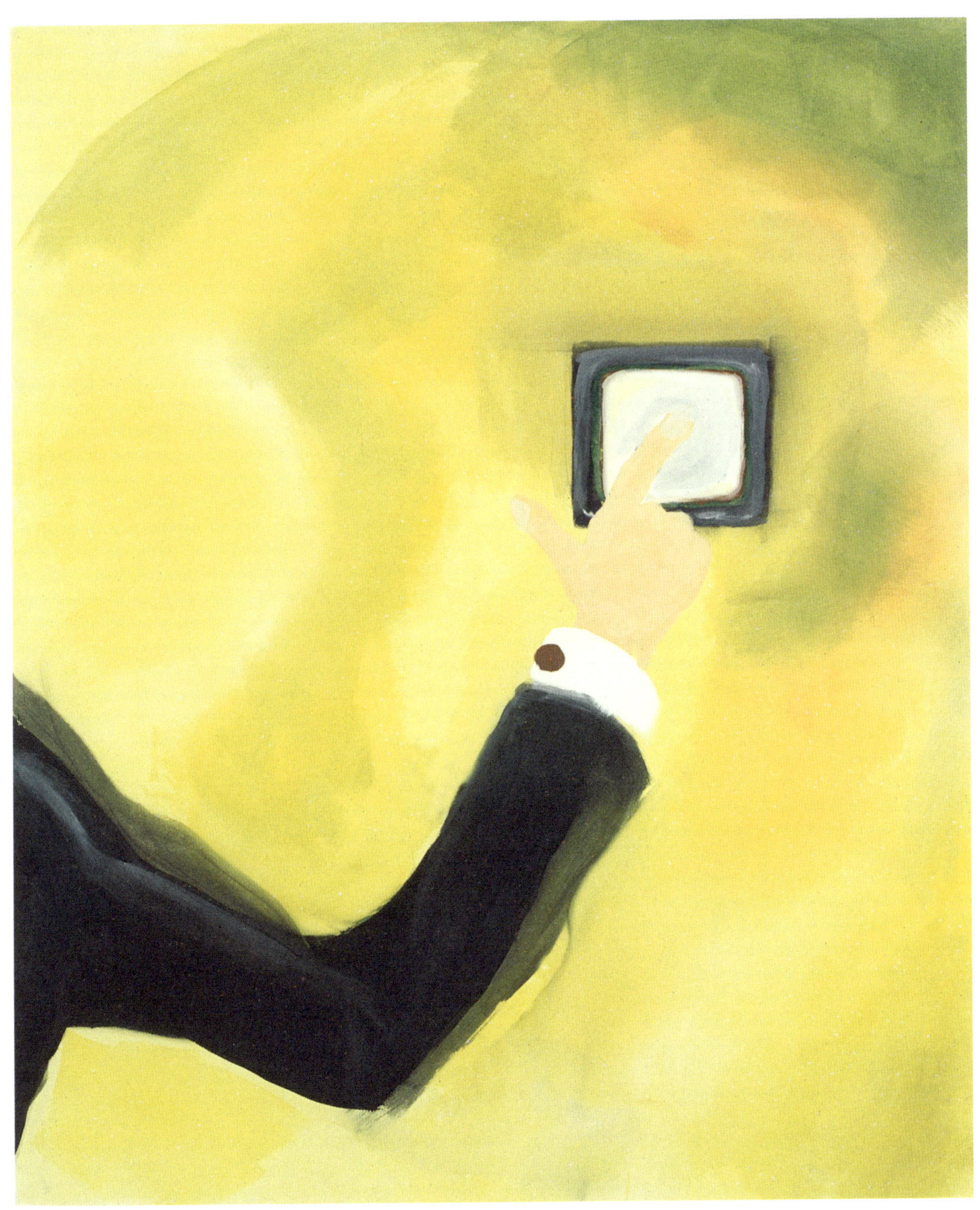

Chum Pain Party I, 2002

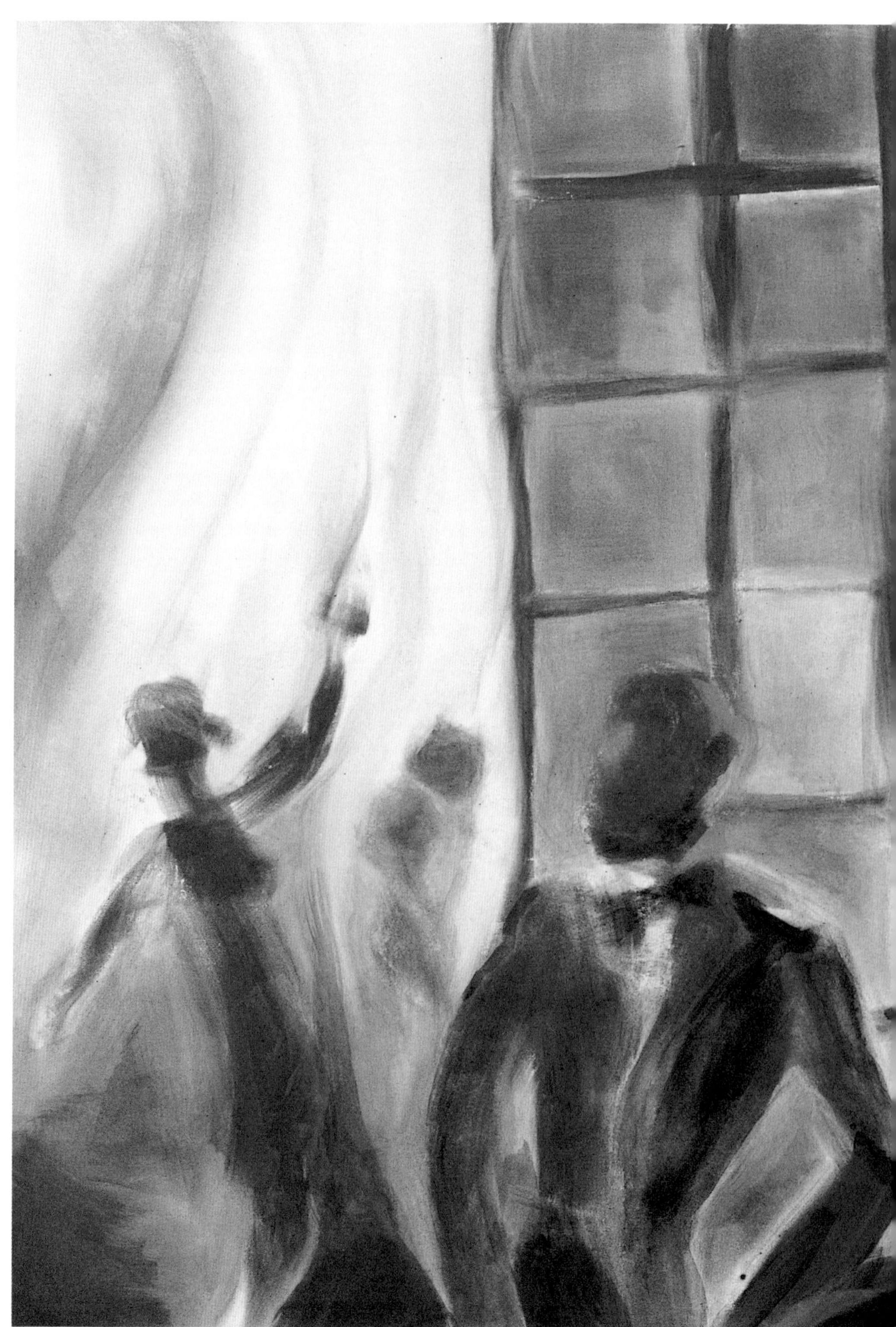

  Chum Pain Party II, 2002

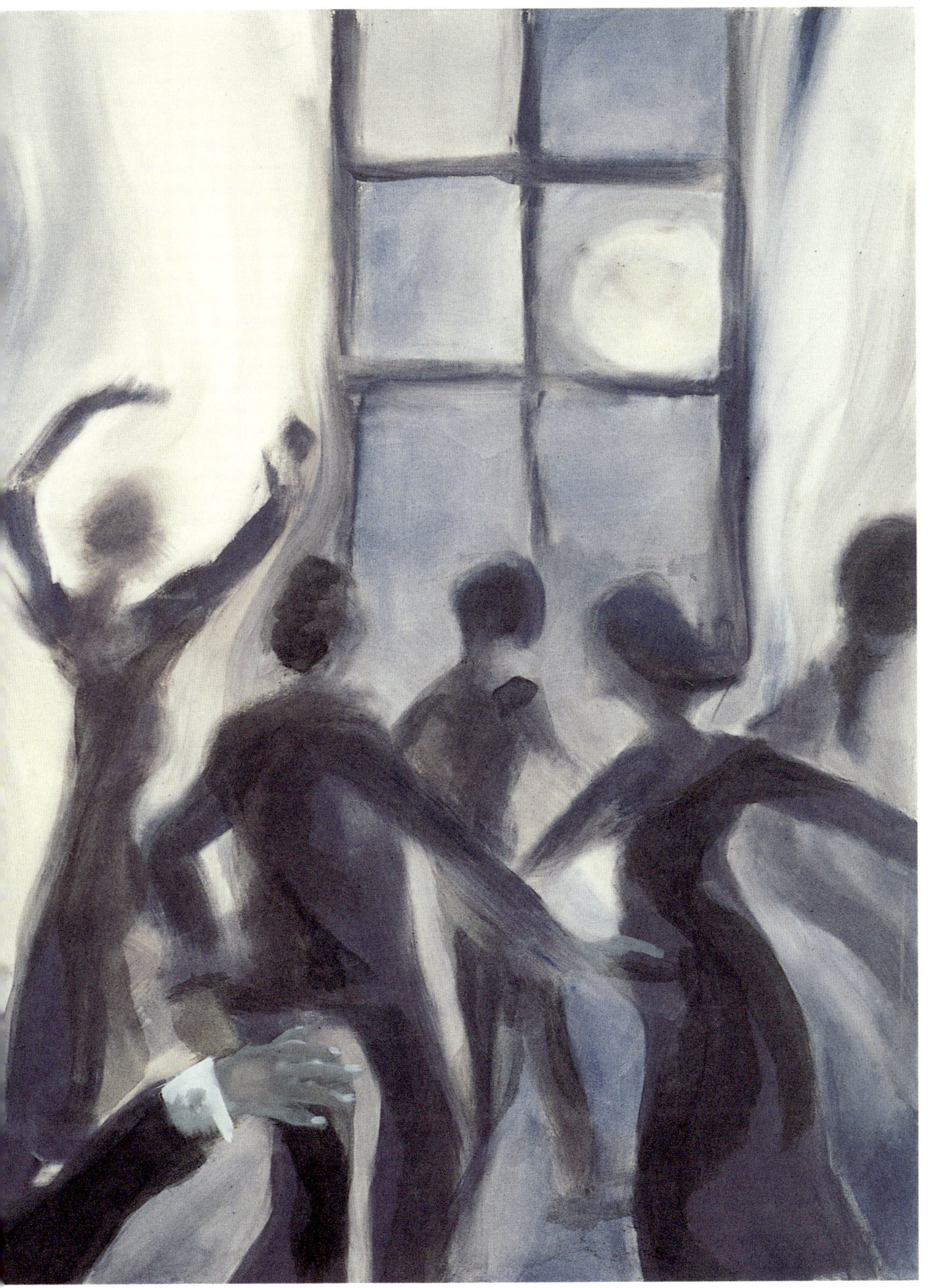

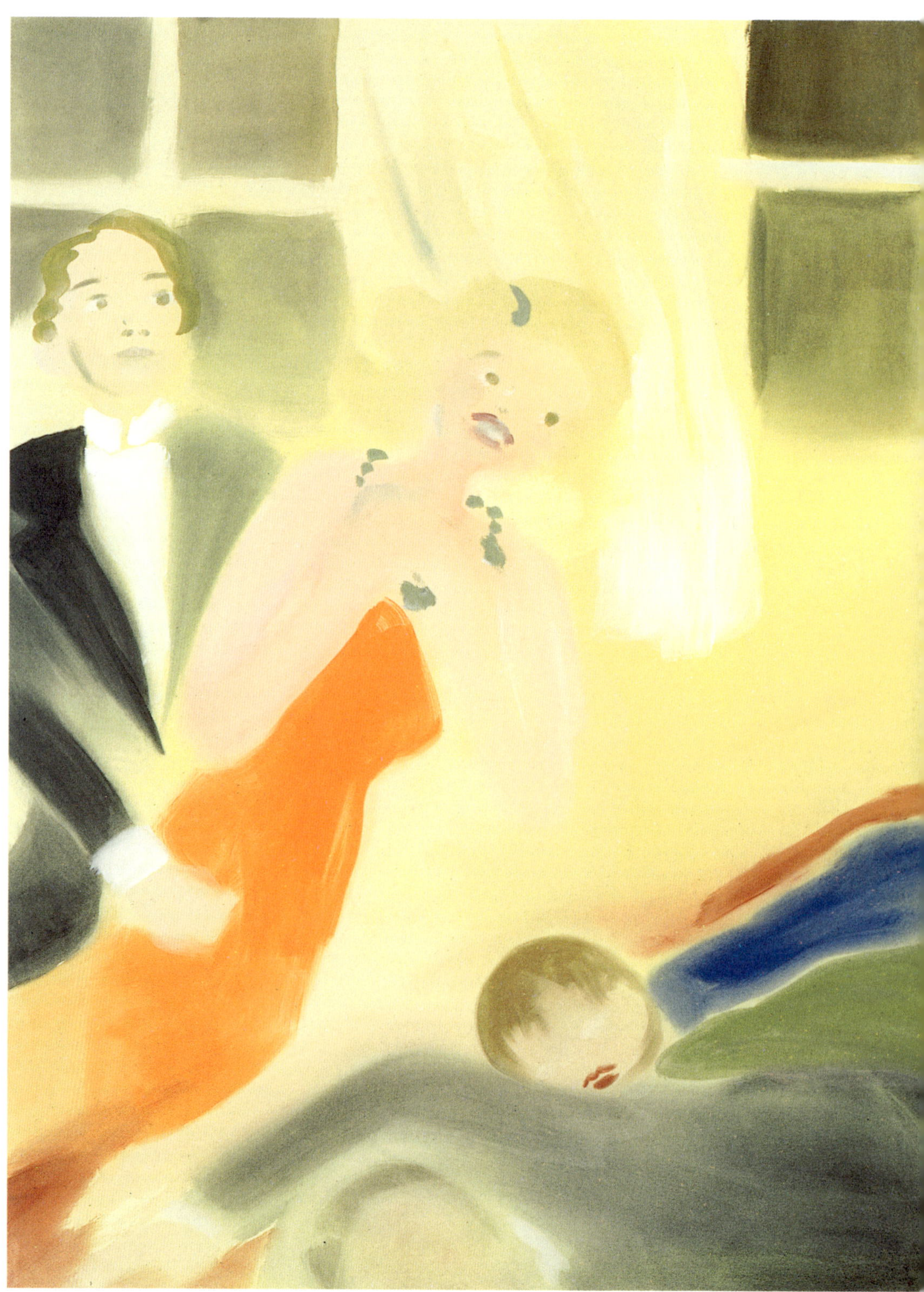

Chum Pain Party III, 2002

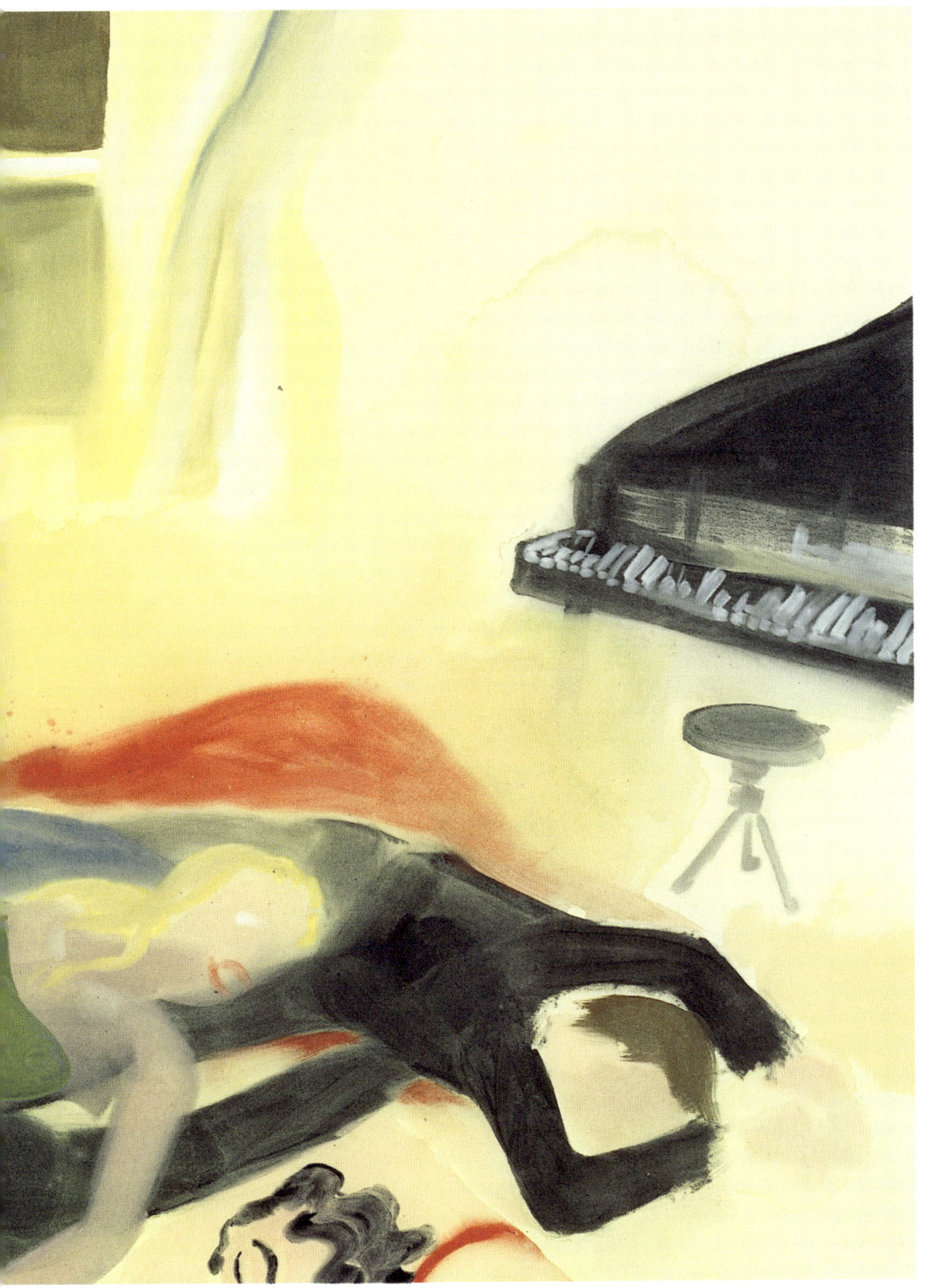

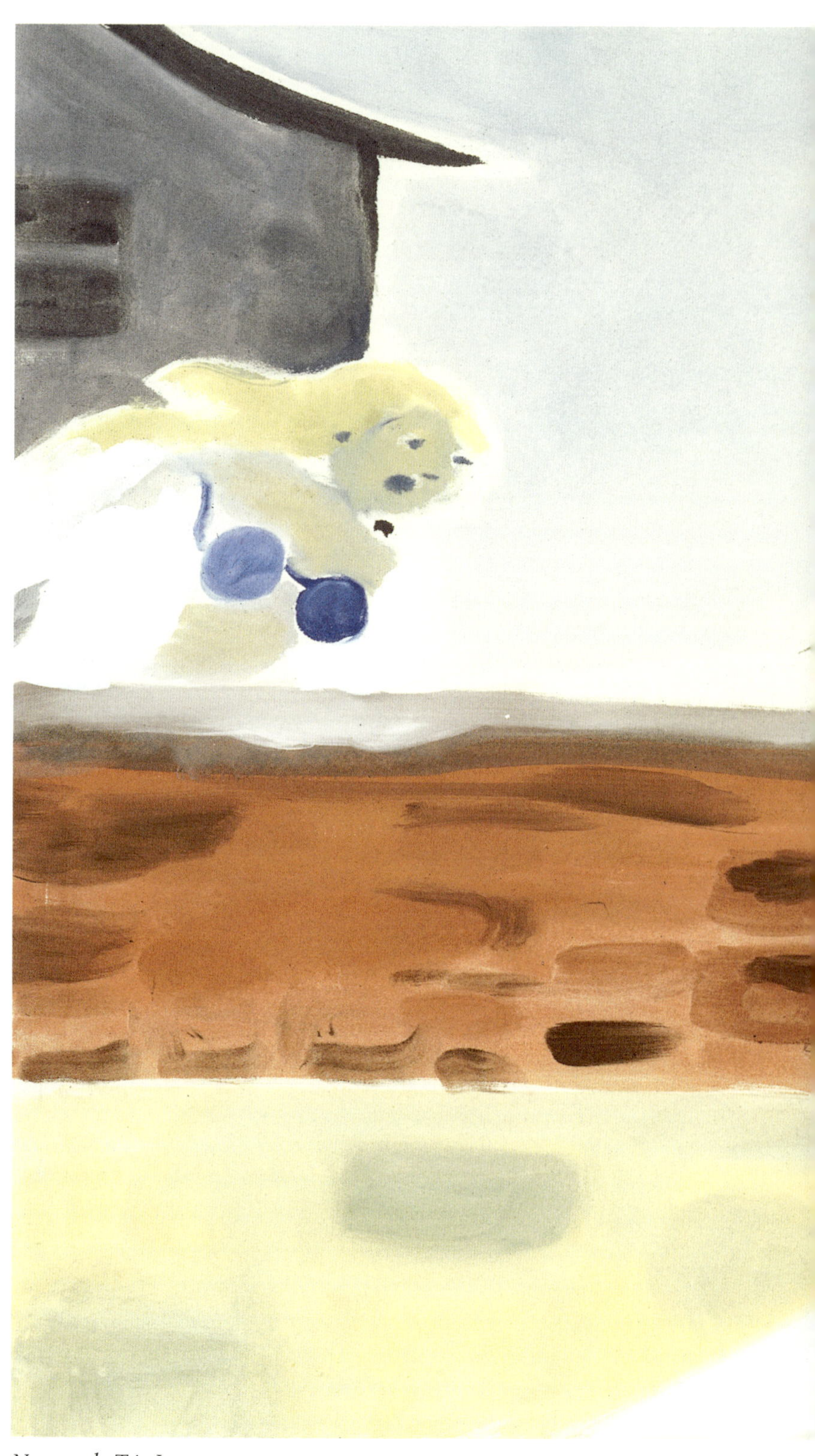

Normandy Trip I, 2002

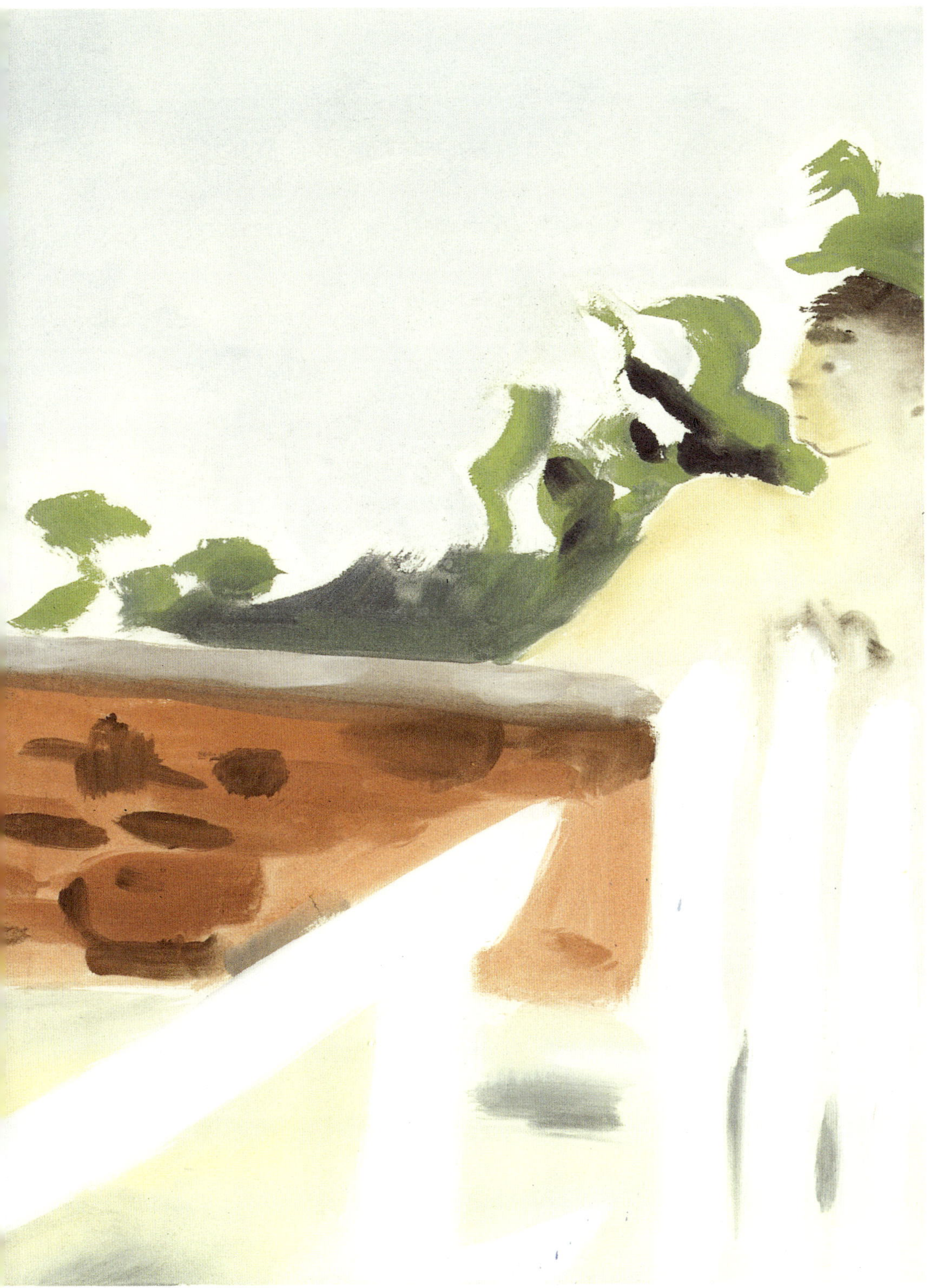

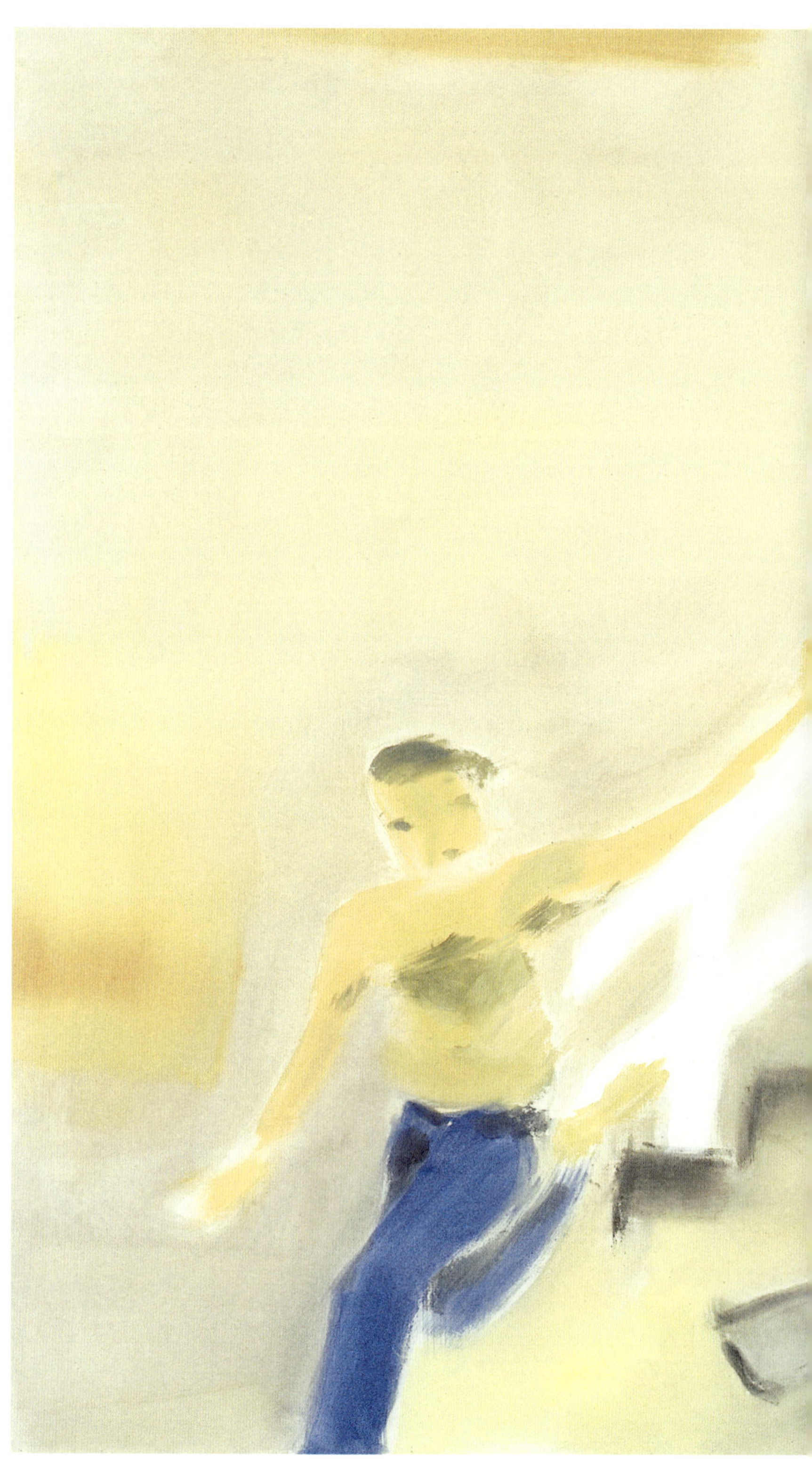

 Normandy Trip II, 2002

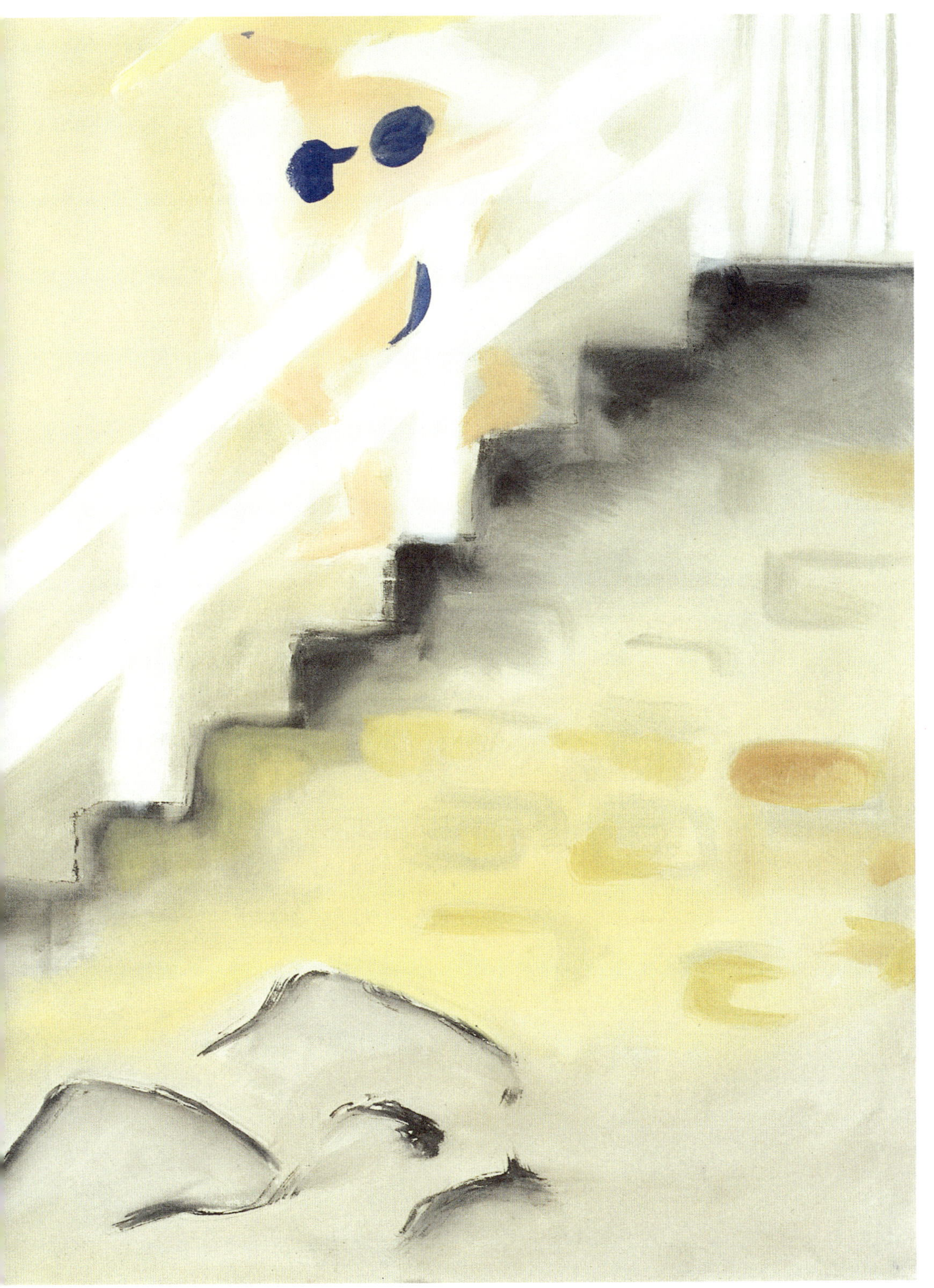

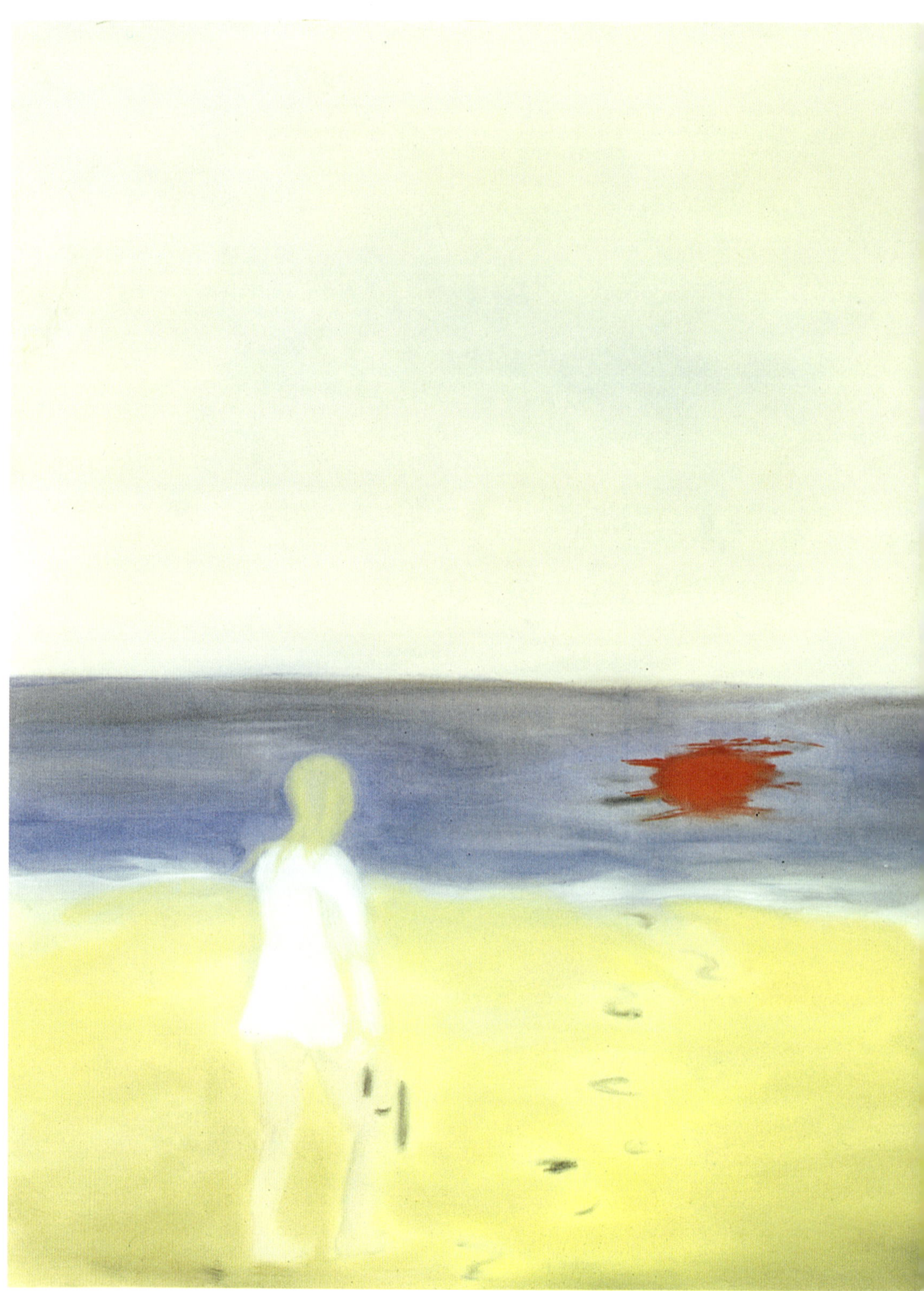

Normandy Trip III, 2002

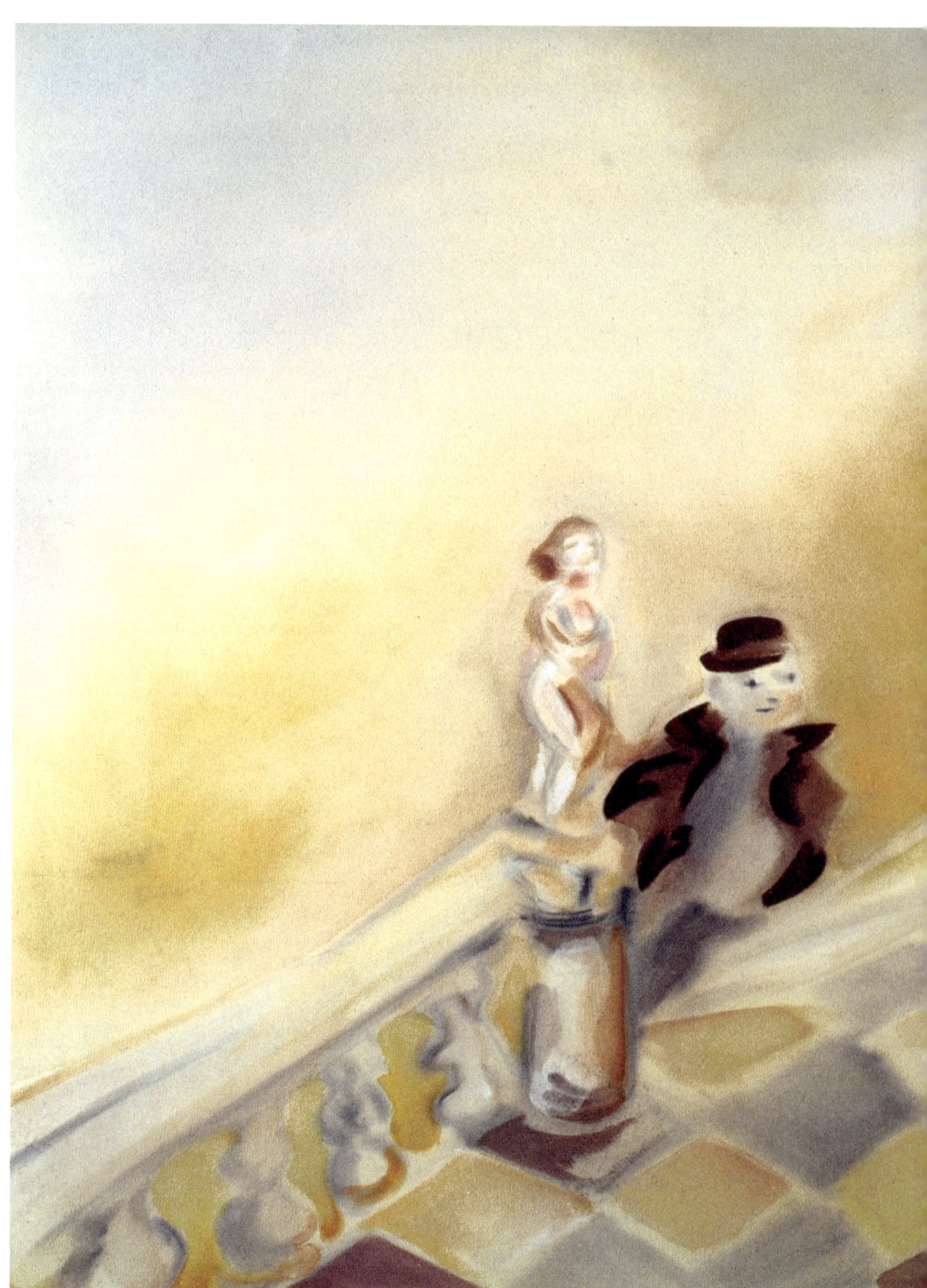

The Rising Detective, 2002

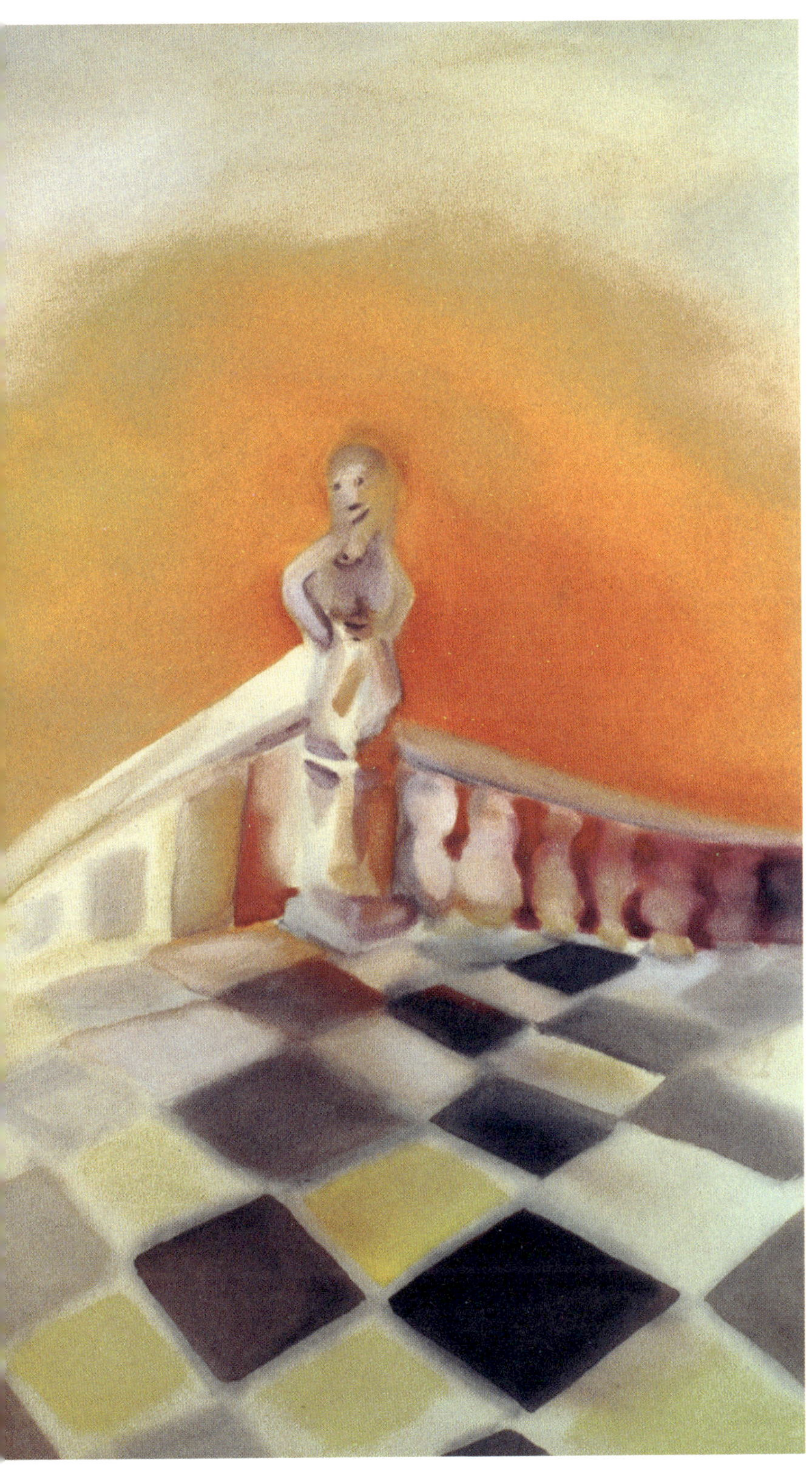

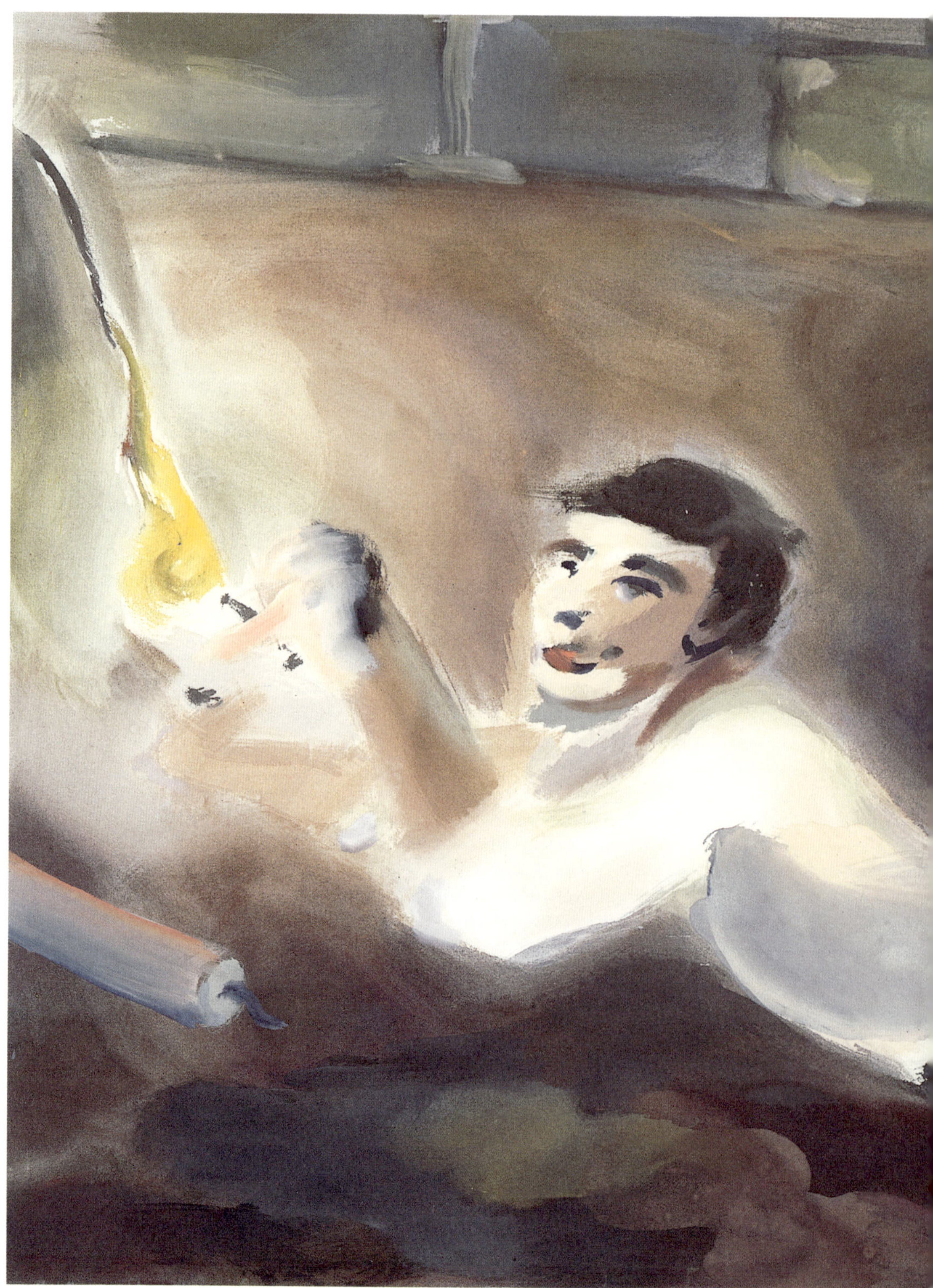

Guy Fawkes, 2002

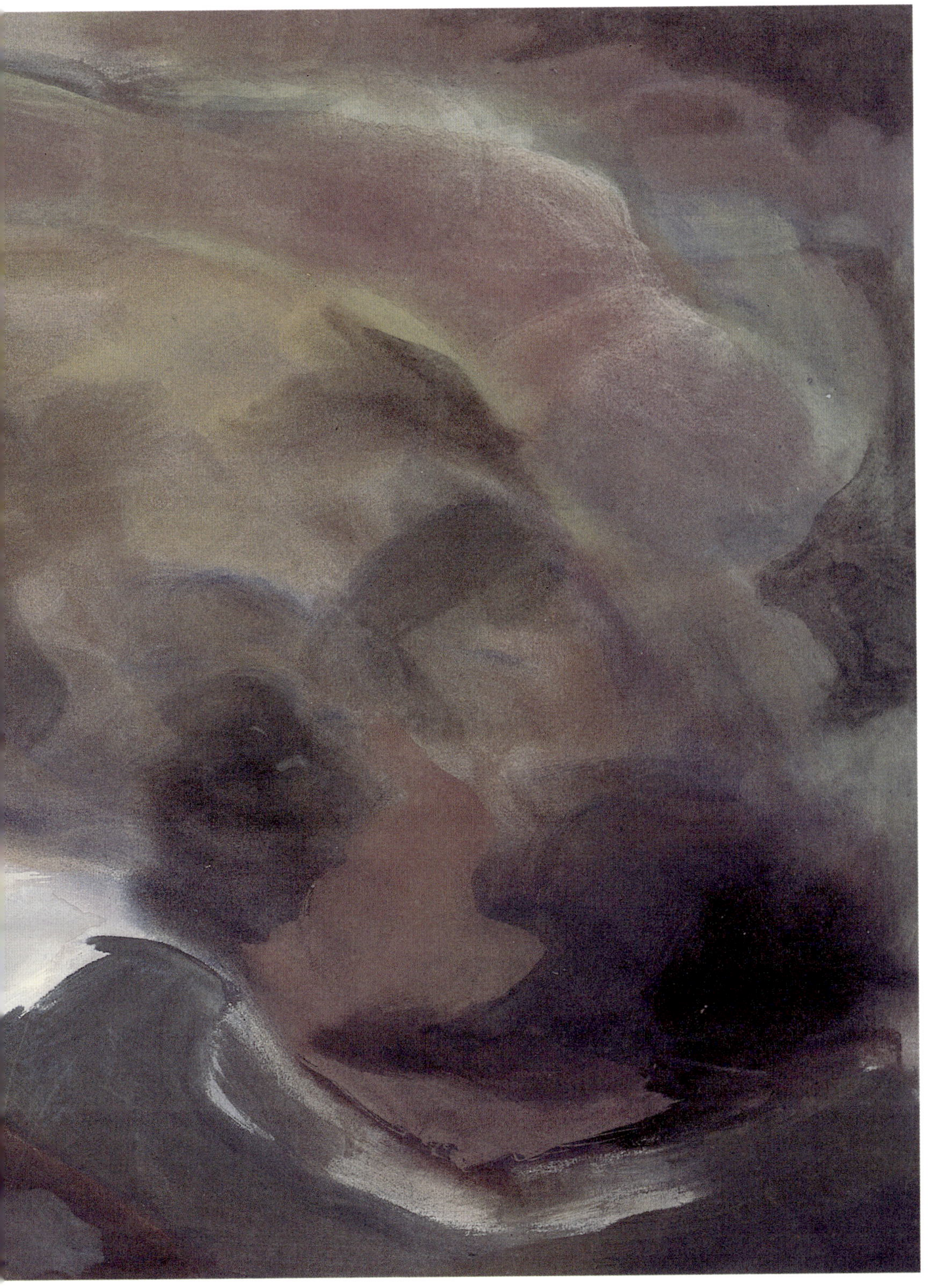

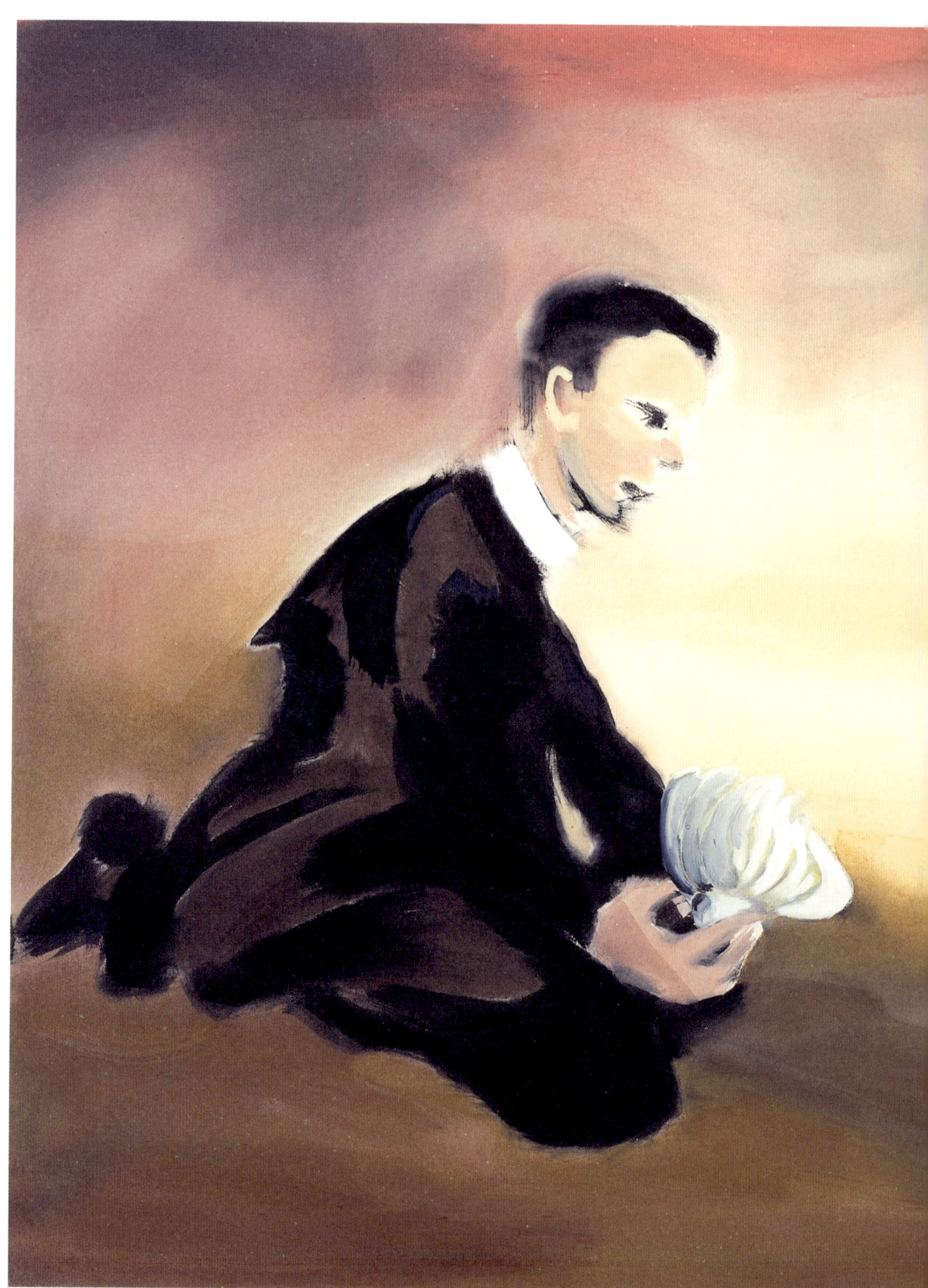

Pot Offer, 2002

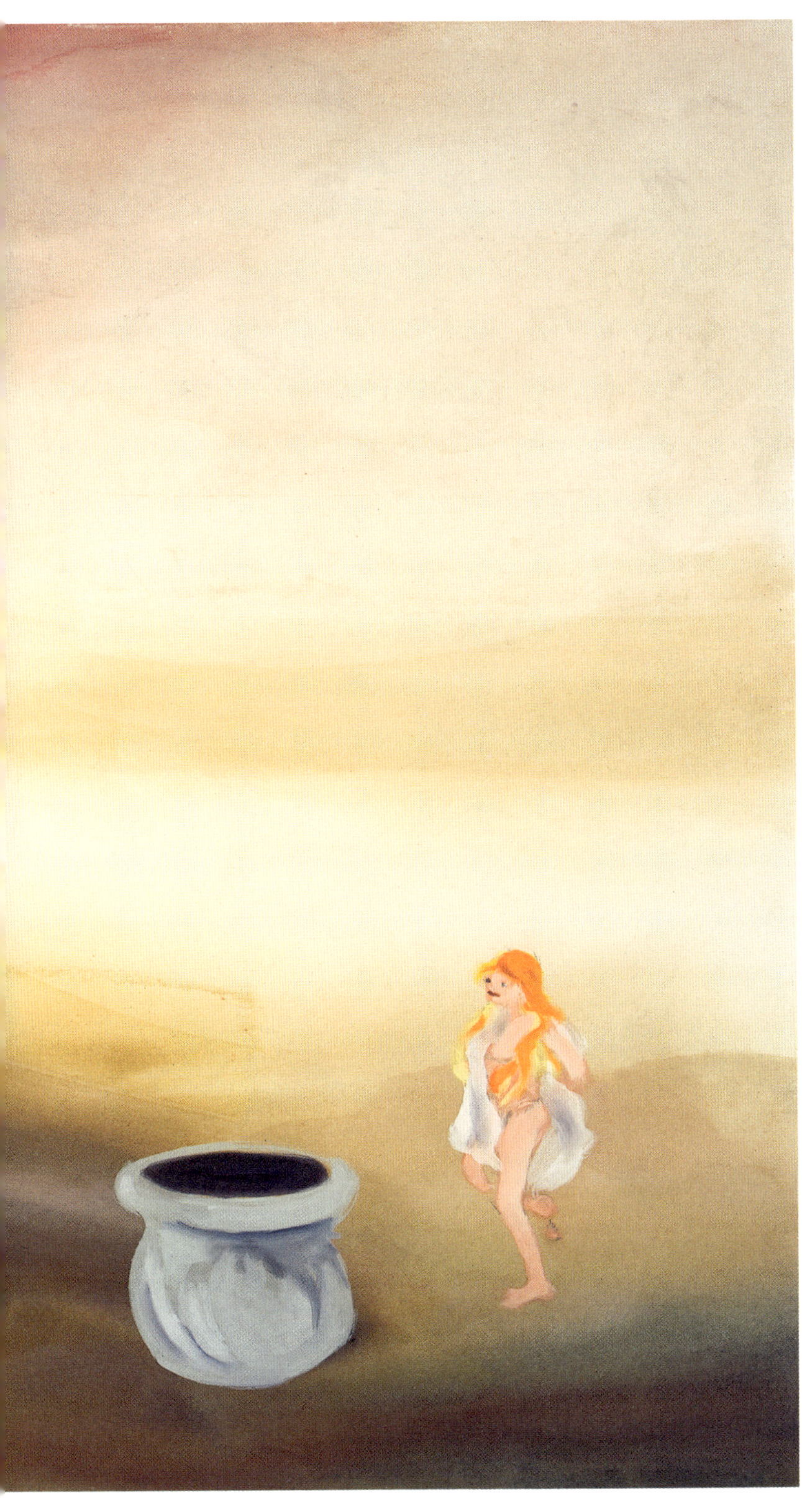

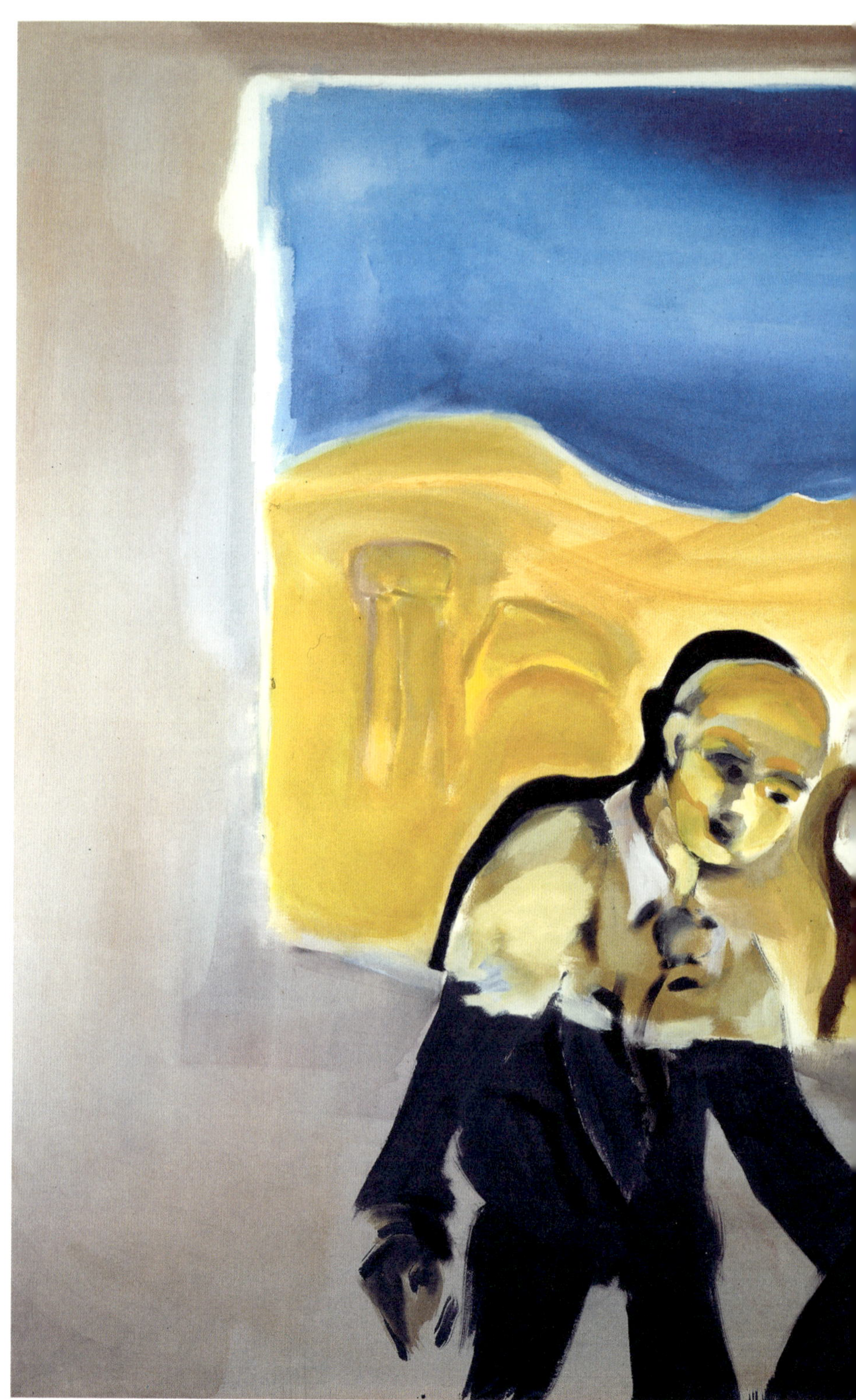

158   *Camel*, 2002

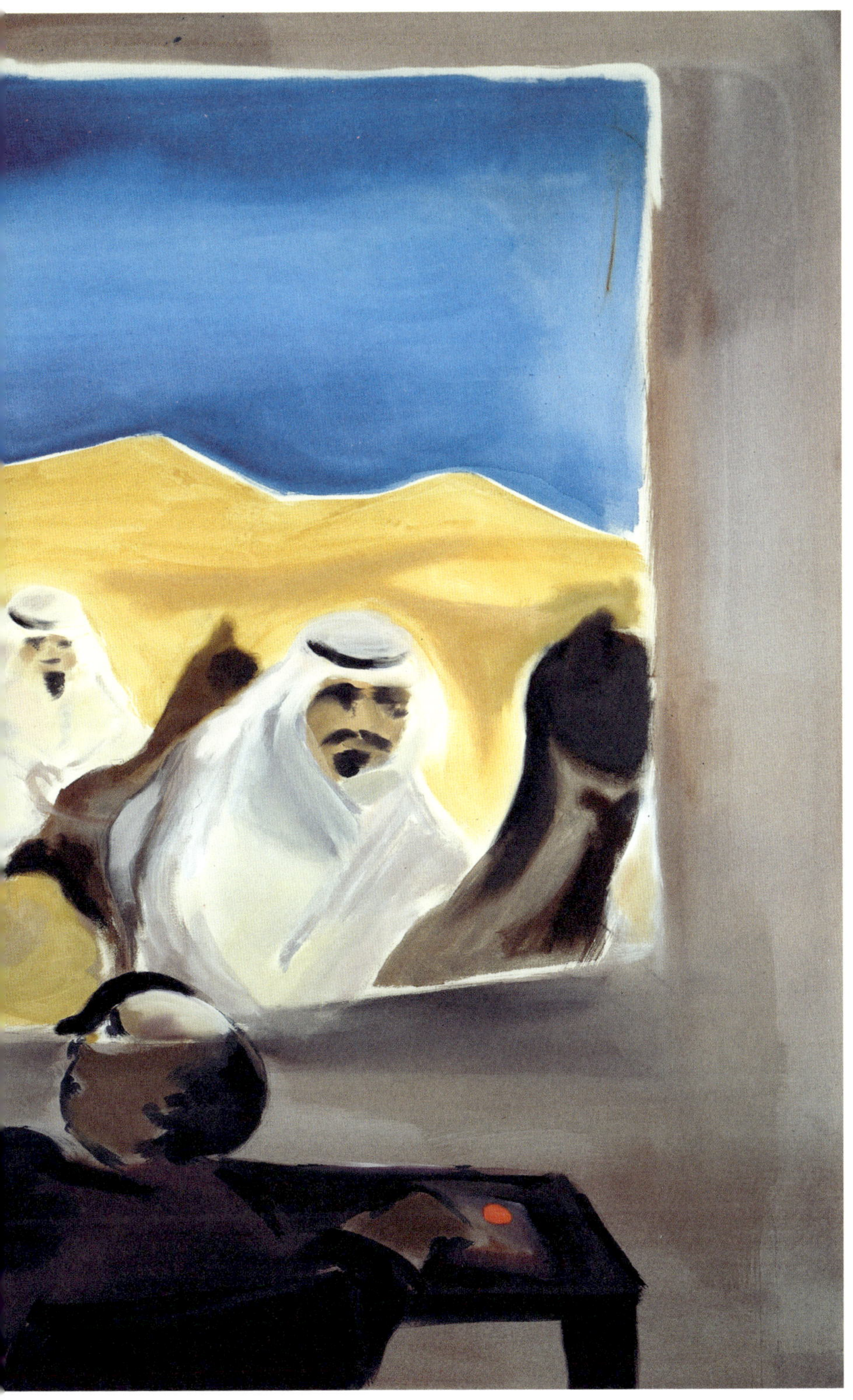

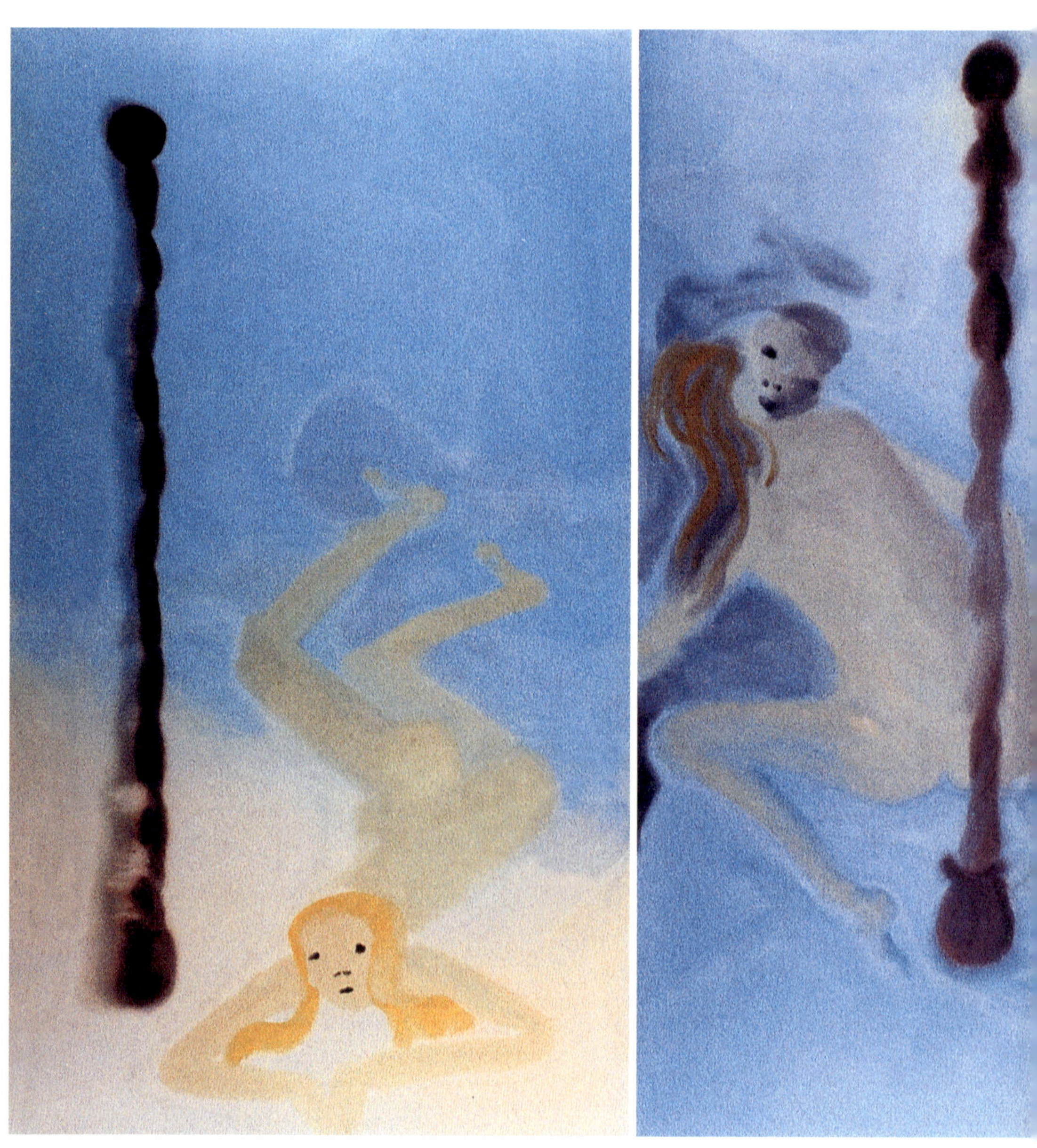

Hotel Flesh (triptych), 2002

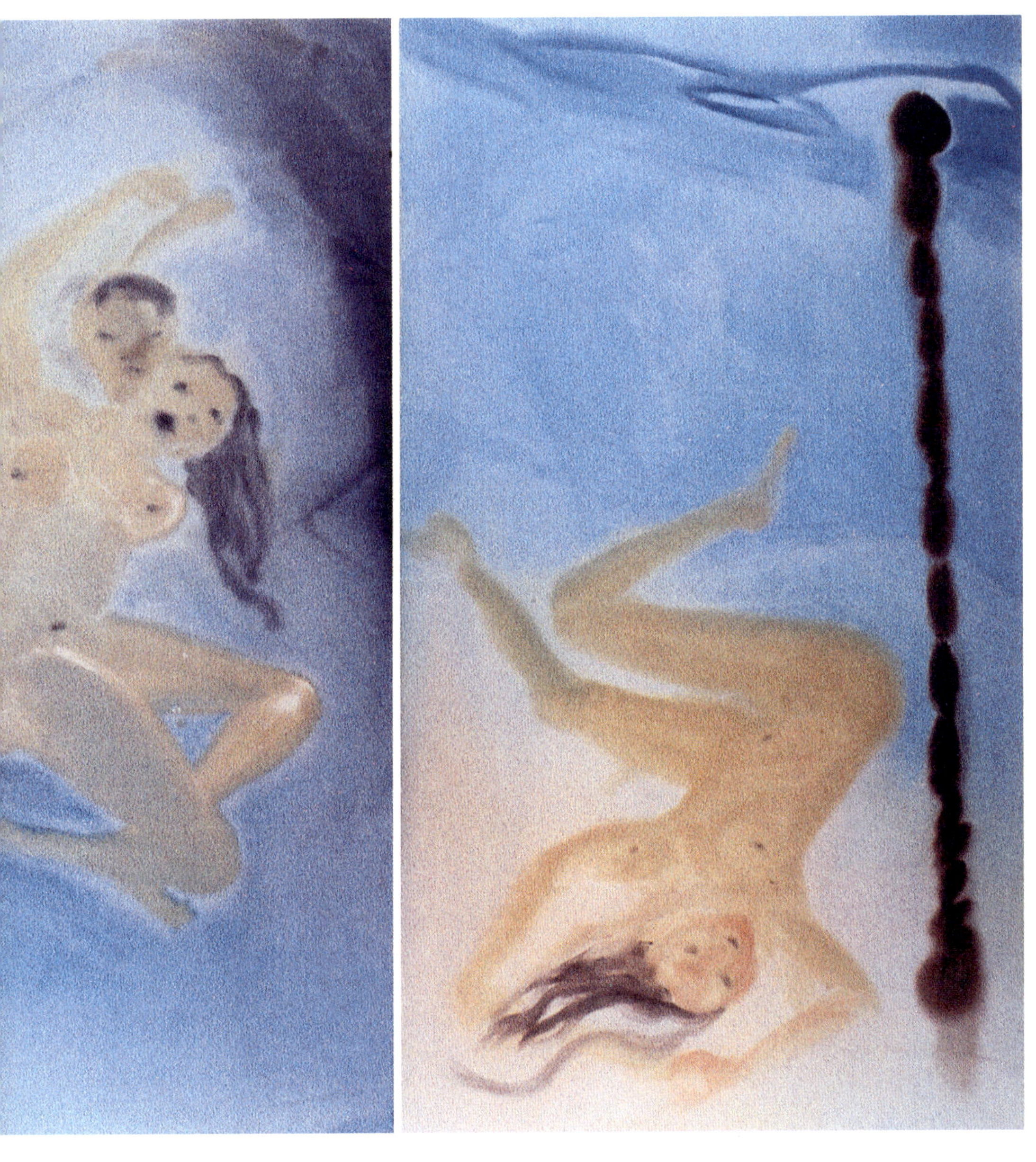

SPACE GIRL AND THE STRANGE CASE
OF BEING IN TWO PLACES
AT THE SAME TIME

C—. Where she might have been able to stay, for a moment; she remembered what it might mean to have been truly content. Or perhaps content is too strong a word for it. Perhaps this was the moment when she felt most conscious; self-conscious, of herself, of her presence, of something more than a transparent apparition.

C—. To what other place could her mind possibly return? One of a series, but this is one in which she feels she once held some stake.

Sun constant in the sky, breezeless summer air, floating over a glass calm sea. And Space Girl and K gazing at each other by the open window. No stir of breeze at all, to such an extent that were this just an image (that is, a purely two-dimensional construction where experience had played no part) it would be impossible to determine that the window was open at all. Tableau all but vivant, save the sound of gulls. Or so she imagines.

Sheltering from the rain and rummaging through her notes, she thought to herself: Could you ever describe, in pictures, what you heard then? You would never know, from the image alone, what you did hear.

But Space Girl knows she heard very little then. It was the silence that mattered as much as anything between them. A palpable silence that seemed to join them together.

[…]

As if a scene drawn at random from a silent film. Like an image made a million times before, reassuring and disconcerting in its familiarity. Silent and still, where perhaps the only sound you might hear is that of the projector itself and the reel of film rattling through its sprockets. The sound would seem to confirm that the image before you is not still at all, but a moving image of that stillness. But as Space Girl remembers the scene, she and K are dead still for moments on end, to the extent that she loses all track of time, even as she plays it through in her head.

And then the switch or change; sudden, cruel, from this dream or recollection to the grey shape of her hunched little frame under the canopy that sends sheets of rain streaming before her like a wall.

There is a moment that fixes itself in the memory, like a stain or score, involuntary in that you never know which moment it might be or when it might surface. A moment you rarely come to understand, since it configures itself with all the lack of naturalism of the *punctum.*

It was never like that, she thinks.

Still. Unnaturally still. Without beginning or end. No pause between then and then, but the pause itself. A split second you might call it, with full deference to the glaring inadequacy of the term. A split second as if to stand for all moments, before and after.

And then to this image; what she remembers now of that scene: sun, lack of breeze, and the silence between herself and K.

They neither moved nor spoke, as far as her memory attests, for hours on end. Except, Space Girl knows, or suspects, that this was the time and place when K must have spoken, must have had something momentous to say. A declaration of sorts. An idea that would project them forwards together, towards another time and place.

For the life of her she cannot rearticulate his words, nor formulate her response, real or imagined. Days like these, in the grey and rain, she tries to reconstruct the scene at regular intervals, as if the passage of time will help with her remembering. Which it does, she believes, from time to time. When she does not try too hard.

[…]

She had once attended a seminar or some such lecture by a legendary doctor of the mind —whose name has long since fallen from her memory—who asserted, between interminable drags of an eternal cigarette, that what most resists summoning in the mind's eye is the very thing that blocks its revelation. What we most desire to picture is the very thing that blocks any image at all. A defence, of course, but one so effective that the image could *stare you in the face* (his phrase) and you would not see it at all.

The Doctor paused for effect, as if he had revealed an extraordinary truth. Another drag on the cigarette. He continued:

You would need to *look aside* (his emphasis). When you pick a book from the shelf, it is *never* (his emphasis) the book you actually need, but rather a near miss or evasion. You persuade yourself that it might serve some purpose by way of substitution or consolation. The book you really seek is almost certainly adjacent to the one you pulled from the shelf.

He continued, the glow from the end of his cigarette amber with the intensity of his inhalation. But now, he proclaimed almost triumphantly, you cannot even recall whence the book came. In vain you search for the break or gap along the shelf, both to replace the one picked in error and to retrieve one of those you must have evaded in a dark moment. But it cannot be found.

Another silence, while he appeared to think on the subject as if it had never occurred to him.

[…]

And her mind switching again back to the perpetual unset sun of C—, its scene remaking itself with unpredictable lacunae upon each recollection, but with few other variants. Because she knows, deep down, that she is attempting to reconstitute a moment before or after. An image cast askance. Because she knows, for reasons stated, that she may well have latched on to the wrong moment.

[…]

She has a way of being in two places at the same time. Two places, two times. Or more.

She finds herself, by some involuntary act forced upon her—at either a physical or subconscious level—mid-step, mid-sentence, in some dimension or plane.

They used to call this time travel, but she is suspicious of the term, since events forced upon her follow no linear trajectory. And they know more about relativity these days. Furthermore, the notion of travel in space or time implies a trajectory to and from. Two points of reference. It is not this way with Space Girl.

She is self-aware in more than one place, a perceiving body in more than one place, like one whose eye moves back and forth between two images, blending them into a complex counterpoint of diverging narratives. As if she could take two turns, two choices, in the game.

She is not certain of her mission, although she is adamant she is obligated to undertake one. Her notes or diaries attest to this much at least. But she senses she is sent back and forth in time and place in search of K, who constantly eludes her. Part love story, part mystery. As it always is.

She moves or is moved seamlessly from time to time and place to place. Slips in and out as if no one sees her. But for her to be able to observe scene after scene, surely she, too, must be visible to the naked eye? She is not convinced, and marks her presence with whatever devices she can.

Space Girl suffers the uncomfortable question of whether she is in or out of the scene she observes. She finds herself at the time and place of some event or consequence no one else could have witnessed. She is almost defeated in her own obligations to bear witness. But for all its absolute ethical imperative, witnessing is also an act of imagination. Not a tall tale, but quite the opposite; an absolute truth of the imagination, where time and place converge, and Space Girl cannot help but observe.

[…]

Dusty crossroads, somewhere in the sand. Thrown again, Space Girl finds herself in anticipation of N. She knows that she must have been sent here for a reason. She arrives a moment before some sort of tragic calamity, but is helpless to intervene, like a ghostly form of no substance, doomed to stand in mute observation.

Sometimes she is convinced that this sense of helplessness is deferred, as in a dream, where indeed she arrives a moment after the event, and constructs an image or narrative of what went before, in anticipation of her belated appearance. The dream, such as it is, ends with the moment of arrival. It is always too late for Space Girl.

This hypothesis sits well with the notion that she never comes upon a time or place of which she has absolutely no knowledge or memory. There is always the sense that she remembers something. As if she has been sent here before, or came of her own accord when she was last free to do so. As if she knows who that face or figure is in the centre of the frame, if only she could put a name to it.

Here, then, at the dusty crossroads, Space Girl appears out of the blue, thrown all of a sudden and suddenly still, as if defying all laws of inertia.

It is as if space itself is running past, she thinks.

Quite unconsciously she starts to sing to herself. Softly sung, almost a whisper, with words barely articulated. A song she cannot place. Or one she did not know she knew.

[…]

She garners her stories as best she can, before she finds herself in another time and place. She never knows when the passage will occur, or where she will find herself, so she works on the assumption that every moment in this place, here, now, might be her last.

But there is slippage from one place to another. While this constant dislocation is disconcerting in the extreme, because she has to live out several stories simultaneously, she takes scant comfort from the accumulation. She carries with her the accumulation of half-configured images. She believes that she might yet be able to make sense of her notes, sketches, snapshots and recordings, by way of list or index. But not yet.

She suspects that were she able to dwell for long enough on these images or evidence, she might be able to call a halt to being shunted from pillar to post. She has the clues with her, sketchily recorded, in real time with all the latest devices and trickery.

She knows by now she is being sent through time and space to solve the very problem of this constant passage. A common symptom of what we have come to refer to as collective memory. A disparate bundle of already familiar possessions that she carries with her.

Space Girl does not grieve, but cannot help anticipate a moment of loss. It is always already lost, at the very moment she recognises it. The moment with K at the window, or when he woke her after so long an absence in that still heat, or on the beach alone, or when they danced at a stranger's wedding in M—, or in V—, when they drifted listlessly afloat.

[…]

Space Girl wonders just how many times she has stood on the same bridge, overlooking the canal. She asks the question of herself not simply because of the over-familiarity of the scene, but because she has no memory of the moment of her arrival or departure, or, more precisely, no sense of approach. She is thrown into a scene already framed and resolved as image without source or progression save what she might observe around her.

At times she harbours the faint suspicion she could never confirm one way or another that the familiarity she so often experiences might not stem from a re-encounter with or re-enactment of her own past, but from a collective fund or consciousness. As if we have all, already, stood on this Bridge of Sighs.

Or another suspicion: that she has indeed been sent here with a specific mission, and it might yet prove to be one of her own making. As if the diaries and fragments she makes and retains of each encounter somehow contribute to the encounter itself. As any Good Space Girl knows, playing fast and loose with the Space–Time Continuum can produce intolerable paradoxes. The most rudimentary relativity primer would state as its first contradiction that were you to travel into the past and alter it by your presence in any way, it would always distort any sense of your present, any possibility of your self. (Space Girl has long since concluded that this is why she so often feels invisible and weightless in every scene she comes to inhabit.)

Space Girl remembers the Advanced Seminar at the Academy, where much was made of the hypothetical possibility of an encounter with oneself. The slightest slippage in time could lead to a seismic shift, where you not only observe yourself in some uncanny refiguring of the self-portrait, but what you observe to be yourself from a moment before or after informs your observation in a perpetual *mise-en-abyme*.

She wonders how many times she has stood on this bridge, at the same spot, at the same hour of the day. And then, as if possessed by some demon, she suddenly tries to upset the cycle, by hurling one of her accumulated devices into the water. Unless that gesture, too, was always to be part of the story.

Andrew Renton

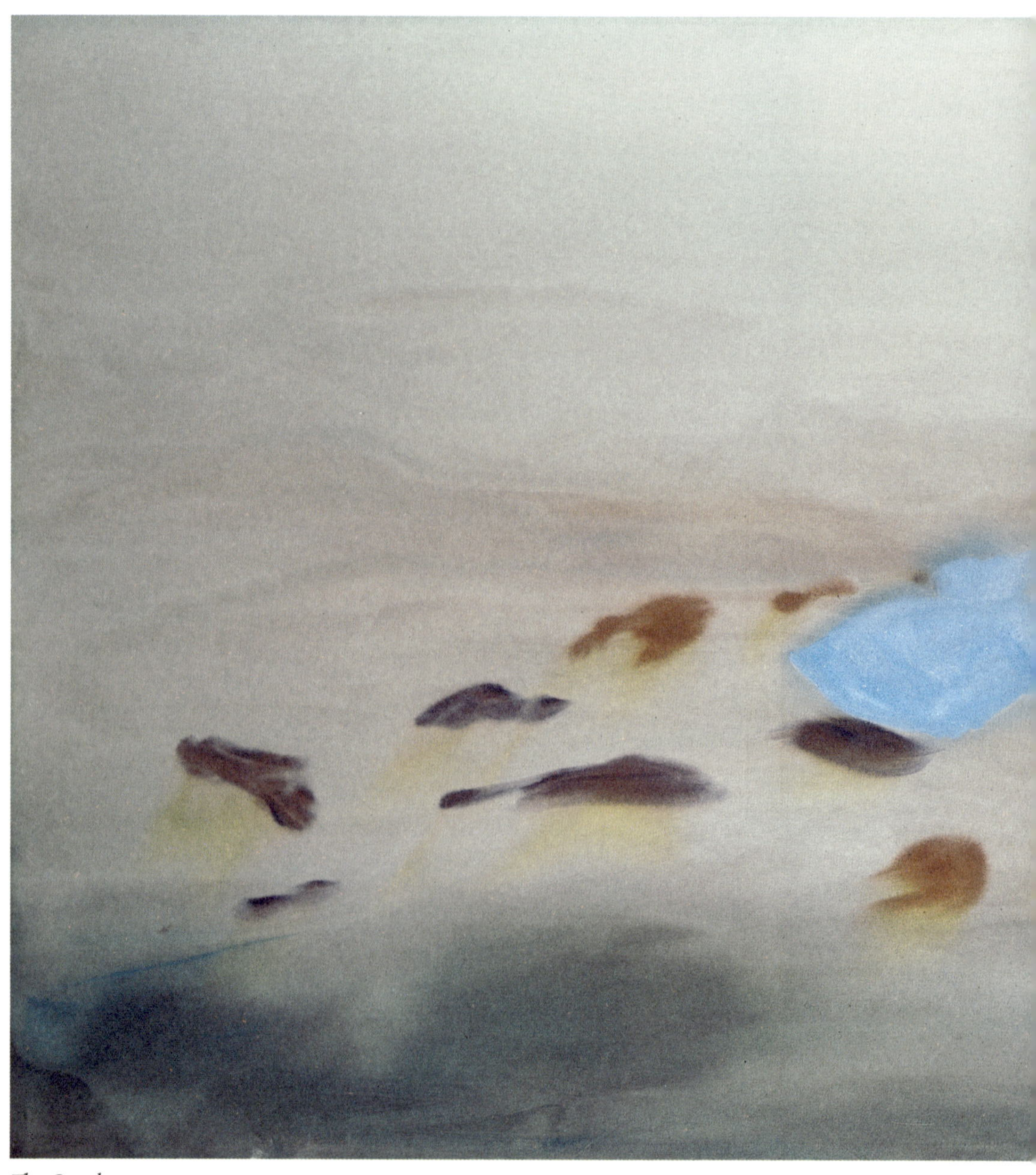

The Canal, 2002

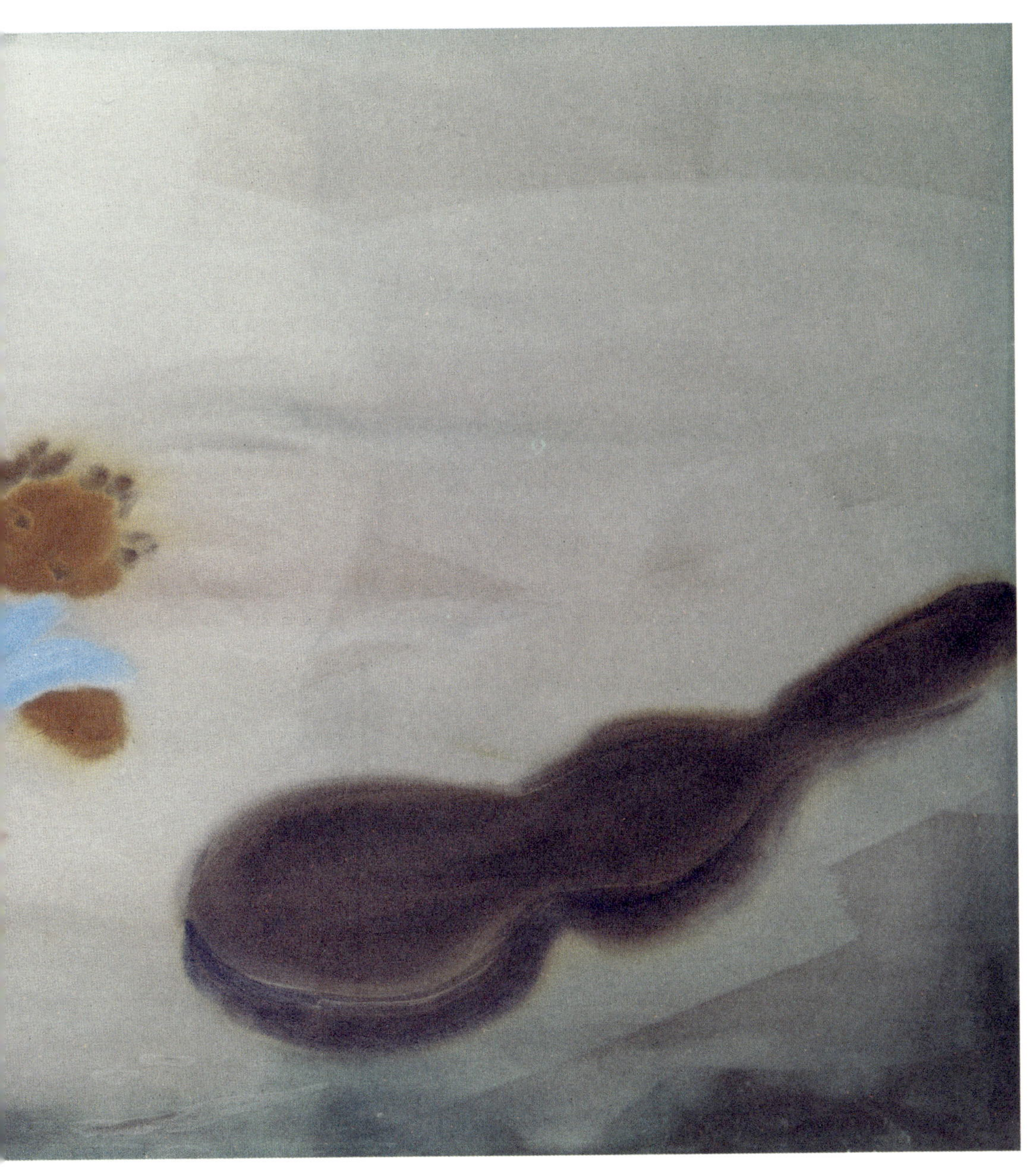

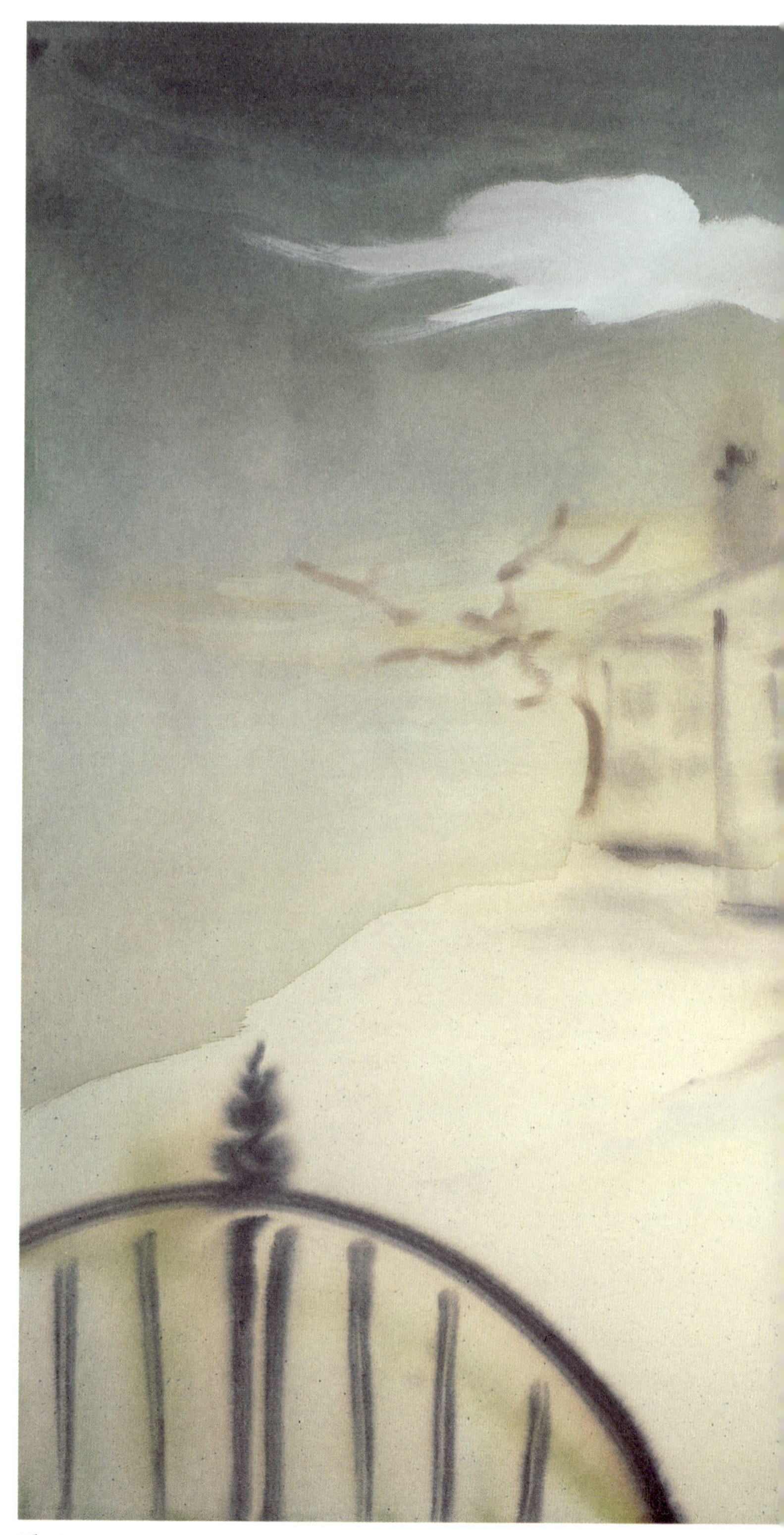

The House, 2002

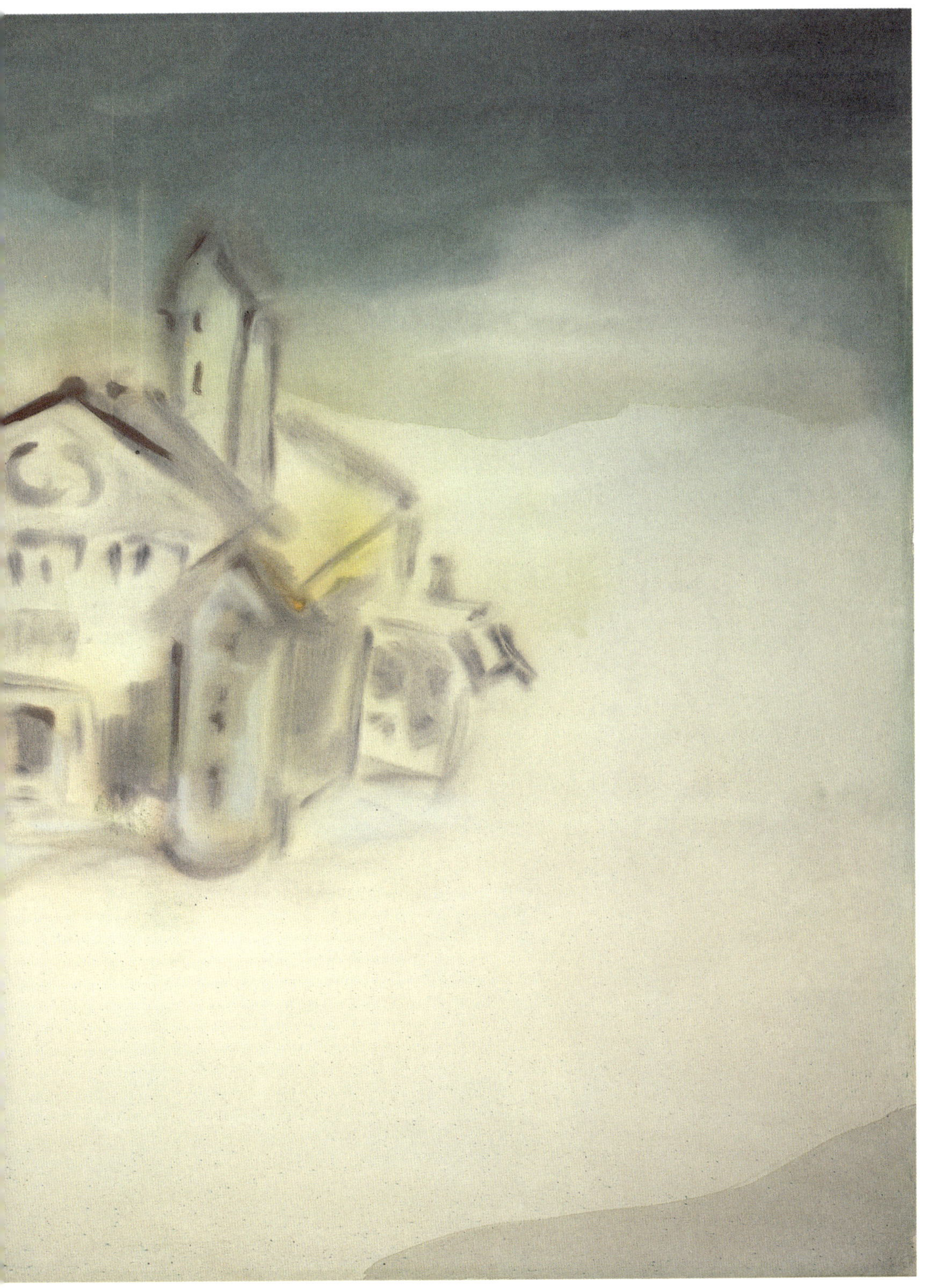

The Chase, 2003

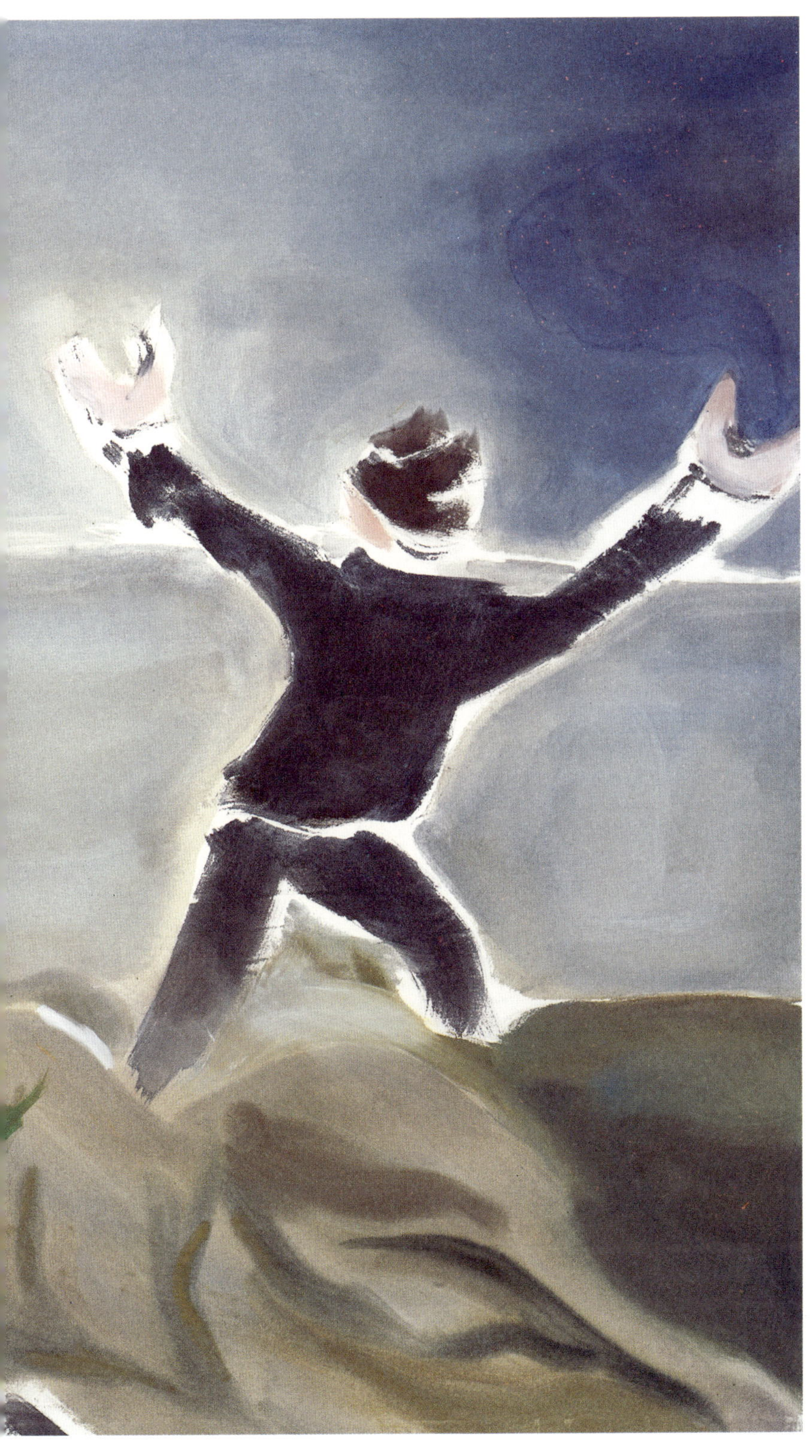

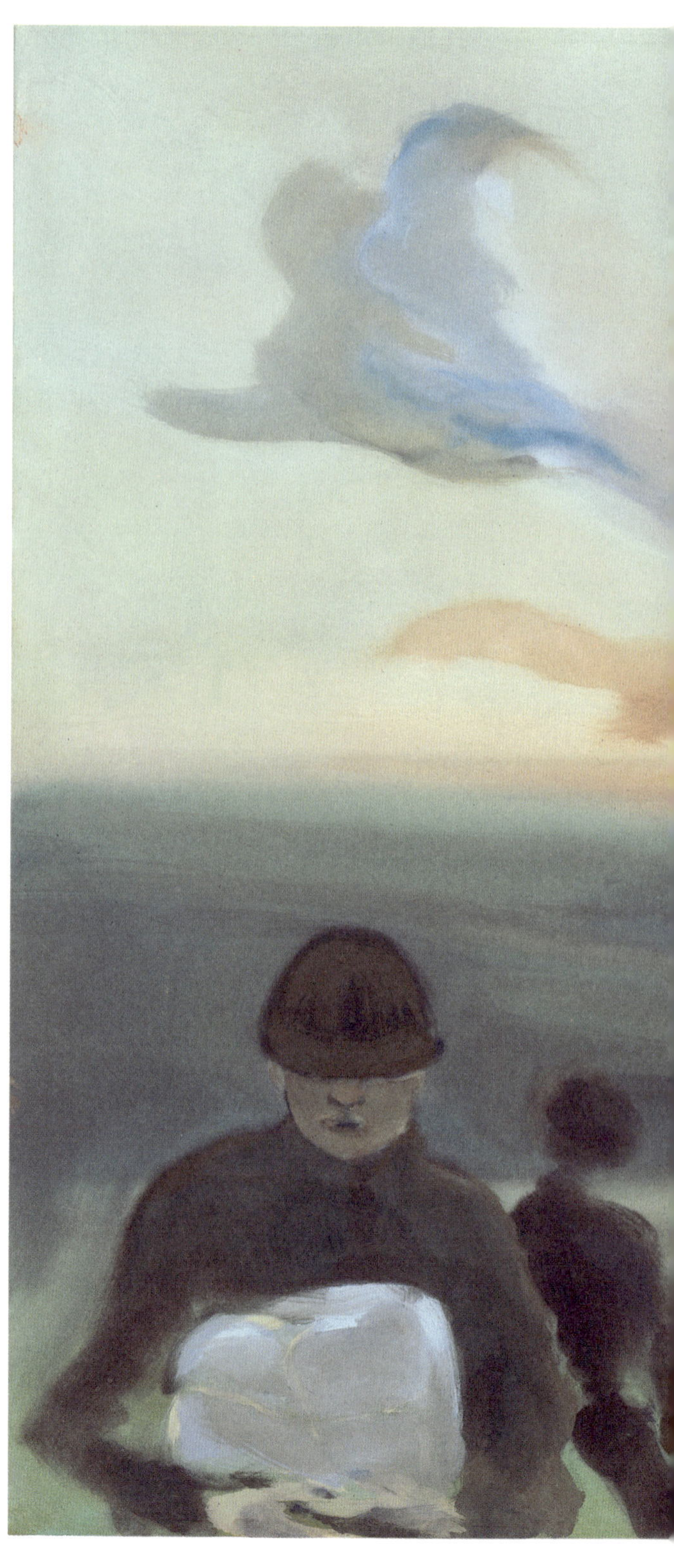

The Smugglers, 2003

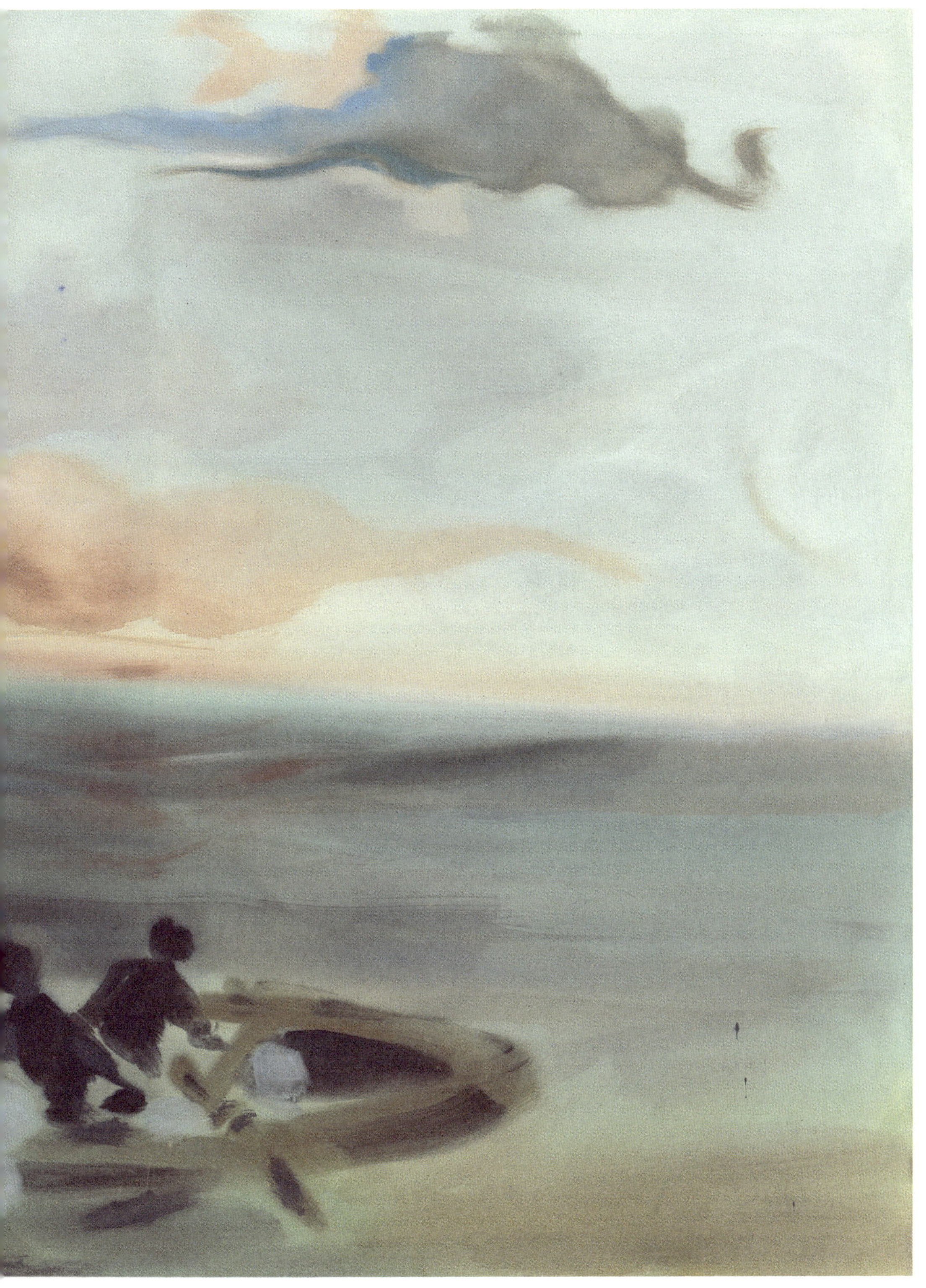

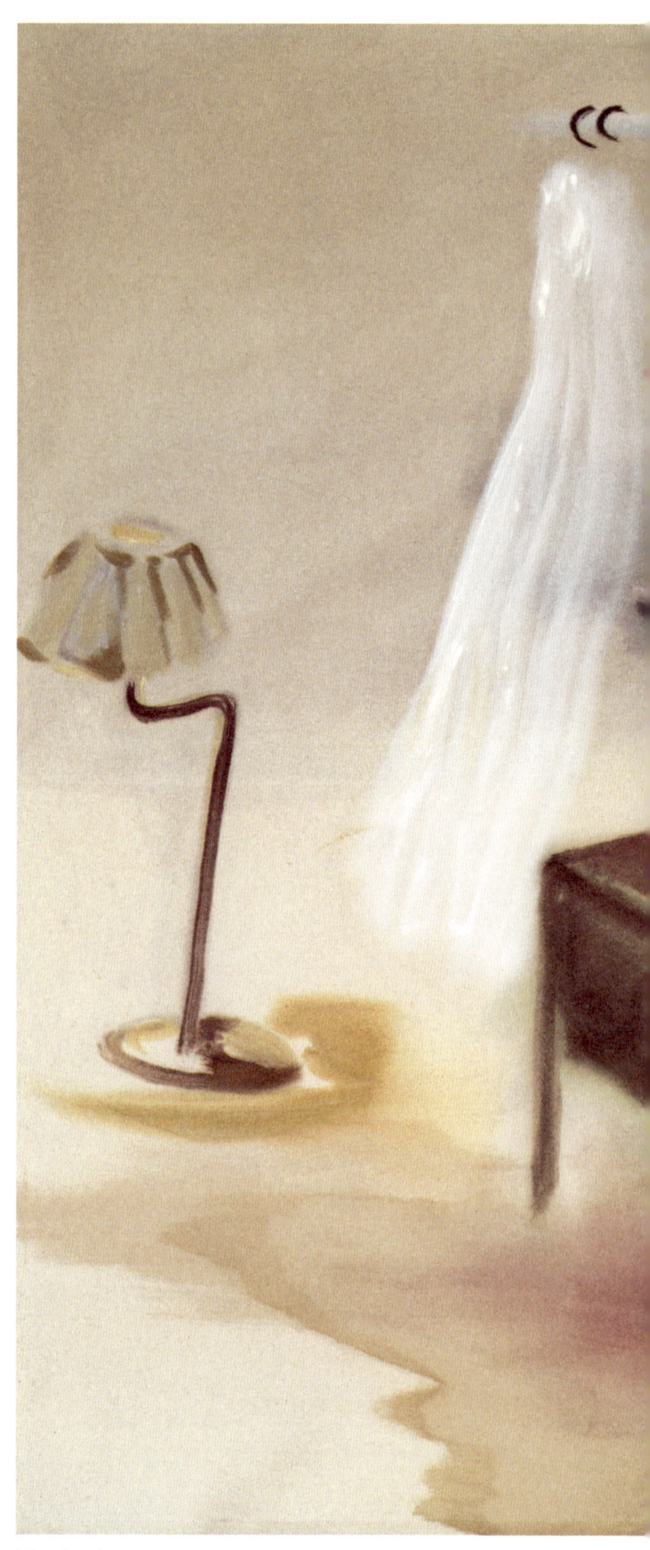

The Study, 2002

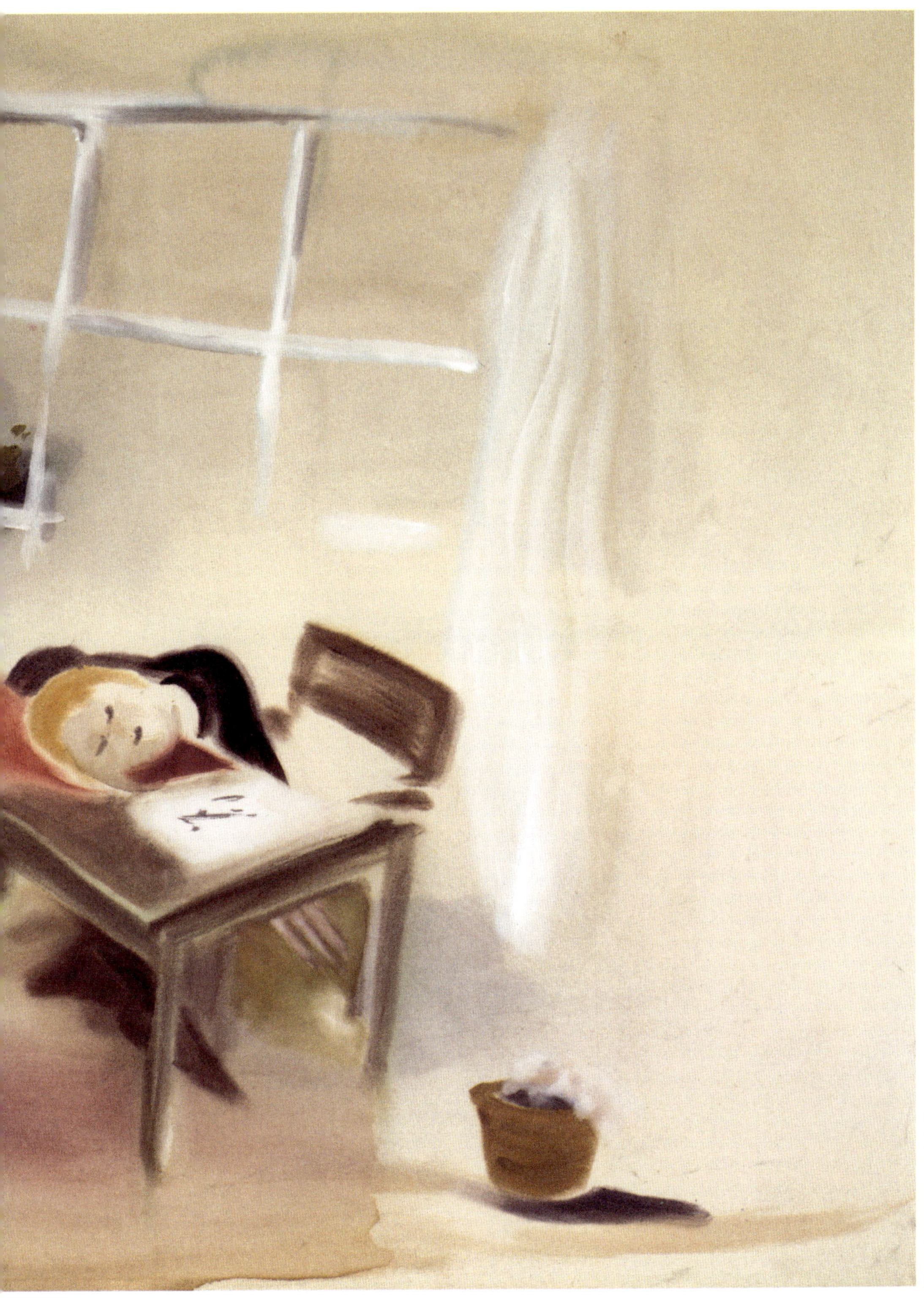

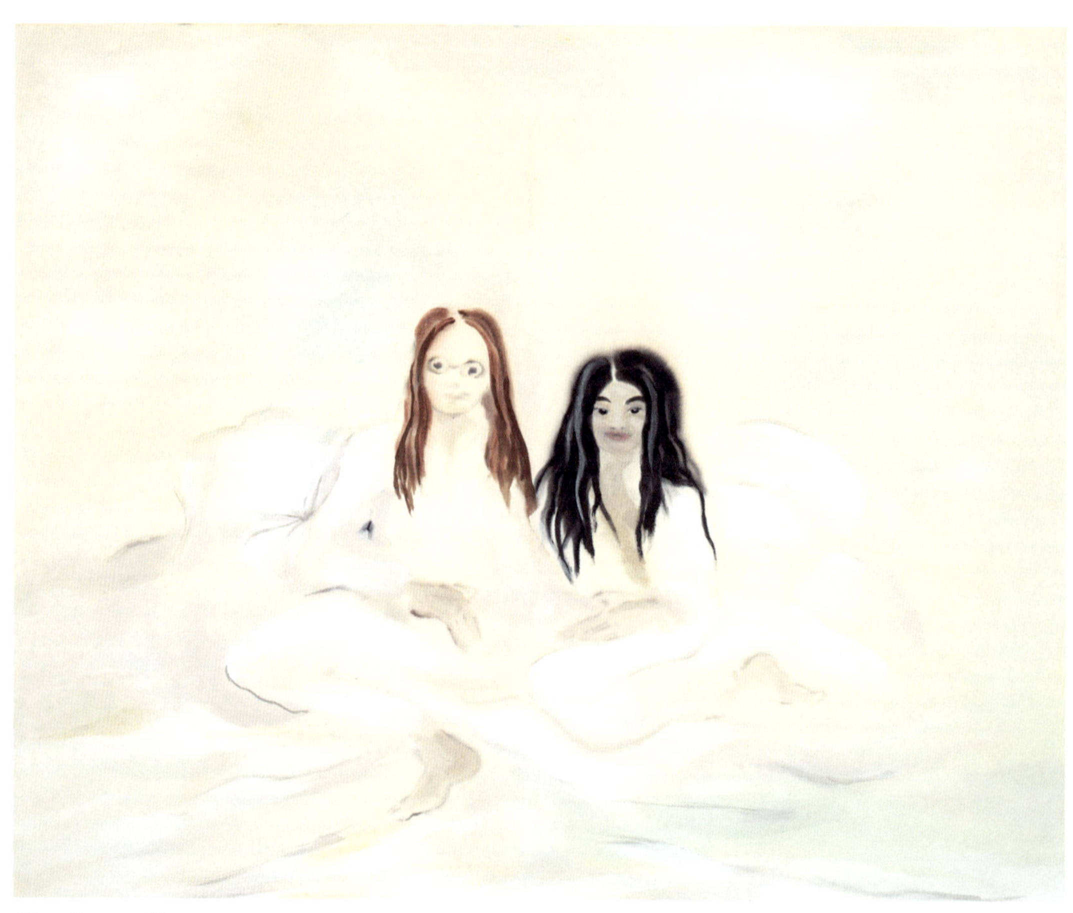

Give Peace a Chance, 2003

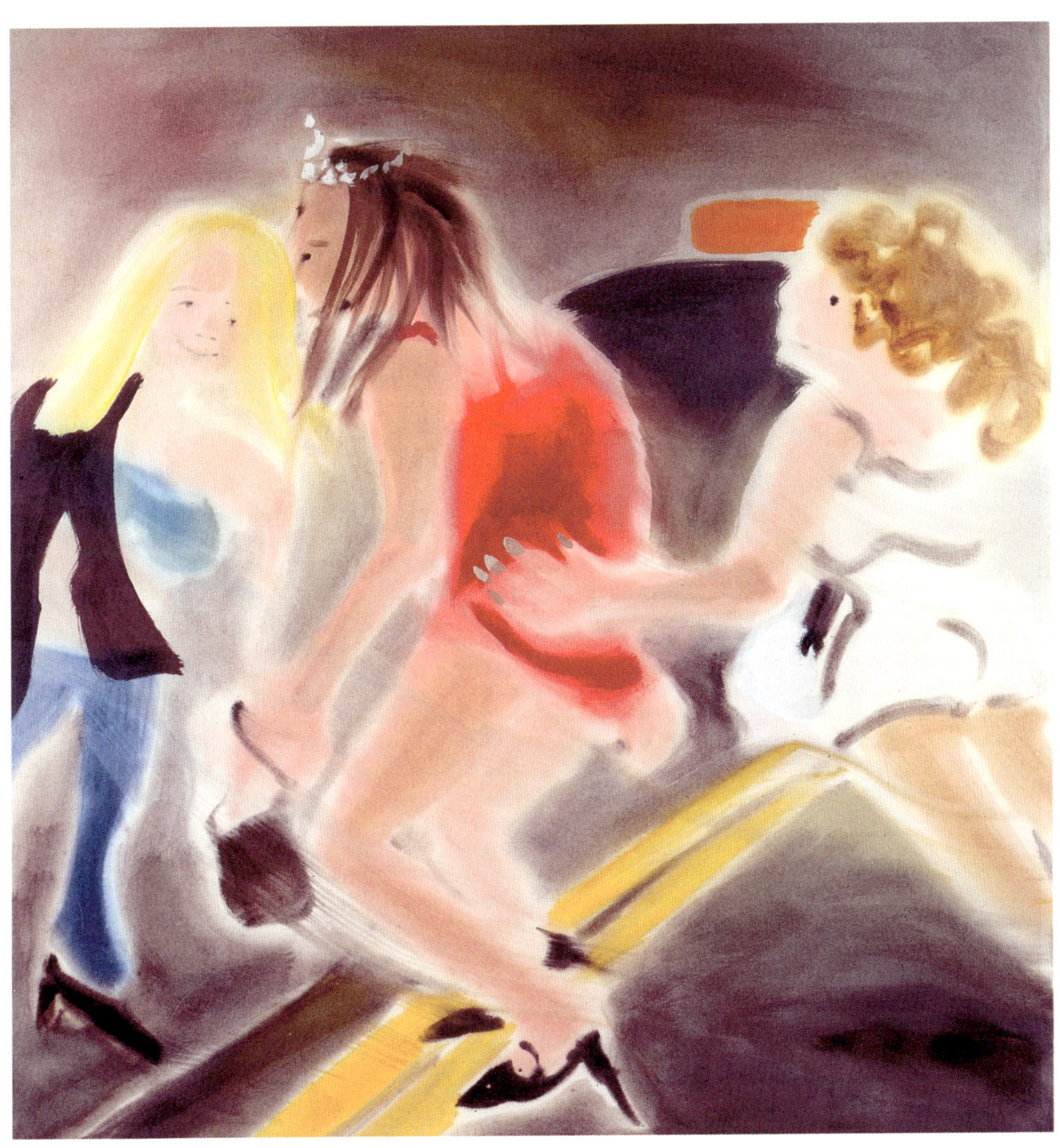

Girls Night Out, 2003

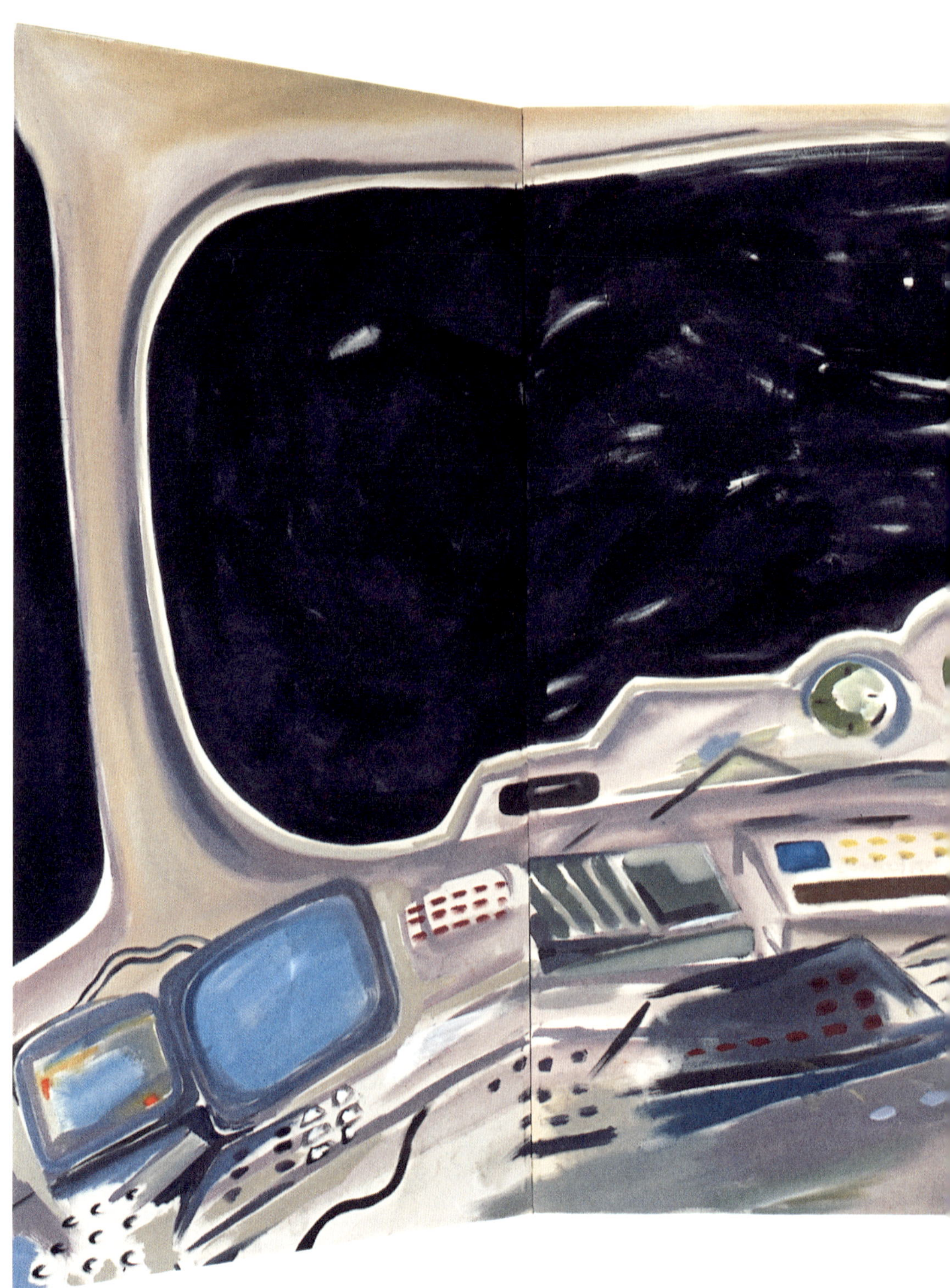

Willküren, 2003

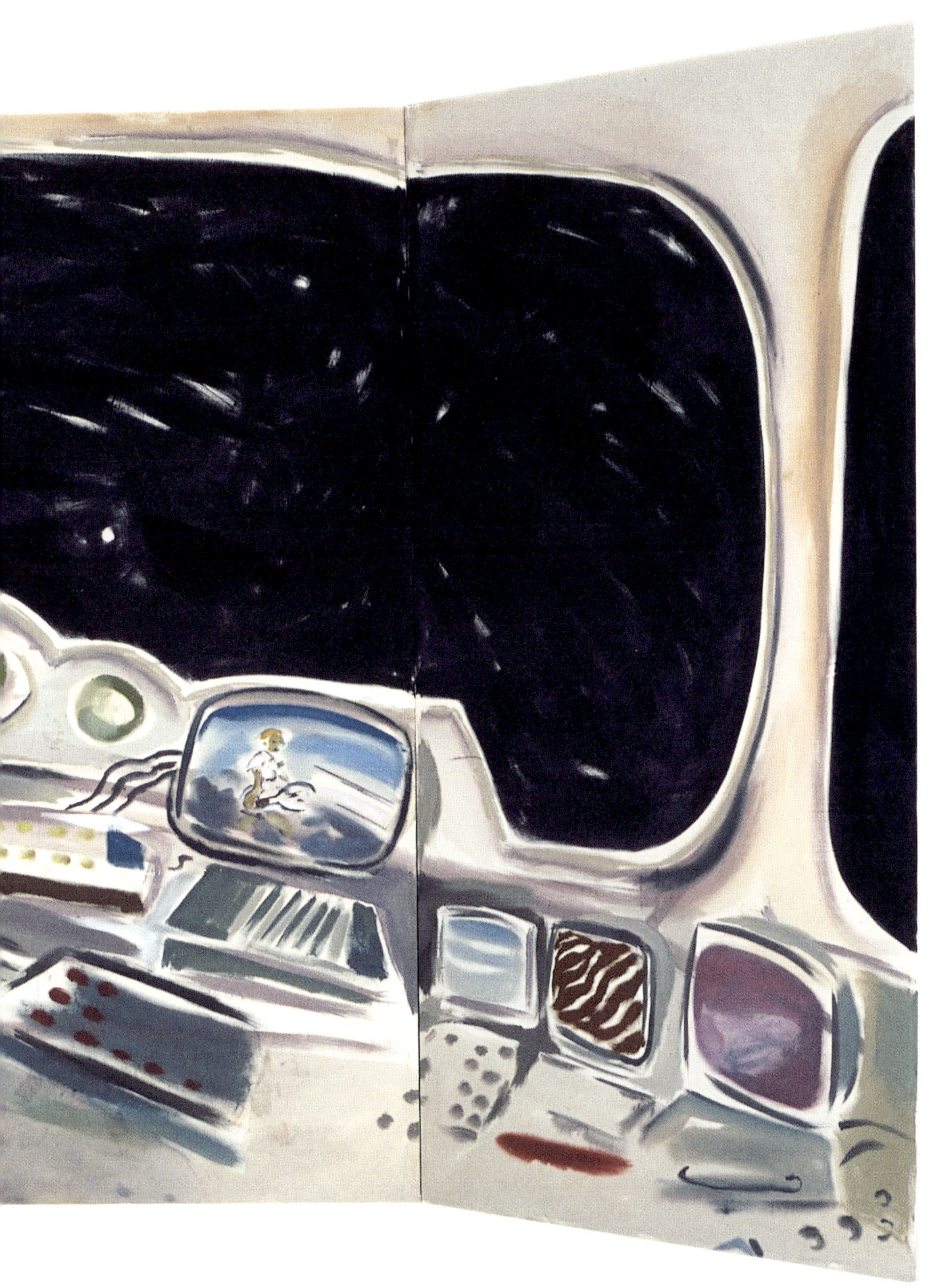

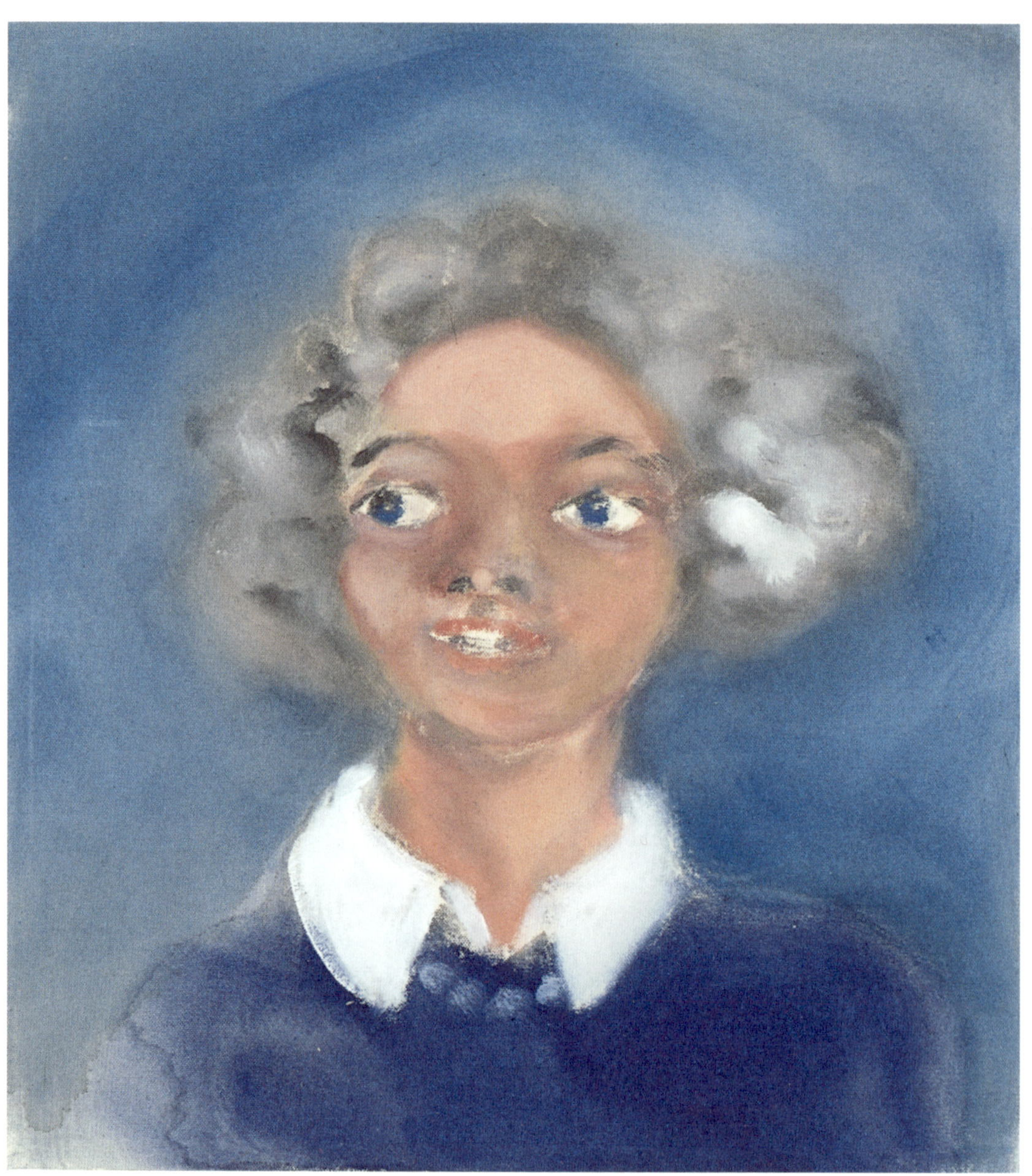

Willküren III, 2003

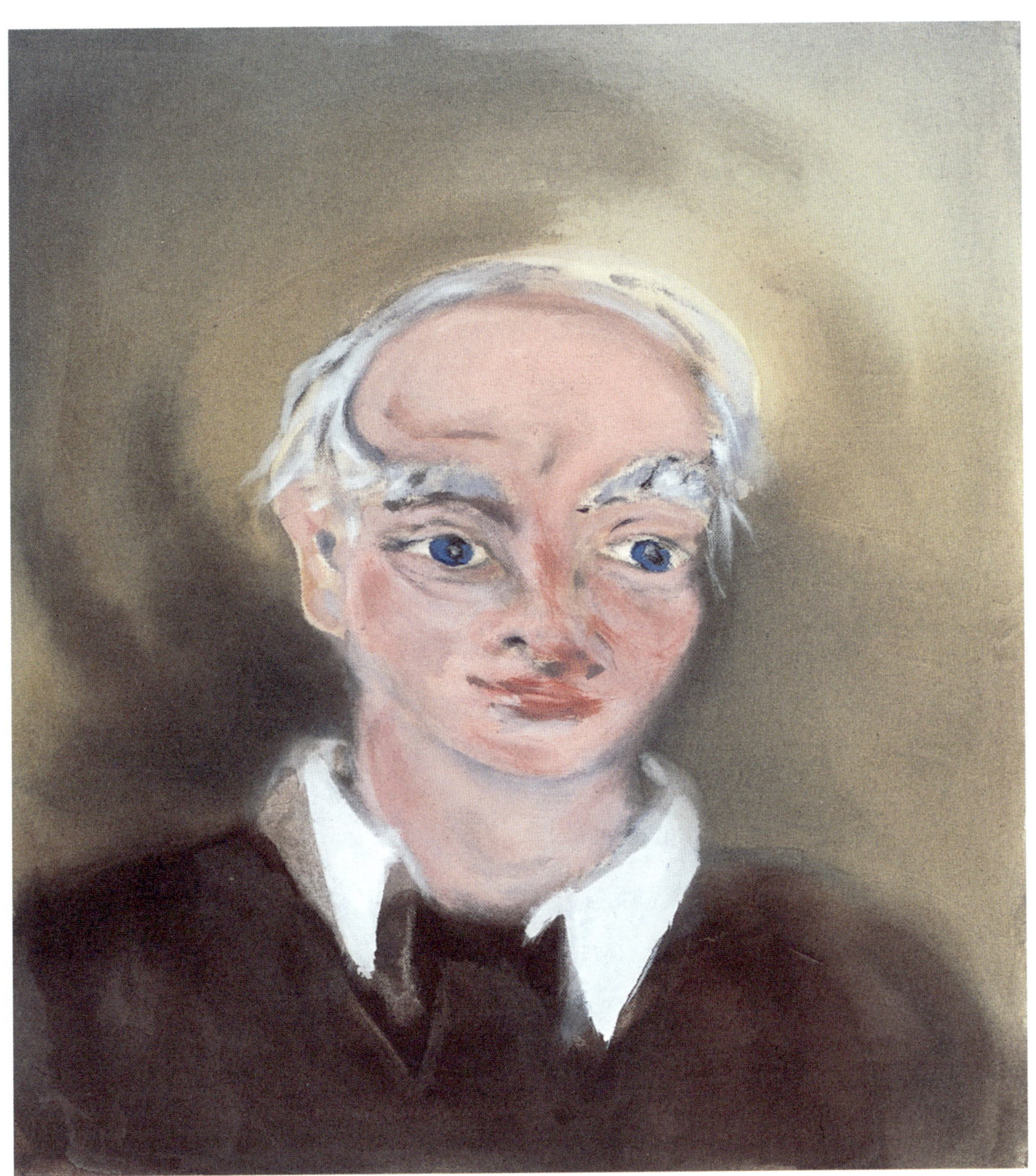

Willküren I, 2003

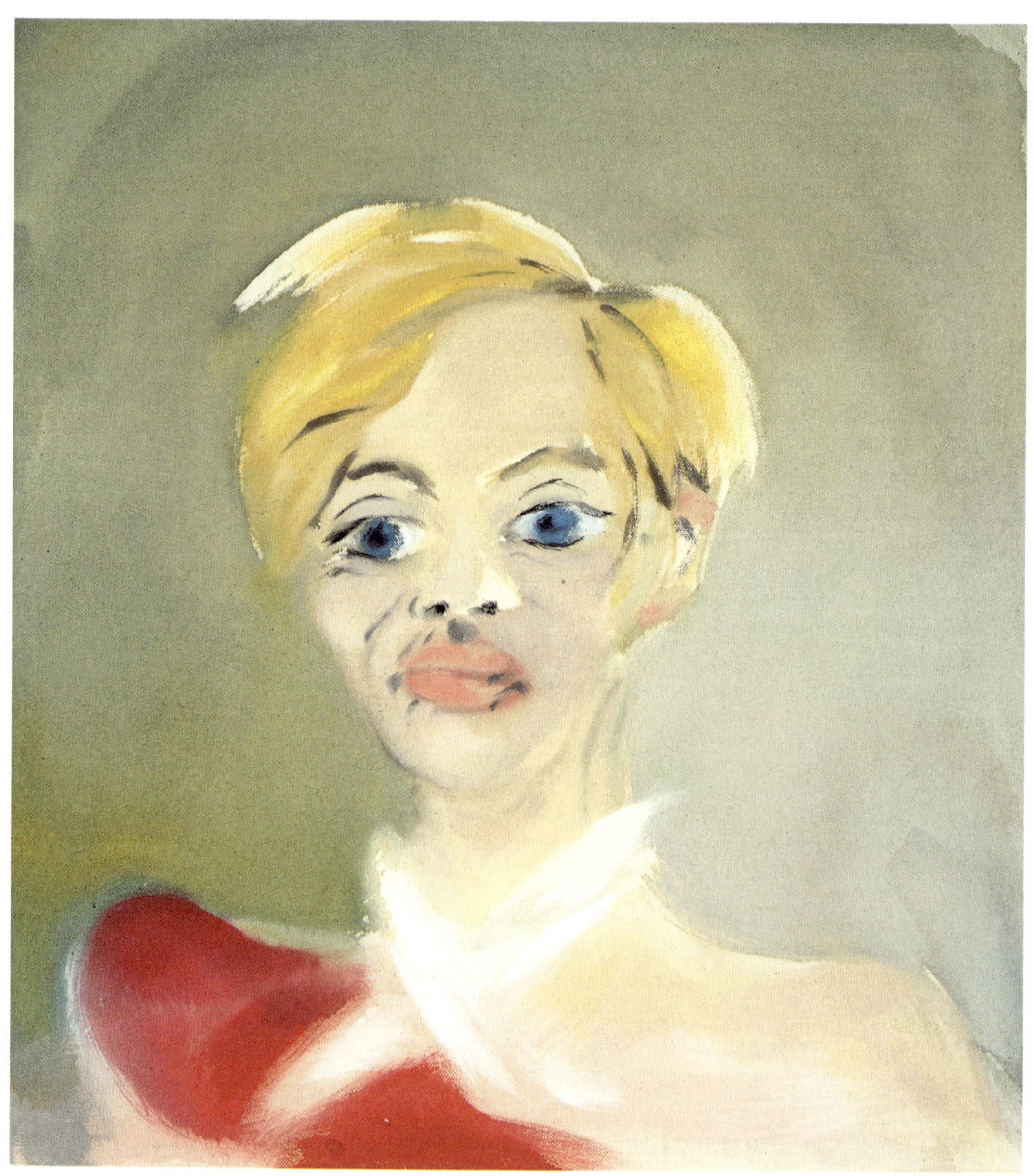

Willküren II, 2003

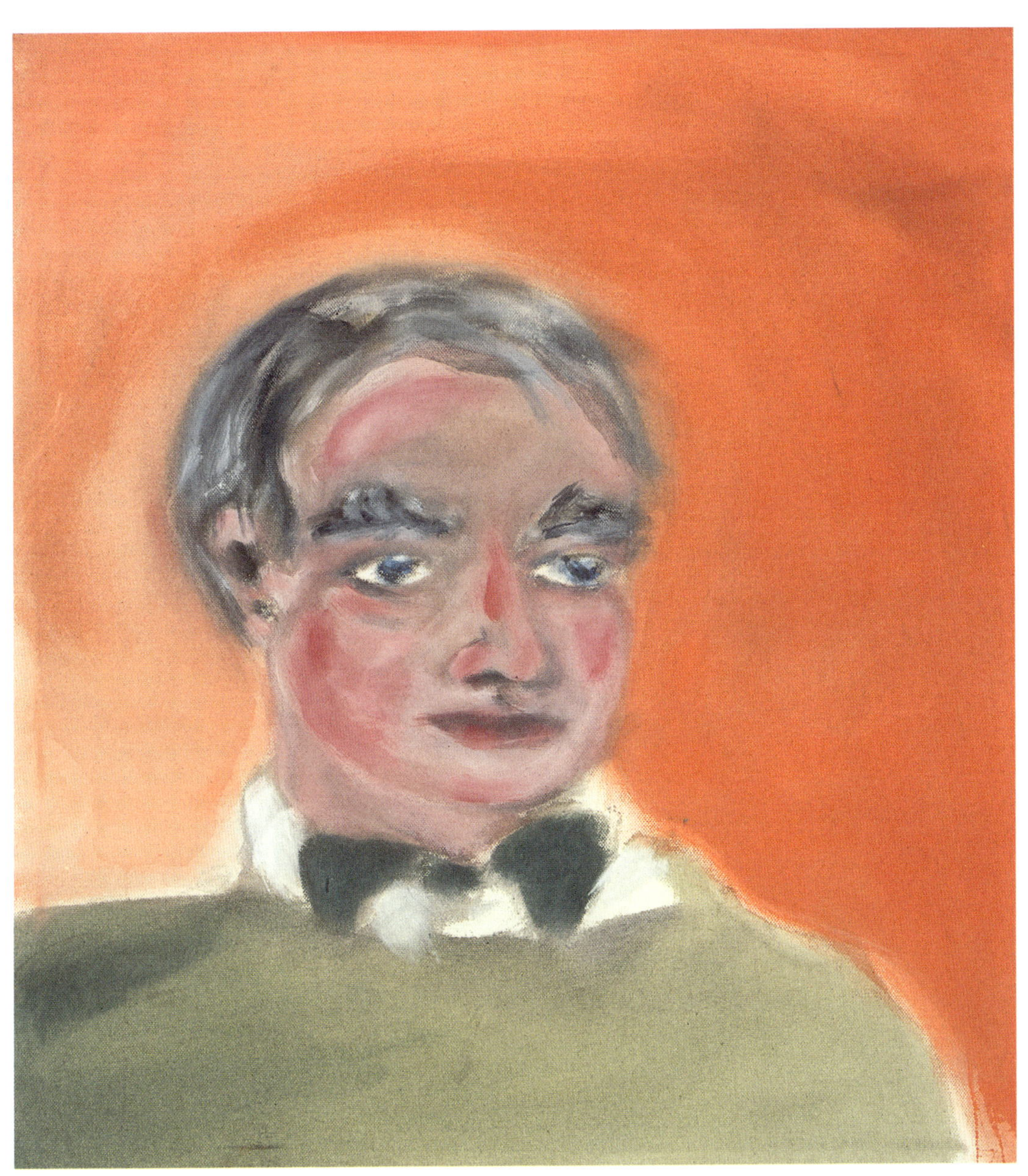

Willküren IV, 2003

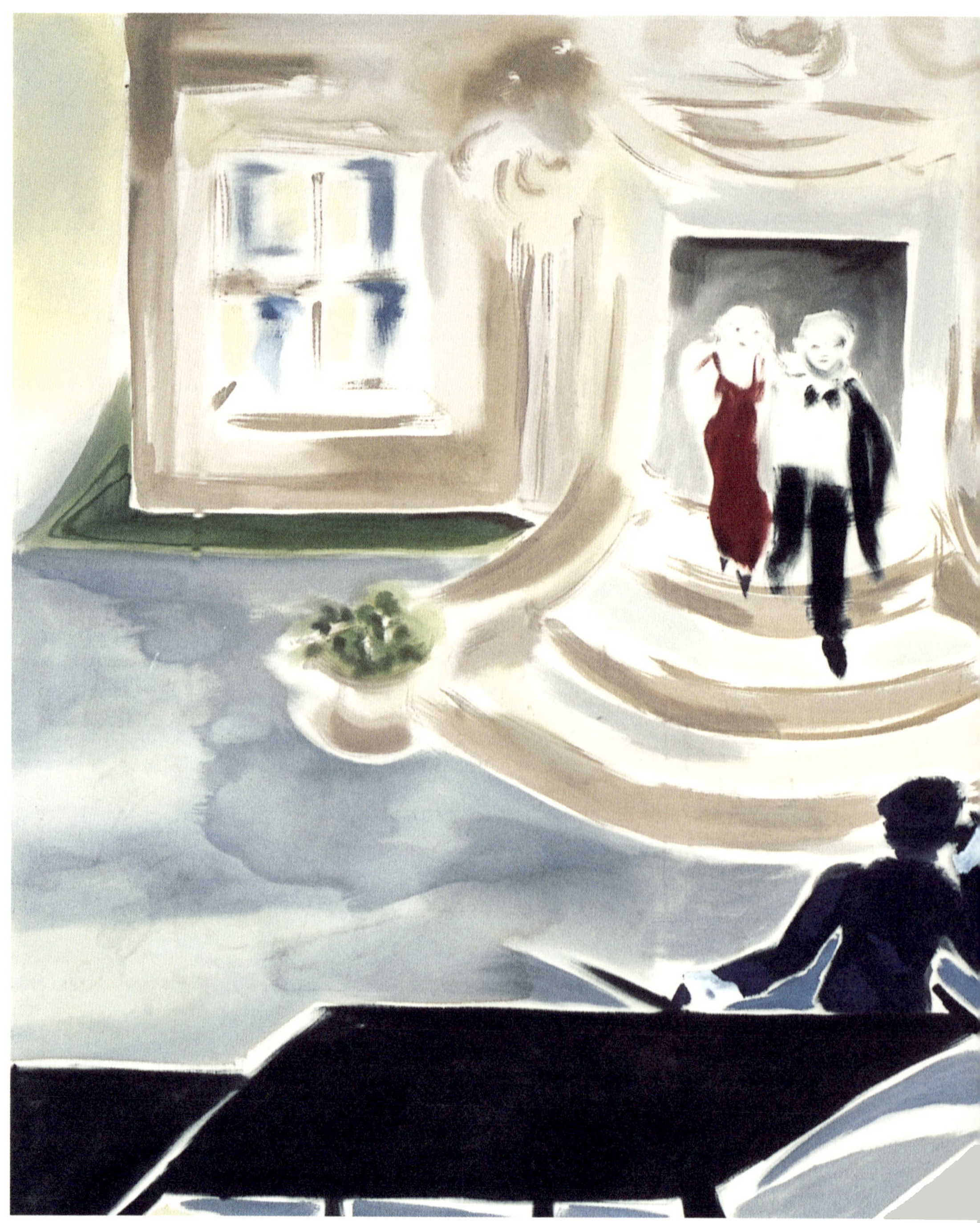

Willküren V, 2003

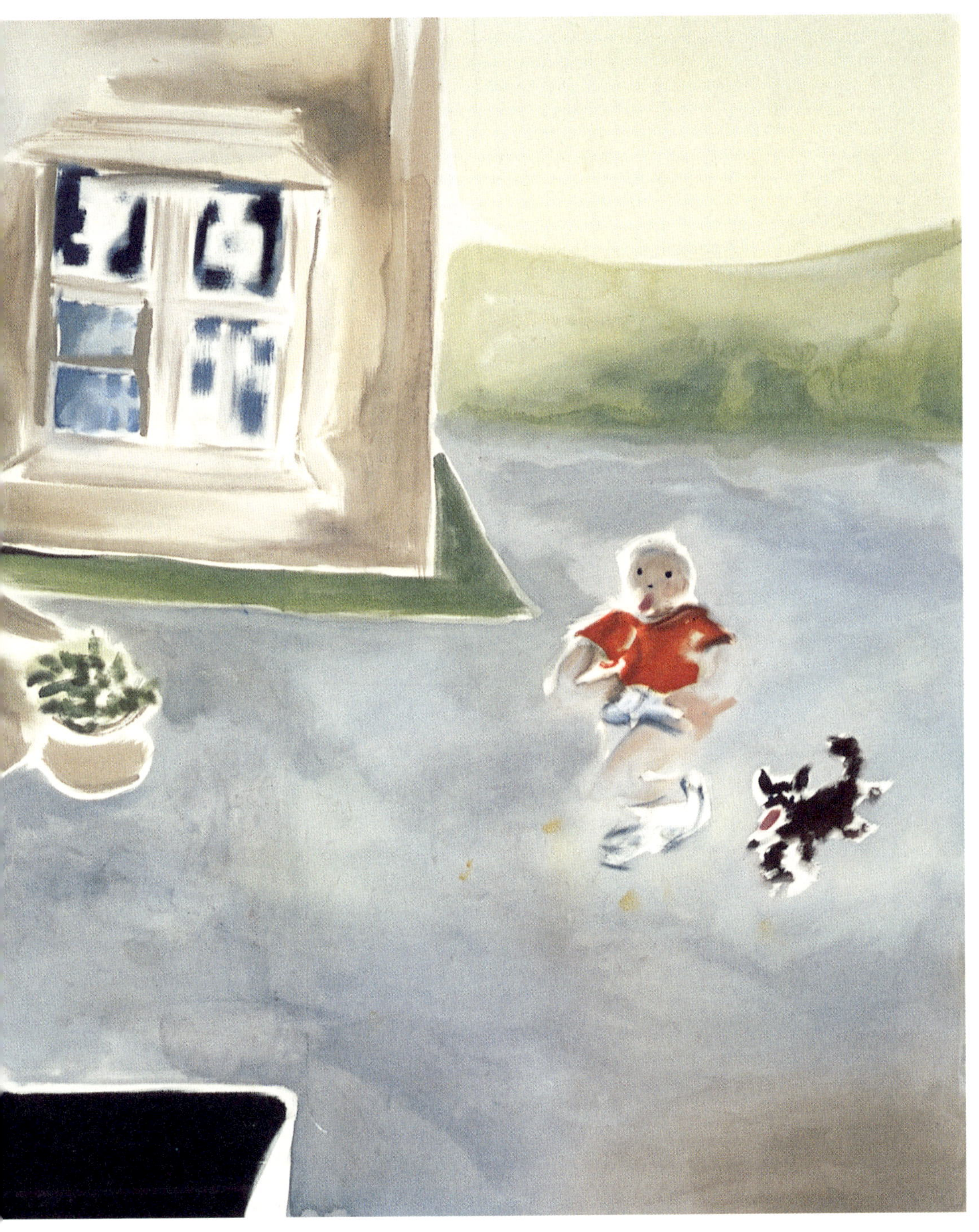

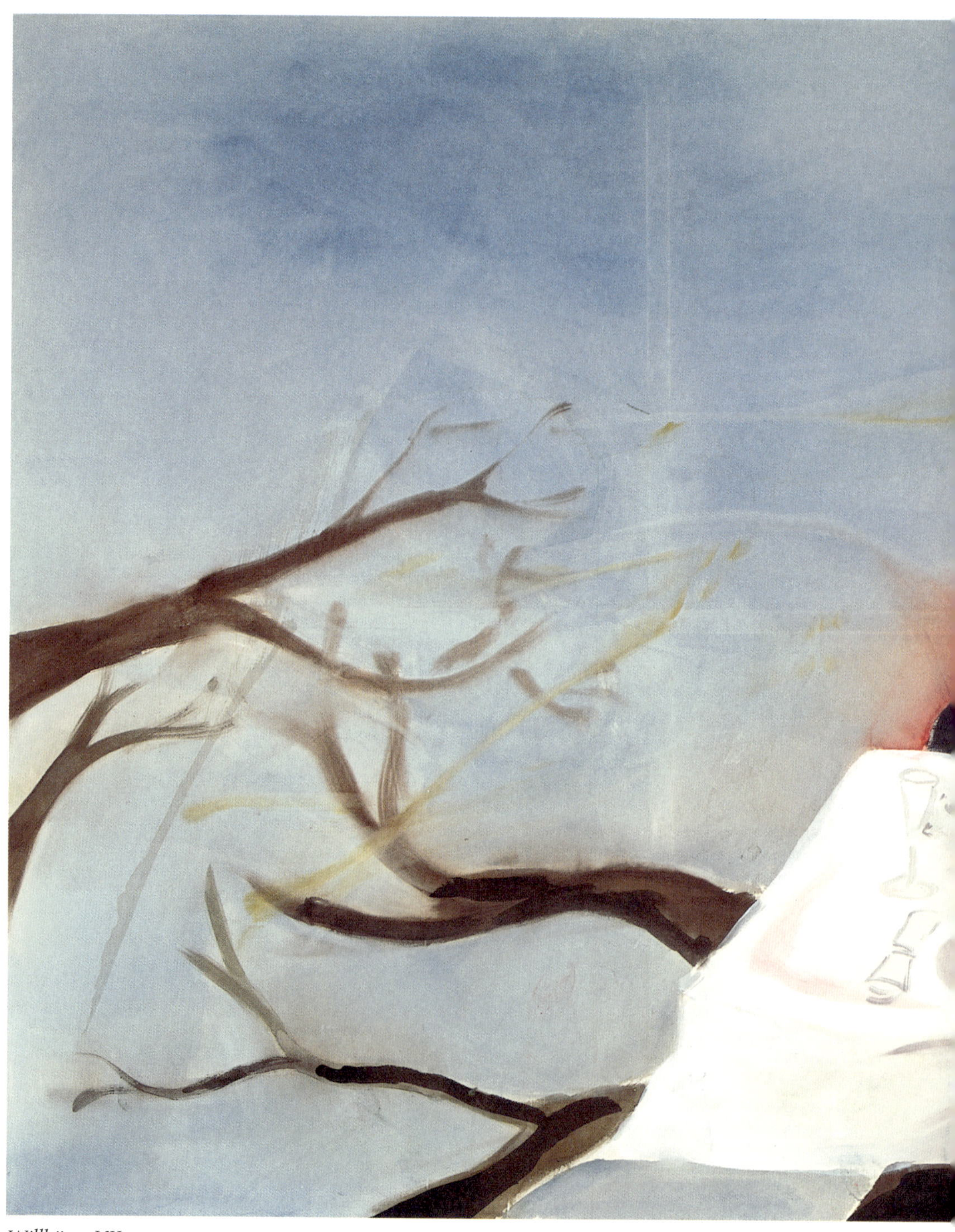

Willküren VII, 2003

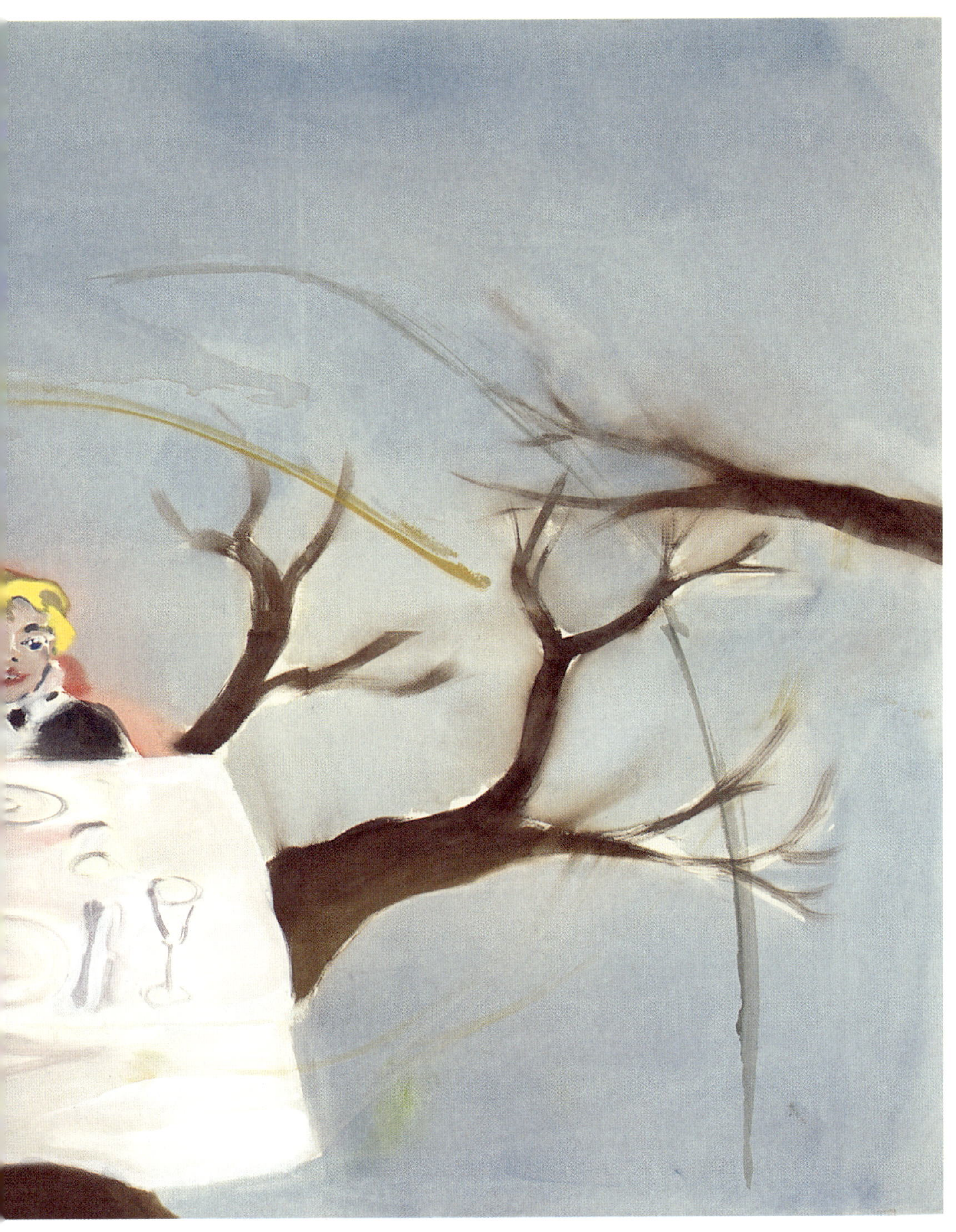

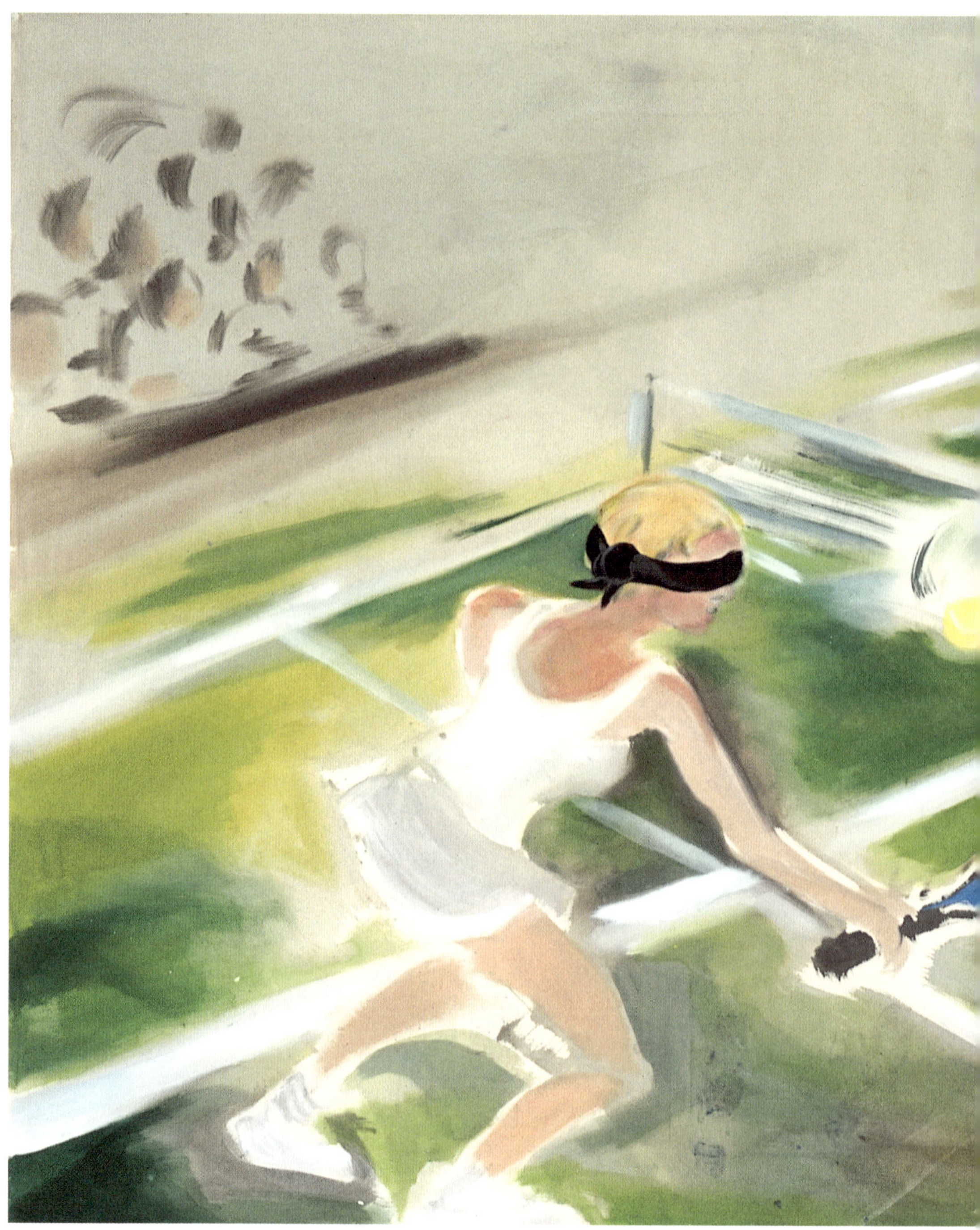

Willküren VI, 2003

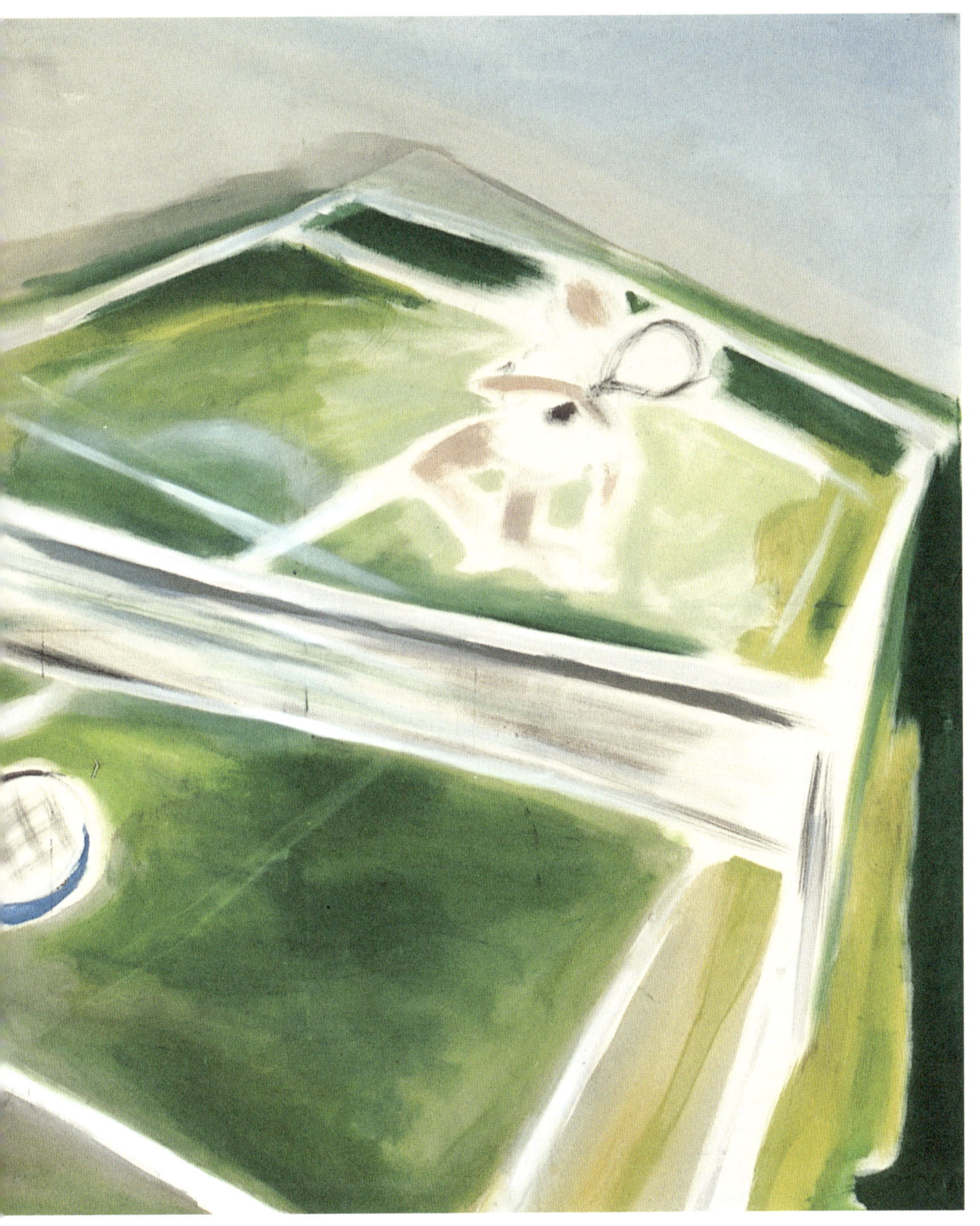

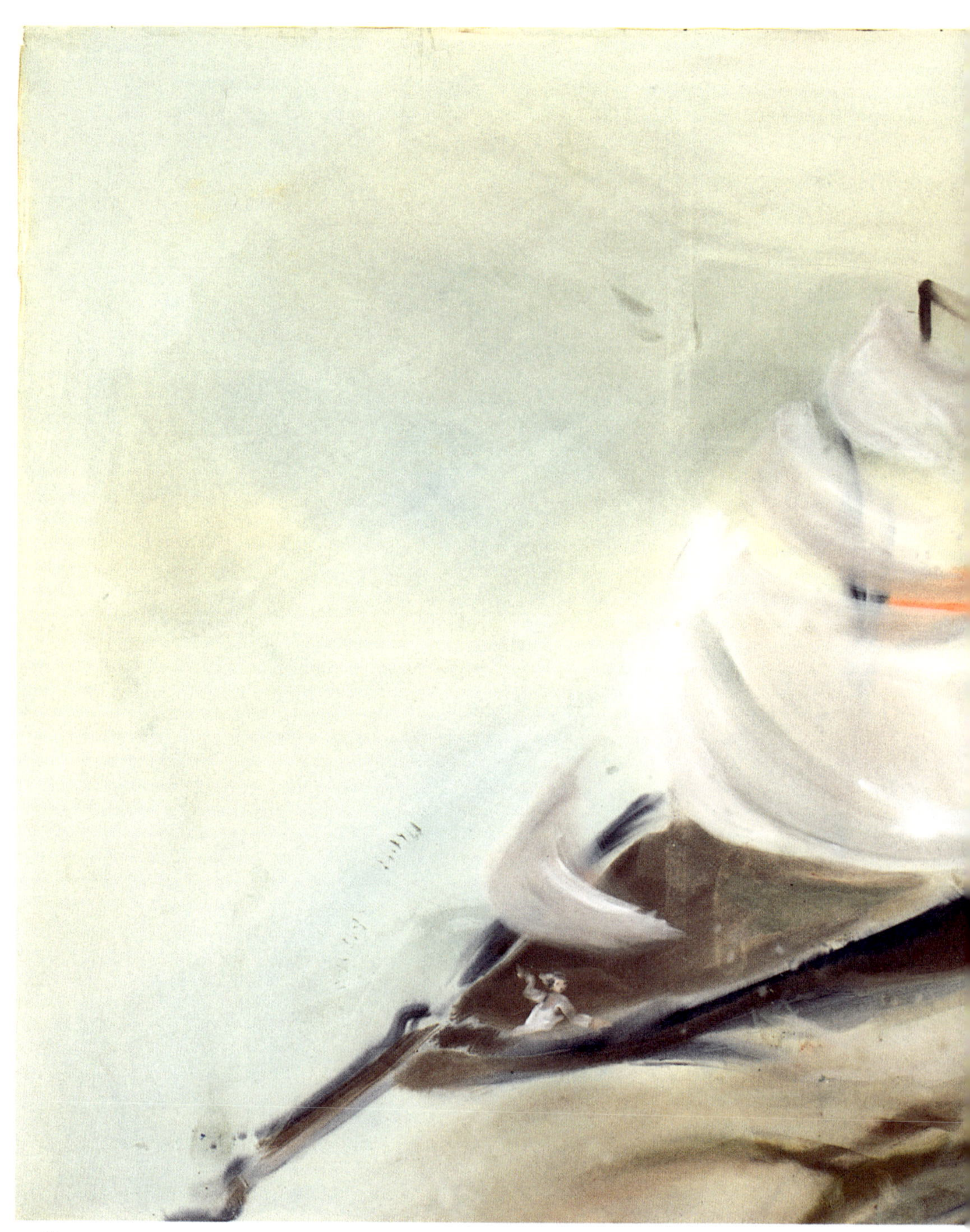

Willküren VIII, 2003

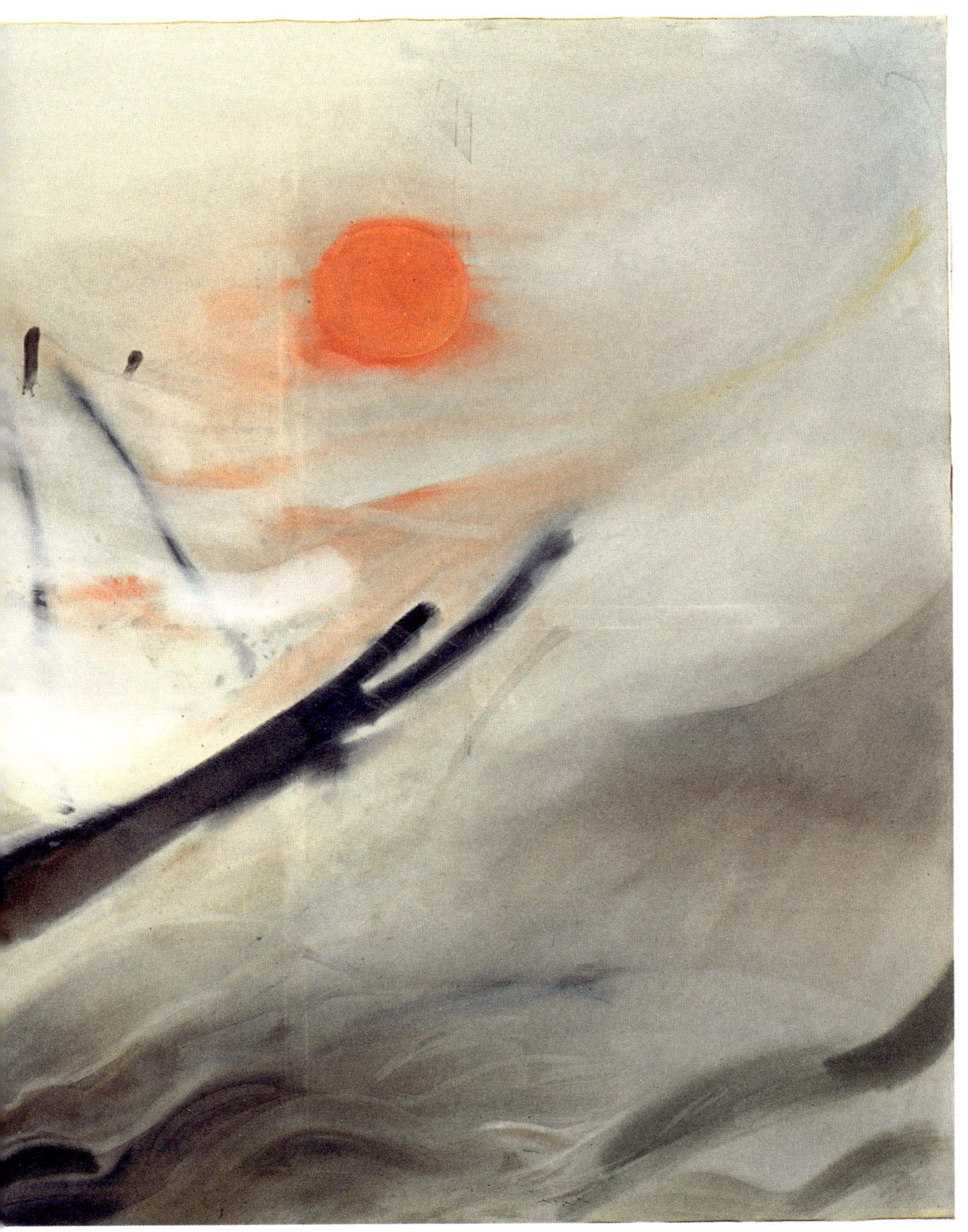

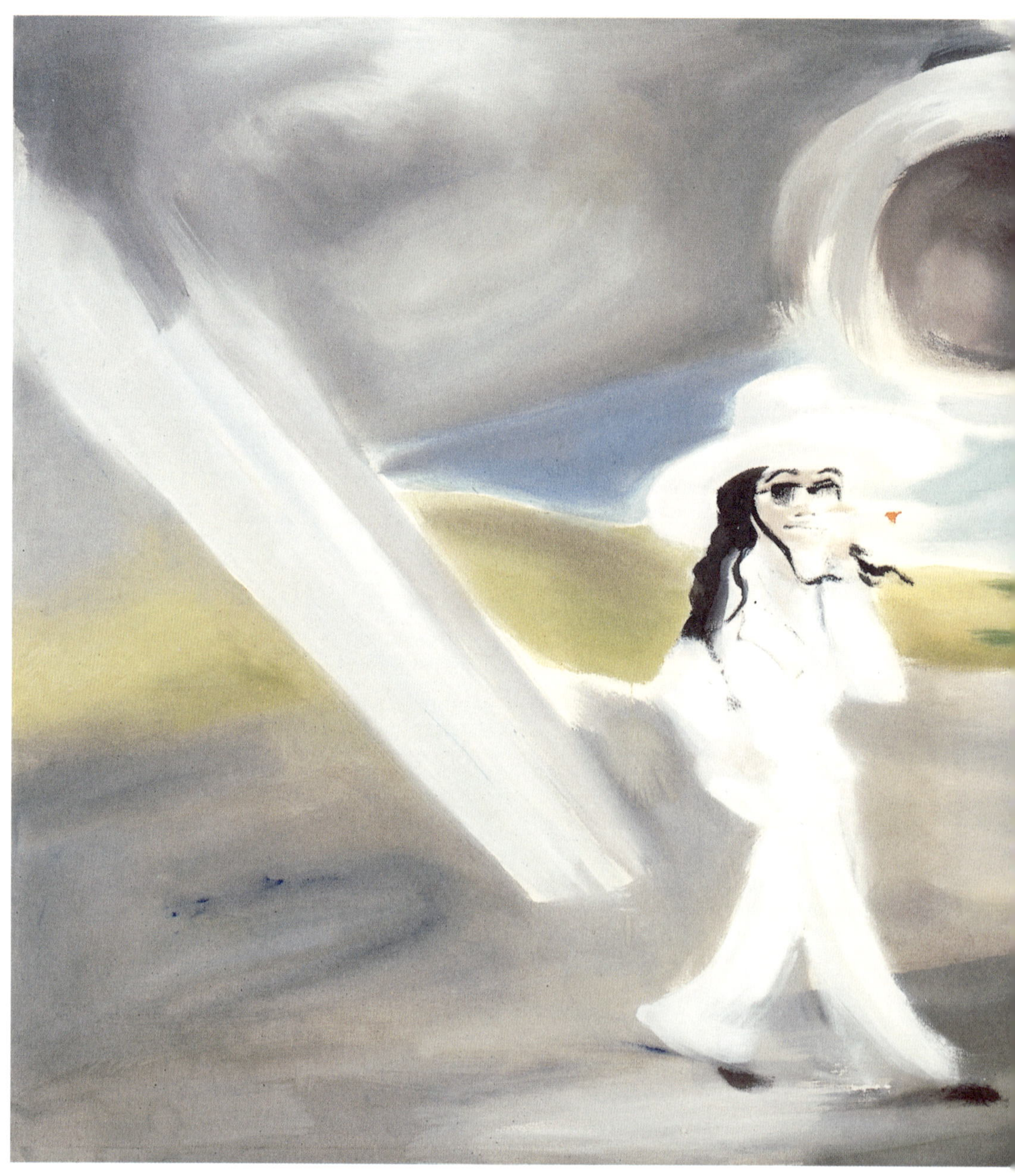

Bianca Jagger, 2003

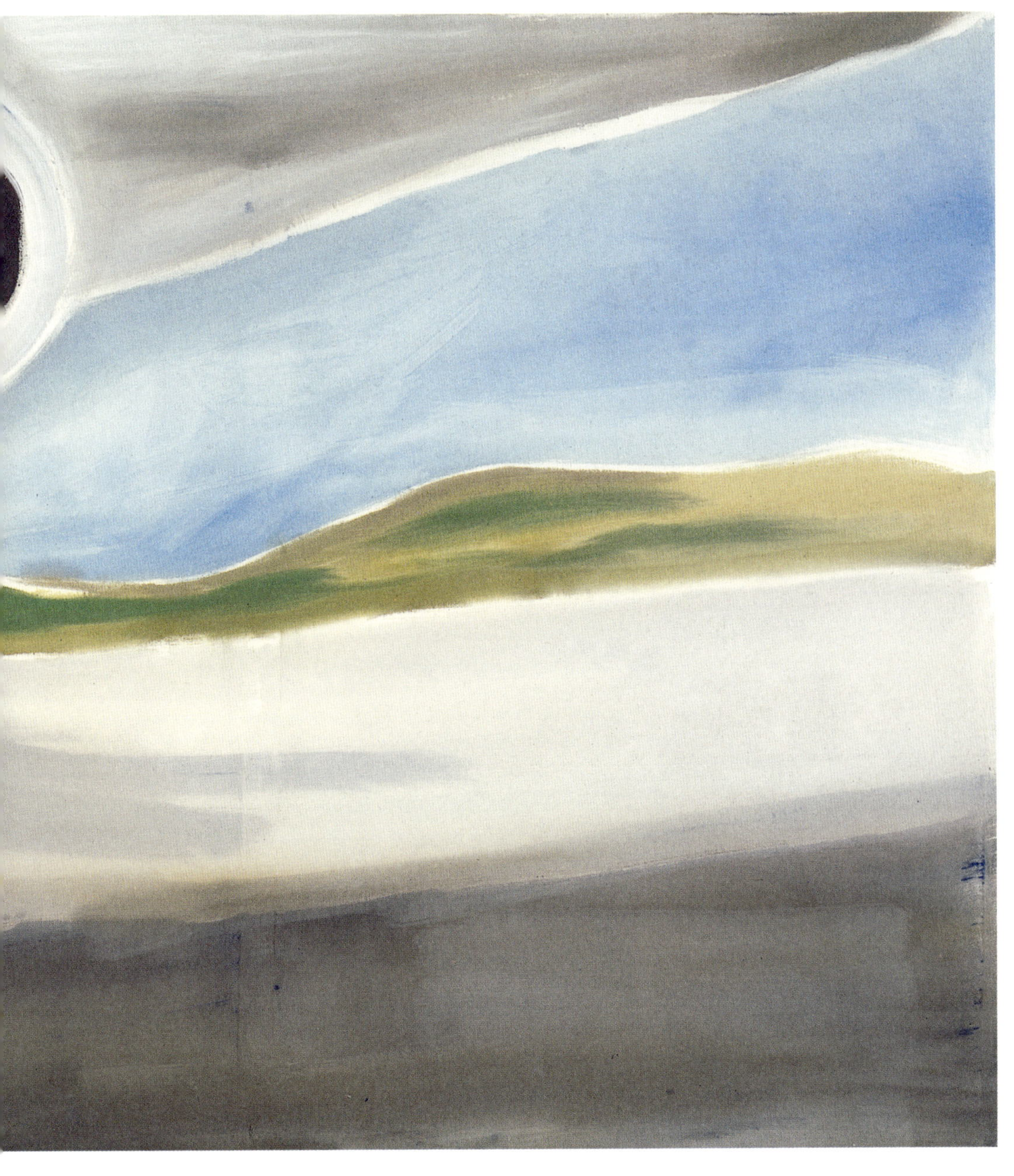

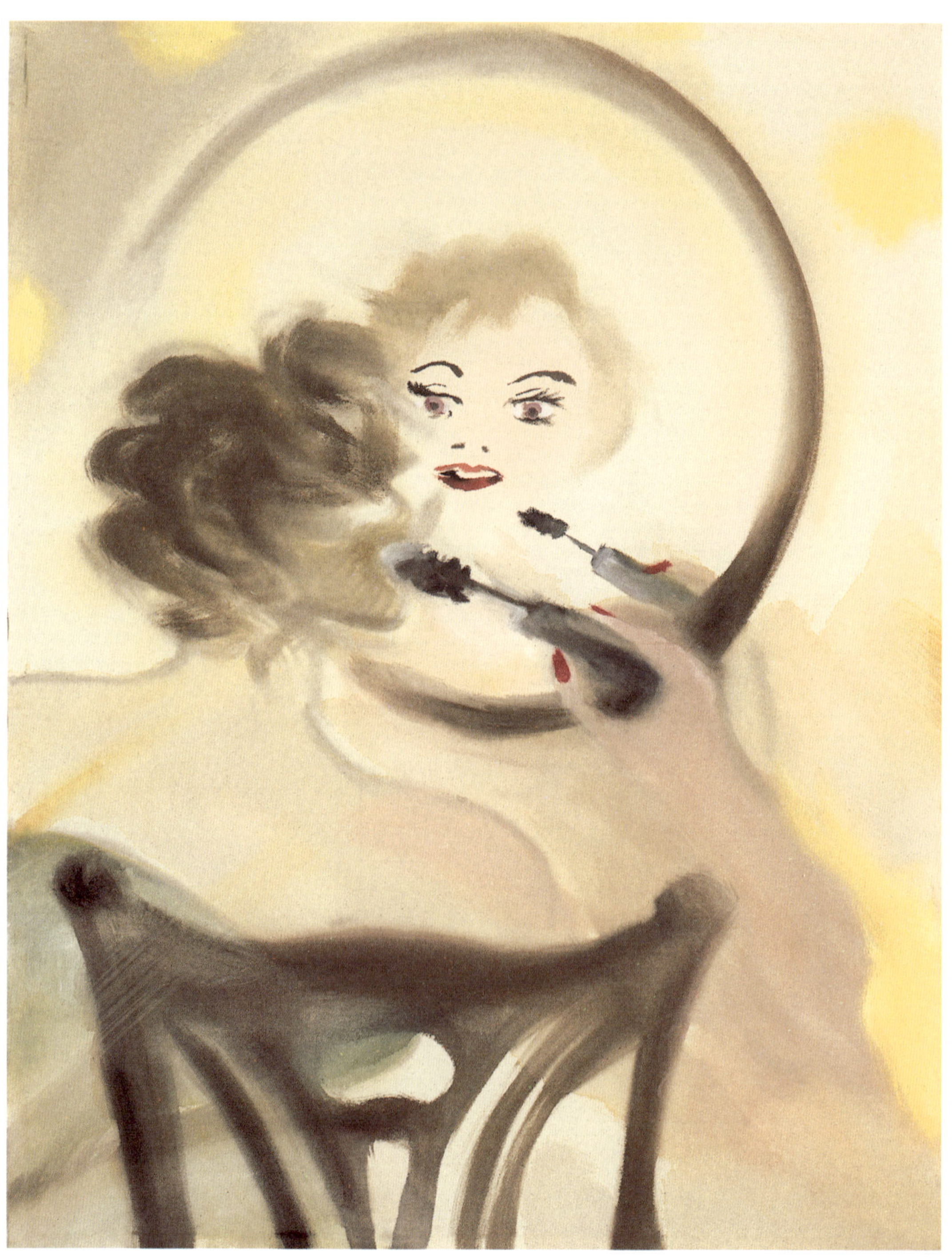

Maaike Schoorel, Hollywood, 2003

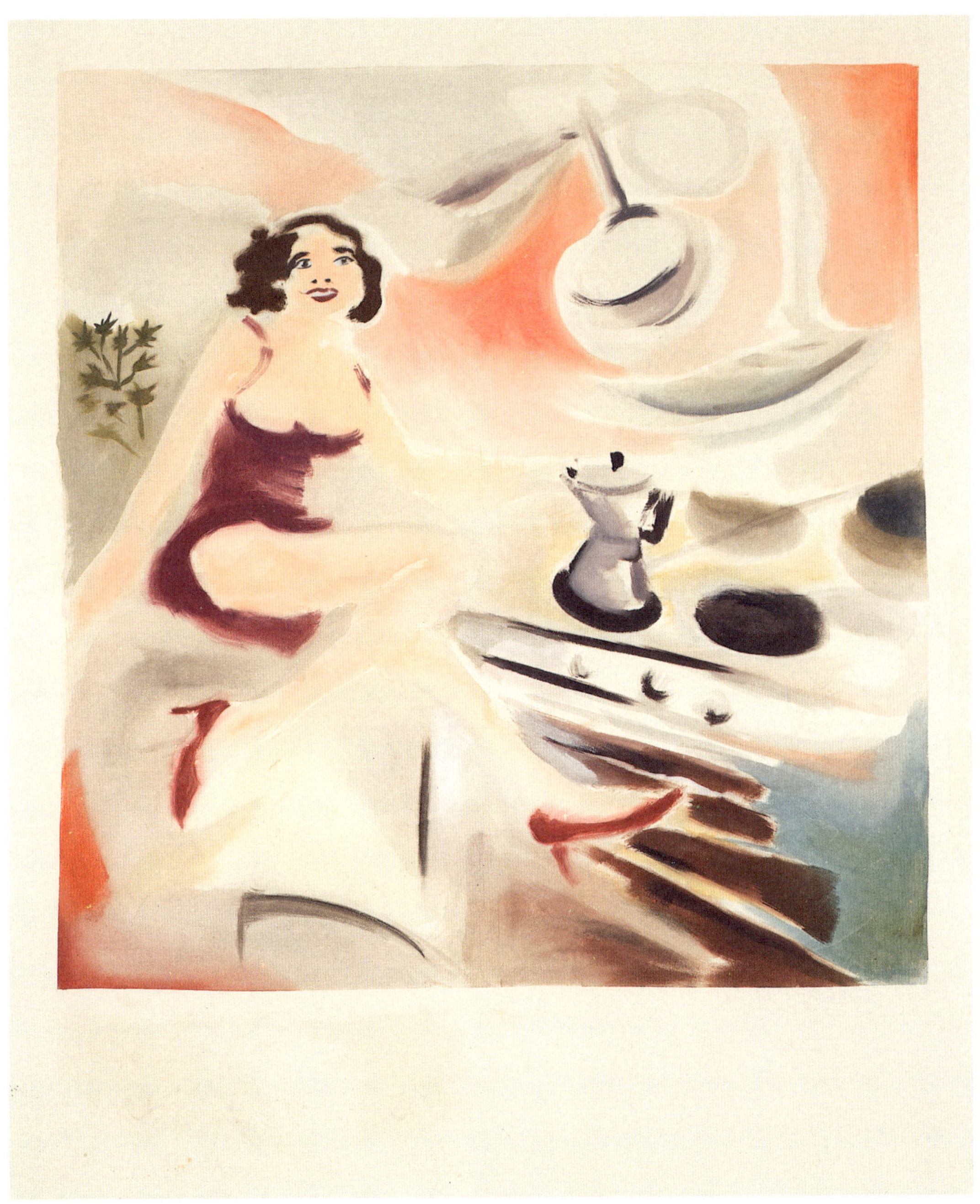

Polaroid Piazza Santa Spirito, 2003

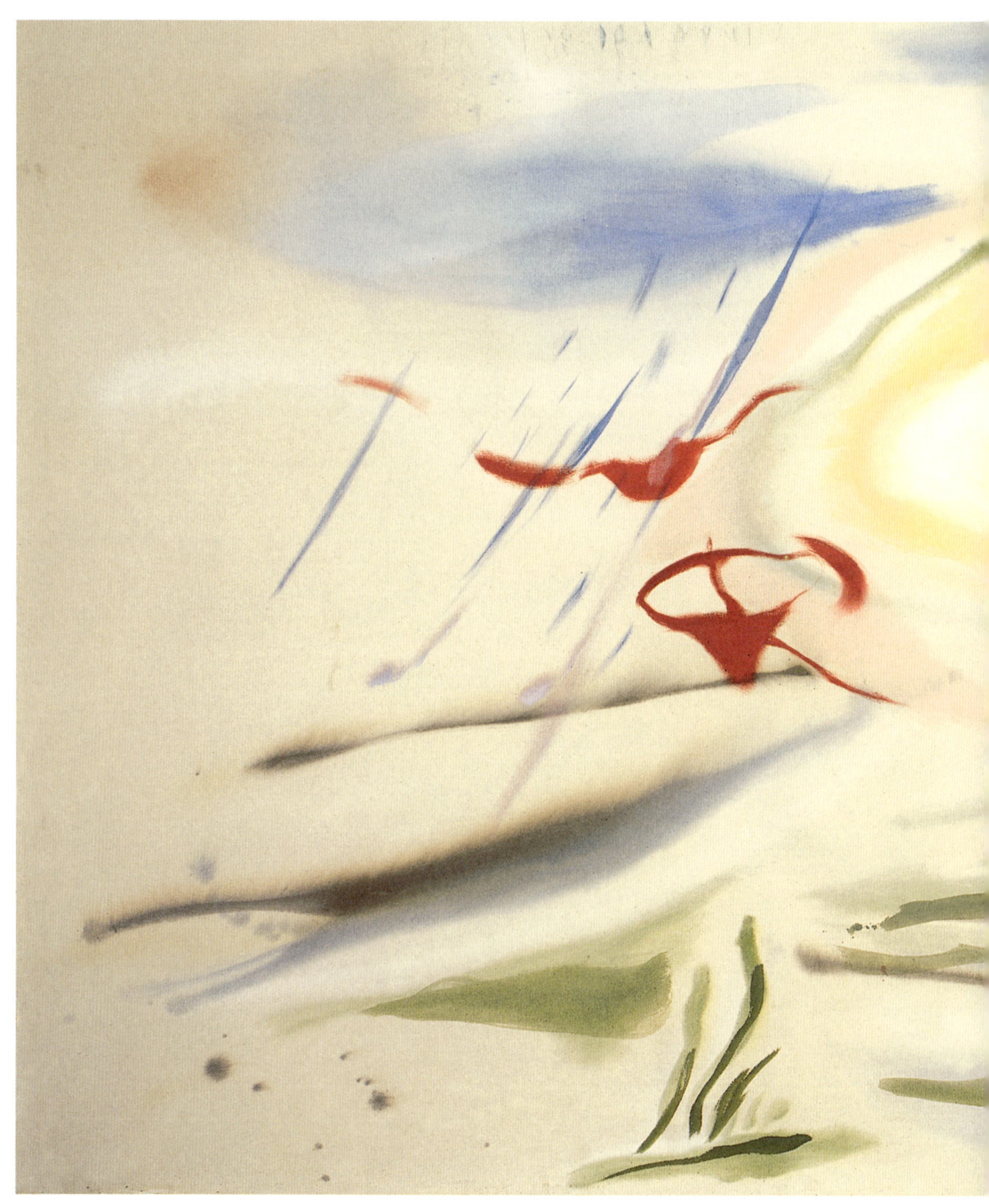

Red Admiral, 2003

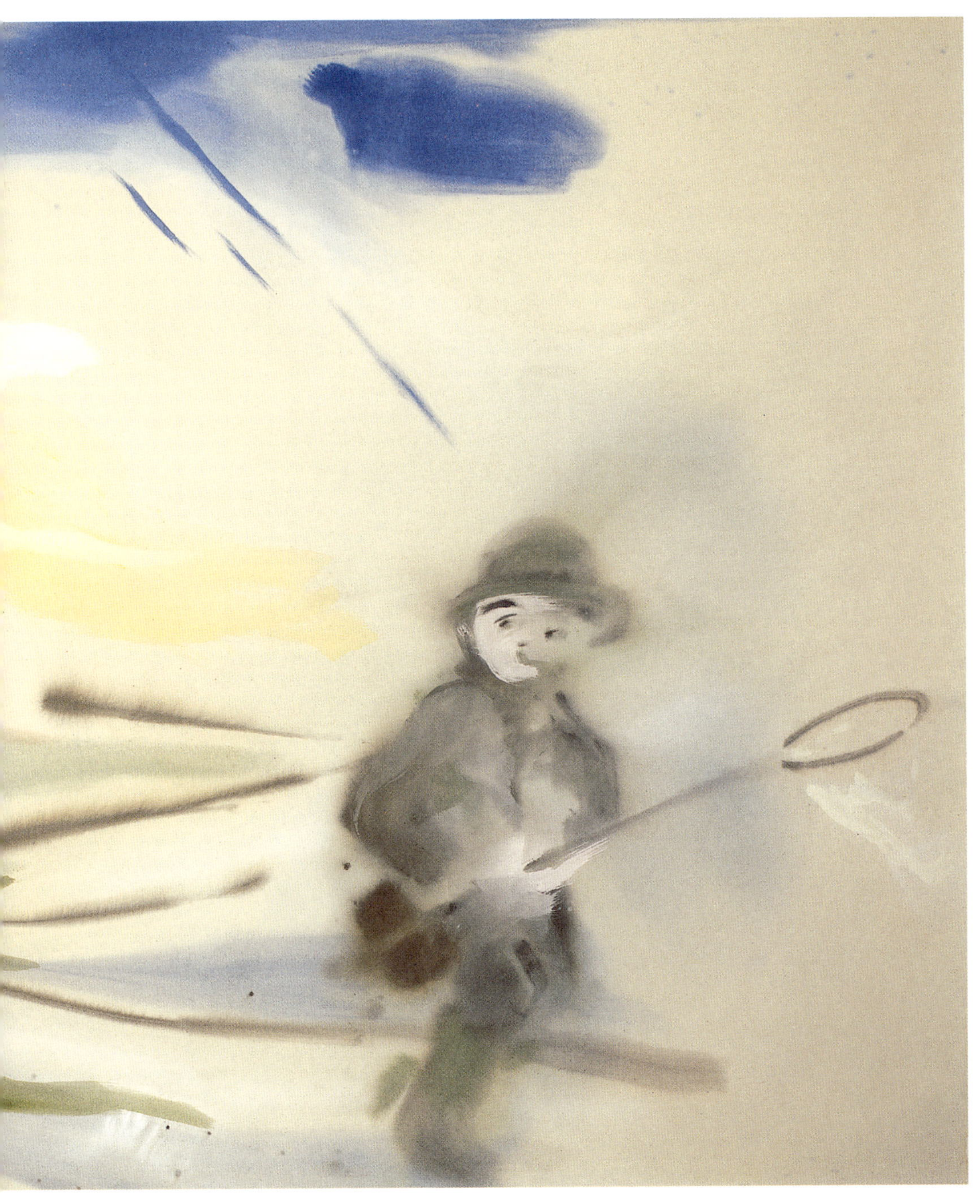

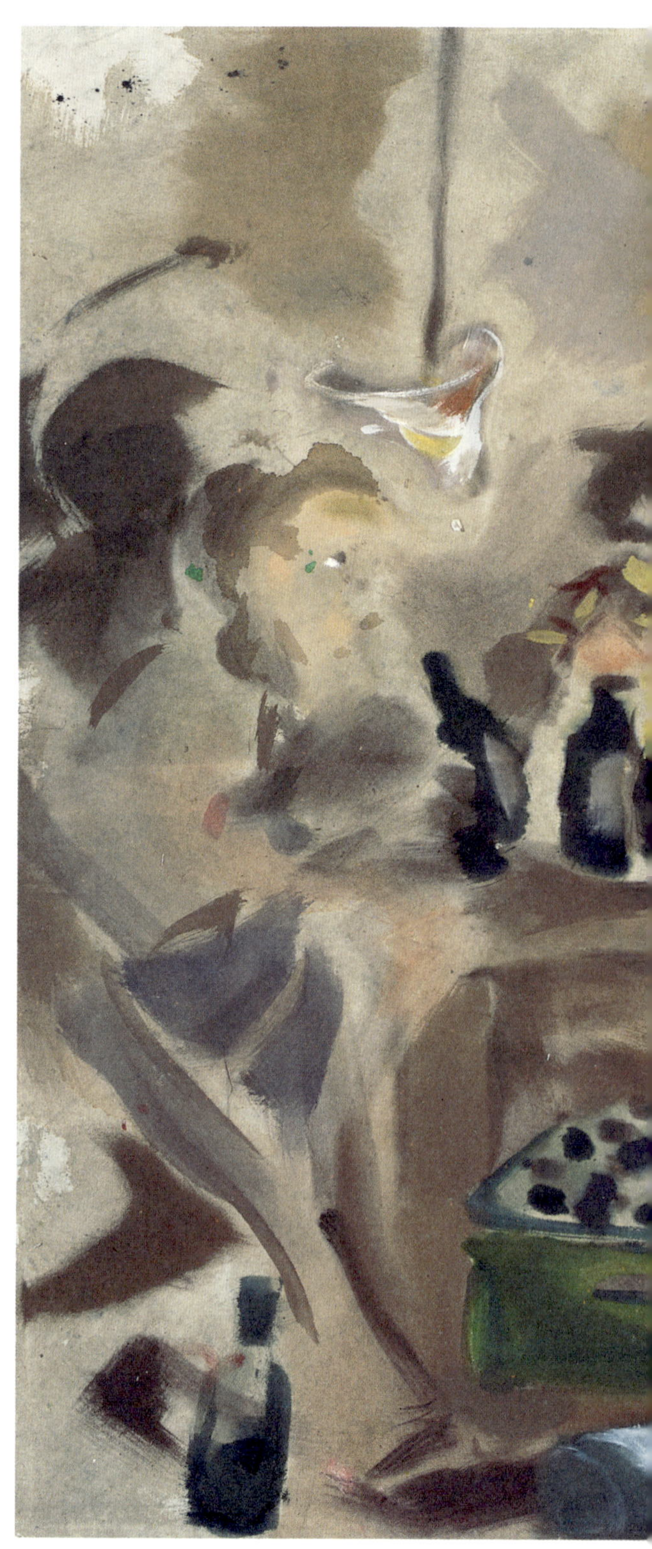

Dirt Bar (Berlin), 2003

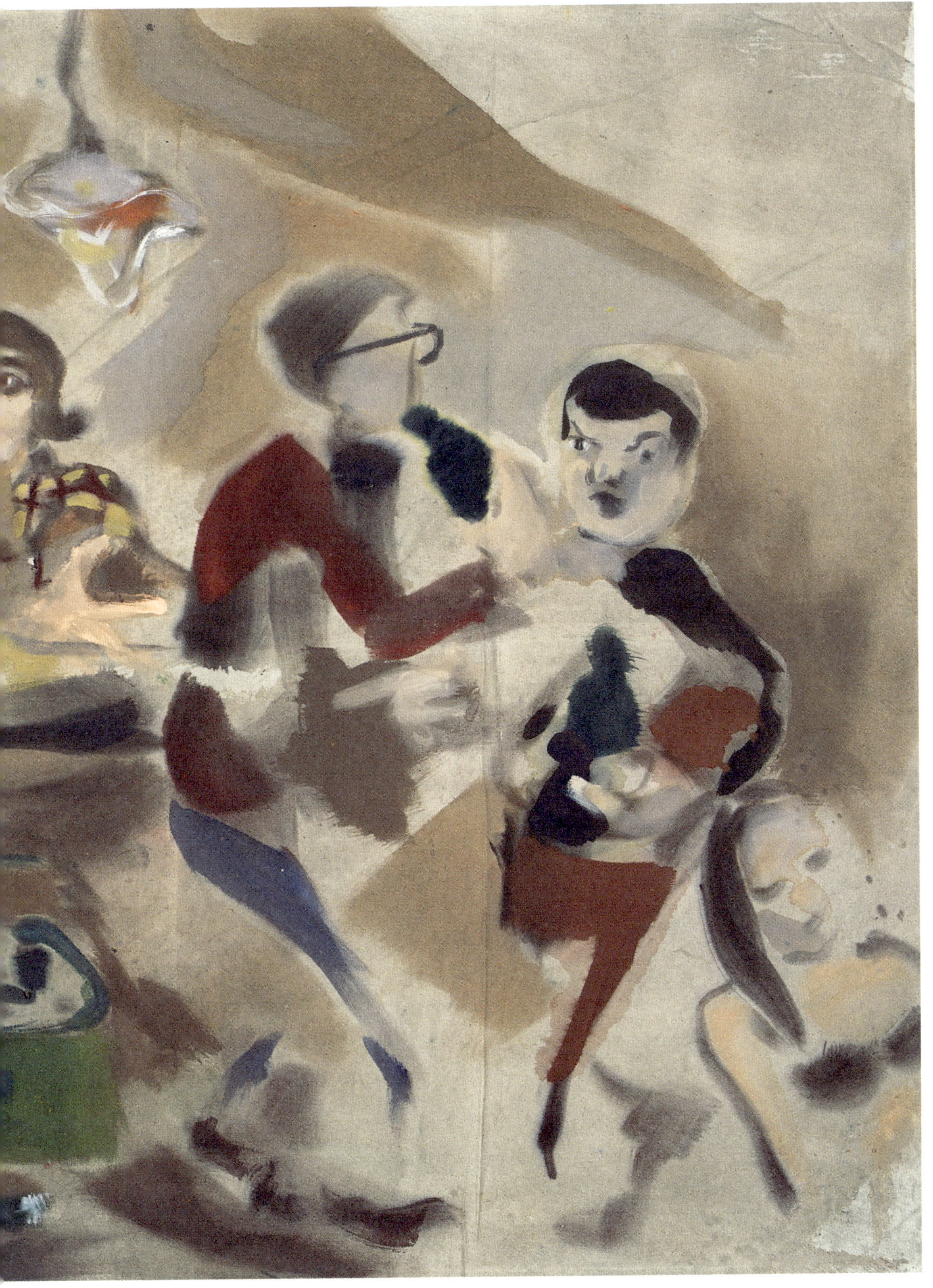

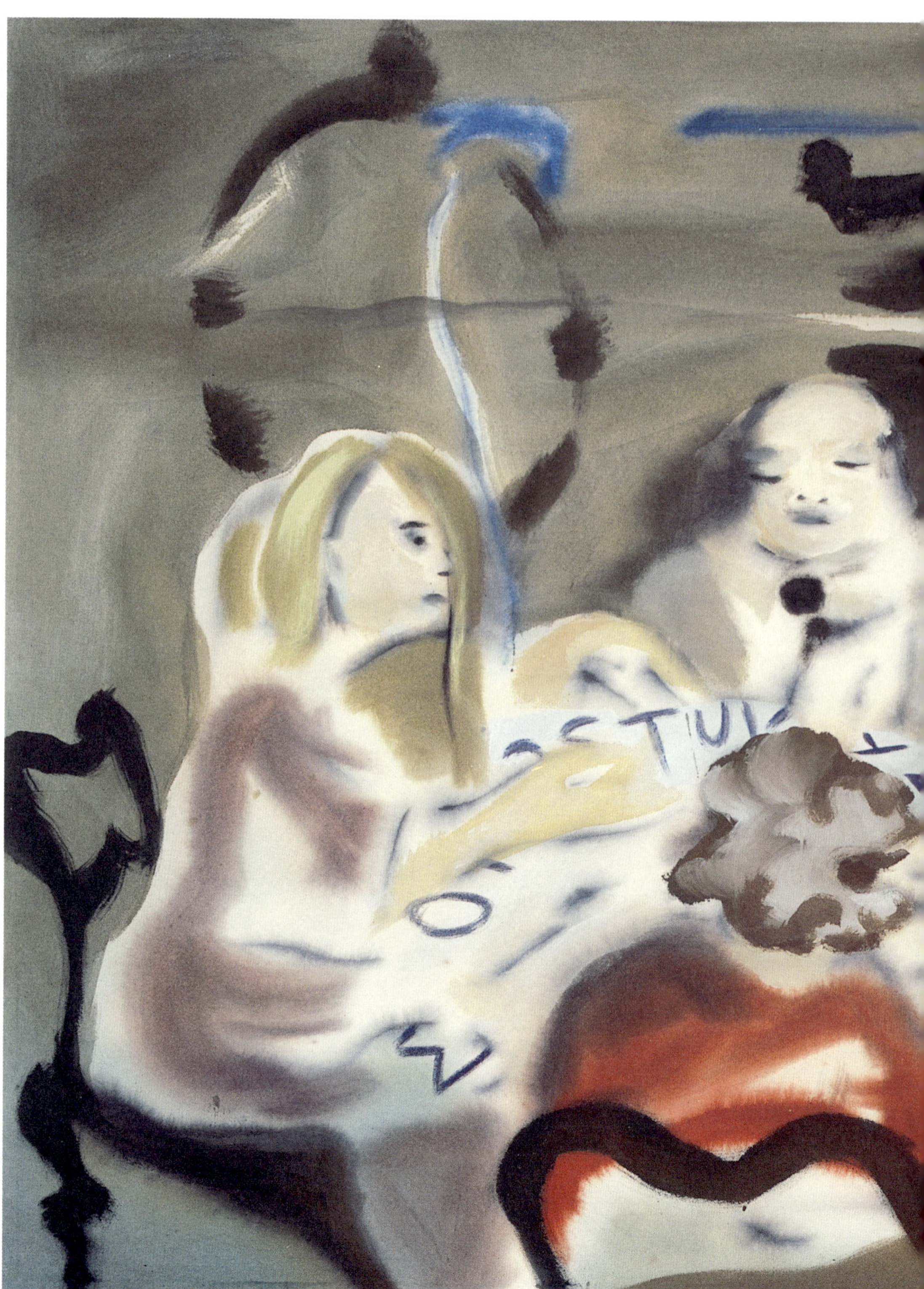

Ouija Board, 2003

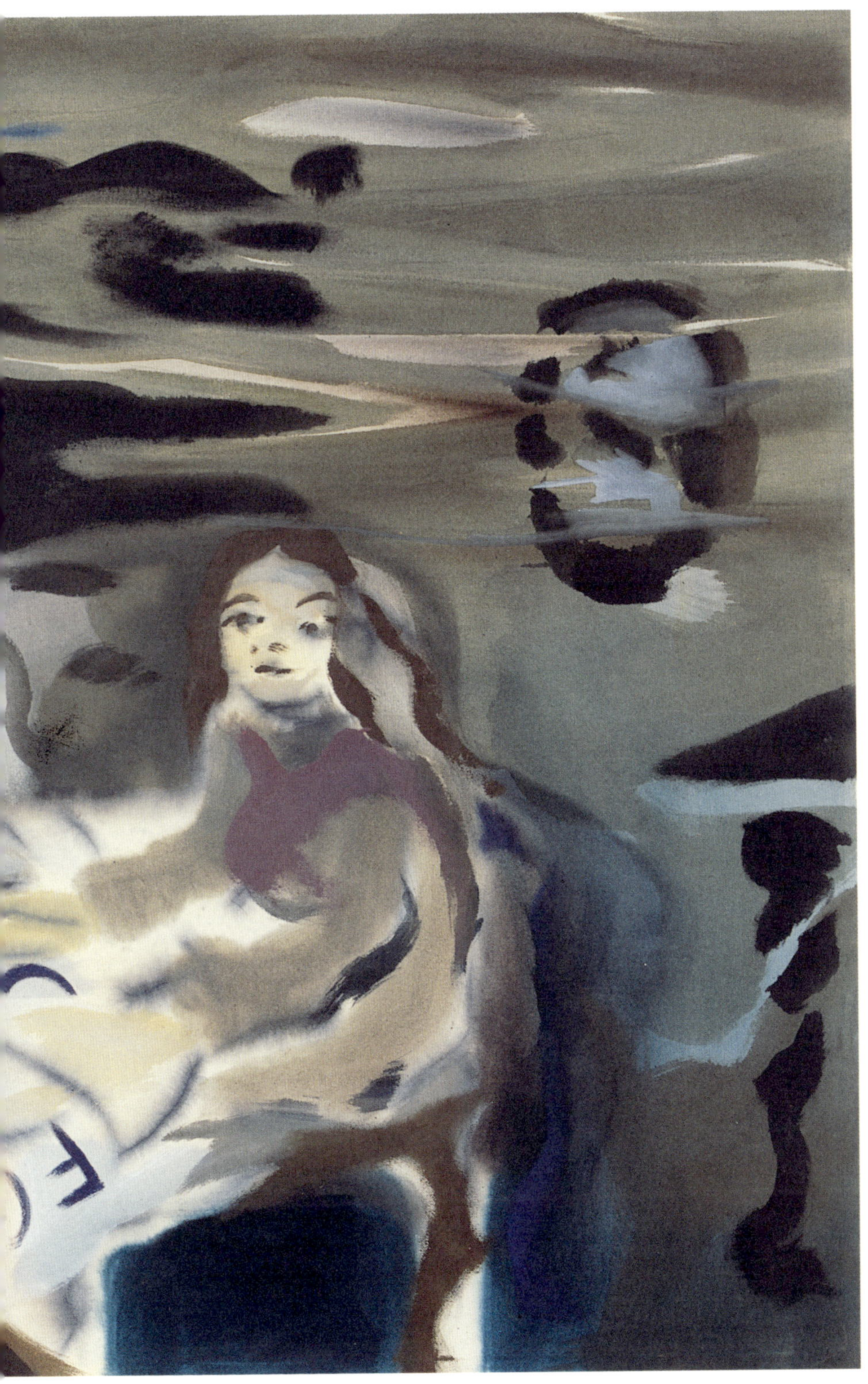

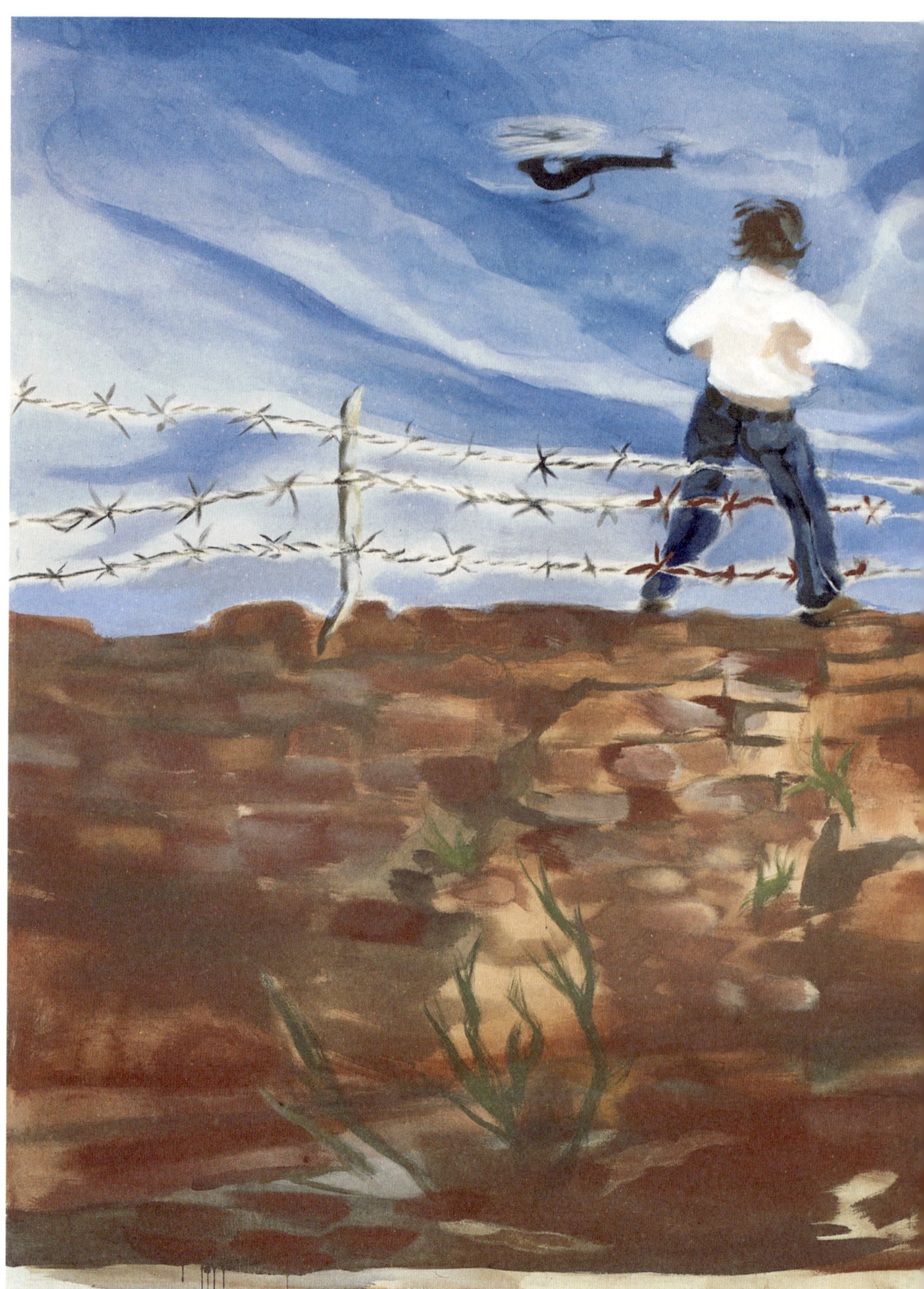

Breakout, 2003

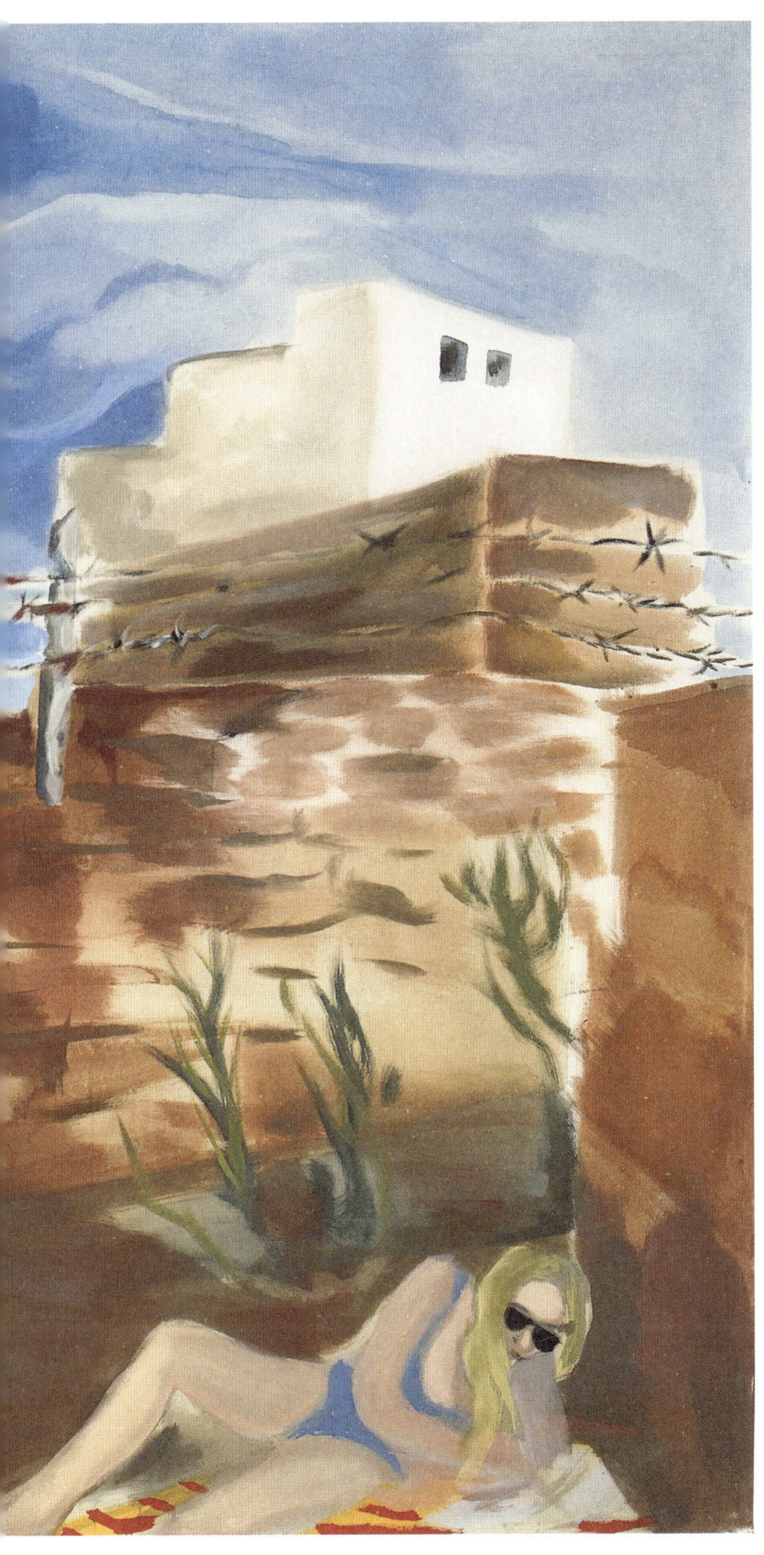

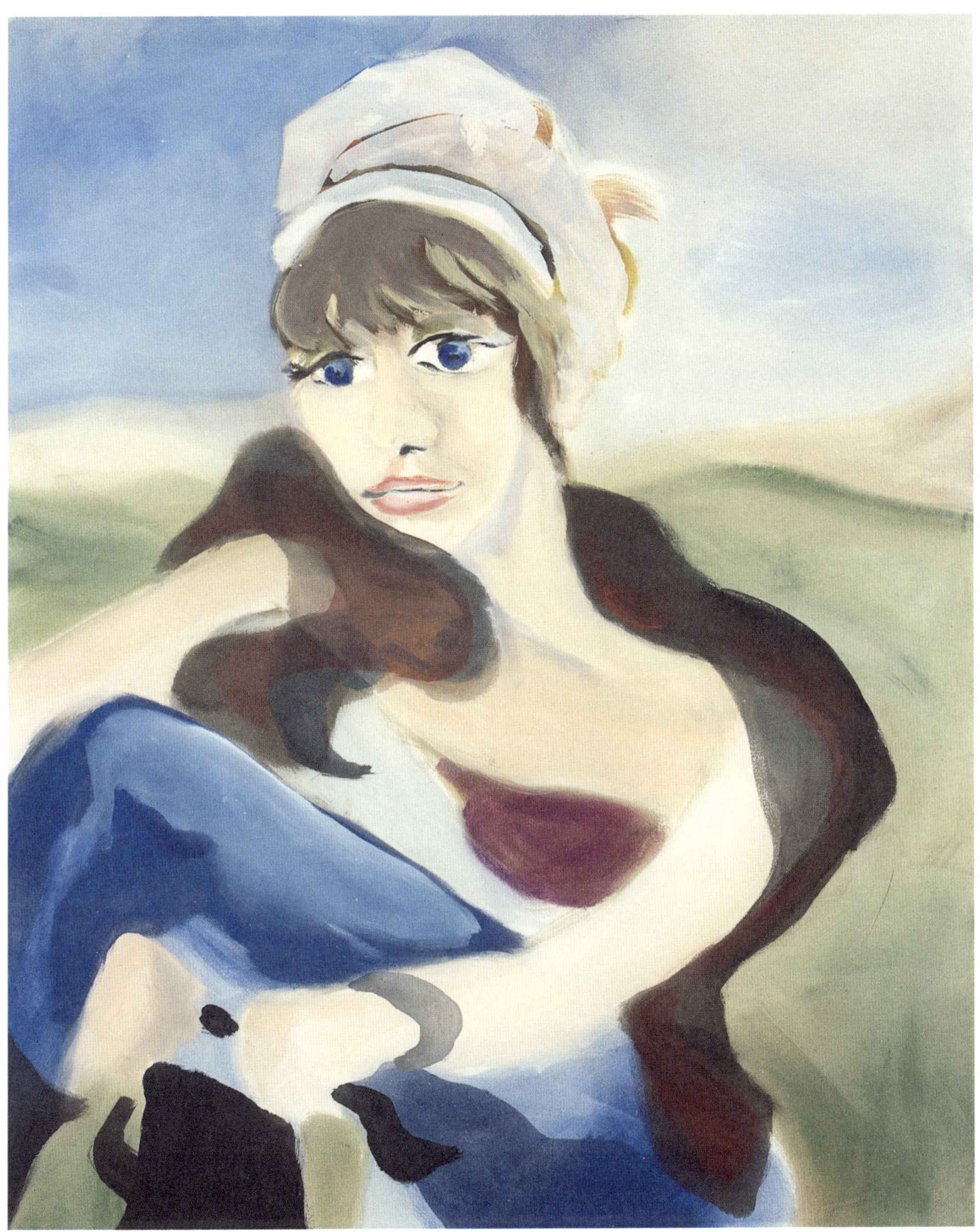

Christa Päffgen, 2003

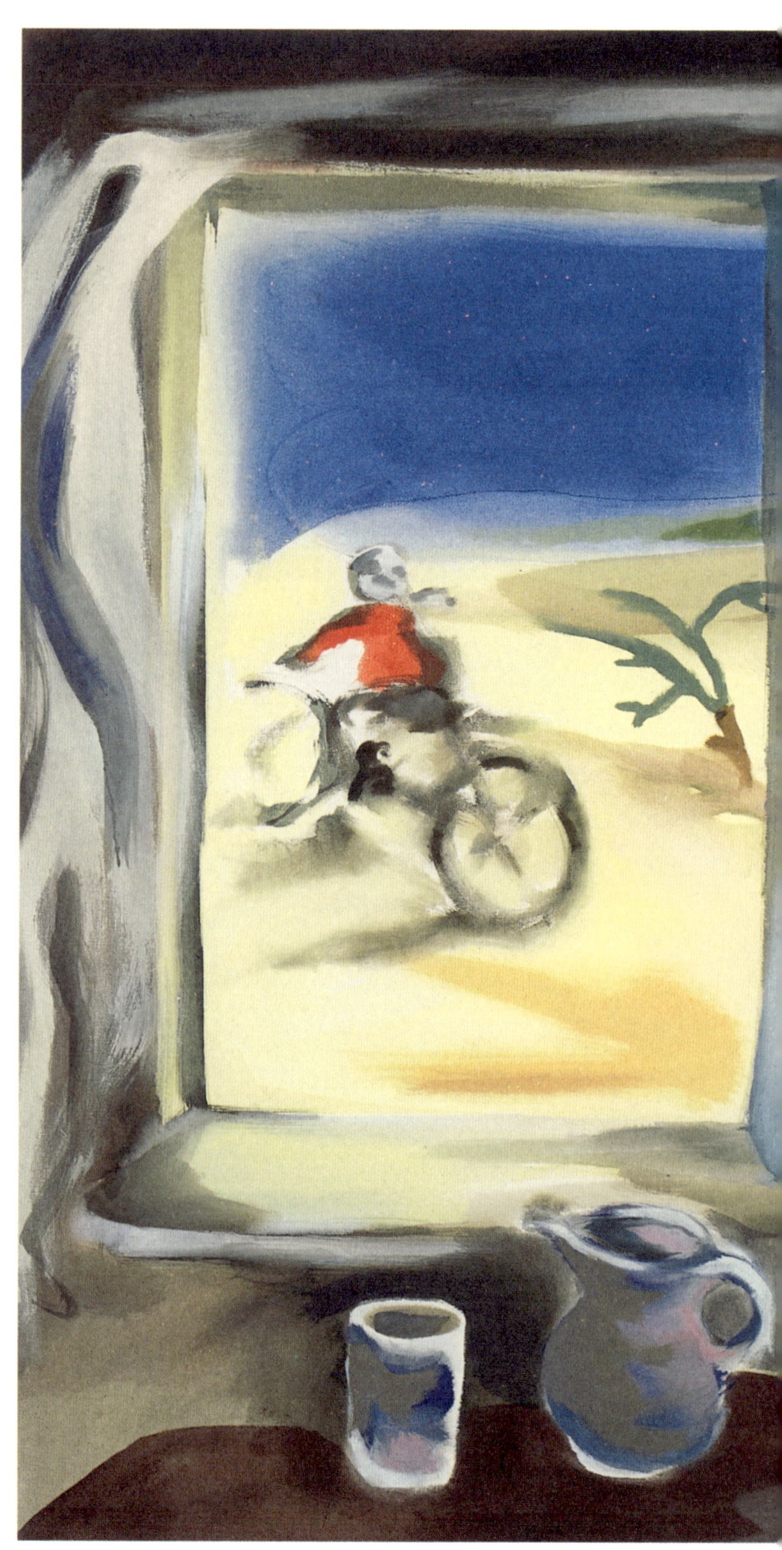

I Need You, I Don't Need You, 2003

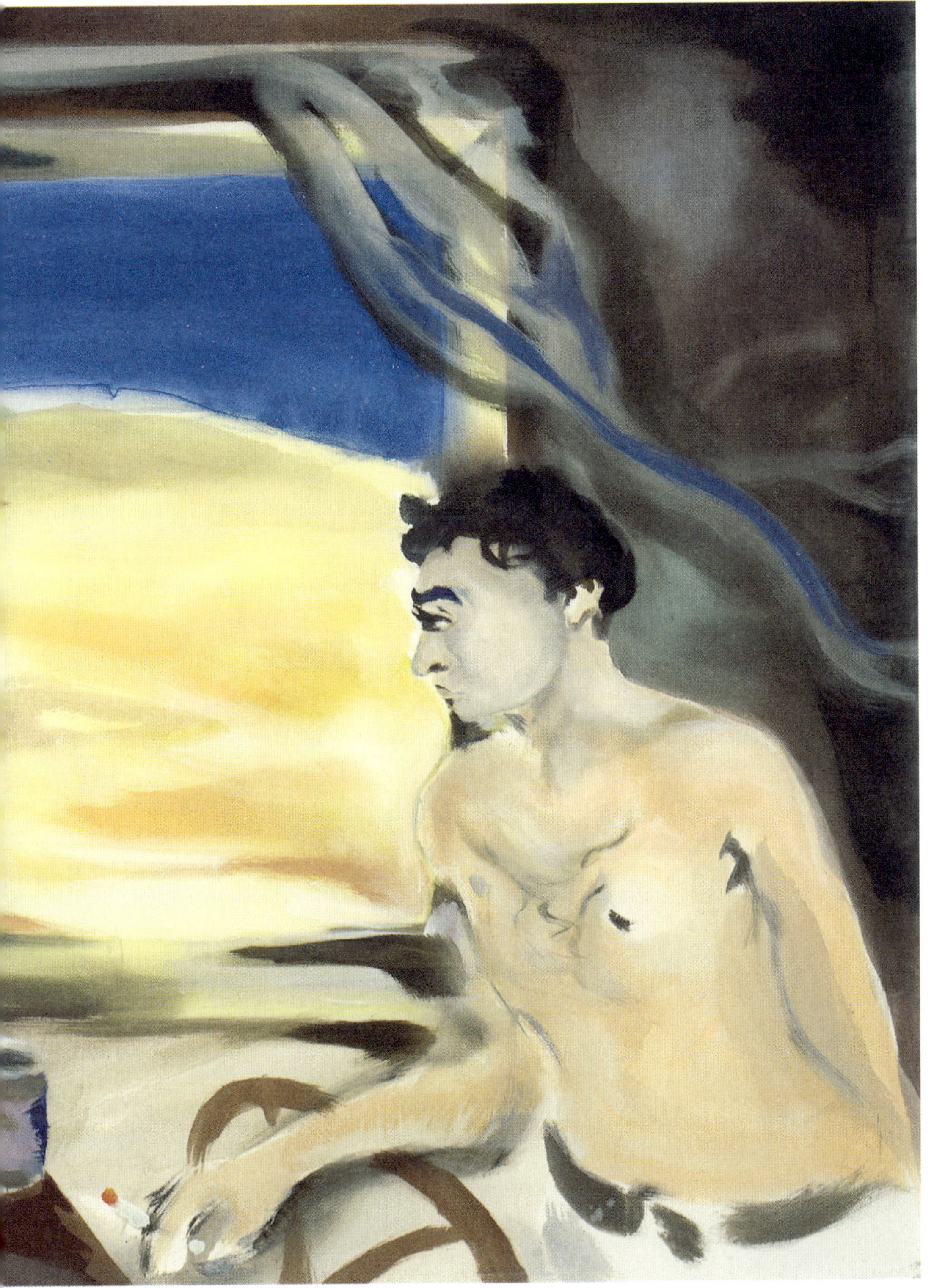

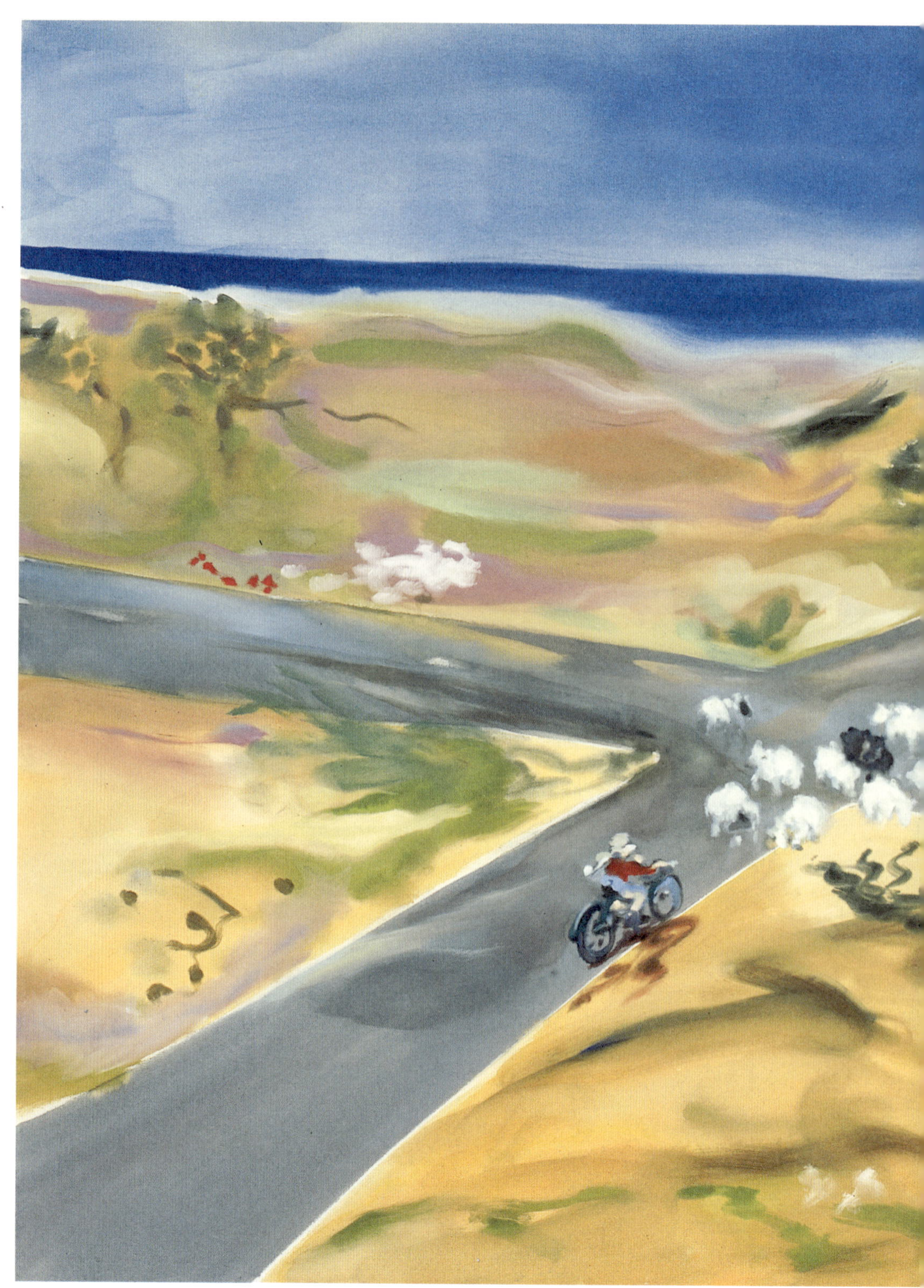

Black Sheep and Almond Blossom, 2003

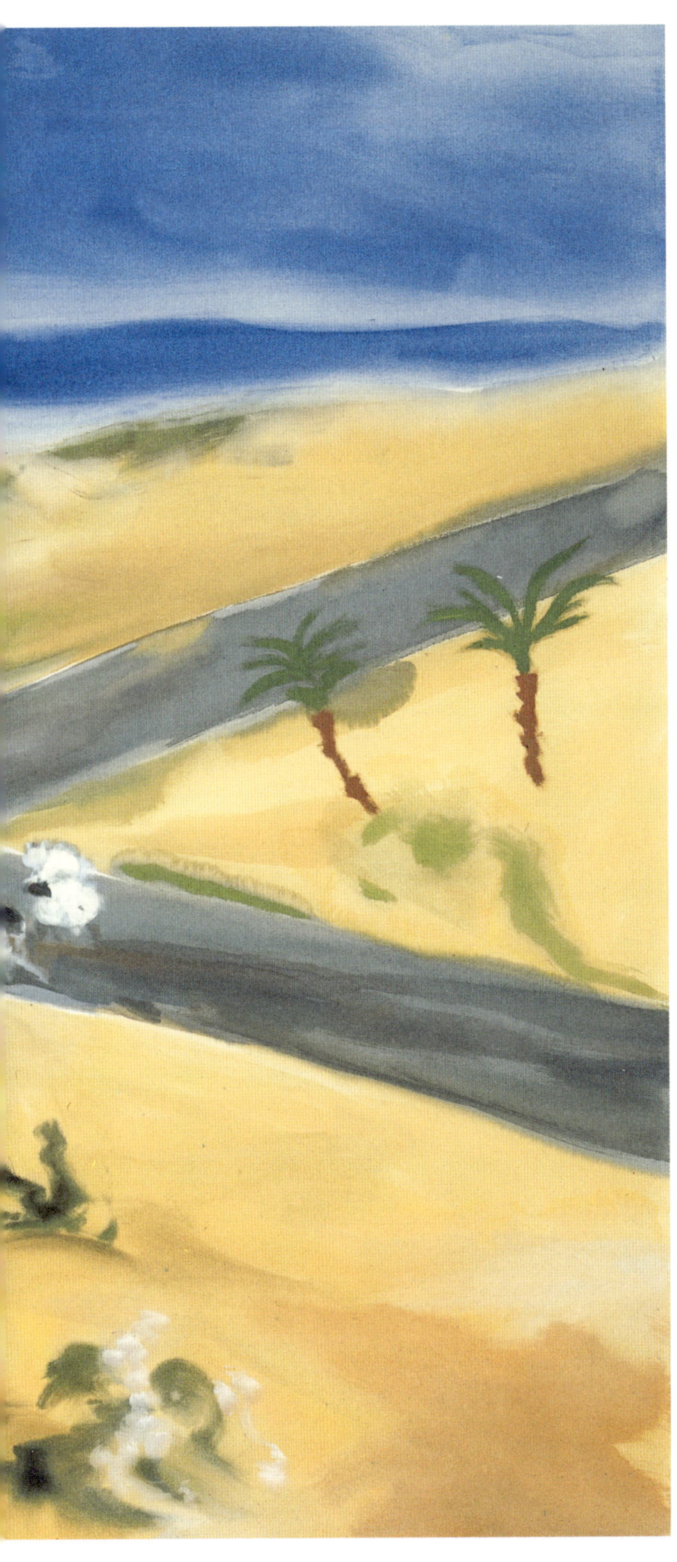

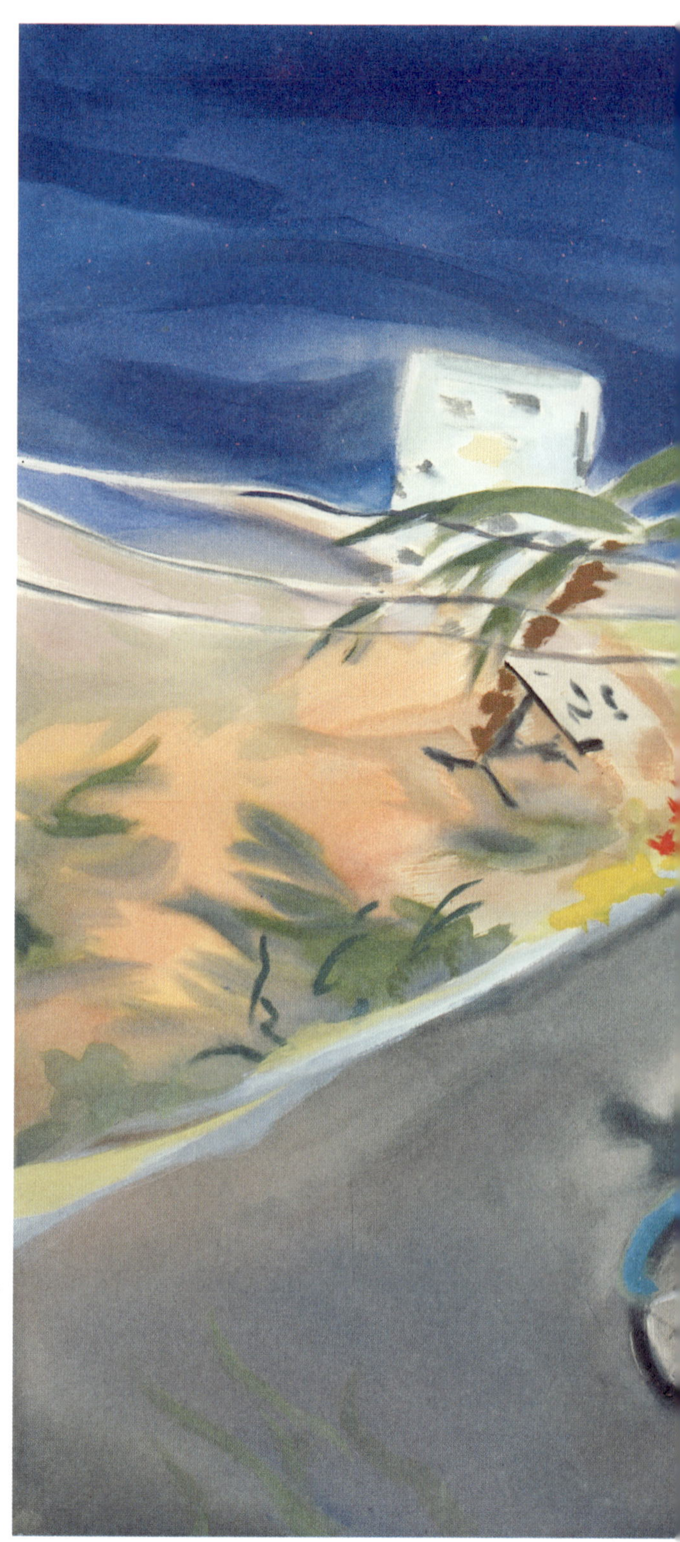

Private Getaway Paradise, 2003

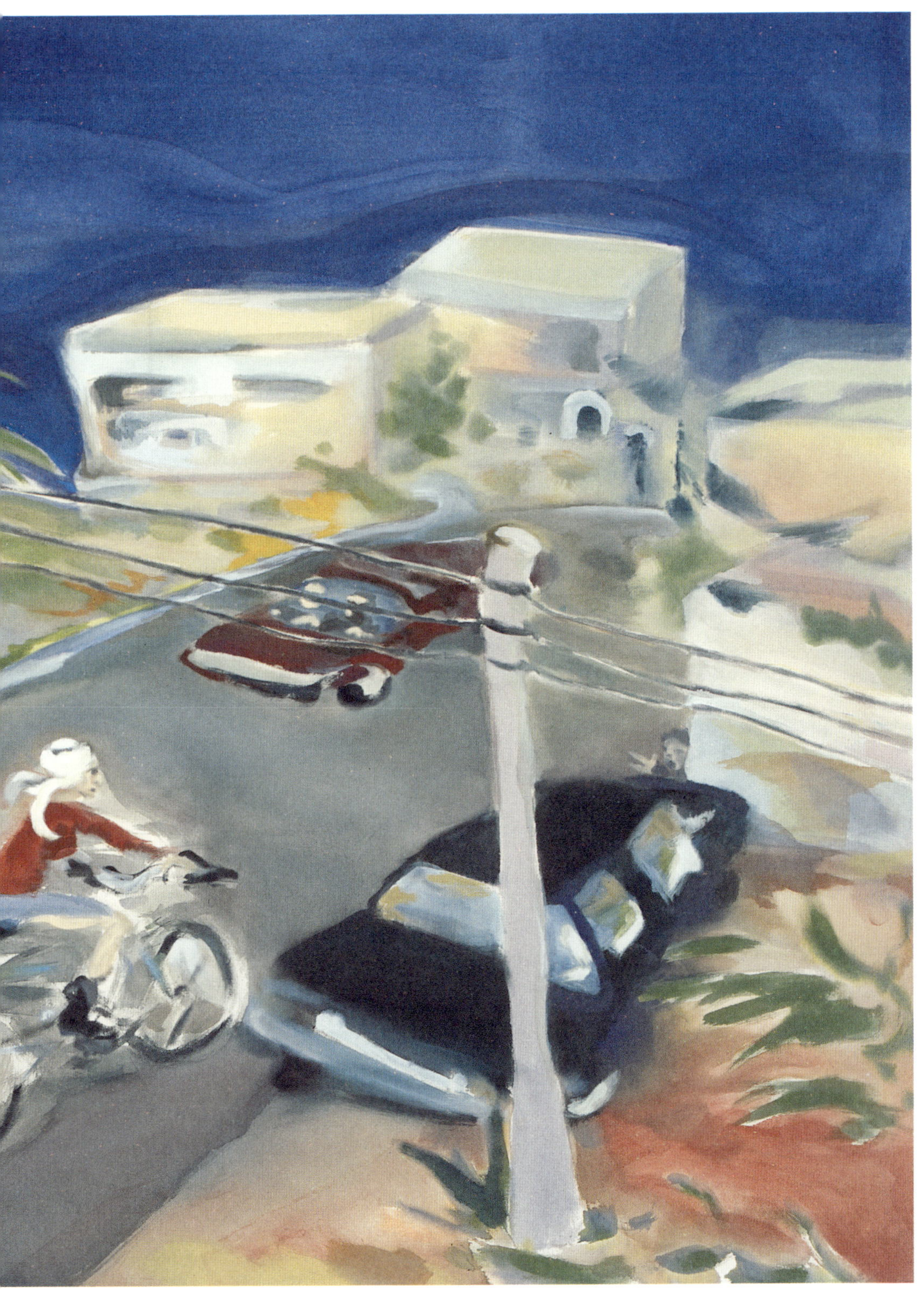

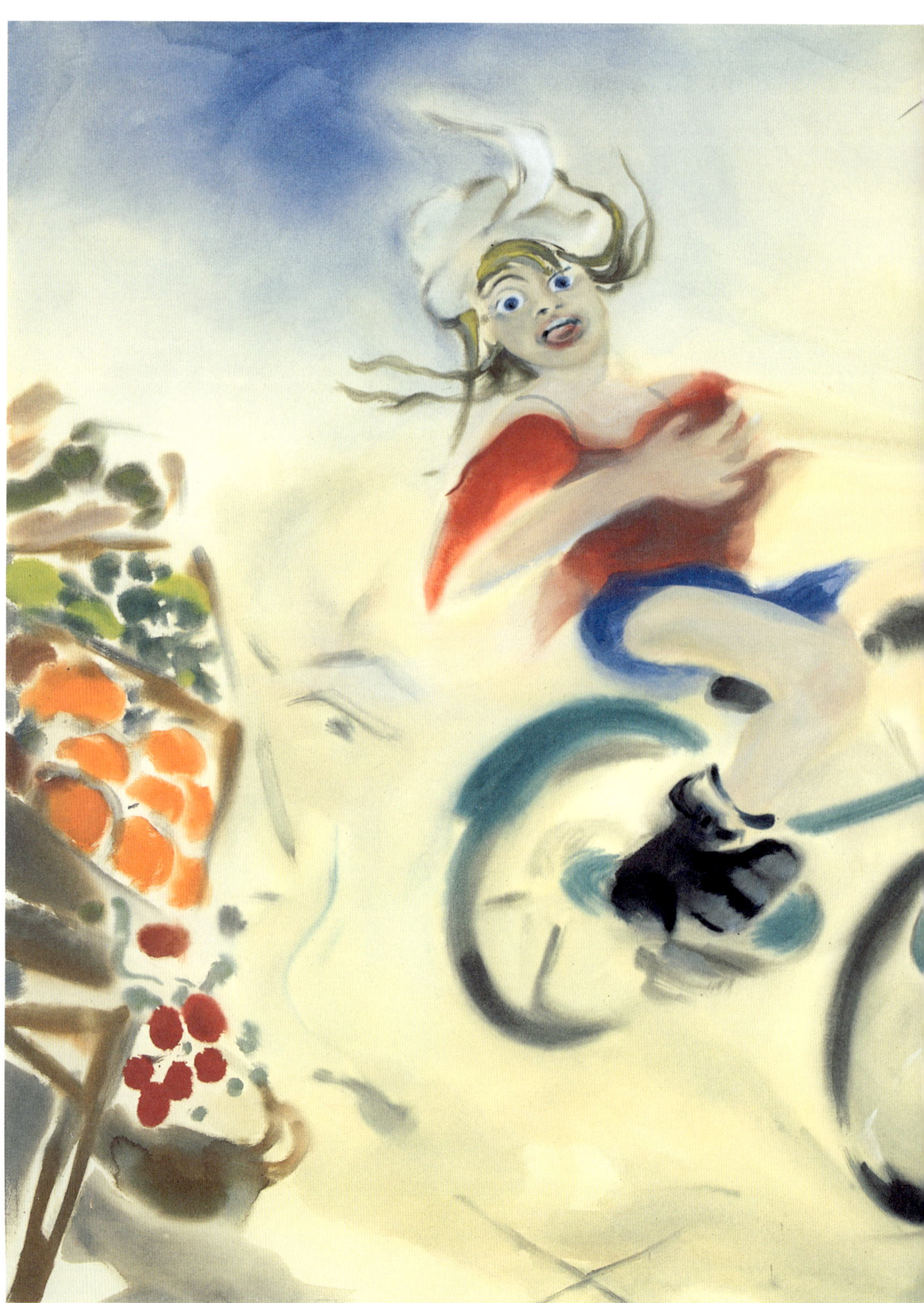

Yellow Scream, 2003

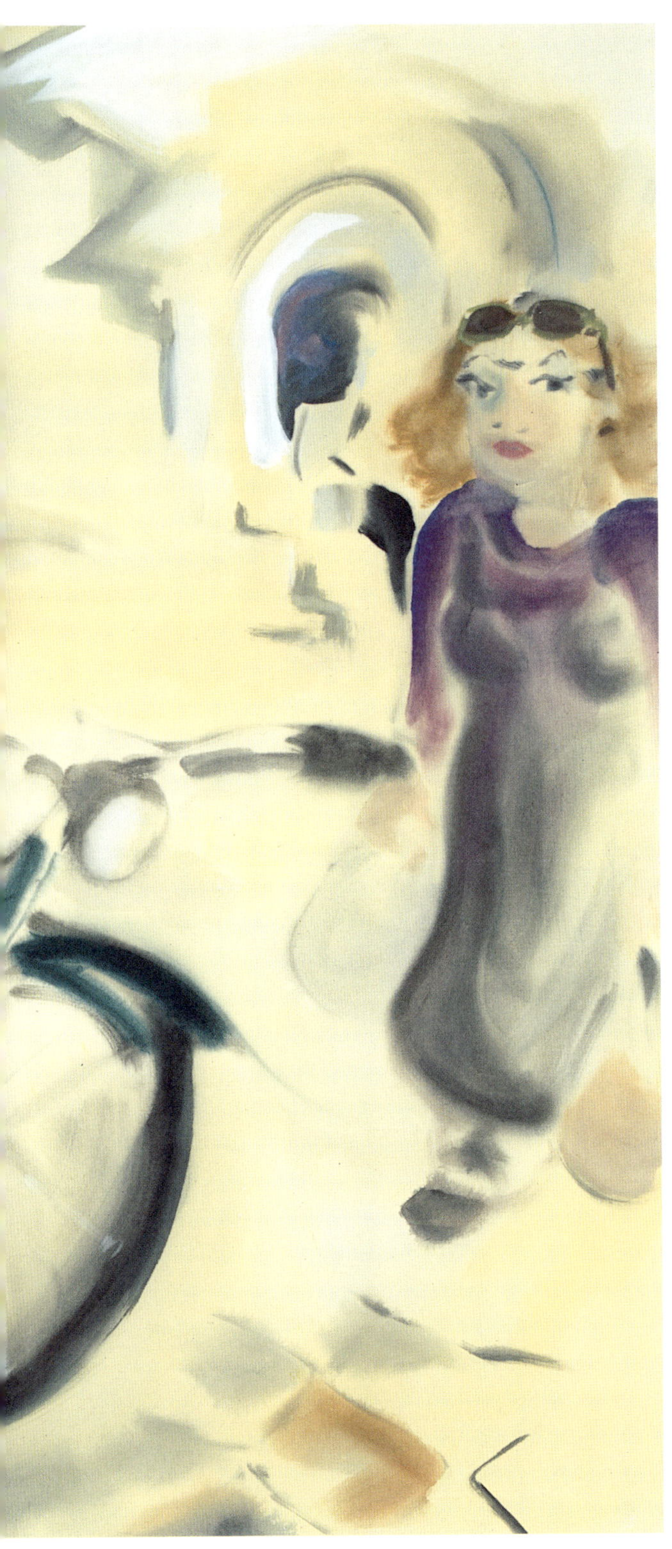

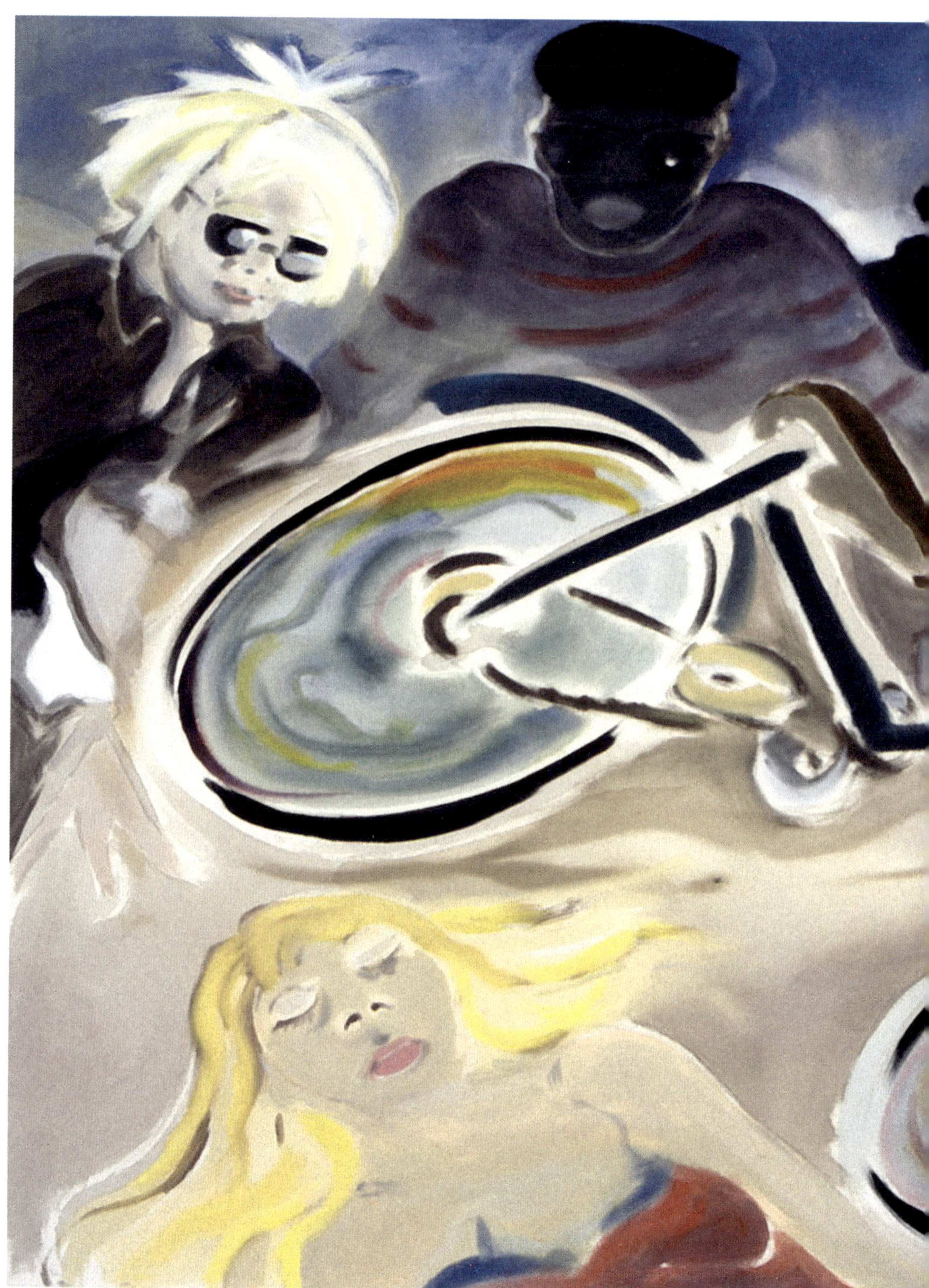

On the Ground, 2003

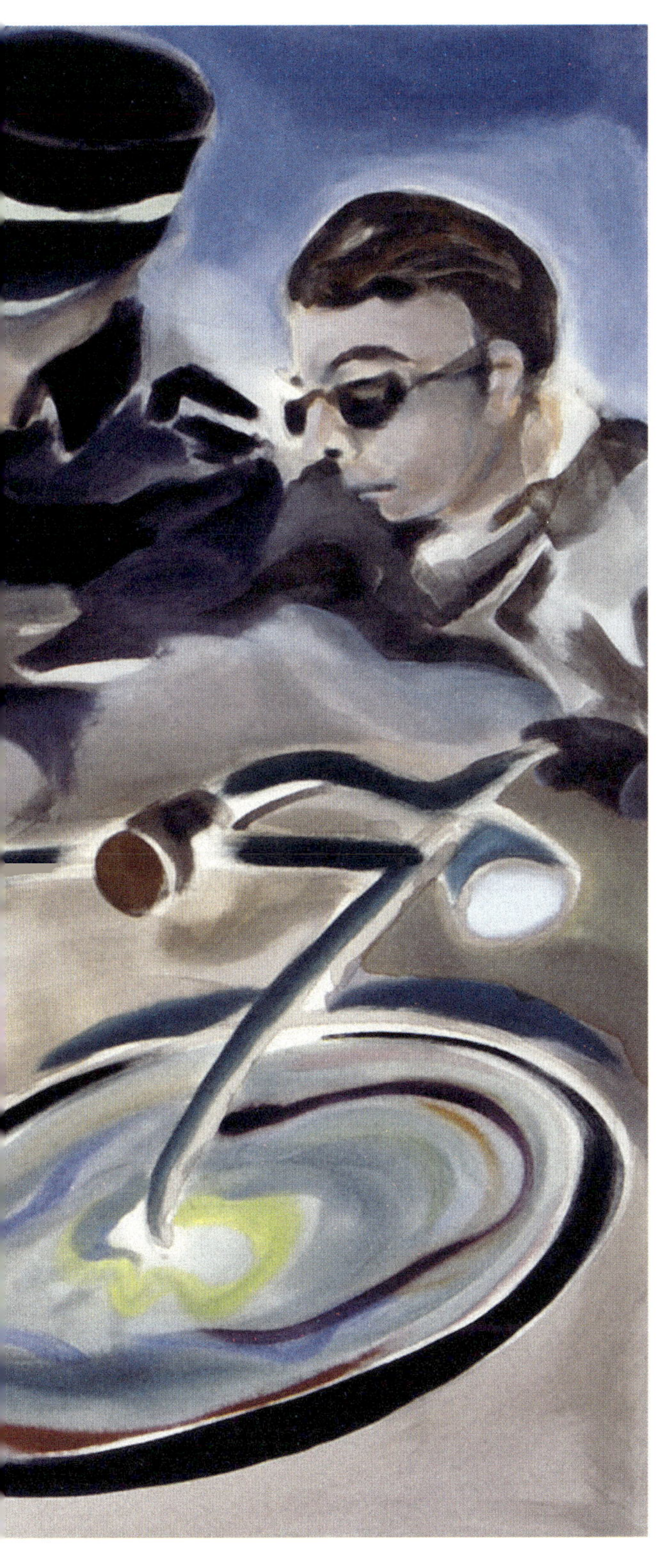

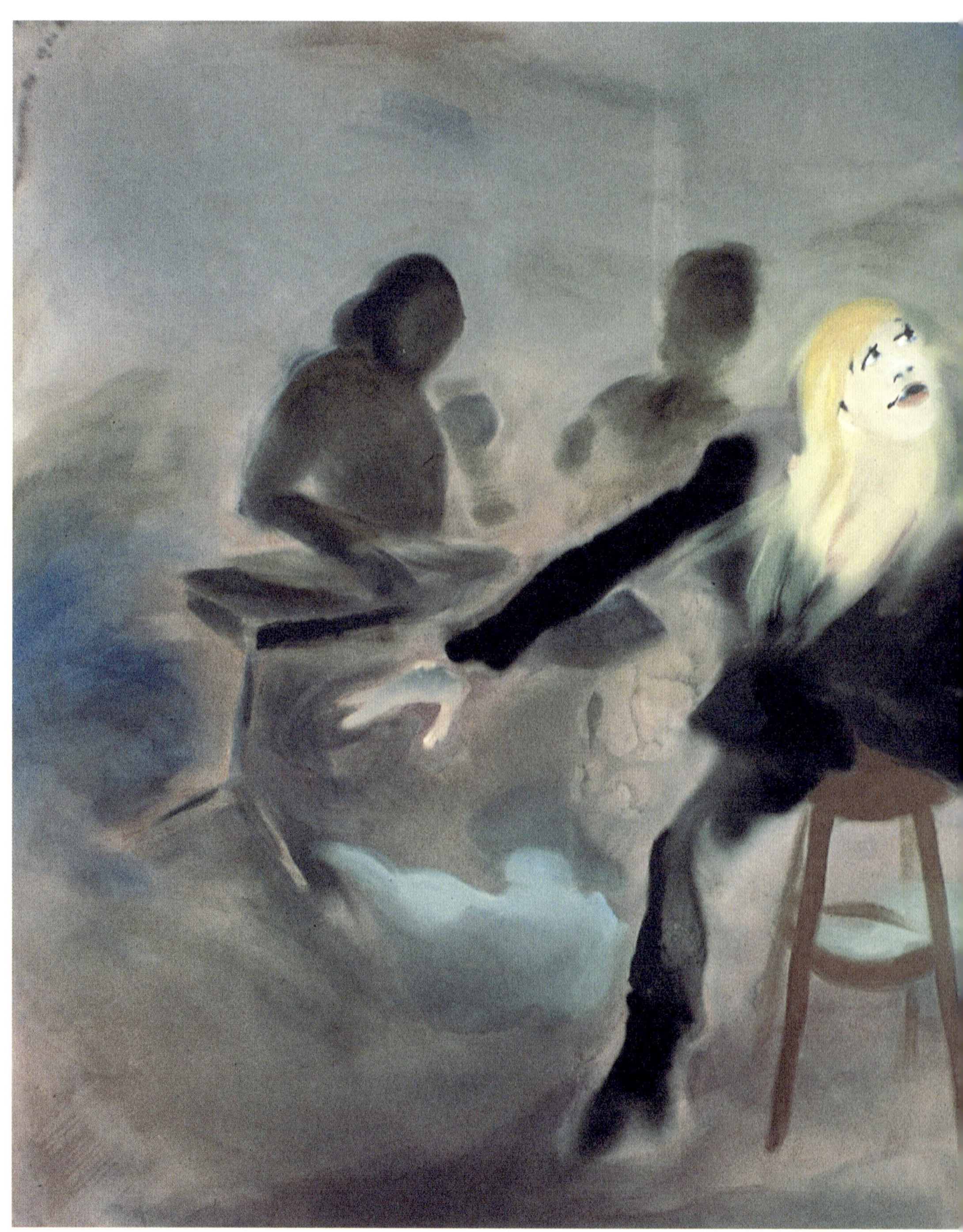

Disembodied Voice, 2003

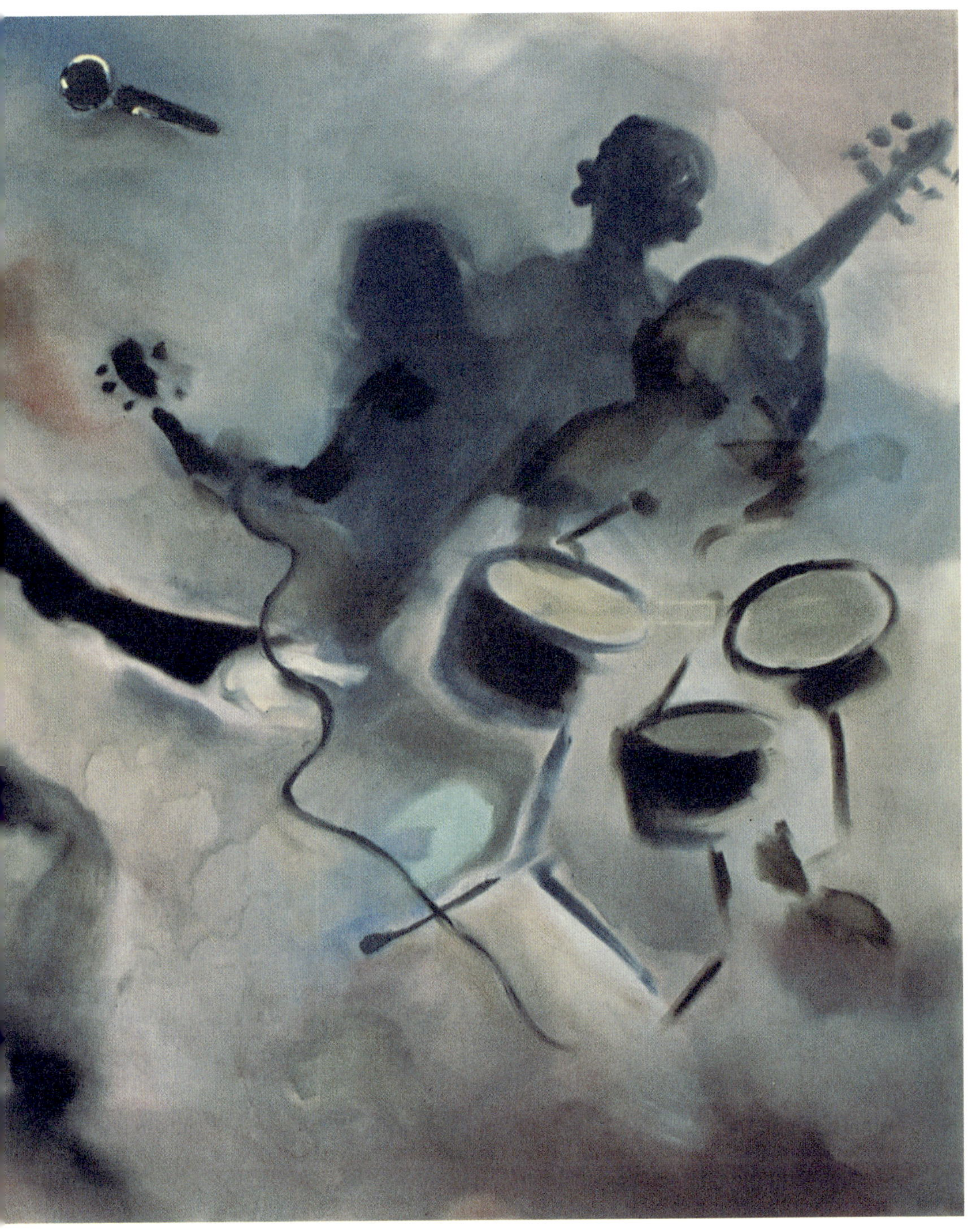

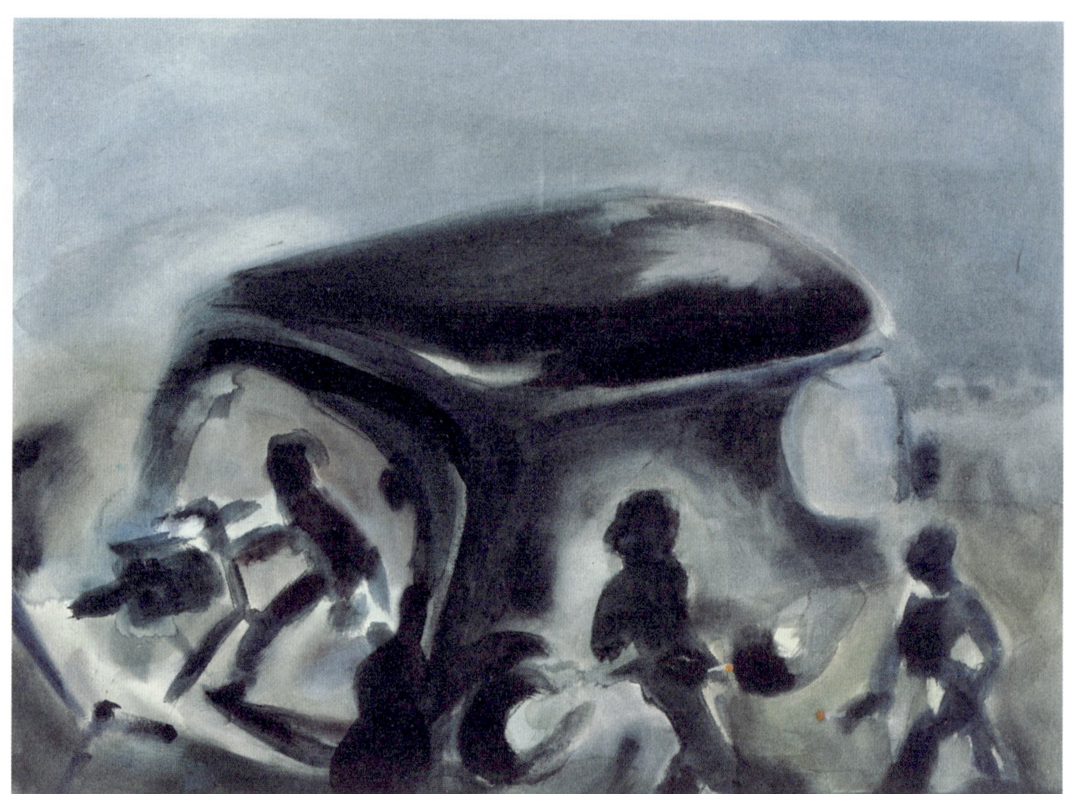

Tour Bus, 2003

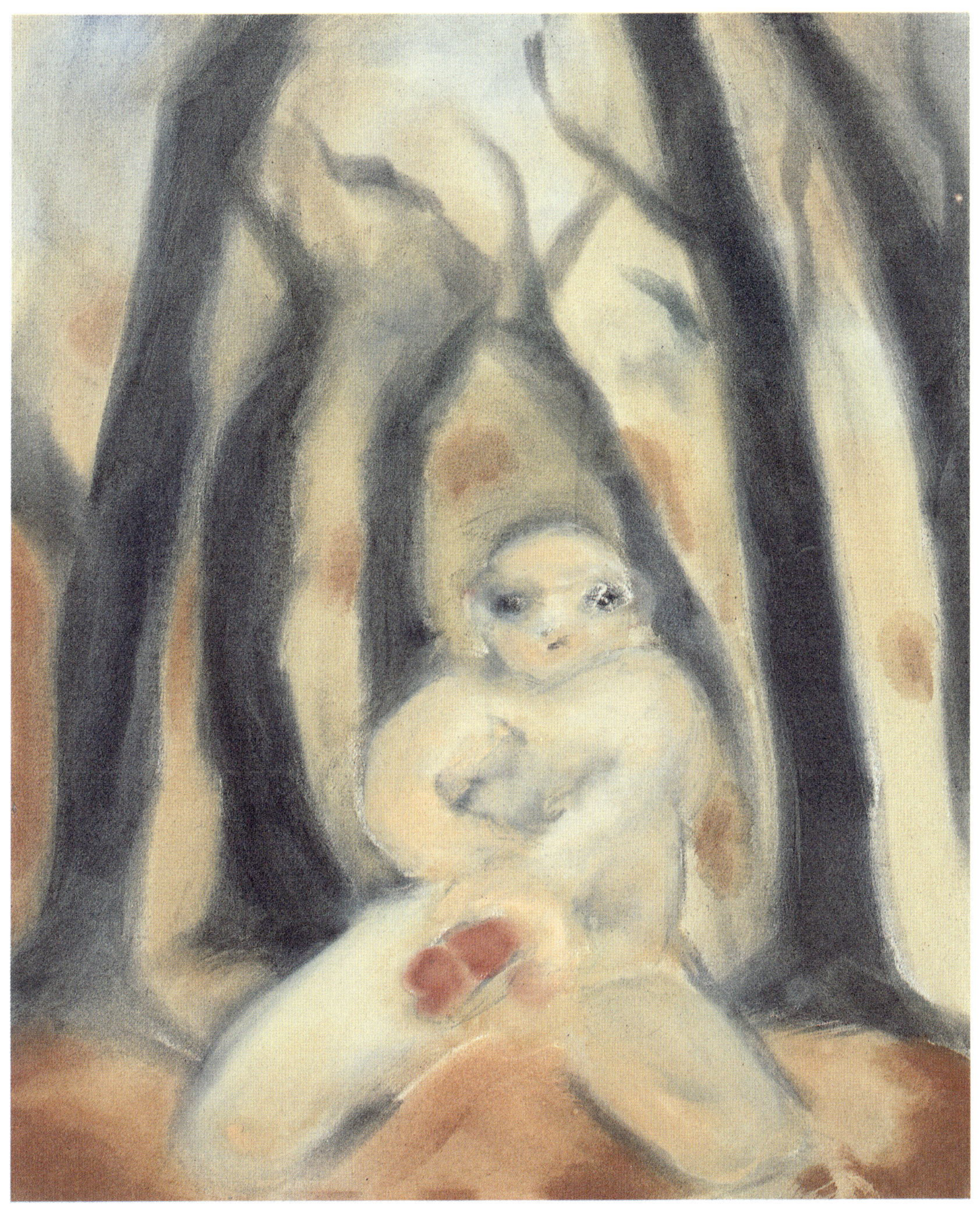

Grunewald, 2003

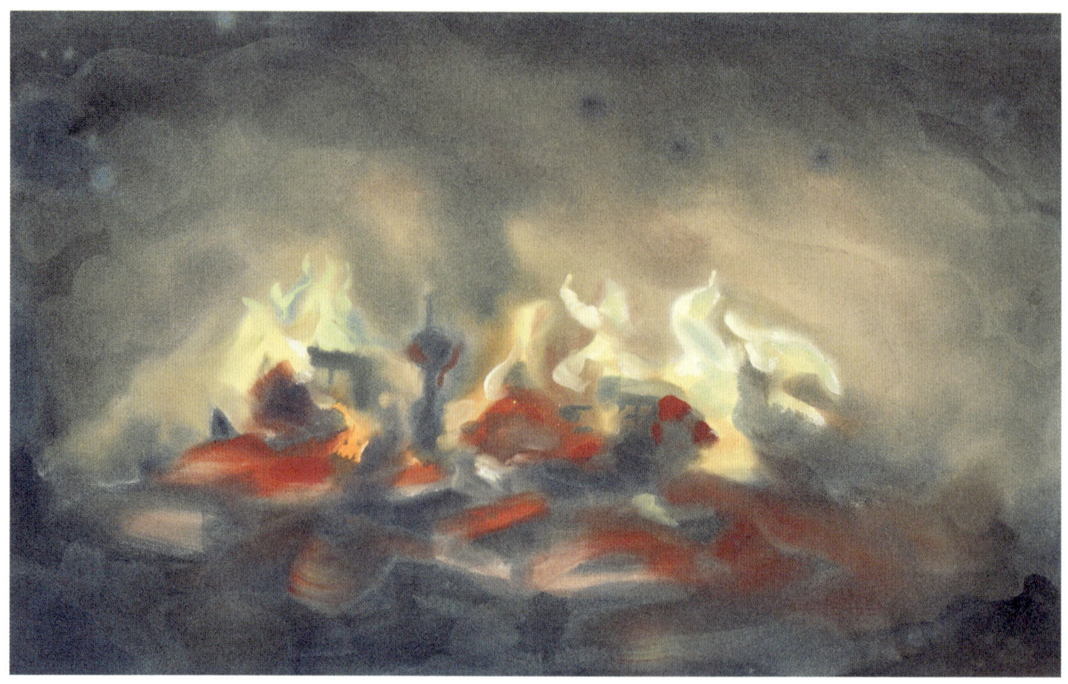

Berlin Burning, 2003

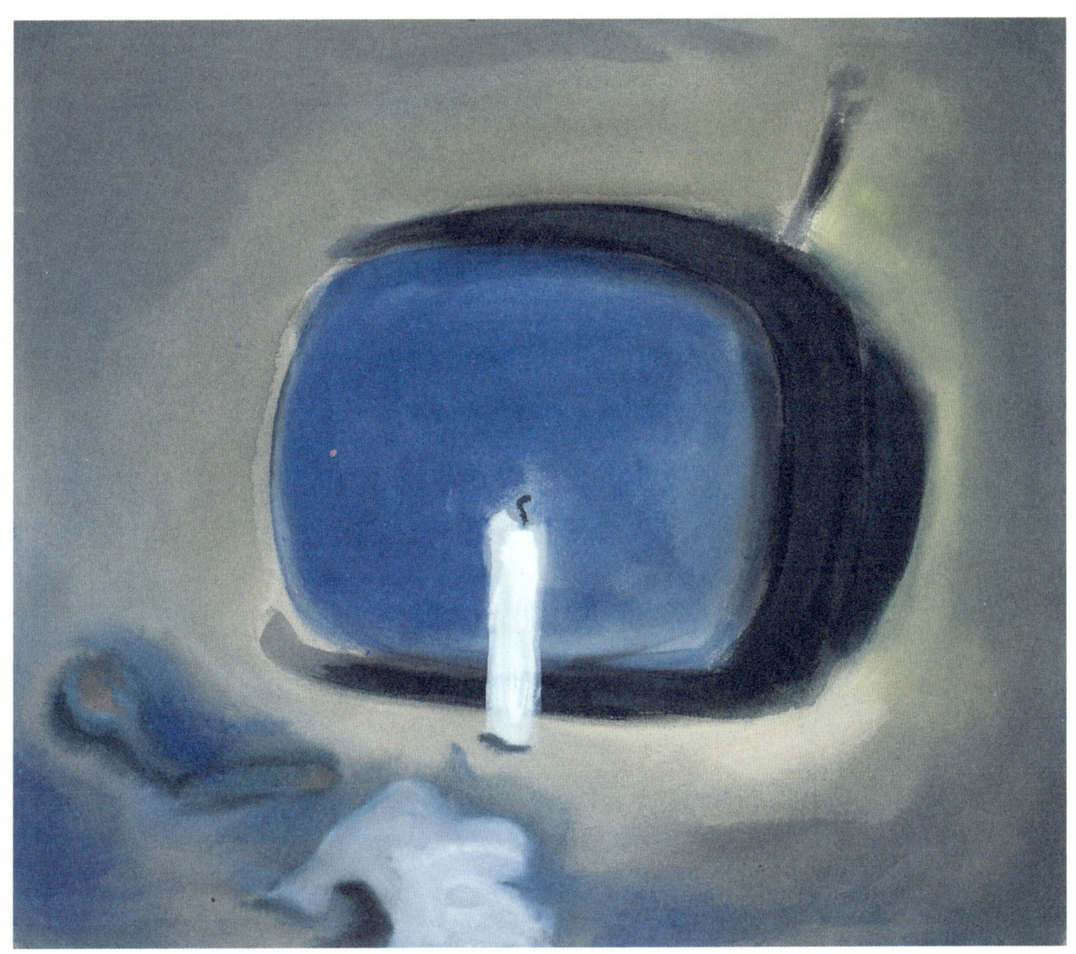

Neil and Me TV, 2003

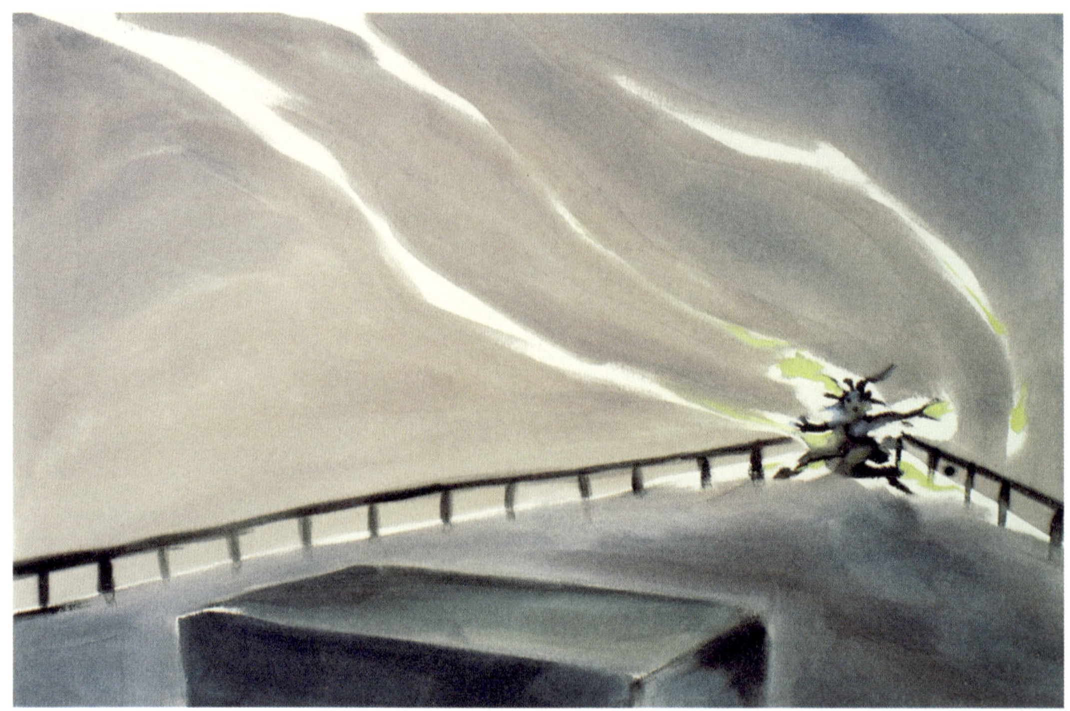

Liquid Sky, 2003

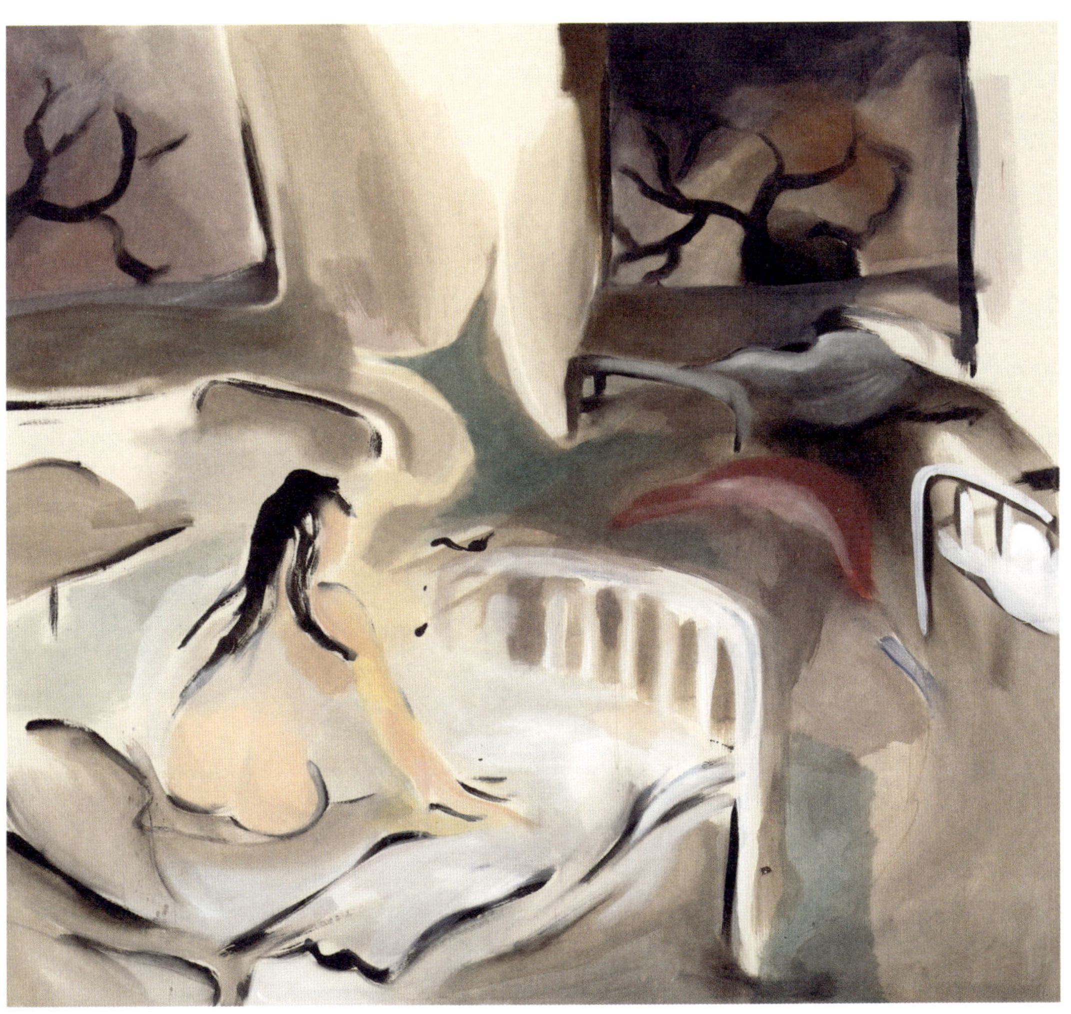

Outside Coming In, 2003

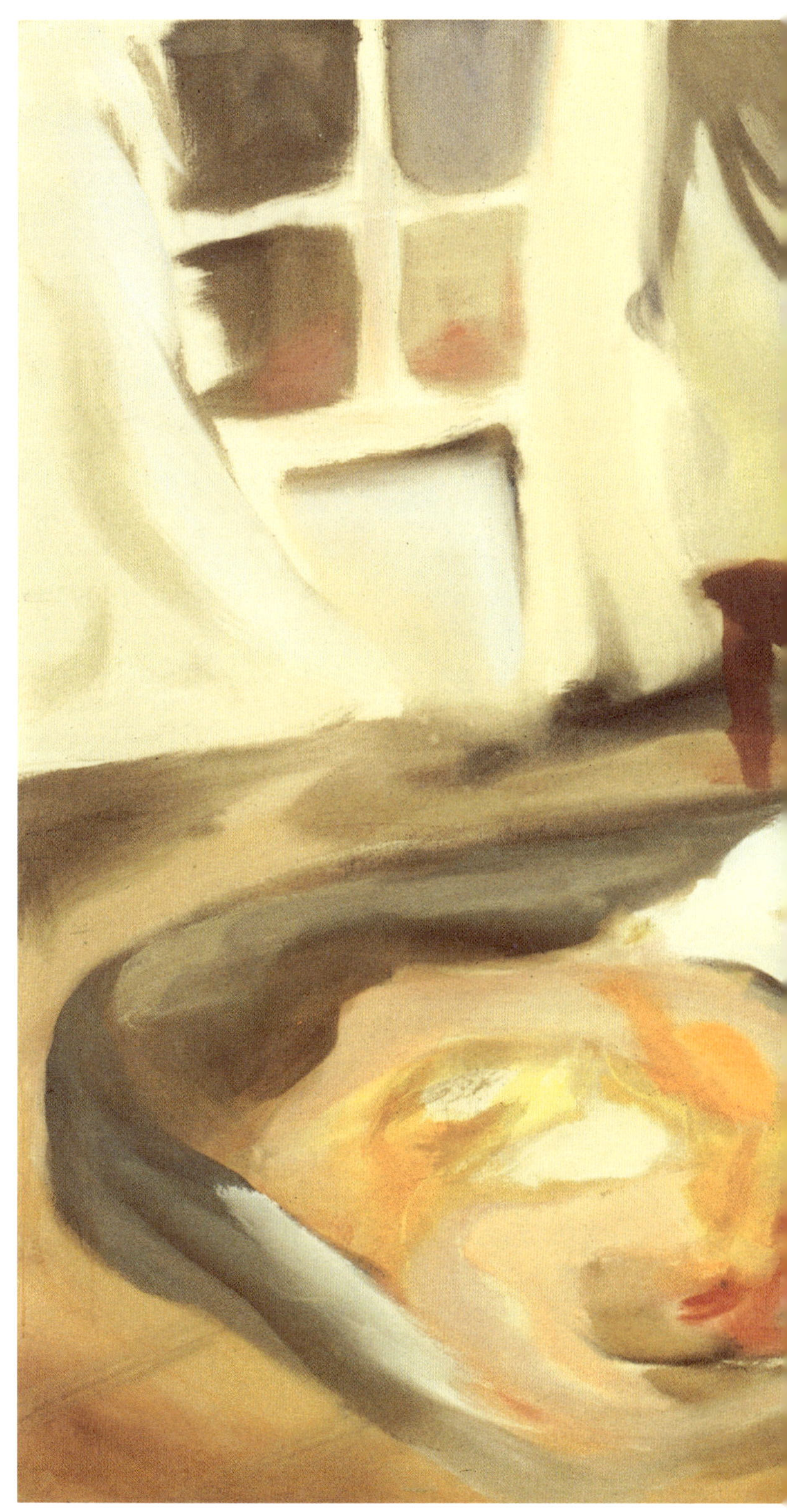

Book of Dreams, 2003

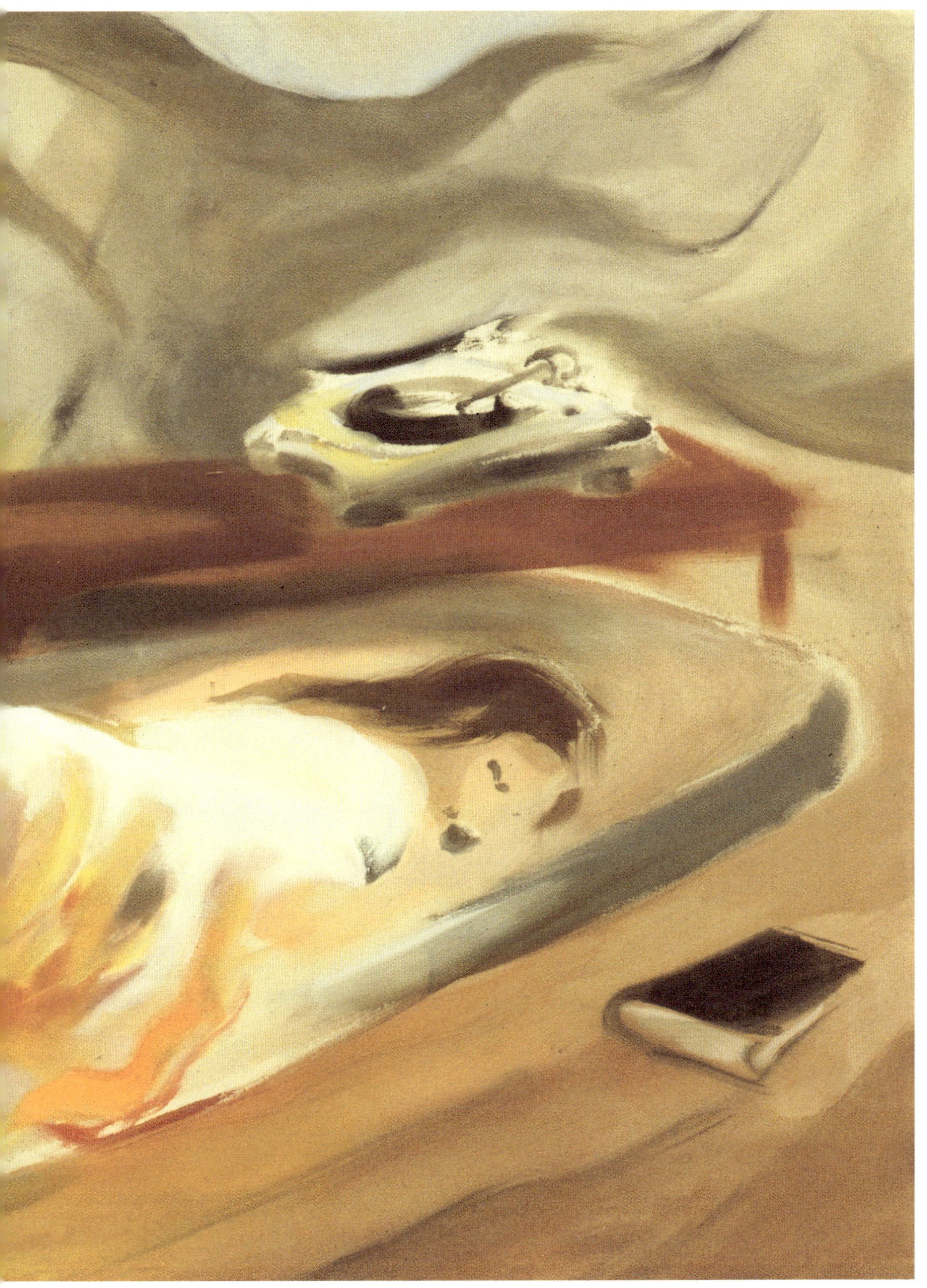

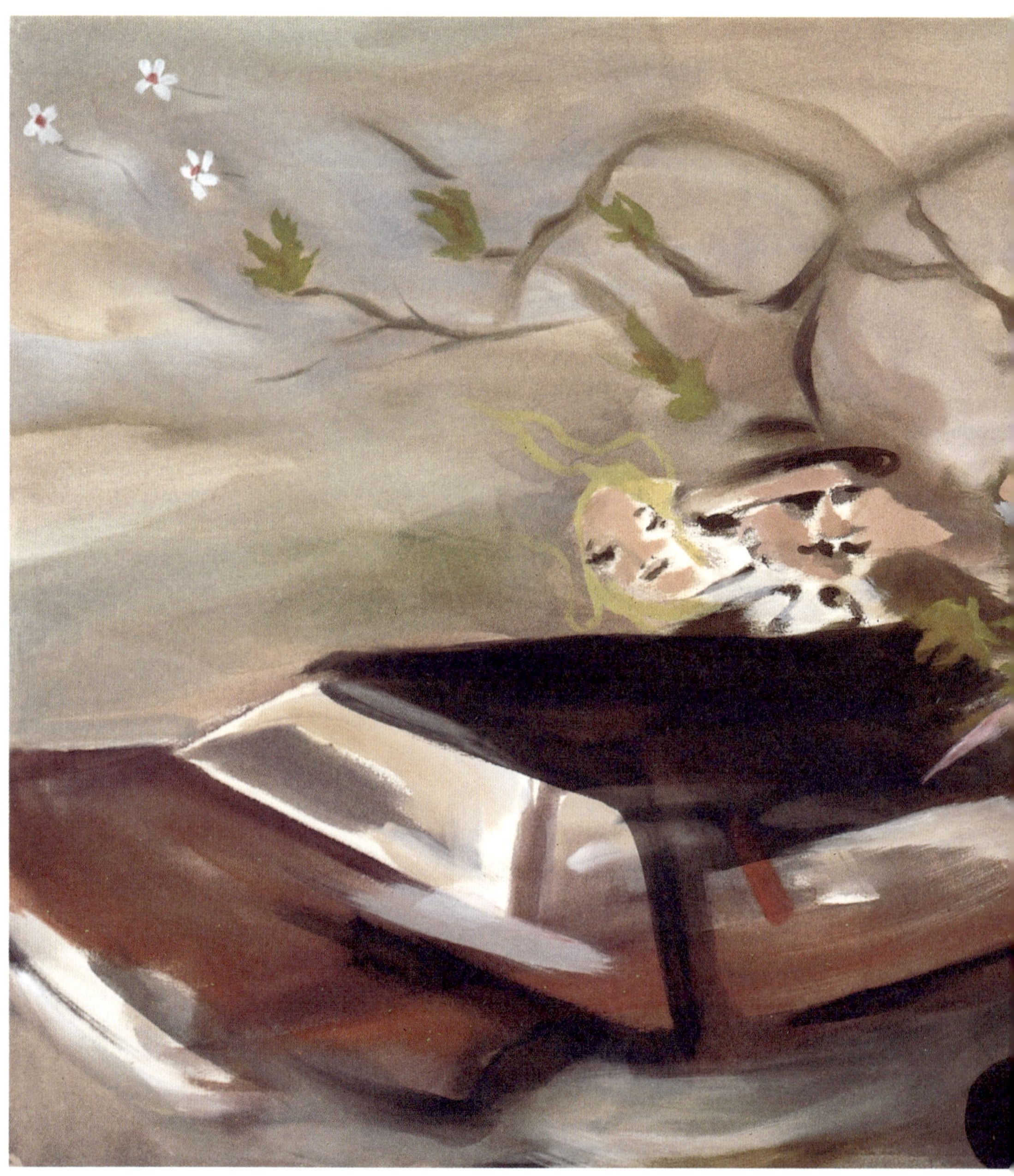

A Man for all Seasons, 2003

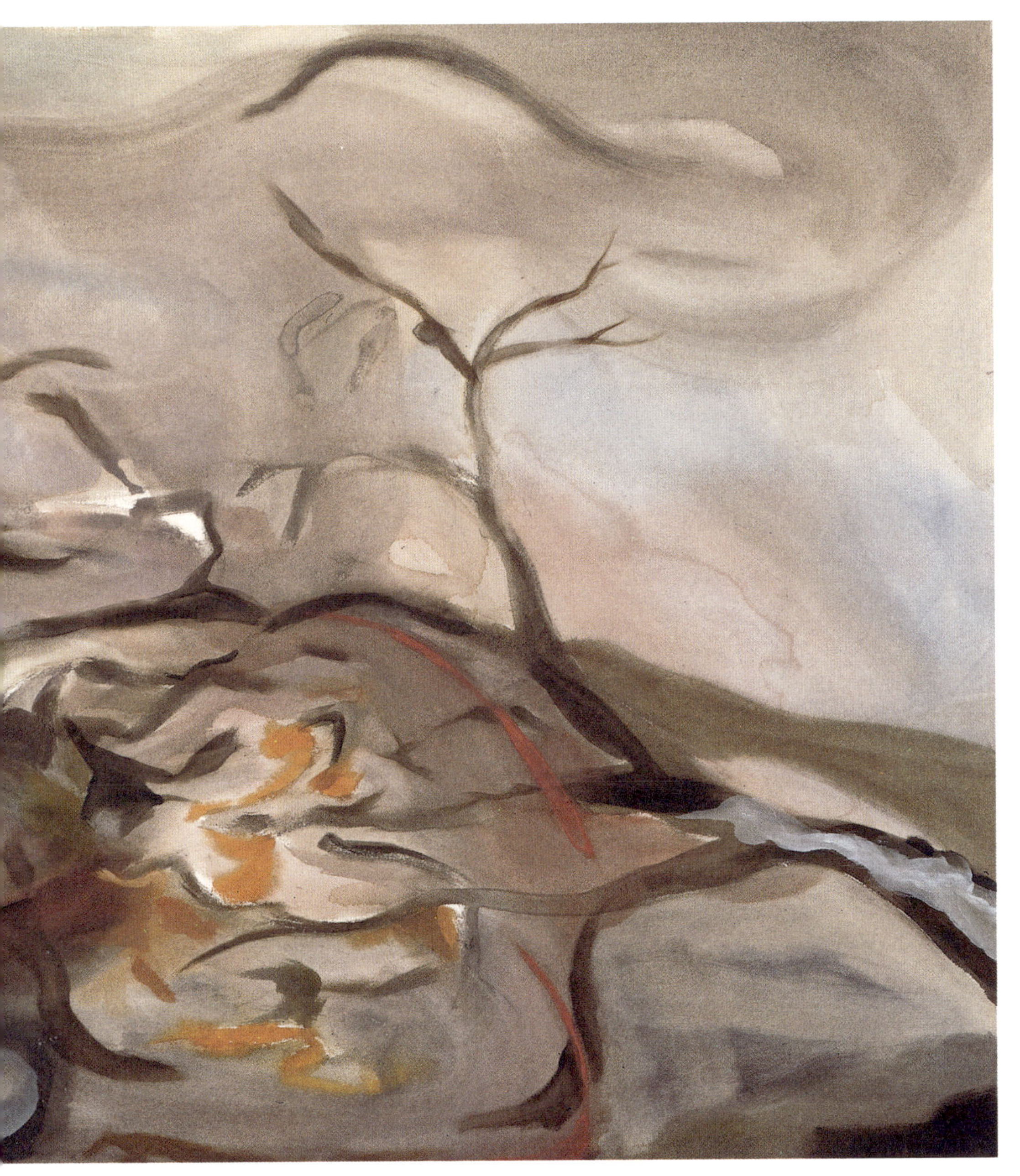

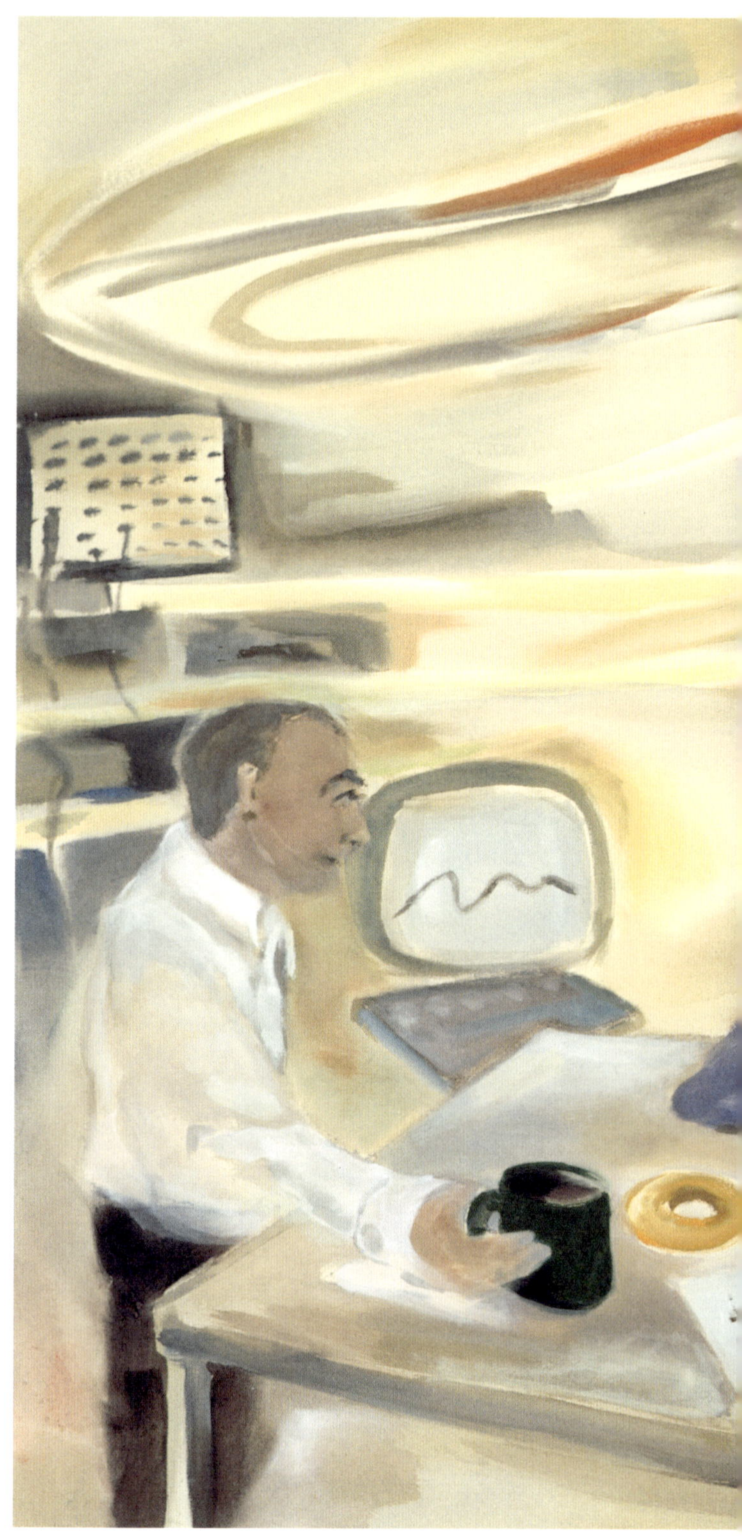

Hot Fusion, 2004

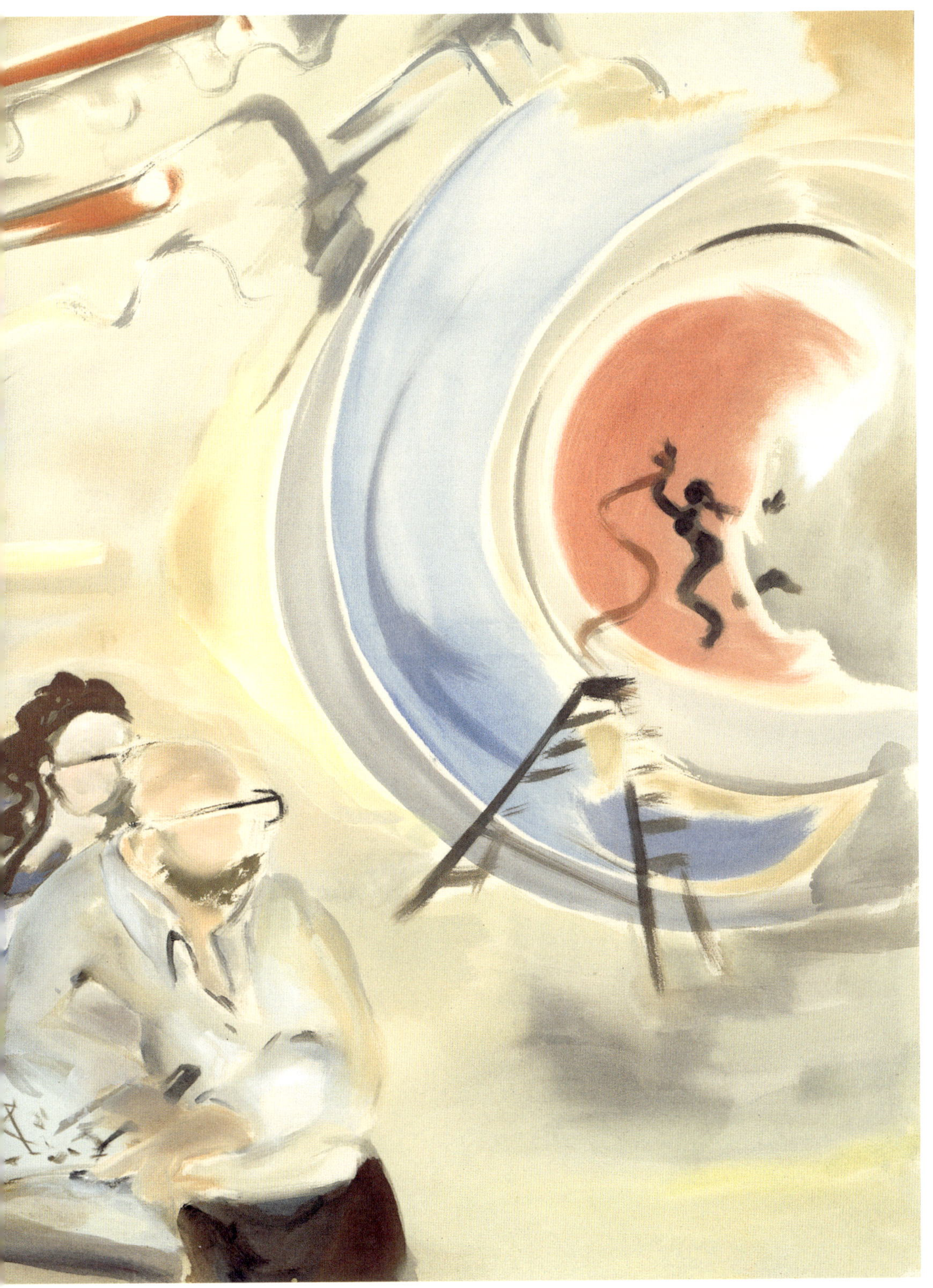

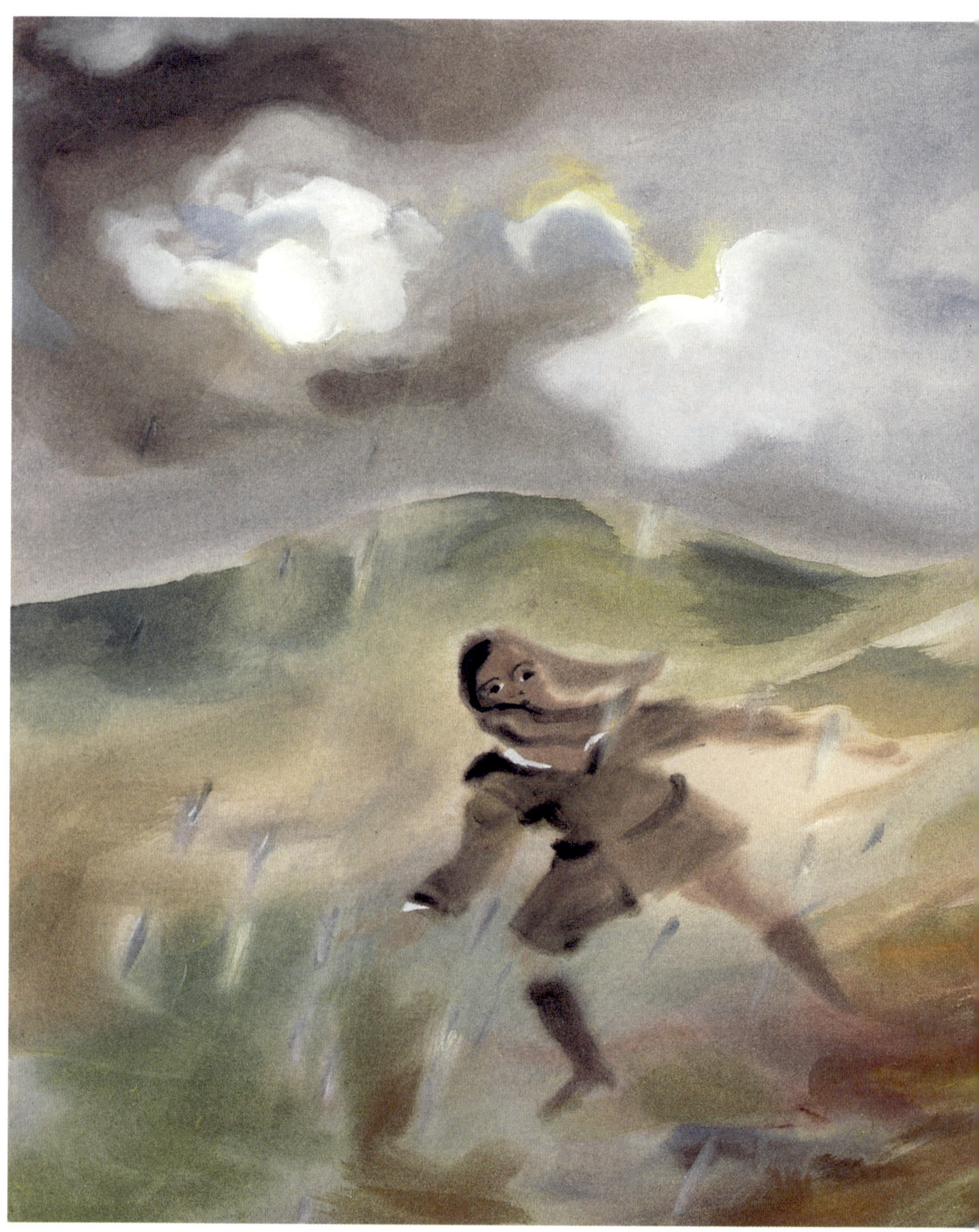

Back on the Stretcher, 2004

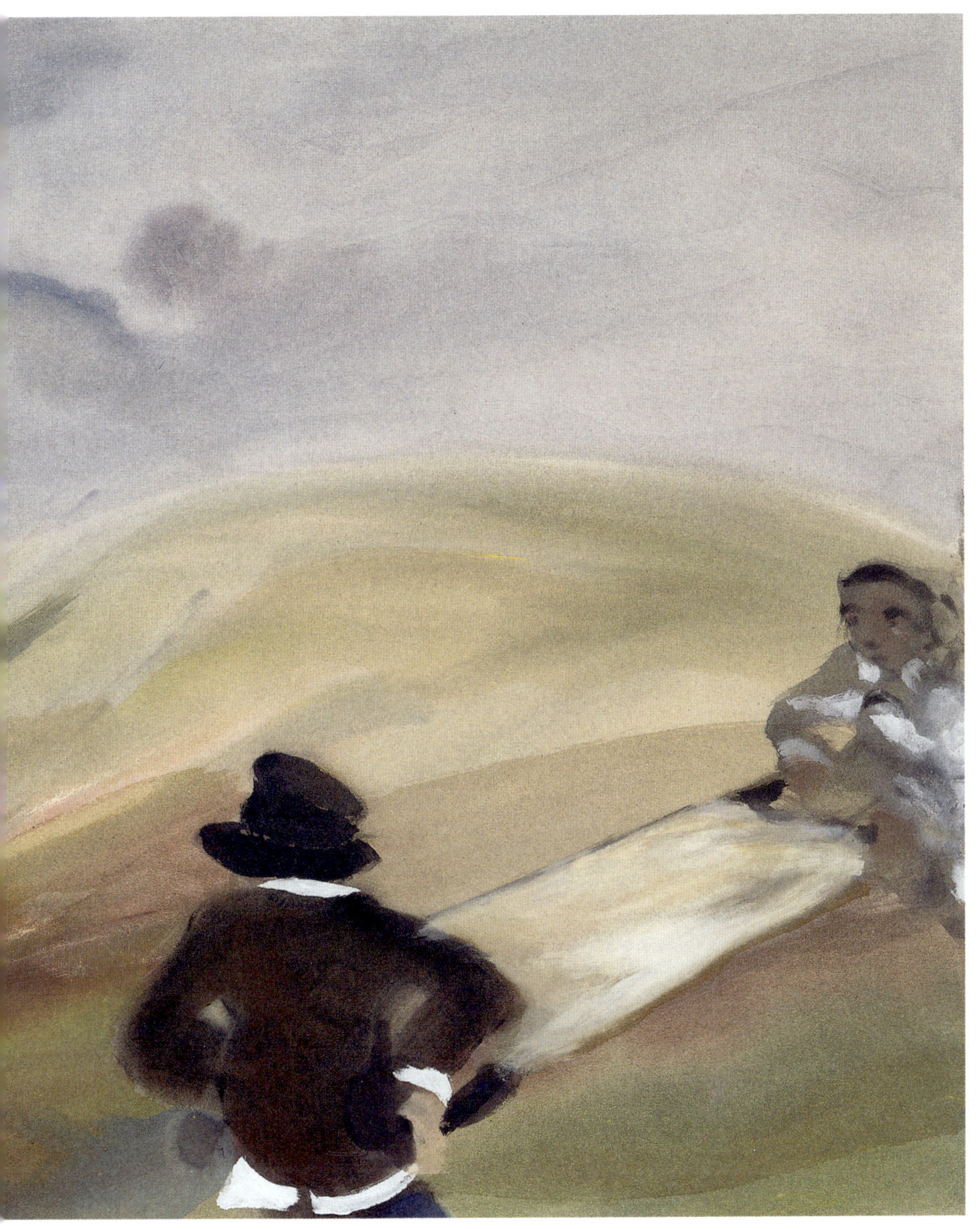

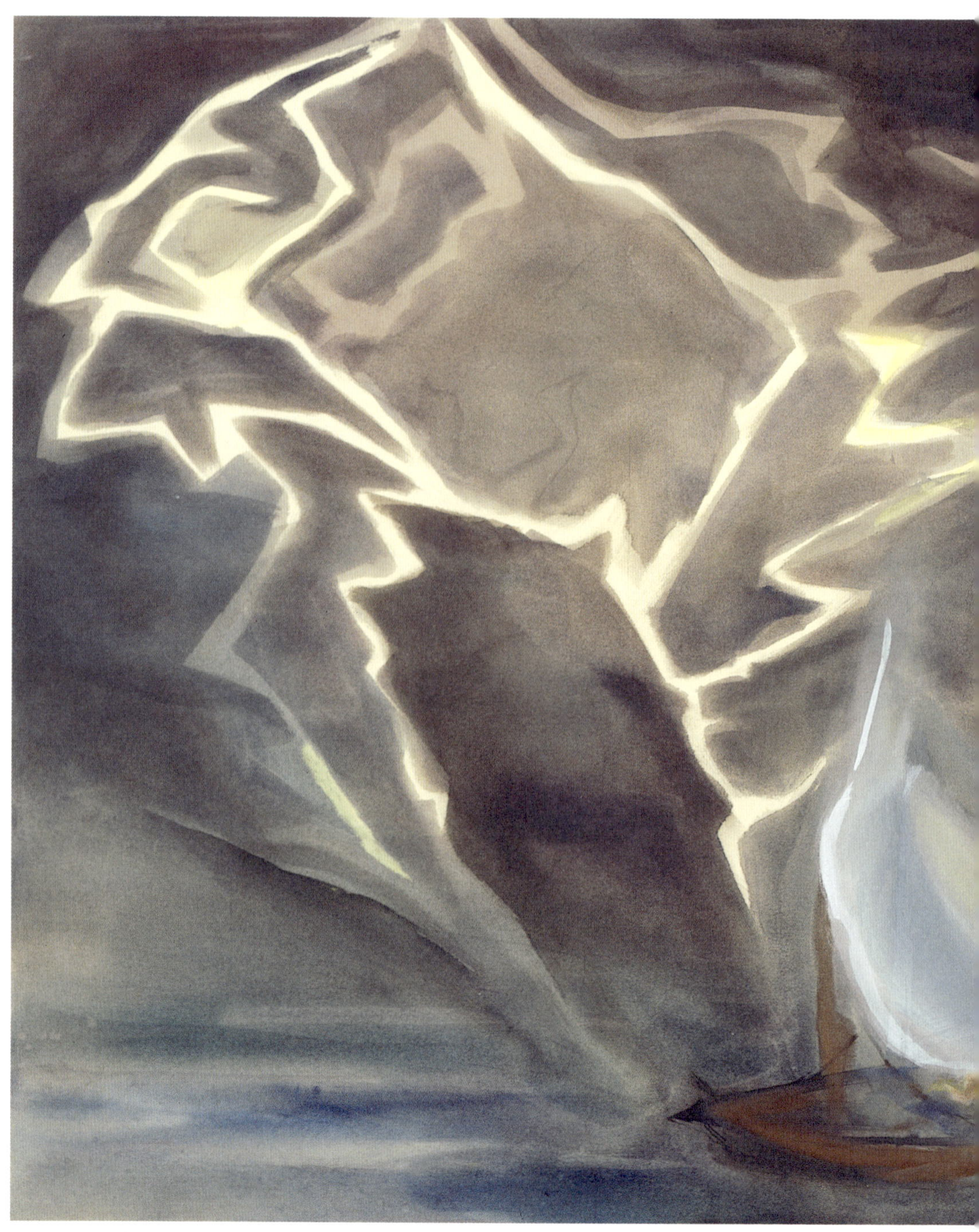

Stormy Weather, 2004

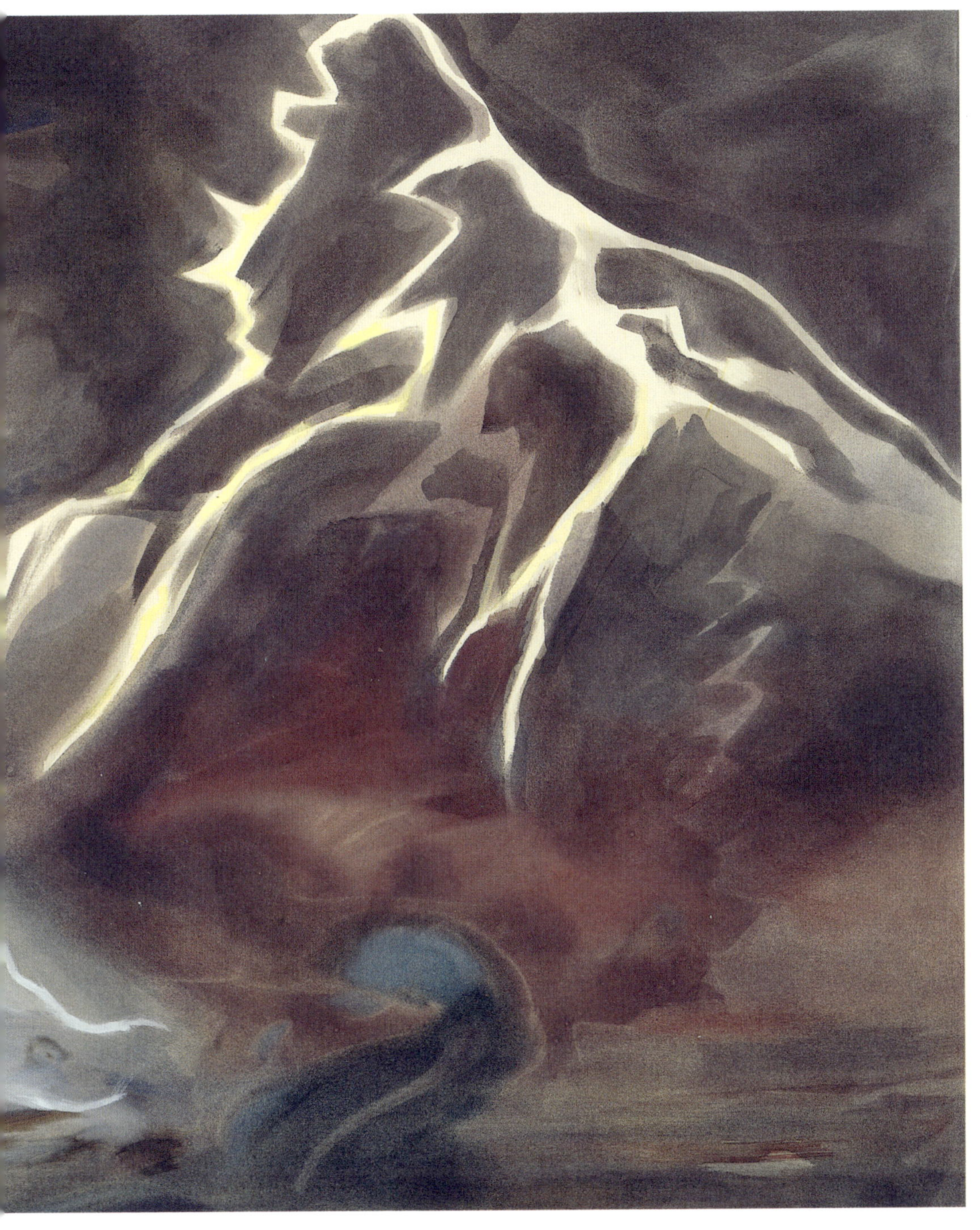

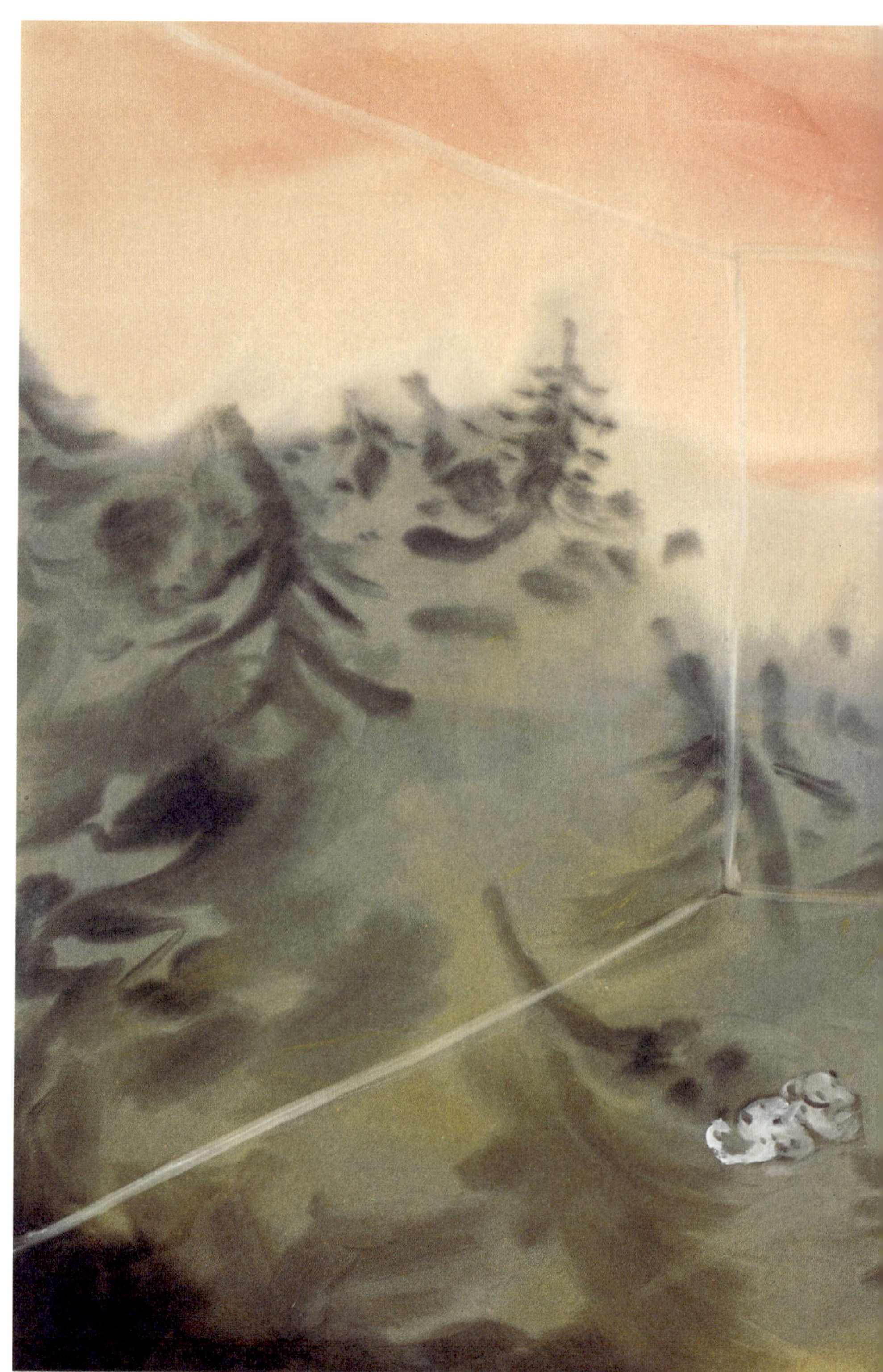

 At Home, 2004

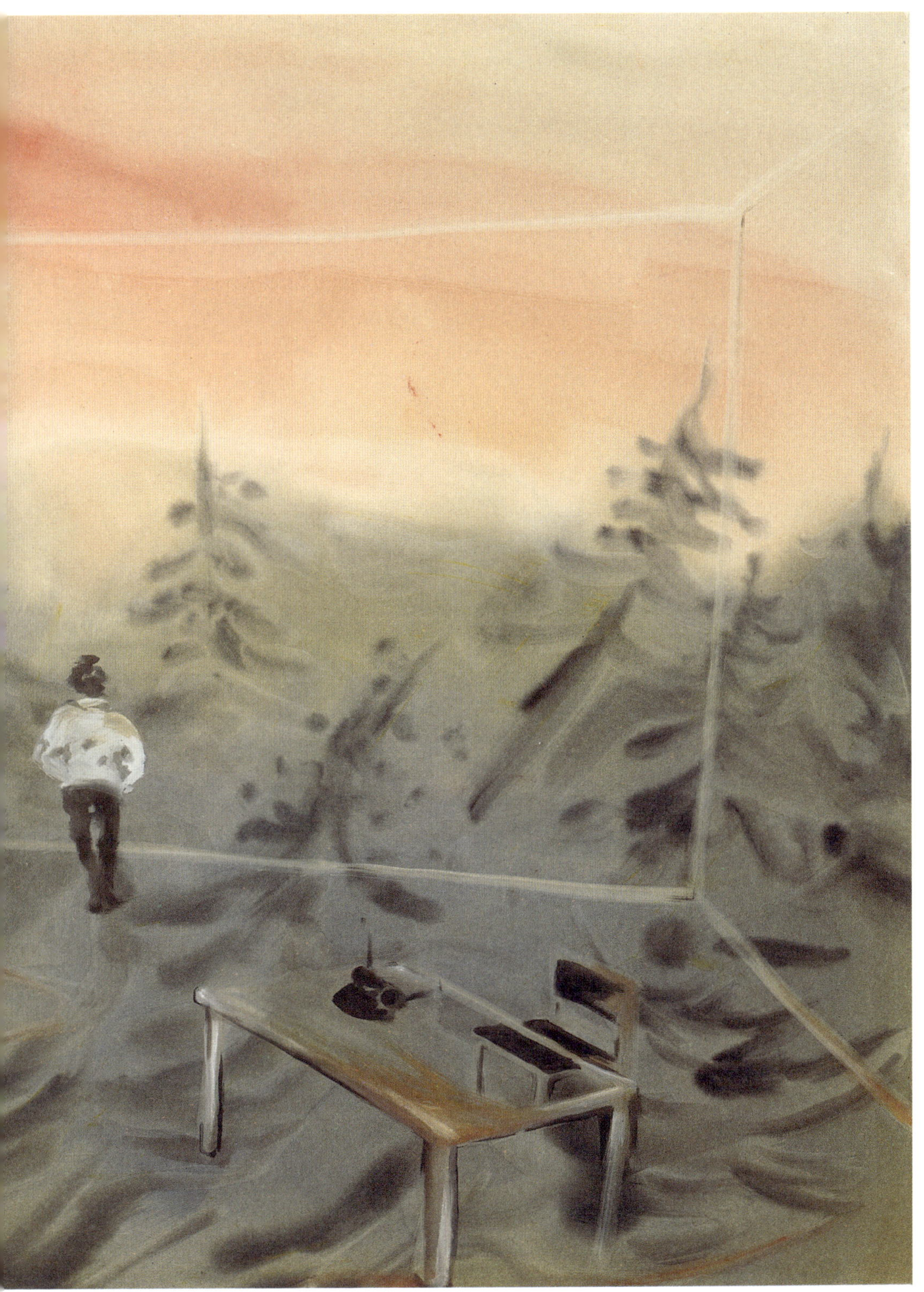

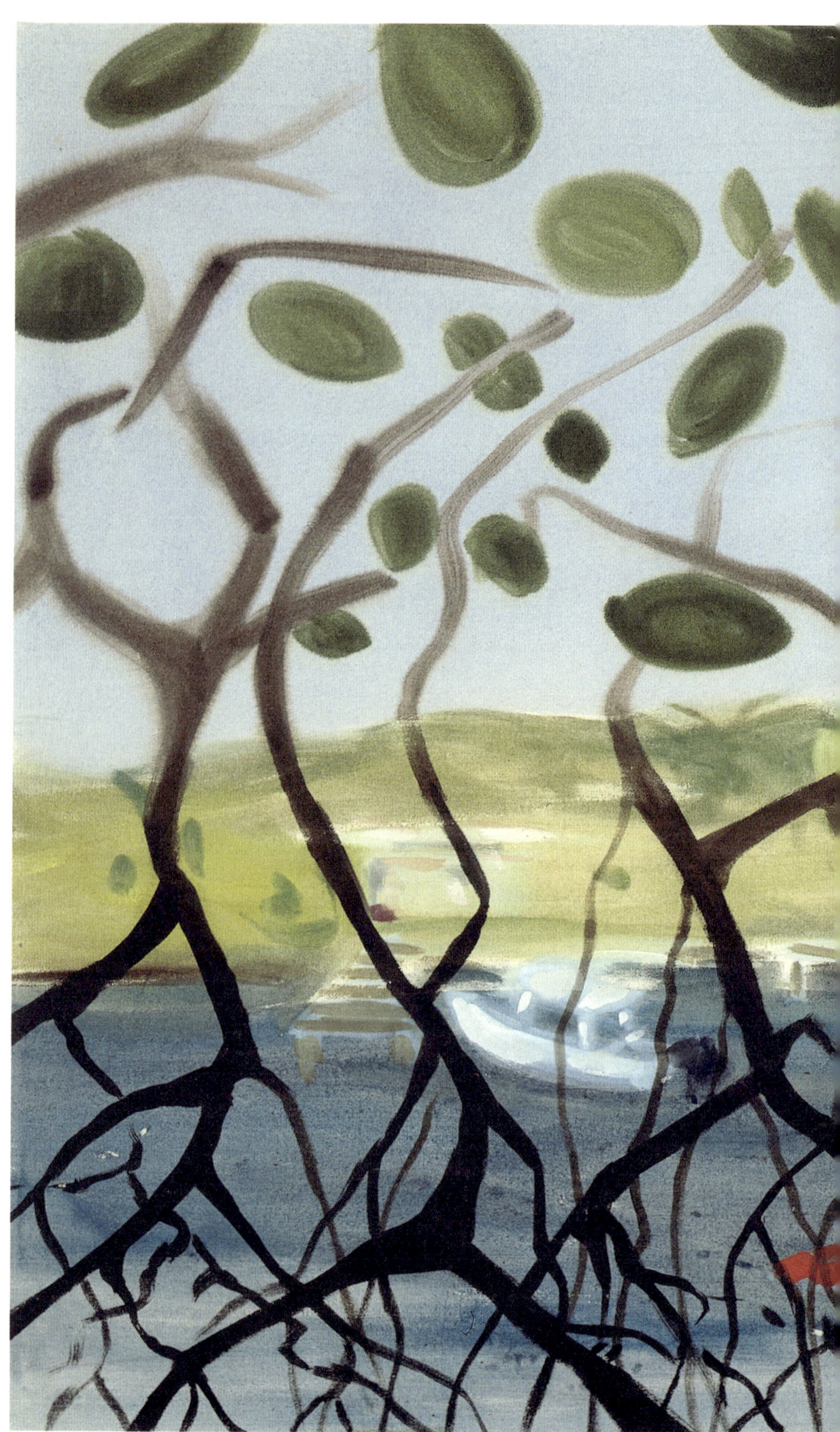

Sans-Souci, 2004

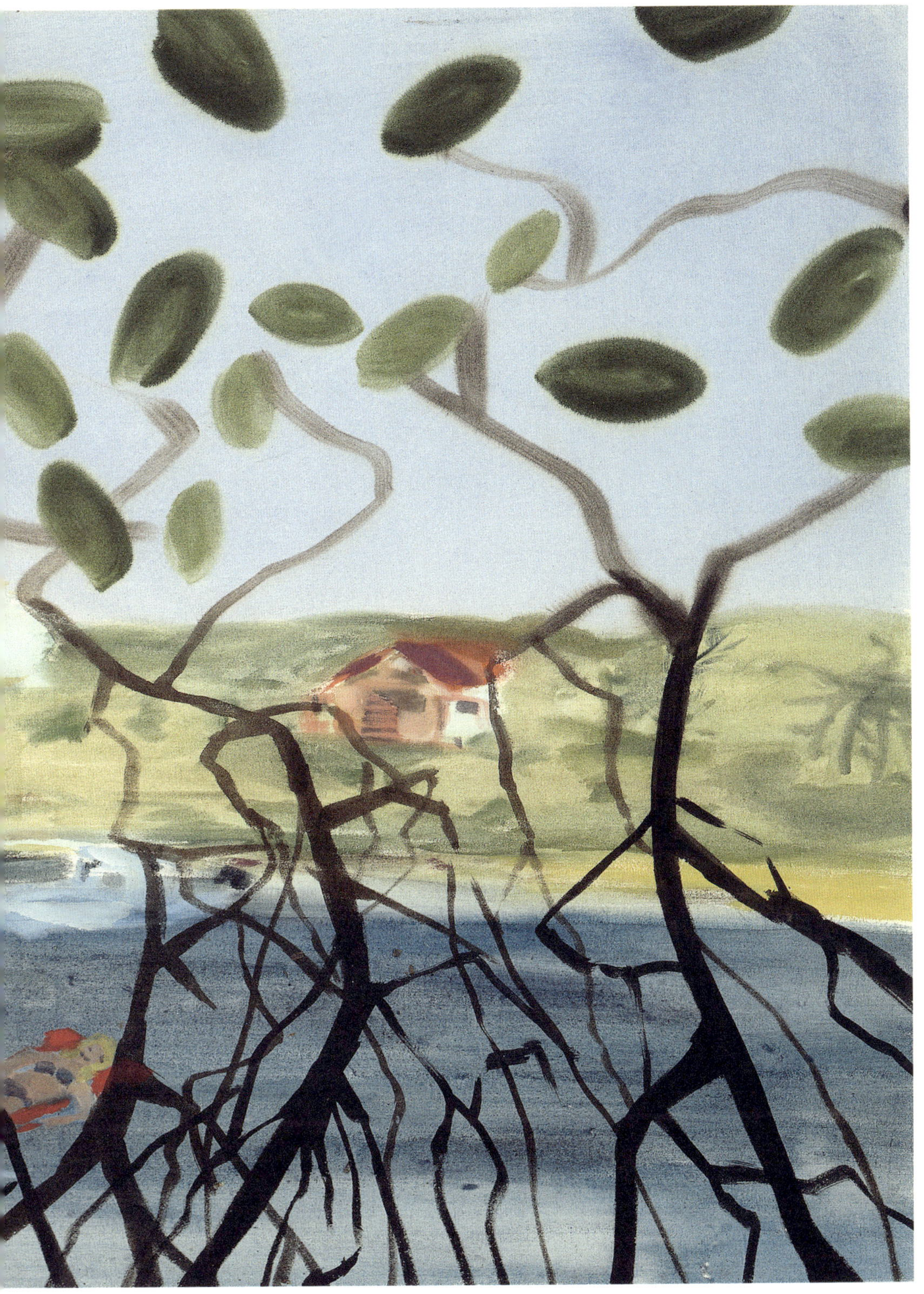

  North Beach, 2004

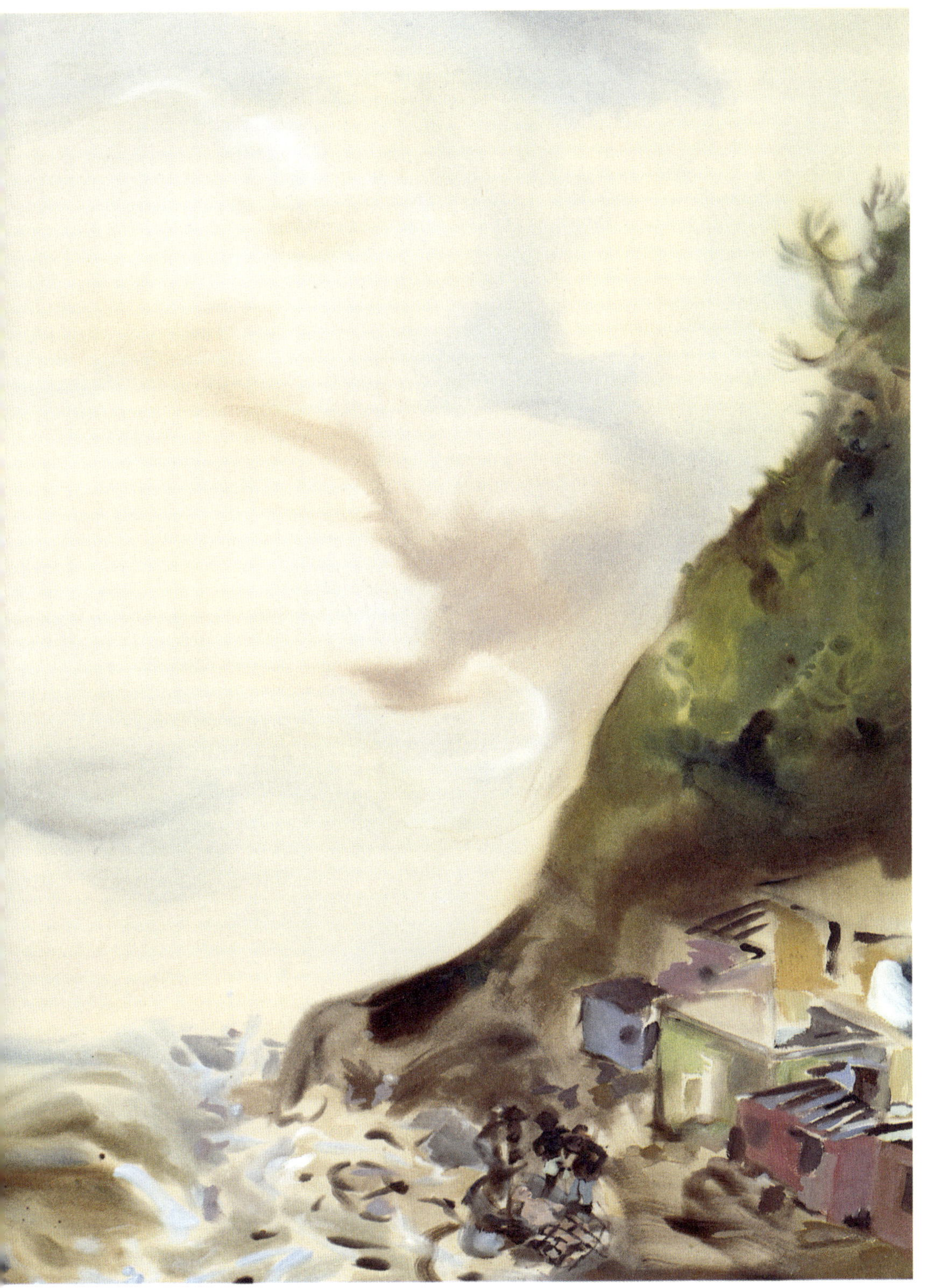

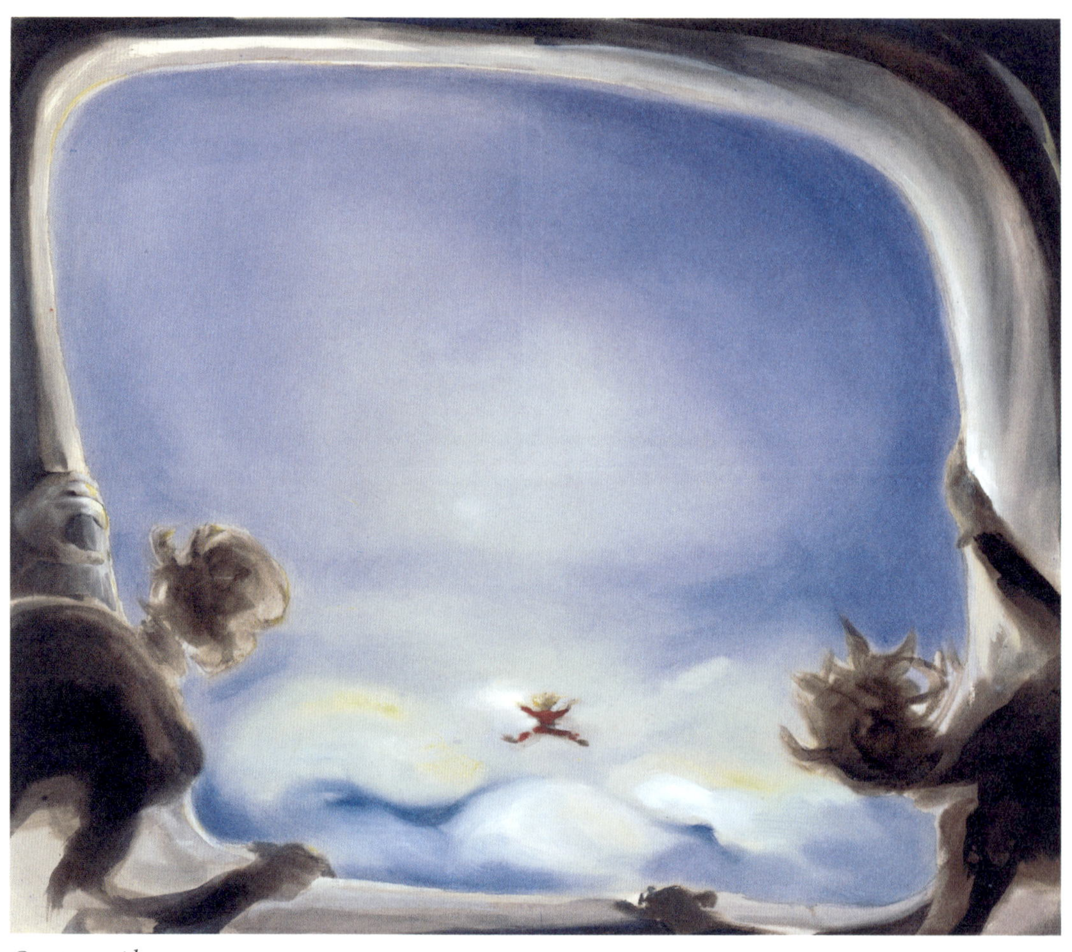

One to a void, 2004

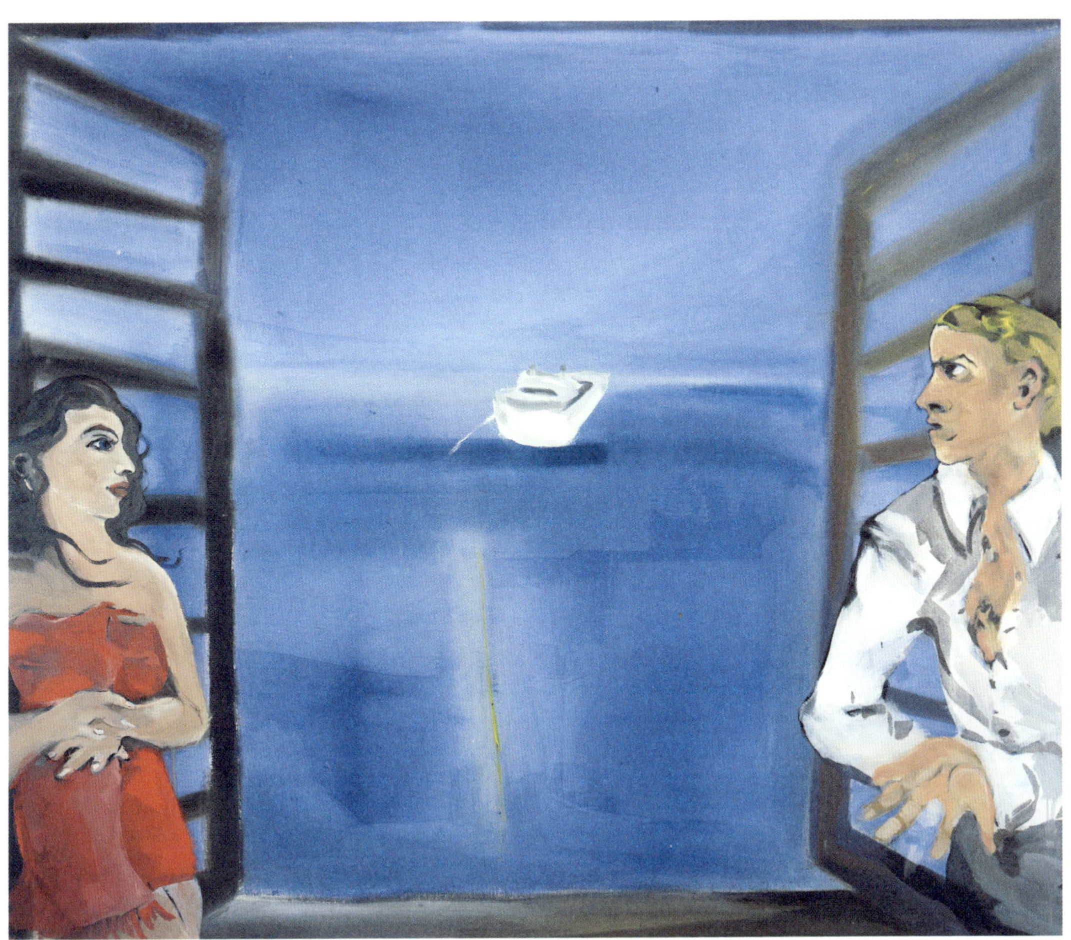

The Proposal, 2004

Bermudas 1964, 2004

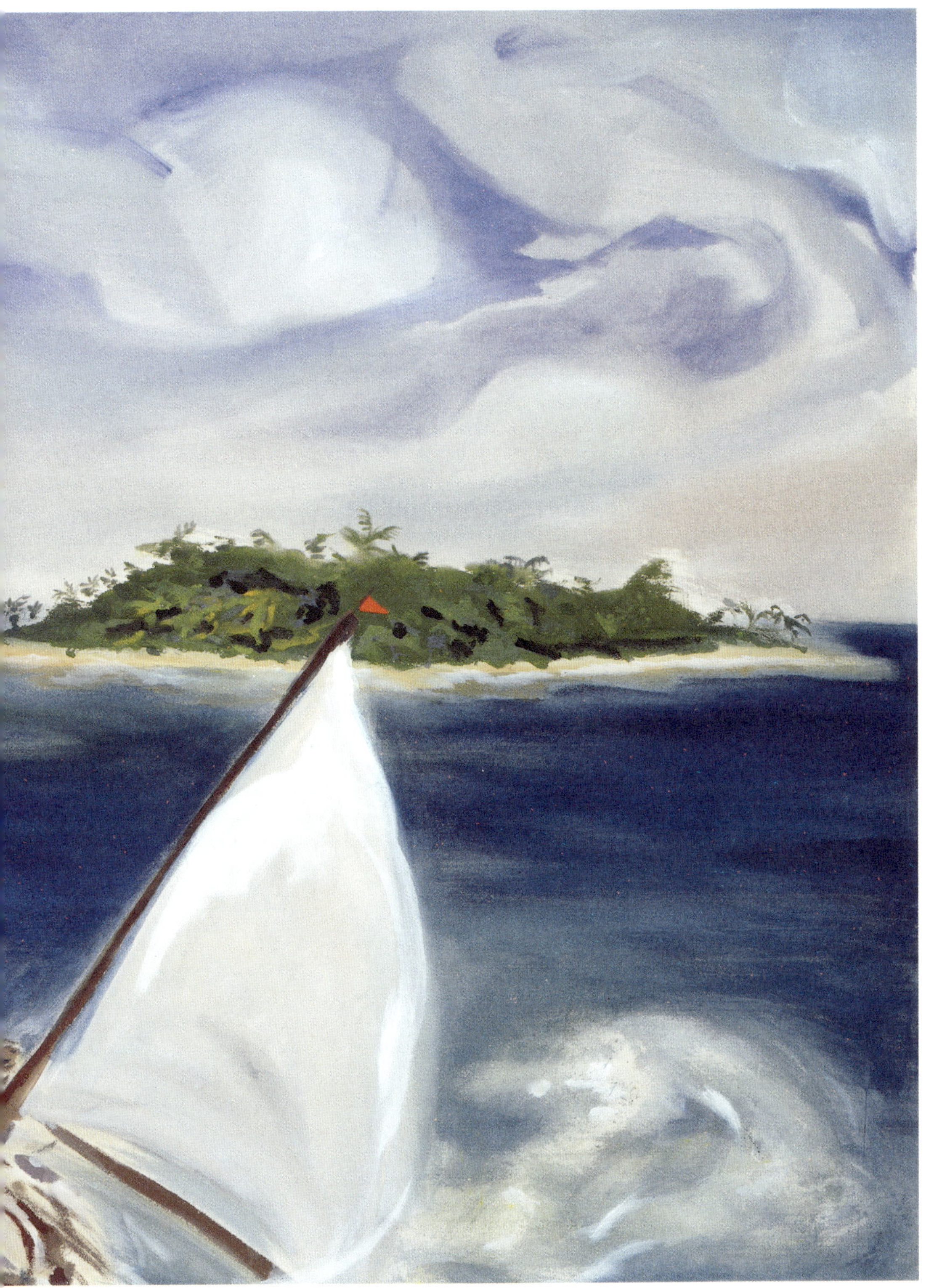

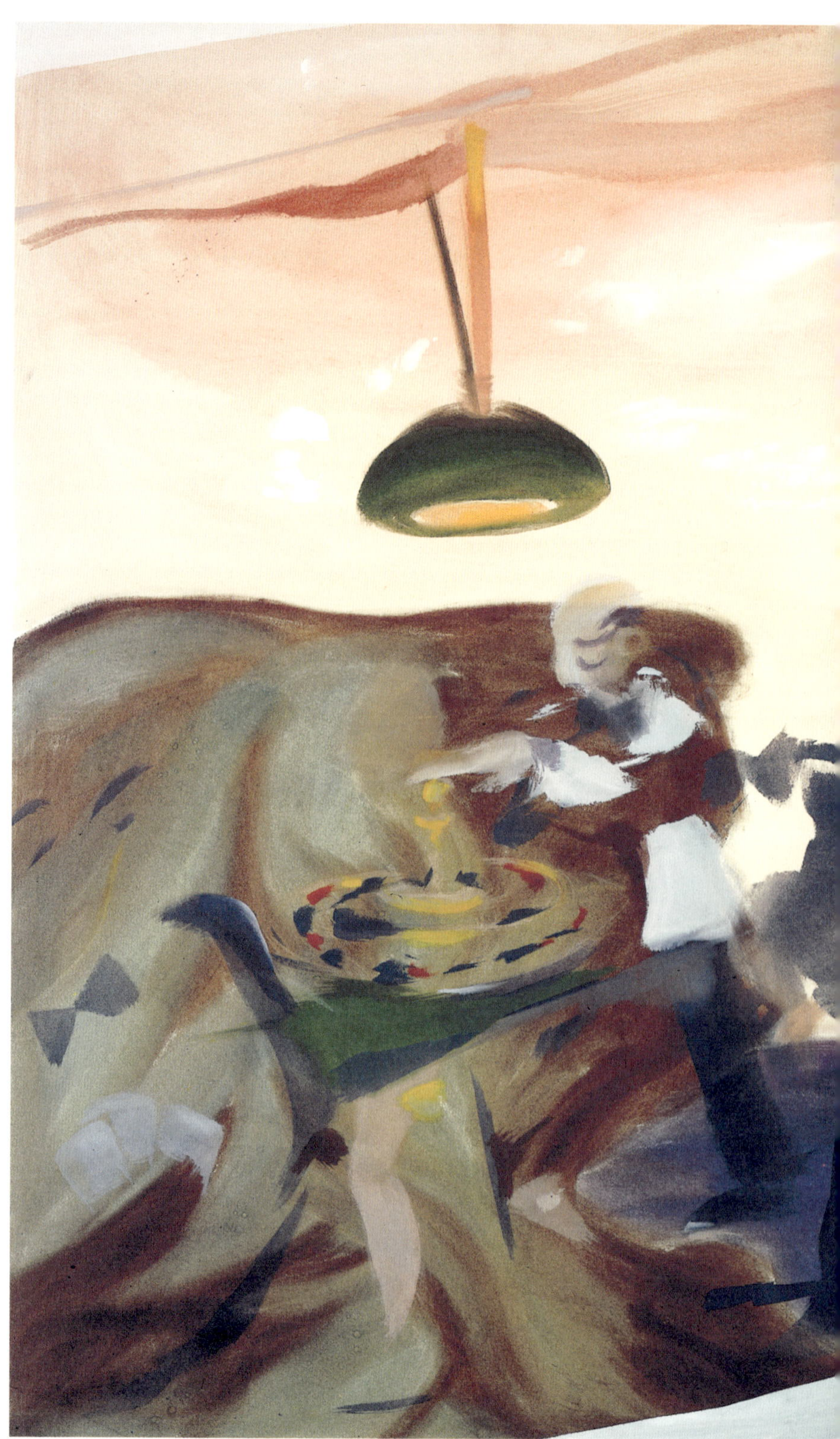

Monte Carlo, 2004

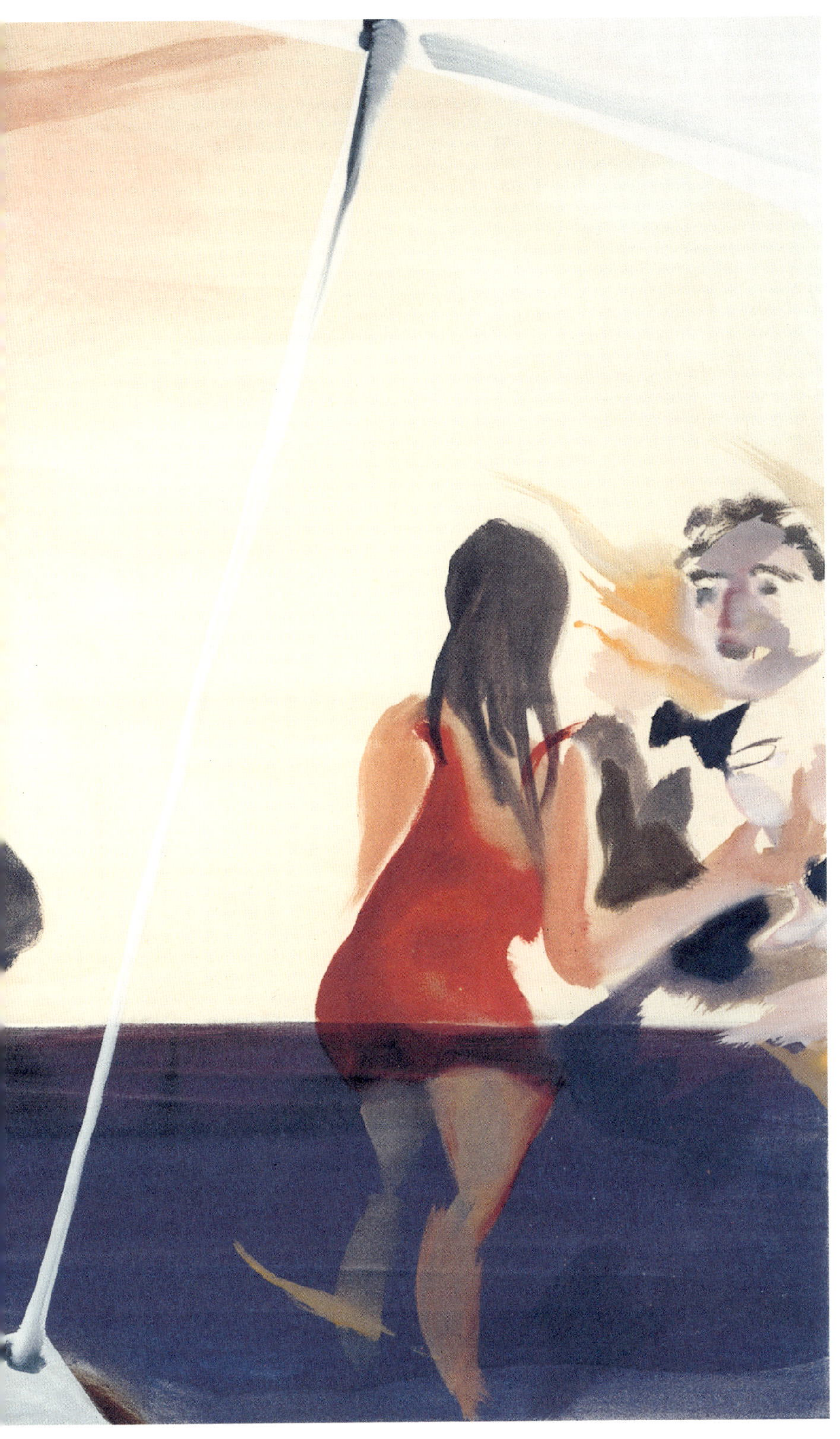

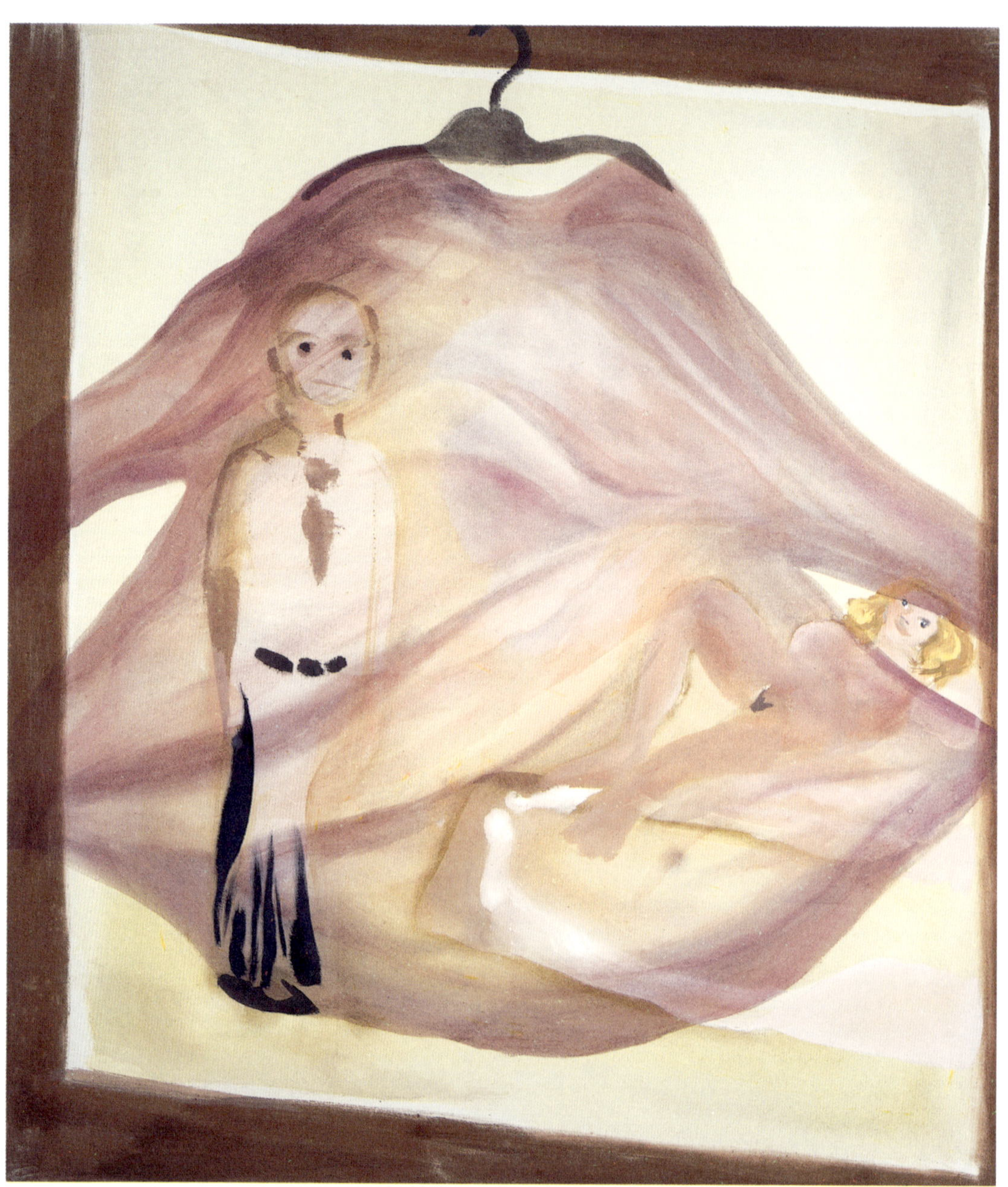

The Negligent Husband, 2004

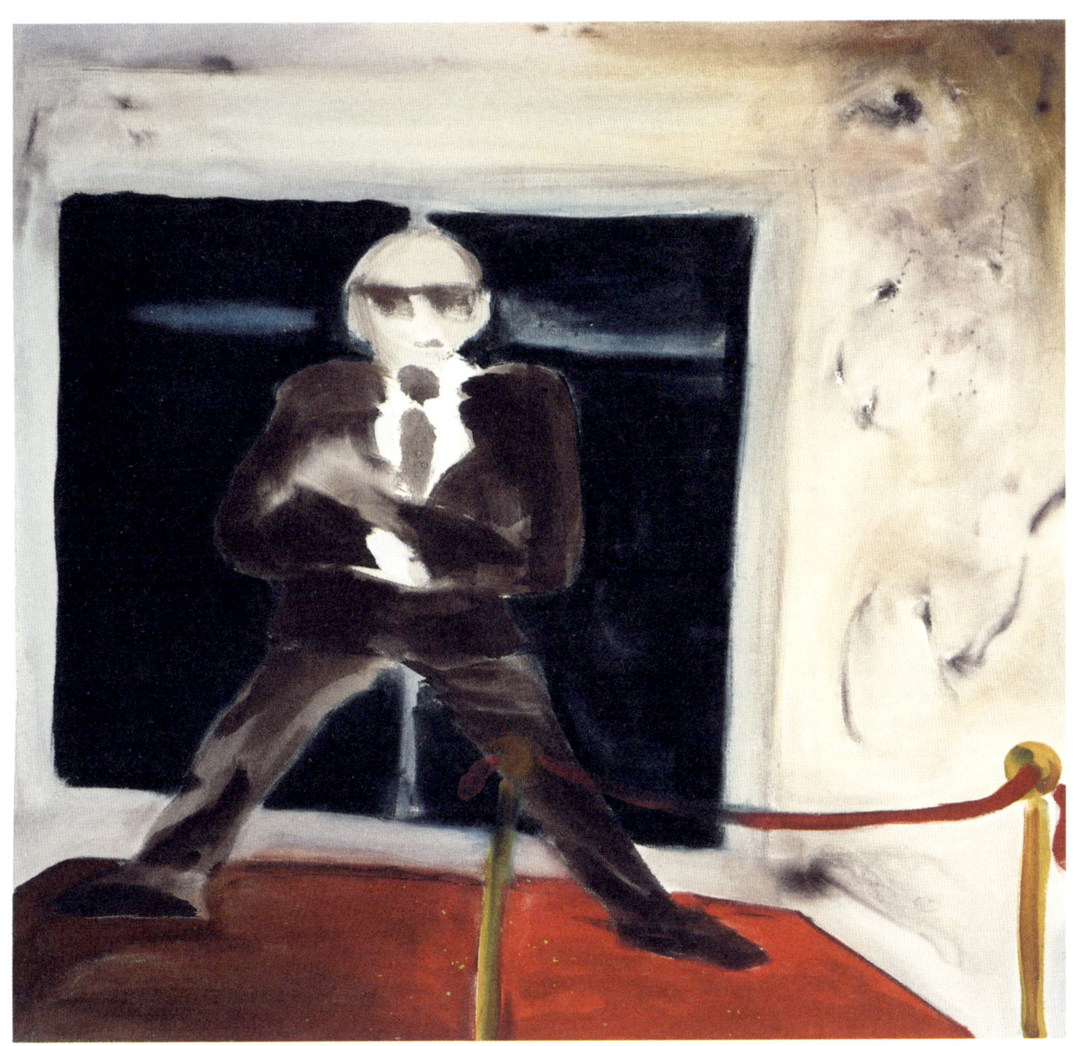

Bouncer, 2004

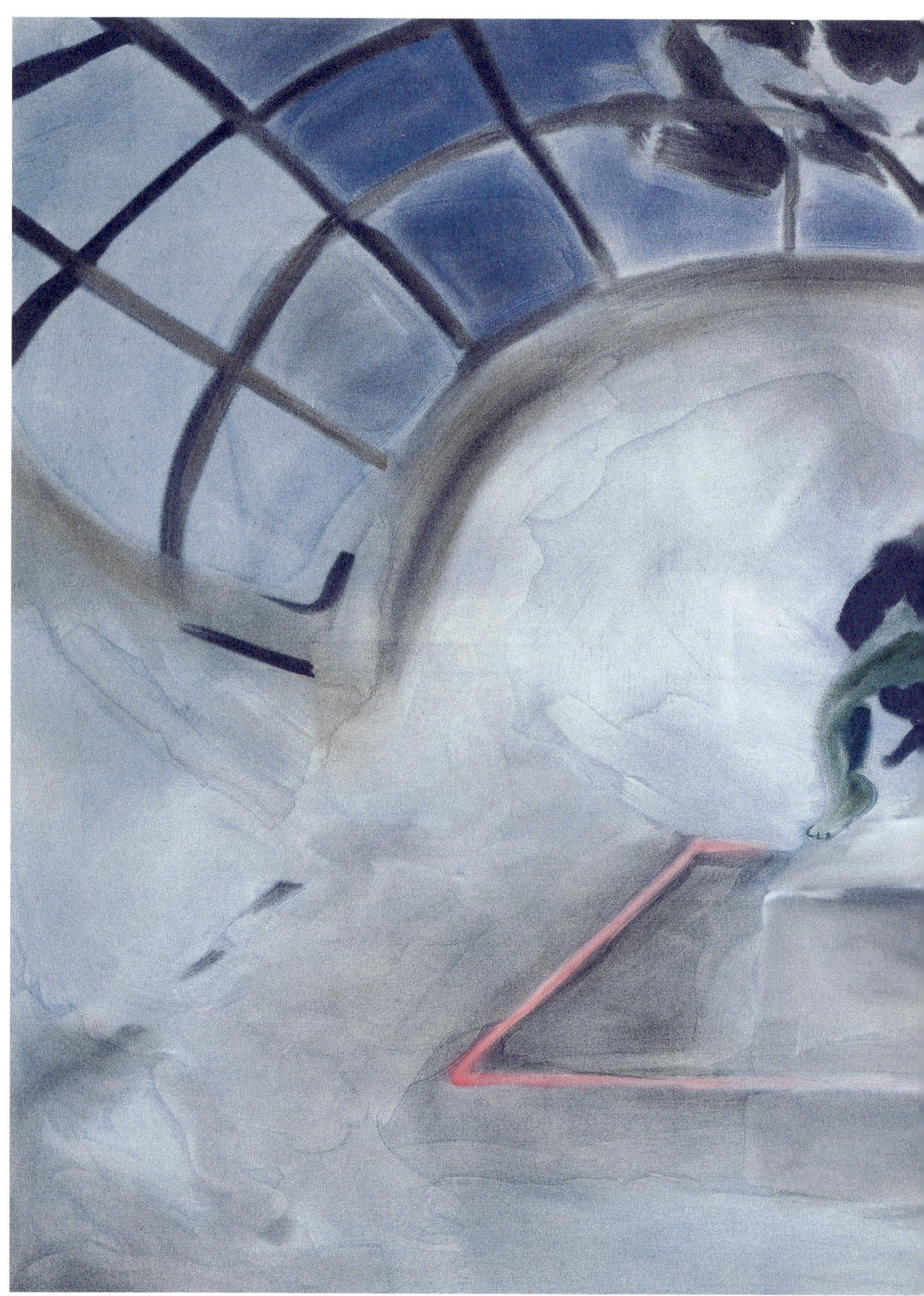

Theft of the Jaded Goddess, 2004

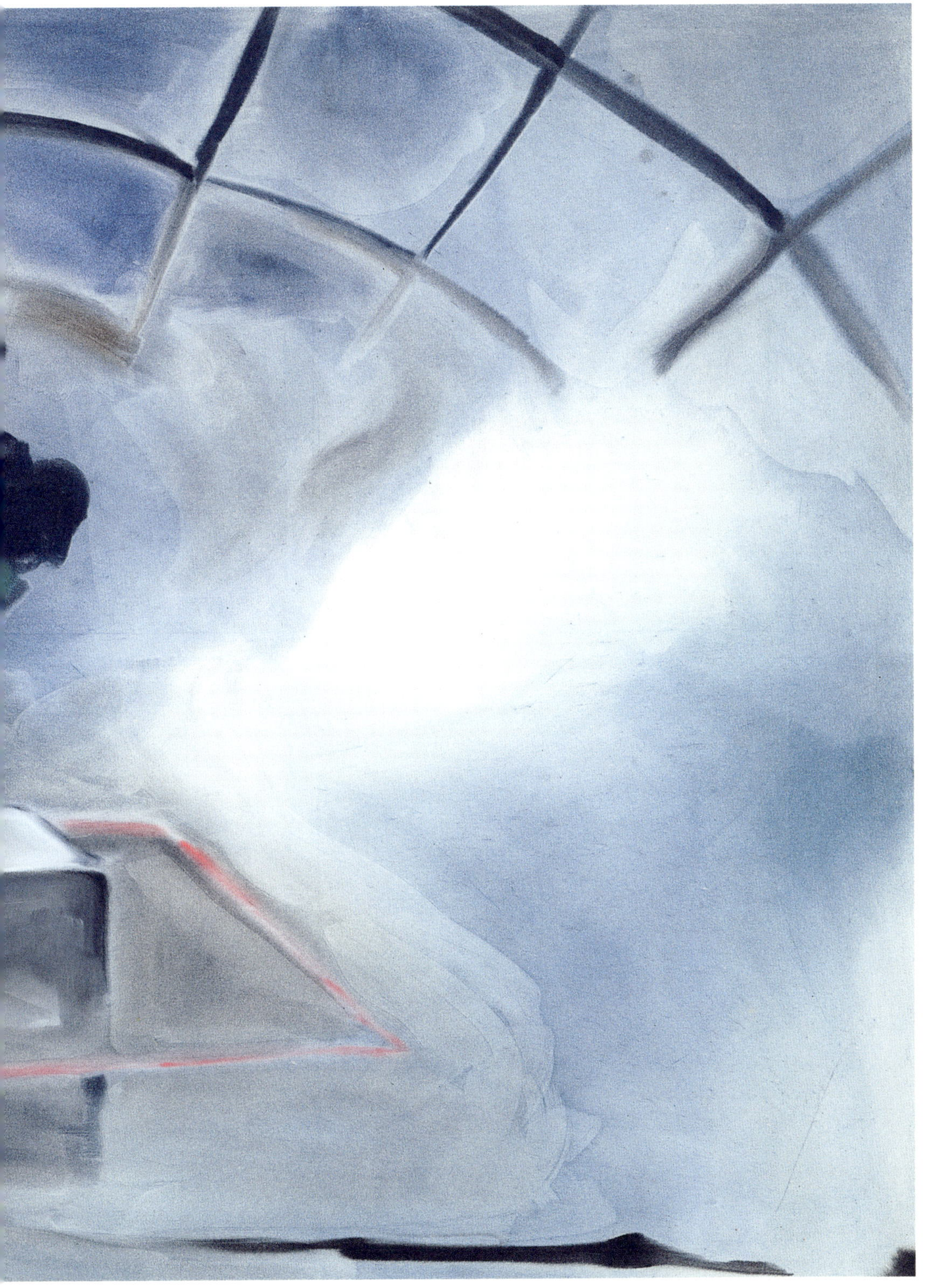

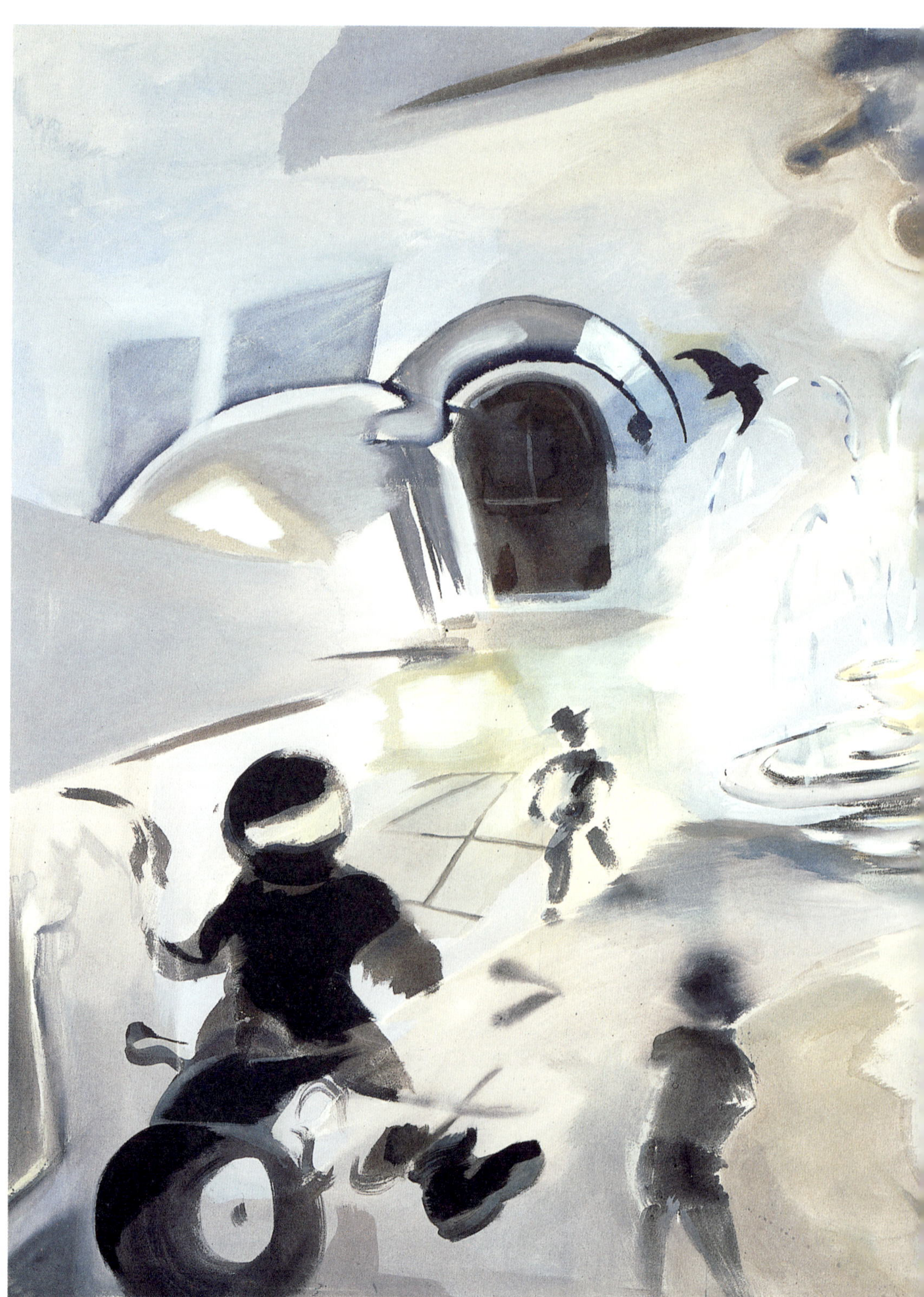

He was very pleased with where he was…, 2004

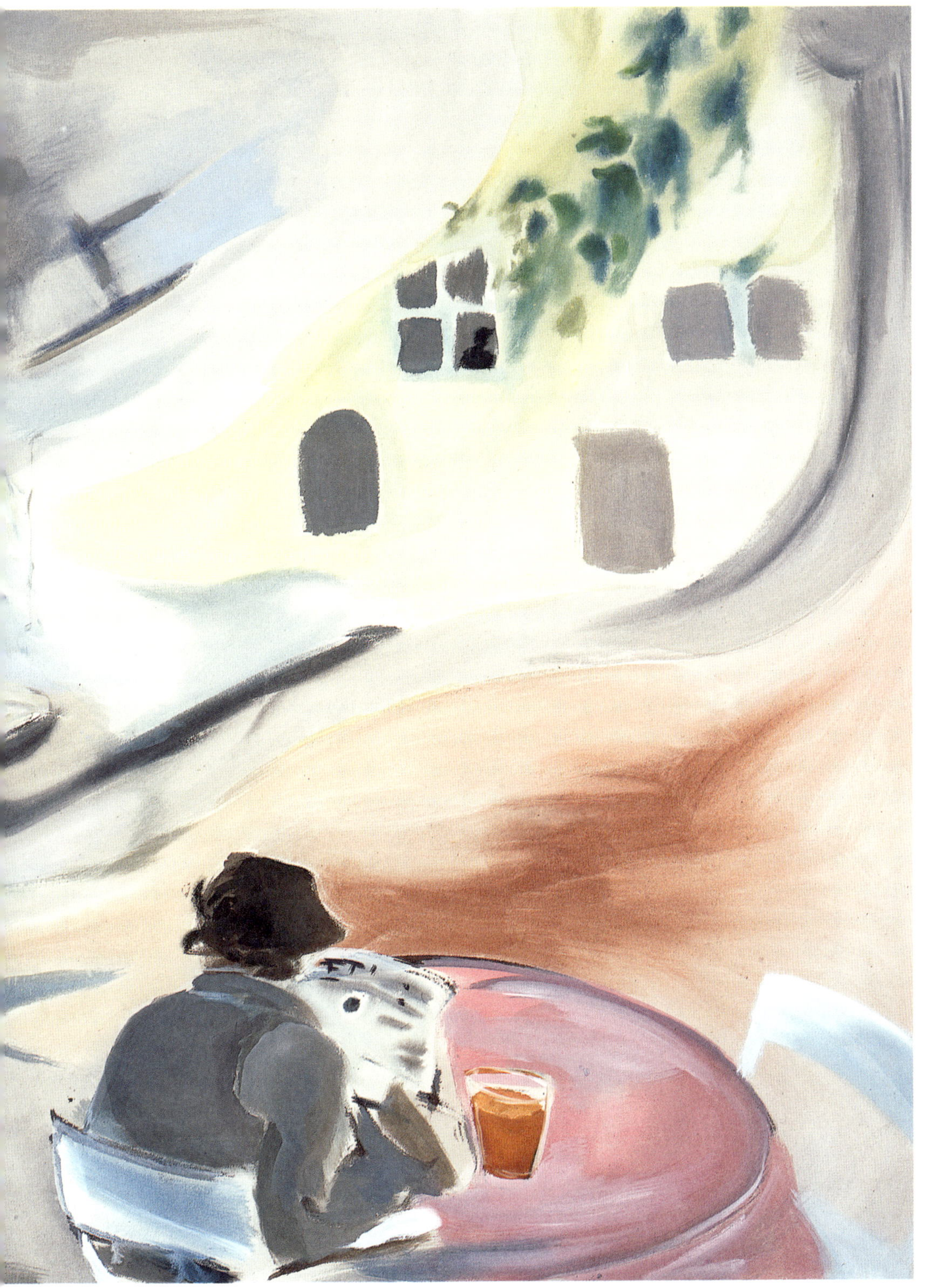

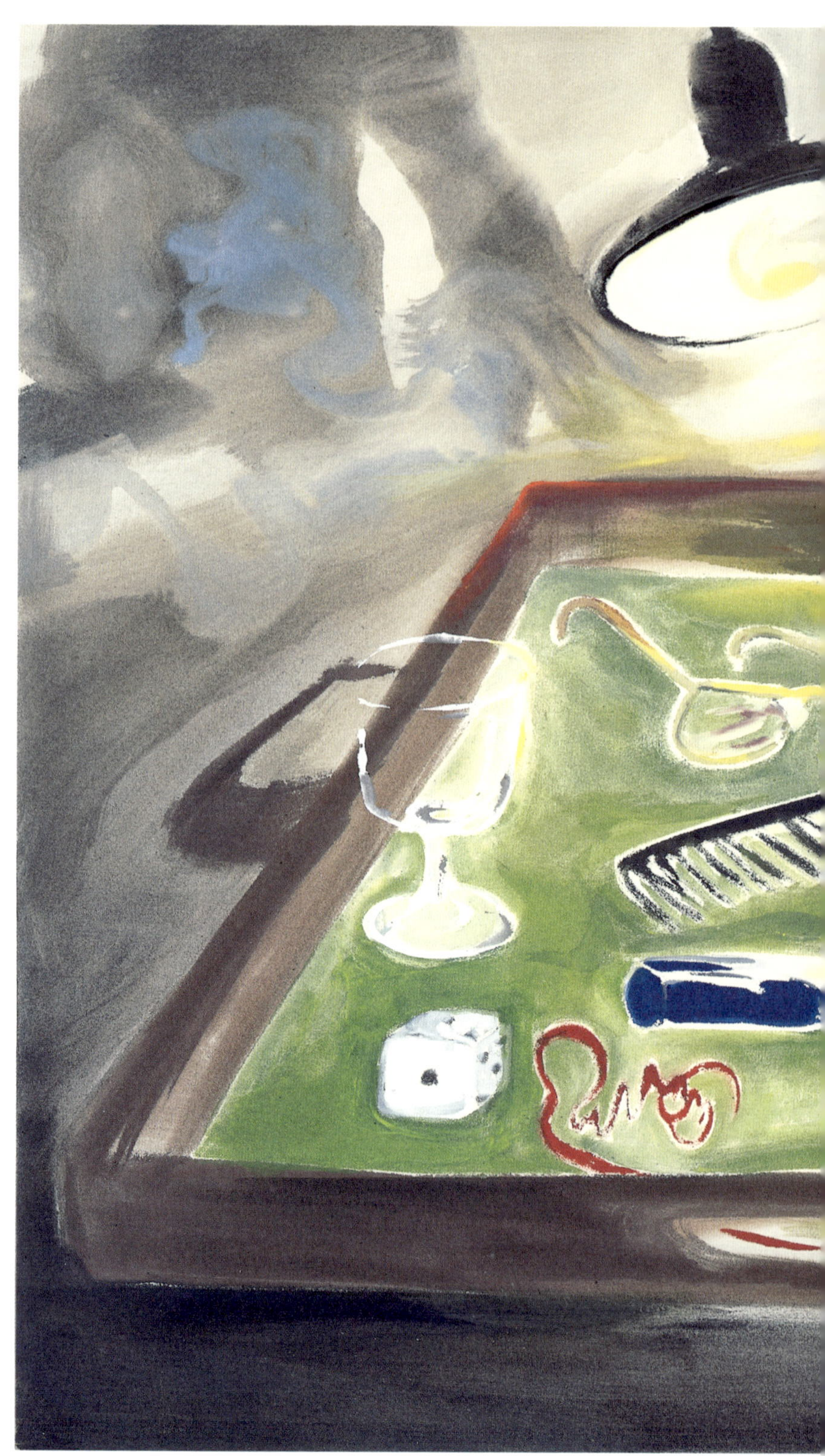

Kim Tray, 2004

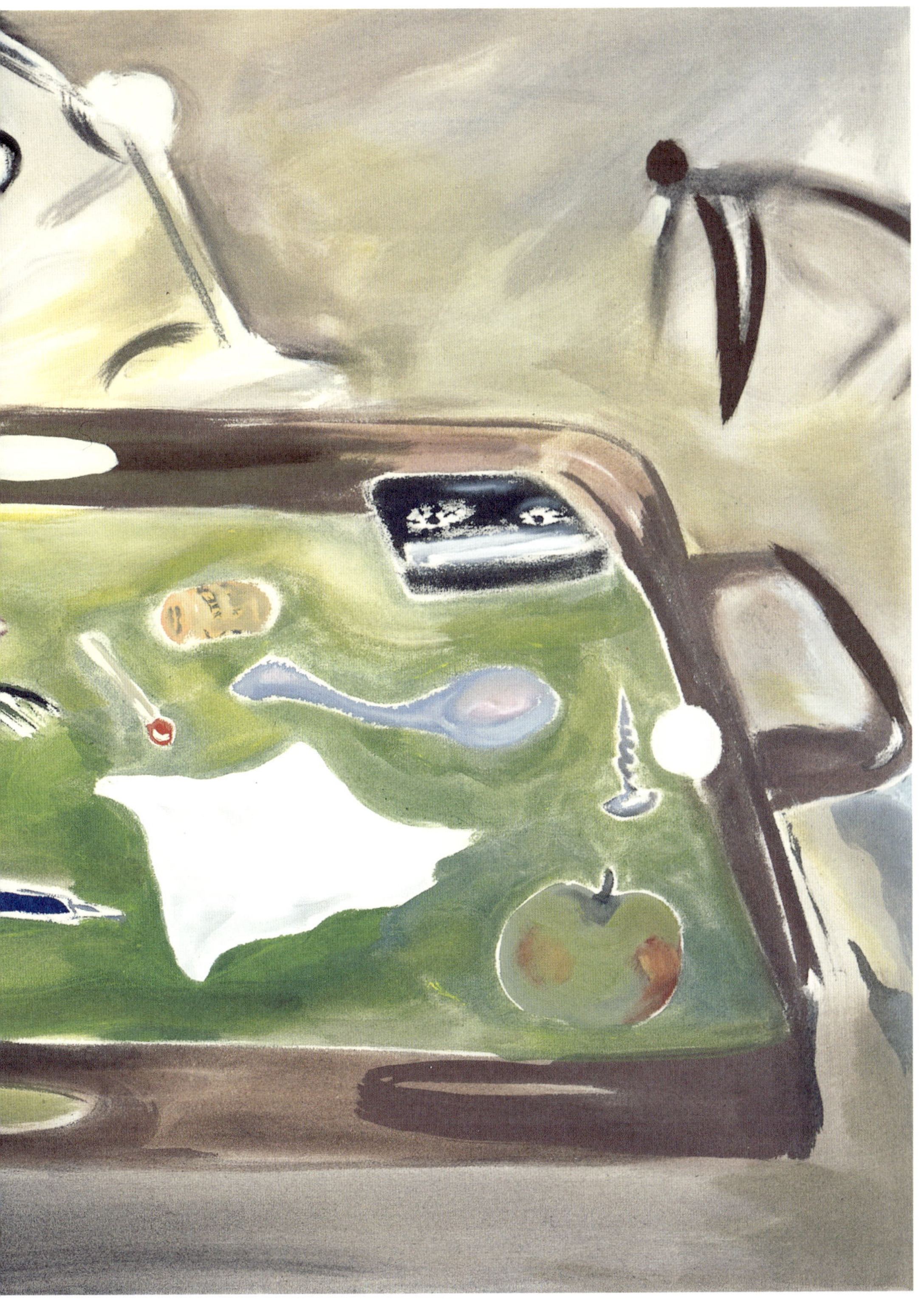

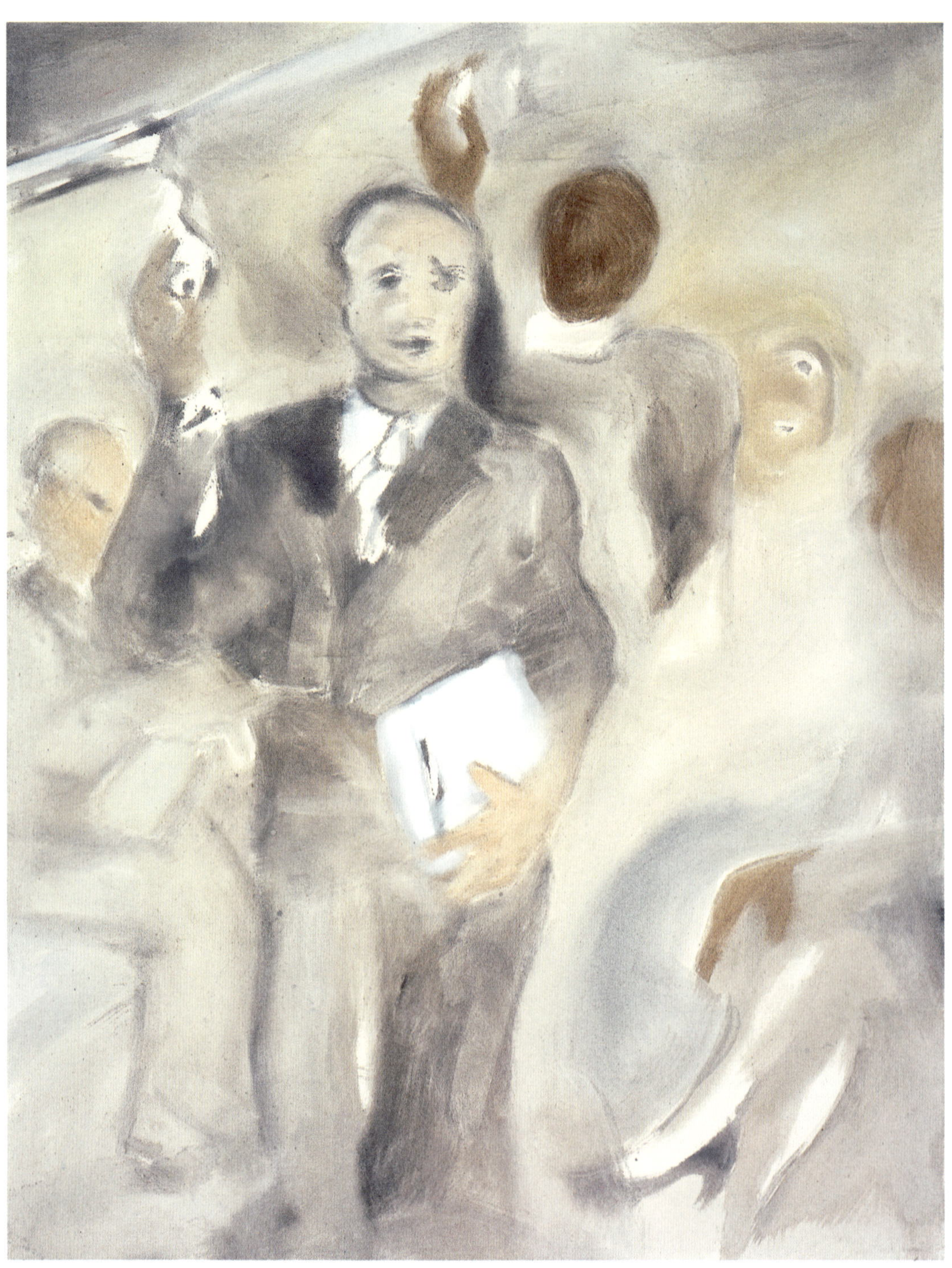

Peter F Shepyct, 2004

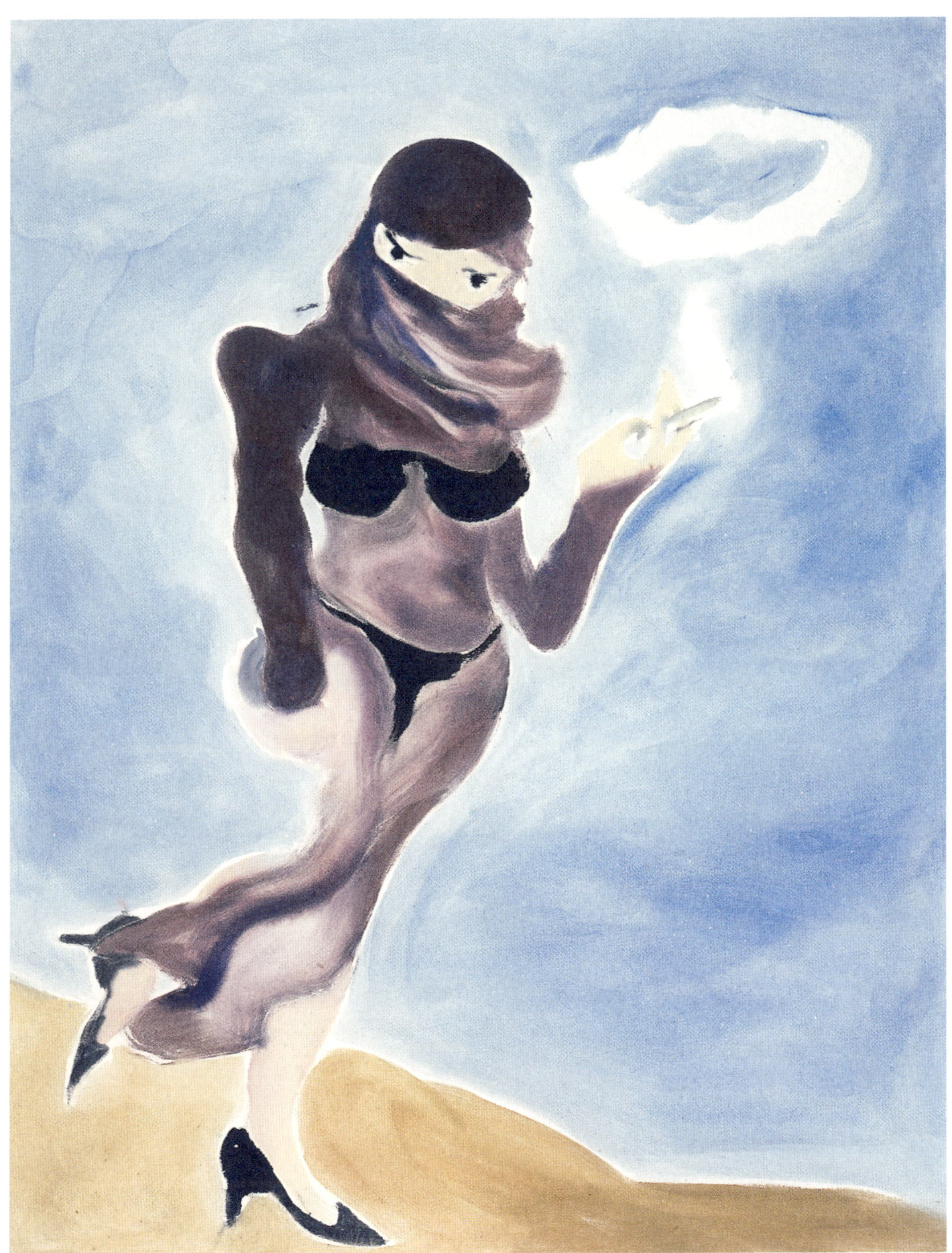

Agent Provocateur, 2004

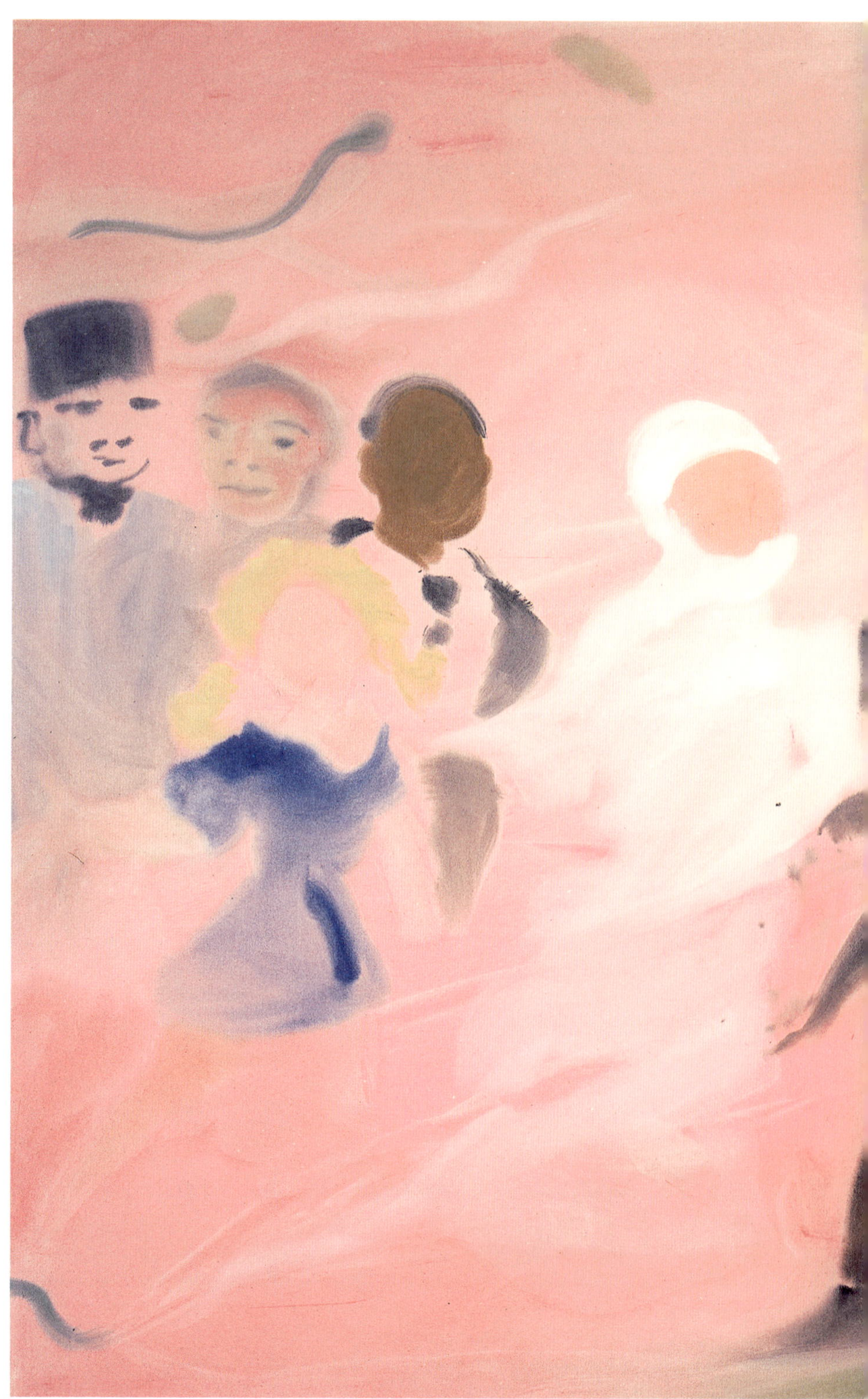

 Wedding, 2004

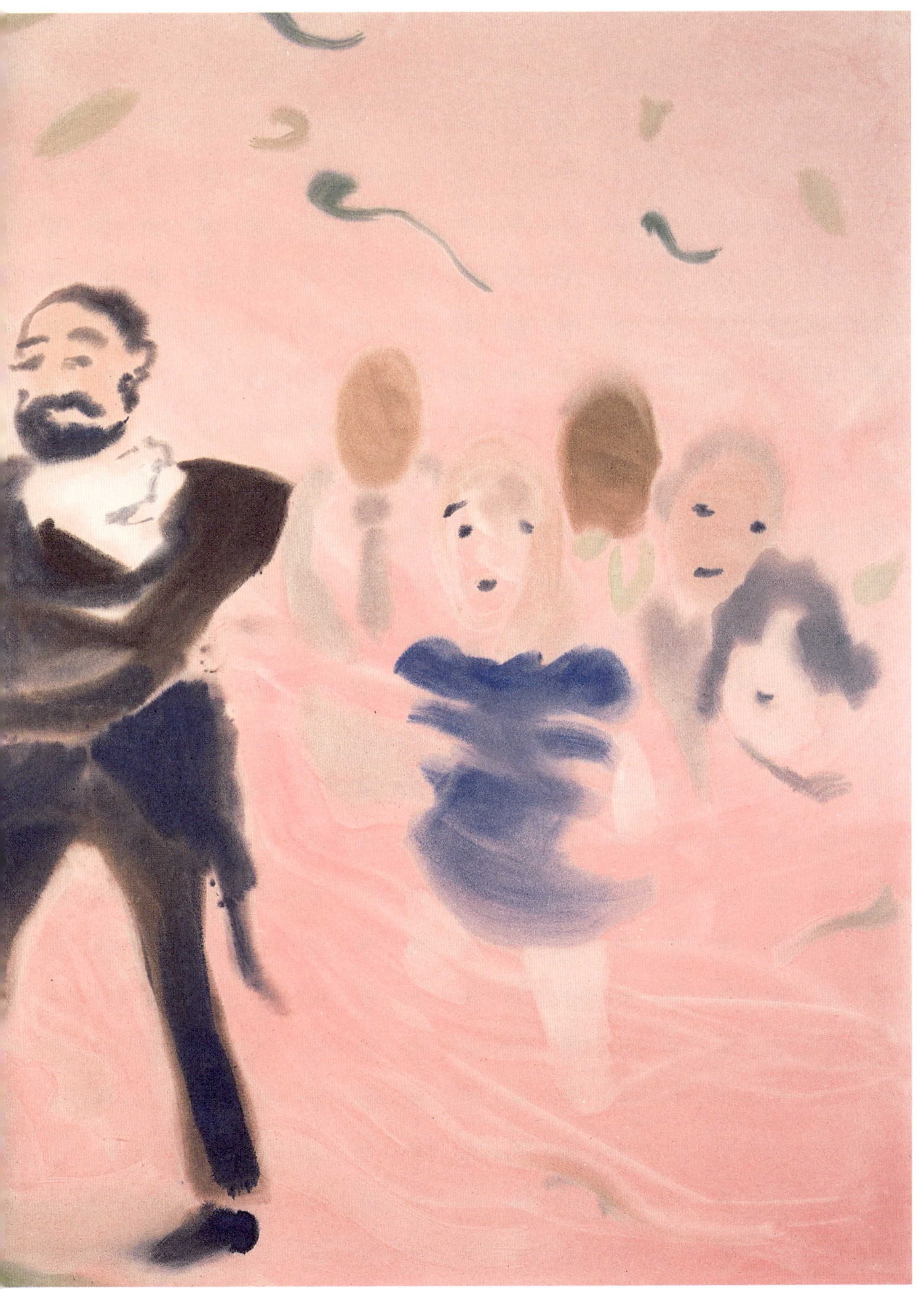

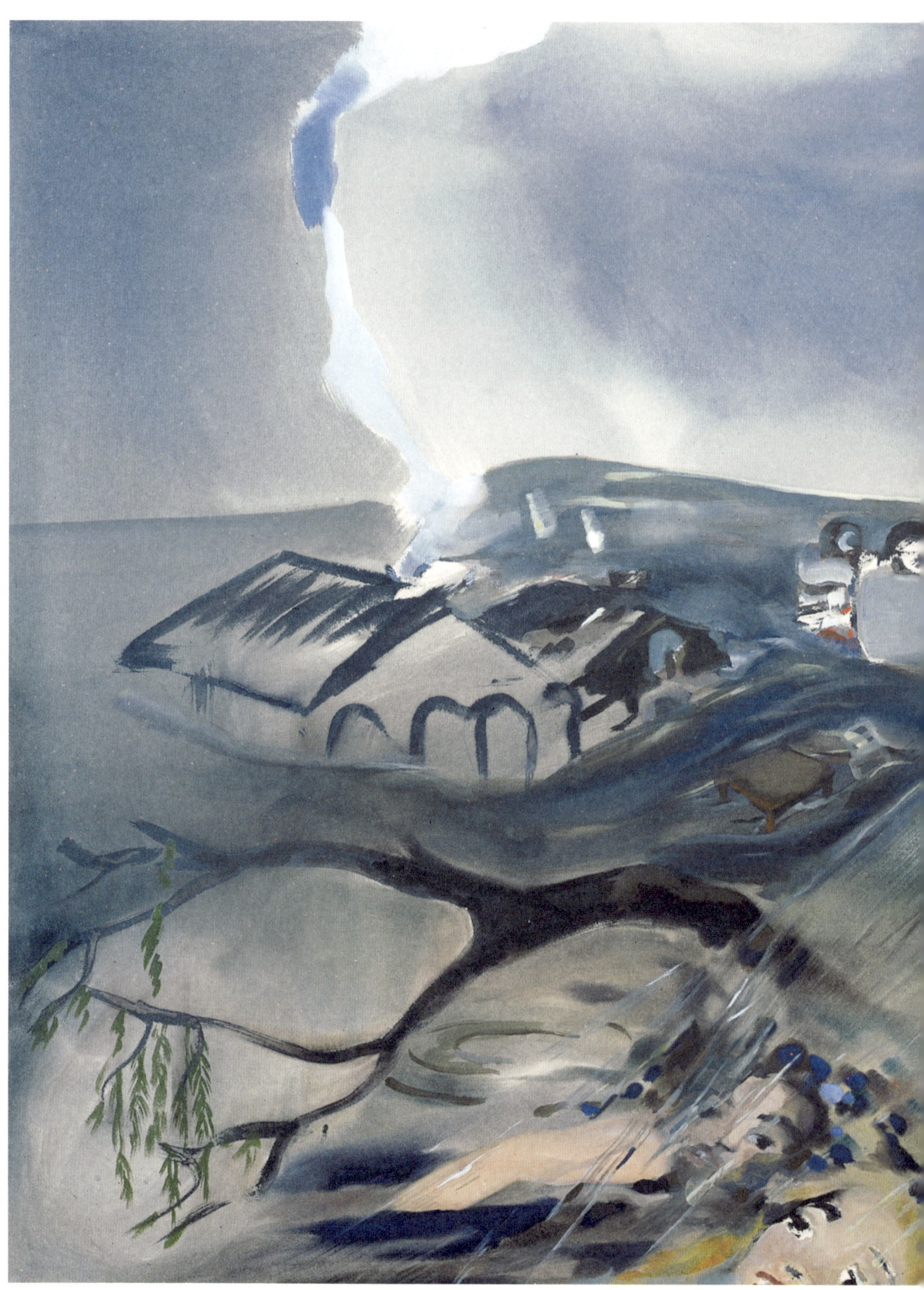

Sinners, 2004

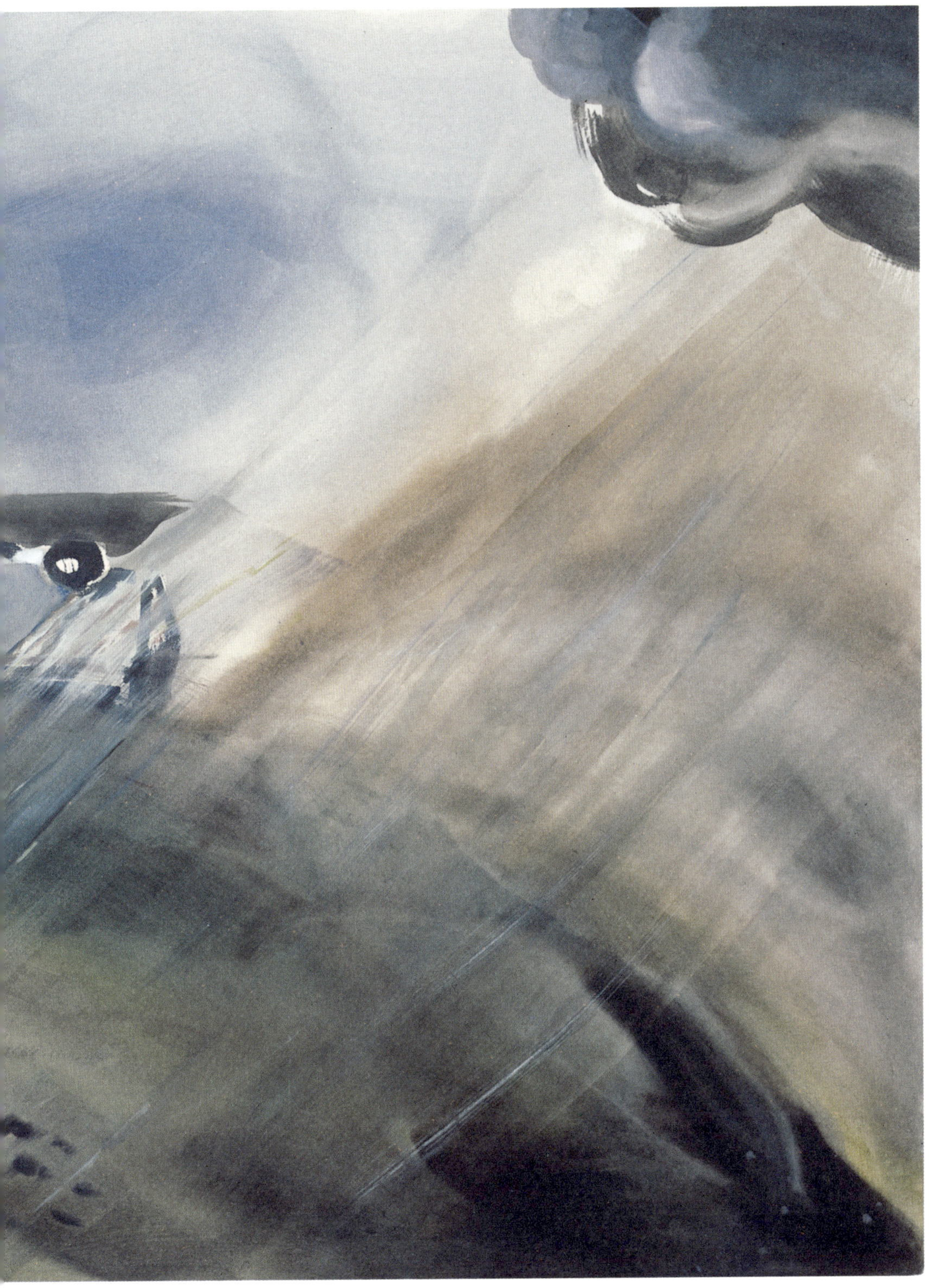

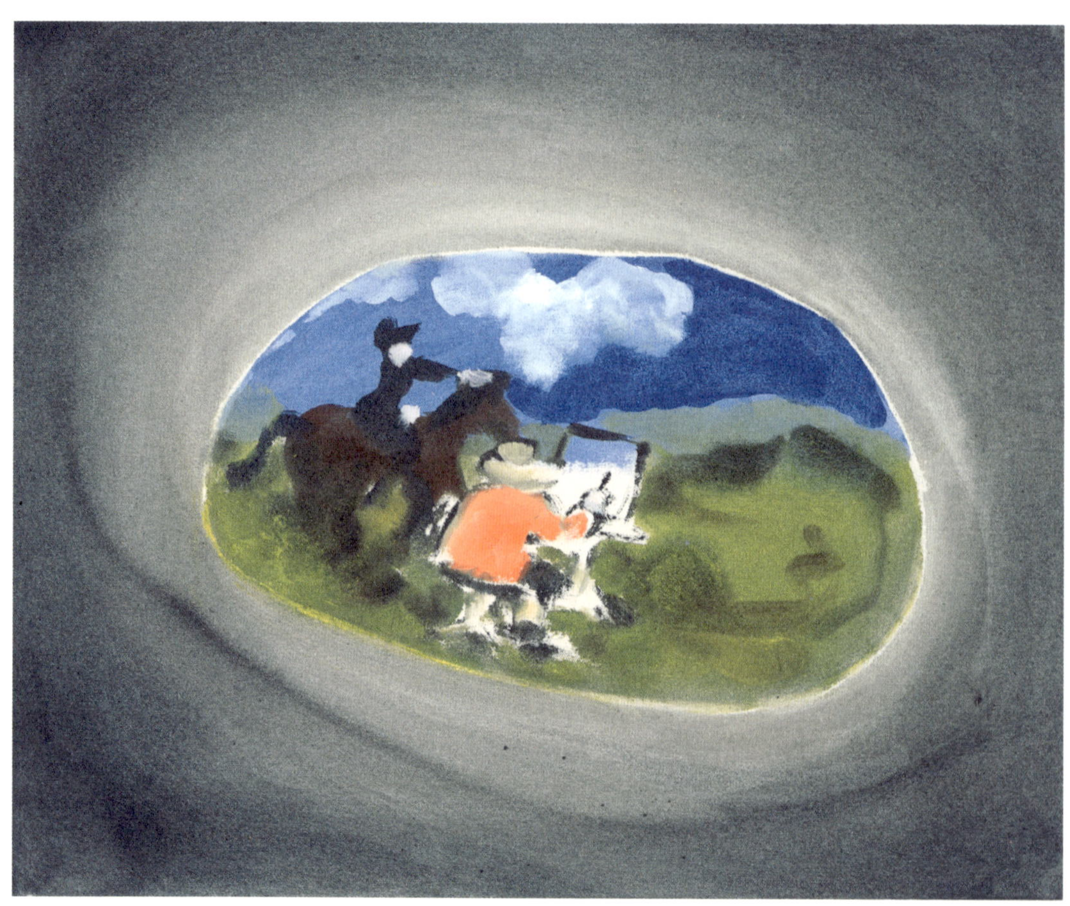

Why I wanted to be a painter, 2004

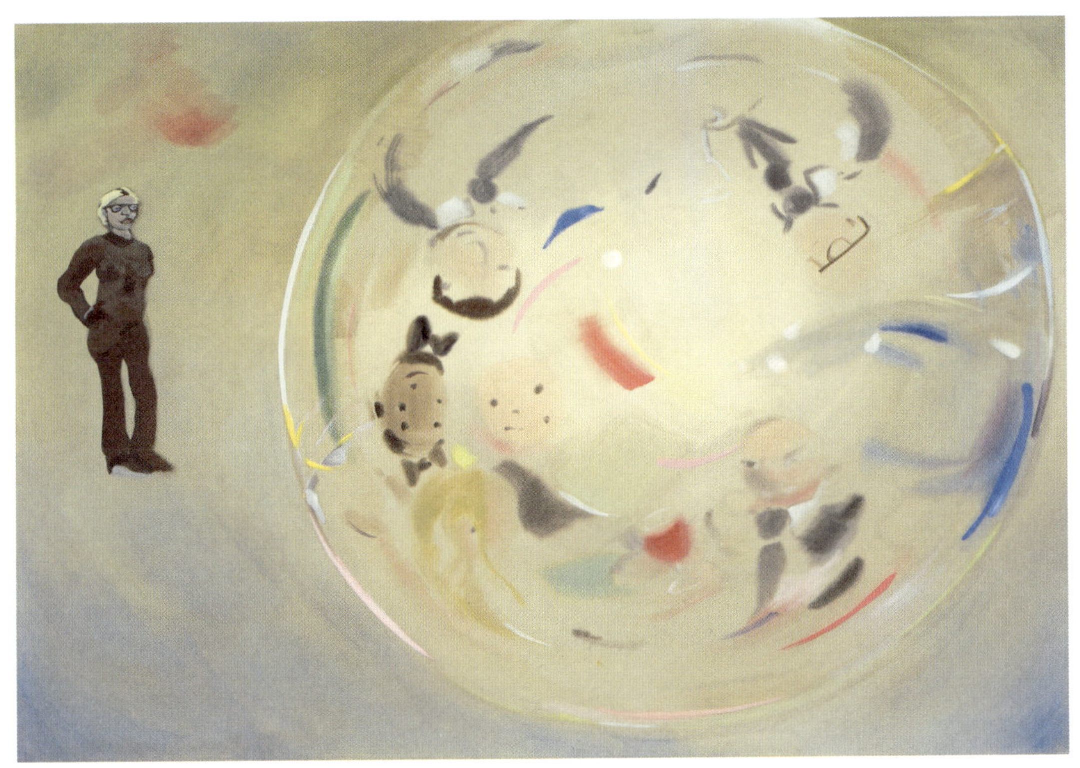

Untitled (Bubble), 2004

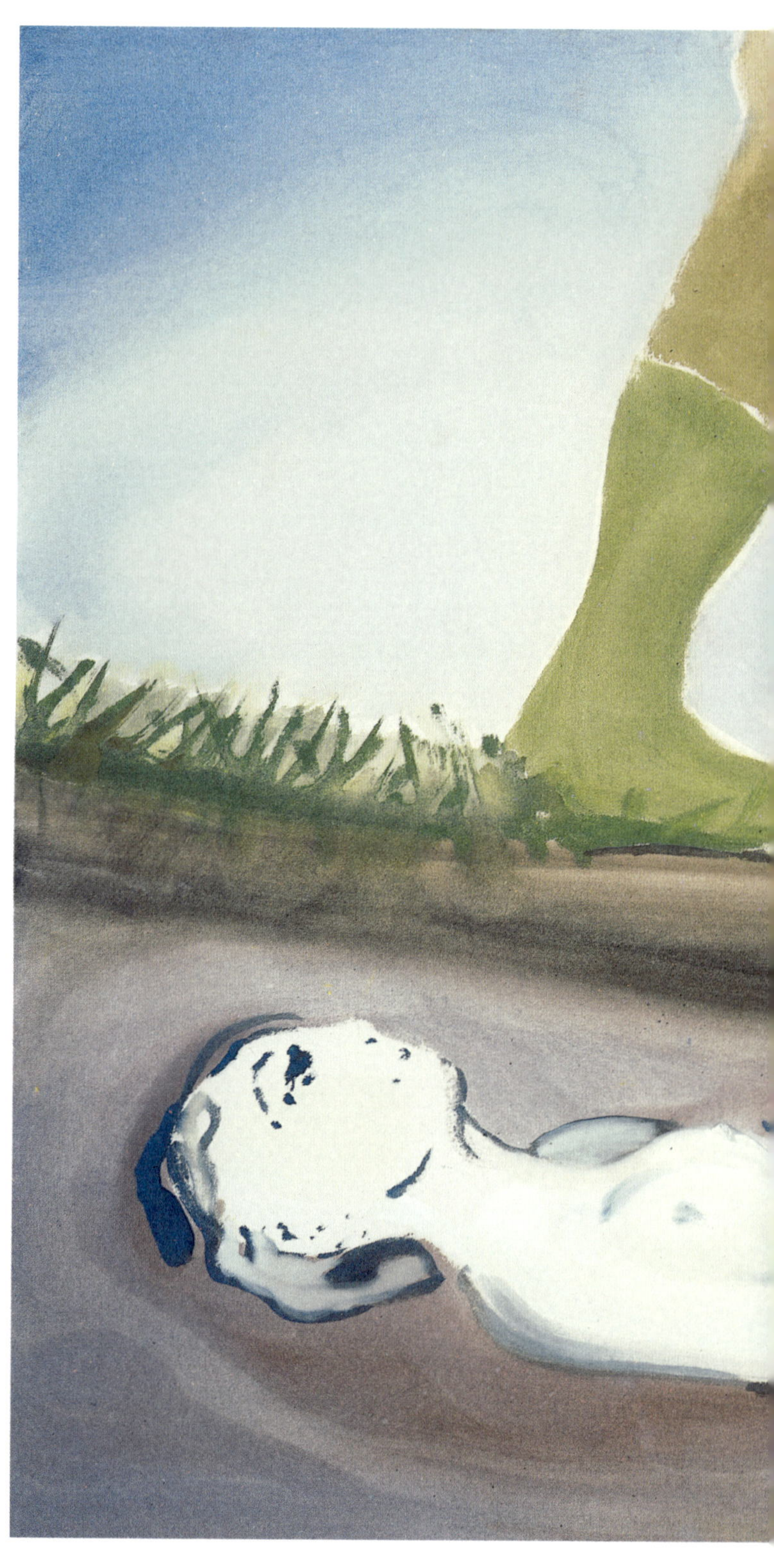

Long Time No See, 2005

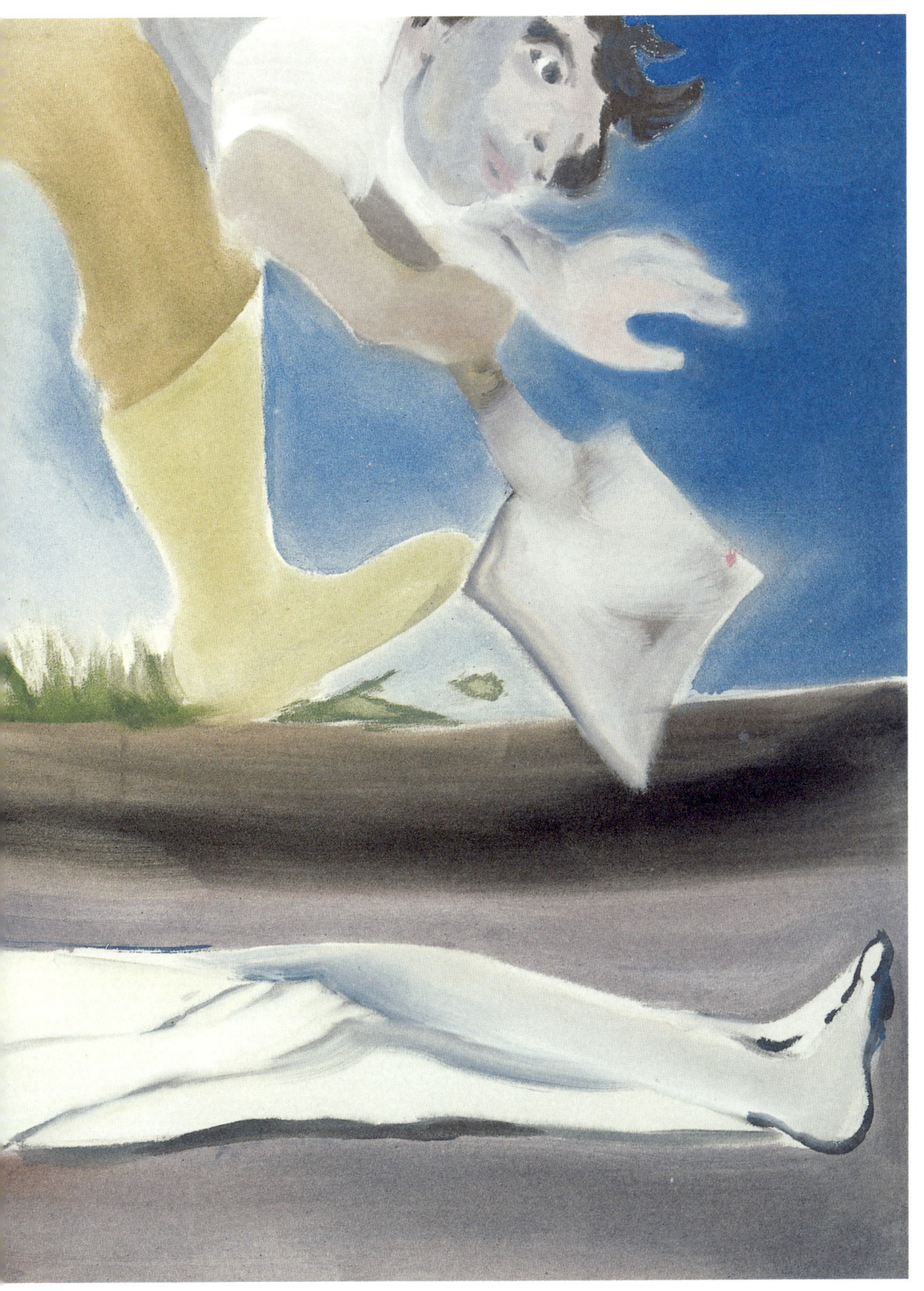

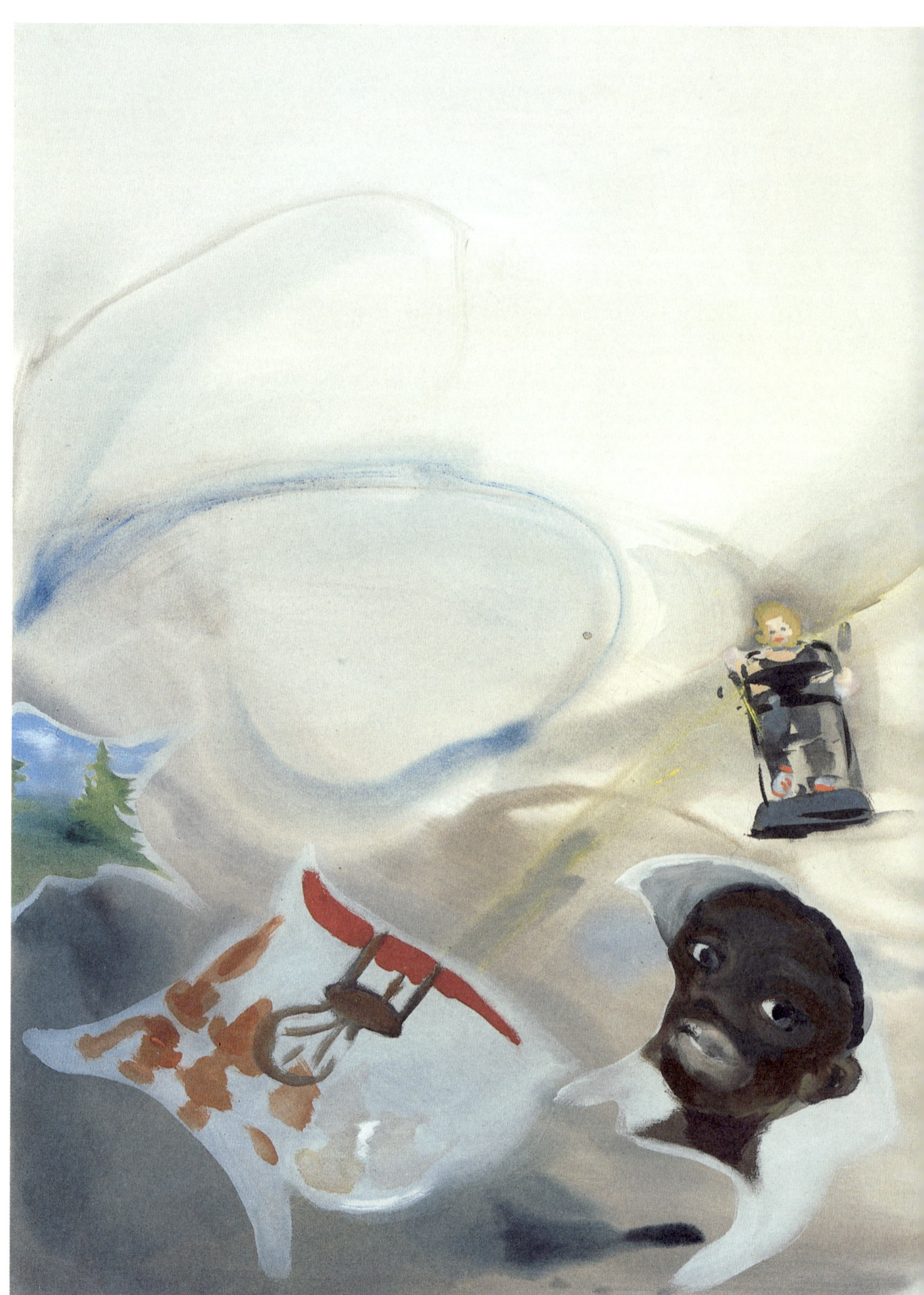

Low Blood Sugar, 2004

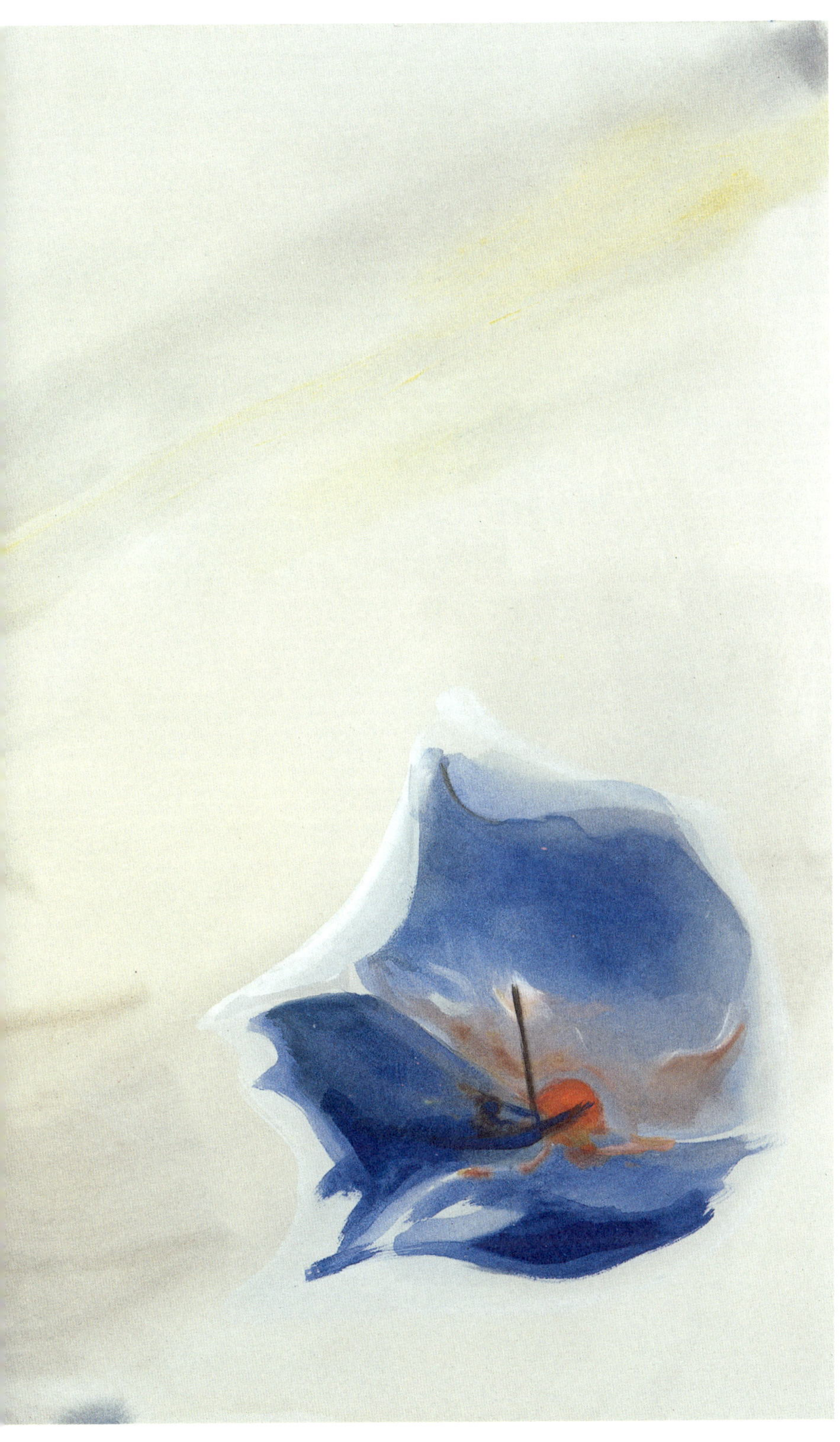

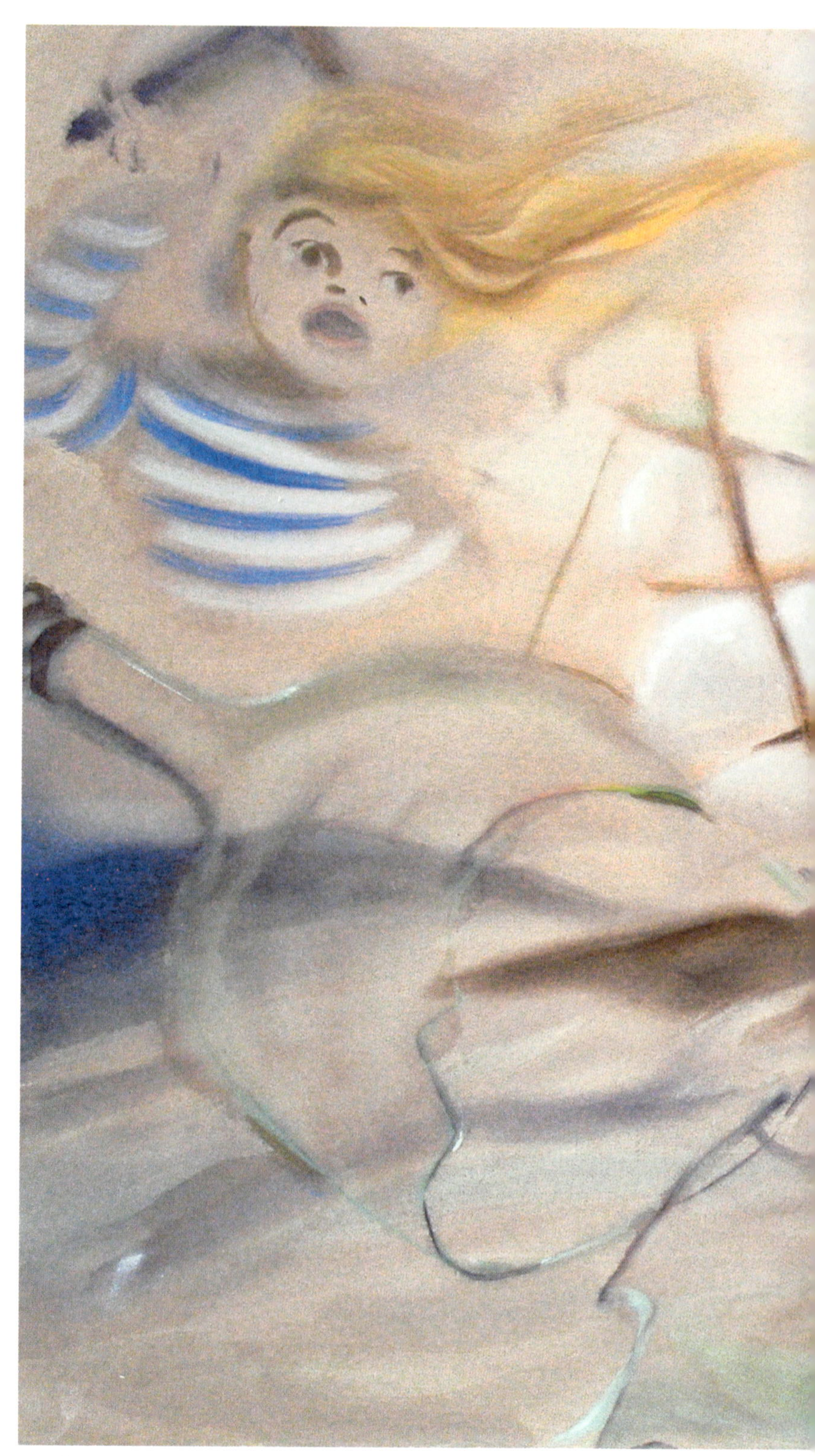

Youth in La Jolla, 2004

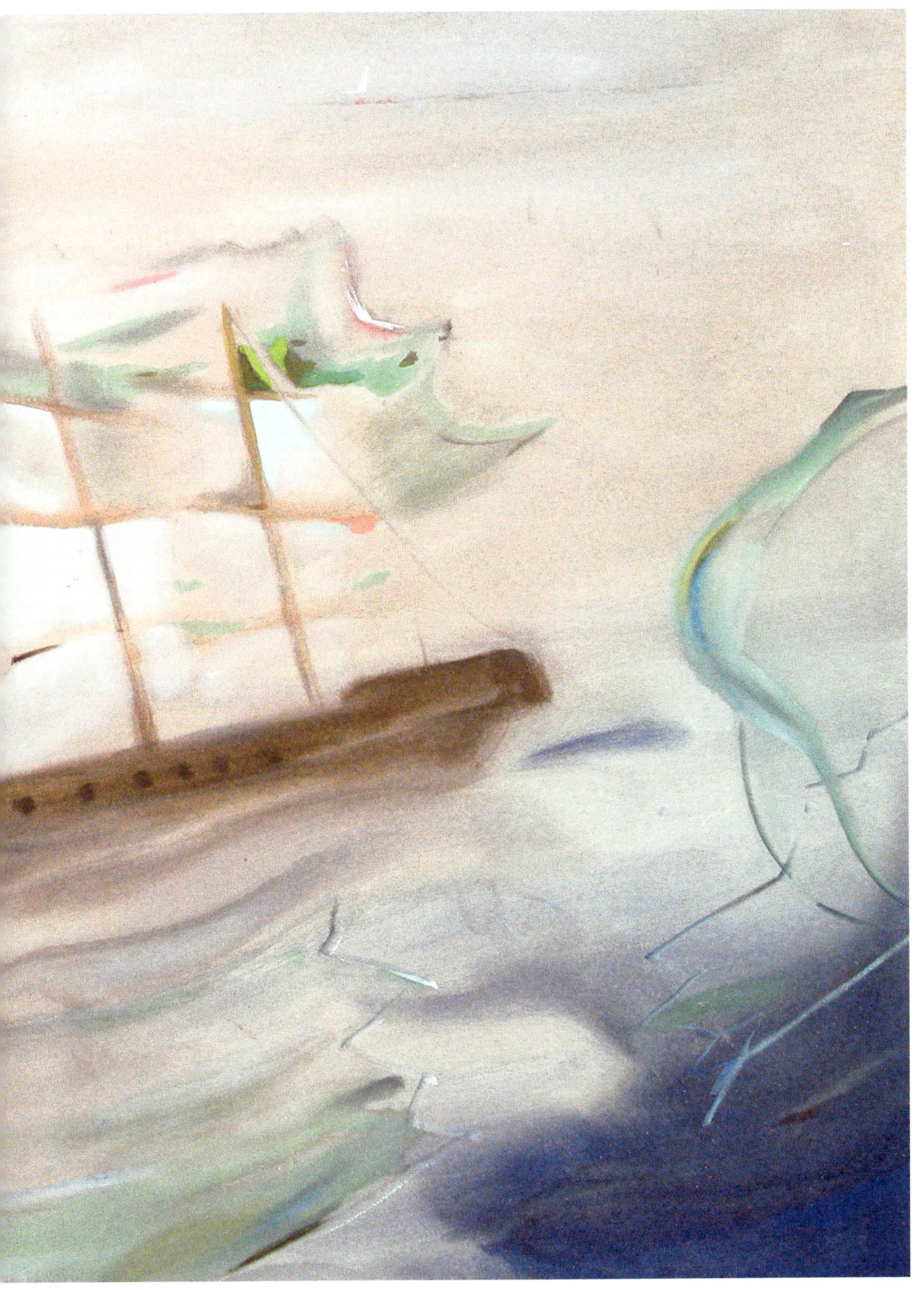

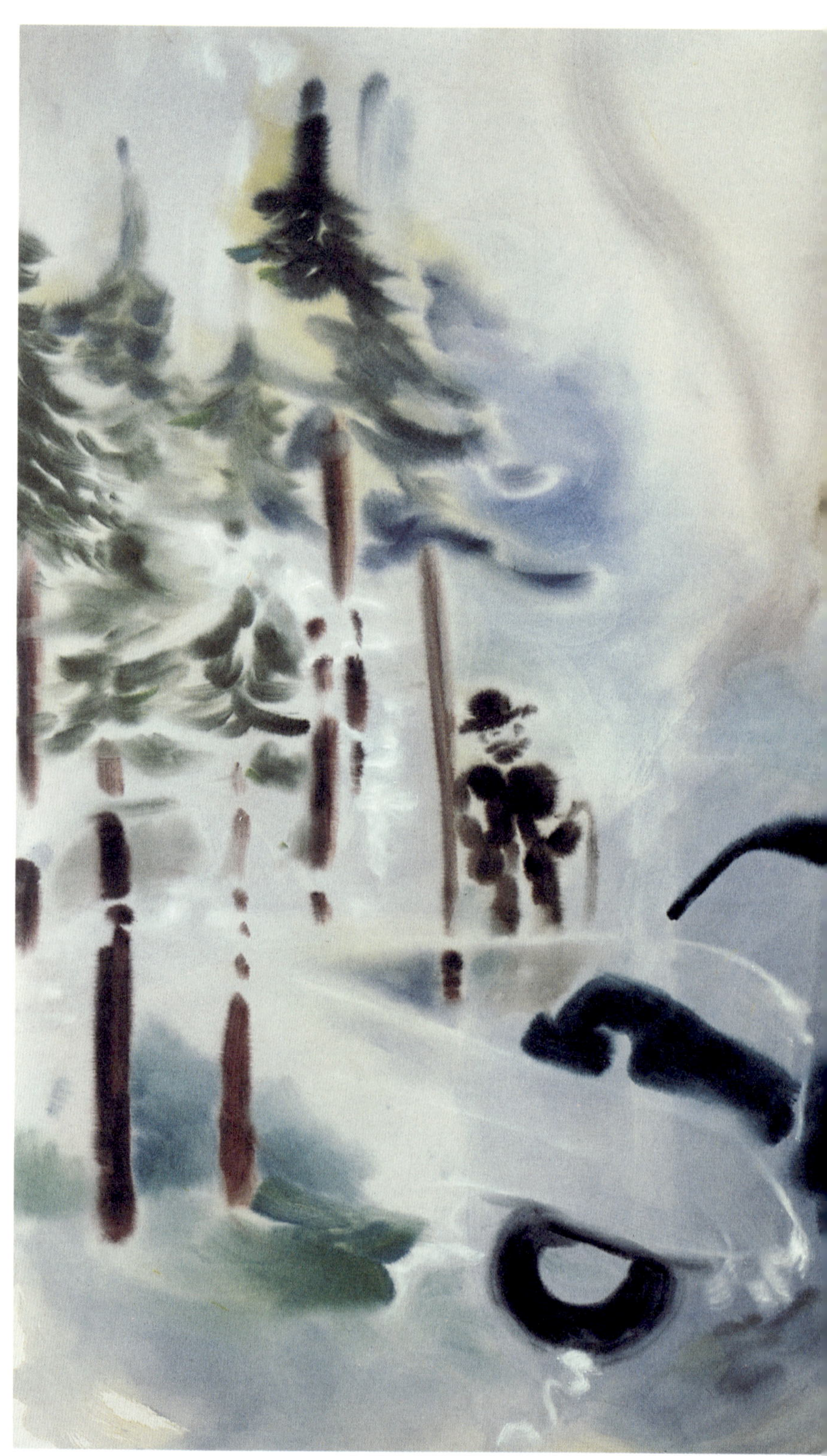

Death of the Maiden (Elfriede Jelinek), 2005

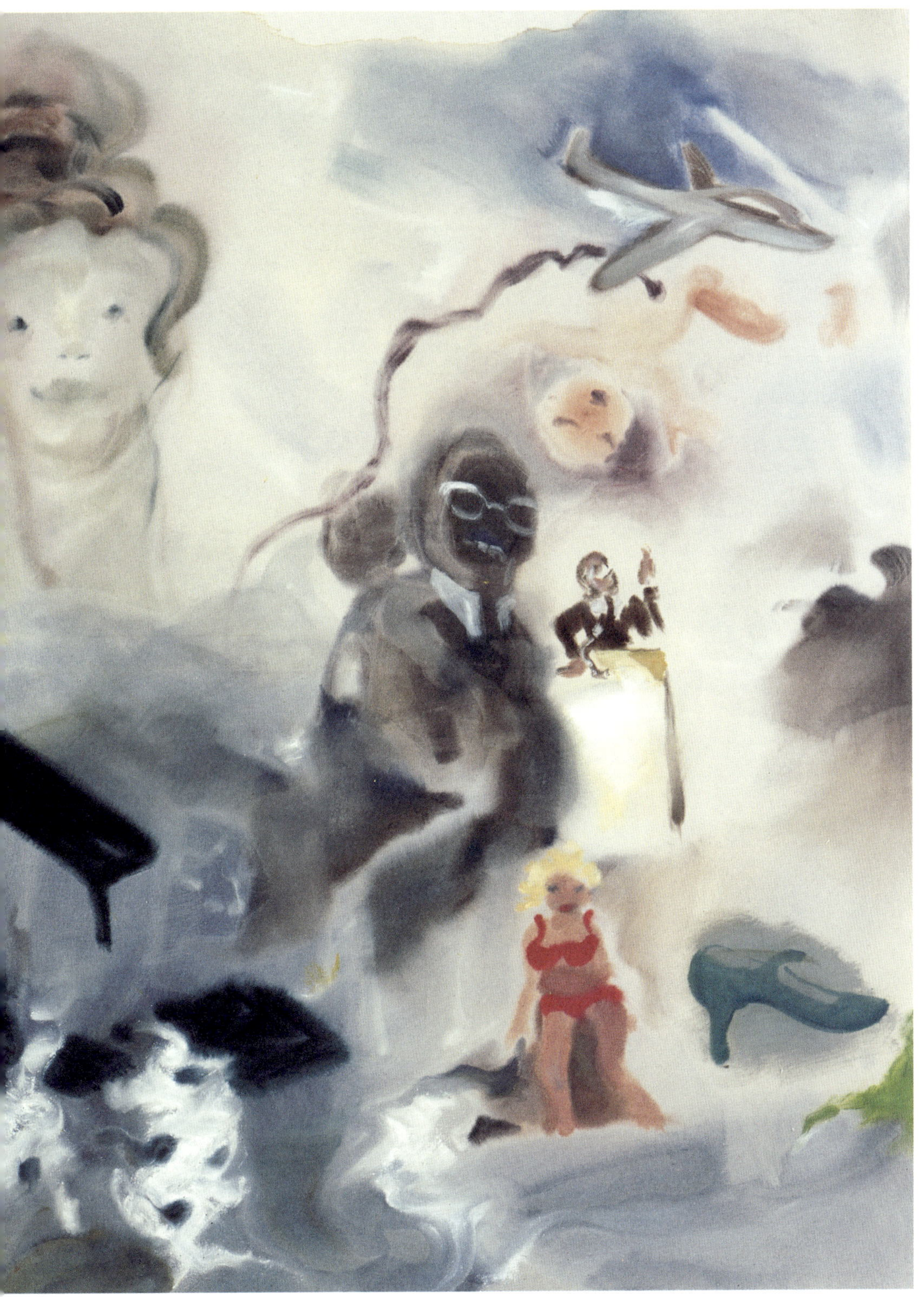

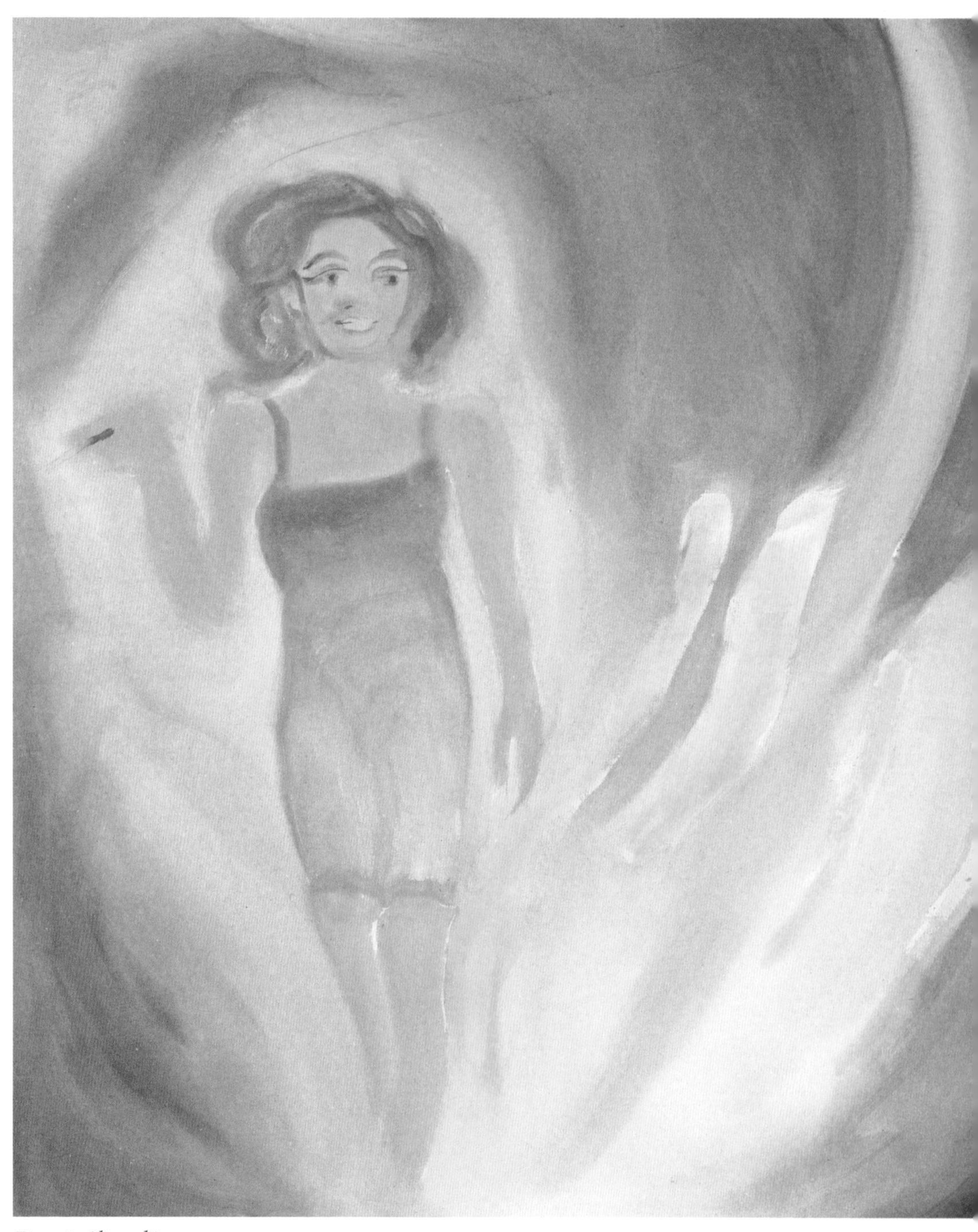

Einstein (diptych), 2005

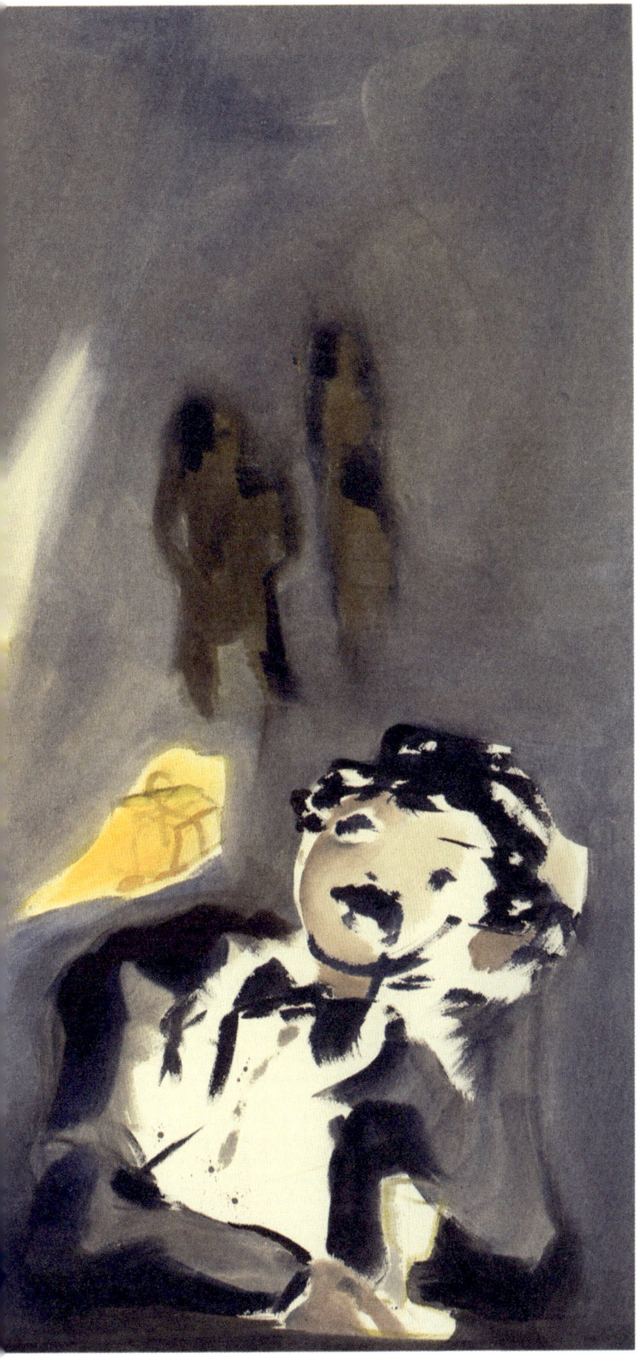

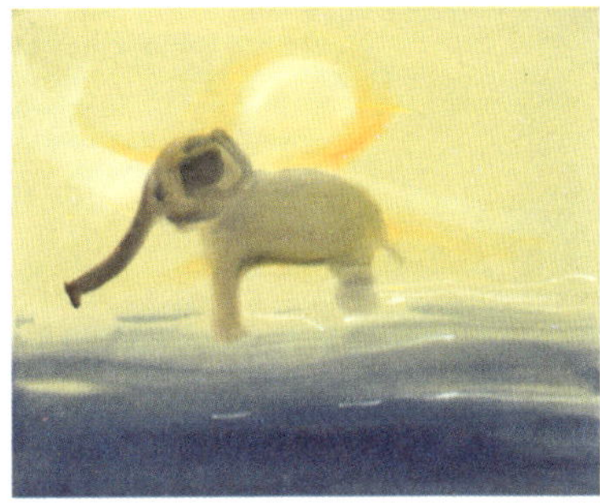

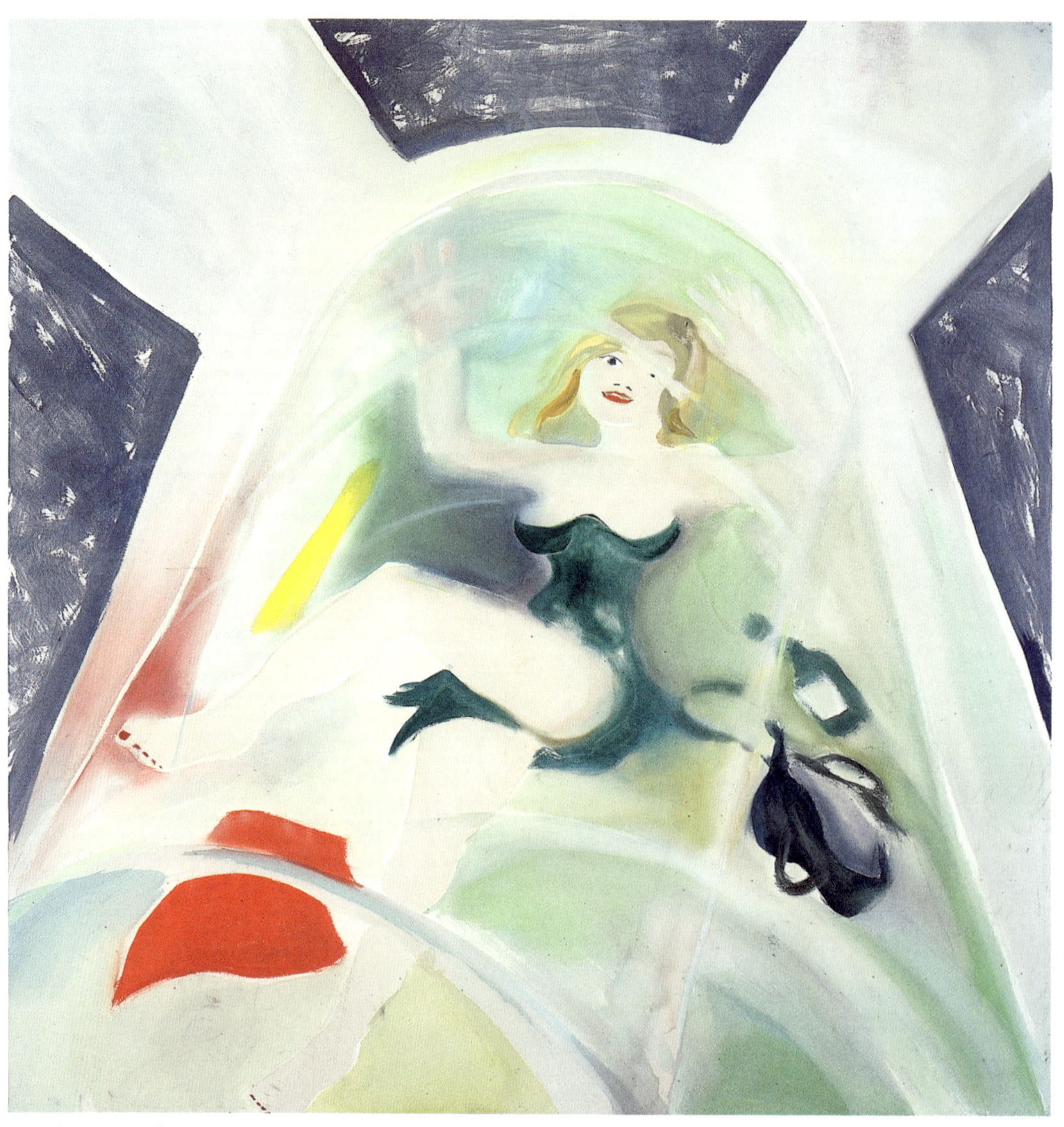

Good Space Girl, 2005

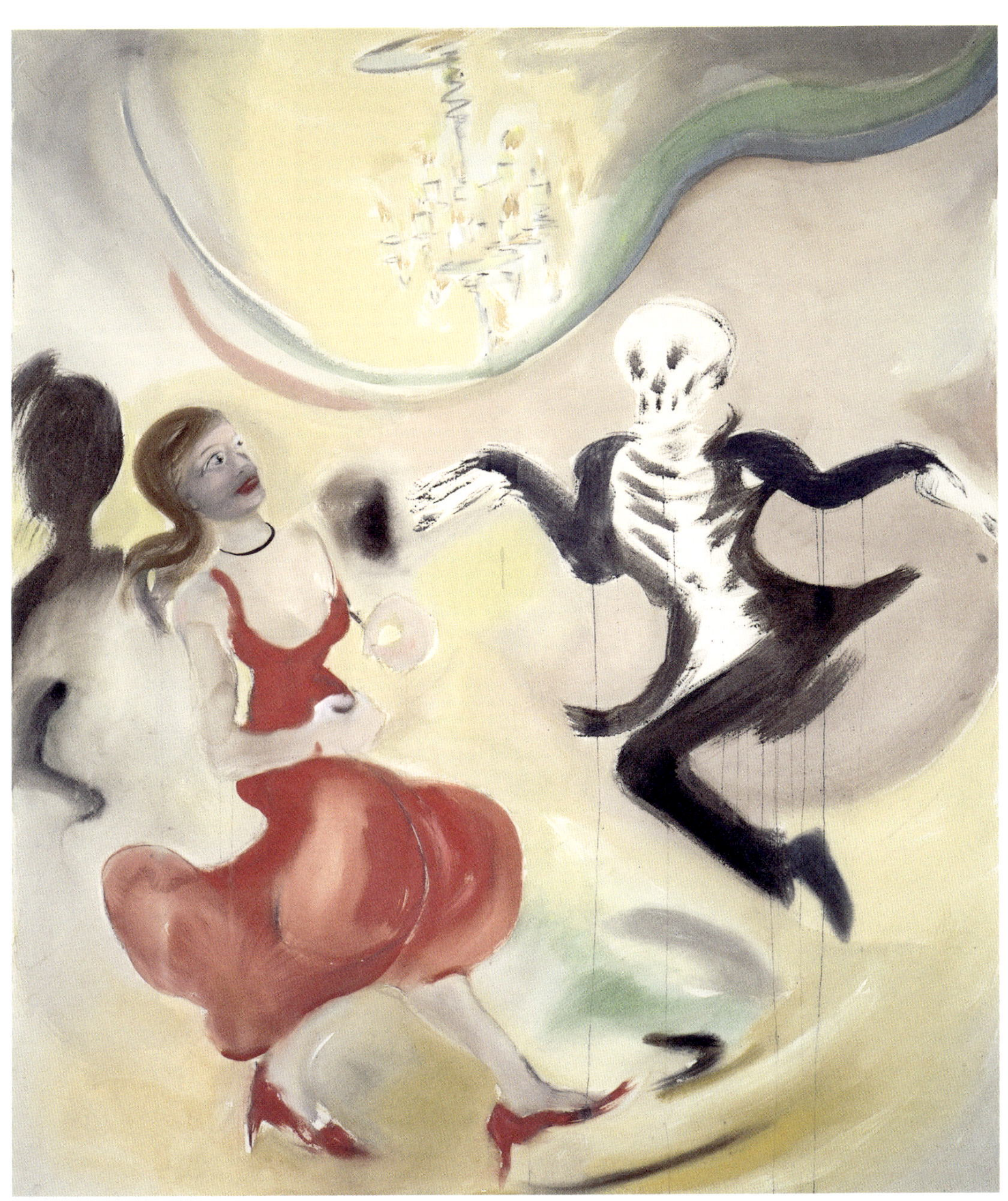

Her Death was Hysterical, 2005

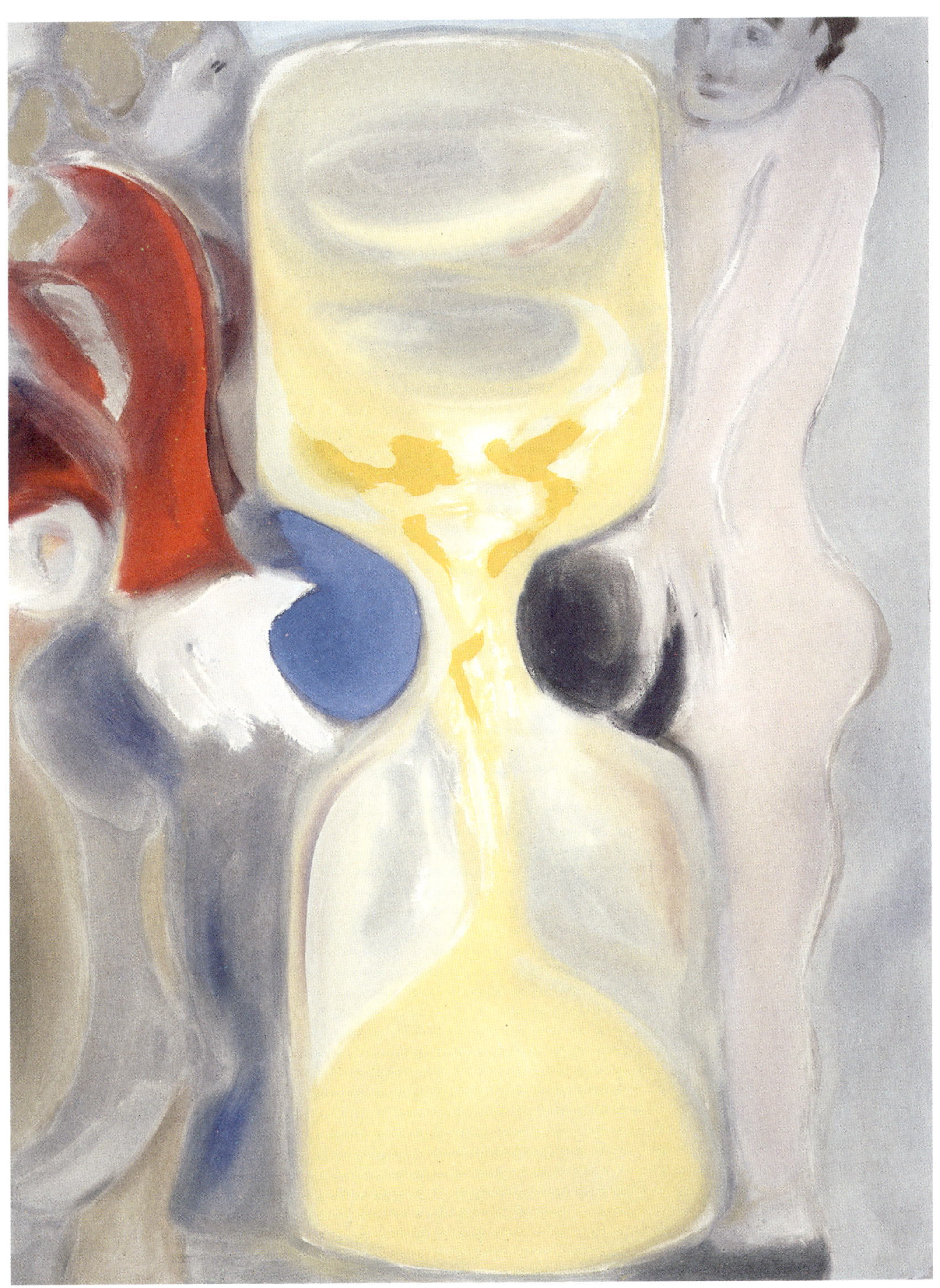

Time is on my side, 2005

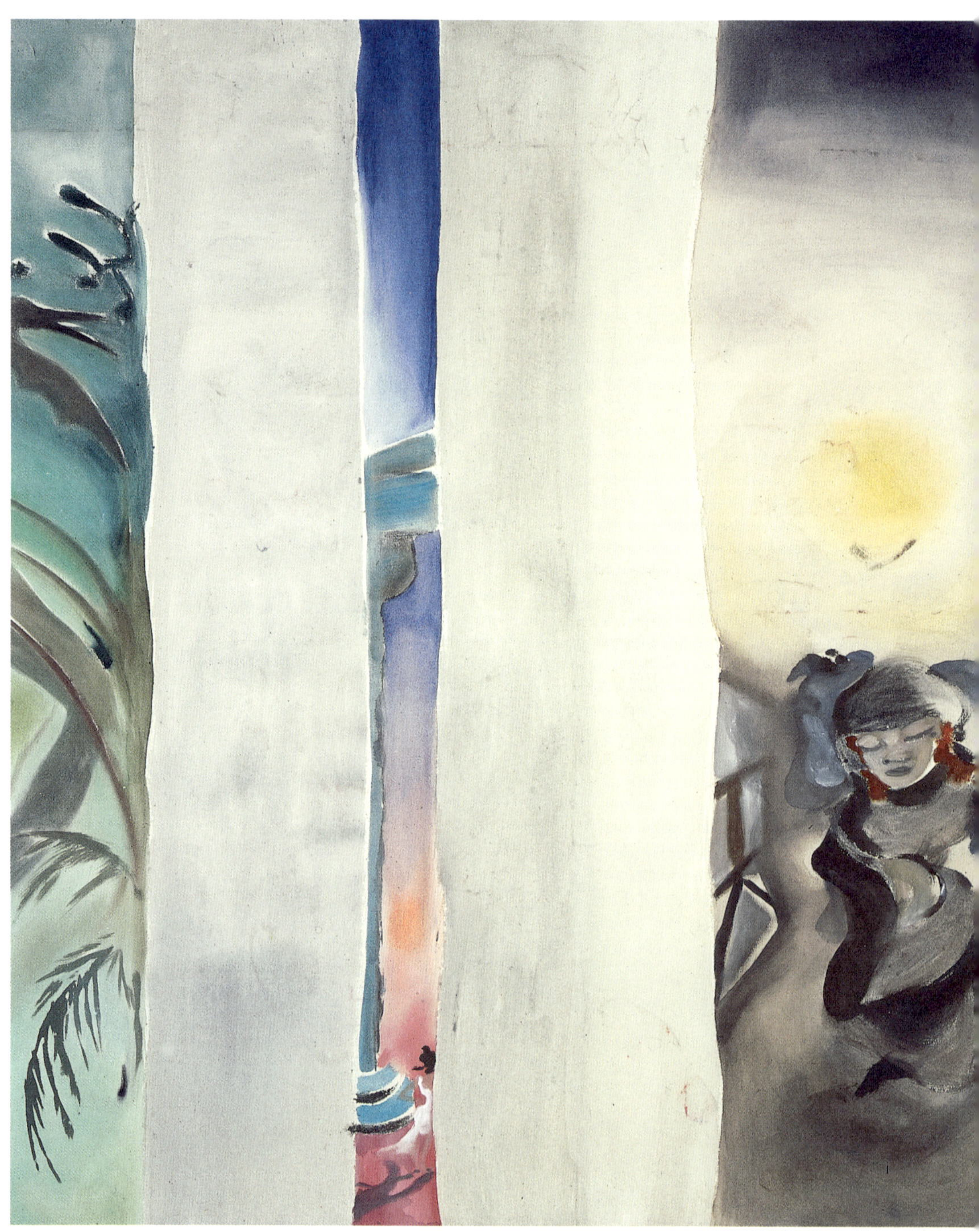

Old Woman, 2005

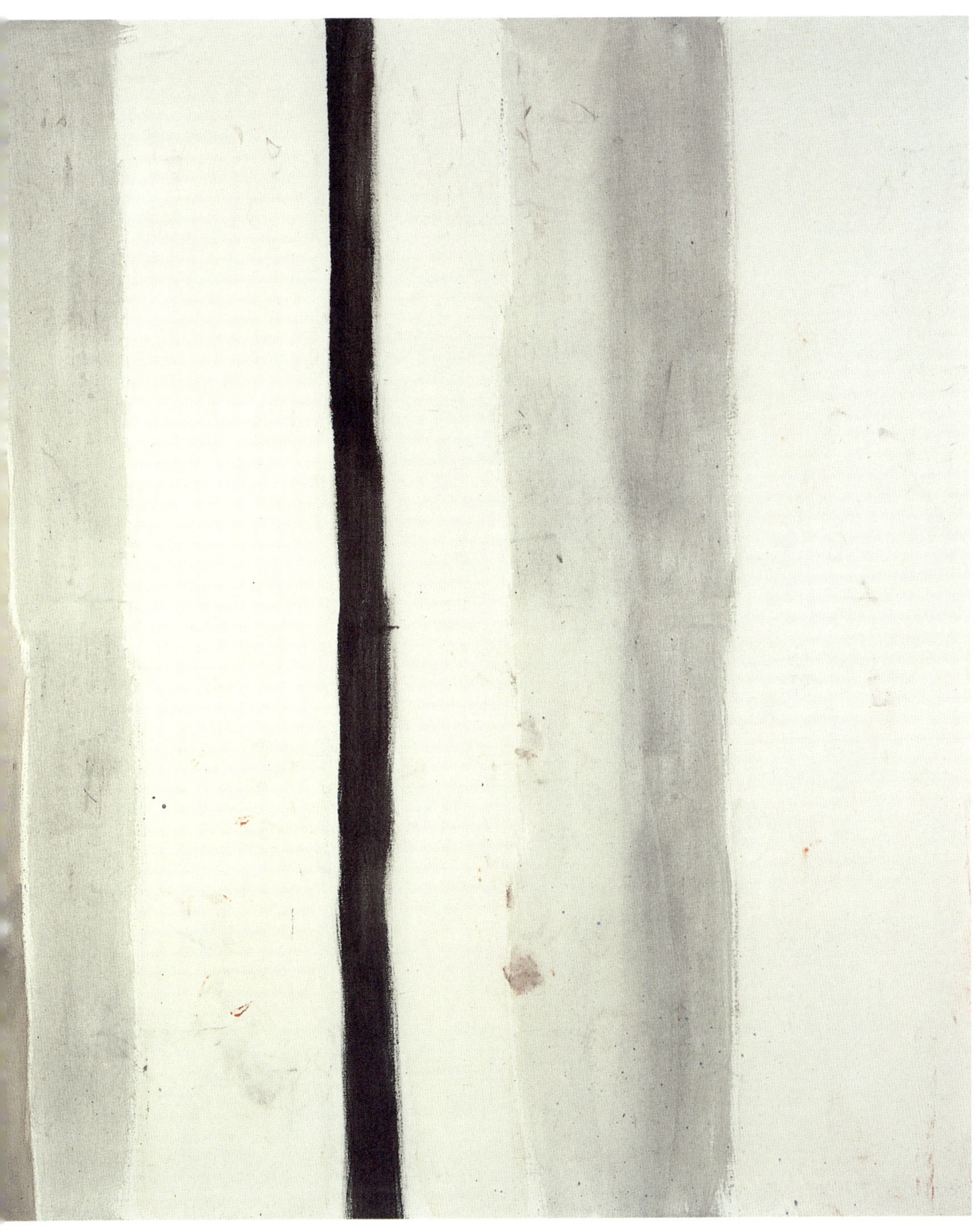

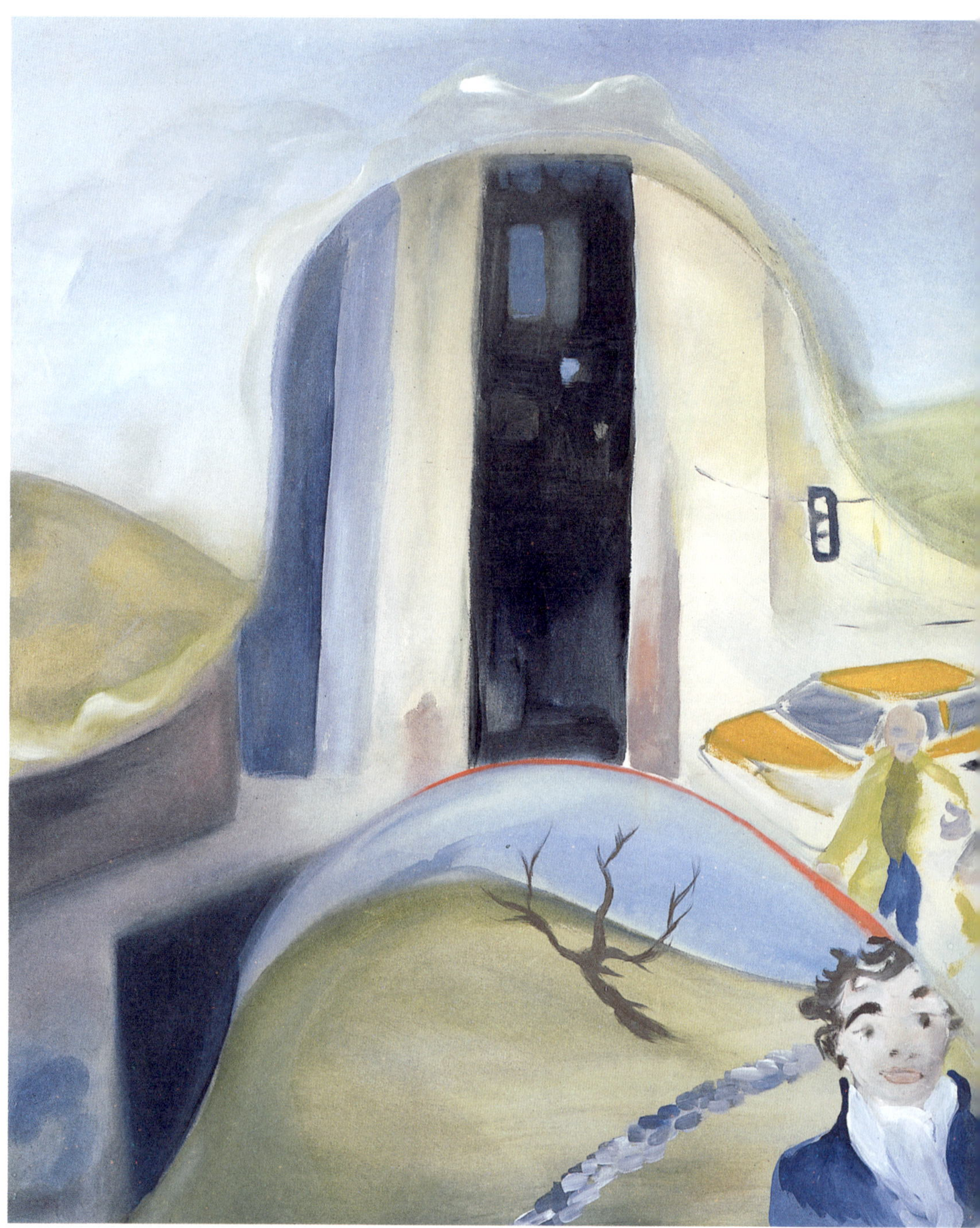

New York Shire Space Time Continuum, 2005

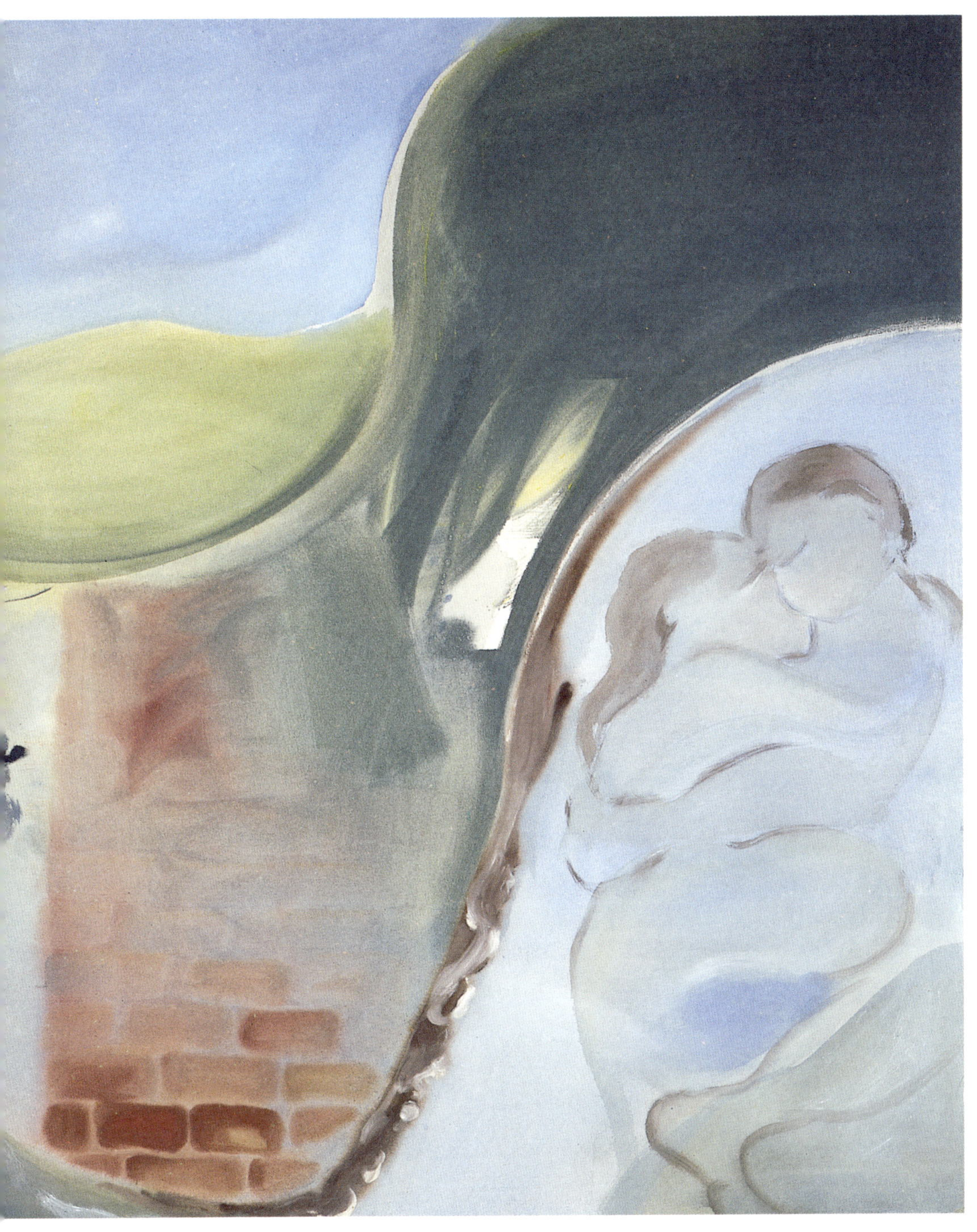

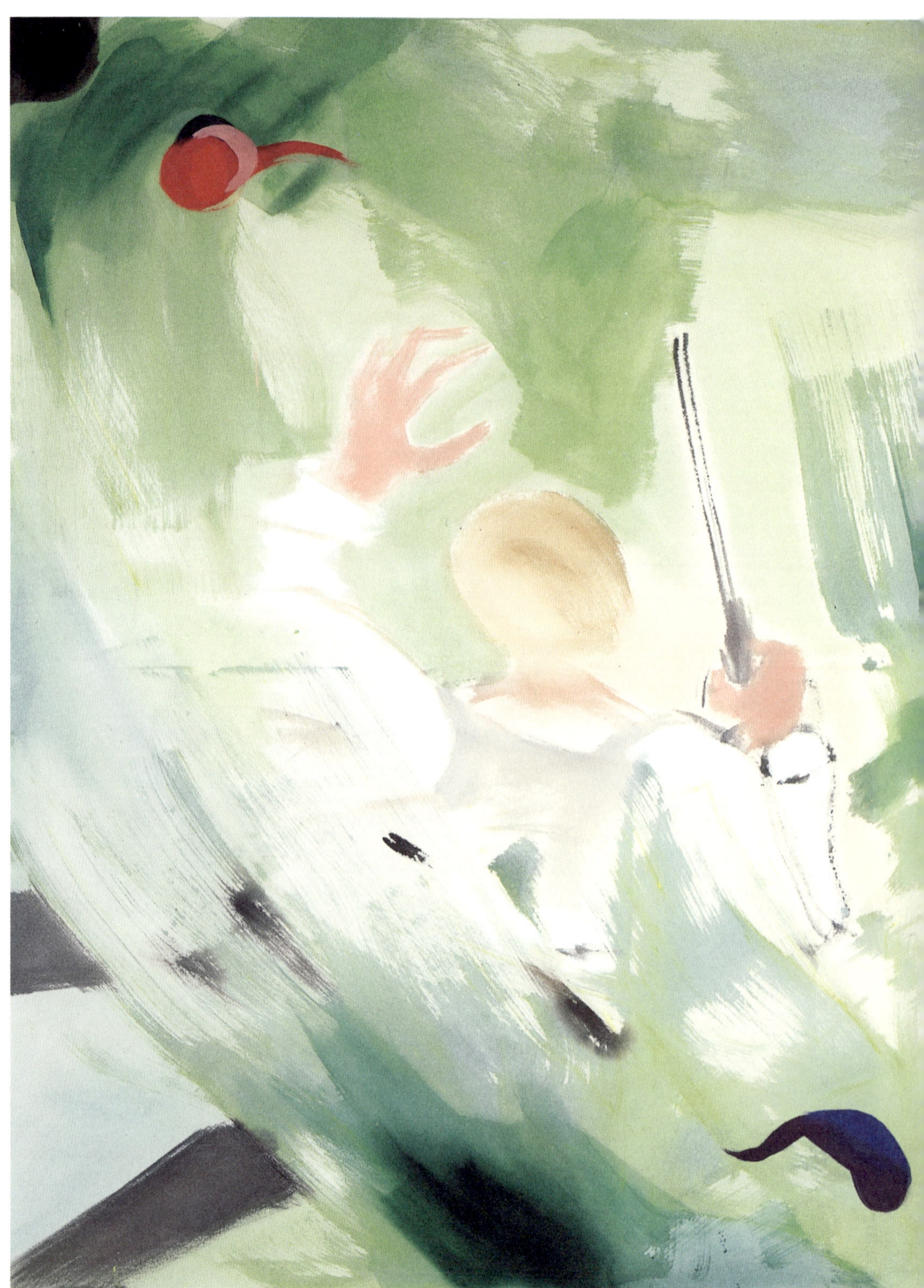

Billiard, 2005

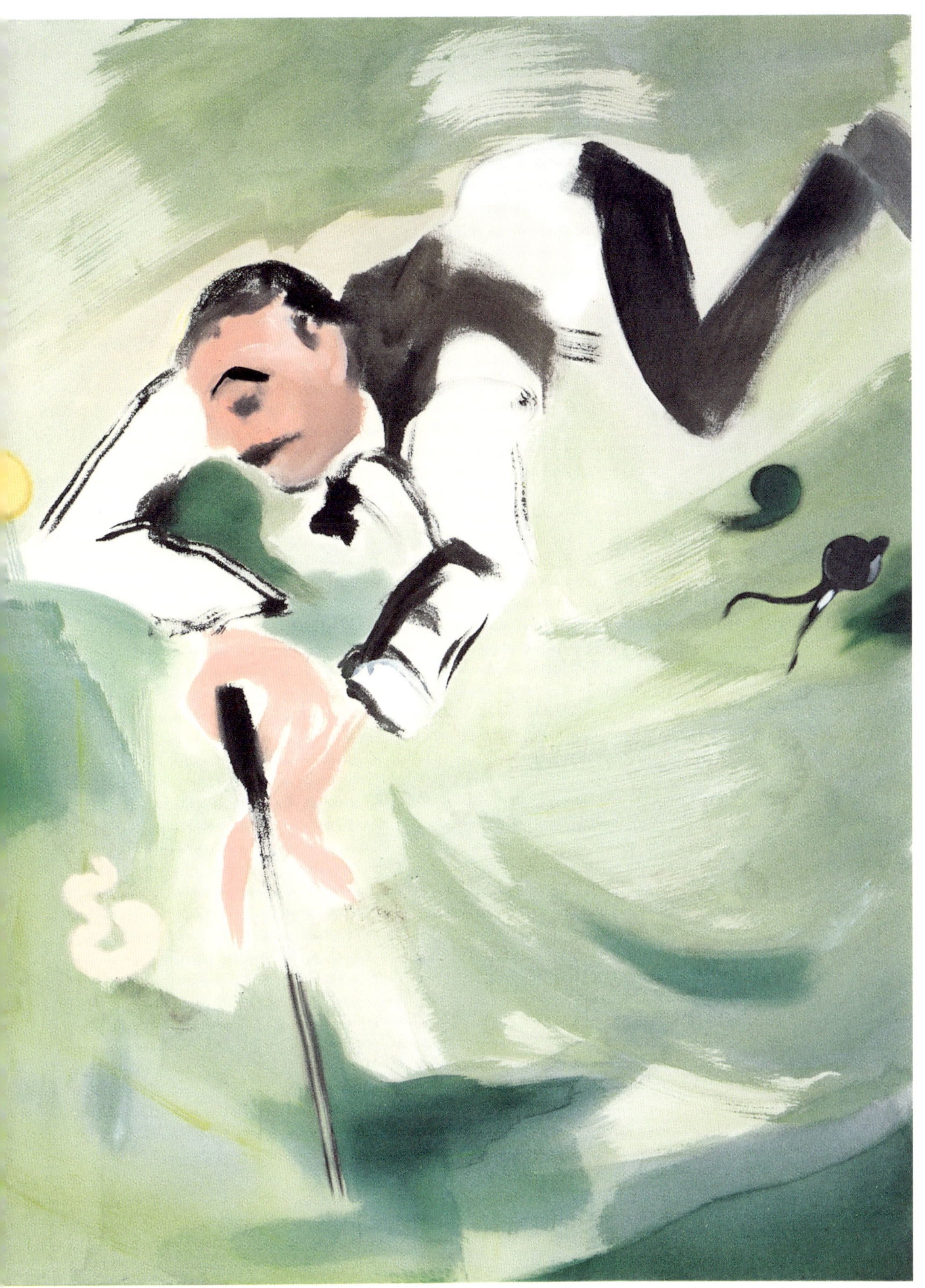

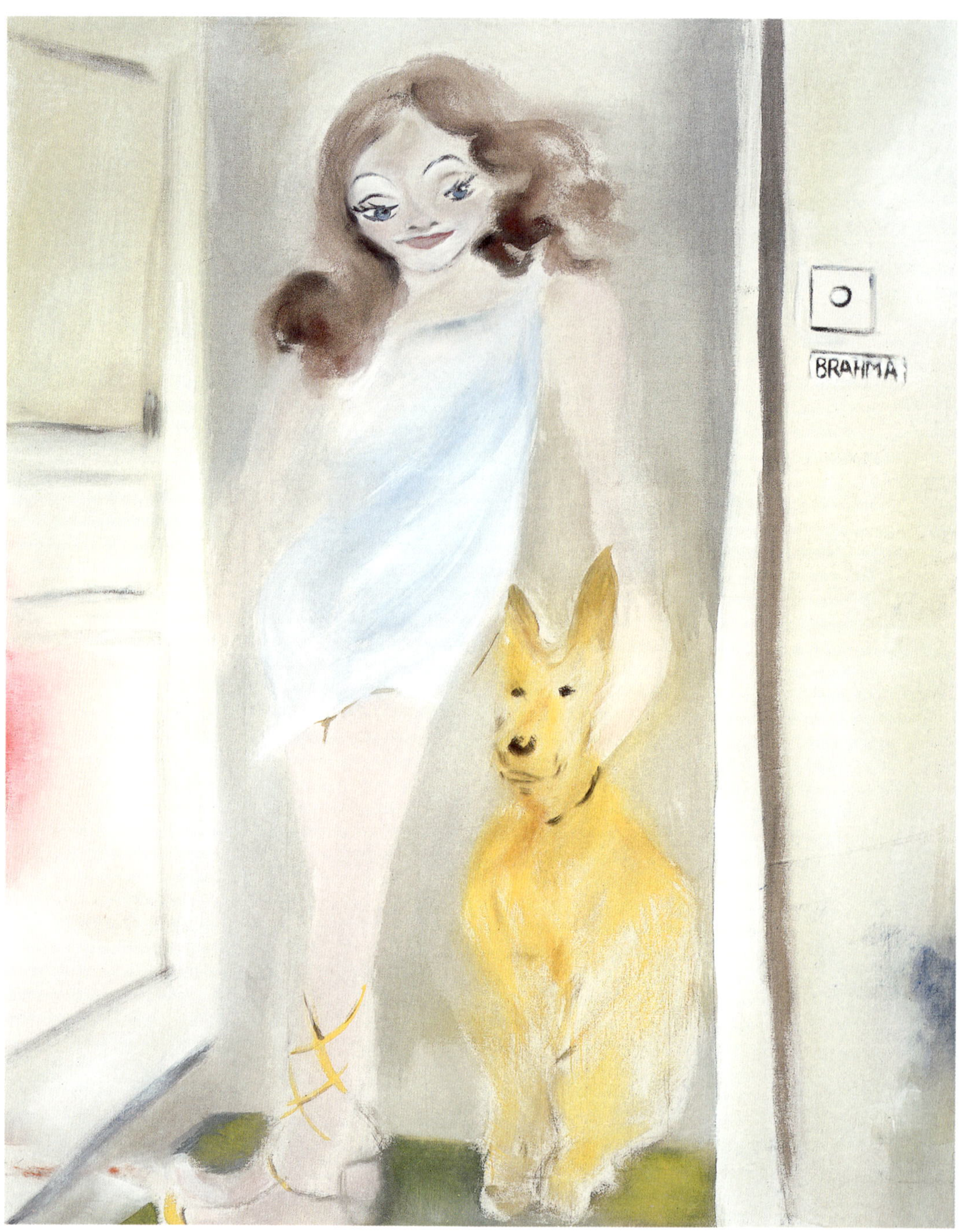

Goddess in the Doorway, 2005

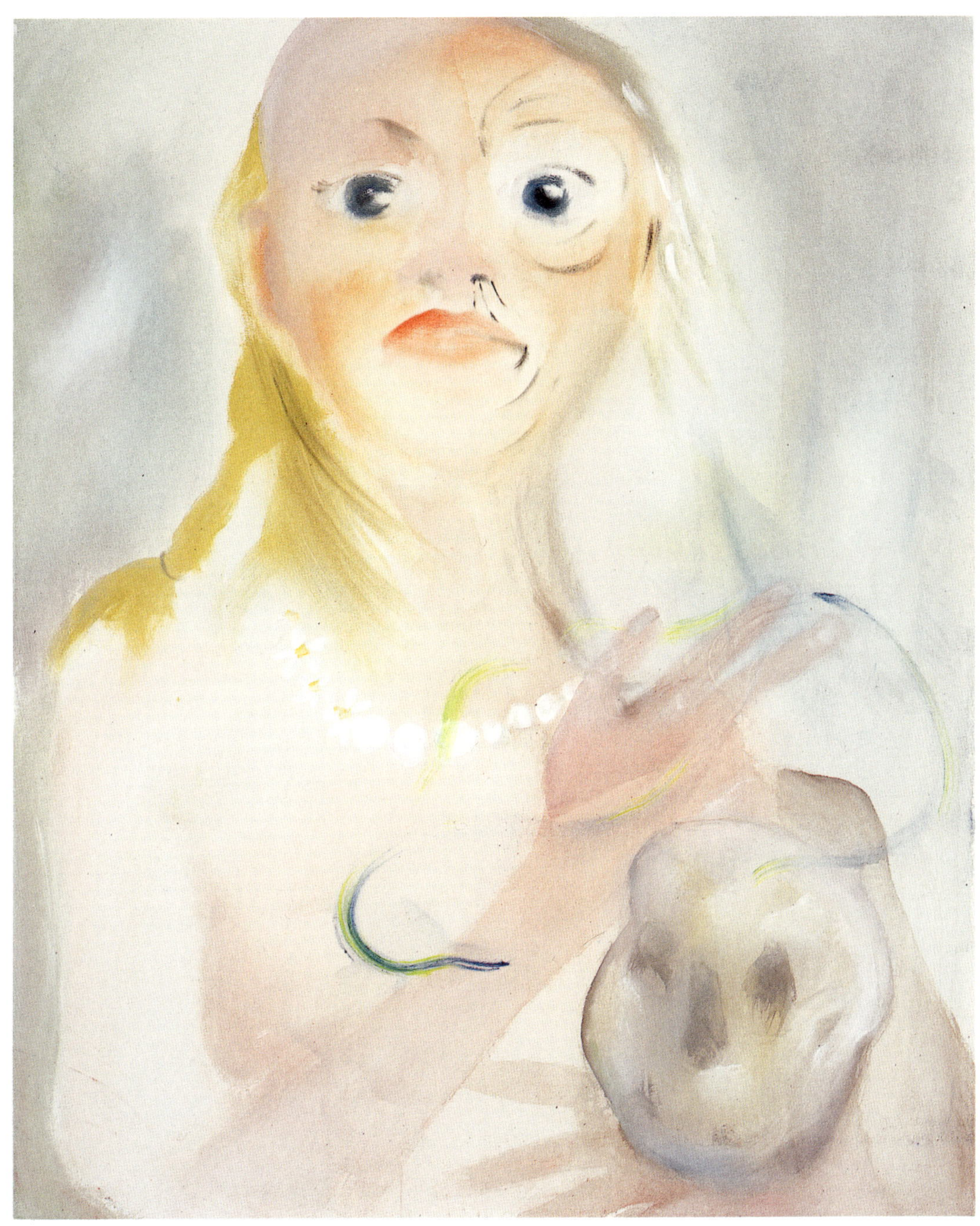

Self-Portrait, 2005

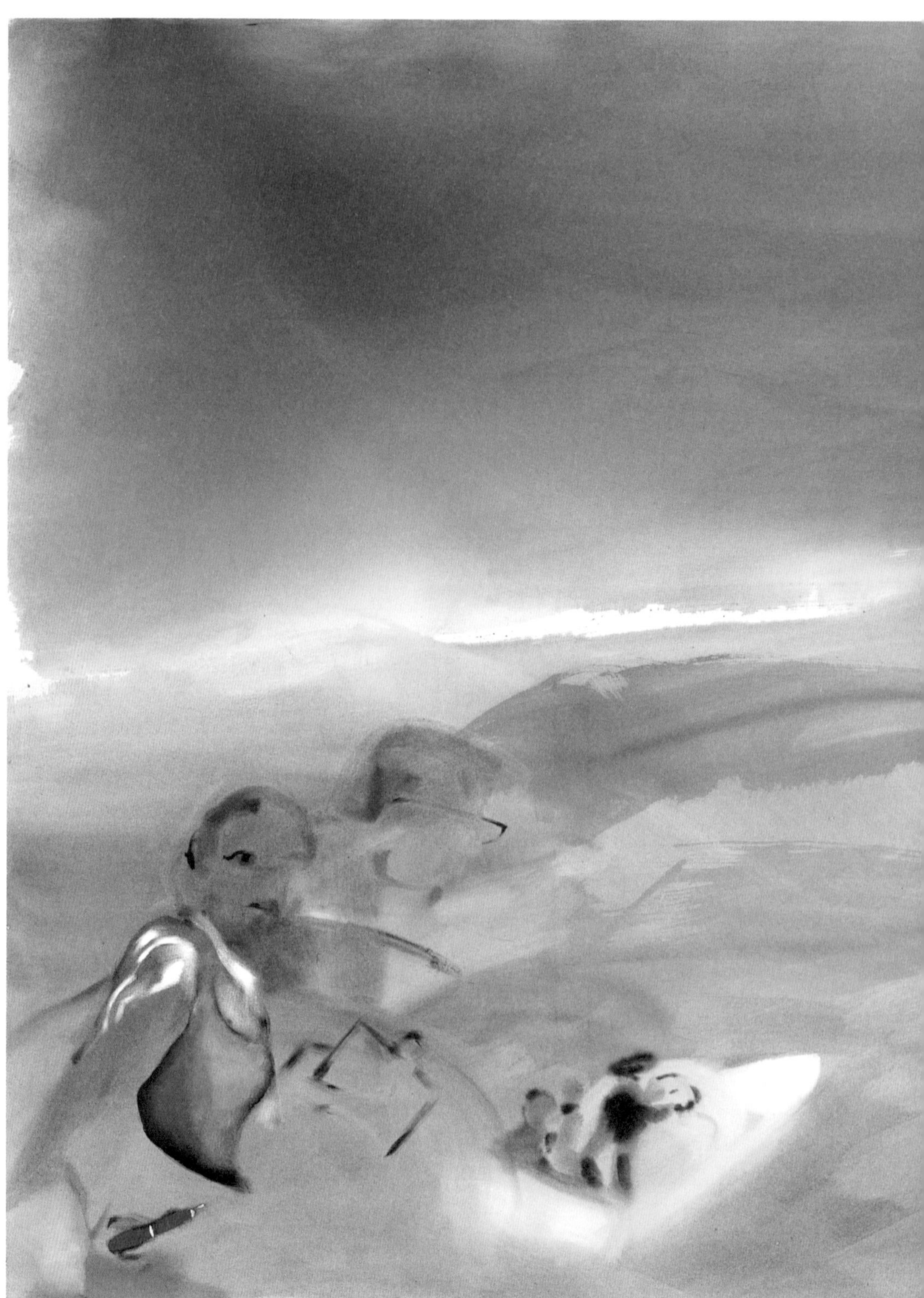

Tinnef, 2005

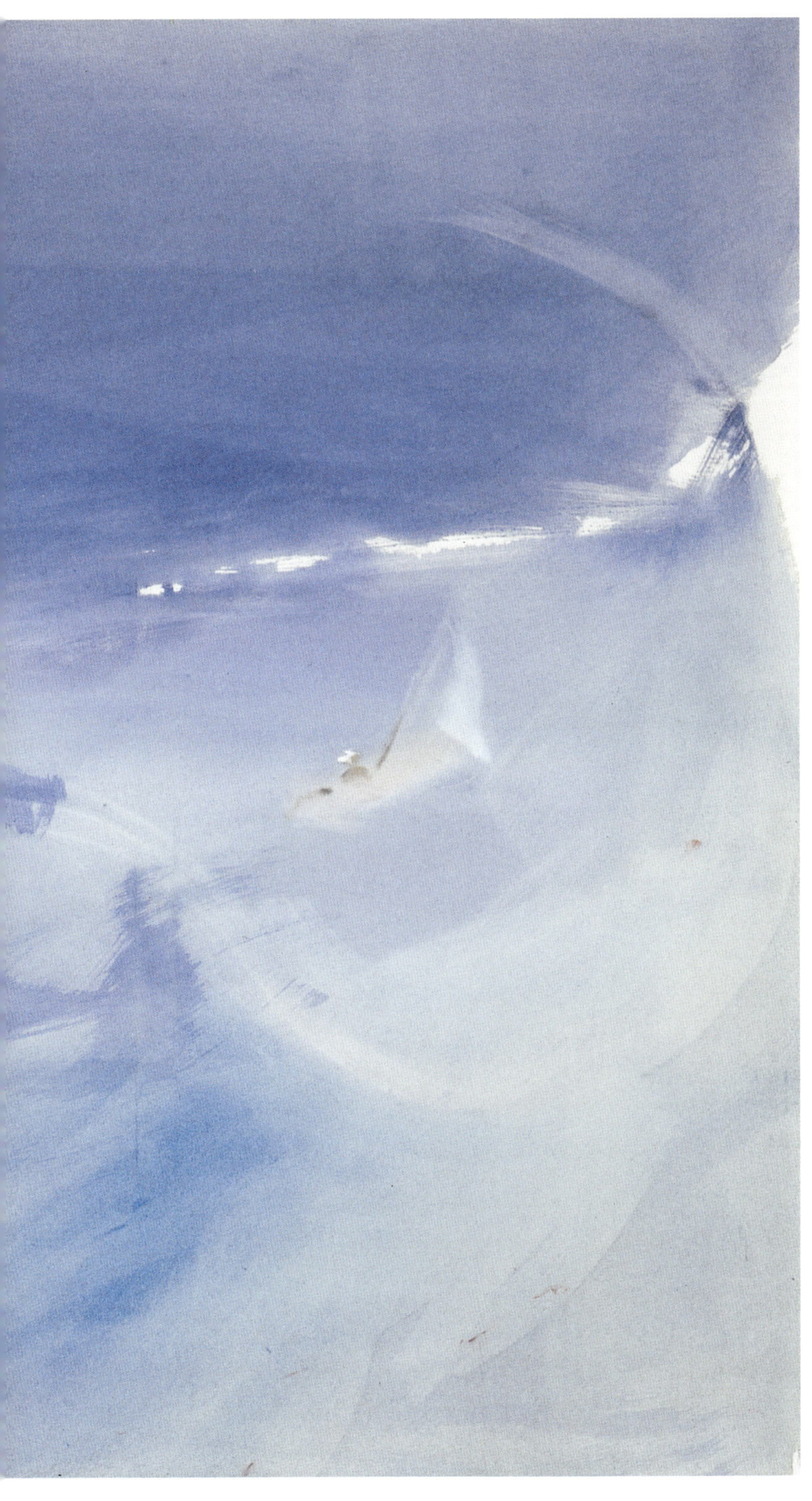

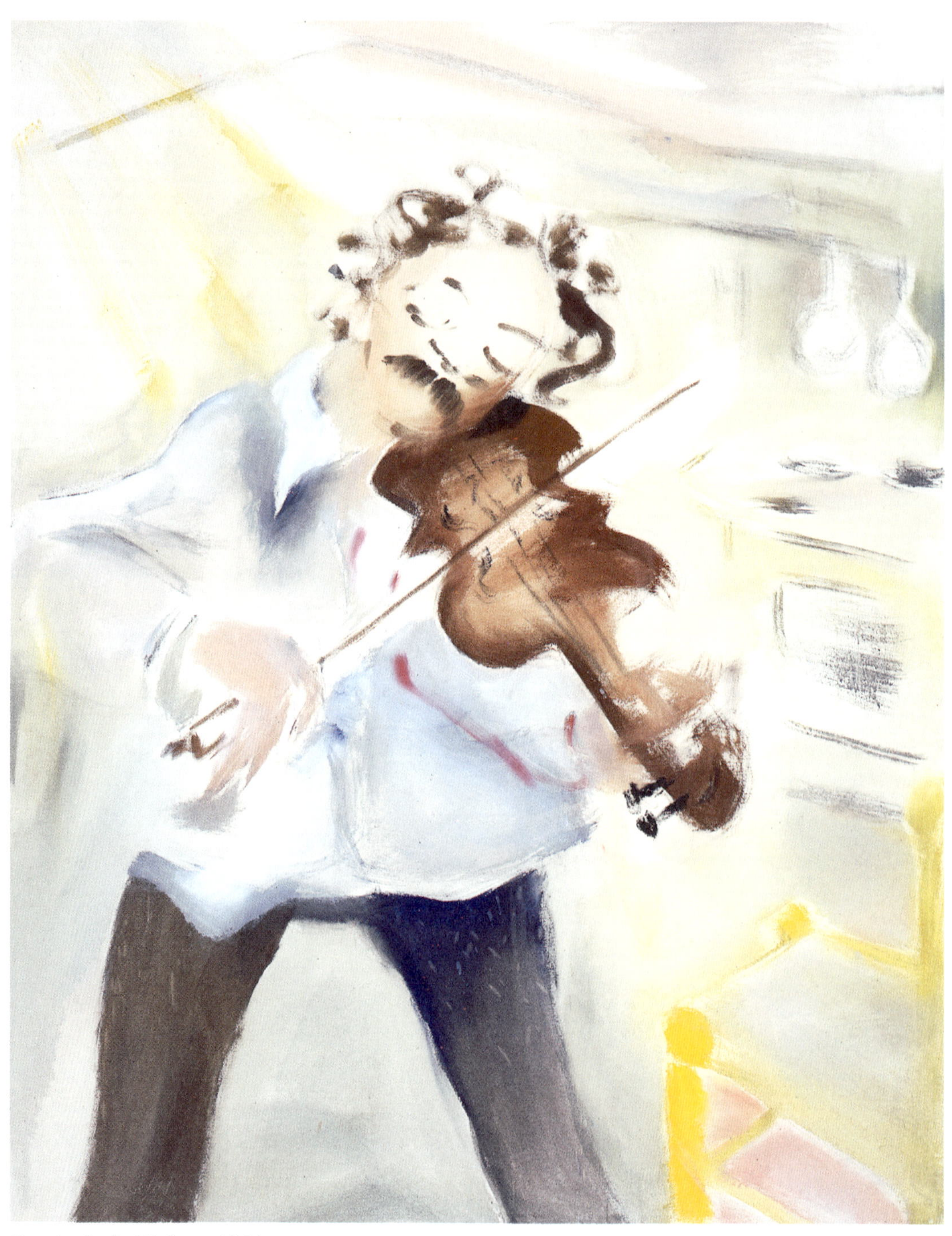

Dancing in the Kitchen with You, 2005

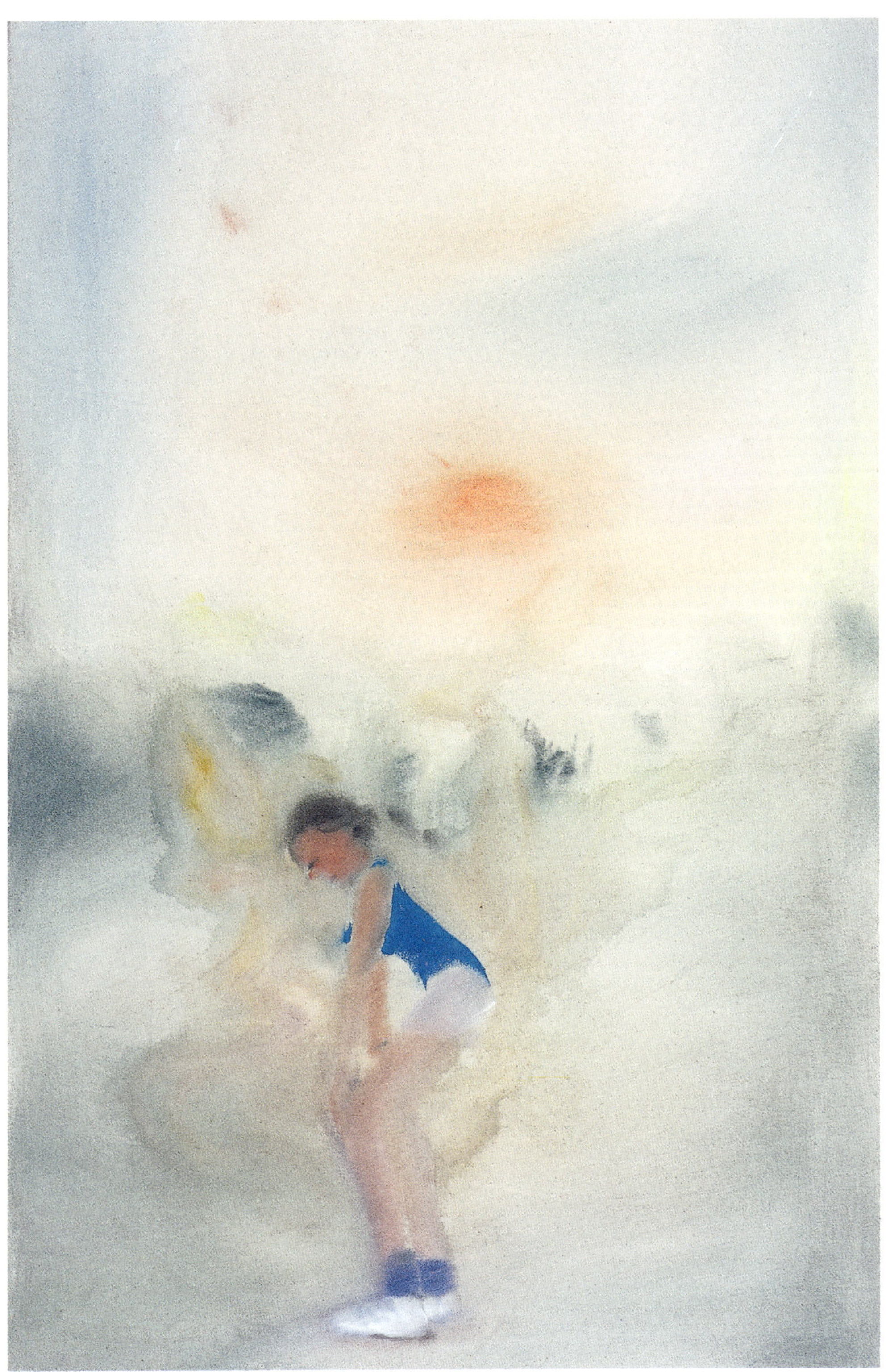

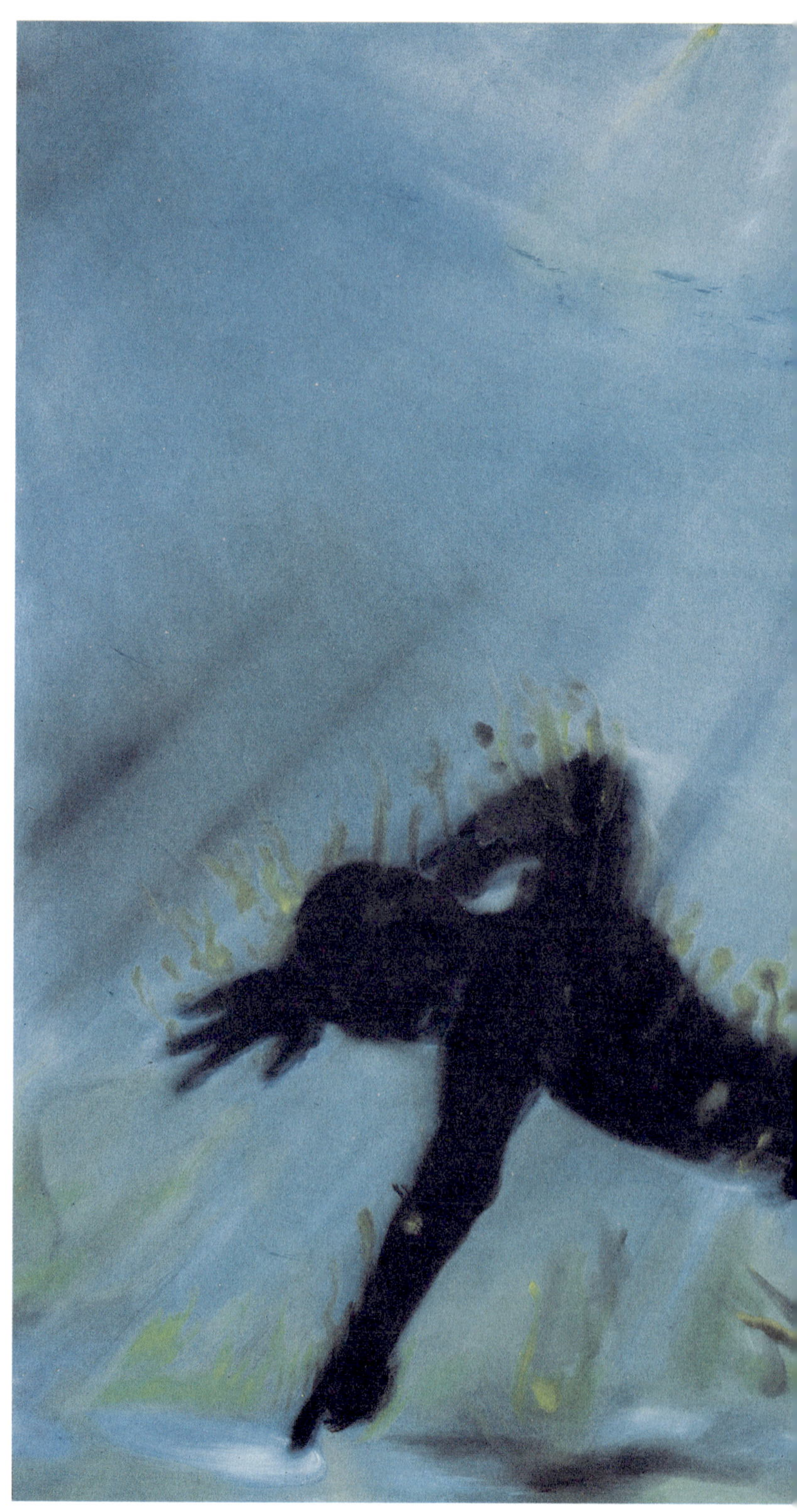

Poseidon, 2005

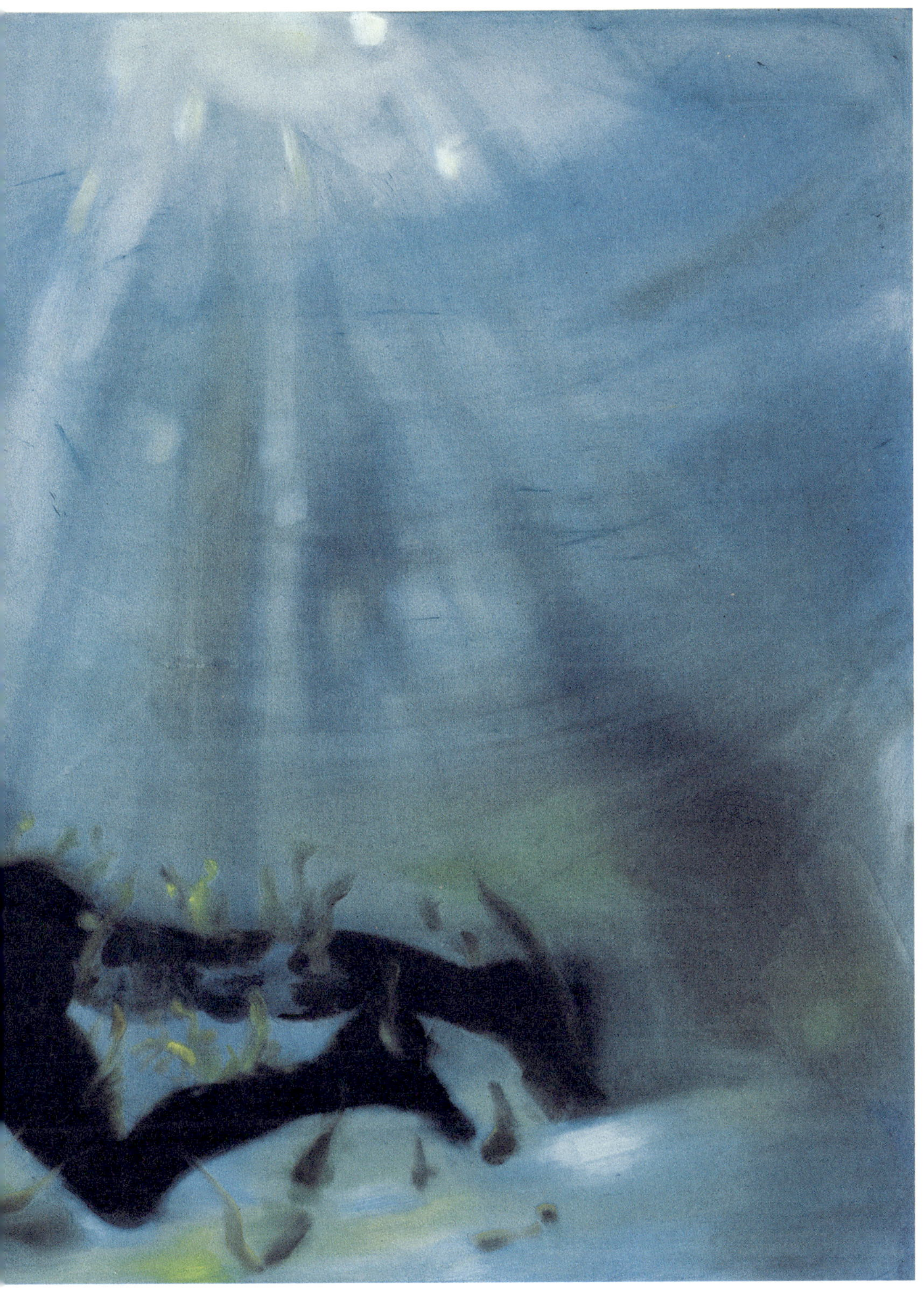

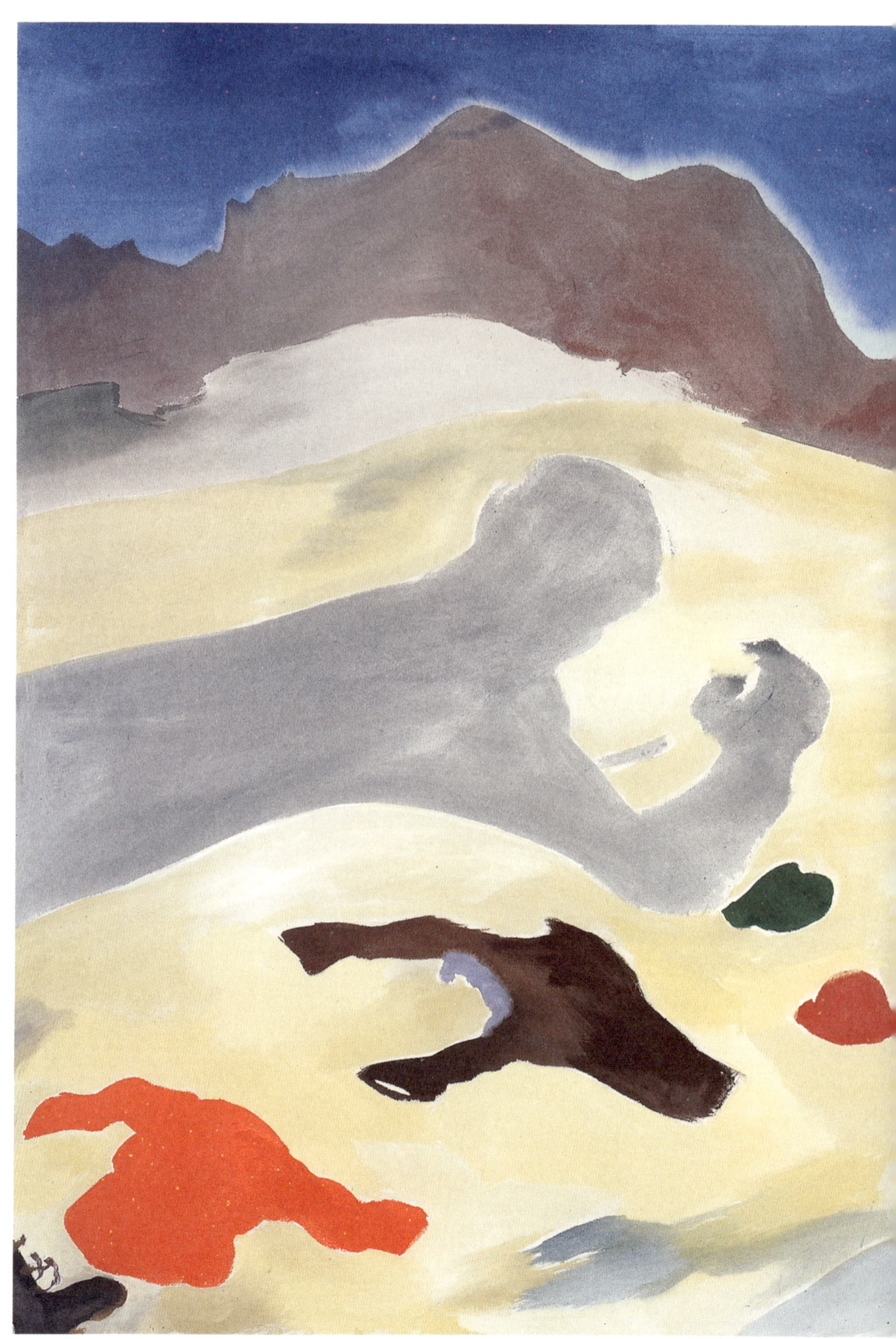

 Hot Air and Short Straw, 2005

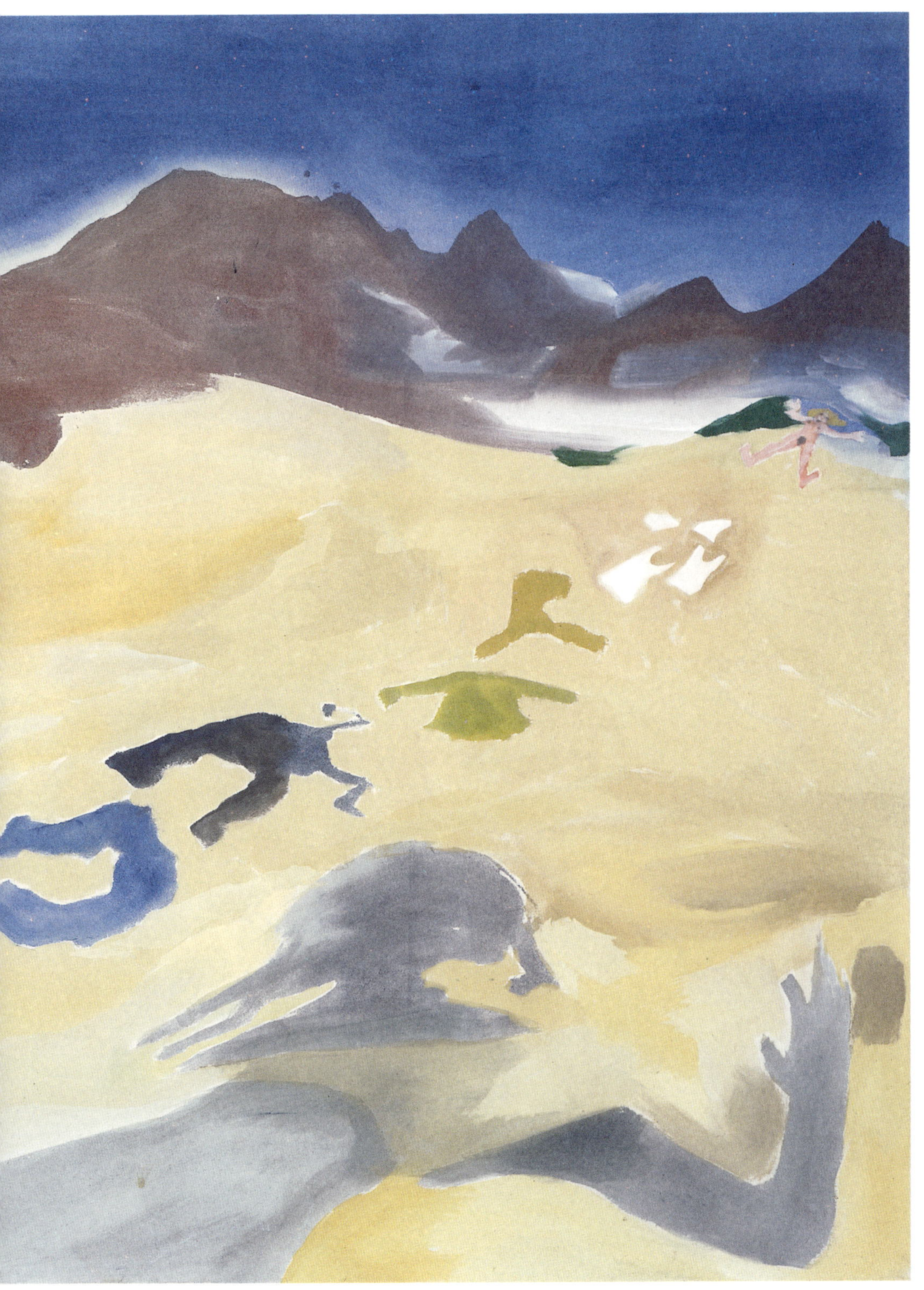

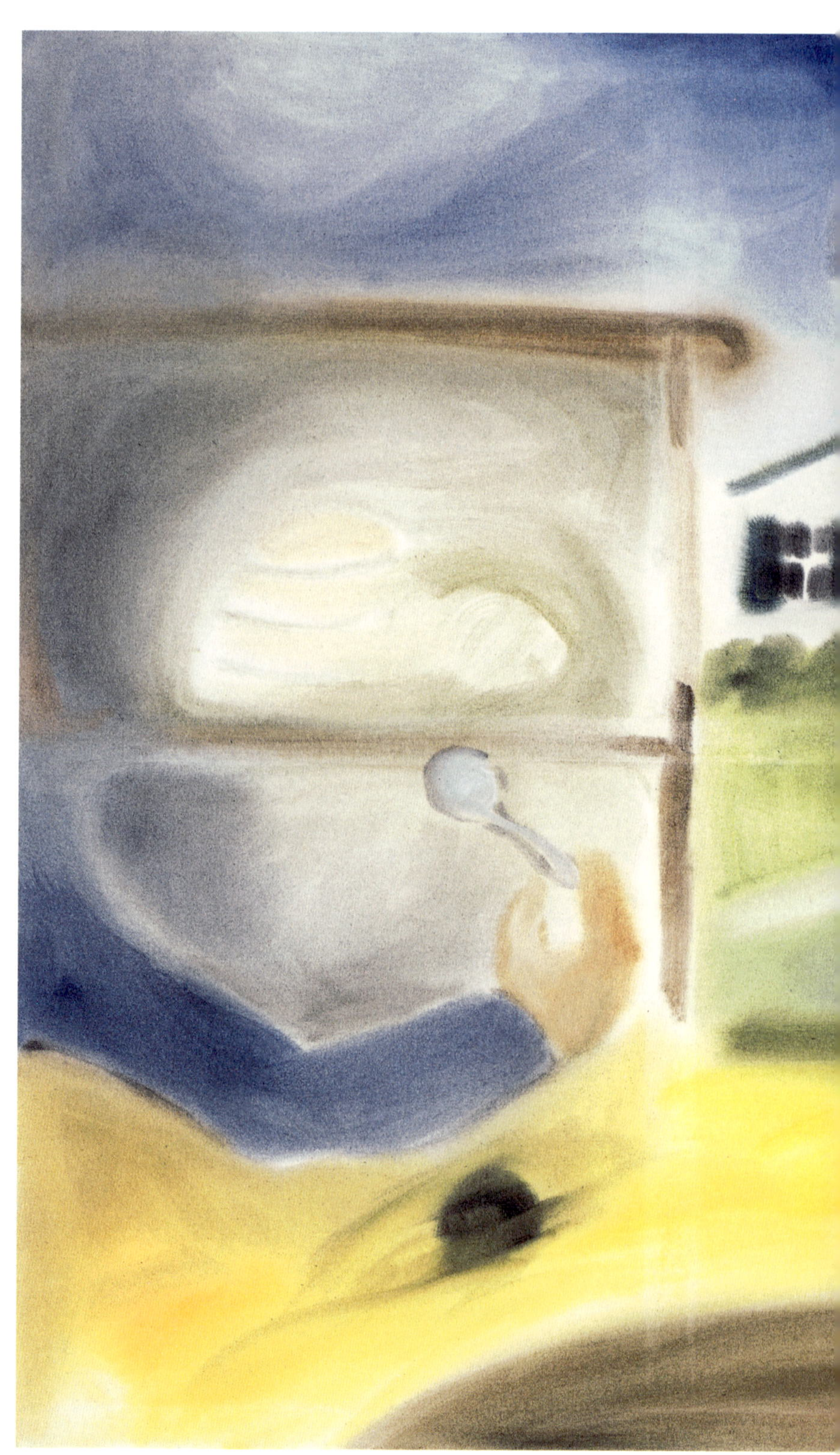

The Painter's Choice: Final Task I, 2005

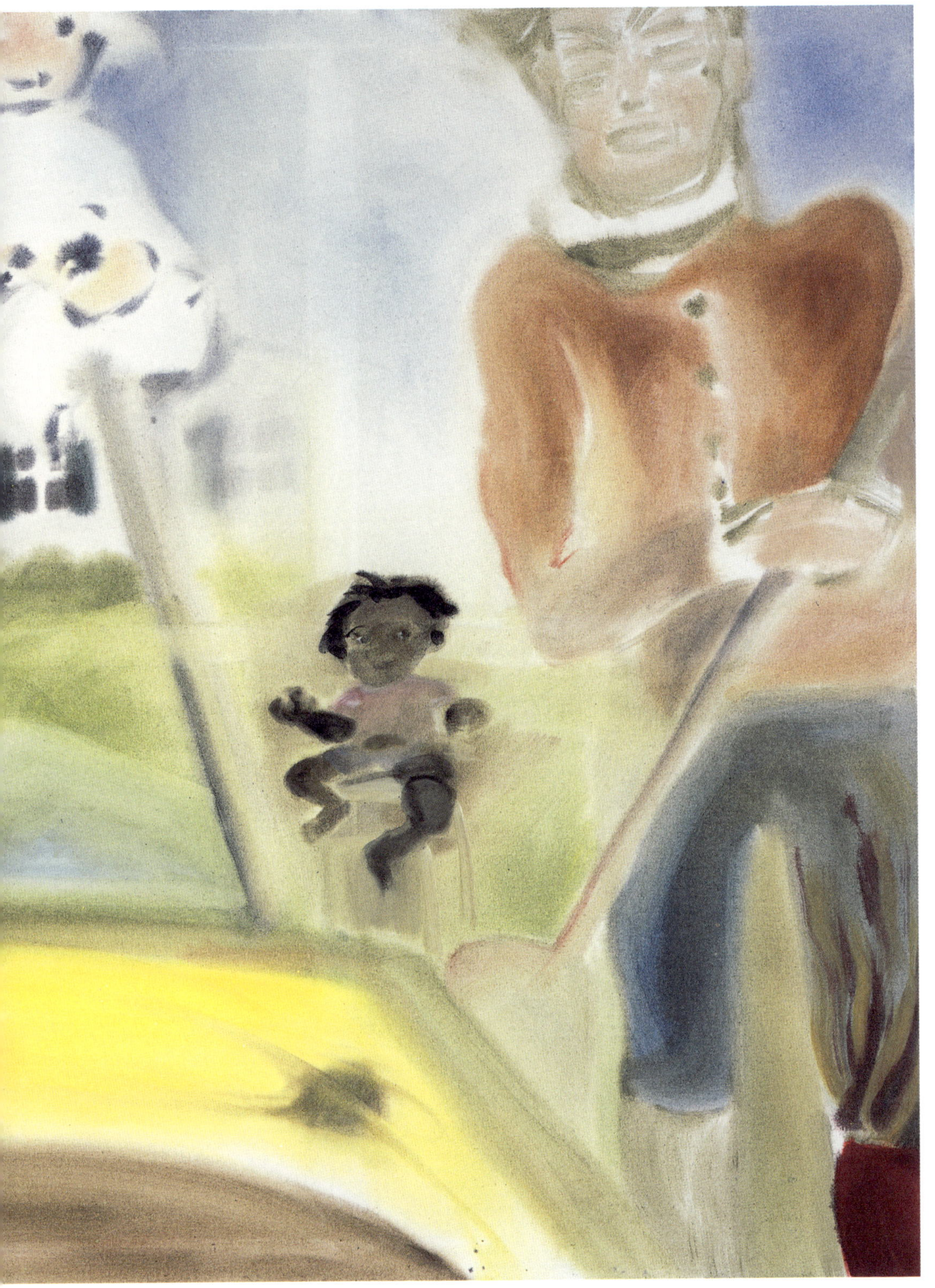

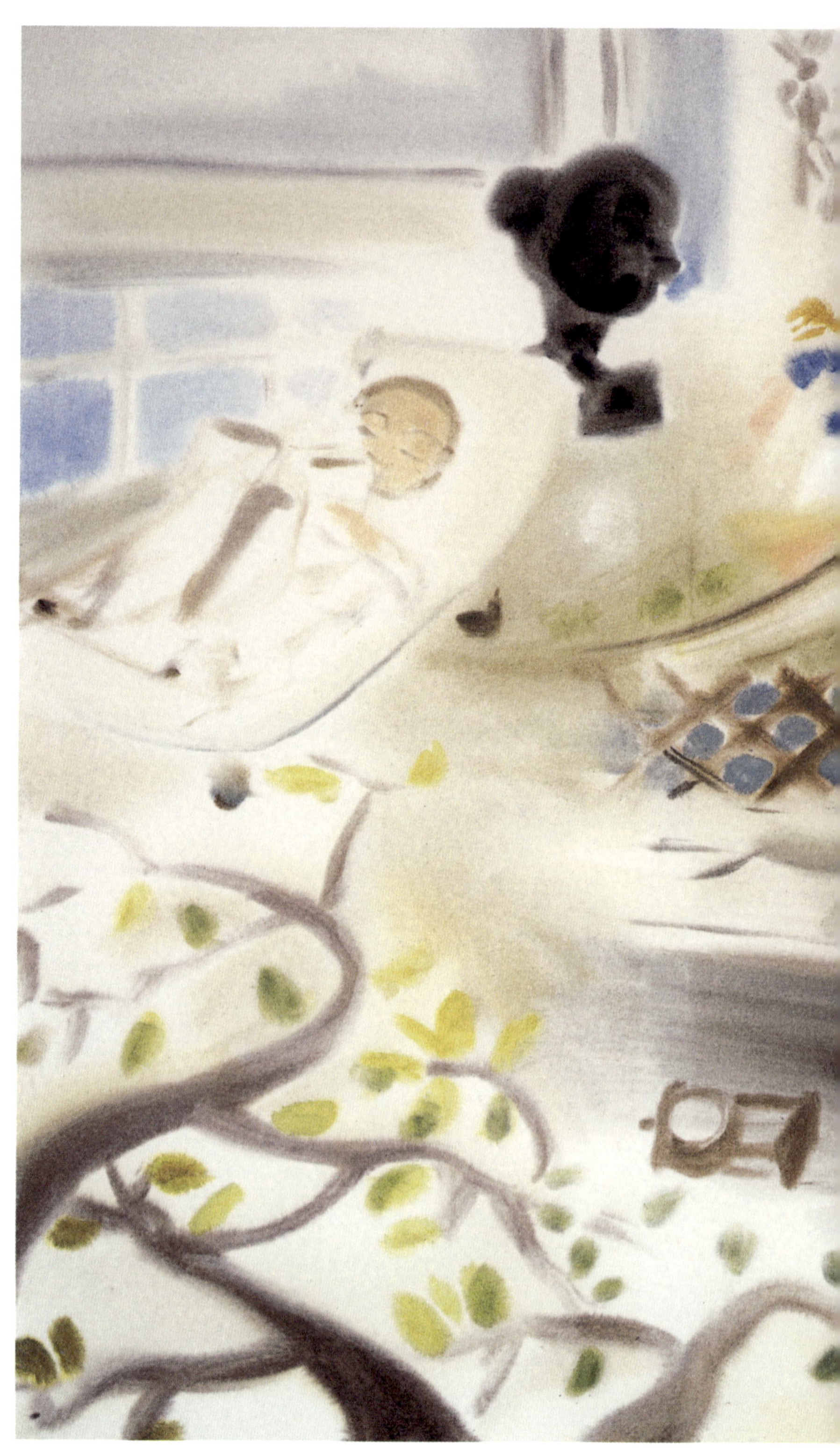

 The Painter's Choice: Final Task II, 2005

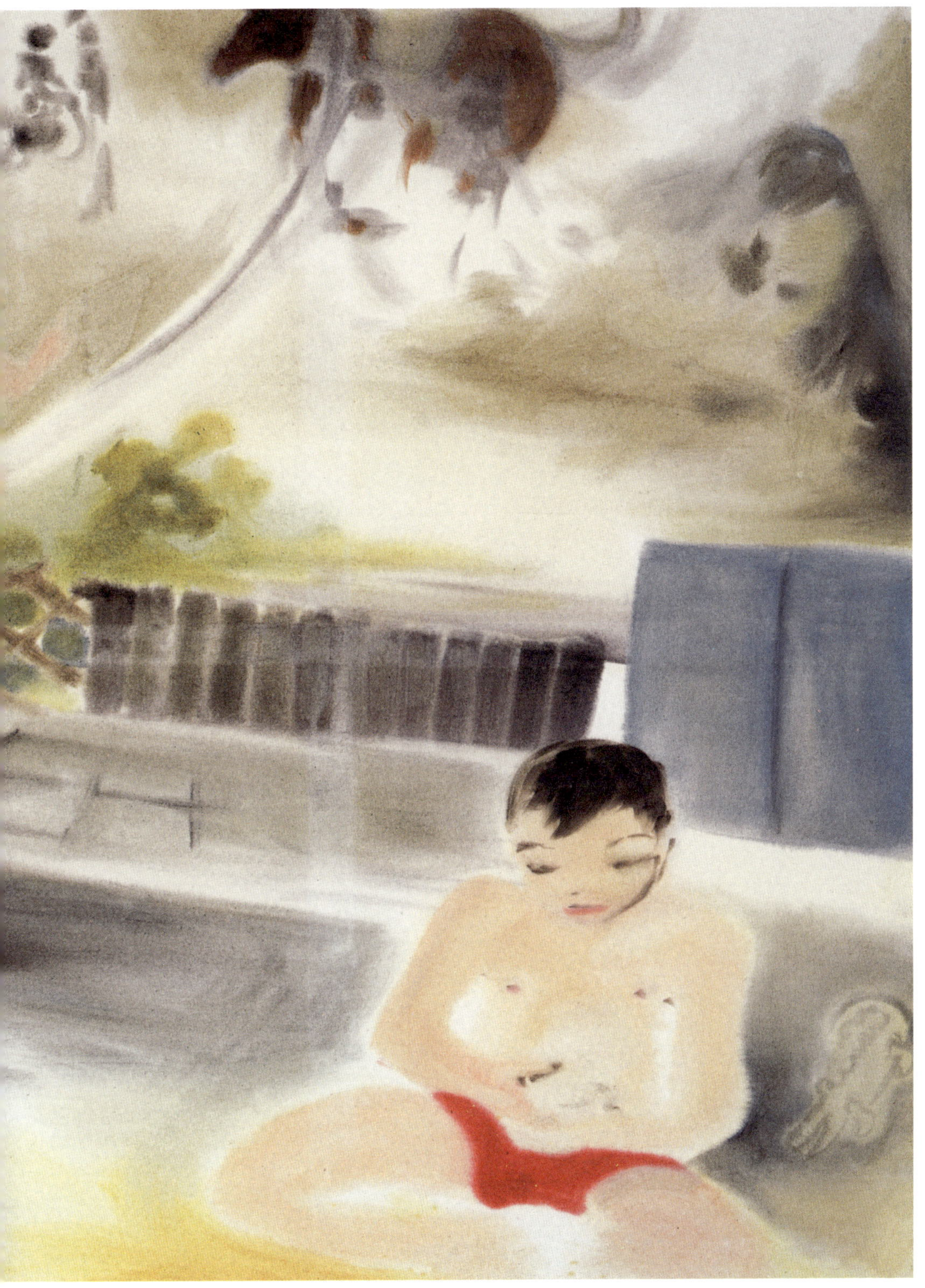

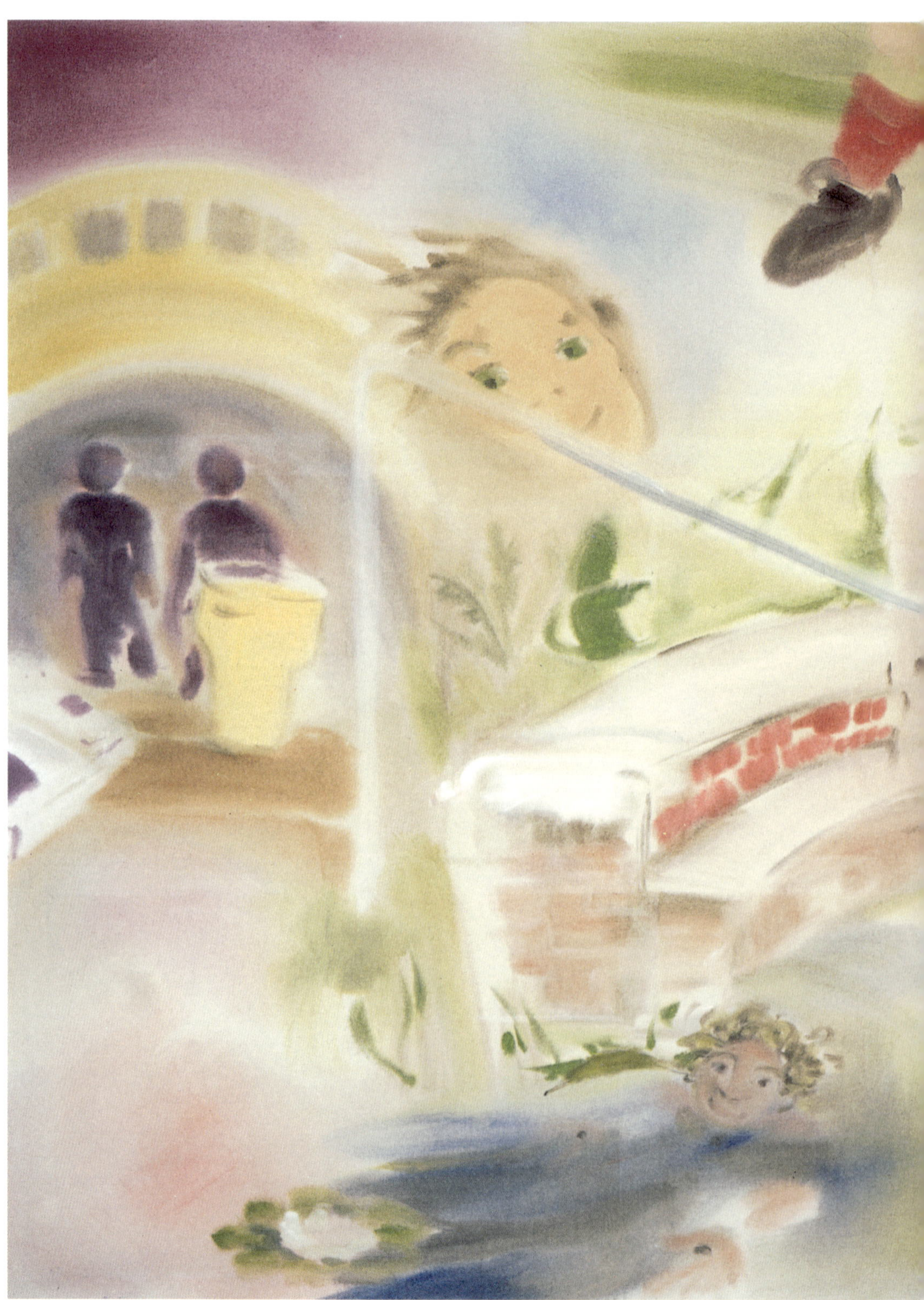

The Painter's Choice: Final Task III, 2005

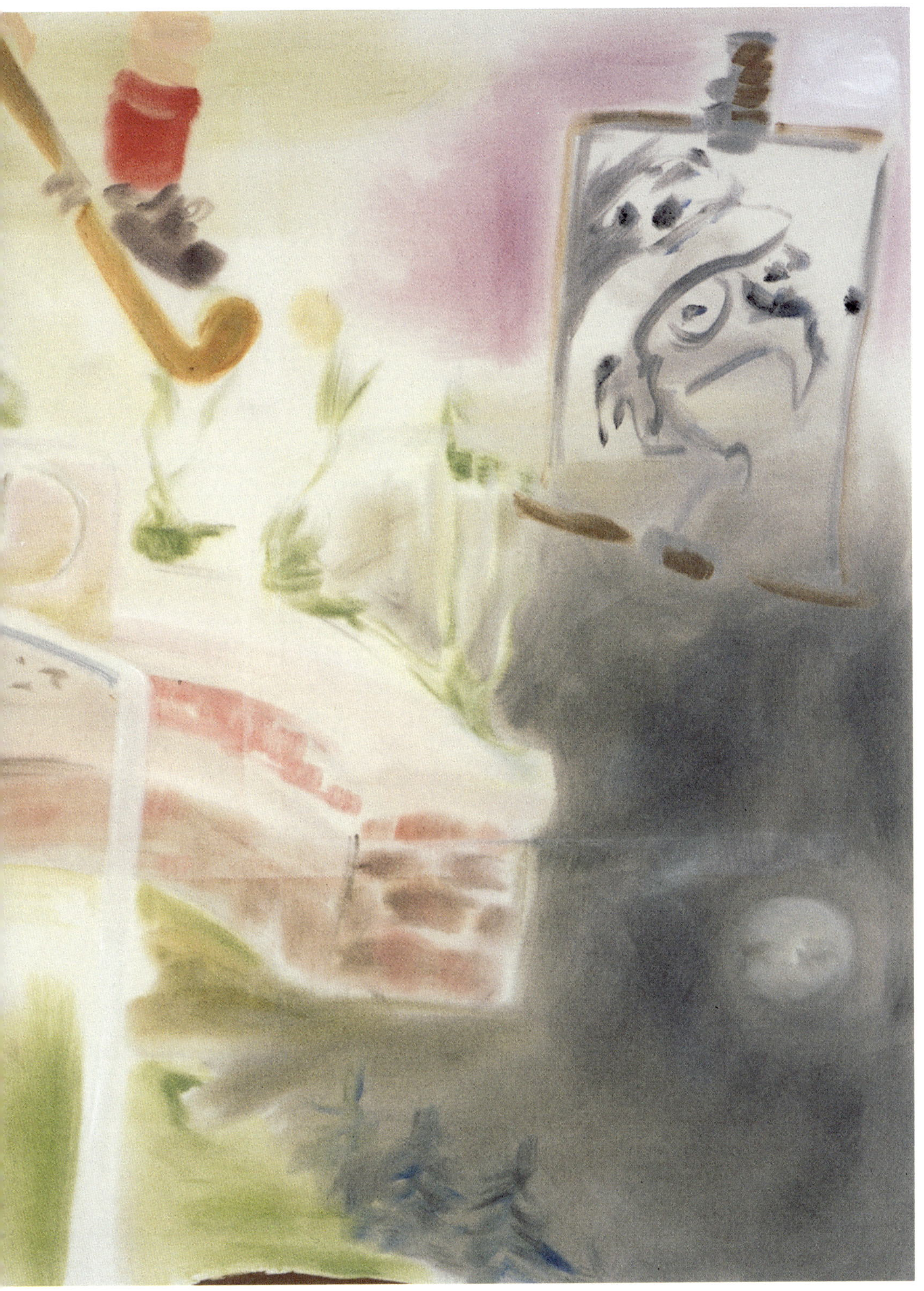

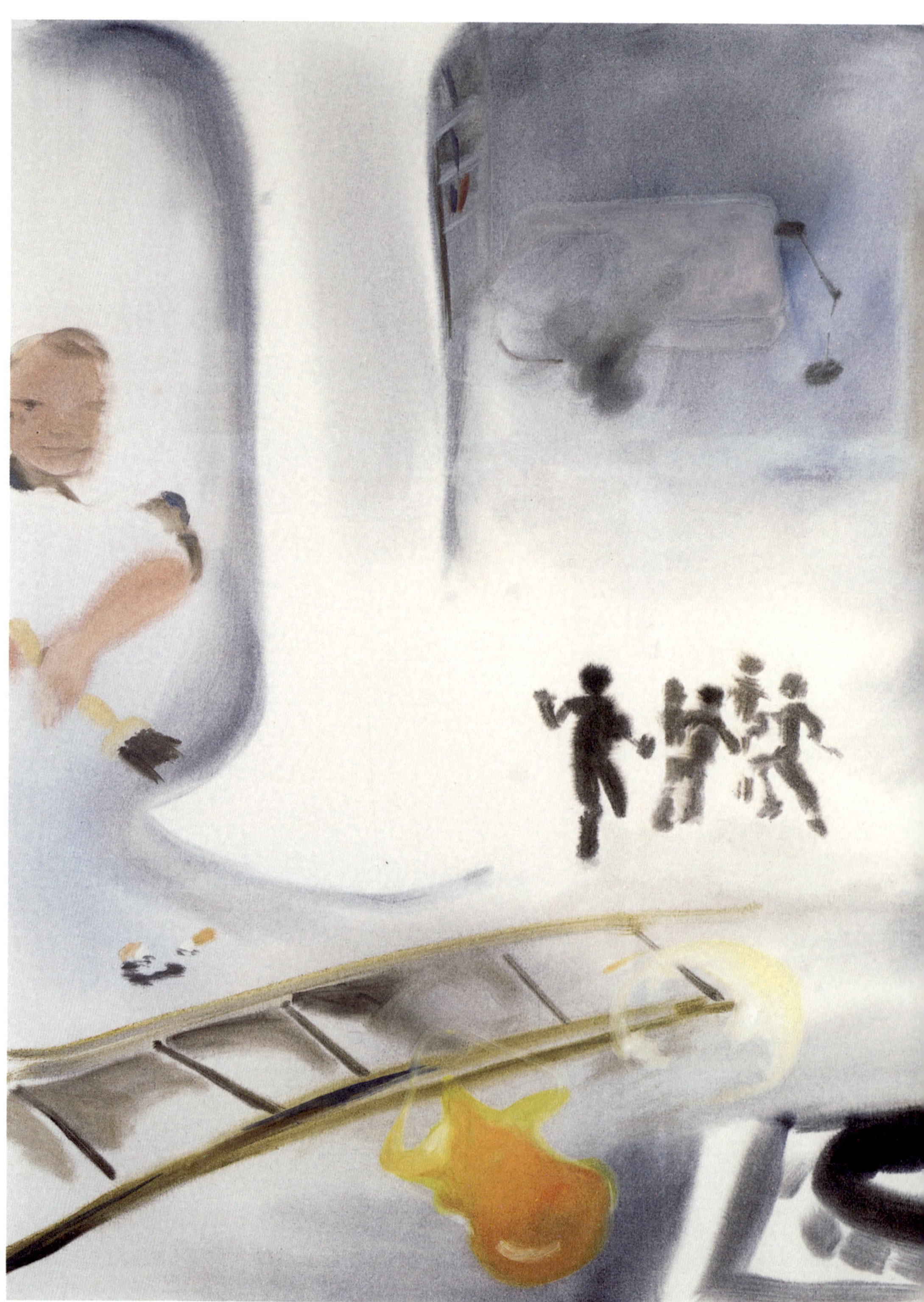

The Painter's Choice: Final Task IV, 2005

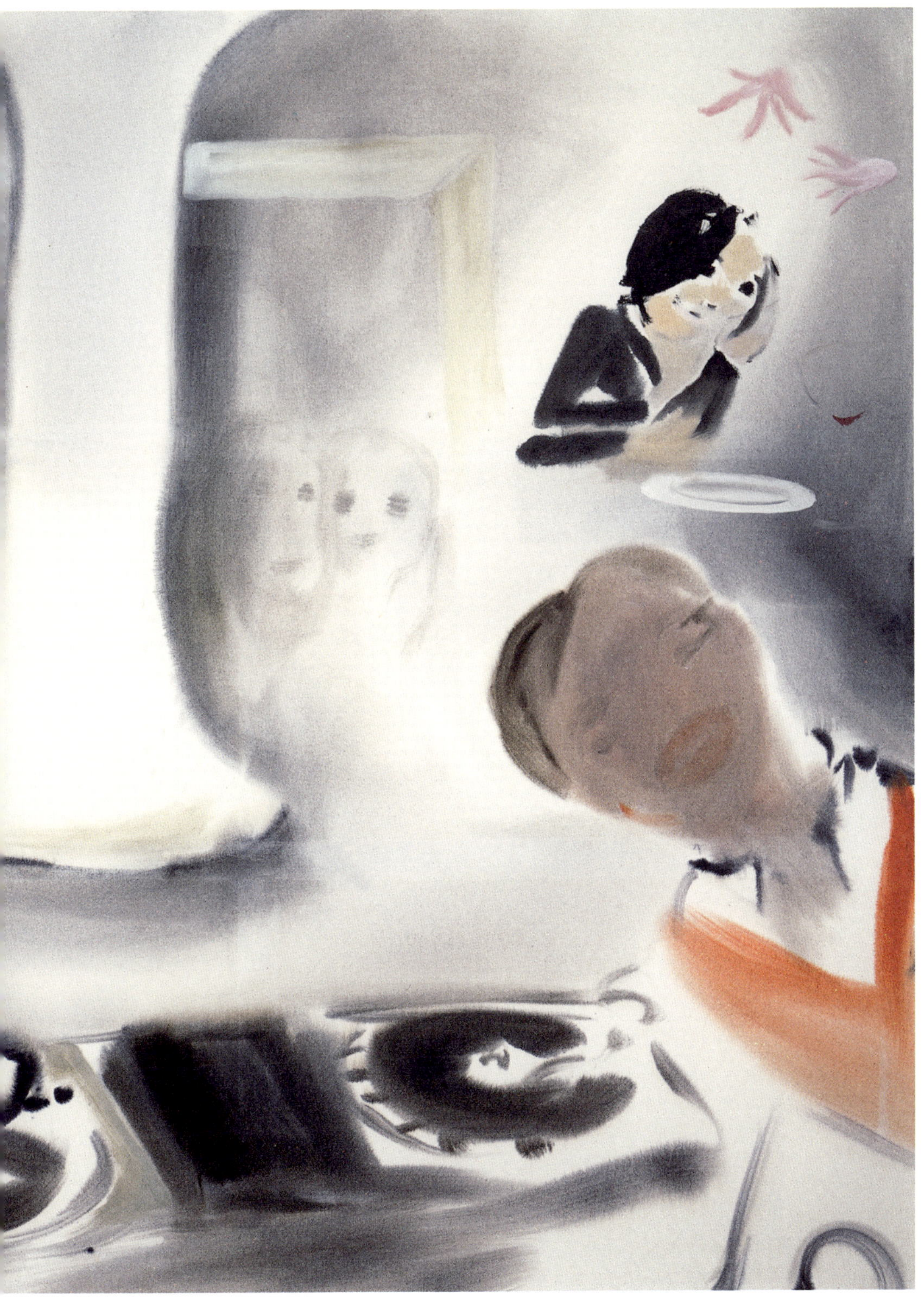

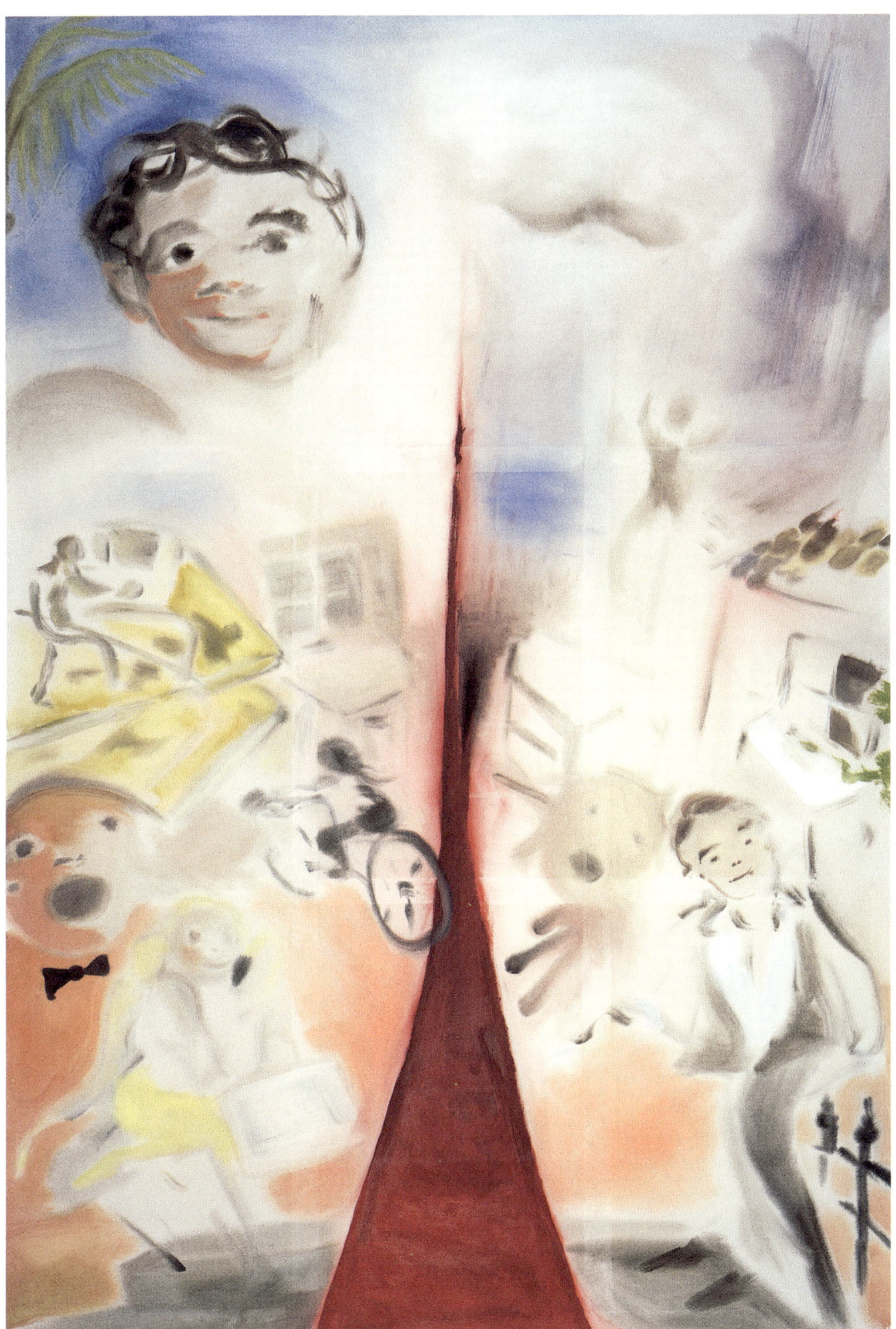

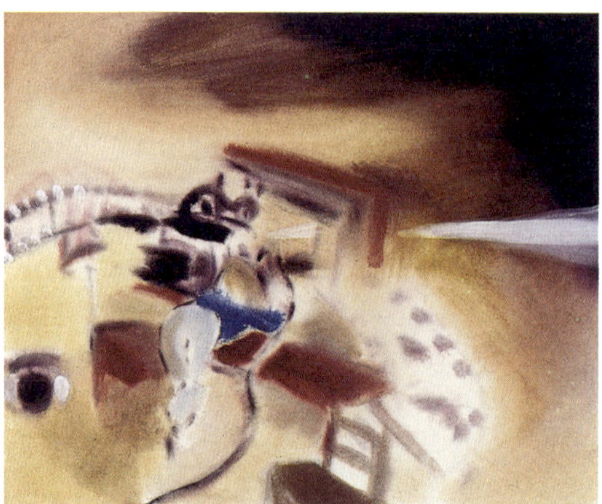

Sucking in the Seventies I, 2005

Sucking in the Seventies II, 2005

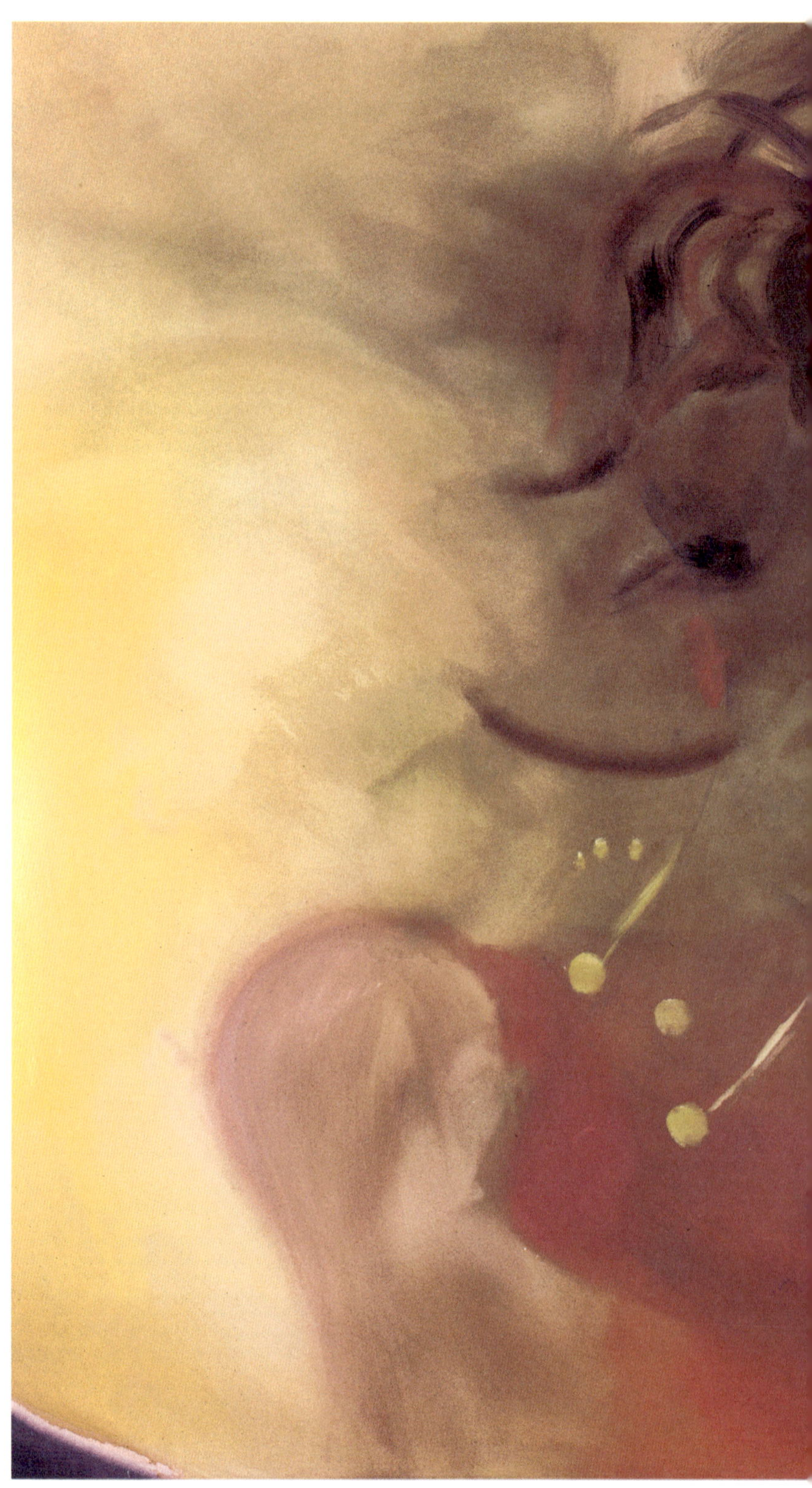

Sucking in the Seventies III, 2005

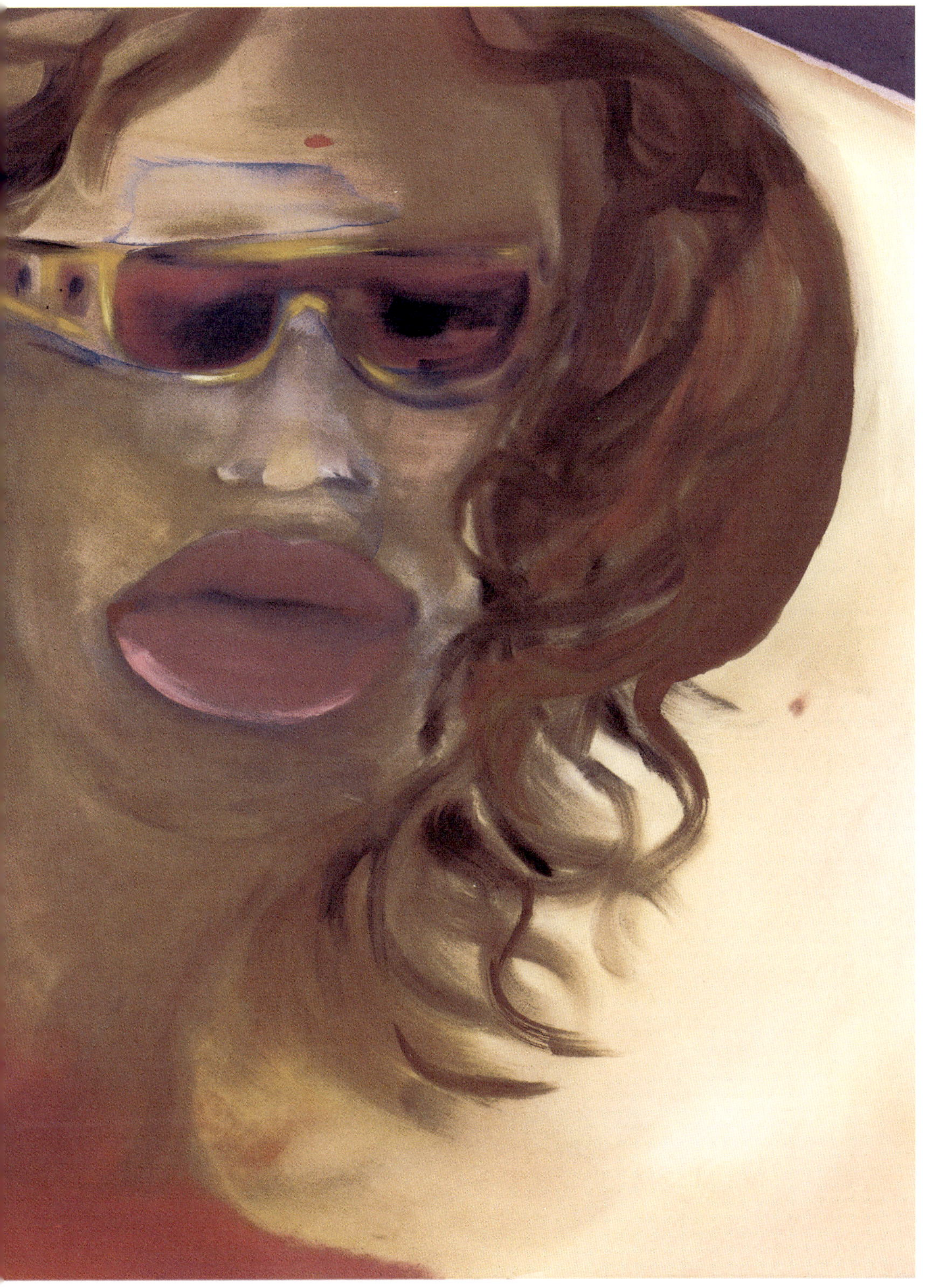

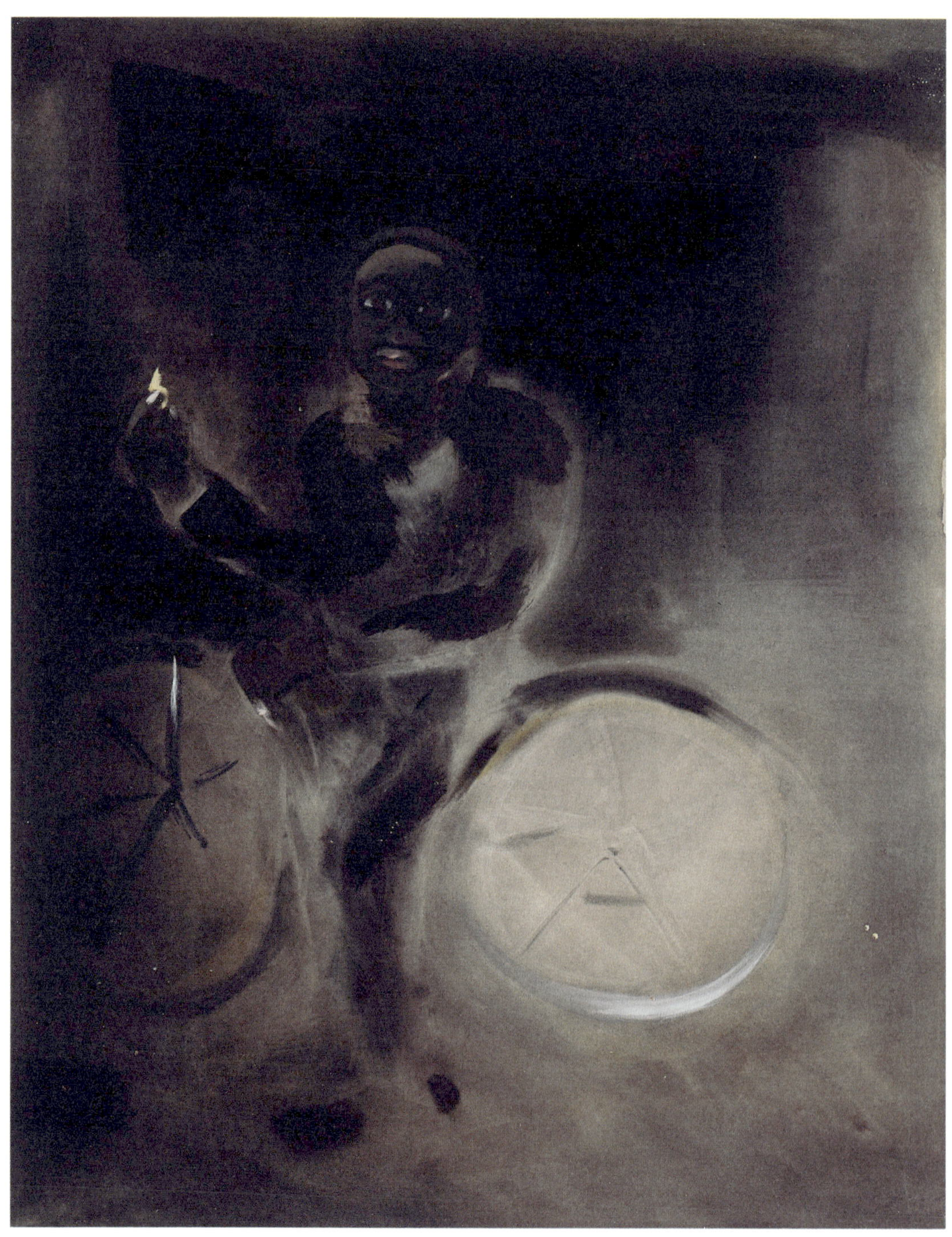

Home Spun, 2005

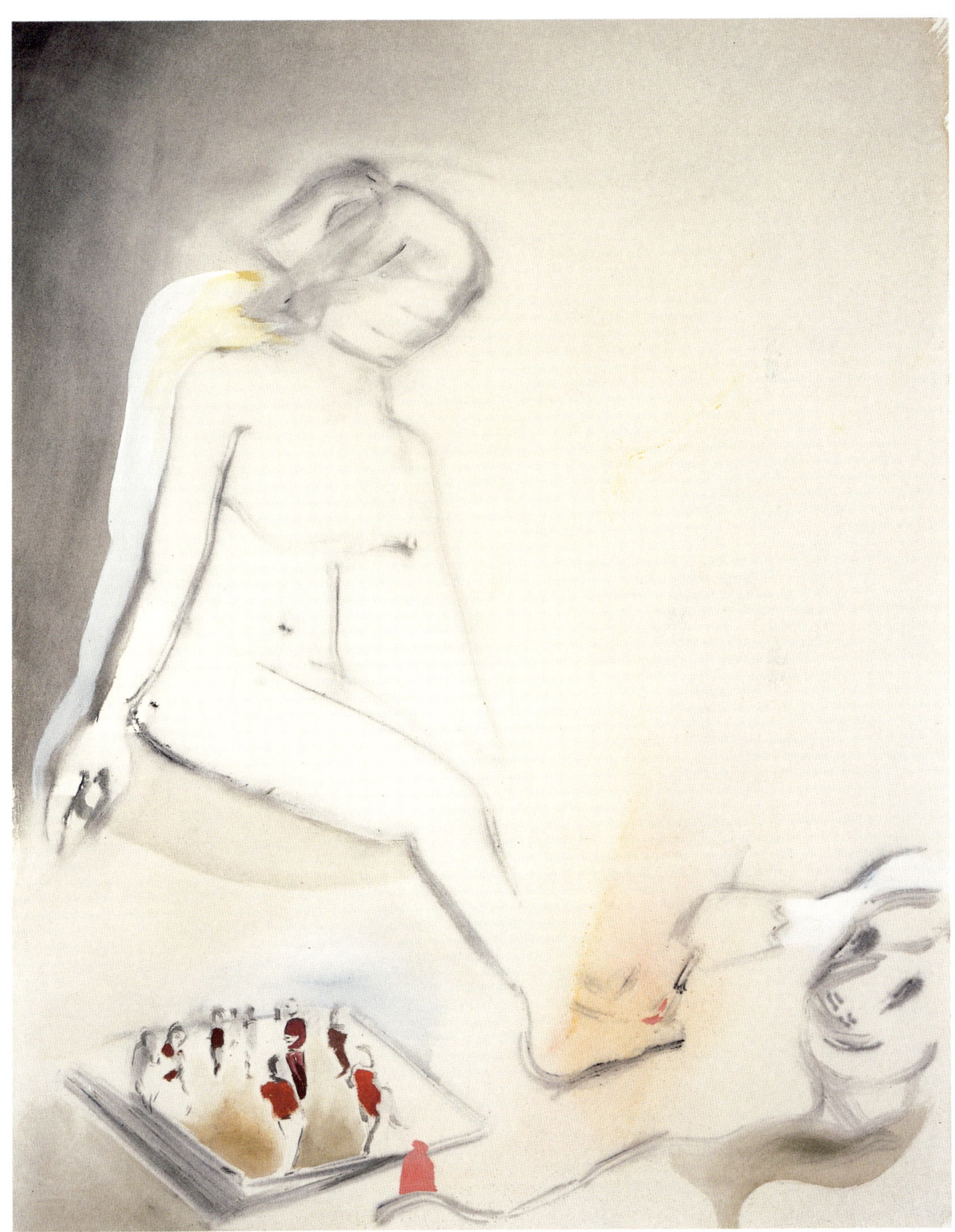

Jessica, 2005

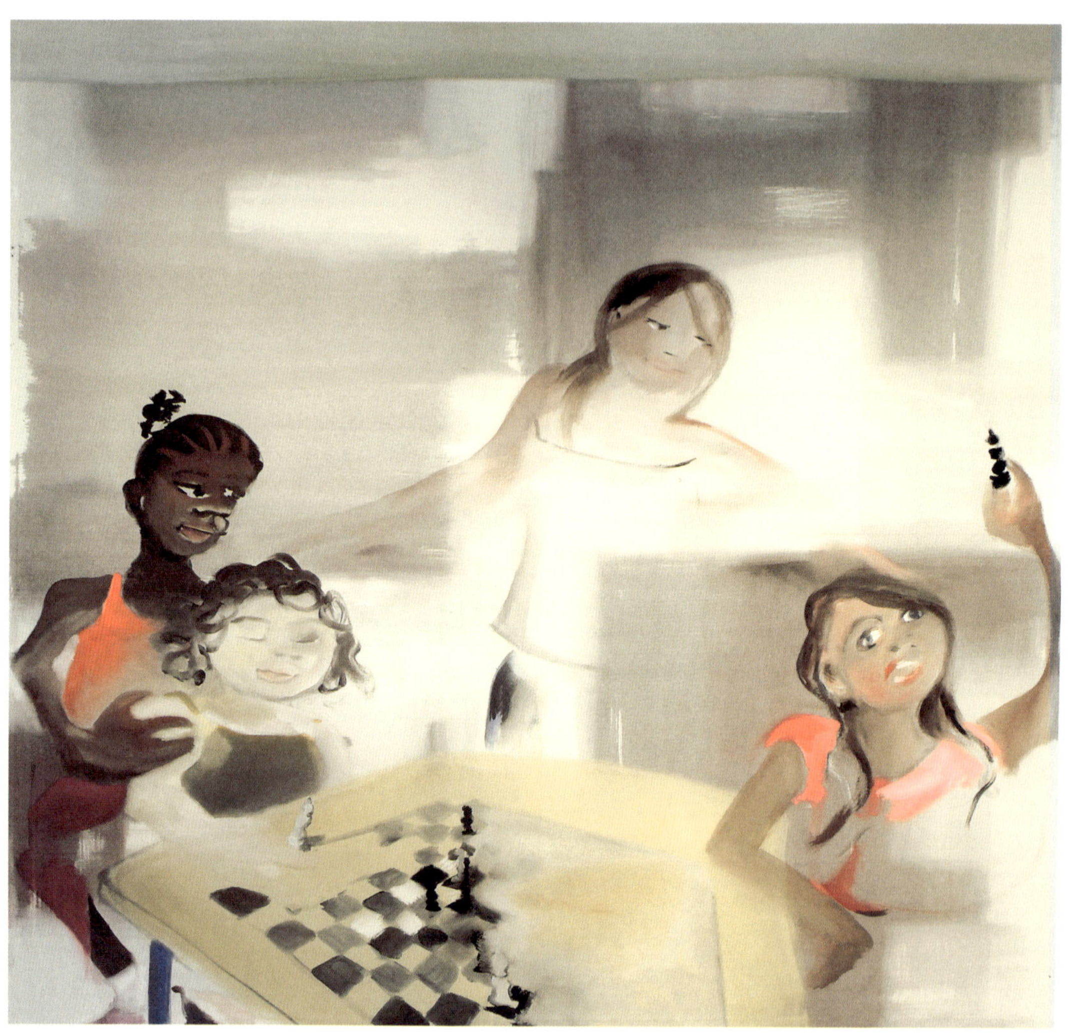

Haute de Lievre I, 2005

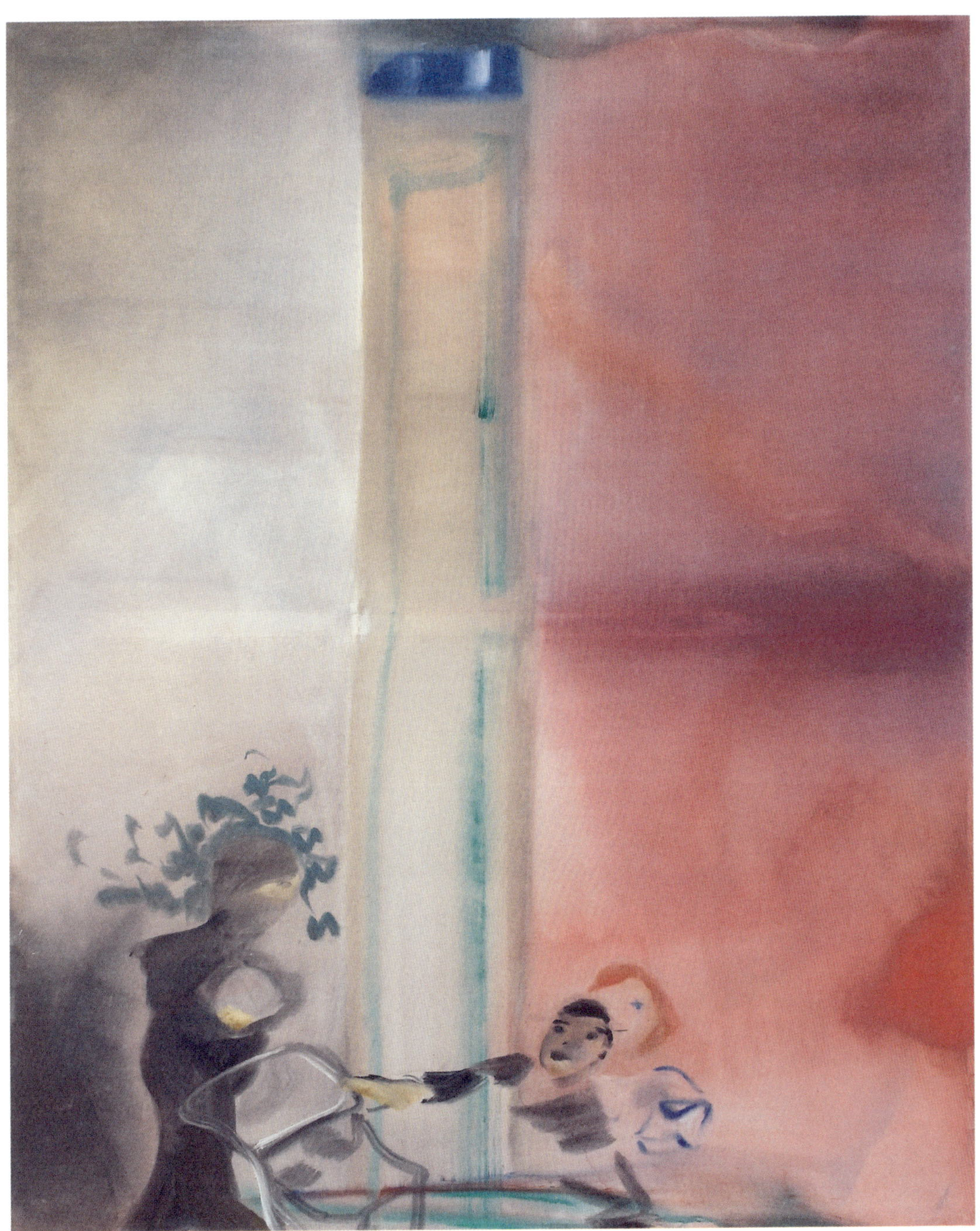

Haute de Lievre II, 2005

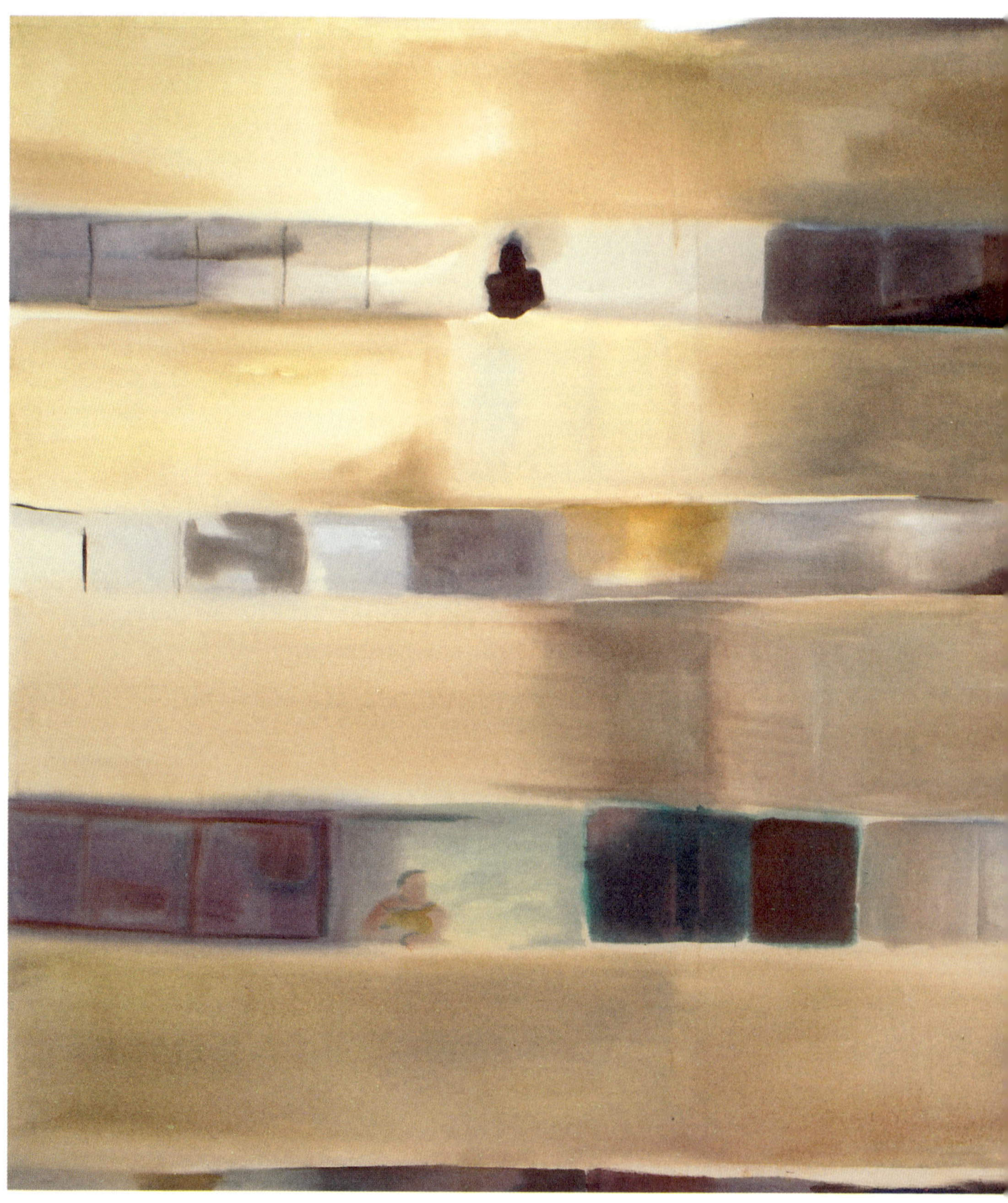

Haute de Lievre III, 2005

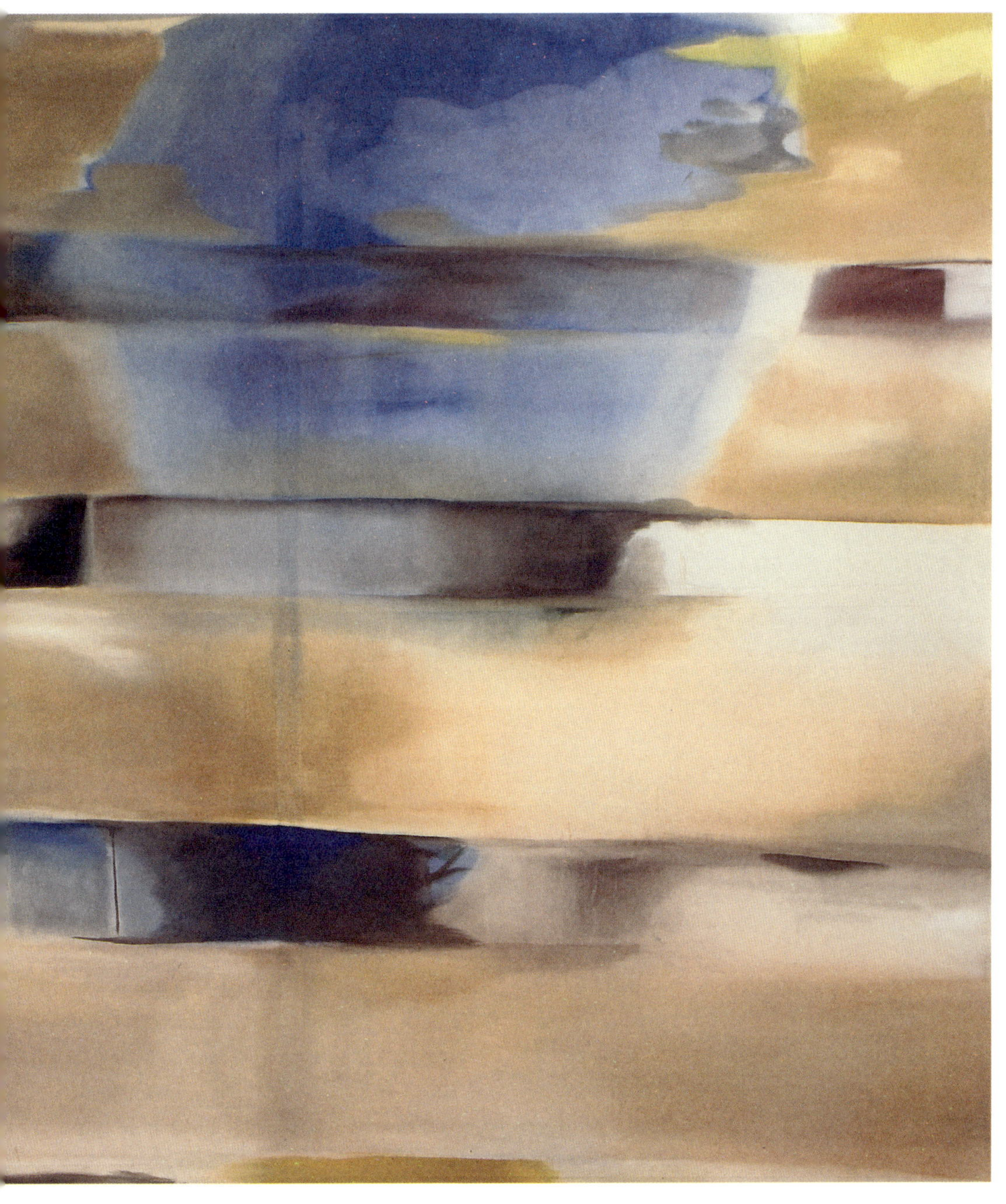

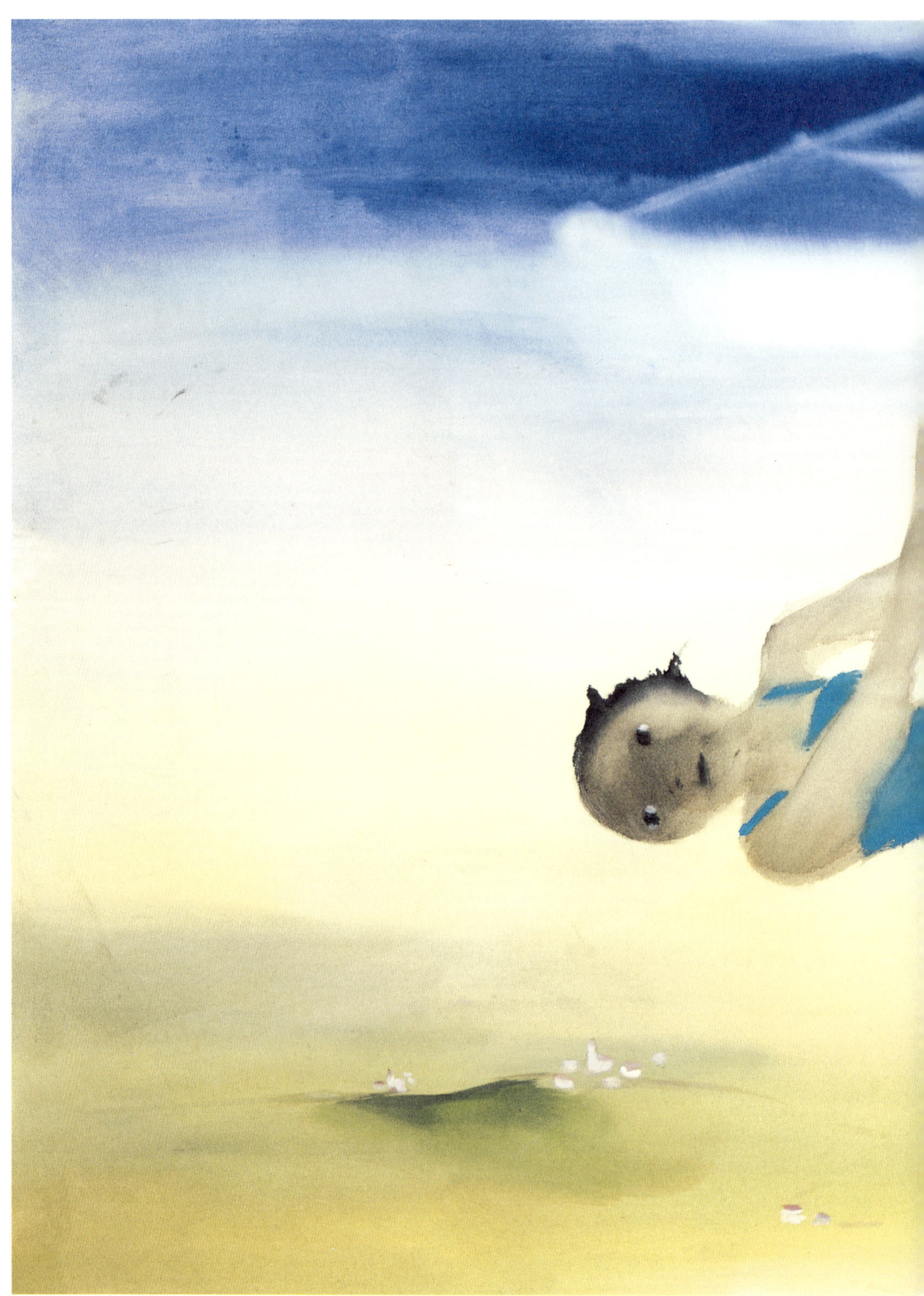

Herbstzeitlos, 2005

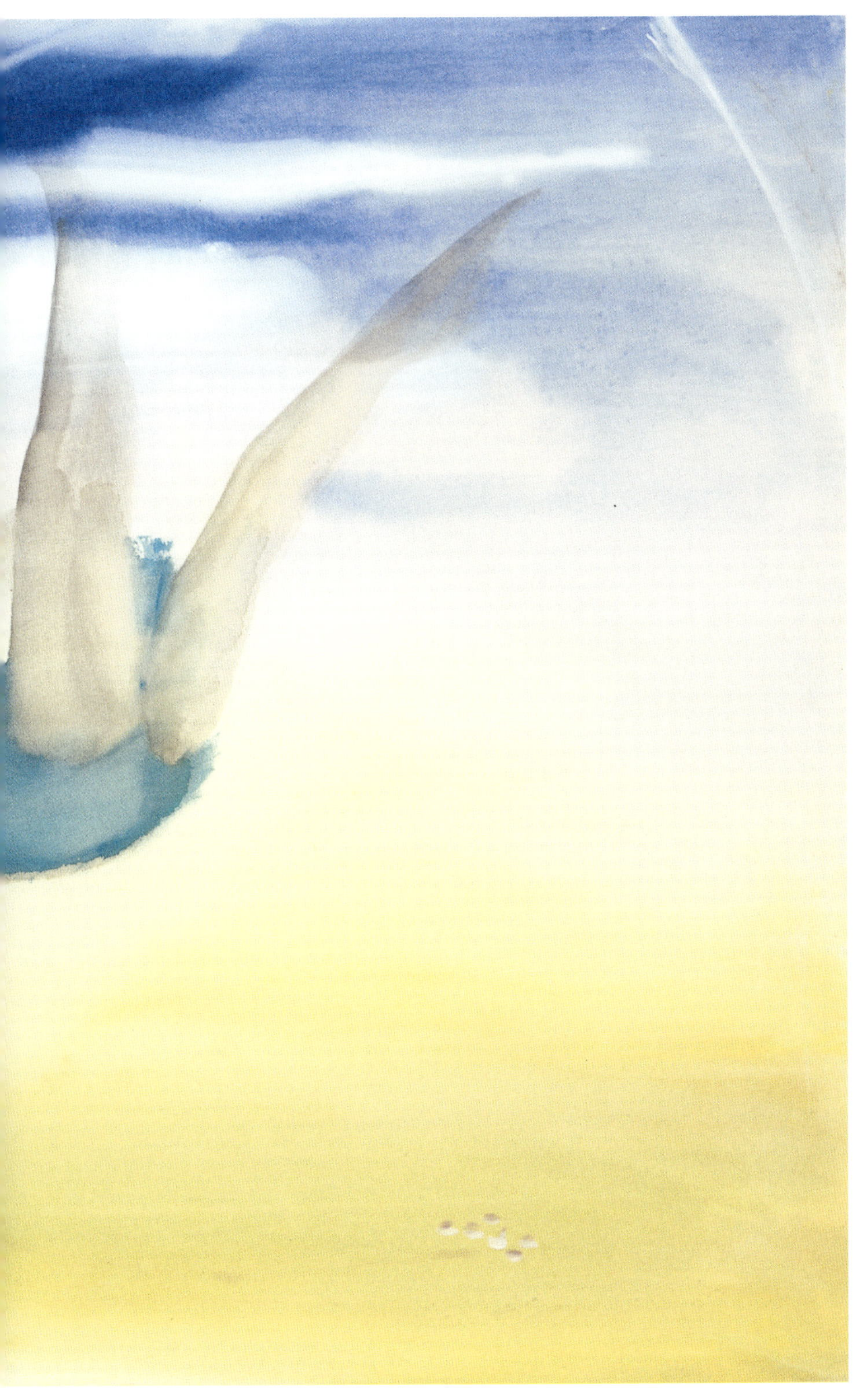

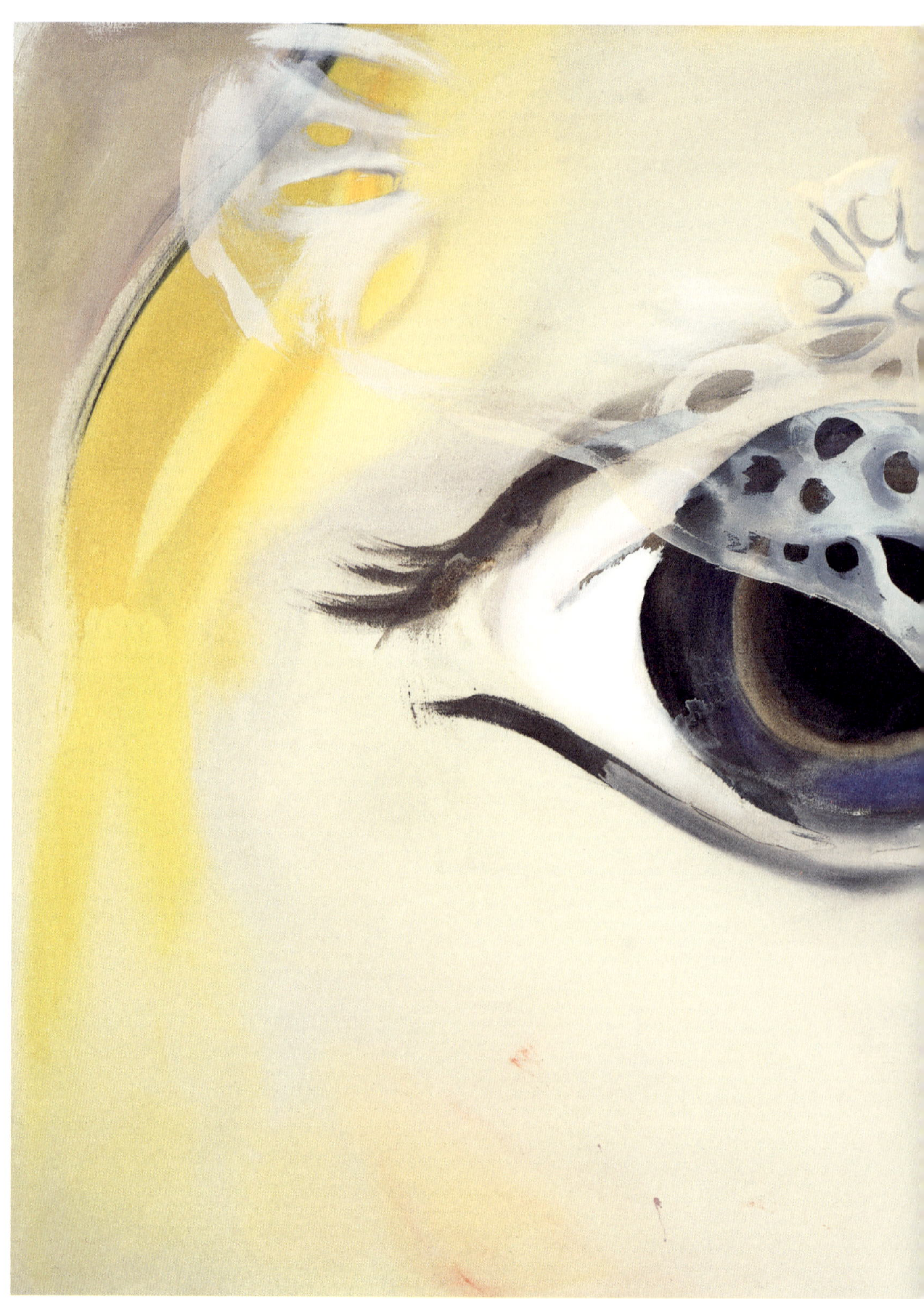

Eyeless in Gauze, 2005

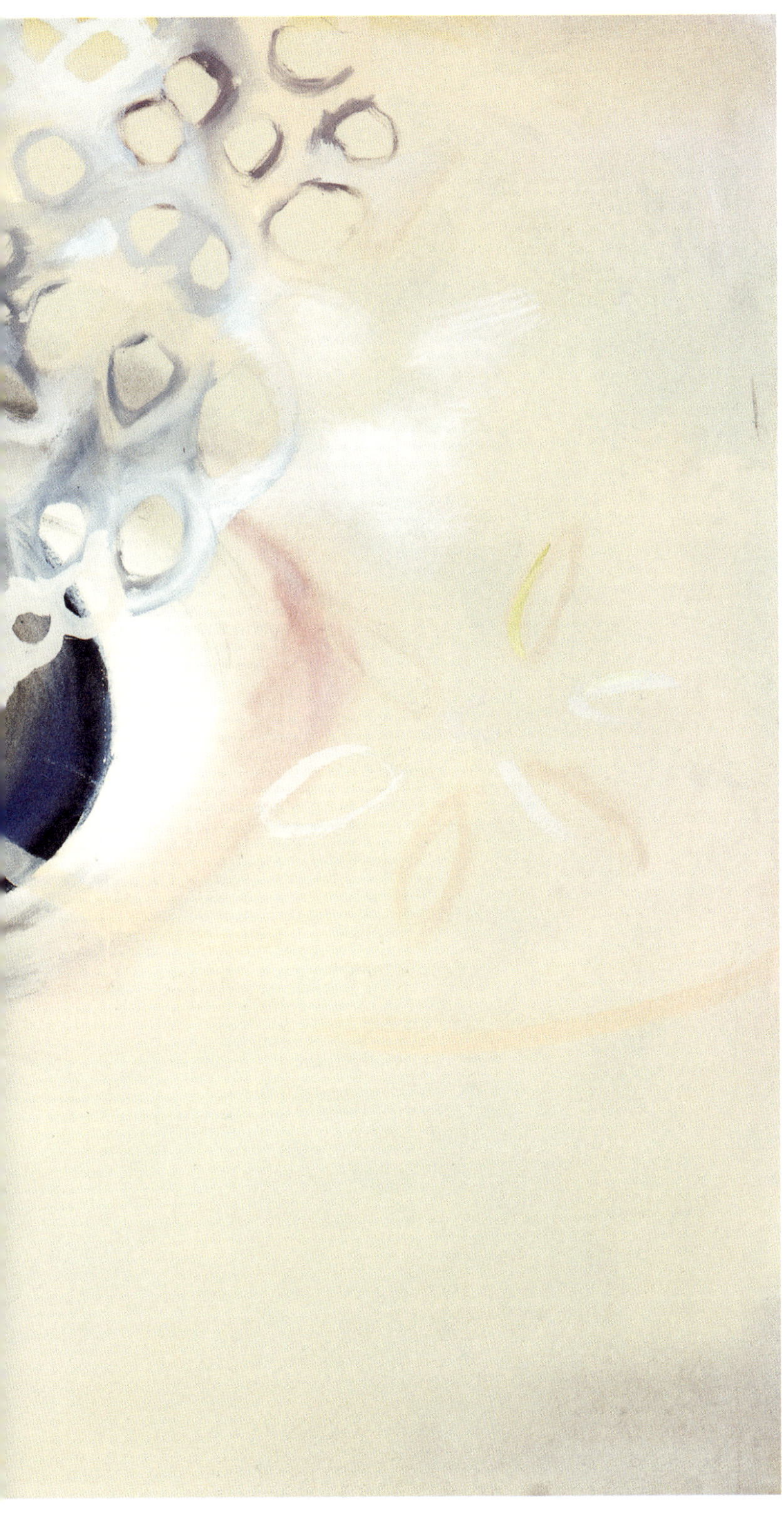

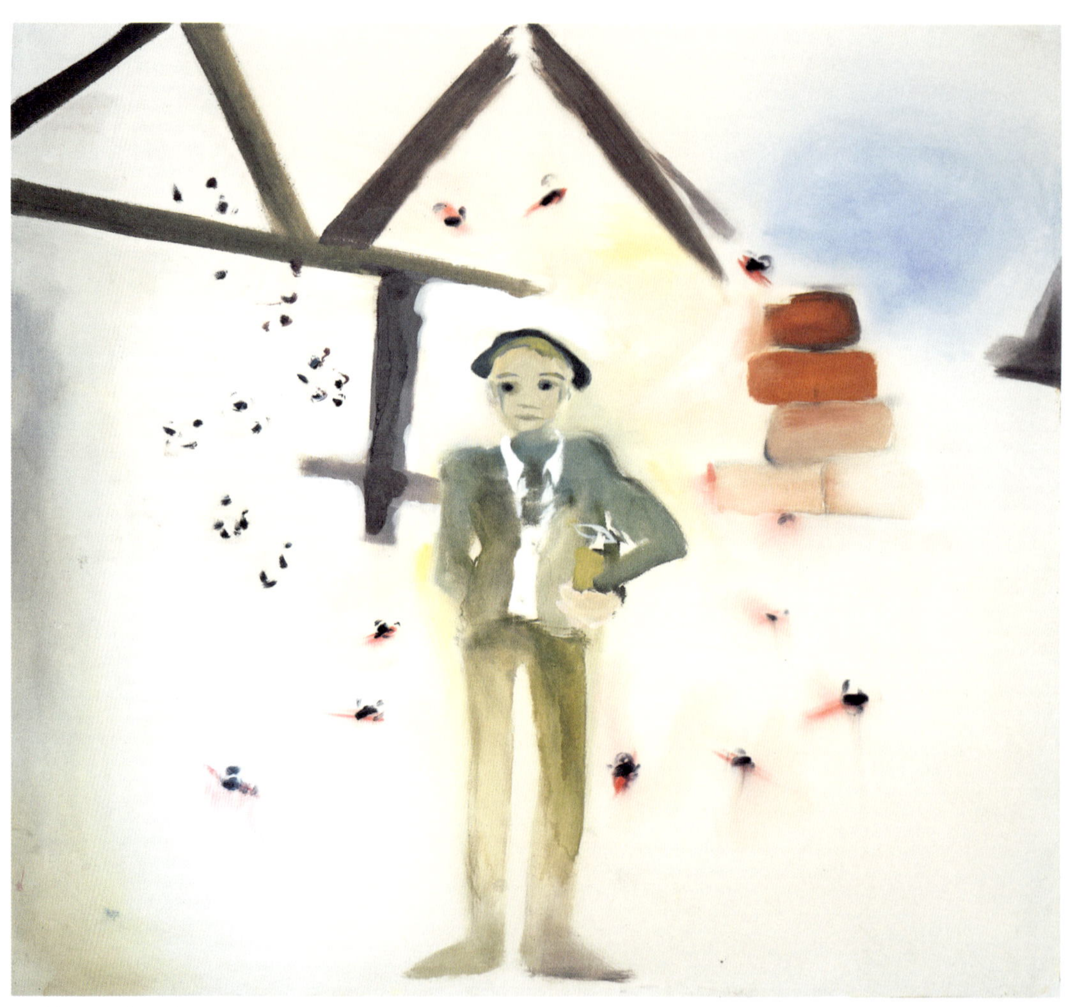

Half-remembered, 2005

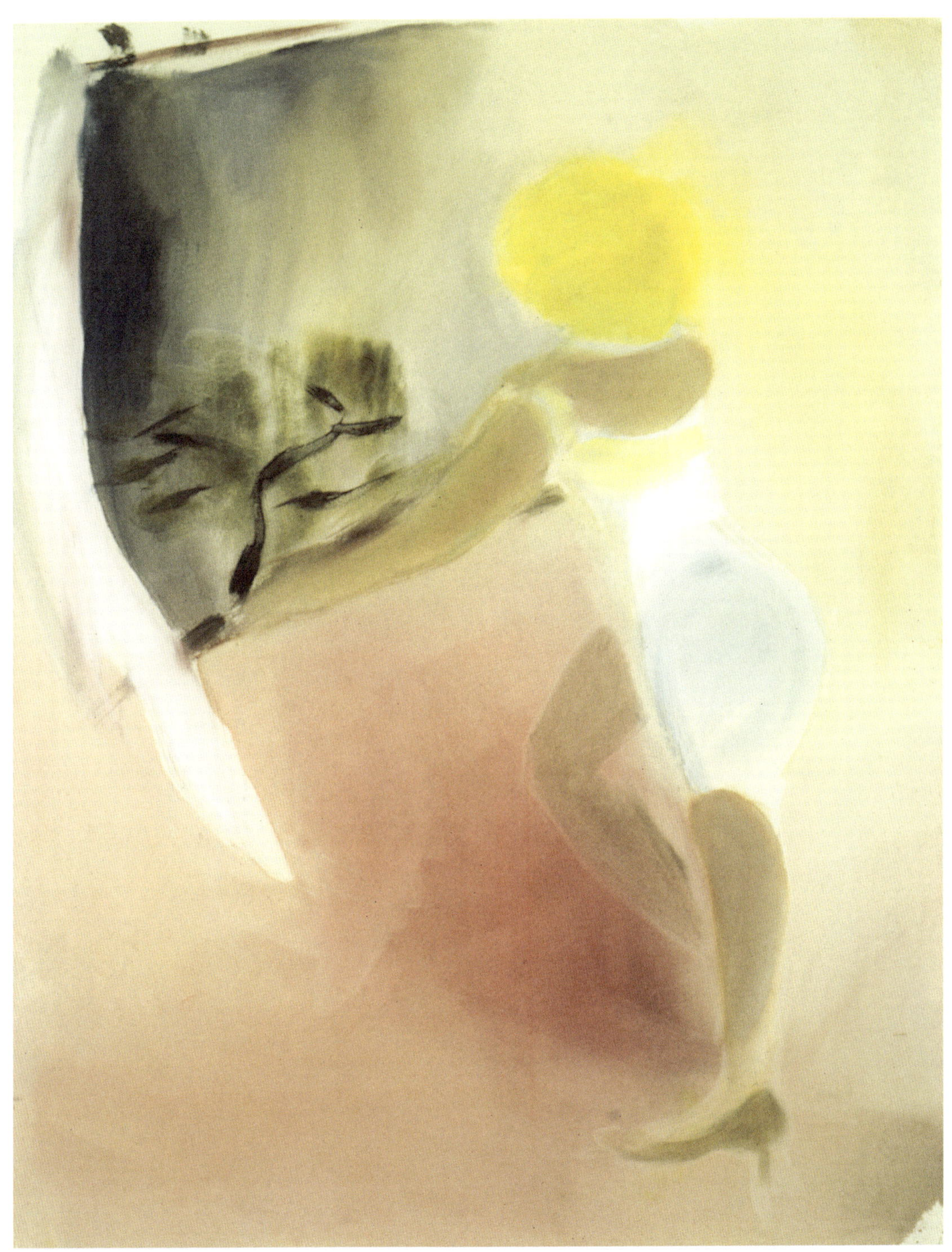

Plötzlich wurde alles gut, 2005

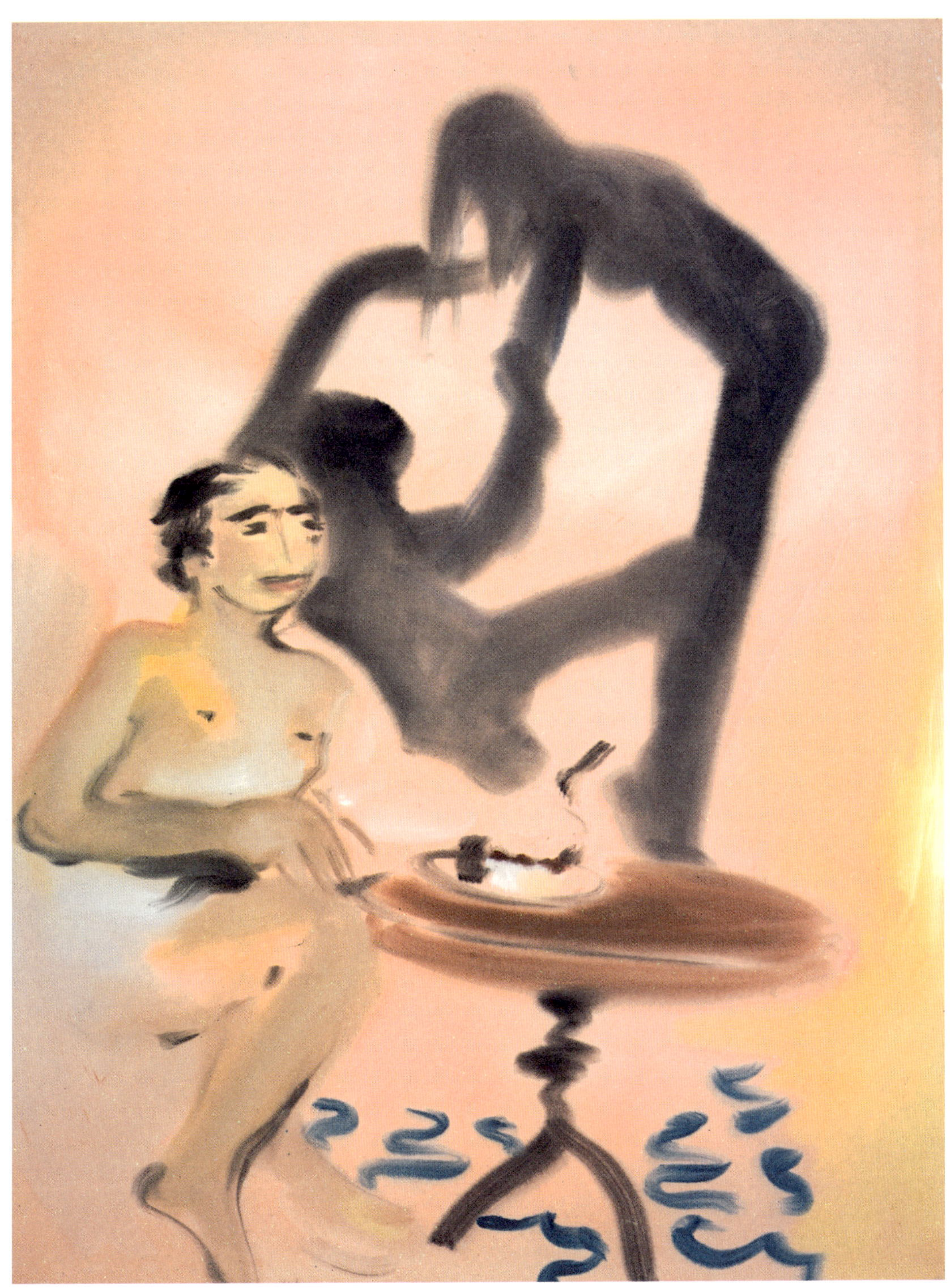

Sweet Pick Me Up, 2005

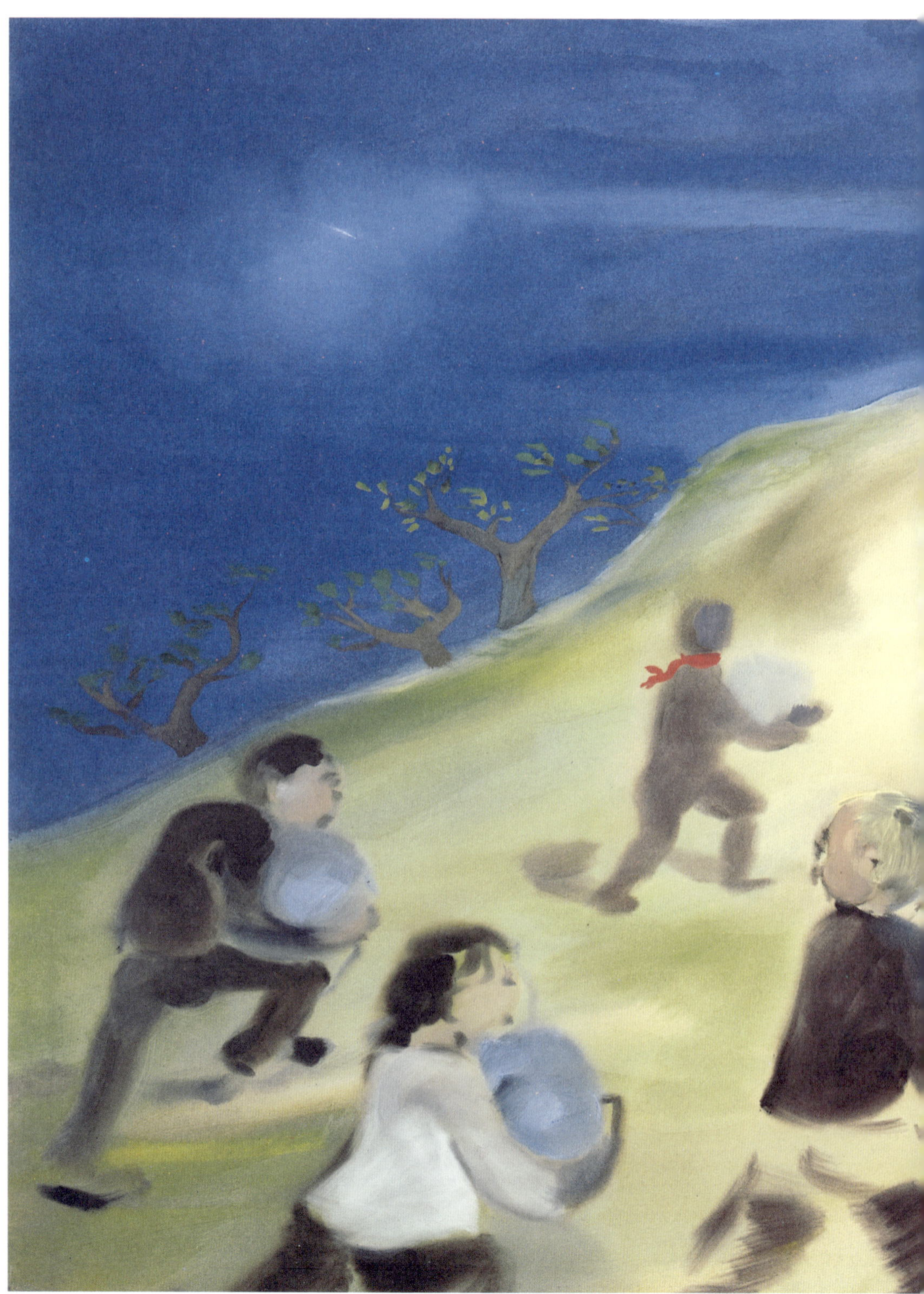

Raging against a myth I, 2005

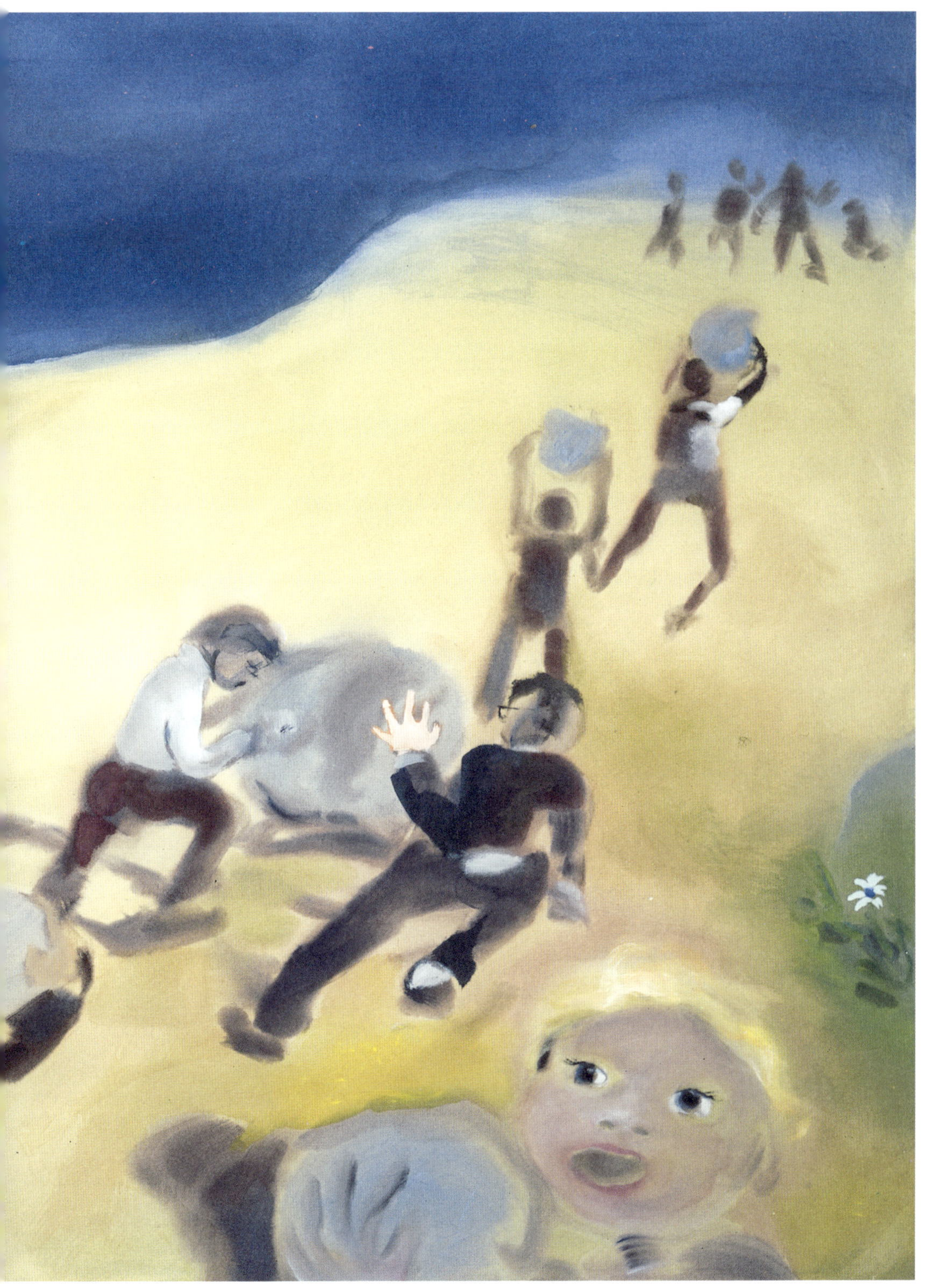

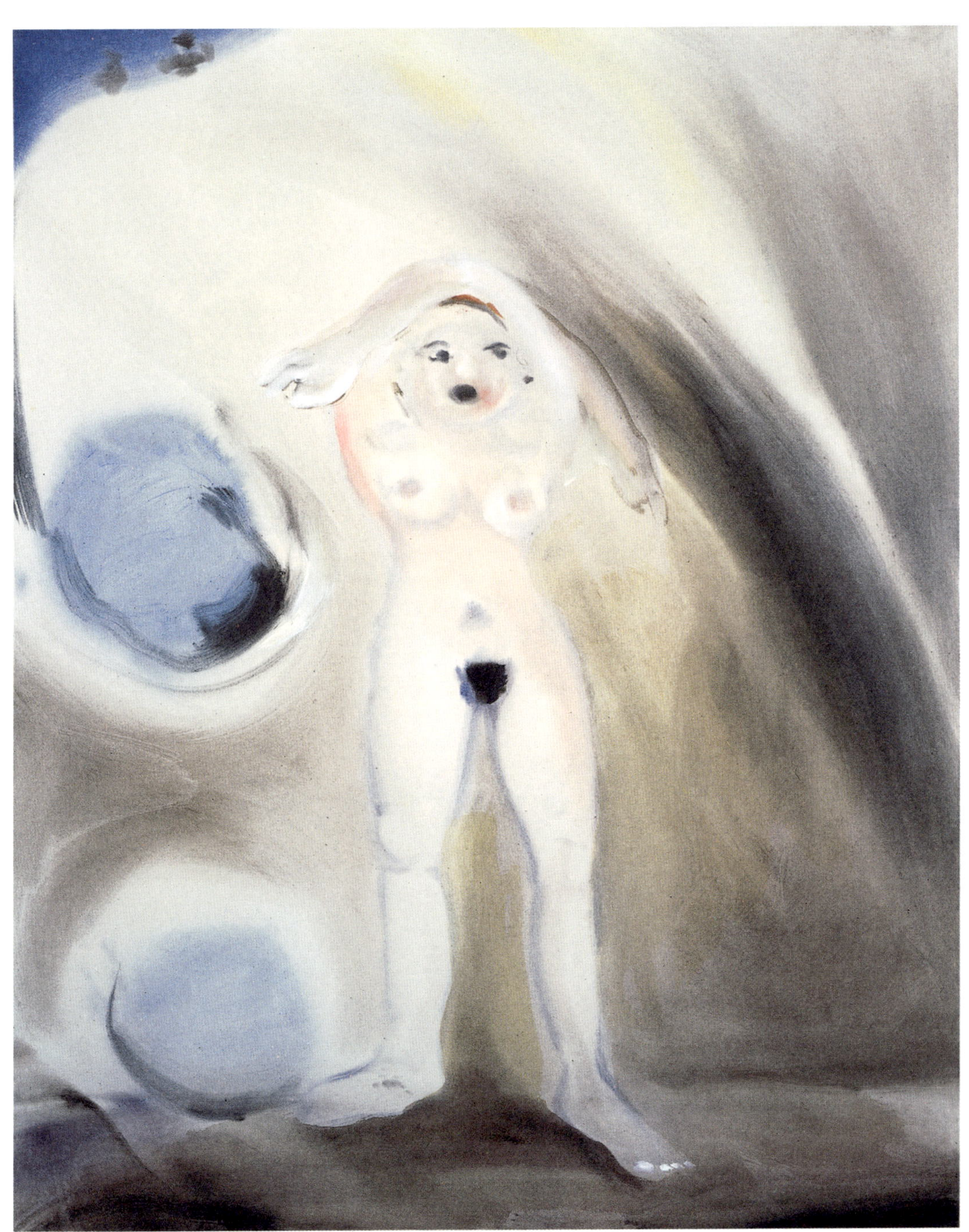

Raging against a myth II, 2005

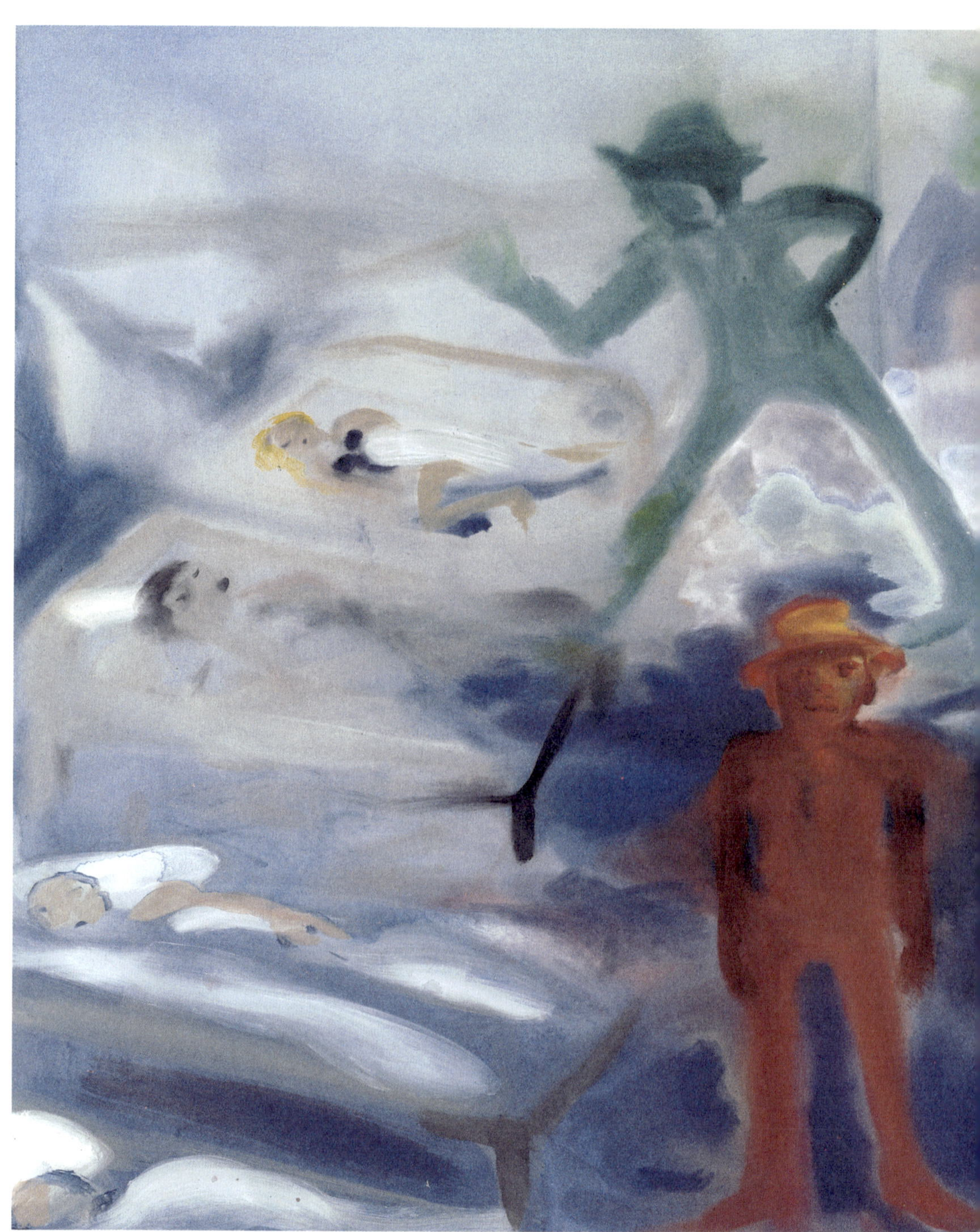

Walk, Don't Walk, 2005

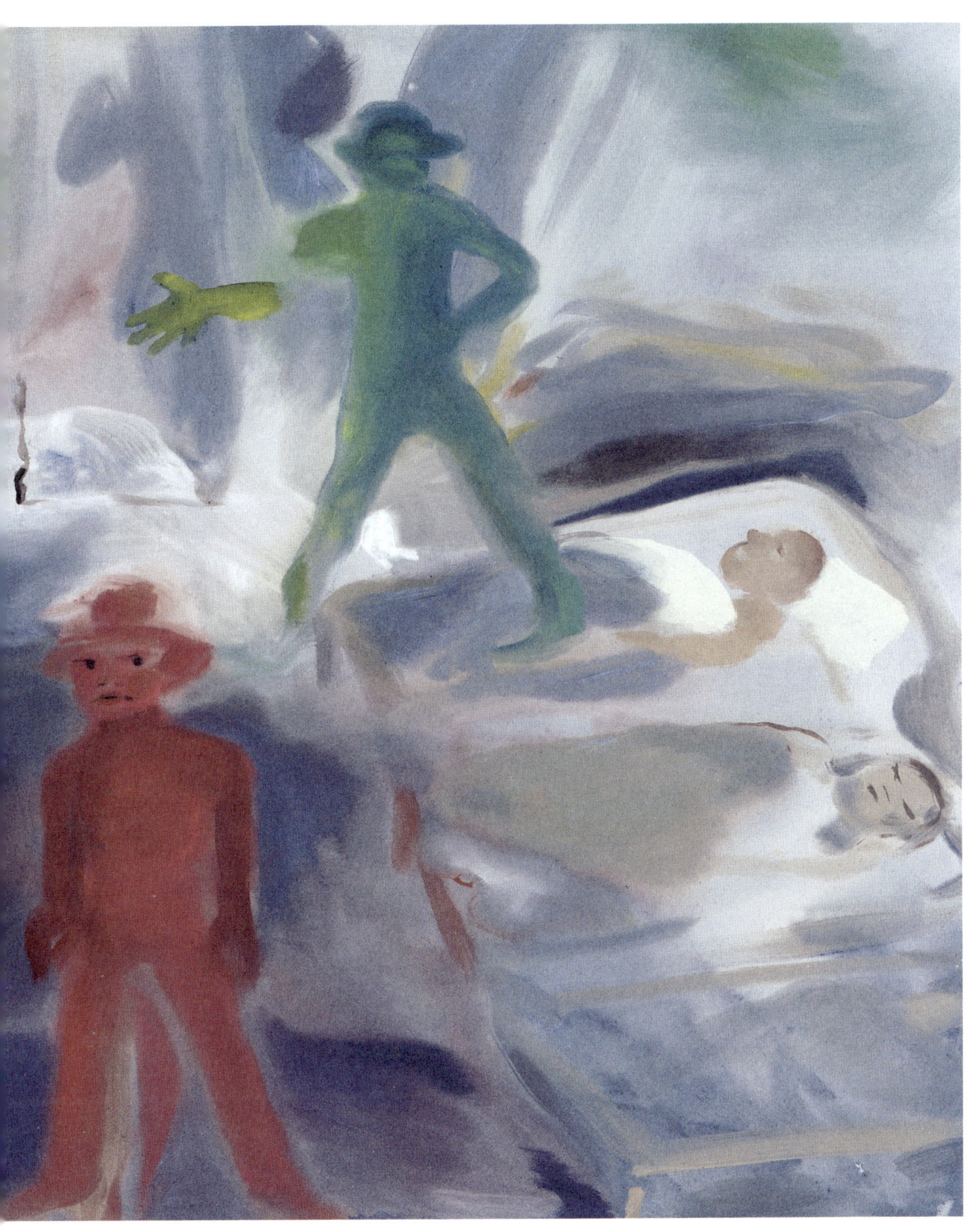

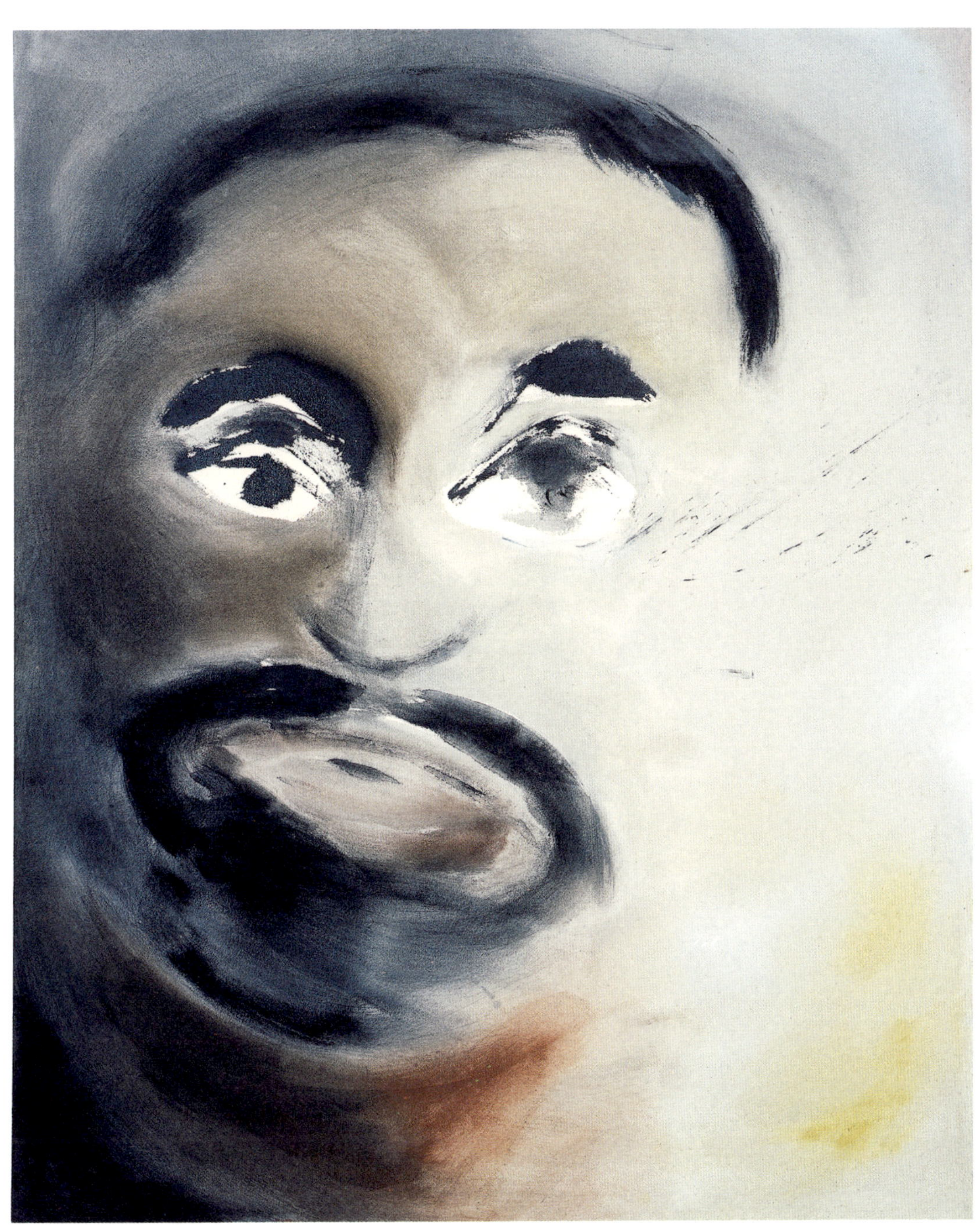

Delusions of Silent Anxiety I, 2005

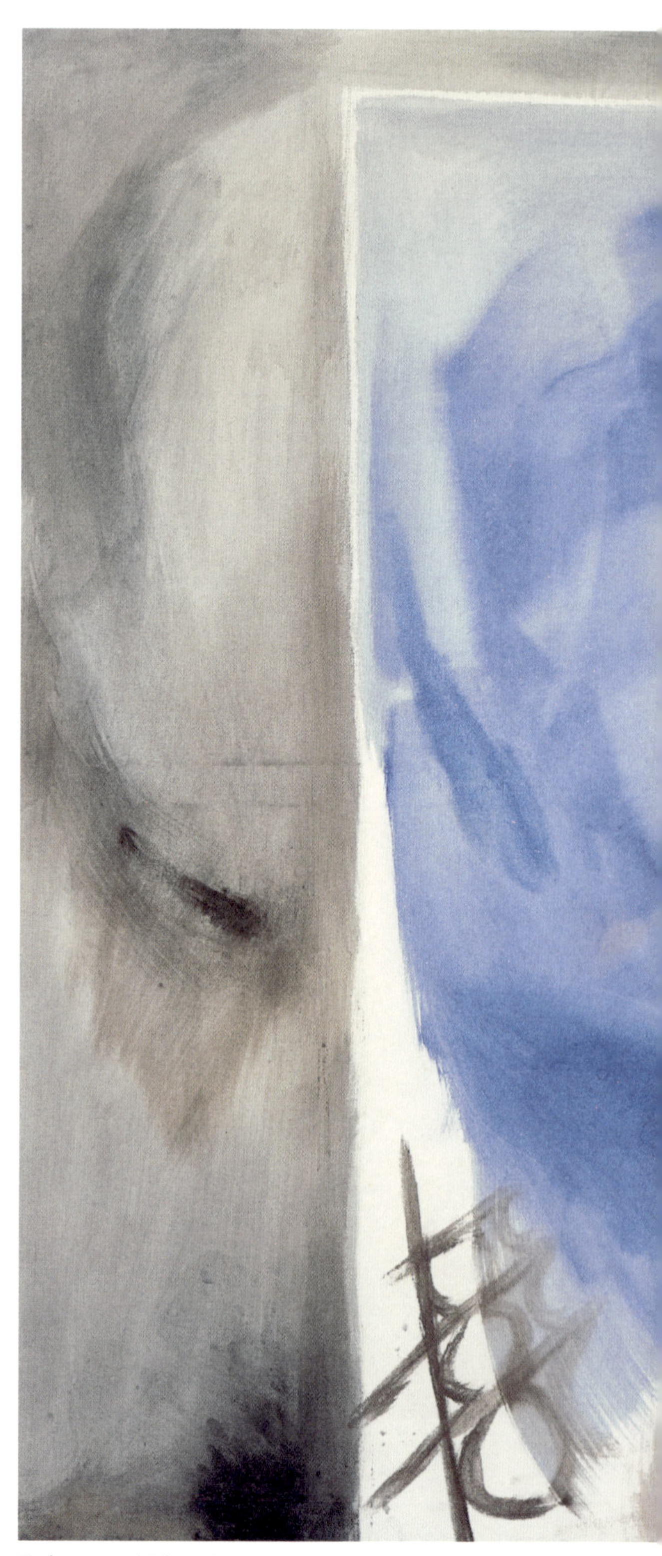

Delusions of Silent Anxiety II, 2005

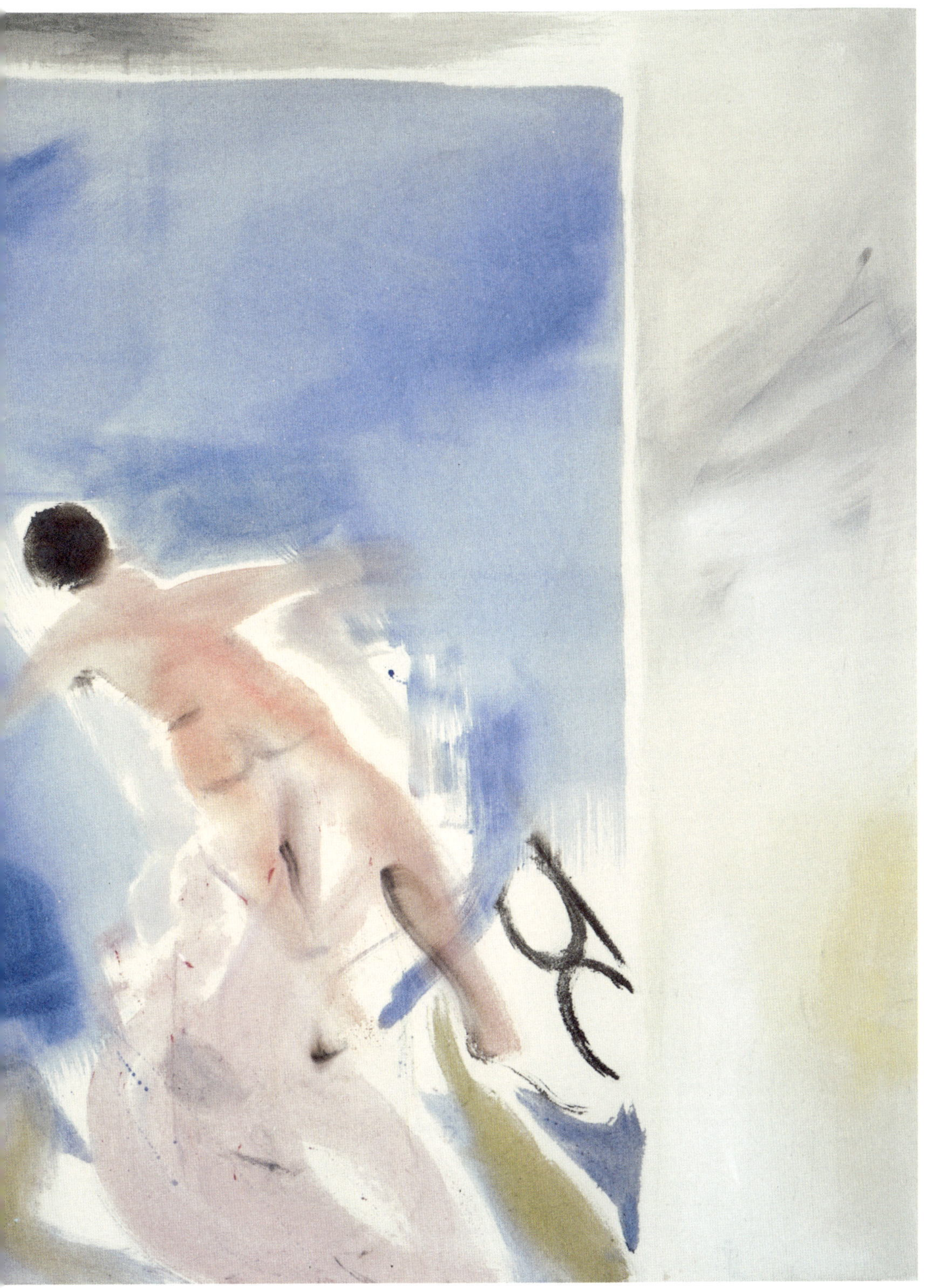

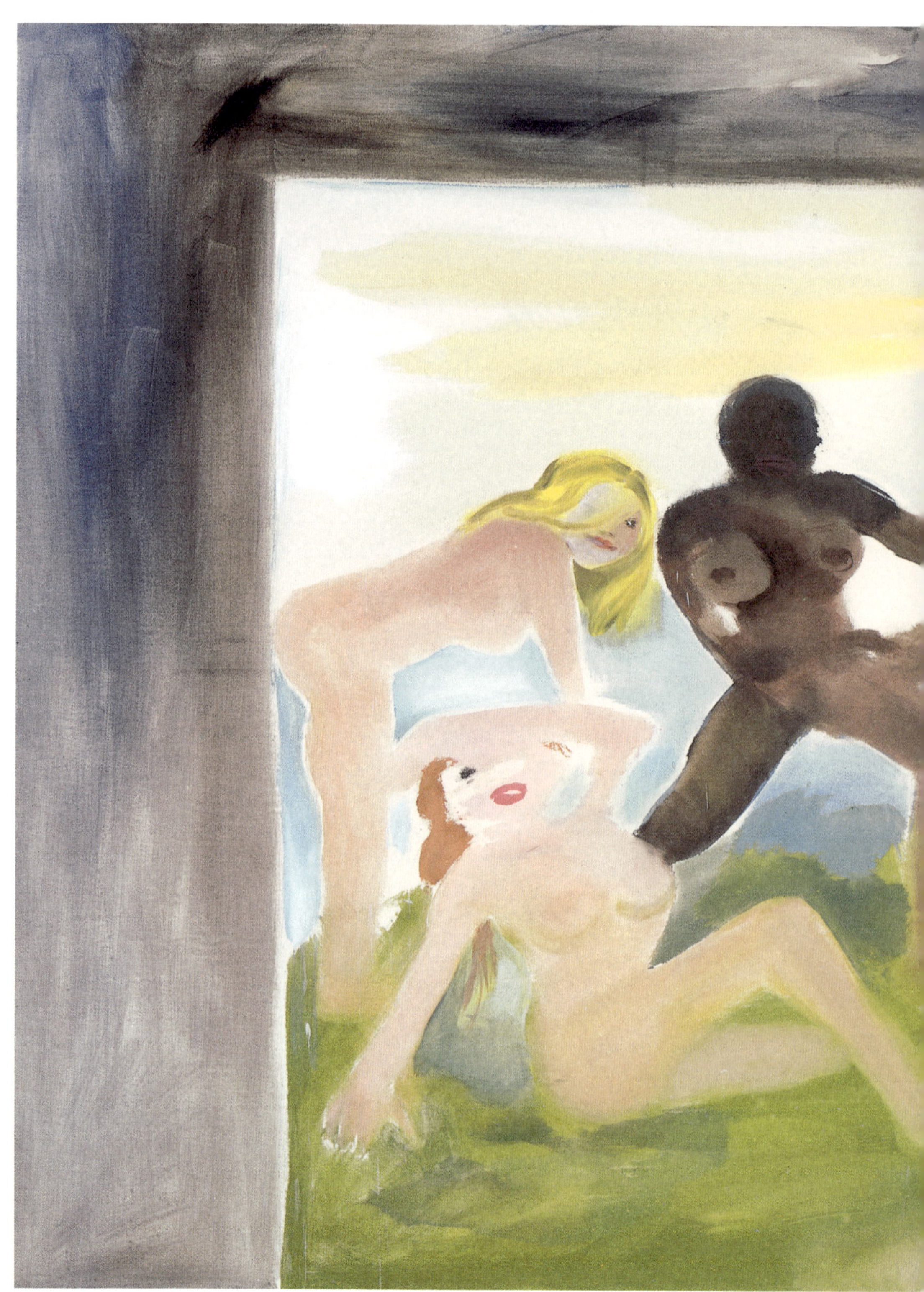

Delusions of Silent Anxiety III, 2005

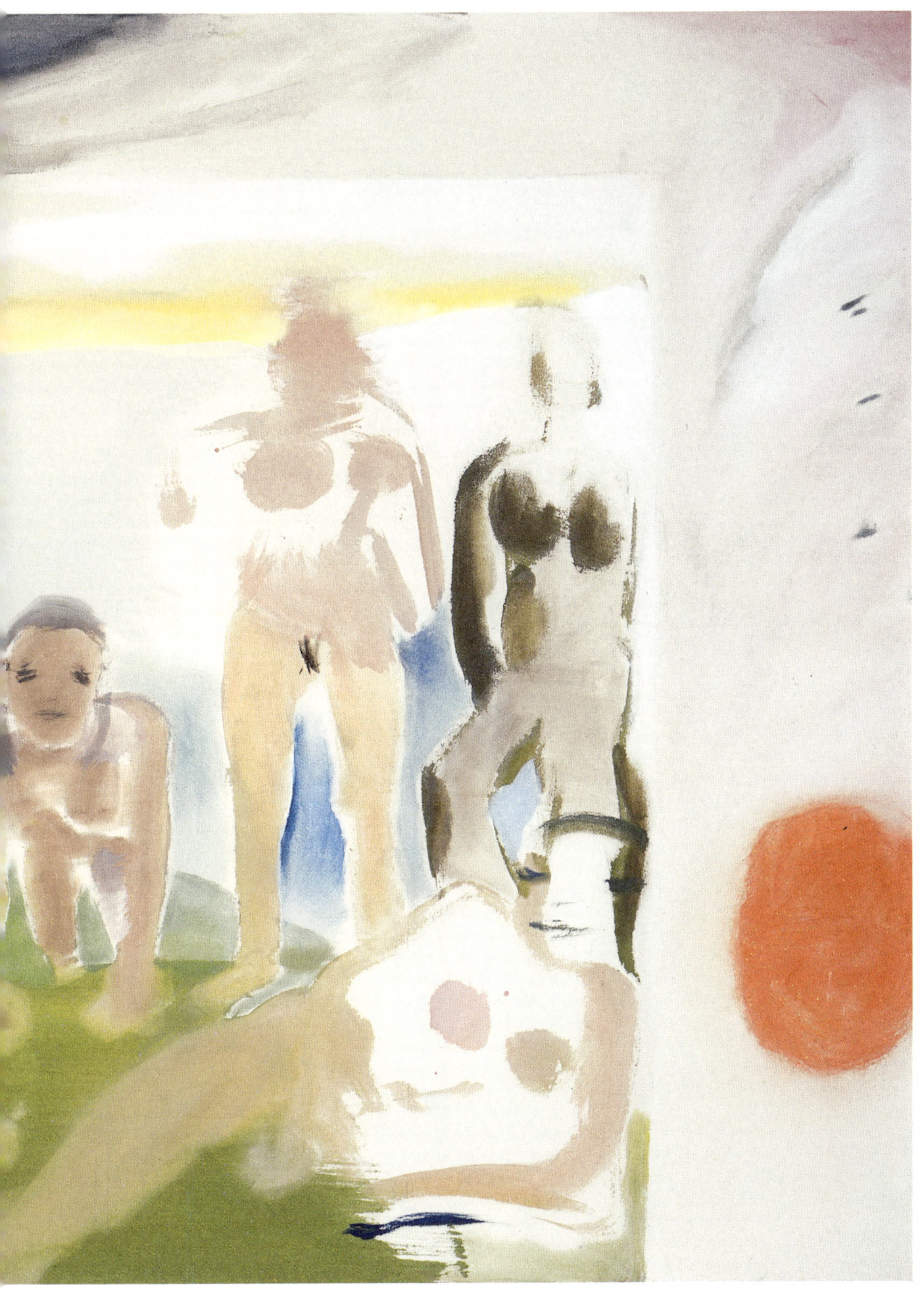

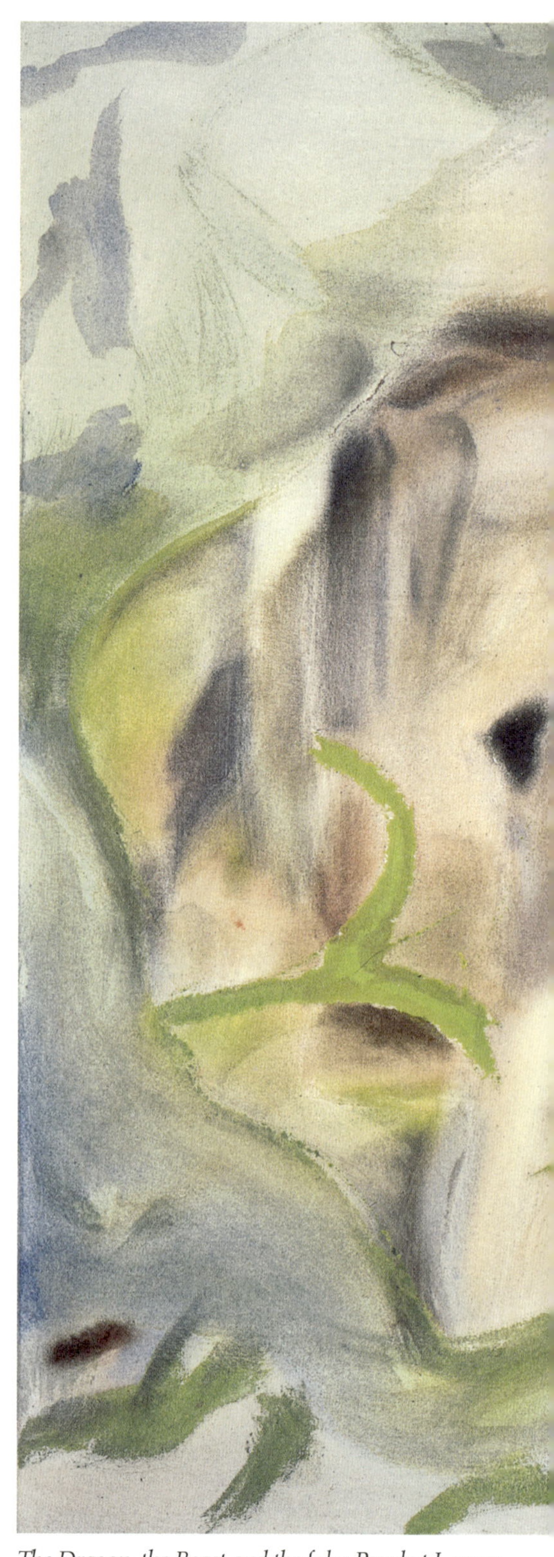

The Dragon, the Beast and the false Prophet I, 2005

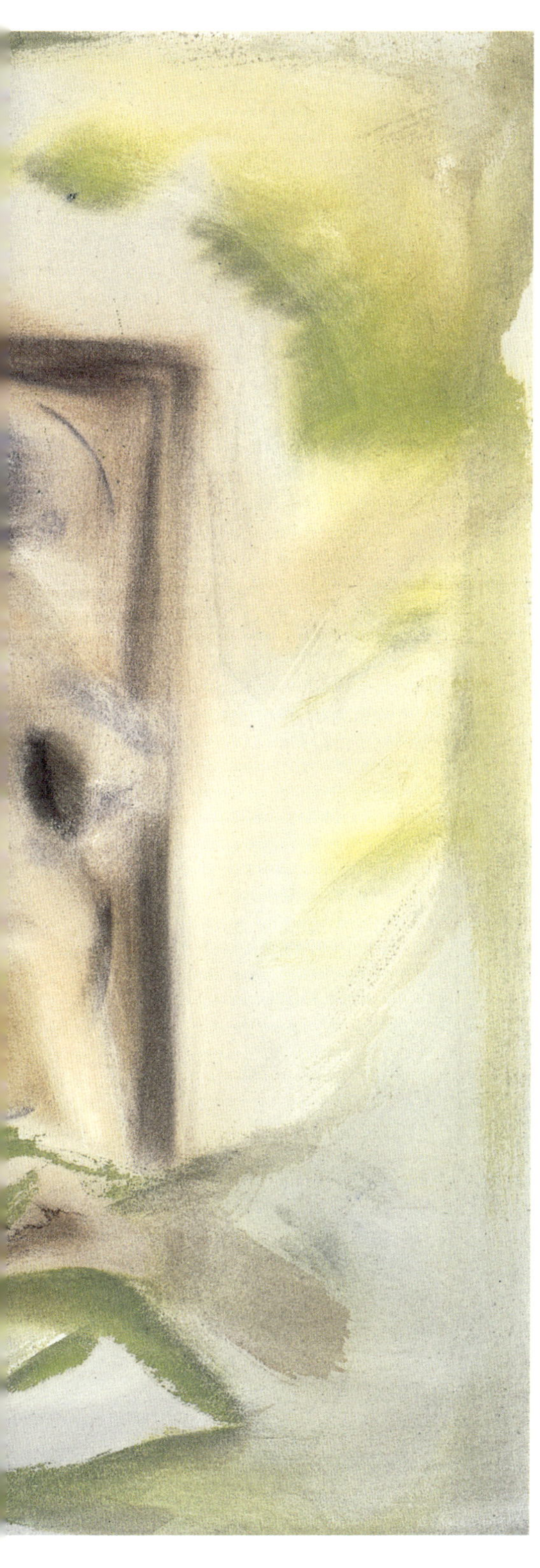

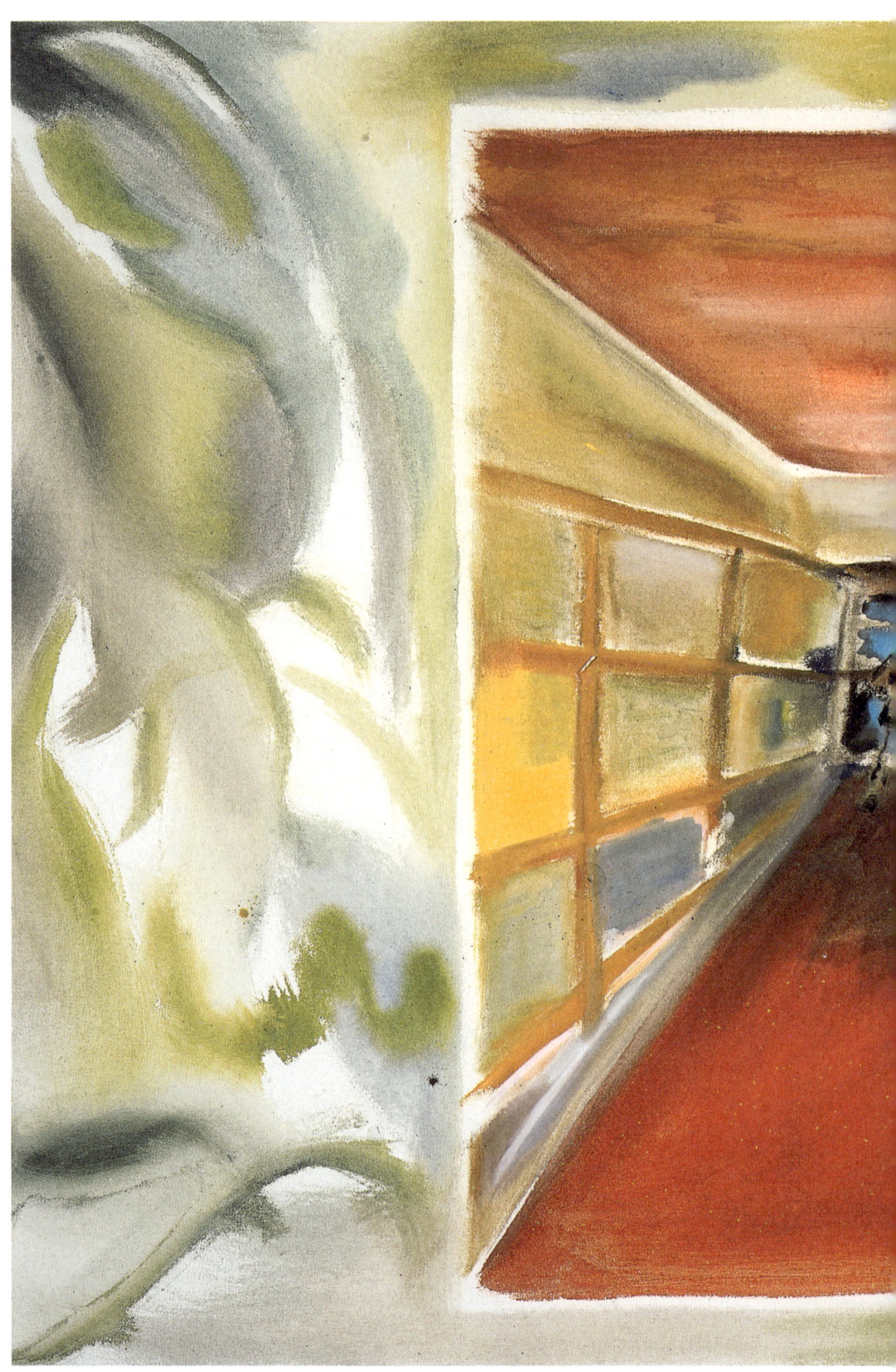

  The Dragon, the Beast and the false Prophet II, 2005

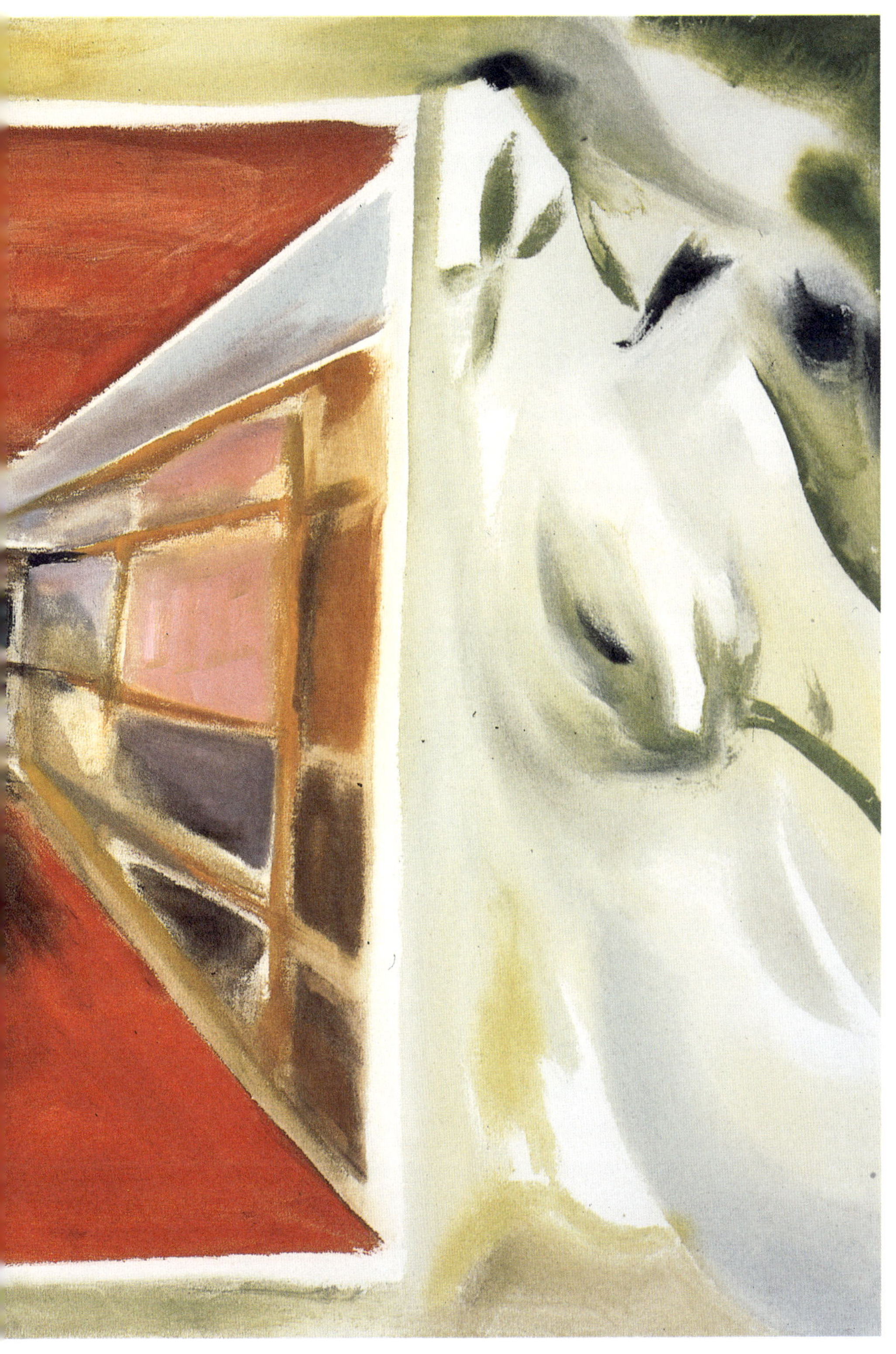

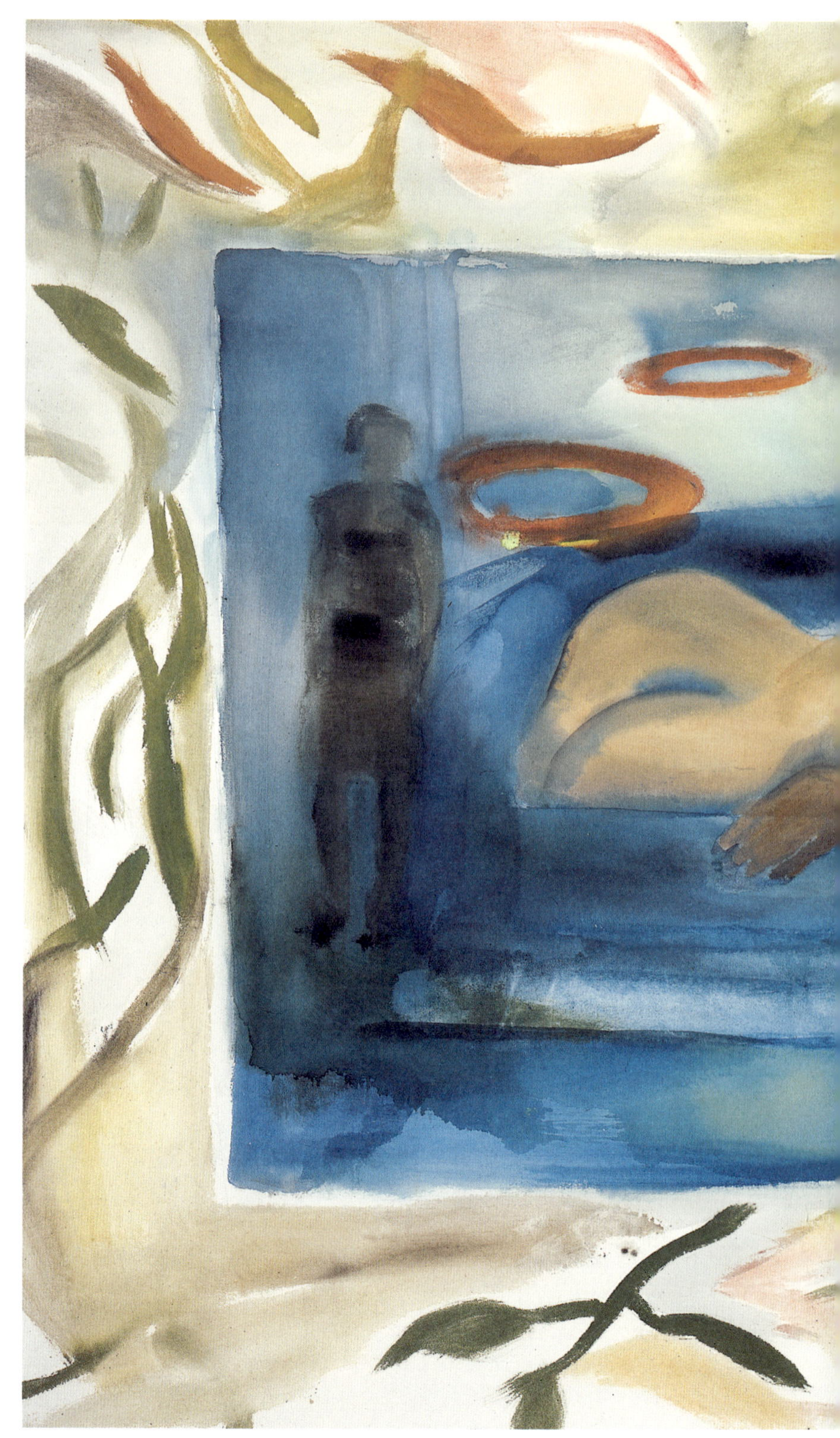

The Dragon, the Beast and the false Prophet III, 2005

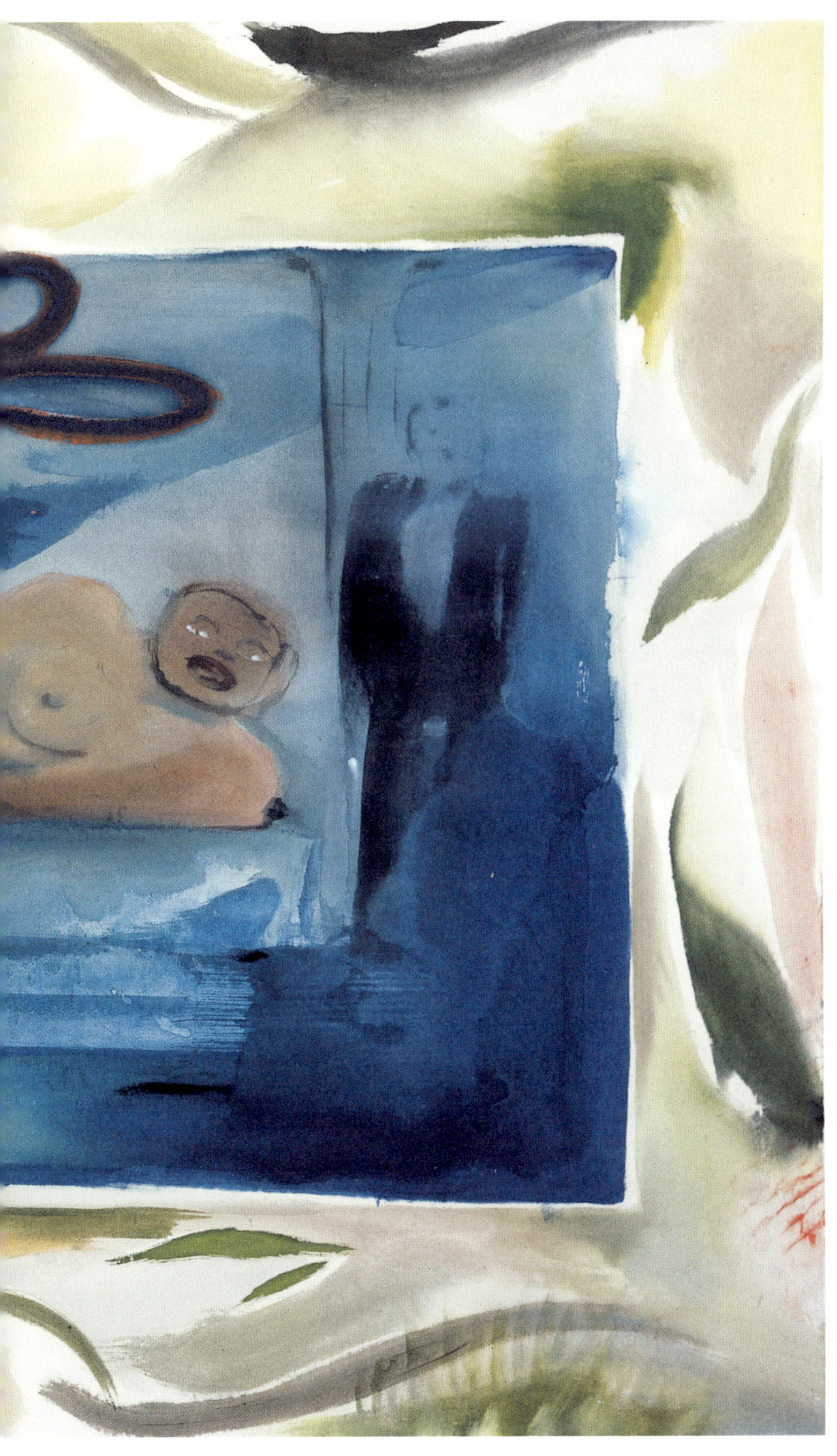

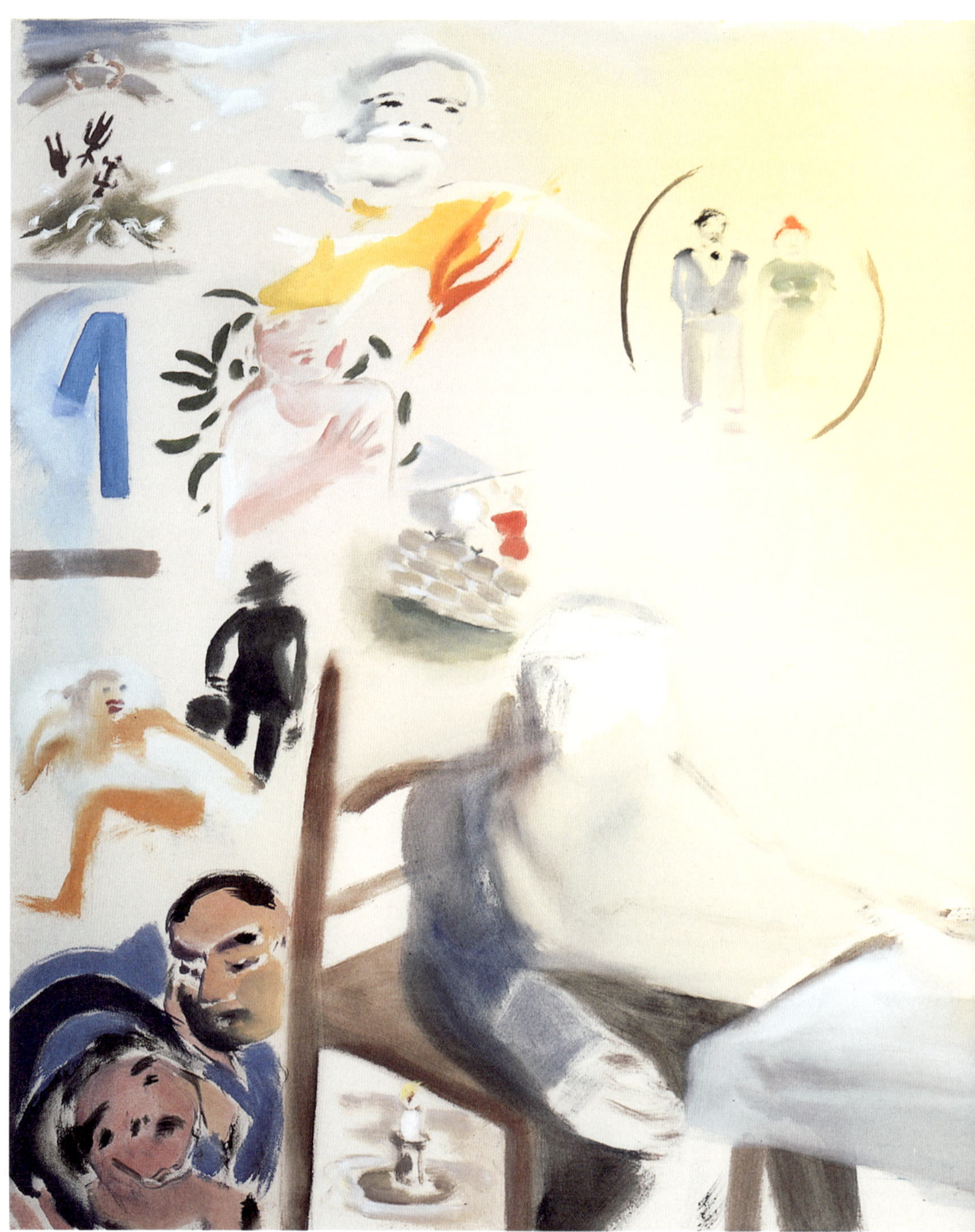

Untitled (Ten Commandments), 2005

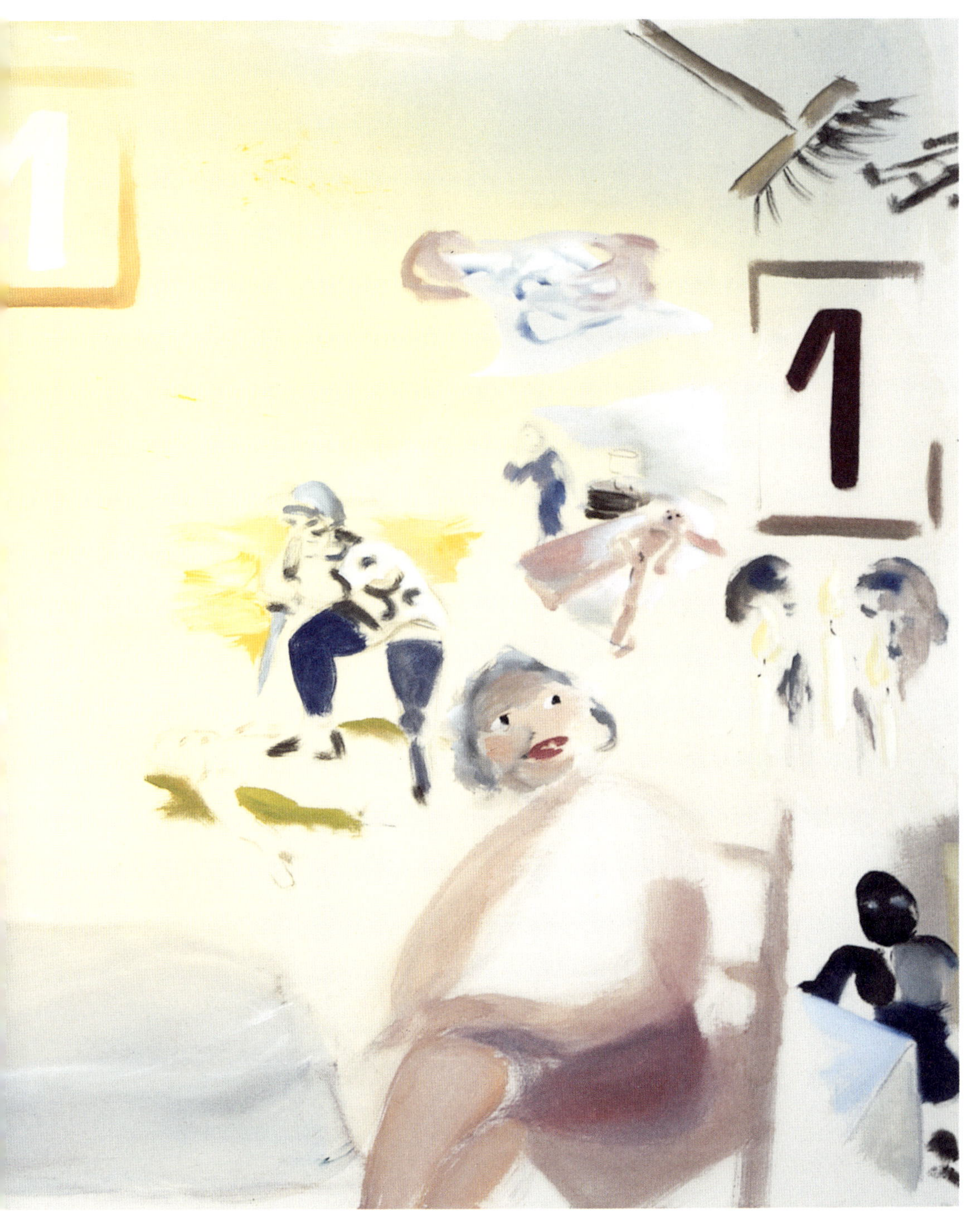

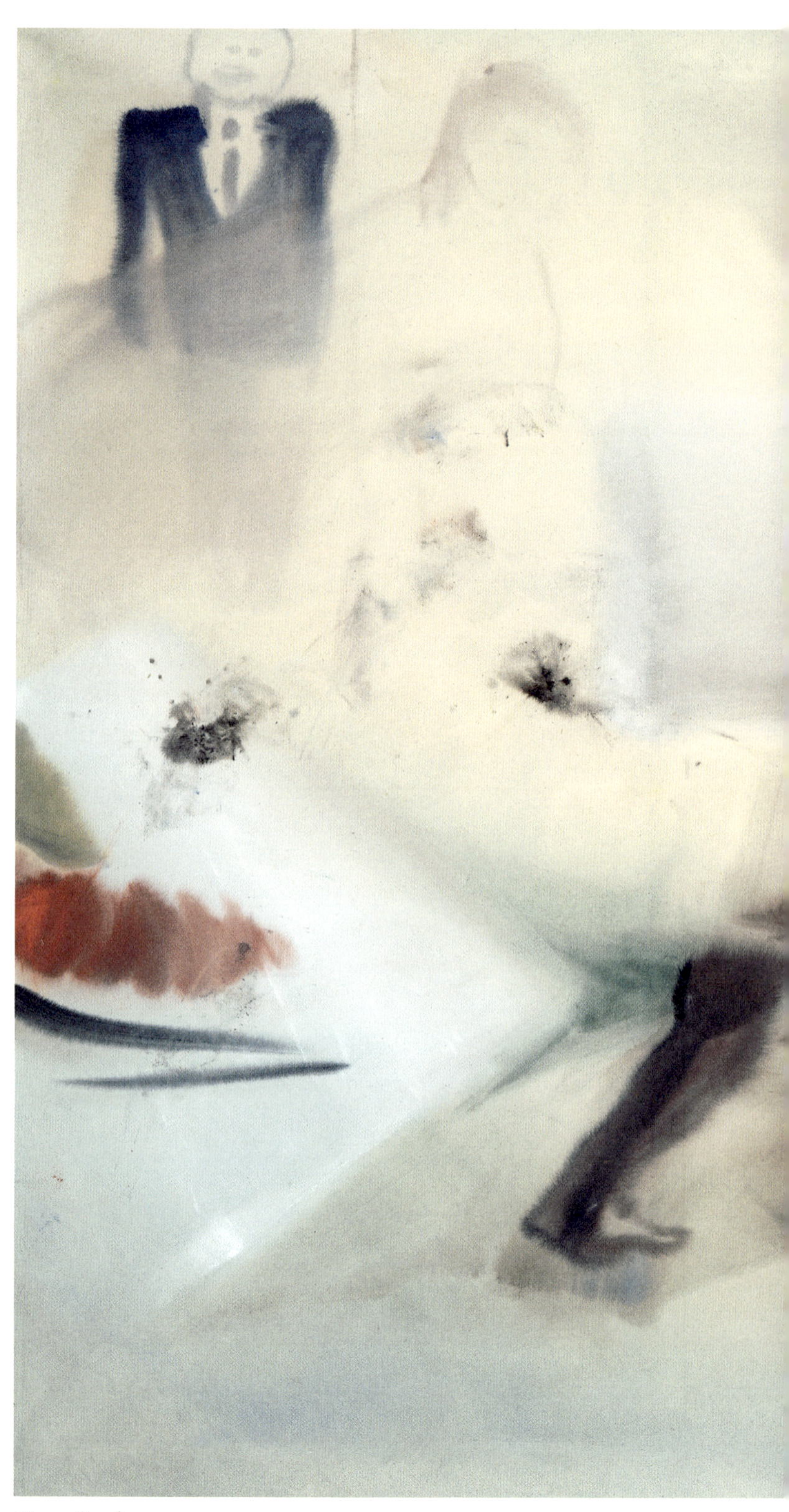

Green Earth, 2005

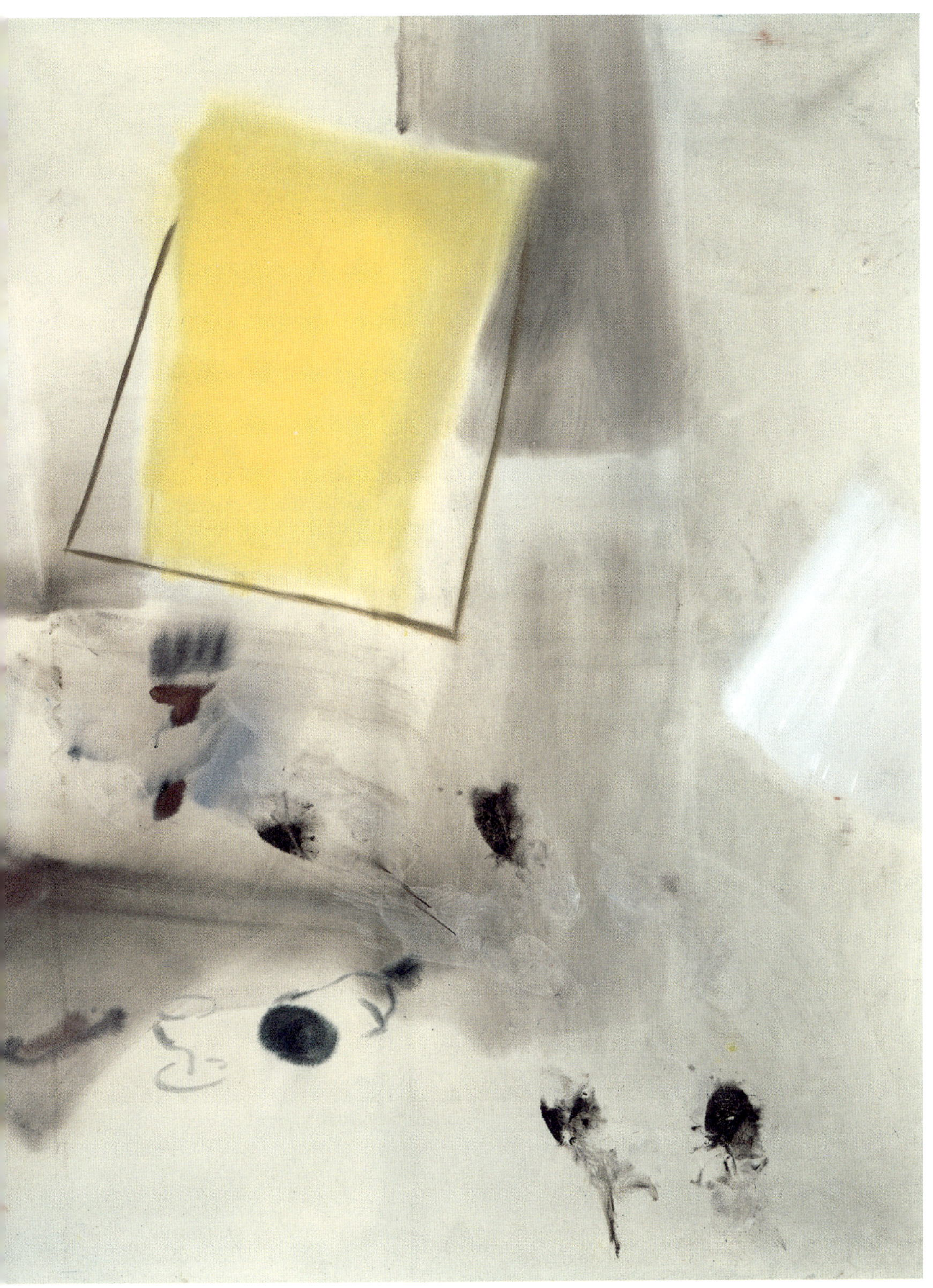

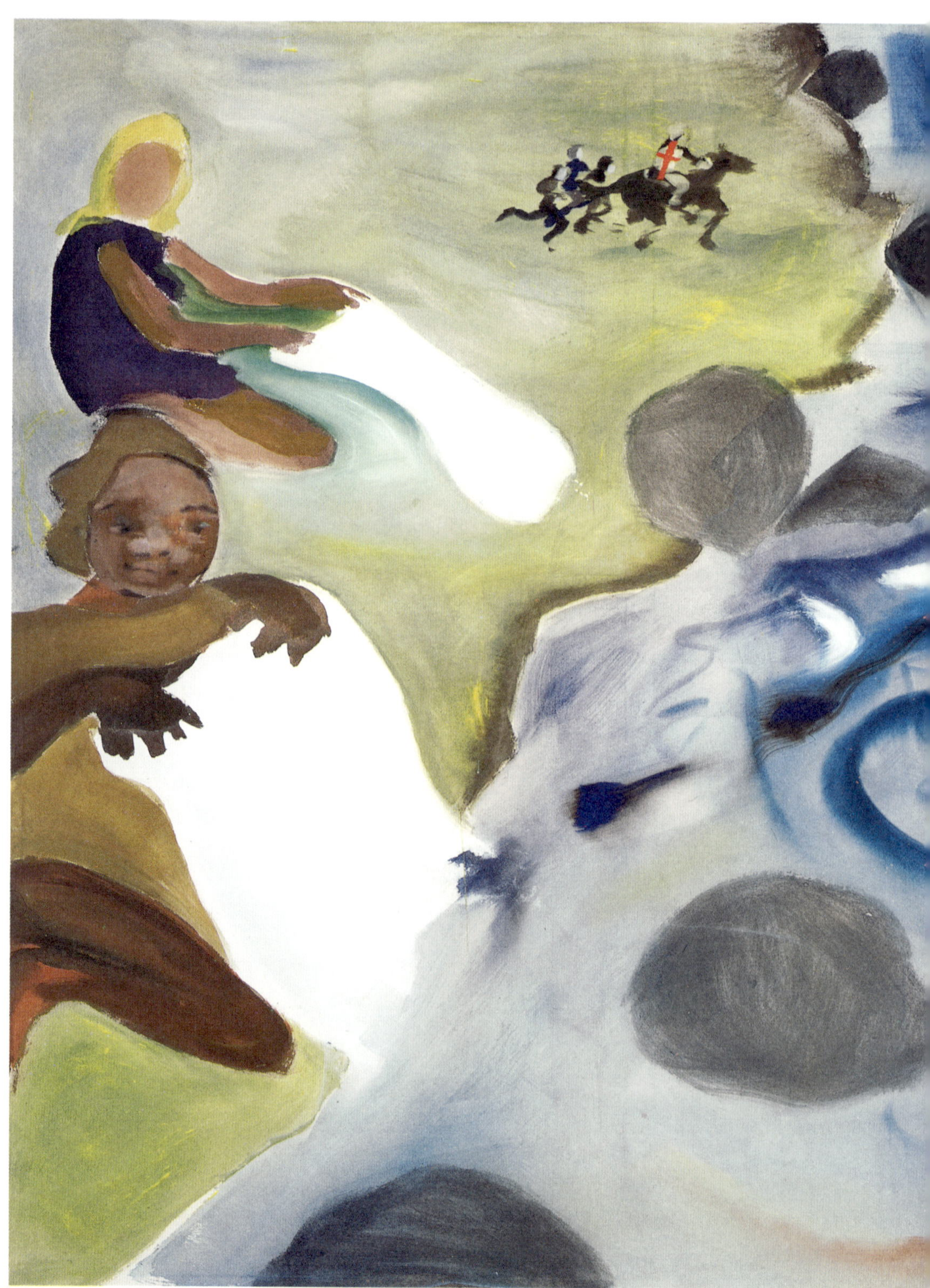

Washing the News, 2005

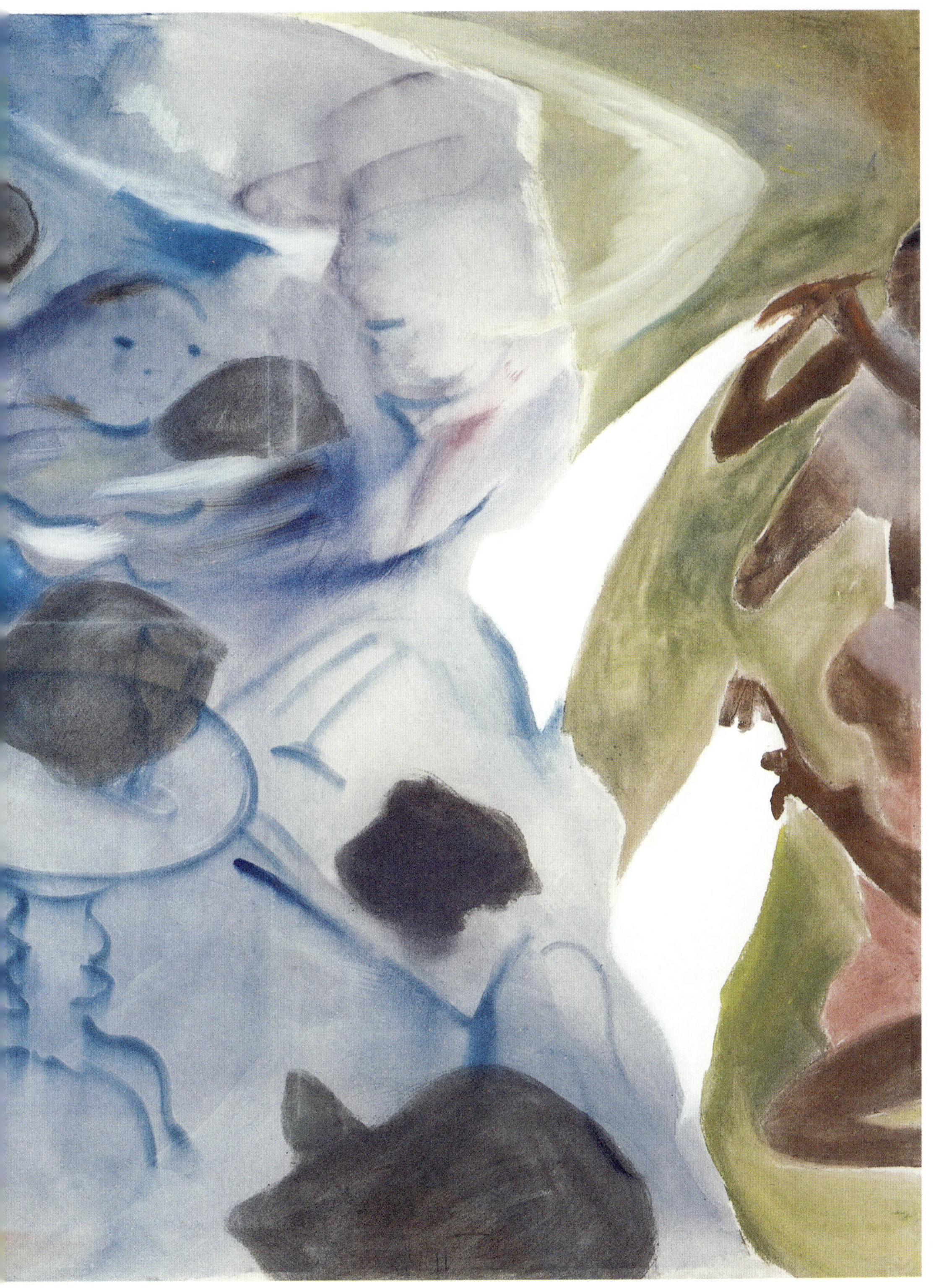

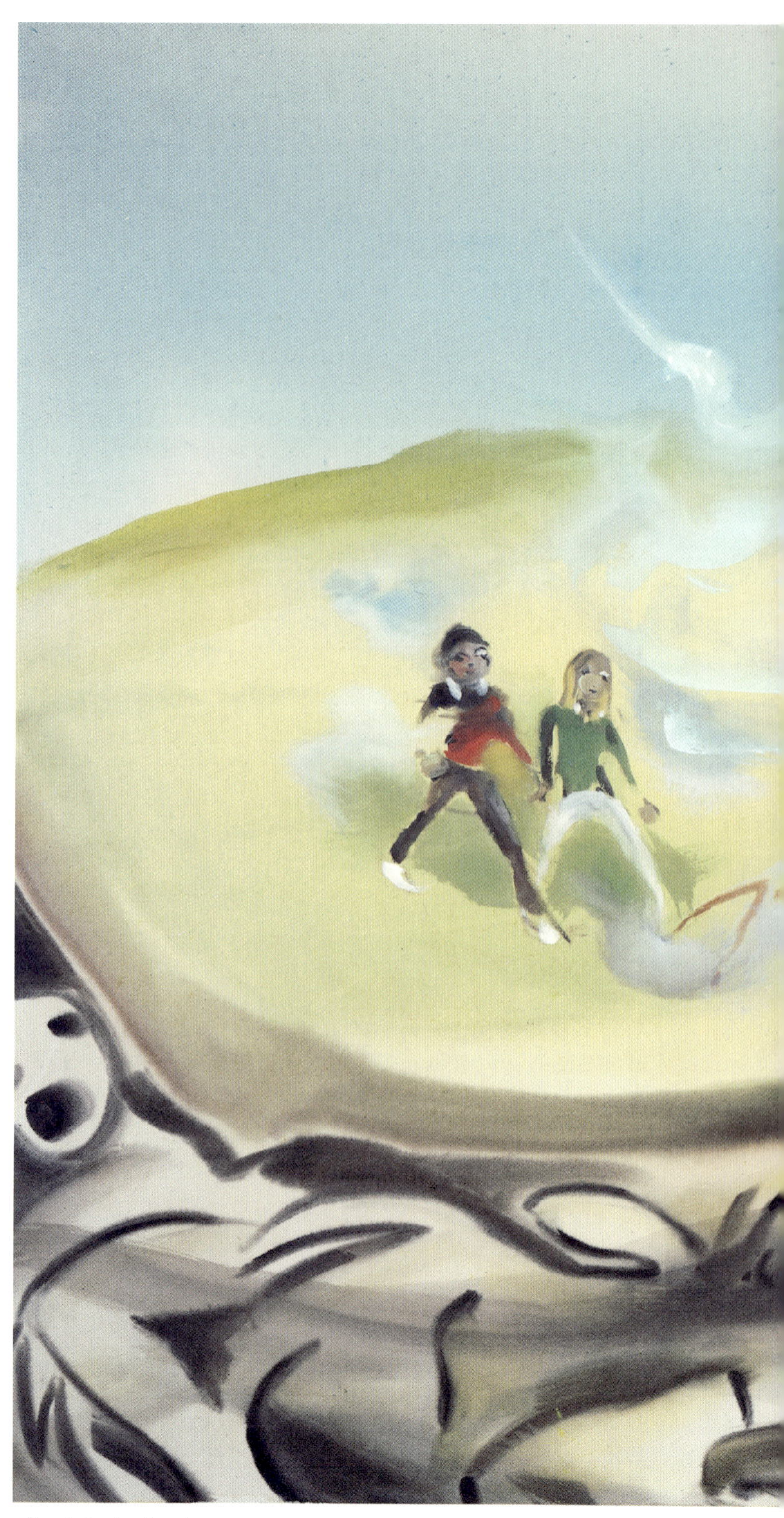

Cloud Cuckooland, 2006

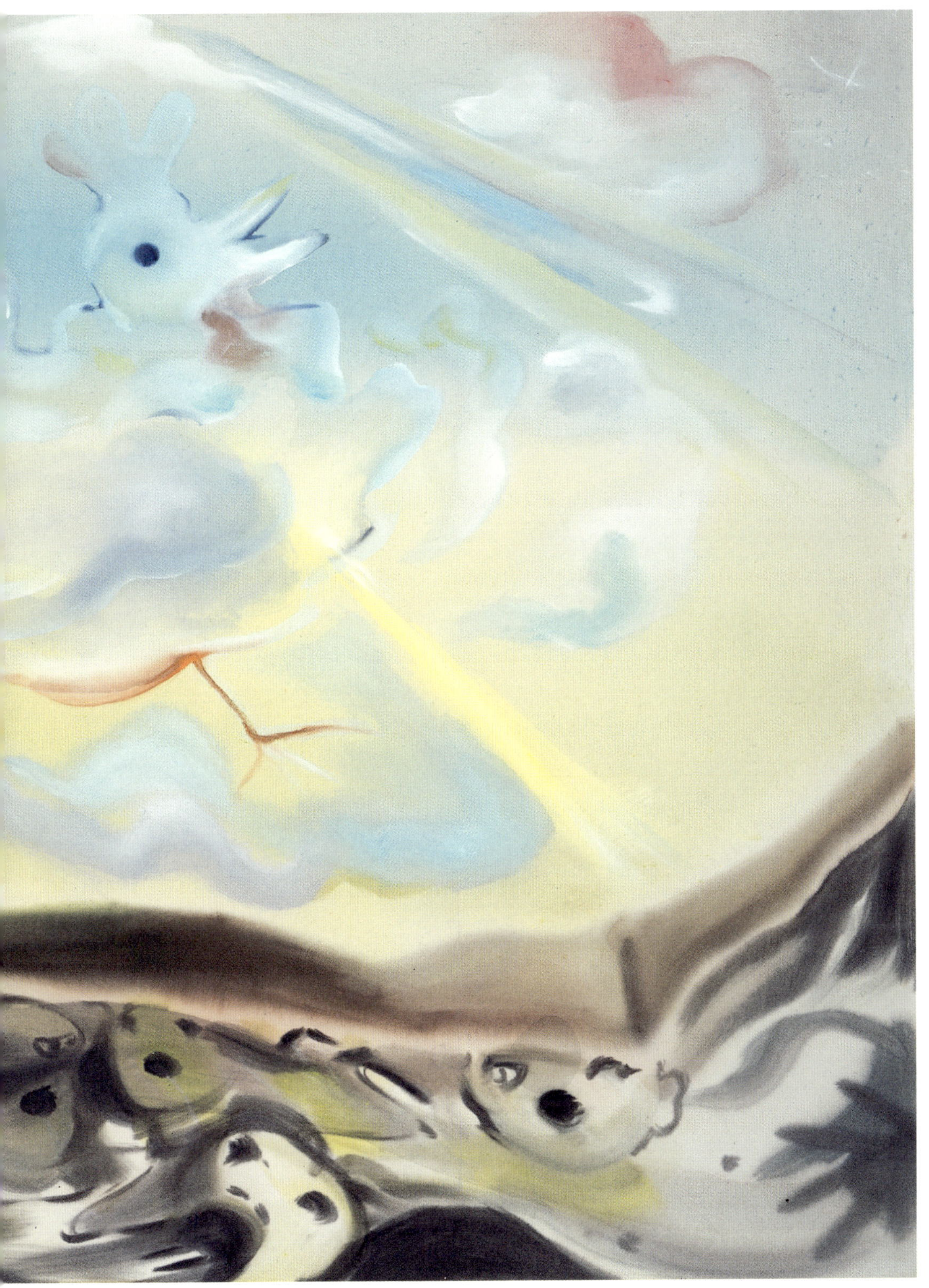

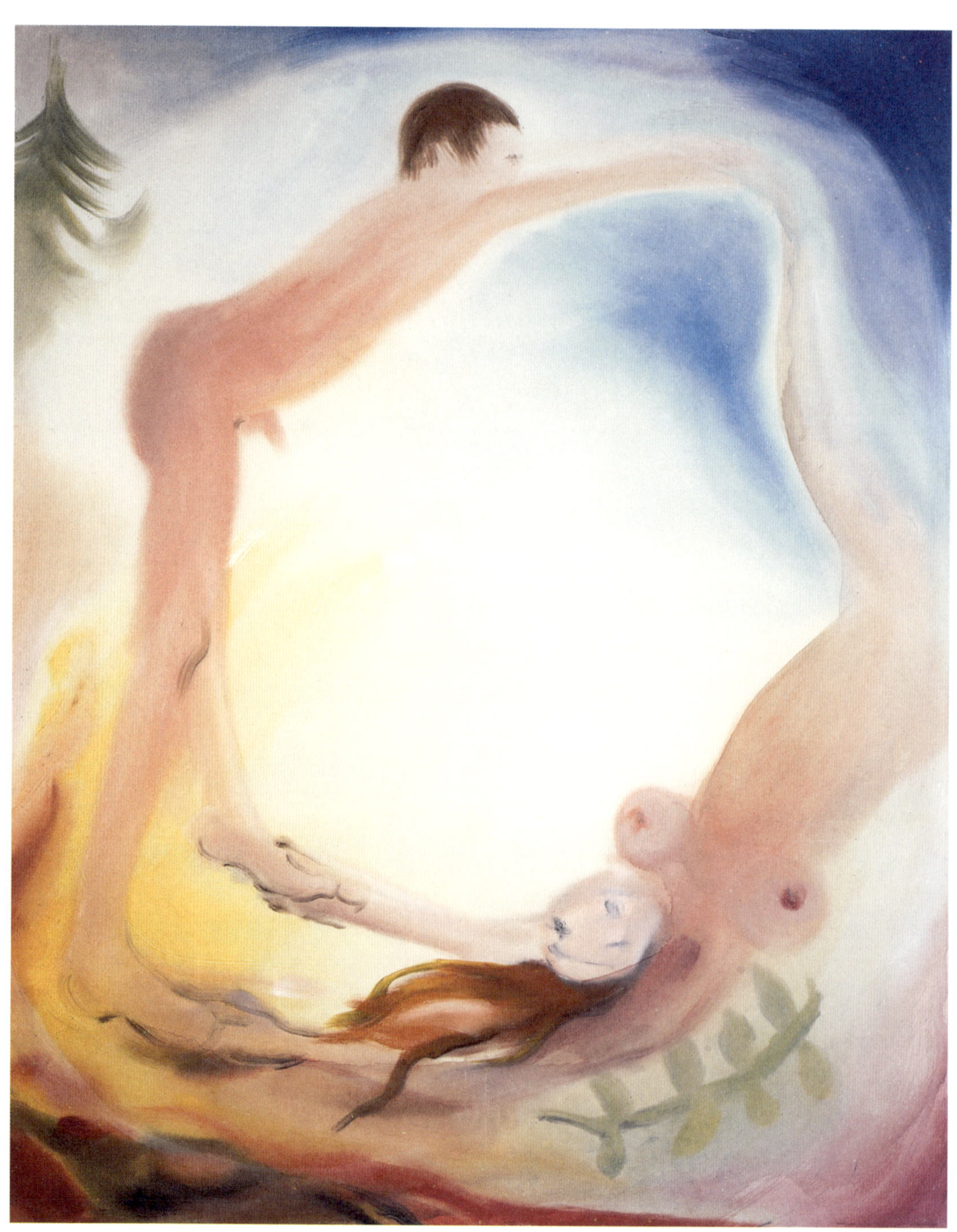

Tugend ist, wenn keiner kommt, 2005

CATALOGUE LIST

Pickel, 1994
Oil on canvas
200 × 130 cm
P. 5

Sitting on the Dock of the Bay, 1994
Oil on canvas
130 × 180 cm
P. 6/7

Untitled, 1994
Oil on canvas
150 × 100 cm
P. 8

Untitled (for Ann Peebles), 1994
Oil on canvas
200 × 150 cm
P. 9

Sherlock Holmes, 1995
Acrylic on canvas
410 × 300 cm
P. 11

Fabio, 1996
Acrylic on canvas
210 × 150 cm
P. 12

DJ Buzz, 1996
Acrylic on canvas
210 × 150 cm
P. 13

Plattenträger, 1997
Acrylic on canvas
210 × 150 cm
P. 15

Kemistry, 1997
Acrylic on canvas
270 × 210 cm
P. 16

Storm, 1997
Acrylic on canvas
270 × 210 cm
P. 17

Mädchen auf Treppe, 1998
Acrylic on canvas
280 × 210 cm
P. 18

Skateboarder, 1998
Acrylic on canvas
210 × 150 cm
P. 19

Der Lesende, 1998
Acrylic on canvas
330 × 210 cm
P. 20

The Young Gallerist, 1998
Acrylic on canvas
210 × 150 cm
P. 21

Hitchhiker, 1998
Acrylic on canvas
210 × 150 cm
P. 22

MC Schäfer, 1999
Acrylic on canvas
210 × 150 cm
P. 23

Car Crash, 1998
Acrylic on canvas
220 × 330 cm
P. 24/25

Goth on the Phone, 1999
Acrylic on canvas
150 × 100 cm
P. 29

Memory Hotel, 1999
Acrylic on canvas
180 × 240 cm
P. 30/31

Anastasia at the Station, 2000
Acrylic on canvas
150 × 100 cm
P. 32

Anastasia on the Train, 2000
Acrylic on canvas
150 × 100 cm
P. 33

Anastasia in Cleveland, 2000
Acrylic on canvas
200 × 150 cm
P. 34

Shoot Him!, 2000
Acrylic on canvas
86 × 102 cm
P. 35

Dutch Landscape, 2001
Acrylic on canvas
110 × 180 cm
P. 36

Emotional Rescue, 1999
Acrylic on canvas
210 × 180 cm
P. 37

I love Boys, Girls, Music, Art, Pleasure…, 2000
Acrylic on canvas
252 × 301 cm
destroyed
P. 38/39

Heidegger, 2000
Acrylic on canvas
185 × 152 cm
P. 40

Karl und Franz, 2000
Acrylic on canvas
110 × 180 cm
P. 41

Housewife Terrorism, 2000
Acrylic on canvas
39 × 27 cm
P. 42

Mourning Electro, 2000
Acrylic on canvas
154 × 169 cm
P. 43

Solo Album, 2000
Acrylic on canvas
200 × 210 cm
destroyed
P. 45

On set go, 2000
Acrylic on canvas
230 × 320 cm
P. 46/47

postproductionerds, 2000
Acrylic on canvas
230 × 320 cm
P. 48/49

Make-up Artist, 2000
Acrylic on canvas
200 × 150 cm
P. 50

Main Actor I, 2001
Acrylic on canvas
200 × 150 cm
P. 51

Director, 2001
Acrylic on canvas
150 × 100 cm
P. 52

Main Actor II, 2001
Acrylic on canvas
100 × 80 cm
P. 53

Leading Lady, 2001
Acrylic on canvas
180 × 260 cm
P. 54/55

Pizza Taxi, 2001
Acrylic on canvas
50 × 80 cm
P. 56/57

Maxim and Rebecca (diptych), 2001
Acrylic on canvas
165 × 233 / 165 × 233 cm
destroyed
P. 58/59

Explorers, 2001
Acrylic on canvas
140 × 110 cm
P. 60

Duellists, 2001
Acrylic on canvas
220 × 170 cm
P. 61

Flesh Records, 2001
Acrylic on canvas
160 × 210 cm
destroyed
P. 62/63

Belle de Jour, 2001
Acrylic on canvas
210 × 300 cm
P. 64/65

Gustav Metzger, 2001
Acrylic on canvas
160 × 200 cm
P. 66/67

A Matter of Life and Death (triptych), 2001
Acrylic on canvas
200 × 160 / 205 × 265 / 370 × 270 cm
P. 69, 70/71, 72

Thou art the man, 2001
Acrylic on canvas
80 × 120 cm
P. 78

Vusering Hites, 2001
Acrylic on canvas
100 × 120 cm
P. 79

Before I came to live here, 2001
Acrylic on canvas
150 × 130 cm
P. 81

Having No Desire to be Entertained, 2001
Acrylic on canvas
160 × 200 cm
P. 82/83

These Things Happened Last Winter, Sir, 2001
Acrylic on canvas
170 × 230 cm
P. 84/85

When He Came…, 2001
Acrylic on canvas
180 × 260 cm
P. 86/87

Come Together, 2001
Acrylic on canvas
200 × 305 cm
P. 88/89

Something, 2001
Acrylic on canvas
150 × 187 cm
P. 90/91

She came in through the bathroom window, 2001
Acrylic on canvas
200 × 344 cm
P. 92/93

Darling, you never give me your honey, 2001
Acrylic on canvas
202 × 149 cm
P. 94

Here Comes the Sun, 2001
Acrylic on canvas
182 × 224 cm
P. 95

Octopus's Garden, 2001
Acrylic on canvas
200 × 315 cm
P. 96/97

Alice in the Diner, 2001
Acrylic on canvas
170 × 220 cm
P. 98/99

Acupuncture, 2001
Acrylic on canvas
104 × 147 cm
P. 100

Alice going down the black hole, 2001
Acrylic on canvas
230 × 182 cm
P. 101

Skate Board, Santa Monica, 2001
Acrylic on canvas
166 × 230 cm
P. 102/103

Marc Foxx, 2001
Acrylic on canvas
182 × 230 cm
P. 104/105

Check In, 2001
Acrylic on canvas
225 × 285 cm
P. 106/107

Director's House, 2002
Acrylic on canvas
190 × 250 cm
P. 108/109

Really Dead, 2001
Acrylic on canvas
200 × 288 cm
P. 110/111

Dirty Bath Water, 2001
Acrylic on canvas
202 × 288 cm
P. 112/113

Devil Lovers, 2001
Acrylic on canvas
236 × 285 cm
P. 114/115

Inspired Shopping, 2002
Acrylic on canvas
140 × 255 cm
P. 116/117

Take Me Baby, 2002
Acrylic on canvas
205 × 270 cm
P. 118

Fitting in Prado, 2002
Acrylic on canvas
240 × 200 cm
P. 119

Deco Morons (Bedford Place), 2002
Acrylic on canvas
267 × 396 cm
P. 120/121

Half a Good Day, 2002
Acrylic on canvas
200 × 280 cm
P. 122/123

Photo Shoot, 2002
Acrylic on canvas
168 × 233 cm
P. 124/125

Mick Jagger, 2002
Acrylic on canvas
190 × 280 cm
P. 126/127

Pink Champagne, 2002
Acrylic on canvas
180 × 290 cm
P. 128/129

Losing Integrity, 2002
Acrylic on canvas
240 × 283 cm
P. 130/131

Untitled (Ballroom), 2002
Acrylic on canvas
120 × 160 cm
P. 132

Chum Pain Party (triptych), 2002
Acrylic on canvas
180 × 130 / 204 × 305 / 200 × 236 cm
P. 141, 142/143, 144/145

Normandy Trip (triptych), 2002
Acrylic on canvas
175 × 235 / 175 × 235 / 200 × 200 cm
P. 146/147, 148/149, 150/151

The Rising Detective, 2002
Acrylic on canvas
177 × 234 cm
P. 152/153

Guy Fawkes, 2002
Acrylic on canvas
100 × 150 cm
P. 154/155

Pot Offer, 2002
Acrylic on canvas
160 × 210 cm
P. 156/157

Camel, 2002
Acrylic on canvas
220 × 260 cm
P. 158/159

Hotel Flesh (triptych), 2002
Acrylic on canvas
280 × 160 / 280 × 240 / 280 × 160 cm
P. 160/161

The Canal, 2002
Acrylic on canvas
150 × 270 cm
P. 168/169

The House, 2002
Acrylic on canvas
185 × 240 cm
P. 170/171

The Chase, 2003
Acrylic on canvas
148 × 175 cm
P. 172/173

The Smugglers, 2003
Acrylic on canvas
177 × 213 cm
P. 174/175

The Study, 2002
Acrylic on canvas
150 × 200 cm
P. 176/177

Give Peace a Chance, 2003
Acrylic on canvas
160 × 200 cm
P. 178

Girls Night Out, 2003
Acrylic on canvas
200 × 180 cm
P. 179

Willküren, 2003
Acrylic on canvas
290 × 150 / 290 × 240 / 290 × 150
P. 180/181

Willküren III, 2003
Acrylic on canvas
80 × 70 cm
P. 182

Willküren I, 2003
Acrylic on canvas
80 × 70 cm
P. 183

Willküren II, 2003
Acrylic on canvas
80 × 70 cm
P. 184

Willküren IV, 2003
Acrylic on canvas
80 × 70 cm
P. 185

Willküren V, 2003
Acrylic on canvas
250 × 410 cm
P. 186/187

Willküren VII, 2003
Acrylic on canvas
250 × 410 cm
P. 188/189

Willküren VI, 2003
Acrylic on canvas
250 × 410 cm
P. 190/191

Willküren VIII, 2003
Acrylic on canvas
250 × 410 cm
P. 192/193

Bianca Jagger, 2003
Acrylic on canvas
185 × 300 cm
P. 194/195

Maaike Schoorel, Hollywood, 2003
Acrylic on canvas
138 × 103 cm
P. 196

Polaroid Piazza Santa Spirito, 2003
Acrylic on canvas
290 × 240 cm
P. 197

Red Admiral, 2003
Acrylic on canvas
170 × 285 cm
P. 198/199

Dirt Bar (Berlin), 2003
Acrylic on canvas
150 × 200 cm
P. 200/201

Ouija Board, 2003
Acrylic on canvas
140 × 200 cm
P. 202/203

Breakout, 2003
Acrylic on canvas
220 × 350 cm
P. 204/205

Christa Päffgen, 2003
Acrylic on canvas
250 × 205 cm
P. 207

I Need You, I Don't Need You, 2003
Acrylic on canvas
160 × 204 cm
P. 208/209

Black Sheep and Almond Blossom, 2003
Acrylic on canvas
205 × 250 cm
P. 210/211

Private Getaway Paradise, 2003
Acrylic on canvas
205 × 250 cm
P. 212/213

Yellow Scream, 2003
Acrylic on canvas
205 × 250 cm
P. 214/215

On the Ground, 2003
Acrylic on canvas
205 × 250 cm
P. 216/217

Disembodied Voice, 2003
Acrylic on canvas
250 × 410 cm
P. 218/219

Tour Bus, 2003
Acrylic on canvas
122 × 165 cm
P. 220

Grunewald, 2003
Acrylic on canvas
100 × 80 cm
P. 221

Berlin Burning, 2003
Acrylic on canvas
85 × 135 cm
P. 222

Neil and Me TV, 2003
Acrylic on canvas
75 × 80 cm
P. 223

Liquid Sky, 2003
Acrylic on canvas
100 × 150 cm
P. 224

Outside Coming In, 2003
Acrylic on canvas
203 × 217 cm
P. 225

Book of Dreams, 2003
Acrylic on canvas
145 × 185 cm
P. 226/227

A Man for all Seasons, 2003
Acrylic on canvas
142 × 254 cm
P. 228/229

Hot Fusion, 2004
Acrylic on canvas
200 × 244 cm
P. 230/231

Back on the Stretcher, 2004
Acrylic on canvas
80 × 150 cm
P. 232/233

Stormy Weather, 2004
Acrylic on canvas
149 × 242 cm
P. 234/235

At Home, 2004
Acrylic on canvas
198 × 280 cm
P. 236/237

Sans-Souci, 2004
Acrylic on canvas
145 × 200 cm
P. 238/239

North Beach, 2004
Acrylic on canvas
202 × 280 cm
P. 240/241

One to a void, 2004
Acrylic on canvas
178 × 203 cm
P. 242

The Proposal, 2004
Acrylic on canvas
180 × 204 cm
P. 243

Bermudas 1964, 2004
Acrylic on canvas
150 × 200 cm
P. 244/245

Monte Carlo, 2004
Acrylic on canvas
178 × 276 cm
P. 246/247

The Negligent Husband,
2004
Acrylic on canvas
182 × 155 cm
P. 248

Bouncer, 2004
Acrylic on canvas
149 × 154 cm
P. 249

*Theft of the Jaded
Goddess*, 2004
Acrylic on canvas
200 × 300 cm
P. 250/251

*He was very pleased
with where he was…*,
2004
Acrylic on canvas
200 × 300 cm
P. 252/253

Kim Tray, 2004
Acrylic on canvas
135 × 180 cm
P. 254/255

Peter F Shepyct, 2004
Acrylic on canvas
180 × 135 cm
P. 256

Agent Provocateur, 2004
Acrylic on canvas
180 × 135 cm
P. 257

Wedding, 2004
Acrylic on canvas
205 × 285 cm
P. 258/259

Sinners, 2004
Acrylic on canvas
200 × 300 cm
P. 260/261

*Why I wanted to be a
painter*, 2004
Acrylic on canvas
55 × 65 cm
P. 262

Untitled (Bubble), 2004
Acrylic on canvas
205 × 285 cm
P. 263

Long Time No See, 2005
Acrylic on canvas
100 × 150 cm
P. 264/265

Low Blood Sugar, 2004
Acrylic on canvas
155 × 205 cm
P. 266/267

Youth in La Jolla, 2004
Acrylic on canvas
175 × 234 cm
P. 268/269

*Death of the Maiden
(Elfriede Jelinek)*, 2005
Acrylic on canvas
200 × 250 cm
P. 270/271

Einstein (diptych), 2005
Acrylic on canvas
178 × 236 / 57 × 69 cm
P. 272/273

Good Space Girl, 2005
Acrylic on canvas
217 × 205 cm
P. 274

*Her Death was
Hysterical*, 2005
Acrylic on canvas
213 × 178 cm
P. 275

Time in on my side, 2005
Acrylic on canvas
213 × 155 cm
P. 277

Old Woman, 2005
Acrylic on canvas
200 × 330 cm
P. 278/279

*New York Shire Space
Time Continuum*, 2005
Acrylic on canvas
199 × 330 cm
P. 280/281

Billiard, 2005
Acrylic on canvas
200 × 300 cm
P. 282/283

Goddess in the Doorway,
2005
Acrylic on canvas
180 × 139 cm
P. 284

Self-Portrait, 2005
Acrylic on canvas
170 × 133 cm
P. 285

Tinnef, 2005
Acrylic on canvas
133 × 176 cm
P. 286/287

*Dancing in the Kitchen
with You*, 2005
Acrylic on canvas
180 × 139 cm
P. 288

Jogger in Battery Park,
2005
Acrylic on canvas
135 × 85 cm
P. 289

Poseidon, 2005
Acrylic on canvas
220 × 284 cm
P. 290/291

Hot Air Short Straw,
2005
Acrylic on canvas
200 × 288 cm
P. 292/293

*The Painter's Choice:
Final Task I*, 2005
Acrylic on canvas
175 × 235 cm
P. 294/295

*The Painter's Choice:
Final Task II*, 2005
Acrylic on canvas
175 × 235 cm
P. 296/297

*The Painter's Choice:
Final Task III*, 2005
Acrylic on canvas
175 × 235 cm
P. 298/299

*The Painter's Choice:
Final Task IV*, 2005
Acrylic on canvas
200 × 300 cm
P. 300/301

*The Painter's Choice:
Final Task V*, 2005
Acrylic on canvas
235 × 175 cm
P. 303

Sucking in the Seventies
(triptych), 2005
Acrylic on canvas
57 × 69 / 109 × 140 /
178 × 236 cm
P. 304/305, 306/307

Home Spun, 2005
Acrylic on canvas
180 × 139 cm
P. 308

Jessica, 2005
Acrylic on canvas
235 × 185 cm
P. 309

Haute de Lievre I, 2005
Acrylic on canvas
290 × 300 cm
P. 310

Haute de Lievre II, 2005
Acrylic on canvas
300 × 200 cm
P. 311

Haute de Lievre III, 2005
Acrylic on canvas
300 × 450 cm
P. 312/313

Herbstzeitlos, 2005
Acrylic on canvas
155 × 213 cm
P. 314/315

Eyeless in Gauze, 2005
Acrylic on canvas
140 × 180 cm
P. 316/317

Half-remembered, 2005
Acrylic on canvas
200 × 200 cm
P. 318

Plötzlich wurde alles gut,
2005
Acrylic on canvas
200 × 140 cm
P. 319

Sweet Pick Me Up, 2005
Acrylic on canvas
195 × 145 cm
P. 321

Raging against a myth
(diptych), 2005
Acrylic on canvas
201 × 288 / 179 × 140 cm
P. 322/323, 325

Walk, Don't Walk, 2005
Acrylic on canvas
200 × 300 cm
P. 326/327

*Delusions of Silent
Anxiety* (triptych), 2005
Acrylic on canvas
170 × 134 / 180 × 214 /
200 × 300 cm
P. 329, 330/331, 332/333

*The Dragon, the Beast
and the false Prophet*
(triptych), 2005
Acrylic on canvas
100 × 80 / 160 × 110 /
200 × 200 cm
P. 334/335, 336/337,
338/339

*Untitled (Ten
Commandments)*, 2005
Acrylic on canvas
200 × 300 cm
P. 340/341

Green Earth, 2005
Acrylic on canvas
210 × 280 cm
P. 342/343

Washing the News, 2005
Acrylic on canvas
210 × 280 cm
P. 344/345

Cloud Cuckooland, 2006
Acrylic on canvas
210 × 280 cm
P. 346/347

*Tugend ist, wenn keiner
kommt (It's virtue when
nobody comes)*, 2005
Acrylic on canvas
300 × 200 cm
P. 348

SOPHIE von HELLERMANN

1975 born in Munich
lives and works in London

SELECTED SOLO EXHIBITIONS
1999 *Super Sophie Solo Show*,
hobbypopMUSEUM, Düsseldorf
2001 *Vusering Hites*, Vilma Gold, London
*Saatchi Gallery Presents Sophie von
Hellermann*, London
Abbey Road, Marc Foxx, Los Angeles
2003 *Willküren*, Kunstverein Konstanz,
Sophie von Hellermann, Jablonka Lühn,
Cologne
2004 *On the Ground*, Vilma Gold, London
Hot Fusion, Marc Foxx, Los Angeles
Sophie von Hellermann, Galerie Ghislaine
Hussenot, Paris
A Perfect Spy, Vacio 9, Madrid
2005 *Goddess in the Doorway*, Greene Naftali
Gallery, New York

SELECTED GROUP EXHIBITIONS
1993 Group show, with Nick Laessing a.o.,
–ism gallery, Oxford
1995 *Coole Bilder*, with Tine Furler, Tatjana
Doll, Dietmar Lutz, Markus Vater,
Ehemaliges Bundesbahnausbesserungs-
werk, Nippes, Cologne
1996 *Drive-in*, with Tatjana Doll, Tine Furler,
Dietmar Lutz, Markus Vater, Former
Factory, Düsseldorf
1997 *Hello Down There*, with Tatjana Doll,
Tine Furler, Dietmar Lutz, Markus Vater,
Gothaer Kunstforum, Cologne
1999 *Spiel des Lebens*, Former Post Office
Building, Düsseldorf
What you buy is your problem, with Dierk
Schmidt, Galerie Fons Welters, Amsterdam
Trouble Spot Painting, NICC New Interna-
tional Cultural Center, Antwerpen and
*MuHKA Museum voor Hedendaagse Kunst
Antwerpen*
Weltausstellung / Robolove, Kölnerstr.,
with Tine Furler, Düsseldorf
2000 *Painting Group Show*, Timothy Taylor
Gallery, London
2002 *Dear Painter, paint me… Painting the
Figure since late Picabia*, Centre Pompidou,
Kunsthalle Vienna, Schirn Kunsthalle
Frankfurt
De La Peintre!..., Galerie Ghislaine
Hussenot, Paris
Immediate Gesture, Lombard Freid Fine
Arts, New York
Mediated Cooperation, collaboration with
Johannes Maier Oberwelte, Stuttgart,
We all Love…, The Mission, London
Electric Show, The Great Eastern Hotel,
London
Paintings, Marc Foxx, Los Angeles
2003 *Art and Mountains*, The Alpine Club,
London
Hydrophobia, Henry Peacock Gallery,
London
Summer Show, Marc Foxx, Los Angeles
2004 *The Drawing Project*, Vamiali's, Athens
Brittania Works, British Council, Athens

Elfriede Jelinek Tribute, Fortescue Avenue,
London
2005 *POST-MoDERN*, Greene Naftali
Gallery, New York
Clarke & McDevitt Present, Hugh Lane
Gallery, Dublin
*No Good Man Island. Sophie von
Hellermann & Brian Griffiths*, Vilma Gold
Project Space, Berlin

BIBLIOGRAPHY
2000 Michelle Grabner, Trouble Spot
Painting, *Frieze*, February
2001 Claire Bishop, Katharina's mice and
men, *The Evening Standard*, 31 August
2001 William Preston, What's Nagging
Sophie?, *Art Review*, September
Martin Maloney, Maloney's Magnificent
Seven, *Art Review*, April
Adrian Searle, Heat of the Moment,
The Guardian, 10 July
Sue Hubbard, The Critics: Visual Art Pick
of the Galleries – Sophie von Hellermann,
The Independent on Sunday, 21 October
Ulrike Knöfel, Jung, blond, böse,
Der Spiegel, 10 December 2001
2002 Carlos Gute, Focus Painting Part One,
Contemporary Painting Today, *Flash Art*,
October
Kate Bush, Cher Peintre, Lieber Maler,
Dear Painter, *Art Forum*, October
Luc Tuymans, Enquête sur l'image peinte
(Dear Painter), *Art Press*, July-August
Johannes Wetzel, Dear Painter, *Financial
Times Germany*, 7 August
Matthias Frehner, Phrasen und
Paraphrasen (Dear Painter), *Neue Züricher
Zeitung*, 31 July
Nick Hackworth, Insider art from the
Germans, *Evening Standard*, 6 June
Kate Bush, Preview Summer 2002,
Artforum International, May
Louisa Buck, Louisa Buck's London Diary,
The Arts Newspaper, March
2003 Morgan Falconer, Hydrophobia,
What's On, 3 December
Adam Brooks, Picabia, the paradigm,
Art in America, March
Helga Meister, Gold – aus Staub und
Wasser, *Westdeutsche Zeitung*,
15 November
Thomas Hirsch, Aus der Erinnerung,
Biograph Düsseldorf, August
Dorothea Breit, Lady, anatomisch schlecht,
Kölner Stadt-Anzeiger, 18 July
Ralph Christofori, Lieber Maler…,
Kunst-Bulletin, Issue April
Alice Koegel, Sophie von Hellermann,
Stadt Revue Köln, July
Belinda Grace Gardner, Fragile
Momente…, *Kunstzeitung*, March
2004 Sue Hubbard, Sophie von Hellermann
at Vilma Gold, *The Independent*, 27 January
Sophie von Hellermann in conversation
with Andreas Leventis, *Miser & Now*,
Issue 03
Pablo Lafuente, Sophie von Hellermann,
Flash Art, July–September

Alison Gingeras, Openings:
hobbypopMUSEUM, *Artforum
International*, March
Leo Benedictus, Here Today Gone
Tomorrow, *The Guardian Guide*, 8 October
–15 October
Jessica Lack, Pick of the Week: Sophie
von Hellermann, *The Guardian Guide*,
19 January
Jessica Lack, Sophie von Hellermann,
The Guardian Guide, 17 January–
23 January
Sofia Sanchez, Wish You Were Here,
(article illustrated by Sophie von
Hellermann), *Interview*, 4 January 2004
2005 Nicole Davis, A New Lease On
Painting, *artnet.com*, 9 February
Christopher Ho, POST MoDERN, *Modern
Painters*, March
Dodie Kazanjian, Bright Ideas, *Vogue*, April
Karen Rosenberg, Show and Tell: Sophie
von Hellermann, *New York Magazine*,
23 May
Suzanne Hudson, Sophie von Hellermann:
Greene Naftali Gallery, *Artforum
International*, September

PUBLICATIONS
Hello Down There, exhibition catalogue
(Cologne: Gothaer Kunstforum, 1997)
Spiel des Lebens, ed. by the artists,
exhibition catalogue (Düsseldorf, 1999)
Trouble Spot-Painting, exhibition
catalogue, (Antwerp: New International
Cultural Center and Museum voor
Hedendaagse Kunst Antwerpen, 1999)
The Saatchi Gallery presents Sophie von
Hellermann, exhibition catalogue
(London: The Saatchi Gallery, 2001)
Bloomberg New Contemporaries,
exhibition catalogue (London: New
Contemporaries, 2001)
Dear Painter, paint me…, Painting the
Figure since late Picabia, ed. Alison M.
Gingeras, exhibition catalogue (Paris,
Vienna, Frankfurt: Centre Pompidou,
Kunsthalle Wien, Schirn Kunsthalle
Frankfurt, 2002)
Britannia Works, exhibition catalogue
(London: British Council, 2004)
I Just Don't Know What To Do With
Myself, exhibition catalogue (Milan:
Marella Arte Contemporanea, 2005)

*For hobbypopMUSEUM biography please
refer to the following publications:*
hobbypopMUSEUM, ed.
hobbypopMUSEUM (Düsseldorf:
hobbypop-editions, 1999)
hobbypopMUSEUM 2000–2002, ed.
hobbypopMUSEUM and Kunstverein
für die Rheinlande und Westfalen
(Cologne: Verlag der Buchhandlung
Walther König, 2002)
hobbypopMUSEUM, Werte schaffen
(Cologne: Verlag der Buchhandlung
Walther König, 2004)
hobbypopMUSEUM, Echo (Athens:
Deste Foundation, 2005)